AMERICAN HARDCORE

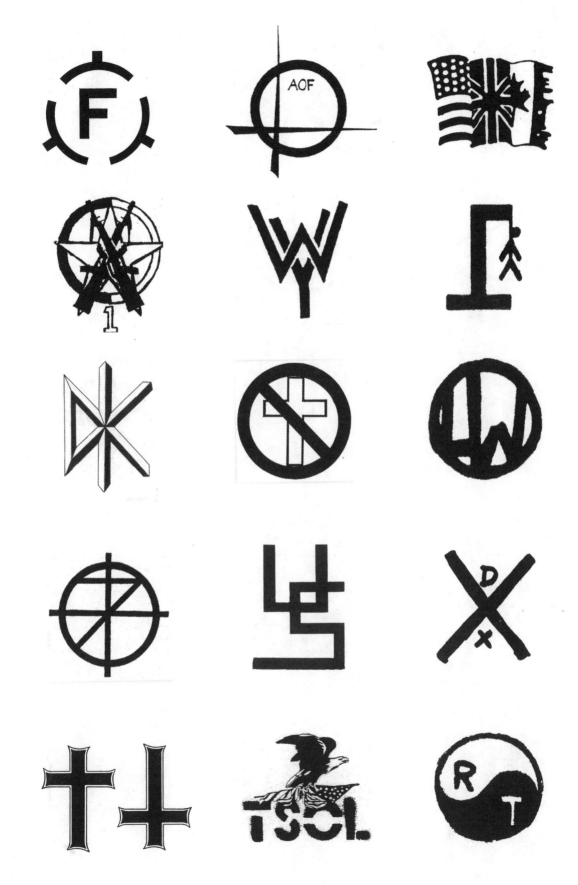

AMERICAN HARDCORE

A TRIBAL HISTORY

by Steven Blush

Edited & Designed by George Petros

FERAL HOUSE
LOS ANGELES · NEW YORK

American Hardcore ©2001 by Steven Blush and Feral House

All rights reserved.

ISBN: 0-922915-717-7

Feral House
P.O. Box 13067
Los Angeles, CA 90013

www.feralhouse.com

info@feralhouse.com

10 9 8 7 6 5 4 3

AMERICAN HARDCORE CONTENTS

HANX!

Christine Aebi, Laura Albert, Leslie Barany, Ray "Raybeez" Barbieri (R.I.P.), Al Barile, Lou Barlow, Marc Bayard, Tom Berrard, Jello Biafra, Brian Brannon, Otto Buj, Dez Cadena, Tony Cadena, Tim Caldwell, Joe Carducci, Spike Cassady, Tom Colbath, Art Chantry, Steve "Mugger" Corbin, Glenn Danzig, Steve DePace, Bruce Duff, Bubba DuPree, Ray Farrell, Maria Ferraro, Harley Flanagan, Al Flipside, Gary Floyd, Glen E. Friedman, Don Fury, Nicky Garrett, Jimmy Gestapo, Greg Ginn, Mike Gitter, Norman Gosney, Jack Grisham, Charlie Harper, Andy Hawkins, Barry Hennsler, James Hetfield, Don Hill, Pat Hoed, Ken Inouye, Ed Ivey, Daryl Jenifer, John Joseph, Tad Kepley, Joey Keithley, Tim Kerr, John Kezdy, King Koffee, Dr. Know, Richard Luckett, Maria Ma, Ian MacKaye, Paul Mahern, Jesse Malin, Parris Mitchell Mayhew, Carlo McCormick, Graham McCulloch, Jeff McDonald, Steve McDonald, Duff McKagan, Roger Miret, Keith Morris, Michael Moynihan, Reed Mullen, Mike Ness, Jerry Only, Hank Peirce, D.H. Peligro, Alec Peters, Raymond Pettibon, Matt Pinfield, Steve Poss, Tom Price, Al Quint, Jack Rabid, Paul Rachman, Jay Robbins, Henry Rollins, Paul Rosin, Danny Sage, Jon Savage, Mike Schnapp, Kevin Seconds, Jon Sidel, Dave Smalley, Winston Smith, Debbie Southwood-Smith, Spider, Spot, Bobby Steele, Pete Stahl, Pete Steele, Adam Keane Stern, Mark Stern, Shawn Stern, Bill Stevenson, Drew Stone, Todd Swalla, George Tabb, Sean Taggart, Tesco Vee, Lee Ving, Ken Waagner, Kim Warnick, Mike Watt, Andy Wendler, David West, Scotty Wilkins, Wino, Adam Yauch

Special Hanx!
Adam Parfrey, George Petros, Mike King, Sal Canzonieri, Edward Colver, Karen O'Sullivan, Eric Hammer, Jerry Lee Williams, The Blush and Radick families

Front cover by Edward Colver: Danny Spira, Wasted Youth, LA, 1981
Back cover by Karen O'Sullivan: Murphy's Law, New York, 1983
Colorized by Eric Hammer

MY WAR

I'M DOCUMENTING THE AMERICAN HARDCORE PUNK MUSIC SCENE BECAUSE IT'S BEING FORGOTTEN. Its history is evaporating as the participants die off or find religion or repress their memories of those dynamic days.

This book addresses the peak years of American Hardcore, 1980 through 1986. Much happened in that short time.

Hardcore was more than music — it became a political and social movement as well. The participants constituted a tribe unto themselves. Some of them were alienated or abused, and found escape in the hard-edged music. Some sought a better world or a tearing down of the status quo, and were angry. Most of them simply wanted to raise hell. Stark and uncompromising, Hardcore generated a lifestyle stripped down to the bare bones. Its intensity exposed raw nerves. Everyone was edgy and aggressive.

Like most revolutionary art and original thought, Hardcore clashed with mainstream society and generated resistance. As a minor subculture it received little attention and commanded even less respect. Hipsters took one look at its adolescent violence and dismissed the whole scene.

Lots of fucked-up kids "found themselves" through Hardcore. Many now say things like, "I grew up thinking I was a weirdo, but I met like-minded people and figured out I wasn't such a freak after all." If that's what "HC" did for them, then the scene succeeded. For some, it served as a valuable social network; for others, it opened a rich musicological mine; but for all involved, Hardcore was a way of life, something that they *had* to do.

The aesthetic was intangible. Most bands couldn't really play that well, and their songs usually lacked craft. They expended little effort achieving prevailing production standards. However, they had IT — an infectious blend of ultra-fast music, thought-provoking lyrics, and fuck-you attitude.

Nobody thought things out too far in advance. We participants were for the most part just kids. Irrational kids. Which in part made the whole thing so intense. The rage often remained unfocused — you'd see kids morph from drugged-out, suburban Metal misfits to shit-kicking skinheads to vegan pacifists over the span of a few years. But let's not over-intellectualize. Accept Hardcore for what it was — something alienated kids created. It taught us to mistrust authority and mass media. It sparked a rebellion that is only now beginning to be appreciated.

I dealt with most of the classic Hardcore bands. I knew "movers and shakers" in every town in America. I watched the great and the small come and go. I saw them turn into the smug commercial Rock Stars against whom they'd supposedly rebelled. I knew those now dead. I experienced it all first-hand. During the scene's formative years I lived in Washington, DC, a place not unlike the rest of America. Nor was my life too unlike those of most of the people in these pages.

As a Hardcore show promoter, college-radio DJ, indie label owner, band manager, and tour coordinator, I hooked up many of the people I will be introducing herein. Did I get enough thank-yous and accolades? In the end, I'm comfortable with my props.

With this book, I give the scene's participants not only their day in the sun but also their day in court. I've spoken with virtually all the important characters of the era — over 150 interviews in all. Participants not represented herein were unreachable or did not respond to my inquiries. There are a few I regret not speaking with, but I did my best. Everyone else cooperated, to varying degrees. They confirmed theories or pointed out my errors. Through this process, I've had to distinguish fact from opinion, forcing myself to rethink preconceptions. I've tried to purge myself of all the punditry, stereotyping, sloganeering, gut feelings, and knee-jerk reaction developed over the years, and I've quit trying to defend my personal tastes. Plenty of petty, shitty attitude persists among Hardcore participants to this day, but I strived to avoid adopting the bad vibe.

As for veracity, both the interviewees and I recount events as best we remember. Those were crazy times long ago; the interviewees, most around 40 at the time of this writing, are recounting the events of often-tumultuous youths. And sometimes the truth gets distorted or misrepresented through nostalgia, embitterment, gossip, poor memory, or brain damage. Having said that, I've done exhaustive fact-checking wherever possible. *American Hardcore* ain't no revisionist history based on what I personally think happened.

My entire life's experiences, conversations, readings and listening has become one massive reference library in my head. I can't always recall the origin of the facts and figures, but I've credited all sources wherever possible. I spent five years making phone calls and driving around America tracking down band members, fans, promoters, and whoever else.

It takes a Hardcore mind to write a Hardcore book. I'm talking about a spontaneous, rebellious, undisciplined, undocumented movement. I wrote *American Hardcore* in pure HC fashion — with everything I fucking had.

As for the current Hardcore renaissance, I don't wanna deny the legitimacy of today's teen angst. I just feel like, "Yo, make your own fucking music! Why just ape the music of my salad days?" I can relate to those old Jazz or Blues cats who played back when it was all about innovation rather than formula, and who now see a bunch of complacent umpteenth-generation beneficiaries claiming the forms as their own. Face it, Hardcore ain't the same anymore. It can still make for powerful music, but it's an over-with art form. It's relatively easy to be into now, but back then it was an entirely different story.

American Hardcore, generally unheralded at the time, gave birth to much of the music and culture that followed. The original fans should feel vindicated. No one today gives a shit about which huge arena act sold ten zillion records in 1983 — Hardcore heroes like Black Flag, Dead Kennedys, Bad Brains, The Misfits and Minor Threat are modern immortals. At the time of this writing, few successful Rock artists are not tinged with Hardcore.

Befitting of all great artists, Hardcore bands "made no money" and "never received their just due" — only subsequent generations of enthusiasts would propel them into "legendary" status.

The world has changed dramatically over the past decades. What occurred in the early 80s can never happen again.

— Steven Blush, New York City, July 2001

PART ONE

America, 1979. Photo by Edward Colver

LIVING IN DARKNESS

Living in darkness
Living in a world
Of my own
— Agent Orange, "Living In Darkness"

Hardcore was the suburban American response to the late-70s Punk revolution. But while Hardcore grew out of Punk, it would be wrong to say, "If you understand Punk, you can understand Hardcore."

Successive waves of style and counter-style characterize Rock history. Reactionary trends constantly arise to strip down, simplify, and democratize prevailing fashions. For example, homegrown teen idols dominated early 60s airwaves. The ubiquitous Beach Boys, Four Freshman, Bobby Vinton and Del Shannon supplied clean, crisp melodies over de-emphasized rhythms. Along came The British Invasion groups — The Beatles, The Rolling Stones, The Who, The Kinks, et al. — throwing away that formula and replacing it with freaky R&B-based rawness. But soon this "revolutionary" new music itself turned into institutionalized mush.

The mid-to-late 70s saw the rise of Disco, the recording industry's unsuccessful attempt to graft a gay, black dance phenomenon onto a staid Rock format. The hip-grinding beat of Rod Stewart's "D'Ya Think I'm Sexy?" or "I Was Made For Loving You" by Kiss — "crossover" songs — generated as much controversy as success.

Suburban twinkies, already irate over having to endure the music of "fags" and "niggers" like KC & The Sunshine Band and Donna Summer, were further agitated by rabble-rousing FM jocks and opportunistic publicists issuing the battle cry "Disco Sucks." Rock stations even staged socially sanctioned Disco record-burnings. If this wasn't racism and homophobia, I don't know what was. Music culture grew even more segregated and reactionary. To fans of heartfelt art, the mid-to-late 70s marked a low point in Pop Culture.

In '76 arose a Second British Invasion, spearheaded by the Sex Pistols, The Clash and The Damned — influenced, ironically, by relatively unsuccessful American artists like The Velvet Underground, The Stooges and New York Dolls. This new, reactionary music was called Punk. It tossed the dominant Rock culture into the garbage can. The only rule was to break the rules. Rough and tough and sarcastic, Punk provided some of the finest and most influential Rock Music of all time. Of course, it soon ran out of steam, becoming pretentious and boring like its predecessors.

A watered-down version of Punk — marketed as "New Wave" — was cranked out by major labels planning to soften the image for mainstream consumption. No conspiracy theory here: that's just the way it was. Clean production, keyboards, sharp suits, angular haircuts, wrap-around shades and skinny ties defined the moment. Perhaps the industry's diversion of "anti-social" Punk into the more palatable New Wave bin delivered a more attractive product to the anxious consumer. Perhaps.

Differentiating between the real and the contrived was often difficult. The industry marketed old-school rockers like Tom Petty and Mark Knopfler under Punk's umbrella. Everybody made a New Wave record.

Late-70s FM radio groaned with minor hits by ersatz New Wave outfits like Fabulous Poodles, Sniff 'N' The Tears, The Sinceros and The Shirts with Annie Golden, star of the movie *Hair*. Skinny-tied success stories included The Knack

("My Sharona"), The Vapors ("Turning Japanese"), and The Romantics ("What I Like About You").

At its best, New Wave attempted to retain the power and conciseness of Punk while mixing in a plethora of arty "isms." Acts like Human League and The Cars represented a danceable, cosmopolitan approach. There arose a generation of disaffected kids who wanted Punk's fury without New Wave's art-school baggage. The seeds of Hardcore were sown.

> *Society is burning me up*
> *Take a bite then spit it out*
> *Take their rules, rip 'em up*
> *Tear 'em down*
> — Circle Jerks, "World Up My Ass"

1976-80 were the Punk and New Wave years; Hardcore happened 1980-86. If Punk peaked in '77, then Hardcore's glory days were '81-82, when it was still undefined and unpredictable.

Hardcore was an American phenomenon fueled by British and homegrown Punk scenes. It began in Southern California. The first HC bands came out of suburban LA beach towns, probably 'cause there they lived as close to The American Dream as you could get. Born of a doomed ideal of middle-class utopia, Punk juiced their nihilism.

The typical Hardcore candidate listened to hard-hitting Brit outfits like 999, Angelic Upstarts and Sham 69, as well as the star-spangled sounds of The Ramones and The Avengers. Such outfits had a violent edge, but Reagan-era kids needed something even more primal and immediate.

Hardcore extended, mimicked or reacted to Punk; it appropriated some aspects yet discarded others. It reaffirmed the attitude, and rejected New Wave. That's why it was *hard-core* Punk — for people who were fed up.

You knew someone was hard-core if they had a shaved head or a crew cut, a threatening demeanor, and a hatred of the mainstream. The few girls into Hardcore appeared severe and unfriendly. What set these kids apart from jocks and rednecks was a vague political consciousness and a vigilante-like do-gooder streak. All in all, it was not a pretty sight.

> *If the kids are united*
> *They will never be divided*
> — Sham 69, "If The Kids Are United"

Sham 69 was a major influence on American Hardcore. Frontman Jimmy Pursey spoke to the hearts of alienated kids with his angry but thoughtful lyrics. Unruly mobs of young males responded to the band's high-powered, anthemic drinking songs. There was a nebulous political component as well. Sham 69 was one of the few Brit Punk groups to tour America.

There's Gonna Be A Borstal Breakout
Sham 69 single, 1977, Polydor UK
Collection of the author

IAN MACKAYE (Minor Threat): For a few minutes, Sham 69 were the truest of all Punk bands. They were populist — really into the kids. The Sex Pistols were ultra-fashion; Sham 69's fashion was work-wear. They were Punk Rockers without the glam. My thing's been anti-fashion: bands like Sham reflected that — a major influence in our direction.

JON SAVAGE (author, *England Dreaming*): I really hated Sham 69; they highlight the problem you have in Pop Music when you start to talk in the language of the man on the street — you actually start mucking down into Right-Wing demagoguery. I always thought Sham 69 were horseshit, though they made two great records: 'If The Kids Are United' and 'Borstal Breakout.' Sham Punk — I'm sorry — is dumb, dumb, dumb.

JACK RABID (editor, *The Big Takeover*): Sham 69 always had a bad reputation back in England because they weren't intellectual enough to fit in with the writers' cultural meaning of Punk. There was a lot of snobbery going on in the British press that Sham were a bunch of yahoos — and the press missed out on some great records.

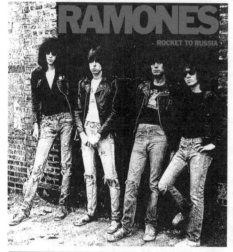

Rocket To Russia
Ramones LP, 1977, Sire
Collection of the author

Guess I gonna have to tell 'em
That I got no cerebellum
— Ramones, "Teenage Lobotomy"

Many Hardcore participants cite The Ramones as an inspiration. Most HC groups adopted their style of loud, high-speed music, t-shirt-and-jeans image, and no-bullshit attitude.

DEZ CADENA (Black Flag): I was in awe when I heard The Ramones' first album, I couldn't believe there was a Rock album like that. It was similar to what I listened to but way faster — and there were no guitar solos.

SPOT (producer/soundman): I'd heard the Sex Pistols early on, but it didn't make a huge impression on me. What made the biggest impression on me was The Ramones' first album. I loved playing that record for people just to watch them cringe. Suddenly, Rock & Roll was fun again.

KEVIN SECONDS (7 Seconds): We'd sit on our bed and play along to Punk records. The best to play along to was The Ramones' first record — if you turned down one side of your stereo, you could just have the bass and drums and on the other side you have the guitar — almost like having this instructional record. We'd tape record ourselves playing to it.

Gimme gimme this
Gimme gimme that
— Germs, "Lexicon Devil"

The first American band to drive its music in a Hardcore direction was LA's The Germs. Frontman Darby Crash (born Jon Paul Beahm in 1958) was America's Sid Vicious. The Germs' chaotic sound eschewed the structure of Punk; their art sprang from rookie enthusiasm and bad drugs. Musically and stylistically, they influenced all Hardcore to come.

DEZ CADENA (Black Flag): I never felt the spirit in any Punk band the way I felt when I saw The Germs. People have tried to emulate it and some have done a pretty good job. What I liked was that everything was a negative but when you put it all together it somehow made a positive. A lot of times they were too fucked-up, a lot of times they didn't play well, a lot of times there was hardly any vocals because the vocalist was too high, or the bass player was out of tune, but somehow they embodied Punk. I saw their singer, even though he was

insecure and had to get high before he played, was a
genius. An eccentric, bizarre drug addict.

JON SAVAGE: I loved The Germs because they
did what the Americans can do so easily and what
Brits can't — which is, they rocked. Although their
'Forming' record is on one level very self-consciously
trying to be arty, on another level it's very
unselfconsciously just rocking out. And rocking out
in only a way that they knew how to — which is not
very well!

**Released on upstart Slash Records in
summer '79, the Germs' album *(GI)* upped the
ante for dissonance and aggression. Celebrity
producer Joan Jett — replacing Mark Lindsay
of Paul Revere And The Raiders fame, who
demanded too much money — played a huge
role in marketing the disc.**

(GI)
Germs LP, 1979, Slash
Collection of Sal Canzonieri

TESCO VEE (Meatmen): The Germs' *(GI)* album is one of those things that stands alone.
Darby Crash has been much lambasted for being this Sid Vicious type but man, that fuckin'
guy was one of the greats. He really was what Punk was all about — snotty, I-don't-care,
shoot-up-till-I-die. He was an important figure in American Culture.

MIKE WATT (Minutemen): Darby went to England and came back and told everyone
Adam & The Ants were gonna be the big band. He got a mohawk and got very heavy. It was
really bizarre. I think he thought the Hollywood scene had no future. He lived and hung out
and skateboarded in Orange County, so actually brought Punk down there.

**Darby Crash overdosed on China White in December '79 — right at the dawn
of Hardcore.**

MARK STERN (Youth Brigade): That record didn't really start selling till Darby died.
They were much bigger when they broke up. There were times when if you were drunk
enough and Darby was drunk enough, it could be an amazing cathartic experience, but most
of the times it was just fucking awful. He couldn't sing worth a shit, and half the time he was
so fucked up he'd be rolling around incoherently. Those shows were never that crowded
either. The big ones had 300 kids; most of the time it was 80 to 100 people.

I don't want no satisfaction
I just want to get some action
— Fear, "Gimme Some Action"

**The first group to generate a Hardcore-style vibe at their live shows was Fear
from LA. Fronted by Lee Ving, a nasty fuck who went out of his way to insult
everybody, Fear did rude tunes like "I Don't Care About You" and "Let's Have A
War." Their early shows saw incredible violence, due in large part to their
popularity with suburban surf jock types. Fear earned infamy for their role in
Penelope Spheeris' cult film *The Decline Of Western Civilization*, police crackdowns
at their gigs, and their controversial '81 spot on *Saturday Night Live*.**

DEZ CADENA: Fear were probably a Metal band before they were a Punk band. They
really knew how to play their instruments. I think the joke around Fear — and it was all

one big joke — was people who took 'em seriously. In its own way, that was true Punk Rock, however twisted.

Critics alleged that Fear dabbled with Right Wing lyrics, symbols and slogans. The fact is that Ving, a foul-mouthed fucker, simply wanted to offend everyone.

The Record
Fear LP, 1979, Slash
Collection of the author

LEE VING (Fear): There really never was a point where my life took an extreme right-hand turn or change of direction. It was a gradual onslaught. I liked the idea of there being no rules. Coupled with that, I wanted to find the best players I could. They called us 'musos' 'cause we knew how to play.

Fear made national headlines in 1980 when bassist Derf Scratch spent four days in Canoga Park Hospital with a shattered face — the result of a severe beating from a few surf jock fans after he spit in one's face. That happened right around the premiere of *The Decline...*, chronicling the violence of the proto-Hardcore scene. Radio ad spots blurted: "See it in the theater, where you can't get hurt!

LEE VING: Derf had some difficulties with some people during the course of the evening, and wound up having some surgery over it. Needless to say, it became very expensive. We had a benefit for him and everything ... He got in a fight with one person — but that person had a glint in his eye that should tell most people to find someone else to fight with.

MIKE WATT : We played The Starwood with Flag, Fear, and Circle Jerks. Derf from Fear was a great bass player, and [drummer] Spit could nail a dude at a hundred feet. So this 6'8 jock grabbed him and pounded him. They put a picture of him in *Rolling Stone*. Remember him, all beat up with the drainage cup on the side of his head? That's from that fucking gig. You gotta watch out who you're spittin' on.

KING KOFFEE (Butthole Surfers): When I saw that *Rolling Stone* with the picture of Derf with a drainage cup attached to his head, I thought he looked really cool. *Rolling Stone* tried to act all horrified, but I was wishing I was there!

We don't need no magazines
We don't need no TV
We don't wanna know
— Middle Class, "Out Of Vogue"

Where does the word "Hardcore" come from? As a term, it's common — "hardcore porn" or "a hard-core football fan." Some in-the-know cite the Vancouver band D.O.A.'s *Hardcore 81* LP. That might be the first official use of the term in music. Regardless of the precise origin, when Punks said, "Hardcore," other Punks knew what they meant. Hardcore expressed an extreme: the absolute most Punk.

JOEY SHITHEAD (D.O.A.): The first time we saw the term 'Hardcore,' this magazine from San Francisco, *Damaged*, talked about 'hard-core' music in an article about Black Flag in late 1980. When we started recording, our manager Ken Lester said, 'Here's an album title for you: *Hardcore 81*.' A lot of people refer to us as the progenitors of 'Hardcore.' It's true in a way.

And the first strictly Hardcore record? That's open to debate. If you lived on the West Coast, you'd say the "Out Of Vogue" single by Middle Class of Santa Ana, who played in an ultra-fast, monotonal style — two minutes per song max. East Coasters would cite the Bad Brains' legendary "Pay To Cum" 7".

LOU BARLOW (Deep Wound): The Middle Class 7" — I'm convinced that is the first Hardcore record. I got it before I heard Minor Threat. I got the first Meat Puppets 7" too — a whole other side. It resonates deeply to me because it's fierce yet melodic ... a real sense of melody and soul. There were so many weird, cool bands for a while. It was people craving noise.

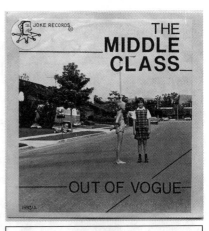

Out Of Vogue
Middle Class single, 1978, Joke
Collection of Sal Canzonieri

JACK RABID (editor, *The Big Takeover*): Anyone who heard 'Pay To Cum' by the Bad Brains had to have a copy. There was nothing like it. Then I heard 'Out Of Vogue' by Middle Class, and around the same time Rhino 39's Dangerhouse single came out. But those groups weren't nearly as good as the Bad Brains. 'Out Of Vogue' may have predated 'Pay To Cum' but it's not all that good — a historical piece, the first of its kind, but it had no impact. Without question, The Germs' album impacted the most. The DC scene owes its entire raison d'être to 'Pay To Cum.'

Rodney On The ROQ

One heard the music of Sham 69, The Germs, Fear, and a host of up-and-coming Hardcore-style outfits on LA Disc jockey Rodney Bingheimer's KROQ Punk/New Wave show, a radical departure from entrenched dinosaur Rock stations like KMET and KLOS. One can't overstate the impact and influence of *Rodney On The ROQ* (Sundays eight 'till midnight) as a cultural lifeline to kids in the boundless LA burbs and as a catalyst for the emerging Hardcore movement.

GREG GRAFFIN (Bad Religion): I discovered *Rodney On The ROQ* in '79. That's how I got into Punk, the real crazy stuff from LA — Middle Class, X, The Dickies, The Weirdos. There were also a lotta forgotten bands like The Gears, good bands from the beach like The Chiefs, our contemporaries like Adolescents. Rodney played other stuff — Dead Boys, Ramones, Buzzcocks and Sham 69. But it was primarily the LA bands that we felt allegiance to, and we were excited to be part of it, so it was our biggest influence.

Flipside

In 1979 the typical Hardcore candidate read *Flipside,* a fanzine out of Whittier, California, 20 miles east of LA. It first appeared in August '77 as a 25-cent, 100-run xeroxed rag documenting LA Punk. By 1980 its coverage expanded to include the entire country, with several thousand copies targeted at those in-the-know. It wasn't a magazine in the traditional sense — rather, a bunch of kids turned on by a scene cranked it out whenever possible. The rumblings of nascent Hardcore fit perfectly into its coverage of acts like Germs and Ramones. *Flipside* scribes with names like Hud, Pooch and X-8 delivered chatty interviews crammed onto the pages in small type accompanying poorly reproduced photos.

AL FLIPSIDE (editor, *Flipside*): It was originally called *Los Angeles Flipside,* intended to be a real local endeavor. Our intention was to carefully cover the LA scene, but we didn't

Flipside magazine #21, December 1980
included with *Rodney On The ROQ Vol. 1*
Rodney Bingheimer, KROQ DJ (holding album),
and Robbie Fields, owner of Posh Boy Records
Collection of the author

have any hard set rules; we just did whatever.

We had no clue what we were doing. I mean, we didn't discover rub-on letters until around the fifth issue. One guy on the staff had worked on a high school newspaper — he kinda had a clue but we just basically patterned it after the English fanzines we'd seen, like *Sniffin' Glue* and *Ripped & Torn* — type it up, xerox it, boom. Then do it again.

The 1980 *Rodney On The ROQ* comp came with a copy of *Flipside* #21. That kicked things off. Within a year came a wave of zines like *The Big Takeover* from NYC, *Ripper* from San Jose and *Maximum RockNRoll* from Berkeley. A grass-roots Hardcore communication network was in the works.

We're just a wrecking crew
Bored boys with nothing to do
— Adolescents, "Wrecking Crew"

Hollywood hipsters were miffed by the rising tide of Hardcore. The music was too fast and too angry. It attracted a younger suburban element that was looking for trouble. A lot of these kids came from beach towns or the heart of Orange County. Those places, safe and boring, spawned angry oufits like Hermosa Beach's Black Flag, Huntington Beach's The Crowd, and Long Beach's Vicious Circle. The meeting ground for "violent surf jocks" circa '79 was The Fleetwood in Redondo Beach. Shows there drew an unsavory audience. Black Flag in particular gained notoriety in the press because the cops would shut down their shows and fuck with their fans.

AL FLIPSIDE: The Fleetwood was a Ralph's supermarket turned into a Rock venue. Some of *The Decline Of Western Civilization* was filmed there. This was around the time when people heard about slamdancing and it was getting really rough and I don't think a lot of the original Hollywood arty people appreciated that. If you had long hair and went to The Fleetwood, you pretty much got beat down. There were gangs beating people, every song. It got nasty for a while. It changed a lot of people's attitude about Hardcore.

JELLO BIAFRA (Dead Kennedys): It was clear that the new vanguard in Southern California had come from outside of Hollywood. It was no longer people who met in art school or who had entertainment industry people for parents. This was a totally different scene, and the Hollywood people made the mistake of shunning it initially. It became antagonistic at first and a lot of those bad vibes remained for the wrong reasons. Namely, some of the people that came into the scene were violent jocks pure and simple, and they brought a real intolerant macho element into the scene.

JACK GRISHAM (TSOL): Hollywood Punks were bummed because a lot of us were 'surfer jocks.' A lot of us did play sports. Hollywood guys were heavier into drugs — we were corn-fed beer kids. Everybody in TSOL was like six-three, six-four — big people. We'd come up and things'd get out of hand. We were more into busting windows and setting the club on fire.

MIKE NESS (Social Distortion): We liked to fight, you know? I remember telling this guy who looked like Adam Ant that I was gonna stick a Les Paul up his ass. That was the older crowd and we were the testosterone crowd.

> *We're just gonna skate*
> *Till the day we die*
> — Gang Green, "Skate To Hell"

Hardcore and skateboarding went together. Both were anti-establishment and home-grown. Both came out of Southern California youth culture.

Asphalt schoolyards and the long, winding roads of housing developments provided early skate-scene meeting places. "Skateparks" appeared — concrete monstrosities of pipes and curves monitored by lifeguard-like assholes anxious to throw out troublemakers. *SkateBoarder* magazine, an offshoot of *Surfer,* was a favorite of aspiring skaters. The mag tended to portray the sport in a clean-cut way. Its earliest coverage focused on the area around San Diego.

Defying the rigidity of skatepark rules, rad outlaw skaters like Tony Alva, Steve Caballero, and Jim Muir (older brother of Suicidal Tendencies' Mike Muir) hit the scene. Writer C.R. Stecyk III and photographer Glen E. Friedman documented

Skateboarding art: Show flyer for Poison Idea and The Fartz at The Met in Portland, Oregon, 1982
Graphics by Henry
Collection of Laura Albert

the streetwise kids of Santa Monica, Venice and West LA making extreme statements on skateboards displaying gnarly art and graffiti. According to local lore, Venice — due to urban blight in the 60s — had "gone to the dogs." Stecyk referred to its skaters as coming from "DogTown." The DogTown vibe influenced rebellious kids nationwide.

IAN MACKAYE (Minor Threat): We read about DogTown and said, 'That's us.' We thought we were a gang, so it made sense Venice skateboarding would appeal to us the most. We wanted to be like them.

TIM KERR (Big Boys): In Texas the early skate scene was considered DogTown. We heard how Tony Alva had his hair green and we loved it. Skateboarding wasn't as much a jock thing as it became. It was a lot of people like me who weren't able to surf — so we skated. A lot of people who grew up in Austin found *SkateBoarder* and started getting into it.

SkateBoarder changed its name in 1980 to *SkateBoarder's Action Now,* then *Action Now,* and expanded coverage into rollerskating, surfing and bike riding. It folded in 1982.

Next came the SF-based *Thrasher*, combining coverage of skate culture and Hardcore. Hitting the stands in '81, it featured the work of Stecyk, Friedman and Brian "Pushead" Schroeder. Pushead was the music editor; his influential HC/Metal column "Puszone" brought the word to kids in far-flung places. J.F.A. vocalist Brian Brannon emerged as an editorial presence. Jake Phelps of the Boston crew followed soon thereafter.

Thrasher promoted a sub-scene devoted to skateboarding — "Skatecore." Some line-ups included big-league skaters — The Scoundrels with Tony Alva, The Joneses with Steve Olsen, The Faction with Steve Caballero, McRad (from Philly) with Chuck Treece, and Duane Peters' outfits (most notably Political Crap). Some Hardcore outfits embraced skateboarding as a philosophy — Big Boys (from Austin), J.F.A. (Phoenix), Gang Green (Boston), Ill Repute and Agression (Oxnard, CA), and Drunk Injuns and Free Beer (Bay Area). Such smart-ass Skatecore outfits exclaimed the rallying cry "Skate or Die!"

BRIAN BRANNON (J.F.A.): On tour, we would never do a soundcheck because we would be cruising around checking out places to skate in every town. We could give a fuck about the soundcheck. For us, it was about doing whatever we felt like because we felt like doing it.

Skateboarding was the only sport that could get you arrested. Delinquents on wheels whizzed down streets, ramps, empty swimming pools — any surface that facilitated anti-gravitational action. Street riders flirted with danger. If they weren't getting hit by cars or breaking their bones in bad spills, cops were nailing them for "trespassing" or "reckless endangerment." Skateboarding spoke volumes about who you were and what music you dug and, most importantly, it said "fuck you" to all.

Flyer depicting President Ronald Reagan and wife Nancy in a nuclear armageddon motif
Collection of Laura Albert

America, land of the free
Freedom and power to the people in uniform
— TSOL, "Abolish Government"

Ronald Reagan, another product of Southern California, won the presidency in 1980. He was the galvanizing force of Hardcore — an enemy of the arts, minorities, women, gays, liberals, the homeless, the working man, the inner city, et cetera. All "outsiders" could agree they hated him.

WINSTON SMITH (graphic artist): Ronald Reagan was a catalyst for the Hardcore scene. Music and art changed radically from '81 to '86 — when Reagan was in his prime. People who were asleep up until then suddenly had their eyes opened. The attitude was, 'Go down fighting if we had to lose, but don't let them get away with it.' I think that had a lot to do with the music — utter rage against what was going in the world.

TAD KEPLEY (Anarchist activist): Reagan said more than once that as a Fundamentalist he believed explicitly in the Book of Revelations. It was a really fuckin' scary time.

By 1982 — the apex of the HC era — Reaganomics dominated. America experienced a recession. Steel and auto factory closings impacted everyday life. Sharp price increases and rampant real estate speculation began. But nothing gets a kick-ass music scene going like repression coupled with recession.

I took a chance on the other side
Got off the downhill slide
Stopped wastin' my time
— **D.O.A., "Woke Up Screaming"**

Across America similar sentiments brewed.
A handful of bands segued into the Southern
California Hardcore sound and style, most
notably Dead Kennedys (SF), Bad Brains (DC),
and D.O.A. (Vancouver).

JOEY SHITHEAD (D.O.A.): A lot of people got
their definition of Punk from The Clash and The
Damned. When the Hardcore thing happened in
1980, it defined a different form of Punk. We played
with The Clash and thought they were wimps.

When Adam Ant was all the rage, there was a
Black Flag show at The Whiskey and an Adam Ant
show up the street from it — all these Black Flag
fans had shirts that said 'Black Flag kills Ants dead.'
That's where we were coming from.

IAN MACKAYE (Minor Threat): We wanted to
have our own clique. We wanted to create our own
culture because we didn't feel connected to anything.
Here was the perfect opportunity for that. You were
instantly devoted to others around you. This was the

Typical proto-Hardcore kid backstage
at the Whiskey-A-Go-Go, 1980
Photo by Edward Colver

first time Rock Music was being written by, performed by, shows being put on by, fanzines
being put out by, networks being created — all by kids, completely outside of the mainstream
music business, for reasons that had very little or nothing to do with economic incentive. It
was a really important time in music history because music actually rose above business; as
you know, music has always been a really insidious marriage of art and business. •

WORLD FULL OF HATE

Violence, does it make any sense?
Violence, can you stop it?
Violence, do you want to?
— **Youth Brigade, "Violence"**

JACK GRISHAM (TSOL): I always thought getting hurt at shows was healthy, because you knew you were having as much fun as possible.

Hardcore's tribalism demanded a new dance. Audience physicality created what became known as slamdancing.

Slamdancing developed in Southern California towns like Huntington Beach and Long Beach. According to lore, Mike Marine, former US Marine and star of *The Decline...*, performed the first slamdance in 1979. Marine created a vicious version of Punk dancing. He'd smash the fucking face of anyone who would get near him — especially some Hippie, who'd get pulverized. Kids referred to it as "The Huntington Beach Strut" or "The HB Strut" — strutting around in a circle, swinging your arms around and hitting everyone within your reach. Slamdancing was significant because it separated the kids from the posers and adults.

Jimmy Gestapo (Murphy's Law) and John Watson (Agnostic Front) doing The HB Strut, A7, NYC, 1982
Photo by Karen O'Sullivan

LEE VING (Fear): Right around the time of our first album, around '81, it changed from the pogo bullshit into the real slam stuff. Pogoing was just jumping up and down. It was less interactive, more benign. The focus changed from Hollywood toward the beaches, and the idea of speed and the slam pit had its birth. We started playing as fast as you could fucking think and the crowd would go as berserk, pounding the shit out of each other in the pit. It was good sportsmanship and all about working up a good sweat.

Stagediving and slamdancing were cool, but a lot of kids hurt themselves. There were broken bones, cracked skulls and bloody gashes either from falling down or as the result of a dancefloor encounter with participants looking for trouble in a hooligan kind of way.

RAY FARRELL (SST Records): Hardcore made it more like a sporting event than music — with like the worst jocks you've ever seen. It excluded women. It became exclusionary only because it was violent — people couldn't handle the physicality. Punk dancing was pretty safe, more communal, almost kinda retarded. With Hardcore, there were a lot more boots flying in the air than tennis shoes — a real aggressive connotation to it. It replaced the arty stuff with an injection of extreme energy, to the point where being a faster band was the equivalent of playing a faster guitar solo in the 70s.

HARLEY FLANAGAN (Cro-Mags): If you weren't down with the people on the scene, went out on the floor and accidentally hit somebody who was down with everybody, you'd get your ass beat. But despite all the alleged violence, most of it was just talk. There were very few instances where people got hurt. Usually, when they did, they had it coming some way or another. When the shit did hit the fan, I was usually one of the active participants. But it was never like there were all these wars in the scene. It wasn't as big as people make it up to be.

Hardcore implied danger and it dabbled in bad shit — making it truly attractive. Hate is easy to harness; you can get into it right away. HC was an incredibly competitive milieu. Everyone talked unity but the scene dripped with division and rivalry and conflict.

PAT DUBAR (Uniform Choice): In the early days there was much more of a community, and much less violence. As soon as everybody started talking this unity shit it all became about segregation. It was twisted all the way down to the way people moved to the music. There was a lot more chaos involved — but it seemed that there was a lot less harm done than when there was more organization and cliques. It got stupid, basically.

There isn't room
For people like me
My life is their disease
— Black Flag, "Spray Paint The Walls"

Members of the Hardcore tribe invited conflict with their confrontational dress and attitudes. If outsiders fucked with them for the way they dressed, it was a badge of honor worth defending.

IAN MACKAYE (Minor Threat): We'd get this hair spray and paint a skunk stripe down the middle of our heads, go to a Roy Rogers and illicit such ugliness that we knew we were onto

Stagediving in LA, 1981
Photo by Edward Colver

something really fucking good. Violence was suddenly such a predicament because everyone wanted to beat the shit out of you — and for what? We were impeccably honest people. We didn't steal. We got into a lot of fights but weren't little assholes. But our appearance was so offensive to people that it made us realize how disgusting the mainstream was, and we were glad to be outside of it. The violence was born of what was going on in this country — things were so dumbed down, to take a position that flew in the face of what was accepted immediately branded you as a fag.

GREG GRAFFIN (Bad Religion): It was incredibly violent for me to go to school every day. Being into Hardcore was a huge threat to them back then for some reason. Maybe they bought into the 'anarchy' element and it scared them, maybe they believed it was a communist plot or nazis returning — who knows? There was such hostility that anyone who wanted to sympathize was afraid to be outwardly supportive.

DANNY SAGE (Heart Attack): It was so not hip to be Hardcore. Guys at school wanted to kill you. It was even beyond liking the Sex Pistols — it was something totally foreign. People didn't know Germs or Circle Jerks or Black Flag. People'd always come up to you in the hall and ask stupid questions: 'Why is your hair cut like that? Why is there a piece of cloth on your motorcycle boots? What does it mean?' It was a big deal.

TOM PRICE (U-Men): I had short hair and a Ramones t-shirt. I'd get physically attacked every day without fail. It was just your standard shit: a Camaro drives up when you're waiting at the bus stop, a bunch of guys yell 'Faggot!' and throw full beer cans at your head. Being an obnoxious Punker, I'd either ignore 'em or yell, 'Fuck you!' Then I'd get the shit

pounded out of me. I'd get stomped all the time. We'd have these houses, and that was where all the local Hardcore kids hung out — and it was routine on the weekend for the house to be totally besieged by frat boys. It would get really violent, people'd get beat up bad — the cops never came to our aid. It was a street war for a while. People had a real violent reaction.

IAN MACKAYE: It was completely violent, to the point where you'd walk down the street and suddenly be chased by hillbillies calling you 'Faggot!' and beating the shit out of you. There was a Georgetown gang called The Punkbeaters, who'd beat up lone Punk Rockers. These were Black and Hispanic kids, although we had plenty of problems with grits — hillbillies. We'd take my brother, who was 14 at the time, and have him walk down the street in Georgetown, and there'd be like ten of us a block behind him, trying to find these kids.

BRIAN BRANNON (J.F.A.): You had to fight against jocks. Even though DEVO had already been out five years they'd say, 'Whip it, man!' One time I wore a shirt that said 'Jocks Suck' in six-inch-high letters to school — as soon as I stepped on campus I could feel all these eyes on me. I knew the jocks were going to mount a charge but tried to play it cool. I

Kenny Ahrens (Urban Waste), looking for trouble on the dancefloor, A7, NYC, 1982
Photo by Fred Berger

had to walk through the cafeteria, past this big Mexican football player, Taco. I was a freshman, he was a senior. He came after me. I walked faster but wasn't gonna run. I almost made it out — a hand reached out and grabbed me back. He let me go with a warning but when I went to lunch later, the whole football team surrounded me. They pushed me around, hit me a few times, lined up to punch me. The first guy didn't punch me that hard but I started hamming it up like, 'You hurt me, I'm gonna die' and got out of it. I was writhing on the ground and they got scared and ran away.

JACK GRISHAM (TSOL): Colored hair was a fucking commitment. Now it's cute, but at that time there was nothing cute about it. Where I lived, there were constant fights going on. It was a big deal to go to the liquor store. You knew you were going to have to fight outside the liquor store to get back home. You had to fight everybody. You're fighting jocks, fighting Hippies — everybody hated you. There was a lot of shit. I don't remember how many times I had to hide from people who wanted to kill me. I mean actual attempts. One time, they sabotaged my car and my car blew up. They cut my gas line.

MIKE NESS (Social Distortion): Where we lived in Southern California, if you walked down the street with a leather jacket and dyed red hair, you were making a decision to get into some sort of confrontation. We were 17 and 18 and there was a generation of 25-year-old Hippies that didn't want this to happen. There were also angry parents, construction workers; they'd drive by and yell 'Faggot!' — we'd flip 'em off and they'd turn around and come back and we'd fight. Back then, you'd see another Punk Rocker from another area and you'd say, 'How you doin'? Where you from?' Then of course it got bigger and Punks would fight with Punks.

TONY CADENA (Adolescents): There was a fight that was so bloody that we couldn't play parties anymore. There were two parties in the same neighborhood. One we were playing; the other had a Van Halen cover band. The two parties clashed in the street. Somebody got cut with a boxcutter, somebody was hit over the head with an ax handle — people hitting each other with baseball bats — when we played, things like this happened.

MARK STERN (Youth Brigade): We went to beat up fucking security people, especially in the old days at The Starwood in LA. They were such assholes. If you danced, dove off the stage, or did anything they didn't like, these big no-neck guys would just throw you out and fuck you up. We'd get so sick of it, we'd wait outside for one — when somebody was throwing a kid

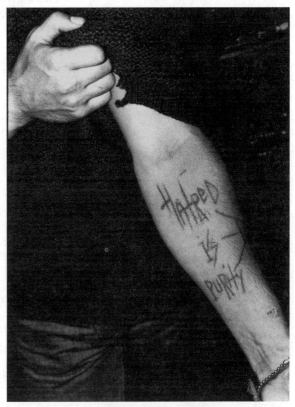

Hatred Is Purity, 1981
Photo by Edward Colver

out by himself, we'd grab him and jump him and beat his ass. We threw a lot of bottles at police back then, too. The violence between Punks was usually pretty rare. In general, the scene was unified in that the violence was projected against those who were against us.

JIMMY GESTAPO (Murphy's Law): Everybody got beat down so much for being Punk Rock that they became Hardcore. We got beat into Hardcore. It was fun running around with spiked hair and bondage belt, but I got beat into shaving my head, putting boots on, and arming myself with a chain belt. I evolved my fashion statement into a function. That's what everyone around me did. I hooked up with my new buddy, Harley. After being beat up for so long, we were ready — eight-ball in a sock, chain belt, knife — whatever. Anybody who said anything to us about the way we looked got wrecked.

HARLEY FLANAGAN: I used to like beating up English people; I thought they had real pompous attitudes. I just didn't like 'em. If somebody walked down to the neighborhood, the East Village, I felt, 'I'm not gonna let every fuckin' bozo come into my backyard.' I'd walk around and get into fights because I was this fucked-up kid. I was into whacking people in the head with a cueball. I was a product of my environment. •

STRAIGHT EDGE

Don't smoke
Don't drink
Don't fuck
At least I can fucking think
— Minor Threat, "Out Of Step"

IAN MACKAYE (Minor Threat): The reaction we got for being straight was so contemptuous, we couldn't believe it. We thought being straight was just like being another type of deviant in this community, just like junkies. I didn't realize it was gonna upset the applecart so much — the reaction we got made us up the ante. That's when I realized, 'Man, I'm saying shit, and people are getting angry. This is really effective.'

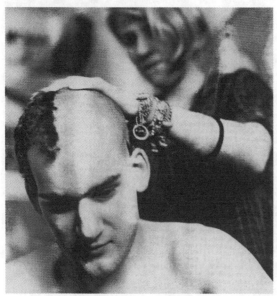

Ian MacKaye (Minor Threat),
the original proponent of Straight Edge.
Xerox copy, origin unknown
Collection of Laura Albert

The song "Straight Edge" inspired the movement known by that name. Straight Edge types set themselves apart from the drunks and drug casualties encountered in school, in Rock Culture, and in everyday life.

At the dawn of Hardcore, drugs were cheap and plentiful. Not groovy drugs like pot and acid — the scene sneered at anything linked to the Hippie legacy — but shit like bootleg Quaaludes (or "714s"), stepped-on cocaine, angel dust (PCP) and so-called "Black Beauties."

Even with the rise of Straight Edge, plenty of Hardcore kids were getting zonked on illegal intoxicants. California and Philly offered easily available crystal meth. Coke was everywhere; groups like TSOL and Gang Green indulged legendarily. New York kids liked angel dust — i.e. PCP. The effect of all this shit on the music lies at the core of Hardcore mythology. Neurological damage only added to the general dementia and intensity.

In one area HC didn't depart from its predecessors: beer abounded — every Rock scene drinks from the same corporate trough.

STEVE DEPACE (Flipper): Speed was the drug of choice for Punk Rockers. It was cheap, it was around, and you could play fast music on it. It also curtailed your appetite. In San Francisco, the Negative Trend guys literally lived on potatoes. The heroin bands just didn't go too far.

BARRY HENNSLER (Necros): We would get roaring drunk at my house and take really bad speed and go crazy on weekends. Straight Edge is cool, but I thought it was one more reason to be a snob. I always hated the cliquish mentality of that shit.

Drugs are part of Rock's psycho-social history — in fact drugs are the star of the show. Straight Edge reacted to that. But don't confuse Straight Edge with sobriety. Drugs set the agenda. It's similar to NA meetings or the DARE program.

One of the most common character types encountered in the Hardcore universe was the guy who was half Straight-Edge, half on-drugs — depending on who was around — and looking to advance either agenda, by violence if necessary.

Straight Edge militancy came out of Ian MacKaye and Boston scene icon Al Barile of SS Decontrol. Ian MacKaye wrote "Straight Edge." Inspired, Barile raised the ante.

AL BARILE (SS Decontrol): The Minor Threat song 'Straight Edge' — I went off on it. I saw all these kids from DC and they were all straight — well, who knows who was straight, who wasn't. These kids seemed to be having a good time and they weren't drinking. That really shocked me. I was still drinking, but out of habit. From that time, I questioned why I was still partying.

I took the message — every song I wrote was about Straight Edge; I was taking it to the next level. At one point I know Minor Threat was sick of talking about it. I went off on the concept — maybe overboard. I just felt that it was an important message; to me it was about enjoying life without being fucked up.

> *Get all your drugs away from me!*
> *Get all those drugs away from me!*
> — SS Decontrol, "Get It Away"

Al Barile (SS Decontrol),1982
Straight Edge rabble-rouser
Photo by Karen O'Sullivan

PAT DUBAR (Uniform Choice): Straight Edge spoke to me because of my total hatred towards the drinking and 'being stupid' environment I encountered in high school. I was never anti-sex or anti-booze. We were really anti-obsession because that's all I saw from people around me — obsession with god, religion, money, drugs, alcohol. All this shit to me was meaningless. It's what pissed me off the most. These people were nothing that I wanted to be about. My reaction was to use everything in my power to tell everyone what was up.

Back when I was a lot more violent, I had this thing — anytime anybody fucked with me when they were drunk, I would hit 'em. I felt, 'Just 'cause you drink doesn't give you license to be a fucking asshole.' Most people still think being drunk is an excuse, but, hey, you're bringing that reality on me, and I'm not a drunk, asshole. I'm not getting in your space, and I'm not interfering with your freedom or your path.

DAVE SMALLEY (DYS, Dag Nasty): We were pretty violent. In hindsight, that's one thing I regret about the past — we were aggressive towards non-Straight Edge people. We hated the stoners and the drinkers in high school so much.

In the wake of Minor Threat and SS Decontrol (eventually known as SSD), by the mid-80s there emerged several true Straight Edge bands — Uniform Choice and Youth Of Today the best examples. That faction of the scene reaffirmed HC "values" by resisting the influx of dumb-ass Metal kids, by avoiding drugs, alcohol, and sex, and by keeping it tediously "real."

Show flyer for SS Decontrol show,
The Club, Cambridge, MA, 1981.
The band promoted Hardcore unity among
Straight Edge types.
Collection of the author

Reaction to Straight Edge within the larger Hardcore scene was predictable. Many kids said fuck-you to the aggressive correctness. Beer-driven songs by Black Flag ("TV Party"), DOA ("Let's Wreck The Party") and Fear ("More Beer") fueled contrarian attitudes against HC's rebellion-within-a-rebellion. Gang Green introduced an ode to excess, "Alcohol."

You got the beer
We got the time
You got the coke
Gimme a line
— Gang Green, "Alcohol"

JACK GRISHAM (TSOL): There was that Straight Edge thing going on, and we were a bunch of beer-drinking fuckholes. We weren't going to be Straight Edge — and if someone says Punk Rock is 'this,' we're gonna say it's 'that.' We were all Skinheads, but Skinheads were starting to become acceptable, so we decided, 'Okay, we'll grow our hair long and hang out with the Punks. We're longhairs and we drink beer and we like to have sex' — and they really bummed on us. With the Straight Edge, it was 'Let's keep our heads straight, let's keep our thoughts straight.' But anytime you mix that with fascism, it defeats itself.

IAN MACKAYE: For people with a tendency to veer to fundamentalism, Straight Edge is a perfect vehicle. But for people who are healthy-minded, it's also worked out well. I think people have done good things with it. And some dumb shit, too. The only thing more ridiculous than a Straight Edge movement is a movement against Straight Edge. What a stupid pastime.

Face it, nothing's wrong with either doing or not doing drugs. Little difference exists between Straight Edge dogma and drugged buffoonery. But to define oneself exclusively in such terms is totally passé. Somewhere along the way, Straight Edge evolved into a mean-spirited, super-strict form of morality in Hardcore's temple of doom.

MIKE GITTER (editor, *XXX*): Hardcore was a rebellion of affluence, mired in suburbia. It was a safer rejection of values. Straight Edge was a declaration of anti-stupidity. It was being an intelligent misfit; it was a positive form of rebellion — it had

Pat Dubar (Uniform Choice), 1984
Straight Edge zealot.
Uncredited photo courtesy of Pat Dubar

nothing to do with nihilism. There was nothing apocalyptic about it. There was no 'We gotta get out of this place so let's burn it to the ground.' I mean, how can you be nihilistic when your college education's paid for and you're looking at taking a position at daddy's firm. It's interesting how a strict puritanical moral code transformed itself into this form of rebellion.

DAVE SMALLEY: There's an old Japanese saying: 'He who is not a radical at 20 has no heart, and he who is still a radical at 40 has no head.' So when you're 17 years old, you're at your most extreme.

We were taking on a value system that everyone around us hated: no drinking, no drugs, almost a Christian kinda life — but at the same time, spitting on society, saying 'Fuck You' to the cops. Kids reacted well to that; everyone hated society as much as we did — everyone had seen their friends burn out on drugs and booze.

The Straight Edge scene was testosterone-fueled — and the "don't drink, don't smoke, don't fuck" ethos essentially assured an all-boy audience.

Members of Gang Green with cocaine, 1983
This is what Straight Edge types despised.
Photo courtesy of Taang! Records

HOLLY RAMOS (NYHC scene): Straight Edge was definitely a cover for guys not wanting to have sex with girls, because they didn't really like girls. That's why I had no time for anything to do with Straight Edge. There was nothing in it for me. •

GUILTY OF BEING WHITE

I'm sorry for something I didn't do
Lynched somebody but I don't know who
You blame me for slavery
A hundred years before I was born
— Minor Threat, "Guilty Of Being White"

Fucked-up but intelligent White kids populated the Hardcore scene. Their legacy included the Cold War, inflation, industrial decline, post-Vietnam trauma, shitty music, bad cops and racial turmoil. They suffered from depression, alienation, and frustration. Some were do-gooders who resented their own relatively high socioeconomic status or harbored guilt over their forebearers' racism. Others seethed with hatred for the outsiders stealing jobs and ruining neighborhoods. Real or imagined, that was the vibe.

Many of those kids turned against themselves as well as others. They craved self-destruction, often committing violence against their own bodies.

TAD KEPLEY (Anarchist activist): Many in the scene didn't like themselves very much. All these people were very authentic in their anger and sense of alienation; you never knew what they were gonna do about it. A lot of these people either drank themselves to death or shot themselves or doped themselves up to the point where they're ineffectual.

Themes of race politics and class warfare dominated Hardcore. Black Flag's "White Minority" and Minor Threat's "Guilty Of Being White" served as anthems of the day. What other Rock genre had such balls?

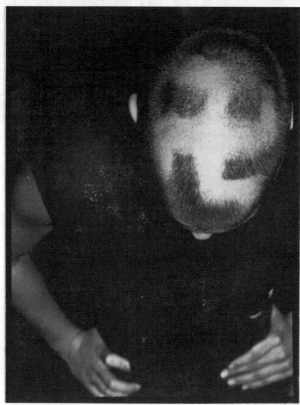

Swastika shaved into a Hardcore head, 1981
Photo by Edward Colver

IAN MACKAYE (Minor Threat): 'Guilty Of Being White' was a song I wrote growing up in DC, being part of the minority — the White population. It drove me crazy — people would beat the shit out of me or rob me 'cause I was White. We had a history class talking about slavery and after class a couple of guys just knocked the shit out of me. It was right around the time *Roots* was on. I got beat up because I was the 'massa.' People were judging me on the color of my skin, so I wrote what I thought was a really direct anti-racist song — I wanted to say something radical. With any of these songs, I wanted to take a strong position. I didn't think anybody outside DC would ever hear this song. It's weird for me to go to Poland and hear kids say, 'Guilty Of Being White is a very good song. We are White

Power.' It played totally different in other contexts. Slayer covered it and changed the last line to 'guilty of being *right.*' It's so offensive to me.

> *Gonna be a White minority*
> *All the rest will be the majority*
> *Gonna feel inferiority*
> — Black Flag, "White Minority"

The rise of Hardcore coincided with the rise of Skinhead culture. In some ways the scenes overlapped. Edgier HC types adopted Skinhead style. A shaved head provided the perfect fuck-you to Hippies and businessmen alike — not to mention moms and dads. The important thing was shock value.

Politically speaking, many HC kids leaned to the Left, but the Right claimed its share of adherents. In other words, Hardcore Skinheads came in two varieties: racist lunkheads and anti-racist lunkheads. Very few embraced the style and remained unfazed by the politics. Some racists' hatred was heartfelt; for others it was just another confrontational tool. The same was true of anti-racists.

JOHN KEZDY (The Effigies): Skinheads cropped up for many different reasons. In California, the Skinhead thing was a surfer thing. Ultimately, what bound all forms of Skinheads is — and I know this will be taken the wrong way — a very male sense of Rock.

The Hardcore-Skinhead connection inspires much debate. Sure, many kids shaved their heads and held threatening Left- or Right-Wing opinions, but that often reflected youthful anti-social inclinations more than coherent racialist doctrine. HC knuckleheads went to shows to beat up other White kids.

Jello Biafra (Dead Kennedys) convinced his fans that nazis and racists were overtaking the scene.
Photo by Edward Colver

> *Ten guys jump one, what a man*
> *You fight each other, the police state wins*
> *Stab your backs when you trash our halls*
> *Trash a bank if you've got real balls*
> — Dead Kennedys, "Nazi Punks Fuck Off"

Jello Biafra sang of such violence on Dead Kennedys' seminal single, "Nazi Punks Fuck Off."

JELLO BIAFRA (Dead Kennedys): 'Nazi Punks Fuck Off' compared goony Surf Punks and jocks to nazis — 'That's what you act like, fuck you.' So many cool people were leaving the Punk underground because they saw somebody jump off the stage to punch people in the back of the head. Some of these people were built like linebackers — they knew how to cold-cock somebody, and they did it for fun. I had to let people know Dead Kennedys wasn't down with the assholes. There was a lot of violence directed towards me and the band because of that song.

That song, perhaps more than any other in the Hardcore vein, served as a lightening rod for controversy.

TAD KEPLEY: It was a boogieman guys like Biafra had thrown out. You have people who do this on the Left constantly. A lot had to do with the scene that guys like [*Maximum RockNRoll's*] Tim Yohannon came out of. They see nazis coming out of the woodwork, when there are none. That's what they do to occupy their time. It wasn't until the mid 80s that I did see a lot of Right Wing politics pop up in the scene; around '85 was when a big Skinhead explosion took place. Early on, I didn't see all these nazis — I always thought the more immediate threat were police and metalheads and jocks.

JELLO BIAFRA: A lot of nazi Punks came into the scene via Agnostic Front, Cro-Mags and their corporate financial backers. I don't think New York has ever recovered from that. You still hear of people winding up at the hospital for going to a Hardcore show at CBGB. The same goes for those giant LA shows. Any subculture with such a fiery reactionary feel is bound to attract reactionaries from all sides.

Contrary to what some people say, there were not hordes of goose-stepping Skinheads at Hardcore shows. But a lot of kids who read about that would emulate Skinhead behavior. There arose such hysteria over a perceived problem that, by the mid 80s, there became one.

MICHAEL ALAGO (music biz exec): Skinheads were kinda scary to me, unless they were cute. Back then, I was absolutely fearless. I loved nasty, tattooed Hardcore boys, and lots of them were filled with so much testosterone that I don't think a lot of them cared whether they got a blow job or had sex with a guy or a girl. So, those Skinheads coming to the scene? I just thought it was sexy. I didn't think about politics. I had my own agenda.

> *No war*
> *No KKK*
> *No fascist USA*
> *— MDC, "Born To Die"*

A lot of the sloganeering that influenced Hardcore came from the Berkeley-based zine *Maximum RockNRoll* and its 40-something Yippie editor, the late Tim Yohannon. *MRR* was an excellent publication that offered comprehensive coverage of the burgeoning national scene, but it quickly got bogged down in brow-beating its young impressionable audience. Yohannon and crew found their boogiemen, and spent endless pages decrying alleged Right-Wingers like The FU's from Boston, Murphy's Law and Agnostic Front in New York, and White Pride from St. Louis.

Top: Zine ad for *Maximum RockNRoll* syndicated radio show, 1981; Bottom: *Maximum RockNRoll* Volume 1, Issue 1, Berkeley, CA, 1982
Collection of the author

RAY FARRELL (SST): Tim Yohannon was a Yippie, aggressively involved in demonstrations, like a lot of people of his age. As Hardcore developed there was an ideological development at *Maximum RockNRoll*, making everything move towards a

Socialist bent. In a way, it's really a continuation of the Yippie movement finding another generation to work with. I think Tim was realizing the aggression of the music and the rejection of society had to step up a bit in terms of its anger, and I think he saw an opportunity for this music and his politics to work together.

DAVE SMALLEY (DYS, Dag Nasty): *Maximum RockNRoll* are fucking idiots. They're fascists of the Left. They turned from something cool — this unifying factor — to this horrible, hate-mongering, isolationist, Left-Wing fascist magazine.

JIMMY GESTAPO (Murphy's Law): There was never a nazi scene in NY early on. *Maximum RockNRoll* hated New York. *Maximum RockNRoll* is fascist yellow journalism.

Hardcore Skinhead pile-on outside CBGB, NYC, 1983
Photo by Karen O'Sullivan

> *Some people look at me
> and talk about me like a clown
> Don't they realize
> it's just my simple way to get down?*
> — Bad Brains, "Supertouch"

Despite its overwhelmingly White demographic and the starkness of its racial politics, Hardcore received important infusions from a few Black kids — most notably the Bad Brains, who were to Hardcore what Hendrix was to Psychedelia; DKs drummer DH Peligro, Skeeter Thompson of Scream, Eugene Robinson from Whipping Boy, Chuck Treece of the Philly skate band McRad, and Sam of Impact Unit (in which The Mighty Mighty Bosstones' Dickie Barrett also played). Their participation testifies to some of Hardcore's better attributes.

D.H. PELIGRO (Dead Kennedys): Being Black and being in Hardcore — I felt I had a fucked-up life and have more reason to be Hardcore than any of these fucking kids. I had it rough. I had two strikes against me every time I stepped out the door. I had to just watch my p's and q's.
I wound up getting arrested in a lot of places. I remember playing in Australia and a Skinhead is yelling, Blacks in the back! while he's waiting in line for the show. Skinheads would be chasing me screaming, Ace of spades! which was one of their anthems. Because there were no pictures on the record, people didn't know what I looked like, didn't know if I was Black or White or what. People kinda tripped when they saw me. A lot of people accepted me and a lot of people had their own twisted views of what I should or shouldn't be. You get in trouble and get fucked with because you're Black, but you might get some of that Rock Star treatment in another sense.

PETE STAHL (Scream): Having Skeeter in the band, we'd have to deal with some asshole in the crowd yelling 'nigger.' But that gave us the opportunity to stand up and say something about it. In a scene that was definitely segregated, we were a statement against that mentality. We'd confront them from the get-go. •

BOYS IN THE BRIGADE

I'm bored of the sleazy make-up
You'd fuck any guy in town
Your life's a total mess-up
Why the hell do you hang around?
— Adolescents, "L.A. Girl"

Hardcore's male-dominated subculture
Mudd Club, NYC, 1982
Photo by Fred Berger

Hardcore was the first Rock Music that sexuality did not drive — for many, it was a relief, like, "Look, I'm not getting laid anyway, so why should I listen to music that says I'm gonna?" If anything, most participants were raging asexuals. Shows didn't end in orgies like psychedelic love-ins, nor were they pick-up scenes — instead they ended in a "pig pile" or a brawl. I'm hard-pressed to remember many women being present.

IAN MACKAYE (Minor Threat): I wasn't anti-sex, but if everybody spent all their time trying to get laid we'd never be able to build anything. I was interested in trying to create a culture. Sex was a diversion every teen did, so I thought it was stupid. It ties into the whole Straight Edge thing. Drinking, every normal teenage kid does; I didn't want to be normal. Groupies were Rock & Roll. Fuck that — it had nothing to do with me.

Hardcore boys saw girls as outsiders, even distractions. Chicks got their best shot at acceptance as photographers, DJs or zine editors. Of course, on the scene's periphery lurked plenty of stereotypical skanks who guys mistreated and/or sponged off.

MEREDITH OSBORNE (LA scene): The Hardcore scene was very adolescent, and teen boys are scared of women. In the Punk days, you could fuck whomever and it didn't matter, but in Hardcore that madonna/whore complex was much stronger. Hardcore guys would vilify girls they fucked.

LAURA ALBERT (NYHC scene): The role of women in the scene was as the sexual outlet or as something that hung on the arm and stood on the side. Women weren't welcome in the mosh pit; girls who did mosh — that was some weird tomboy thing. You weren't welcome in the bands. Girls didn't welcome each other, either; there was no camaraderie. The only thing you could really offer was sex. It pissed me off that I had to do it, but I was also grateful for it 'cause I got in there in a good way. I wanted that power, too, so I learned to play the game. I did what I had to.

HOLLY RAMOS (NYHC scene): It was a real guy thing; I think it was a real gay thing, too. Girls weren't involved whatsoever in bands. The appeal of Hardcore was as a high school for dysfunctional kids. There was that whole male bonding/sweating/being-naked/doing-that-dancing going on.

LAURA ALBERT: I was always aware of this very male sexual energy going on, and since I wasn't a boy, I couldn't be a part of it. I wanted something from these people but I knew I didn't want to actually have sex with them. I had this feeling that I would've gotten more if I was a boy.

Most Hardcore chicks rejected femininity. Their ideal was the tomboy — in contrast to the big-haired bitches you'd find sucking dick backstage at Metal concerts. The truth is, few gorgeous women participated in Hardcore — many of them were nasty, ugly trolls.

MARIA MA (Raleigh scene): If you were a girl and acted a certain way that the guys could deal with — like you were asexual and you got in the pit and stagedived and knew the music — they could accept you. On the flipside of that, if you wore lots of makeup and leather minis, they could deal with that, too. The girls in DC were clean, whereas the New York girls were into scrungy fishnets and stuff. Then you'd have those Hardcore dykes, who I associated with San Francisco.

Unidentified chicks at Hardcore shows
Top: Photo by Fred Berger
Bottom: Photo by Karen O'Sullivan

CYNTHIA CONNELLY (author, *Banned In DC*): We were big into Hardcore. I had a really great time, at least for a while. But when moshing became violent and extremely masculine, there was nothing funny about it. I hated going to shows when it became so violent and insane. As it got more and more Hardcore I got more and more disinterested. By '83, I was 100% disinterested. Most women I knew bailed.

Why did Hardcore, allegedly open-minded and egalitarian, involve so few women? And is it politically correct to write women into the history, to pretend they had an active voice, when in truth they didn't?

IAN MACKAYE (Minor Threat): You can say it was total misogyny, or that here were these boys who forced an issue and made it possible for an era where more women are in bands than ever before. If you walk into a show now and see a band with three women and a boy, do you even think twice about it? No! So shoot some props out to the Hardcore kids.

Like Hardcore itself, chicks earned respect through sheer force of will. Kira Roessler of Black Flag was a role model for many, just for surviving hellacious touring conditions. The few all-girl groups — The Wrecks (Reno), Frightwig (SF), Mydolls (Houston), and Raszebrae and Anti-Scrunti Faction (both LA) — presaged the Riot Grrl movement. Suzi Gardner, later of L7, dated Flag's Chuck Dukowski (and groaned the backup vocals to "Slip It In"); Courtney Love hung out with Bruce Loose of Flipper — those women clearly picked up that die-hard aesthetic.

For the most part, HC guys never figured out that they had to respect the opposite sex — nor did they figure out how to get laid.

Hardcore kids dancing, LA 1982
Photo by Edward Colver

Out — just an act
His parents love him
They send him money
But he won't come back
Forget him, just forget him
— Hüsker Dü, "Pride"

Critics who hated Hardcore claimed it was comprised of, among other things, homophobic jocks who went fag-bashing every weekend. But that was not always the case.

GARY FLOYD (Dicks): There was a lot of queer shit going on — tons of closet cases. Tons of people running around. This was before AIDS. I know it's gonna be hard for people to believe, but there was a time before AIDS when people were doing a lot of fucking. A lot of straight guys were getting their dick sucked — and I was sucking a little bit too — because it just was happening. It was every place — people were just doing it. Totally it was going on! I got my share of action.

Did a scene dominated by bare-chested boys jumping atop each other serve as an outlet for repressed homosexuality, or was it a straight tribal free-for-all, like football and wrestling — an expression of natural urges to get physical?

TESCO VEE (Meatmen): I never sold my butthole — but gay porn mags were onto us. They thought we were hot! Both Henry Rollins and I were in this gay magazine from LA called *In Touch*. I posed in my bare ass with a milkbone sticking out — an action shot of my 140-pound Hungarian guard dog biting the milkbone. Henry was shot live as 'Stud Of The Month.' I guess they were onto me 'cause I was in a Hardcore band and hung my ass out. I was dressed in one of my early caveman outfits. My wife hates those *Dutch Hercules* pictures, where, in my underwear, you can see the outline of my penis.

Photos of Henry in a gay porn mag launched one of the most frequently asked questions of the era: Is Henry Rollins gay? The truth is, he just does a lot of "gay" things, like poetry and bodybuilding.

Went to the shoestore lookin' to meet
Some young boy with a pair of nice feet
He's fourteen and I'm looking for work
— Dicks, "Little Boys' Feet"

A few powerful HC outfits starred militantly gay frontmen. The best, for some reason, came from Austin: the Big Boys' Randy "Biscuit" Turner, The Dicks' Gary Floyd, and Dave Dictor of The Stains (later MDC). Floyd and Dictor were America's worst nightmare: foul-mouthed homosexual communists. While Hüsker Dü certainly never announced themselves as gay, "Pride" — off their noted *Zen Arcade* album — sounds like a gay HC anthem.

TIM KERR (Big Boys): The fact that Biscuit and Gary Floyd were gay wasn't an issue. We had no songs about being gay. Biscuit never pushed that agenda; we could care less. I can't say Hardcore wasn't a homophobic scene; there were people who fucking hated gays, blacks or whatever. Everybody was thrown together in this 'us-versus-them' thing.

GARY FLOYD (Dicks): I'm not that big of a puss and if anybody ever fucked with me, its like, 'Yeah, I'm queer, fuck you — I'll beat your fuckin' ass!' Luckily I had some tough guys in the band who'd back me up on that. I was always up-front about it. I want everybody to know, 'I'm a big fag, and I'm not gonna try to slip my hand up your ass,' but at the same time I'm not gonna refrain from saying, 'Hey, that's a cute guy...'

Randy "Biscuit" Turner (Big Boys):
It was a big deal to be out back then
Photo by Bill Daniel

Paradoxically, fag-bashing sometimes took place at or near HC shows. I witnessed incidents of it and am sorry to report I did not "stop the violence." I saw Wendell Blow of Iron Cross and some Skinhead types beat the pulp outta some poor hustler who made the mistake of cruising 'em outside of The Bayou in Georgetown. Cro-Mags members and friends perpetrated notoriously vicious fag-bashing sprees.

My HC homosexual encounter occurred after a show in '83, while out on tour with No Trend. We were exhausted by the time we hit San Francisco, yet had to wait to play until 2 A.M. at an after-hours party with DRI, Urban Assault, C2D and The Fuck Ups. After the show, we accepted an offer to sleep at some filthy flophouse. I awoke at daybreak to some scrungy Punker guy blowing me. The worst part was having to sit around with him and his foul-ball friends in the morning, as if nothing happened.

Broken home, broken heart
Now you know just how it feels
To have to cry yourself to sleep at night
— Hüsker Dü, "Broken Home, Broken Heart"

Street Punks and runaways abounded in New York, San Francisco and Hollywood. You'd see plenty of damaged people and abused kids with anger, rage, and pain. The Hardcore scene offered them hope.

Many of the kids living marginal existences said awful shit about "fags" — sometimes because they were gay themselves. In NYC, starving young Skinheads would make 20 bucks blowing old men in the West Village — then, to "right themselves," would return to the East Village to fag-bash.

LAURA ALBERT (NYHC scene): A lot of homeless kids in the New York scene turned tricks. Most were abused children. Some weren't even sexually abused — it was emotional abuse. If you come from a dysfunctional family and a man comes along, you realize that you have something that somebody wants intensely; it's a huge sense of power. It's hard not to be a part of it.

MICHAEL ALAGO (music biz exec): That was their own way of releasing tension and saying to themselves, 'Ah, I just rolled that fag.' Most of the Skinhead kids I hung out with tell ya they've done that before. I don't mean to psychoanalyze these kids, but they went and got or gave their blow job, got the 20 or 30 bucks they needed, and to make them feel more like heterosexuals, they needed to go back and beat the shit out of somebody. That stuff definitely happened.

A cadre of rather discreet, leather-clad predatory gay men did their best to blend in. There'd always be one or two older guys at any given show who'd chat up

young boys, a situation not unique to Hardcore — they would've been there if it were a piano recital or a Boy Scout jamboree.

JEFF McDONALD (Red Cross): Yeah, there were always a few chickenhawks around. When we started going to shows, we were 14; these people would say, 'Hey, you dig this music? Well, if you need a place to stay, you can stay at my house!' I used to think that was so great, these people were so nice. I quickly figured out to stay away. But we weren't from a broken home and weren't susceptible to needing a place to crash.

STEVEN McDONALD (Red Cross): I recall being so young and not knowing what they had in mind, but having this feeling you're being looked at like in a cartoon, when someone starving looks at someone that turns into a T-bone steak. There was speculation about our first record contract because someone actually paid to put out a record by us before anyone else we knew. Everyone speculated that Robbie Fields of Posh Boy had it in for us big time because I was like 12 years old.

MICHAEL ALAGO: I wasn't the only one. One person I remember — whenever we got together we talked about all the cute little boys — was Patrick [Mack] of The Stimulators. We'd carry on about the boys. It was always very hush-hush, like 'Let's get a few beers and go somewhere.' In fact, that's what made it kinda sexy, not telling anybody else. But if there's a Hardcore matinee, you can still find me there, and I still go because of the energy of the music and I'm hoping to see some big-dick-swingin', tattooed loveboys to put over my shoulder and take home.

GARY FLOYD (Dicks): I never tried to fuck kids, and I never tried to take advantage of drunk people; that's the actions of assholes. I didn't use my sexuality, my music, and my drinking to fuck kids. I do know that type of person that would get somebody drunk and try and stick their finger in their ass — and you know what? Karma'll get those people. I'm a big follower of the Hindu religion — I think karma will eat your butthole open. •

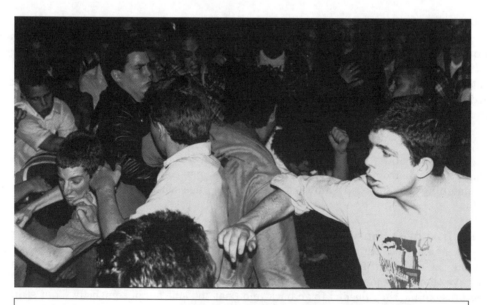

Kids gettin' physical in the pit, LA, 1981
Photo by Edward Colver

THEY HATE US, WE HATE THEM

This fucking city is run by pigs
They take the rights away from all the kids
Understand we're fighting a war we can't win
They hate us, we hate them, we can't win
— Black Flag, "Police Story"

Hardcore kids weren't the only violent assholes back then. The cops were out of control, too. As enforcers of the status quo, the police represented HC's most identifiable enemy. Every scene vet relates tales of some cracker pig fucking with 'em for no good reason.

AL FLIPSIDE (editor, *Flipside*): The cops were bad. I don't know if they hated us or it was just their free ticket to practice riot control. They would come fuck with us because nobody cared. Their usual tactic was — instead of closing a hall and telling people to go, they'd close the hall and force people out faster than humanly possible. As you tripped over each other, they'd beat you, keep you from your car, keep you running around. It was chaos; it was stupid.

Today you'd call what the police did to Hardcore kids harassment or even a form of "racial profiling." They busted shows, accumulated dossiers, gathered evidence. The authorities recognized the threat of violence, real or perceived, when Black Flag and Dead Kennedys came around. Cops didn't want a new movement, so they tried to kill it before it grew.

LAPD crackdown at Hardcore show, 1981
Photo by Edward Colver

HENRY ROLLINS (Black Flag): The cops would always do unlawful things to fuck with you — they'd put guns in your face. We were scared of cops. What were you gonna do, beat them up?

DEZ CADENA (Black Flag): The police, especially in LA, have always been pretty *fascismo*. The cops thought Punk was a rebellion that threatened them, the American Family, and society in general — and they wanted to stomp it out.

TIM KERR (Big Boys): When the Bad Brains visited us in Austin, the neighbors called the cops a few times; there was Reggae playing outside. One time when the cops came, they asked me when we were playing next, so I told them. That's when I realized they were keeping tabs on this shit, trying to make sure it didn't turn into this huge youth movement or something. A friend of mine got taken to jail once — when they opened the book, he saw photos and files on all of us: Big Boys, Dicks, MDC. It's weird to talk about — you start sounding real paranoid, but there's a history of that type of J. Edgar Hoover-style shit.

LA cops no longer bust heads at Rock shows like they once did. In the early 80s they'd find out where Black Flag was playing, and 200 cops in riot gear would turn up, plus helicopters. They'd rush in and beat up 16-years-olds in what were essentially "police riots," where cops instigated trouble and caused damage.

LAPD crackdown at Hardcore show, 1981
Photo by Edward Colver

GEORGE ANTHONY (Battalion Of Saints): You'd have riots; people were getting maced and arrested. These poor kids would go to see a show and come out with their nose in their ear, and the cops did it. Everyone would be inside having a good time and the cops would come in and say, 'We've got to shut it down,' and take the money. In the early 80s, it was madness. There was an Exploited show in LA — the cops came in and everybody sat down. They were just golfing with their clubs on these poor kids — girls, it didn't make a difference. There's nothing you could do — the cops have their orders and they think they're right.

PAT DUBAR (Uniform Choice): The police in LA — any opportunity they had to beat your ass, they would. What better targets than Hardcore kids? Most of these kids were either runaways or from dysfunctional families or had parents who didn't give a shit. So it was a safe bet that if they wanted to beat the fuck out of someone, they could — 95 percent of the time nothing would happen. So, it was a chance worth taking, and they did. They did it a lot. They fucked with me a few times. Cops in Orange County were even bigger dicks because, at least until the county went bankrupt, OC was a well-protected, 'nice' place to live. It was really hard to have shows there, and if there was ever any trouble, and you looked like a Punk Rocker, you were the first one to get hassled or to go down — on a level so scary they wouldn't even do it to most gang members now. They wouldn't put a gun to a gang member's head, but they would do that to Hardcore kids.

Copulation
Anti-cop compilation LP, Mystic, 1983
Collection of the author

D.H. PELIGRO (Dead Kennedys): I recall an incident — I think DOA was playing — that was like an acid nightmare: tear gas came in, windows were smashed in, people were grabbing their jackets and putting them over their faces and running out. Cops with helmets and shields came in and just bum-rushed the crowd and started beating people and pushing them out the door. There was a line of cops just beatin' the piss outta everybody who was pushed out. They tried to club me in the head and I kept putting my hands up and they smacked my arm and it swelled up and I had a gig the next night. It was madness. It was mayhem.

HC abounded with "Fuck Tha Police" motifs. There were the songs "Police Story" by Black Flag, "Police Truck" by Dead Kennedys, about a paddy wagon gang-rape, and tracks on *Copulation*, the anti-cop comp. But MDC (Millions Of Dead Cops) delivered the ultimate vent of that rage; their anthem "Dead Cops" summed up the anti-authoritarian mindset:

Whatcha gonna do
The Mafia in blue
Huntin' for queers, niggers and you."
— MDC, "Dead Cops"

LAPD crackdown at Hardcore show, 1981
Photo by Edward Colver

HOW WE ROCK

Time to break from this verbal poison
By creating a new sound reverberation
That infiltrates the cracks of the nation
— Bollocks, "Meditteran"

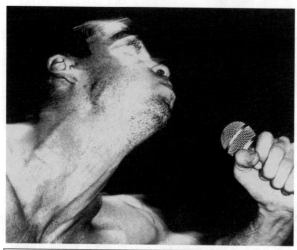

Henry Rollins (Black Flag), 1981
Photo by Edward Colver

BARRY HENNSLER (Necros): Hardcore was a negation of all traditions. The anger of Punk accelerated to fit into where everyone's head was at in the early 80s. It was a cleansing.

LOU BARLOW (Deep Wound): There is a pure Hardcore formula — and it's not The Ramones and it's not Heavy Metal.

Hardcore music was totally unique, focusing on speed and anger. Although the philosophy implied "no rules," the music wasn't avant-garde, experimental, nor did it have unlimited possibilities. It was all about playing as fast as possible. The more talented bands occasionally implemented mixtures of mid and fast tempos. HC guitarists — with their new-fashioned style of attack — ripped as fast as humanly possible. Soloing represented traditional Rock bullshit and was forbidden, so they developed previously unheard rhythmic styles. Singers belted out words in an abrasive, aggressive manner. Drummers played ultra-fast, in an elemental one-two-one-two. That insistence on speed imposed limitations, which soon turned into assets.

Participant's inexperience and lack of technical proficiency only added to the mix. For example, had SS Decontrol played in '82 as well as they could in '85, there would've never been the classic *The Kids Will Have Their Say* album. Most outfits made it on sheer energy. Removed from social contexts, many sucked. Fans were more into the vibe than the quality of the music.

Hardcore is like any other specialized, self-perpetuating musical genre. Take the Blues, for example. B.B. King or John Lee Hooker, Texas Blues or Chicago Blues — they're all playing the same basic licks. You'd think they'd get tired of the so-called limitations. But Blues survived because there's always gonna be someone who thinks they can play those same chords in a new way. HC bands played the same chord progressions over and over — while no doubt imagining themselves creating something different.

One might say, "Hardcore groups just played simple chords and it was all the same beat." But distinctive sounds arose. If you asked someone to paint a picture with a thousand colors, they'd probably try to use most of 'em. But with only three colors they might do some real interesting work. That's how Hardcore worked.

ED IVEY (Rhythm Pigs): For me, Hardcore is Folk Music. As an amateur musicologist, I can watch a young band play and know what they're gonna do because they're following the form. When they play those bar chords a certain way or go back to that repeated chorus —
this is Folk terminology being passed down the line. This made us into this cohesive group of people that shared something private that made us, in our minds, better than everybody else.

You don't understand a word we say
You don't listen to us anyway
— Big Boys, "Fun Fun Fun"

Hardcore fans didn't want their beloved bands to grow beyond established parameters. They wanted their heroes to sound exactly the same, over and over again, forever.

ANDY WENDLER (Necros): Hardcore was just big enough and we were big enough in Hardcore that we found we couldn't change. People wanted to hear the same songs from '80 and '81. Hardcore, even more than Rock and Jazz, was limited. It was starting to die in '86. People'd see us if they knew we were gonna play early stuff but didn't want to hear anything new.

Hardcore may be the only music whose pioneers turned on it and, later, were even embarrassed by it.

Springa (SS Decontrol), 1982
Photo by Phil In Phlash
Courtesy of Taang!

GRANT HART (Hüsker Dü): I got bored with Hardcore very fast. Over time, a lot of other people started doing what we were doing — it lost its uniqueness. We didn't wanna sound like anybody else. I didn't like a lot of the shit that was status quo Hardcore. After having encircled ourselves with the counterculture, it was time to carry on the revolution within.

LOU BARLOW: In '84, I went on a trip with a friend, and we listened to Neil Young the whole time. I was like, 'Wow, that was really good!' Also it was restlessness: we just wanted to play something different — we started listening to a lot of British stuff. So many influences were converging on us. We couldn't play Hardcore anymore.

KEVIN SECONDS (7 Seconds): My whole thing was to make melodic, hard-edged music that had something to say — I didn't want this goofy bullshit that a lot of bands — especially on the West Coast — were coming up with. Bands were starting to become more 'musical,' which was good in itself, but it definitely veered away from the early-80s Hardcore sound.

JACK RABID (editor, *The Big Takeover*): There were an awful lot of good Hardcore bands, but there was a limitation placed on it by youth. Things having to be hard and fast — and inevitably harder and faster — took out one of the elements that make Rock & Roll great, which is the ability to expand on the form. Like the Bad Brains. After their original twenty-five songs, I always wondered where they'd go after that. Where do you take it?

As time went on, a few outfits poked fun at the scene's growing rigidity and codification. "Anti-Hardcore" groups, whose modus operandi was to fuck with the

doctrinaire, included Flipper (SF), No Trend (DC), Mr. Epp (Seattle), Culturcide (Houston), Kilslug (Boston), Mighty Sphincter and Sun City Girls (Phoenix) and End Result (Chicago). They pointed out the stupidity of scene politics, and used noise as a weapon.

AL FLIPSIDE (editor, *Flipside*): There were some great anti-Hardcore bands — Flipper, No Trend, Negativeland, Frantix, Culturcide. They were more interesting to me because they were actually taking things a step further. By '84, I was listening to No Trend and not paying attention to Hardcore. It all got old after awhile.

KING KOFFEE (Butthole Surfers): I thought bands who played straight-ahead Hardcore music missed the whole point. Playing Hardcore became like being in a Rockabilly band, aping a style that happened years ago. You're not creating anything original at all. The ritual became retarded. •

Ian MacKaye (Minor Threat), NYC, 1982
Photo by Karen O'Sullivan

ANTI-FASHION

Colored hair and funny clothes
They are the menace of today
And they won't listen to what you say
But don't forget that they're your future
— Social Distortion, "All The Answers"

KEVIN SECONDS (7 Seconds): I didn't buy into the whole thing of walking around like a peacock, with big blue-green mohawks. The kids I knew that were into that gave me shit 'cause I'd always just go for a shaved-head look. They'd say, 'Aren't you proud to be Punk?'

AL BARILE (SS Decontrol): By 1980, whoever was into Punk was hanging onto something that wasn't there anymore. I wanted to be into something not built around fashion. For me, that was Hardcore.

Hardcore fashion constituted a defensive posture — a warning to enemies and an attempt to look tough. Such displays are common in the animal kingdom — many creatures try to make themselves look larger or meaner.

DAVE SMALLEY (DYS, Dag Nasty): The first time I shaved my head, I didn't really shave it — I did it with scissors. I cut it all off in little splotches and walked into H&R Block to pick my mom up from work. I

Boots, 1982
Photo by Edward Colver

was wearing combat boots, a dog collar and chain around my waist, probably a shirt that said, 'Fuck You.' The whole office was like, 'Oh man...' My mom just said, 'Go out in the car. We'll discuss it later.' She cried and I felt bad, but you have to do what's inside of you at that age.

If you wore Hardcore apparel in '81, it was most likely ripped-up old t-shirts on which you wrote the name of your favorite band. At shows, acts with "mass produced" t-shirts dared only charge five bucks — max — per shirt.

"STRAIGHT EDGE" HANK PIERCE (Boston scene): A great thing was being able to make your own shirts, which no one does anymore. Springa [SSD] used to make shirts with a marker. There was a radio spot in which Ian MacKaye pretended to be Springa's mom: 'You ruined another shirt!'

All regional looks were variations on the working-class Punk thing: jeans, flannel or t-shirts, boots, maybe chains. Everyone had a worn-out leather jacket. Onstage it was either dirty jeans or used work wear. Rugby and Oxford shirts were not uncommon.

KEVIN SECONDS (7 Seconds): On the West Coast, you had kids from beach towns; they had engineer boots with bandannas wrapped all over the chains, and the plaid shirts. In San Francisco, they looked like the Goth kids now — dark thrift-store clothes. Skaters of course always had their own thing, wherever they were from. Even if it was kind of silly when you look back on it, it was important to try, to stand out a little and do your own thing.

CBGB matinee crowd, NYC, 1983
Photo by Karen O'Sullivan

JACK GRISHAM (TSOL): None of *us* wore chains on the boots and that kind of crap. When you're running from somebody or jumping fences, that'll hang you up. That always cracked me up about the bandannas — that's the type of shit that gets hooked on a fence. We were into the combat thing — we'd go to Army Surplus and get black combat gear. We'd go on missions.

"STRAIGHT EDGE" HANK PEIRCE: There was something in Boston —DC had it too — butt flaps. It started having the name of a band on the back of a flannel shirt. You'd take a piece of cloth and write a band name on it. You'd wear this butt flap, this cape that hung off the back of your pants.

Females developed a parallel fashion statement, reacting to the Punk coquette vibe with an asexual style: big black boots, a ratty dress worn like a t-shirt, and often a partially-shaved head with a tuft upfront. At East Coast venues like the Wilson Center or A7 first appeared that sleazy schoolgirl look: kilt, engineer boots, leather jacket and beret.

HOLLY RAMOS (NYHC scene): Hardcore defined the fashion of the time. We were Hardcore, we were severe. Cuteness had no part. I didn't wear my boots with little frilly things. It was serious. We were fucking militant. I wore plaid skirts, real dirty ones I never washed. I'd wipe my hands on 'em; they were green and white with bloodstains. I was really into being filthy and loving it. The private school I went to had a dress code: you had to wear a button-down shirt, so I'd rip the cuffs off like Patti Smith on *Horses,* with tight plaid pants over combat boots. Big plaid overcoat, Doc Martens and messy hair — spiked but unstyled, short and mangy. God, you were tortured in high school for looking like that.

Kids who didn't shave their heads bleached, colored, and spiked their self-cut hair, which was often fucked-up from chemicals. They got into piercing and

tattooing, precursing Modern Primitivism. Tattoos of band names and logos adorned guys as well as girls — even their bald heads. Henry Rollins and the guys in the Cro-Mags first popularized "ink."

Hardcore functionality influenced the later Grunge look: shirt wrapped around the waist, simply as a matter of utility, gigs being sweaty affairs without coatchecks.

RAY FARRELL (SST): I remember asking Mike Watt of the Minutemen why he wore flannel shirts. I told him I was into flannel shirts as a kid — I wore 'em because John Fogerty of Creedence Clearwater Revival wore 'em. He said, 'You've got it right there.' It's his tribute to John Fogerty. Who knew that'd become the flag for so many things to come? •

These guys had the look down: The Outpatients, 1983
Courtesy of Scott Helland

HÜSKER DÜ

F.U.'S

D.O.A.

MISFITS

ANTI

BLACK FLAG

Circle Jerks

CORROSION

MINOR THREAT

S.O.A

OF CONFORMITY

MARGINAL MAN

*THE EFFIGIES

BAD BRAINS

MDC

POISON IDEA

SSD

tHE FARTZ

BUTTHOLE SURFERS

CH3

NECROS

PART TWO

Unidentified Hardcore type after a fight outside CBGB, NYC 1983. Photo by Karen O'Sullivan

BLACK FLAG & SST: THIRSTY AND MISERABLE

We are tired
Of your abuse
Try and stop us
It's no use
— Black Flag, "Rise Above"

If the Ramones and Sex Pistols defined Punk, then Black Flag defined Hardcore. Inspired by the Germs, but unashamed to display gnarly Rock influences like Black Sabbath, ZZ Top and The Grateful Dead, they were the most important band of American Hardcore.

Black Flag kindled a unique, identifiably American response to Punk. Their punishing music, tireless work ethic, and independent attitude — as opposed to prevailing LA Punk egomania — became the inspiration and archetype for all who followed. Few others in Rock history could've survived the conflict, turmoil and opposition these guys faced. Flag stood defiant in the face of unimaginable odds — and for a few years were the greatest band on the planet.

Black Flag, 1981:
(L to R): Robo, Dez Cadena, Greg Ginn, Henry Rollins, Chuck Dukowski
Photo by Edward Colver

IAN MACKAYE (Minor Threat): Black Flag was the vanguard, the new band. I could tell those guys represented the youth culture. Reading about them, they sounded like the Sham 69 of America. The pictures of them were incredible. Then we heard the single and I listened to I've Had It a thousand times in a row. We weren't artists anymore, we were kids. Germs, The Weirdos and The Dickies were great but they weren't *kids!"*

PAT DUBAR (Uniform Choice): Everyone related to Black Flag because they directly connected with all our subconsciences, saying what we felt. Everything that they were saying was going on in my life. 'White Minority' had nothing necessarily to do with me — but the anger behind it was exactly what I was experiencing. Their whole approach to shit inspired me into action. Prior to that, I had no reason to be a musician. What I saw was unapproachable. I saw Black Flag and said 'I want to do that, like those guys.'

The Punk vibe was urbane, elitist and exclusive. Everyone preached D.I.Y. but few practiced it. Black Flag, on the other hand, merged the basic constructs of aggression, anti-stardom and alienation with a blue-collar mindset. Basically enlightened suburban Rock dudes when they first showed up at hip Hollywood shows (at clubs like The Masque), they got treated like total losers. That sense of loathing and isolation only inspired them to go out and destroy everything in their path. They pushed so hard they changed the face of Punk — and Rock — as we knew it.

HENRY ROLLINS (Black Flag): Flag never assimilated well with the Hollywood Punk scene — The Weirdos, X, The Bags. They might tell you one thing now but they didn't like Black Flag. Flag, the stoners from the beach, would show up in jeans and T-shirts, long hair, a joint behind the ear, and Budweisers. By the time I joined, Black Flag had this whole attitude about Hollywood. We'd fuck with them. We wanted to bum people out, especially anybody with a mohawk, any 35-year-old guy with a blazer and eye makeup doing a Bowie-meets-the-Dickies thing. We'd go, 'Hey Punk Rock faggot!'

MIKE WATT (Minutemen): Hollywood shut us out. We were forced to make things happen on our own because the Hollywood people were tight about their scene. Maybe I don't blame those Hollywood guys — yeah I do, fuck them — but they really inspired us. When we wanted to play gigs, they were elitist and wouldn't let us play. This was like 1978 or '79. We were Punk fans and we went there; there was no Punk gigs in San Pedro, none in Hermosa Beach; they were only in Hollywood. Hollywood was all of these LA people who were the misfits and the losers from their high schools all coming together. You'd meet people that you'd never meet in Pedro! I met artists for the first time. I got turned onto all this music and culture.

Rollins stagedive, LA, 1981
Photo by Edward Colver

Black Flag were from Hermosa Beach and cultivated a notorious "Surf Punk" following. They were the first to induce ferocious slamdancing at gigs. All across America, kids were starting to hear of this dangerous LA outfit with spurs on their boots, into Charles Manson, and living in an abandoned church.

In existence since early '77, by the summer of '81 Black Flag were already breaking in their fourth lead singer. By the time of their summer '86 breakup, they burned through at least 15 members. That constant flux manifested itself in their sound.

Their story actually goes back to late '76, when Glen "Spot" Lockett, a local musician, became staff engineer at a small Hermosa recording studio called Media Art. Spot also worked part-time at The Garden Of Eden, a local vegetarian restaurant, where he became friends with Greg Ginn, a regular customer from the 'hood. Spot wrote music reviews for a lame local Hippie rag called *The Easy Reader*, so he and Ginn got into spirited musical debates. Greg was so inspired by the first Ramones album that he'd just started playing guitar in his own Punk group, Panic. Spot later became Black Flag's producer and soundman, essential to the band's primal presentation.

Panic featured Greg, brother Raymond "Pettibon" on bass, local Metal drummer Brian Migdol, and fiery frontman Keith Morris, a record-store clerk whose dad was the bait-and-tackle king of the Hermosa pier.

RAYMOND PETTIBON (artist): I kinda played bass and learned their songs but I was never in the band. There's nothing I could do that would deaden the mind more than play bass in a Punk band. Especially that band.

SPOT (producer/soundman): At first, I thought they were hilarious. They only knew six songs, each a minute long. That was back when Keith Morris was singing. I worked on the first single but I wasn't in control. I guess *Jealous Again* was the first one I did. But at that point, the band was more sophisticated, unlike their Panic days.

Around then, Greg bought an amp from South Bay burnout Gary McDaniel, who played in Würm, a garage band. McDaniel soon replaced Pettibon in late '77, and assumed the alias "Chuck Dukowski" — a nod to Beat poet Charles Bukowski. Colombian army defector Robo, an illegal alien who came to the US in '75 and stayed with an expired student visa, replaced Migdol on drums a few months later.

At Media Art in January '78, Panic recorded their "Nervous Breakdown" single for Greg Shaw's popular Bomp! label. But Bomp! was more interested in the Power Pop sound of The Beat, The Pop and 20/20, so Panic asked for and got their tapes back. Then they learned of a UK Punk act called Panic. Pettibon proposed they rename themselves after the symbol of Anarchy — the black flag. Greg and Chuck agreed; the roach spray of the same name evoked nihilism. Raymond, a prodigy who graduated from UCLA with an Economics degree at 19, designed the oft-spray-painted Black Flag "bars" logo.

Chuck Dukowski, 1980
Xerox copy, origin unknown
Collection of the author

RAYMOND PETTIBON: The symbol is my version of the black flag. I was into politics early on: I was a card-carrying anarchist when I was 14. Black flag is a symbol of Anarchy. Depicting that as pistons seemed to have some visual power, plus convey the actual form of the flag.

Pettibon's art complimented Black Flag and others on their SST label. His incendiary work left its mark on legendary posters, flyers and record covers. Brothers Greg and Raymond fell out over the rights to those graphics, an ugly score still unsettled at the time of this writing.

RAYMOND PETTIBON: As far as I'm concerned, SST is not even a part of my past. For one thing, it was dishonestly procured. I was never paid for any of that stuff. I mean, why don't you talk to the people at SST about it? If you talk to them it's like Stalinist Russia, rewriting history. Somebody is some big commissar and the next day he's purged and all traces of his existence are literally written out of the official history.

Before picking up a guitar, whiz kid Ginn invented electronic products and held many patents, the most profitable of which was for an antenna tuner. At age 13, he put out an amateur ham radio zine — *The Novice* — and began selling ham

gear and FM reception boosters.
He then formed SST: Solid State
Transmitter.

Greg probably would have
succeeded had he stuck with it,
but when Punk hit, the
electronics went straight into

SST Records: The label that put Hardcore on the map

storage. Selling the business late in '79, Ginn applied his acumen to a record
label. SST Electronics became SST Records. SST 001 was Black Flag's classic
"Nervous Breakdown" 7" EP, with "Nervous Breakdown," "Fix Me," "I've Had It,"
and "Wasted."

After playing a few beer bashes, Flag first
officially gigged at a free outdoor event, part of
a Sunday afternoon "Lunch on the Grass"
program at Hollywood Pond. Greg duped the
Manhattan Beach Parks Department into
thinking they were some quasi-Fleetwood Mac
tribute ensemble. Suffice it to say, they
wrought havoc on an unprepared public.

GREG GINN (Black Flag): Our first gig was
outdoors and there were 2000 people there. They
started throwing food at us, but I liked the music we
were doing. I wasn't doing this to make people angry
or get some kind of reaction — but I learned early on
that I did, and that people hated to see that kind of
freedom. The more uptight people were, the more
angry they'd get at what we were doing. It all went
from there.

CHUCK DUKOWSKI (Black Flag): They threw
everything from insults to watermelons, beer cans,
ice, and sandwiches. Robo's head made a great target.
Afterwards I enjoyed a lunch of delicatessen
sandwiches I found still in their wrappers.
(Everything Went Black)

Example of Raymond Pettibon's art
Show flyer for Black Flack and Fear, LA, 1981
Collection of the author

Flag next played San Pedro with The Plugz and a local outfit playing their first
gig, the Minutemen. Black Flag's alliance with the Minutemen — guitarist/vocalist
D Boon, bassist Mike Watt, and drummer George Hurley — lasted for years, the
apex being the joint *Minuteflag* EP (SST 050).

MIKE WATT: Greg sees our first gig and asked us to be SST 002. That was *Paranoid Time*,
seven songs recorded and mixed in one night for $300. It was at that point we realized all you
had to do was pay for pressings, that records weren't a gift from Mount Olympus. The Punk
thing before that was safety pins and writing names of bands on clothes, but making a label
and getting in a van and touring, actually playing other towns? A lot of Hollywood bands
never toured — I think only The Dils had a van. Maybe it was from Greg's experience with
ham radios, but he believed that if you try, you can get things beyond your little group. He
said, 'Fuck it, let's sell records, let's go on tour. Let's make the rowdiest music. Let's not make
mersh records. Let's not hide this as a secret. Let's get out and play.'

Mike Watt and childhood pal D Boon were working-class kids who grew up on
Classic Rock. The pair attended shows in Hollywood, then would return home to

play in a cover band, Starstruck — led by cheesy Mark Weisswasser, who'd sit up front with a chrome drum set while Watt, Boon and a female singer stood behind performing Queen's "Tie Your Mother Down" or "Dust In The Wind" by Kansas. Musically, they were headed back to their day jobs — they hadn't yet made the connection between proficiency and self-expression. In late '78, Watt and Boon started The Reactionaries. Their original material was a sped-up version of what they listened to: Blue Oyster Cult and Alice Cooper.

The Minutemen as they appeared on the cover of *Flipside* #32
(L to R): D Boon, Mike Watt, George Hurley
Xerox copy, courtesy of Al Flipside

MIKE WATT: We didn't know what was gonna happen at the next Punk show, there was so much excitement, but we didn't feel brave enough to try that ourselves. Finally, in '78, I told D Boon, 'Man, fuck this with Mark, we just gotta go for it.' So we tried The Reactionaries, which was me and George [Hurley] and D Boon. And then we got this guy named Martin to sing. But it was too Rock & Roll. It wasn't us, even though we had no idea what we wanted to be, It was like fast Blue Oyster Cult! But that's all we knew.

You see, when Punk came, we were real embarrassed that we knew how to play. The other Punk bands were writing as they were learning. For us, we couldn't turn back the hands of the clock, so we tried all these real extreme devices to hide it, which we picked up from the English group Wire: you don't need verse/chorus, you don't need solos, you don't need shit. We thought Punk meant that no one was supposed to know you can play well! Then it seemed some Punk bands, as they played better, turned more Rock & Roll, and the joke was on us! We didn't give a fuck — no matter what we played, you could tell it was The Minutemen.

SST groups played wherever they could, house parties and basement bashes the norm early on. Playing New Wave in the LA burbs made one the subject of total hostility. So imagine what a hard-core Punk show was like. At one blue-collar gig near the Standard Oil Refinery in El Segundo, rowdy rockers almost killed members of Black Flag and Minutemen. But abuse from rednecks, cops, Punks and hipsters only spurred the drive to achieve.

SST outfits lived in working-class towns: Hawthorne, Lawndale, Redondo and Pedro. Their work, their lives said, "We don't want to be in Hollywood, with the fashionable leather jackets and all that bullshit." They practiced twelve hours a day, every day. That's all they did.

BILL STEVENSON (Descendents, Black Flag): Our music had a real blue-collar element, which is what I like about it — music made by people that aren't afraid to get their hands dirty. And that's not very Hollywood.

South Bay rehearsal studios 86ed Flag and Minutemen. They practiced for a few months of '79 at a run-down Hermosa Beach bathhouse known as "The Worm Hole," before the city council ran 'em out of town.

MIKE WATT: We were thrown out of one practice pad after the next. See, in LA's 140 towns and Orange County has lots of towns, so when you moved across the line, they had that small-town police department mentality. They'd call Long Beach and say, 'Hey, these assholes are there now.' They'd kick in our doors, raid us: we had a lot of problems. At the gigs, the pigs would show up, ready to fight, for nuthin'.

Few people outside LA ever saw the first Black Flag lineup with Keith "Spiderman" Morris. According to those in the know, they did some of their most over-the-top gigs with Keith (a.k.a. Johnnie "Bob" Goldstein). Morris wasn't the most talented vocalist, but he was incredibly entertaining.

DEZ CADENA (Black Flag): If you talk to anyone involved with Black Flag, they'll have their favorite singer. Keith was my favorite; he was the initial singer, part of the initial fury. They hit me with a pure vengeance — straight between the eyes. Keith was intense. I saw them at a Moose Lodge in Redondo in early 1978. Black Flag played twice, opening and closing the show. I remember the people there got mad — Keith was wearing a Hippie wig and yelling 'Fuck You!' to everyone. When he grabbed the American flag, that's when they really bummed. Later that night, he took off the wig and they played again — the old men couldn't tell one band from the next. The bill was Black Flag, Rhino 39, The Alleycats.

In August '79, tired of working hard for no reward, Morris quit, dealing Black Flag — just beginning to gain Hollywood acceptance — a major setback.

KEITH MORRIS: I was a real jerk back then. I did tons of coke and booze and was always in the middle of some stupid shit ... I split with Black Flag 'cause I just couldn't deal with it anymore. The feeling was clearly mutual. A few weeks later, we started Circle Jerks.

Red Cross drummer Ron Reyes was brought in to replace Keith. Reyes's turbulent half-year stint included a role in *The Decline Of Western Civilization* and the fierce vocals on Flag's legendary second record, the *Jealous Again* 12" EP, with "Jealous Again," "White Minority," "Revenge," and "No Values." Credited as "Chavo Pederast," Ron delivered dramatic interpretations of Greg's caustic lyrics, but never fit in with Greg and Chuck's intense "dude vibe." An antisocial headcase, Ron dressed and acted all Punk, with "Crass" on his jacket and shit. After a while, Flag was just a pain in the ass for him.

Black Flag, 1980: Greg Ginn and Ron Reyes
Xerox copy, origin unknown
Collection of the author

JEFF McDONALD (Red Cross): Ron Reyes was a very troubled, angry young man. He was a bit older, around 18 at the time — he had a rough life. All of us in Red Cross came from the suburbs — he was the first person we ever met from a severe broken home situation. He was the first to let you know about it, too. He'd make you feel really bad about having a homelife. As kids, we didn't know how to deal with him.

PAT HOED (Adam Bomb of KXLU): In terms of raw intensity, the lineup with Ron, Chuck, Greg and Robo was the best. All I gotta say is: put on *Jealous Again* — nobody can top that. It was totally over the top, and you could hear what the guy was talking about, the rage in his voice. With Ron, I think that's when Black Flag really took off, with *The Decline*....

In March '80, during the recording of *Jealous Again*, Black Flag played a particularly violent gig at The Fleetwood. Ron quit after two songs, so Chuck, Greg

and Robo carried on with a 55-minute "Louie Louie," inviting audience members on stage — and all hell broke loose. From that point on, Flag launching into the opening of "Louie Louie" cued crowds in the know to storm the stage and wreck shit. Reyes returned to finish *Jealous Again* some weeks later, which all things considered was very cool of him. But for the next few months, they searched for his replacement.

Black Flag, 1981:
Dez Cadena and Chuck Dukowski
Xerox copy, origin unknown
Collection of the author

DEZ CADENA: After Ron quit, Flag tried for several months to find a new singer, and they'd booked a West Coast tour. So finally one day at The Church, Chuck came up to me and said, 'Dez, you know our band well, you know the words —' I thought about it for ten seconds and went for it. He asked me on a Saturday and I think the next Friday they were on tour to play Vancouver. As a singer, I had to throw caution to the wind and go for it. Sometimes I'd lose my voice and sometimes I'd have an amazing show.

In June 1980 ex-Red Cross guitarist Dez Cadena replaced Ron Reyes as singer. Dez's father, noted A&R man Oscar Cadena, produced, arranged, or recorded over 300 albums in the 50s and 60s with Yusef Lateef, Hank Jones, and Lightnin' Hopkins, Sonny Terry and Brownie McGee, for labels like Savoy, Blue Note, Prestige and Fantasy.

DEZ CADENA: I remember the Minutemen wanted my dad to produce them because he has a name in the Jazz world — those guys were fans. But when I played him the demo, he goes, 'These guys are too loud.' And for what my dad did, that's probably true. He's used to doing music where there's more dynamics and subtleties, and here's the Minutemen doing 'Fascist.' I don't think it was his ear to listen to that type of thing.

Ron Reyes saw Dez as a traitor. Ron's vibe was "You have my job, fucker!" That caused great tension between the Hispanic Hardcore titans.

DEZ CADENA: Me and Ron were friends and neighbors from Redondo, but we had differences because of Black Flag. During the six months he was in Flag, I'd only seen one of their shows, and they played a ton. I think he felt I was jealous, but I just didn't like his singing as much as Keith's. Anyway, during that first week up in Canada, when we got to Vancouver, there was Ron, who'd already been out of the band for like four months. It'd been close to a year since we'd spoken, and I noticed a change in him. During that time, Ron developed a kinship with people up there — he met D.O.A. and the Subhumans, he had friends and a girlfriend.

Anyway, we were passing out flyers out in front of a Pere Ubu show as we were playing the next night at a bar in the Indian part of town where Hendrix used to play, and Ron came up, drunk out of his mind, to pick a fight. Needless to say, he became an even bigger and better drinker in Canada. I think he felt threatened, but I hadn't even sang a note with the band in town yet; it wasn't like I'd stolen his job. So, he confronted me in a fighting manner and blind-sided me. He came back again; I stuck my arm out because I was tall and he was short; I didn't wanna fight. But after he landed a couple of blows, I had to respond — and I bloodied his nose. This kept on for a half-hour period, where his friends would drag him away, he'd come charging up to get me again, I'd duck his running swings, he'd fall down. It was comical. At one point, he took a brick — cheap Canadian brick — and he hit me in the head. The brick didn't knock me out; it didn't even cause a bump. We ended up making up somehow, although I never did find out the reason for it. It was all so ridiculous, looking back at it. I don't know if Ron would laugh at it or what. That's my side of the story.

In 1980 and '81, Flag started gaining serious notoriety, partly for the members' ceaseless spraypaint spree — the "Black Flag" tag appeared on virtually every highway overpass in the Los Angeles area. They played at The Vex, in a dangerous East LA 'hood where even cops feared to go. But it took police riots — at The Whiskey and The Bulgarian-American Cultural & Education Society (BACES Hall) in East Hollywood — to make the band truly infamous.

DEZ CADENA: The Whiskey booked us — we were to play two shows that night, but we never got a chance to do the second. Two months before ... we went to every high school, like Huntington High and Hawthorne High, and hit every single locker with wallpaper paste and a flyer. So we had maybe a thousand people in The Whiskey, and another eight hundred people outside blocking Sunset Boulevard. This one riot started — called the 'New Riots on Sunset Strip' — when one Punker went, 'Fuck the cops!' and threw a bottle at them. They called the vice squad, and then it got real ugly.

I've seen a few riots — in that case, I was well-protected up in some Rock Star backstage area where I could view the carnage — and it scared me every time it happened. It doesn't happen much anymore. It was always a scary feeling, like 'What's gonna happen? Are they gonna take us away? Are they gonna take our equipment? Are they gonna start hurting people?' Punk Rock violence had already started to cook up in '79, but it seemed to gel with our band. It seemed that we were destined to have problems like that. All we wanted to do was play; we didn't care who did what to whom.

Show flyer for Black Flag and Adolescents
LA, 1981. Art by Raymond Pettibon
Collection of Laura Albert

Black Flag became synonymous with Punk violence. There were many incidents where Flag would try to play and the police would be there to break up the show. Eventually, cops were shutting down gigs before they even started, threatening audiences, like "Don't come back! You shouldn't be here!" Police would beat the shit out of kids for no reason other than that they were at that Black Flag show. *BAM* and *LA Times* features decried "Black Flag violence."

Flag's survival was no small feat. Undercover cops with binoculars staked out SST, and even tapped their phone lines. So Flag turned their energies inward to become a self-sufficient unit. They self-promoted — flyers, graffiti, stickers, cheap radio spots — and toured relentlessly.

MIKE WATT (Minutemen): The Torrance Police thought SST was a heroin ring. They had us under surveillance; they'd stop us all the time. When we'd drive records around in the van, they thought we were making heroin drop-offs. Darby Crash had just died; Flag was going on tour — they thought that was code for the big deal. They came with the fucking police captain, searched the whole place. I had to go to court four times. They found a firecracker, like an M-80; the cop goes, 'Where you keep the rest of these?' I showed him where we made records. It was also the practice pad — an old dentist office, a narrow but long storefront. Eventually, the judge brought me and the arresting officer — some longhair narc guy, bald on top — into his chamber. He goes '50 dollar court cost.' I had to ride down in the elevator with that fucking pig. I didn't say shit, but I wanted to kill him. I was like, 'You motherfucker!' The pigs were afraid of their kids turning into us or something because they had us tailed for months, and were still convinced we were a drug ring, that no way could guys just wanna fuckin' tour around and make records. There was a real hair up their ass about how we were gonna wreck their kids. Maybe we did. I doubt it.

Show flyer for Black Flag's first East Coast gig
Peppermint Lounge, NYC, March 1981
Art by Raymond Pettibon
Collection of the author

HENRY ROLLINS: There was never a problem for me — I didn't have my name on the bottom line of everything. But Greg, always. Sometimes the sheriffs would come into our place at night. You'd hear the perfect idle of a cop car and the spotlight would come through the window. Door opens, flashlight on us. 'Which one of you is Greg Ginn? Step outside please.' Every time they'd walk him outside and twenty minutes later he'd come back. 'What happened?' 'Nothing.' After the Unicorn Records case, him and Chuck were found in contempt of court and taken to LA County Jail for a week. He never talked about it once. That was impressive.

Flag first toured the US with Dez, truly peaking during his one-year run. A scrawny kid with huge pipes, Dez was the screaming voice behind the throat-shredding attack on seminal shit like "Clocked In" (off the classic *Cracks In The Sidewalk* comp), the "Six Pack" 7" (from an aborted attempt to record an LP), and the "Louie Louie"/"Damaged I" single.

SPOT: My favorite singer was Dez. He was unique. He was just being himself. He wasn't trying to be a Punk Rock frontman. Dez was just a goofy guy with this amazing voice — but he didn't really want to be a singer. It's too bad — I always felt he really had something to offer. The last thing he recorded as the vocalist was 'Louie Louie.' Live, he was amazing.

Black Flag first played the East Coast on March 14, '81, with Mission Of Burma at the Peppermint Lounge in New York. Maybe 75 kids showed up, including Ian MacKaye and Henry Garfield who'd driven up from DC. A few days later, 50 or so kids attended Washington's 9: 30 Club for Black Flag, Youth Brigade (DC) and Henry's group, S.O.A. Flyers wheatpasted around DC hailed it as "The St. Patrick's Day Massacre." I saw that show and Flag were unbelievable. Later they crashed at Ian's parent's house, where everyone bonded.

Black Flag twisted young minds everywhere they went.

BARRY HENNSLER (Necros): Flag came through Lansing in '81 — the Necros opened. We hung out with them: it was like living on a desert island and having someone visit that knows all sorts of cool shit. They weren't dicks; they were very cool. It made us practice hard and think that if they could get in a van and traipse across the country playing the music they did, then it could be done. The roots of Hardcore as a national thing can be traced to those tours. I saw The Clash on the *Give Em Enough Rope* tour and they were Rock Stars with a bus. Joe Strummer kicked his roadie in the chest. It was no different from a normal Rock concert, other than the hairstyles. I remember seeing The Ramones, thinking they were a hundred years old. It still wasn't our thing. Black Flag was *our* thing.

Over time, Greg and Chuck convinced Dez to switch from lead vocal to rhythm guitar. No one will ever know why — though a solid guitarist, Dez made a far better frontman. But in July 1981, when the group hit NYC, they auditioned singers in the East Village, deciding then and there to offer the gig to 20-year-old Henry Garfield.

Henry, now sporting the Rollins surname, doubled as roadie for the rest of that tour, while Dez trained him on fronting Black Flag. Henry had to get a handle on the material, so they slowly eased him in, all five laboring on vocal and guitar parts at soundchecks. Dez sang gigs while Henry worked the stage and sang two or three encores a night — usually "Louie Louie," "Gimme Gimme Gimme" and "Police Story." Dez taught him the phrasing of new stuff like "TV Party," "Thirsty And Miserable" and "Room 13," while inventing rhythm guitar parts for all the songs; for instance, in "White Minority," Dez came up with a melodic riff giving the song way more wallop. The transition went on for two weeks — in Chicago, Detroit, Madison, Minneapolis and Salt Lake City.

Henry Rollins and stage-diver, LA, 1981
Photo by Edward Colver

DEZ CADENA: I quit singing because I was always a guitar player, and that's what I wanted to do. Greg and Chuck made the decision to get Henry in the band. Henry was a big fan; there were correspondences in the past. They approached me late one afternoon on tour in New York, and I was 'two sheets to the wind' — I was feeling good. They go, 'Henry is reluctant to do this because he doesn't want to make you feel bad, and we tried to explain that you're really a guitar player.' See, Henry at that time was kinda shy. Then they said, 'Look, we're in New York, let's go to Manny's, pick you up an amp and a guitar, practice, and have Henry ride with us halfway home, and by the end of the tour he'll know what to do by watching you.'

So, I called him up and didn't know what to say. I'd only met him a few days before in DC. It was bizarre, but it was something I had to do, kind of my obligation, especially since I did want to play guitar. I said, 'Hey dude, come down and jam with us!' I was all drunk and shit. I think he thought that was weird. But he came down, rode with us, helped us out, watched me sing. I don't know if it helped him much — I lost my voice all the time.

HENRY ROLLINS: Here's what happened: They played Irving Plaza with Bad Brains and UXA. They weren't gonna play DC so I said, 'I work hard, I've got money in the bank. What if I do a road trip and go see Flag?' After the show, they said, 'We're going to play an after-hours party at A7.' I drove from Irving Plaza to A7 and helped them load in their equipment. It was down-home — thirty people following the band. So they set up and started playing the set again in this tiny room. I knew I had to get in my car, drive back to DC, stick my head under

Black Flag logo by Raymond Pettibon

the work sink, put on my cap and apron, go work an all-day shift and do inventory that night. So I requested they play 'Clocked In' which is about going to work. Dez goes, 'This one's for Henry, because he's got to go to work soon.' The band was tuning up and I looked at Dez and the band was like, 'Henry's going to sing.' I knew all the words and sang it the way I thought it should be sung. I laid into that thing like I had blood in my eyes. We were playing — the guys in the band were looking at each other and looking at me going, 'Fuck!' because I was like a pitbull on a chain. The guys from DC were like, 'Yeah! Never knew ya had it in you!' Forty seconds later the song was over, and I gave the mic back to Dez and said, 'Thank you.' I got in my little VW and went back to DC.

A few days later I get a call from Greg Ginn. He said, 'We're up in New York. We wanna know if you wanna come up and hang out.' I thought, 'They must be bored.' He goes, 'Dez is moving down to rhythm guitar and we're looking for a singer — maybe you want to come up and, uh, we'll pay for the trainfare.' I said, 'Audition?' He goes, 'You know, come up and hang out.' He was vague. I said, 'Lemme talk to Dez — Dez, what's up?' 'Well, I want to play rhythm guitar so we're looking at singers.' So I got on the train, met the band at the Odessa, and said, 'What's up?' They said, 'We're auditioning a few singers and we saw you the other night and we thought it was cool.' They liked the S.O.A. record and dug the fact that I told them my favorite song was 'Damaged I,' the slow one. I said, 'Yeah, when you guys play that I have to keep myself from killing people.'

So we went to Mi Casa, a rehearsal room where the equipment was all set up. They handed me a mic and said, 'What song do you want to play?' I pinched myself 'cause I was standing there with Black Flag and they were looking at me to call the tune. I said 'Police Story' which starts with Ginn, and that feedback. He had no volume setting on his guitar, just an on/off switch. That's how the guy is — either asleep or all over you like a cheap suit. Whenever he turned the switch on, it'd feed back. If you hear those early Flag records, every time a song would begin you'd hear that screech because that was him turning his guitar on. I got through the set the best I could, then we played the set again — a whole 90 minutes of music. I shouted myself hoarse and they said, 'Wait here. We're gonna have a band meeting.' They came back in the room a little while later and said, 'Pack your bags. You're going to LA.' I said, 'Whadda ya mean?' They said, 'Do you wanna be in this band or not?' I'm like, 'Yeah!' 'Alright then, quit your job, get rid of your shit and let's go.' They handed me a handful of lyrics and said, 'See you soon. Here's the tour itinerary. Find us.'

I got on the Amtrak and went back to DC, stunned. I went to work and started calling people. The first call was to Ian: 'Ian, they want me to be the singer in Black Flag. What do you think?' I'll never forget what he said: 'Right on, Henry. You're the man. Go.' No hesitation on his part. I was at a major crossroads. I worked an ice cream store 50 hours a week. I'm from a little band that has an 11-minute set and no bass player. I was frustrated. I looked up to people like DKs and Flag, who lived like pirates in the van, and here I was in my job. All of a sudden, here was the call.

Henry's entrance was not seamless. Considerably younger than the others — he was in his very-early 20s, they were approaching 30 — Rollins was an outsider who left his whole world behind to join his favorite band.

SPOT: It took a while for Henry to click — he was very awkward. He came from one style and learned to plug into a whole other thing. Mentally it all worked; physically it took time. About the time *Damaged* was done, he'd pretty much settled in. As far as how the band changed, I don't think it had as much to with him as it did with the direction the band was going. Everything started slowing down and getting more exaggeratedly heavy.

DEZ CADENA: Henry was a little stiff at first, he was trying really hard, you could tell. S.O.A. was different than Flag — it was more Thrash — while Flag was a bit more pounding. But it's awkward for anyone joining a band — it was awkward for me. It didn't take him long, though.

BILL STEVENSON: Henry gets an 'A' for effort. He tried harder than anybody. He just forced himself to become a good singer — just by trying so hard. He forced himself to have a sense of rhythm, which he didn't have when he started. He forced himself to have a strong voice, which he didn't when he started. When he first joined Black Flag, he would sing one song and his voice was shot. He overcame all his weaknesses.

Black Flag live at Peppermint Lounge, NYC, December 1981
(L to R) Henry Rollins, Greg Ginn, Chuck Dukowski
Photo by Fred Berger

While Morris, Reyes and Cadena were nerdy and frenetic, Henry exuded a brooding vitriol previously unseen, though he was in a no-win situation.

AL BARILE (SS Decontrol): I remember meeting Henry Rollins at Irving Plaza and in hindsight, I gave him more credit than he deserved. He was a messenger, not a prophet.

DANNY SAGE (Heart Attack): With Henry it's a whole different band — they started doing Black Sabbath songs done by guys who couldn't play Sabbath. Henry grew his hair real long, wore just shorts, and was covered with tattoos. Even his version of 'Police Story' sucked. Henry reminded me of guys in my gym class that hated me because I liked Flag.

TAD KEPLEY (Anarchist activist): Like so many other people, the band that struck a major chord for me and really got me started was Black Flag. I first heard them with Dez singing. Rollins could never compare. He was a joke and a poseur — it was Greg Ginn's band to begin with. Greg Ginn *was* Black Flag, while Henry Rollins is the *Details* Magazine idea of what a rebel should be. And he always was. He always seemed insincere and full of himself, so I was never a huge fan of them during that era.

TONY CADENA (Adolescents): If I put on a Black Flag record before Henry Rollins joined, I get shivers up my spine from it.

Rollins met serious physical confrontation at every gig; even in the group's latter days, Henry fell victim to spit, cigarette burns, and sucker punches. It was rough.

HENRY ROLLINS: Oh man, they'd light your balls on fire, cigarettes on the legs, lots of lighters. You're on stage singing, all of a sudden some guy is lighting your earlobe on fire. People should have their fingers broken for that shit. A lot of it was directed at me. I got bottles bounced off the head — after a while, you become very wary, ready for someone to fuck with you — you get into you-versus-me situations. To this day, I take shit. 'What's your problem?' I go, 'I don't have a problem, man.' 'You have this attitude.' 'Yeah I have an attitude. You weren't subjected to what I was subjected to, so don't try to tell me how I am.'

BILL DOLAN (NYHC scene): I remember trying to speak with Henry after this show in DC, and he was such an incredible dick to me, I couldn't believe it. I understand he's bombarded with stupid people, but nonetheless, it did not feel great.

In summer '81, Flag returned to LA with Henry, went into the studio as a five-piece, and with producer Spot recorded *Damaged*, one of Rock's most important records. You judge music by its legacy: in *Damaged* you hear the future, a punishing Punk/Metal fusion in the style that now dominates. Henry wrote no lyrics, but delivered ferocious interpretations.

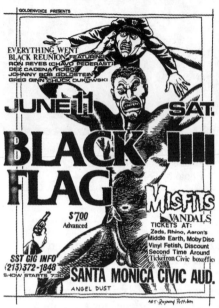

The sonic chaos on *Damaged* made *The Clash* or *Never Mind The Bollocks* seem tame in comparison. The Ginn/Cadena guitar tandem fueled Rollins's larynx-ripping performances. From the opening notes of "Rise Above" to the climax of "Damaged I," the disc stood as the standard to which every HC musician aspired.

Damaged is also famous for Ed Colver's arresting cover photo of Rollins punching (and breaking) a mirror — from his fist oozed a "blood" mixture of dishwashing liquid, instant coffee, and ink.

Show flyer, Black Flag and Misfits, LA, 1983
Everything Went Black reunion gig
Art by Raymond Pettibon
Collection of the author

ED COLVER (photographer): That was something that Henry Rollins and I did together. We put tape all over the back of the mirror before he smashed it. I love how weird and obscured that photo was — how it showed the side of his head, up into his fist. Unfortunately, no transparencies are left from those sessions. It's been totally lost to history.

To get *Damaged* into stores, SST cut a deal with Unicorn Records, a fly-by-night operation under the aegis of MCA. Greg and Chuck met the Unicorn guys while checking out LA recording studios. The label put out three or four records — all huge money-losers, as it turned out.

The deal was doomed from the start. A week before the release of *Damaged*, the *LA Times* quoted MCA's distribution head: "As a parent, I found it an anti-parent record." Some said MCA was looking to dump Unicorn — and they thought they could score moral points by appearing to refuse *Damaged* for ethical reasons. The band had already printed album covers, so over the MCA logo they placed a sticker bearing the "anti-family record" quote. Business had started terribly — Flag, stuck on Unicorn, had no major distribution.

JOE CARDUCCI (SST): Plan was to get MCA distribution at a time you couldn't even hope to get any of those creeps to listen to your demos. You'd send big labels your stuff; it would come back; they didn't even open it. But Flag thought they could be insulated from the majors yet have the distribution. They intended to do enough on their own so that MCA wouldn't have to do anything. When I got there, everyone in the band and extras like me and Spot and Mugger spent downtime on the phone, calling hundreds of stores around the country, asking if they had the new record. The idea was this was gonna be written as a store request — there'd be pent-up demand from buyers, so MCA wouldn't hafta do shit; the record would fly, the band would tour, that whole wheel'd be moving. But it didn't work that way.

Amid this controversy, Flag embarked on a disastrous Xmas '81 UK tour. Illegal alien Robo's visa troubles prevented his entry into Britain. Greg, in a pinch, called friend Bill Stevenson of the Descendents and flew him over.

DEZ CADENA: We played one show on a tour with the Exploited, GBH and Chron-Gen. Then Exploited quit the tour leaving us stranded and totally fucked. Ian MacKaye was on tour with us and even though we were cold and starving, nobody even offered us a place to stay. Back home, even if you were making no money, you'd always find someone who'd offer a place for the night. If it wasn't for two American girls who were friends of Chuck, who knows what would've happened. Brits were not good to us at all.

Drummer Bill Stevenson
(Descendents) replaced Robo
Photo from *Minuteflag* EP

IAN MACKAYE: We were in England with no shows, no money. Ten of us stayed in a one-room flat with two women from LA — one runs a bakery now in Boise; the other married Gilbert Hernandez from [comic book] *Love & Rockets*. Flag played with The Damned and Anti-Nowhere League at The Lyceum on the Strand. We met the women backstage, and went back to this one-room flat. We were desperate. The only food we got each day was two rolls, two pieces of cheese, an apple. I had a little money — but those guys kinda ripped me off that tour. I'd paid for my own ticket to get there — I was working for them, but they kept taking my money. I'd saved a few hundred to bring with me but my dad hid my cash because he thought I'd go to England and get robbed right away. He figured I could get money through American Express but of course this was before you could get cash on a credit card. So we were all broke; we ended up doing about eight shows. Fuck, Black Flag was so great.

When Black Flag returned to the US in early '82, they resumed intensive *Damaged* touring, playing cities no previous Punk or New Wave act had. Bill Stevenson had helped hugely, but clearly wanted to return to his own group. And no one could deal with Robo anymore. So Flag enlisted Emil, a DogTown skater from Marina Del Ray who played with Paul Roessler in Twisted Roots. A dark-skinned Germs-style drummer with blond dreads and a joint behind his ear, Emil stood out like a sore thumb. You couldn't imagine him in Black Flag. And he didn't last long, recording only the A-side of "TV Party." I saw them play four times that tour, and they were incredible.

JOE CARDUCCI: Emil decided halfway through the tour he was gonna quit, he didn't like it. He was from Hollywood, connected to the ex-Germs people. He was friends with Kira and Paul Roessler, these nature people that looked like Hippies and smoked a lot of pot. The Roesslers were from the Caribbean; their father was an underwater photographer. I don't know where Emil came from but he was great. Greg really liked him but Greg asked a lot from anybody who was in Black Flag, that's for sure.

When Flag with Emil hit Vancouver, they found his replacement in former D.O.A. drummer Chuck Biscuits. The new five-piece lineup recorded the amazing *My War* demo.

JOEY SHITHEAD (D.O.A.): We did a D.O.A. demo and Chuck argued over how to play a song. He had a hard time arguing with his older brother [Dimwit], an excellent drummer. Dimwit told him, 'Make it simpler, you're too busy!' Chuck said, 'Well, fuck you guys. I quit.' It so happened Flag was in town that weekend and were trying to get rid of Emil. They

Gaideavoice & ▬▬ PRESENT

BLACK FLAG ▚▚

45 GRAVE
DOA
DESCENDENTS
HÜSKER DÜ
UXB

$8.50 & 9.00
TICKETS AT
TICKETRON
& DOOR

SATURDAY
JULY 17

OLYMPIC
AUDITORIUM

Show flyer for Black Flag, Olympic Auditorium,
LA, 1982, depicting brief lineup with drummer
Chuck Biscuits (Left). Art by Raymond Pettibon
Collection of Laura Albert

stayed at our house and were sheepish — they said, 'We'd like to ask Chuck to drum for us.' We treated it like a sports deal. I said, 'You can have the rights to Chuck Biscuits, but you've got to pay the six hundred bucks he owes us for his drums!' — like selling Wayne Gretzky but instead of fifteen million we got $600. Chuck jumped in the van and stayed with them for six months.

Biscuits was excellent, but Greg fired him right after the demo for not aspiring to their work ethic. The search for a drummer resumed. Luckily, with the Descendents on hold while singer Milo Aukerman went to college, Bill Stevenson could return. Chuck Biscuits went on to Circle Jerks, Danzig and Social Distortion.

In summer of 1982, Black Flag released "TV Party," that quirky paean to early-80s couch-potato culture — unfortunately it's their best-known song. Fall '82 saw the final SST/Unicorn release, a promo-only interview record with KLOS-FM DJ Frazier Smith. It displayed caustic humor and wry social commentary — the last words from Flag for quite some time.

Fall '82 through spring '84 were trying times. In late '82, SST went on the legal attack, serving notice on Unicorn's bullshit business practices. The ensuing wrangle left Flag unable to work — they didn't stop practicing but California state judge Thomas Gearnhart restrained them from touring and putting out records. They tried to sidestep the injunction in mid-'83 with *Everything Went Black,* a two-LP set of pre-Rollins demos whose cover didn't mention Black Flag. This led to Greg and Chuck serving five days in LA County Jail.

GREG GINN: Unicorn went bankrupt. They were going down; they had lawyers involved who wanted to bleed the assets by running up huge legal bills. They were stripping the company down to where we couldn't get any money out of them. It was a lesson in how people manipulate corporations. It's a bizarre twist in the law that we weren't able to release a record for a certain period. Chuck and I went to jail for contempt of court. In LA, we were too well-known and the judge didn't like us. We released *Everything Went Black* without the name of the band, but the judge said it was Black Flag. Now, if somebody does something and won't put a name on it, there's nothing to stop it. But Unicorn were going bankrupt and had nothing to lose. It cost us a lot of money that we owed a lawyer until way after the band broke up. I'm sure he was surprised when we came back and paid him.

BILL STEVENSON: Unicorn had us fucked. We couldn't release our music, so Greg and I basically became paralegals. We had this pretty cool lawyer who said, 'Okay, look, you guys, you don't have any money. You can fight this case yourself — I'll just sign the papers — but you have to do all the work.' That was cool … and we fucking destroyed them in court. We got them in so much trouble; we got the FBI on their ass. You see, Greg only plays offense, he never plays defense ever. So, he looked at all their other court cases pending in the public record, and he found one where there was some supposed shrimp-boat shipment from South America or something for $790,000, and determined it was probably cocaine money. He threatened those guys and told them to never bother us again or they'd end up in jail. That was the last we saw of them.

JOE CARDUCCI: We caught them moving checks around. They were sellin' records to distributors that we dealt with. They'd filed Chapter 11, and we found out they were taking checks that were supposed to go into the Chapter 11 account and putting them into one of their non-bankrupt corporations. When they did that, the judge threw them into Chapter 7 and foreclosed on 'em and that freed us — much to the judge's consternation, 'cause he fucking hated us. He looked at those Raymond Pettibon drawings on *Everything Went Black* and wanted to lock us up. The whole thing took over a year, maybe two. Greg saved money by doing all the research. Our lawyer pointed him to all the legal books, that way we wouldn't get billed at a hundred bucks an hour, which was 50 percent off anyway. Bill also did a lot of legal work. If Bill hadn't put the Descendents on hold and done what he did, I'm not sure the band would've stuck around. Greg had reason to see it through 'cause the music was all written, all the way up to *In My Head*. There were so many bills to pay, it would've been unconscionable to not deliver the music after investing all that time and bullshit.

Though impoverished, Flag couldn't go out and tour again on the same album with the same set — they would've burned out audiences. But if they played new material they couldn't release, imitators would've ripped them off. So they were stuck — and broke. Well before the court threw out the Unicorn injunction, they had the next album, *My War*, in production.

JOE CARDUCCI: The Necros came to LA, and wanted to come to the practice place. Greg put them off, thought about it, and decided not to have them over — the band was practicing *My War* and *Damaged* but were barred from recording due to Unicorn bullshit. He wasn't about to let these other bands, these imitators, snake his new material — and you know that would have happened. As soon as Flag added a second guitar, everybody added a second guitar. Soon as they got rid of him, everybody got rid of the second guitar! And good bands doing that, like Minor Threat. I suppose people had their reasons, but it was noticeable. That was Greg's musical dilemma.

SST's freedom from Unicorn came at a huge cost: insolvency and inner turmoil. A real ugly era lasted most of 1983: Greg wasn't gonna fire Chuck and Chuck wasn't gonna quit. Chuck didn't just play bass, he played "lead bass," jamming like a lead guitarist. For a while, Greg thought of adding a second bass so Chuck could "go off" and do his thing. The tension led to Dez's departure for a solo career focusing on his guitar work. With Paul Roessler, Dez formed D.C.3, shocking Hardcore crowds with two-hour sets of Deep Purple and Mountain-infused Rock, as heard on their four SST albums.

Black Flag singer Dez Cadena
became a guitar hero and formed D.C.3
Photo by Mike Malinin, D.C.3 SST press kit, 1984
Collection of the author

DEZ CADENA: I quit Flag 'cause I was playing guitar every day, gettin' better and better. I started feeling, after songs like 'Thirsty & Miserable,' I wanted to start writing songs in a different style. I told Greg I wanted to start my own band, make my own mistakes, and take my own chances; he totally understood. He gave me my rig to take — that's when I did D.C.3.

By the end of 1983, Dukowski was out. He started to work full-time as Black Flag's booking agent/manager while playing with SWA (along with vocalist Merril

Ward and guitarist Sylvia Juncosa), who made six hard-to-handle discs for SST. With Dukowski gone, Ginn played bass on *My War* under the alias "Dale Nixon."

HENRY ROLLINS: Dukowski wasn't really booted. Dukowski quit and simultaneously got vibed out. Rhythmically, he was very wild, more like a lead guitar player — listen to the basslines, he wasn't laying down rhythm, he was all over the neck, and this drove Ginn nuts. At the time we started *My War*, Greg said, 'I'm having a real hard time with Chuck. I'm having to play to the drums. I'm not a rhythm player, I'm a lead player.' Sometimes we'd practice 'Can't Decide' all afternoon. Ginn's music had all these off-time holds; it was not straight time. He insisted 'Gimme Gimme Gimme' was never played correctly. Greg, Bill and Chuck would do the intros to the songs, I'd be there with the mic waiting for the vocal, and Greg would go, 'No, no, c'mon Chuck!' You'd see Chuck practicing to a click track, trying to get himself more in line. Finally, they could no longer play together, so Chuck said, 'I'm quittin'. I'm gonna manage the band.' I said, 'Do you want me to come with you?' because at that point I was more in line with Dukowski spiritually. He was more the *My War* guy, Greg was the *Loose Nut* guy. Both were cool but there were two clearly different brains going on. One guy was going for a Darwinian/Nietzschean thing, while the other was going for the more introverted, intellectual, less-tactile Ginn thing. Chuck was about getting blood flowing. When I said, 'Do you want me to go with you?' he went, 'No, you should stay in Black Flag.' So I did.

Show flyer for Black Flag, Houston, March 1984, *My War* tour
Art by Raymond Pettibon
Collection of Perry Webb

Legal problems behind, Black Flag released the long-awaited *My War* album in spring '84 — its seven-minute Metal dirges and Fusion-style time signatures proved too much for many fans. By that point Flag weren't even listening to Punk anymore — they dug post-Ozzy Black Sabbath of the day like *Heaven And Hell* or *Mob Rules* — with Ronnie James Dio singing — or *Born Again* — with Ian Gillan. Henry got heavily into post-New Wavers Nick Cave and The Birthday Party, opening some minds at SST, where otherwise they'd to Rush-style FM Rock all day.

BILL STEVENSON: Around the time of *My War*, we were listening to Black Sabbath's *Born Again*. I loved that — it sounds more like a bulldozer about to run over your head. They took *Volume 4* to its absolute extreme. Songs like 'Thrashed' and 'Disturbing The Priest' were ideal: Black Sabbath with a real singer! We were into *Heaven And Hell*, *Mob Rules*, *Born Again*.

HENRY ROLLINS: The post-Ozzy Sabbath with Dio and Gillan was a big deal for Greg Ginn. He got ahold of *Heaven And Hell* and the first Dio album simultaneously, and once Ginn got into something, man, that was it. He'd play *Heaven And Hell* every minute. When I heard it, I felt like, 'It's gotta be Ozzy or nobody,' but they played it in the van so much, I eventually realized, 'This stuff fucking rules!' I was a convert. After we lost those tapes we got into ZZ Top *Eliminator*. That was our soundtrack for 1984. I think we wore out that cassette three times. We played it before every gig, and we played it in the van all the time. It was our wake-up-and-drive tape. All the ZZ Top records were in the Flag lexicon, as well as

MC5, Velvet Underground, early Nugent, Sabbath, AC/DC
with Bon Scott, Captain Beyond — Stoner Rock. Not
much Punk Rock. The only Punk you'd see around would
be SST stuff and our friends. Otherwise, Punk was too
lightweight for Ginn and Dukowski. They'd look at Punks
and go, 'Pussies. You're too busy with your eye makeup to
get crazy.' I was coming from a Punk thing. I'd play The
Damned, and these guys would look at me and say, 'Are
you fucking kidding me?' They thought Nick Cave was a
poser, they thought Einstürzende Neubauten was
bullshit. They thought so much was weak.

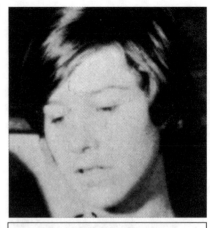

Bass player Kira Roessler
replaced Chuck Dukowski
Photo from *Minuteflag* EP

**Flag eventually lost interest in the Hardcore
movement that worshipped them as kings. This
self-contained touring/recording outfit instead took
their cues from The Grateful Dead, for whom Greg
dreamed about opening; most of the SST crew were
Deadheads. More and more, Flag emphasized the
jams rather than the songs. And no one — not even those Rasta-fried Bad Brains —
smoked more herb. By 1984, they'd burn an ounce or two a week (a fringe benefit of
working with Goldenvoice promoter Gary Tovar, who later served a lengthy prison
sentence for marijuana distribution).**

DEZ CADENA: I'm not a big Grateful Dead fan. Greg loved them, Chuck respected them. A
lot of it had to do with their whole concept — all their fans were dedicated, being
underground while selling tons of records. I have my own opinion about that band. I take
my Psychedelia seriously, and I know they can get pretty trippy, but I'm more into
cyberspace than cowboy-space. They were a Country band.

**They brought in Paul Roessler's sister, 22-year-old Kira, to replace Chuck; since
age 16 she had played in minor LA acts such as Waxx and Sexsick. Few groups
worked harder than Flag during Kira's two-year stint.**

HENRY ROLLINS: Kira was infinitely more talented
than anyone who ever walked onstage at an L7 gig. It was
cool to have a skinny girl bass player in Black Flag. That's
where our band was at. You'd hear, 'Black Flag are macho.'
'Oh yeah — check out the balls on our bass player!' She
was a damn good player. We used to go out but I broke up
with her, which pissed her off to no end because *no one*
breaks up with Kira Roessler. Six months later, she was in
the band. Greg came to me, 'Uh, we're going to audition
Kira. I really like her; I want her in the band. Are you
going to be okay with that?' I said, 'Greg, sure. I've got no
problem with Kira. She's a great bass player and I respect
her.' She was never very friendly to me in the band. Later
on, she mellowed out a bit, but we were never pals. I gave
her 110% respect but she came in when Black Flag was up
against a wall, financially and culturally. We went through
some of the gnarliest tours any American band has ever
been through. Guys quit and went home crying and Kira
never complained once. She was intense and played her
ass of every night with precision and determination. You
can't fuck with her.

The hairy Henry Rollins
Photo by Laura Albert

BLACK FLAG

SLIP IT IN

ST. VITUS

TOM TROCCOLI'S DOG

WEDNESDAY
DECEMBER
19, 1984

167
CHURCH
ST.

TICKETS:
$7 now $9 door
at
record peddler
records on
wheels

Y'ALL AGES

Show flyer for Black Flag
Slip It In tour, December 1984
Art by Raymond Pettibon
Collection Of Laura Albert

For all their work, Black Flag never made money. Their tours were brutal jaunts in a beat-up, spraypainted van — if it broke down, everyone panhandled. They did over 200 dates a year, rarely making more than a few hundred bucks a show. I set up some gigs in DC, and they — plus two SST support acts — never netted more than $1500, even at 80% of the door after costs. Bandmembers survived on $10 per diems. They set the standard for non-economic success.

BILL STEVENSON: Greg taught me that work ethic is cool, but that work ethic and 75-cents will get you a cup of coffee. You have to succeed, not just try. It doesn't matter if you try, it's gotta happen. I'm talking about the music — I don't give a fuck about the economics.

At the SST office, guys slept under desks or in refrigerator boxes. For a typical dinner, Carducci, who ran the operation, heated and served a can of V-8 as tomato soup; Mugger rolled catfood into whitebread balls. They'd steal from all-you-can-eat buffets, visit food shelters, and "dumpster dive." After bringing them by Matt Pinfield's WRSU show in '84, I took a few Flag guys to my parents' house in Jersey to let 'em raid the fridge.

RAY FARRELL: I'm often introduced as 'the SST guy,' which is like having been in 'Nam. Like 'This guy's been in battle, he's slept on floors, with rats crawling on his chest working at a record label.' Inconceivable stuff to people in the music industry. These seem like romantic stories in retrospect — but how romantic it was at the time, I don't recall.

Black Flag's "look" featured the ridiculous outfits Greg's dad Regis bought by-the-pound at thrift shops ("Ginnwear" or "Regiswear"). The guys wore baggy versions of Ben Davis polyester pants, bell-bottoms or flairs, just cut badly. But they never could've survived if not for the generosity of the elder Ginns.

HENRY ROLLINS: Mrs. Ginn is a saint, her and Mr. Ginn. If the Ginns weren't around, Black Flag would've broken up. They basically floated the band, and these are not rich people. They loved their kids. I'd do anything for Mrs. Ginn to this day — World War II concentration camp survivor, lost a lot of her family to Russian bullets. A woman you cannot front on. I have great respect for them. They put me up for a few years, fed me and would not allow me to pay rent. Me and D Boon helped build their new house and they said, 'Henry, we have a bedroom for you.' When the band broke up, Greg told me, 'I want you out of my parents' house.' I said, 'I wouldn't think of staying there.' Greg will always think I have it in for him and don't like him but I have nothing but respect for him. I don't care what he says about me. The fact that I keep in touch with his parents really bums him out.

The hard work began to pay off. What began as a subsistence mechanism developed into a formidable commercial enterprise. SST's stable included Hüsker Dü, Minutemen, Meat Puppets and Saccharine Trust. Fans wondered how SST could put out so much product — Flag could put together an entire album for under $1500; Minutemen did the two-record *Double Nickels On The Dime* for less.

RAY FARRELL: SST was into the idea of spreading money as a family. You'd get into the lifestyle of what SST was about — like, if you were into Flag, you should check out Saccharine Trust. You were getting all kinds of music, all points of view, and at the same time, all very uncommercial and disconnected from any other scene. People were down on Flag and SST — they weren't as interested in sharing the 'burgeoning Punk explosion' with everybody: they had their own thing intact. They were also having fun with it: coming into a city, basically setting it on fire. An SST package was like the circus coming to town. I liked the approach, nobody was doing that.

SST knew what marketing was all about. They really got into promoting — Henry wrote letters and answered mail, Chuck was on the phone to radio and retail, Spot was in the studio — nobody just sat around. When they weren't working, they were practicing. Eventually they got enough money to get a storage place and rehearsed in there. They'd finally beaten Hollywood and started getting respect.

MINUTE**FLAG**

Minuteflag
Joint Black Flag/Minutemen EP, SST
Art by Joe Baiza (Saccharine Trust)
Collection of the author

Steve "Mugger" Corbin, their roadie, went on to oversee the entire operation. He ran away from home at 13 to escape an abusive father, and through Punk Rock, eventually became a CPA and a computer industry mogul. Mugger also fronted Nig Heist, one of the most vile outfits ever, with Ginn, Dukowski and Stevenson either onstage in Hippie wigs or playing behind the amps. Songs like "Put My Love In Your Mouth" (off *Snort My Load*) really fucking upset people. An infamous cassette of a Denver show featured promoter Barry Fay throwing them off stage, announcing to the crowd, "I promise, you'll never hear another piece of shit like this on my stage again!" When Nig Heist played, they got beaten up, chased out, or fucked with. But when it came to SST, everything was dead serious.
Not only didn't Black Flag want the credit "Gods of Hardcore," they did everything they could to run away from it all. With time, they went further and further out of their way to alienate audiences. In 1984, the guys grew their hair long. Their music had developed into this twisted Rock experience, evolving from the brattish Punk of "Six Pack" and "Nervous Breakdown" to the gnarly Metal of *Slip It In* and *Who's Got The 10-1/2?* They became heavy and intense and, in a strange way, very sexual — uncommon in the HC milieu.

GLEN E. FRIEDMAN: They grew their hair long to get back at Punkers. They started putting down Punks because they though they were getting cliché. But it's like, 'Why are you putting down what propagated you?' You can challenge people's views but don't put it down and take advantage of your position. I began to see that happen a bit with them. You heard these long instrumentals and songs like 'Slip It In' — it wasn't the old Black Flag philosophy. To talk graphically about sex was not their style. They were becoming campy and the metaphors were no longer interesting. There were a few good songs on *My War* but I started liking the music less. A whole album comes out and I don't give a fuck about any one song and I see them developing this direction I'm not too keen on? And Dukowski is kicked out? That hurt me so much. Greg was the major force but Dukowski was a big part of the philosophy. Greg said Chuck couldn't keep time but fuck that, Chuck was a real motivator. He was psychotic in an important way.

Tour poster for Black Flag, 1985
Who's Got The 10 1/2? tour
Collection of the author

Make no mistake about it: Black Flag was Ginn's group. In such cases, if one person makes all the decisions, they also make all the mistakes. In general, less compelling work develops than with a confluence of personalities. Hey — Paul McCartney was awful without John Lennon; Paul surrounded himself with sycophants, so no one put the brakes on his half-baked ideas. It was usually bad news when Greg got everything he wanted.

HENRY ROLLINS: Basically, it didn't matter who the singer was — it was Greg's band. Greg didn't want a singer; he wanted a mouthpiece for his ideas. People'll say, 'Henry hurt Black Flag,' but you could've had Dez the whole time — Greg would've still done an instrumental record. Greg didn't want bandmembers, he wanted people to do what he said. He wanted a metronome for a drummer, a metronome for a bass player, a singer who would not be a frontman. Anyone who had any personality up front was not welcome. Even at the end, if I'd go, 'Yeah!' while Greg was doing a lead he'd say after, 'Don't step on my leads.' 'What'd I do?' 'You were talking while I was playing.' 'When I went Yeah? Okay, Greg, I'm sorry.' It was weird.

And it was not the greatest idea to have Greg produce Black Flag records. When I hear them now, I go, 'What I would give to get a good engineer in there to remix this.' I don't think Spot was much better. At the end of the day, Spot was more fun than functional. He got bummed out when Black Flag no longer recorded 16-track at Media Arts, and it was no longer his lab experiment. When Ginn got ambitious, Spot got dissed.

JOE CARDUCCI: When you look at it, by '84, a lot of the bands were changing, as was the audience. When you look at the groups on SST, I feel the Minutemen were less interesting; I didn't think they were gonna last. I'm talking about *Three Way Tie (For Last)*, which is sub-par. Hüsker Dü had peaked already. By '84, Flag were structurally much more of an arty band, with Kira, Bill and Greg. They were not giving the same physical kick they had given, and they were approaching things in a more abstract way.

In 1985, Black Flag released their final two albums, *Loose Nut* and *In My Head*. The latter sported their glossiest studio production and featured the great tunes "Drinking And Driving" and "Retired At 21."

BILL STEVENSON: *"In My Head* is a cool record, as close as anybody's ever got to fusing totally aggressive heavy Rock with super-progressive riffing and also a sorta Pop song structure. I don't dig the way it sounds, but musically we finally arrived.

JOE CARDUCCI: The last record, *In My Head*, is the record Greg was trying to make from *Damaged* on. Greg was frustrated with the band. Well, he was frustrated for other reasons too; everything was pent-up. *Damaged* is an album full of songs written for one guitar but recorded with a two-guitar line-up — it doesn't sound how it should. *Everything Went Black* is the way it should sound. *My War* and *Slip It In* are written for two guitars but recorded with one. So, their whole discography's fucked up. I mean — we're lucky the stuff exists, considering the fucked-up situations.

In summer '85 Flag came apart at the seams. The early days had been difficult, but at least the guys had each other. Now, Greg couldn't stand anyone he was working with. Some good shows happened, but not enough to keep things going. Drummer Anthony Martinez replaced Bill Stevenson.

BILL STEVENSON: Greg and I weren't getting along, and things were getting ugly. Henry was getting into all his poetry shit, or whatever that shit is. I just felt like it wasn't really focused, so Greg and I talked, and he was just as glad for me to go as I was to go. It was definitely mutual.

D Boon (Minutemen)
His death signaled the end.
Photo from *Minuteflag* EP

By the end of '85 Kira left, too. Like all other Flag alumni, she'd toiled hard for scant reward. A guy named C'el replaced her. With this lineup, they did one final tour, perhaps the most arduous of their career, but drew less interest — and smaller crowds. They also had a noticeably different vibe: you'd always find either Anthony Martinez or C'el, the macho Hispanic dudes, fucking some skank in the back of the van after a show.

JEFF McDONALD: Black Flag: they used Hardcore until they got bored of it, went off on their weird trip, and basically alienated themselves to the point where they could barely draw a few hundred people at the end of their career. But they were doing some interesting music near the end, so they were willing to sacrifice it all for art.

SST took a huge psychological blow in December '85 when D Boon died in a car wreck. With the Minutemen on the verge of success, this avoidable tragedy numbed all who knew them. Ironically, the Minutemen had recently teamed up with their hero, Rock scribe and BÖC associate Richard Meltzer.

MIKE WATT: The day D Boon got killed — he and his girl went off to Arizona. Richard Meltzer gave us ten songs; we were going to record with Meltzer. We couldn't believe it — Blue Oyster Cult! We'd just gotten back from the R.E.M. tour; D Boon was red with fever, really sick. I said, 'D, man, don't go. Look, here's the songs, we have the ten lyrics.' One was about a ticket, 'Dead man found in car, ticket on windshield.' They were short and hilarious. We were really into it. I gave him the lyrics, and he goes, 'Don't worry Bones, I'm gonna just lay in the back; when I get there I'll read 'em.' She fell asleep at the wheel, the van rolled, and that was the end of it.

> --------PRESS RELEASE--------
> 12-24-85
> We regret to inform you that Dennes Dale Boon (D. Boon) singer guitarist and founding member of San Pedro's MINUTEMEN was killed in an automobile accident in Arizona late Sunday night or early Monday morning December 22, 1985. D. Boon was born in Napa California on April 1, 1958, was a lifetime resident of San Pedro, and graduated from San Pedro High. This is all the information available to us at this time. Ray Farrell can be contacted for additional information.

Everything falls apart, December 1985:
SST press release announcing the death of D Boon
Collection of the author

The SST family splintered. The death knell came in early '86, when Warner Bros. signed Hüsker Dü — the first Hardcore outfit to ink to a major.

GLEN E. FRIEDMAN: Where I realized it was getting unhealthy was when Hüsker Dü signed; I started hearing rumblings that Hüsker Dü sucked because they left SST. Like, 'You

BLACK FLAG

photo: Ed Colver

SST RECORDS
(US) P.O. Box 1, Lawndale, CA 90260
Office: (213) 575-0110
Booking: (213) 618 0797
(UK) 208 Bravington, London W9
Office/Booking: (01) 278-3331

SST press shot of the final Black Flag line-up, 1986
(L to R): Henry Rollins, C'el, Anthony Martinez, Greg Ginn
Photo by Edward Colver
Collection of the author

used to love them — now because they're not in your family you don't like them?' You could feel them losing their power in the community; they weren't happy about that. I didn't like their prejudice to the outside world. A new SST brainwashing was going on. If you weren't on SST, Black Flag wouldn't like you. They began to only stick to their own kind. They began to put down every other band. Anything they weren't a part of was fascist or fucked up. Lists of places to play were no longer public information. Black Flag started to hoard that stuff to themselves; they were treading new territory around the country, but they got hardened and decided to keep to their own more.

Ginn had become a bitter, paranoid pothead, obsessed with instrumental music: Flag made the all-instrumental *The Process Of Weeding Out* (note the pot reference); on the final tours, they'd start with an instrumental number, after either Greg's instrumental trio Gone (with the Trenton, NJ tag-team of bassist Andrew Weiss and drummer Simeon Cain) or his Prog Rock jam combo October Faction opened; and in early '86 Flag even played a few instrumental gigs without Henry at select LA clubs. Greg and his friends would get stoned, go onstage — and no one gave a shit. Even the merchandising guy, Tom Trocoli, got into the act with his own band, Tom Troccoli's Dog.

MIKE WATT: I thought Tom Trocoli was a sidemouse. He weaseled his way in. He didn't have anything to offer. October Faction, I had no respect for. I saw these stickers on tour that said, 'October Faction Still Sucks.' It was just a jam-fucking-session — I couldn't be part of that on wax. That, to me, was when they were abusing too far. It's enough to bring your own bands on tour, but then to have a jerk-off? I didn't dig that.

By this time, Rollins had gotten established on his own, doing Spoken Word tours and writing *Spin* articles. That's where he was at. Ginn decided to break up the band after their last show in Detroit on June 28, 1986. Appropriately, Black Flag stopped when Greg said so.

BLACK FLAG

INSTRUMENTAL

BLACK FLAG

THE PROCESS OF WEEDING OUT

Black Flag without Henry Rollins: SST press kit for instrumental Black Flag EP, 1986
Collection of the author

GLEN E. FRIEDMAN: Black Flag made their fans think but I don't think they were trying to energize their audience. It was all just for their own personal interests. They just wanted to play music a different way. You should be selfish as an artist, you shouldn't be doing it for the people, but don't take 'em for granted either. I grew apart from them. There was this whole brainwashing, where I saw how they put down Hüsker Dü and Minor Threat and other important bands. I saw it as jealousy. Everyone was sick of their whole attitude. Black Flag started playing smaller gigs and no one came out to see them. When Black Flag broke up, it was like, 'It's about time.'

Ginn immediately focused on Gone full-time, but things never panned out. They did an excruciating tour: small shows, every day, sometimes a few times a day. In NYC they did six sets in one day (I saw two). Mercifully Greg called things off that December. In February '87, Henry rang up Sim and Andrew and, with guitarist Chris Haskett, formed Rollins Band.

SST press shot of Gone, 1986
(L-R): Simeon Cain, Greg Ginn, Andrew Weiss
Photo by Naomi Peterson
Collection of the author

SST did not remain an important force. In 1984 SST was poised for long-term success as a defiant indie. They laid the groundwork, and paved the way for everyone. But SST went from a channel for essential artists to a ineffectual barrage of mediocre shit like Zoogz Rift and Das Damen — to the point where no one cared anymore. SST released a few decent off-beat ensembles: Always August, Saint Vitus — but by then, with Ginn resentful and out of the loop, the label couldn't move forward. Flag and SST eventually just frittered away their originally infectious and inspiring D.I.Y. vibe. •

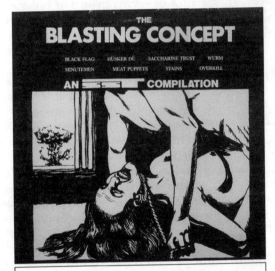

The Blasting Concept
SST compilation with Black Flag, Minutemen, Meat Puppets, Saccharine Trust, and Hüsker Dü, 1982
Cover art by Raymond Pettibon
Collection of the author

LOS ANGELES:
HOW COULD HELL BE ANY WORSE?

Hate my family, hate my school
Speed limit and the golden rule
Hate people who ain't what they seem
American dream, it's gonna swallow you whole
— Bad Religion, "American Dream"

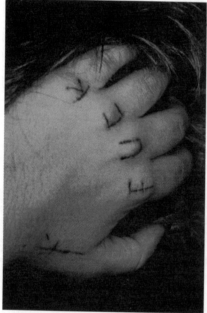

"Mr. Fuck Hand," LA, 1981
Photo by Edward Colver

Aside from a few urbane hoods like Downtown LA and Hollywood, Southern California is one giant, sterile suburb. To the east of LA, endless burbs fade to desert. To the west, endless ocean. North is the San Fernando Valley. Southward lie boundless clusters of families trying to live the American Dream. A half-hour south of Downtown LA are the beach towns collectively known as the South Bay, then Orange County, and still further is San Diego and, finally, Mexico. Hardcore was born of that suburbia.

The South Bay hosted a minor Punk scene of a non-descript group of bohemians in tune with the Hollywood movement, featuring local group The Last. Many of those South Bay types were ex-surfers and Heavy Metal glue-sniffers.

JEFF McDONALD (Red Cross): There was a small group of about 200 Punk Rock-type arty weirdos. But the cops shut down shows in the South Bay areas immediately. It was very conservative. Part of the fun of going to shows was watching 'em get busted up. There'd be 30 people there; it'd be real exciting. They tried shows in San Pedro where it was a little more liberal, but in San Pedro you had low rider gangs. They'd see weird-looking people and assume Punks were rival gangs — so there'd be baseball bat fights and all that. So even though there was this new scene of South Bay musicians, it was hard to play there until many years later.

Most SST outfits, like the Minutemen from San Pedro and Black Flag from Hermosa Beach, came from the South Bay, working-class and relatively diverse, in comparison to nearby Orange County (affectionately called "Reagan Country"). Seemingly everyone in OC had that weird sense of twinkie unity that exists when everyone comes from the same background, with the same uniform and attitude.

MIKE WATT (Minutemen): The kids from OC came from money — they all lived at their parents' house. You'd have these parties when the parents were out of town and shit in the swimming pool. We weren't as bad off as the Hollywood guys, with thirty guys shootin' heroin in a bathroom. We all had jobs. I don't think D Boon had a weekend off right before he died.

MILO AUKERMAN (Descendents): In the South Bay where we're all from, it was more like the predecessors to slackers — kids in T-shirts and jeans. OC was more violent than our scene, but those kids would drive up to all the Flag shows and wreak havoc.

MIKE WATT: The Orange County guys were not enlightened dudes — they weren't so faithful: you'd see them in parkas doin' the fuckin' Mod thing or Rockabilly thing. They were the first good-lookin' guys on the scene. They didn't put out their own records. Posh Boy, this guy from the Hollywood scene, ripped them off. TSOL had a manager! OC bands got into makeup and dressing up. Bands in places like DC wore T-shirts like us — I'd equate DC Hardcore more with the SST thing.

In addition to Flag and Minutemen, other notable South Bay groups were Red Cross (Hawthorne), Saccharine Trust (Wilmington), and Descendents (Manhattan Beach). They all kinda watched each other's backs.

MILO AUKERMAN: Black Flag were the first band on the block, so to speak, then Minutemen started around the time the original Descendents lineup started. The nice thing about those bands is that whenever we played, we were all on a bill together; there was this one-big-happy-family thing; we would support each other's endeavors. Minutemen put out our first record. I look back at those days with fond memories because I see the way music is run today, and I don't think that stuff could ever happen again.

JOE CARDUCCI (SST): There's a unique mix of bohemia, blue-collar, redneck and Hippie/Beach culture in the South Bay, from San Pedro to Manhattan Beach, which you don't find anywhere else in the country. There was no fear in Black Flag or The Minutemen or The Descendents or Saint Vitus or Saccharine Trust. They can be embarrassed, and they make fun of themselves for their dorky moves or whatever, but they don't really care how they look or what people are gonna say.

"The Church," venue and hangout where the earliest LA Hardcore shows took place, Hermosa Beach, CA, 1980
Photo by Edward Colver

The South Bay scene came together at a vacant church in Hermosa, then known as the Creative Craft Center, called by kids "The Church." Lots of HC types hung out, did drugs, and got into overly dramatic situations. Much of *The Decline...* was shot there. Ron Reyes lived down in the storage room, which doubled as a practice space. Guys in Black Flag and The Last lived in that crazy place, too.

TONY CADENA (Adolescents): The Church was really fun. You'd go downstairs to this little room where the bands played. When I went, there were no problems, no police. If you went to a club, you'd always run the risk of getting popped for drinking outside. There wasn't that problem at a party where the music was deadened by the earth. I saw The Klan there and Black Flag with Keith singing; that was amazing. The room was electrified — even the walls seemed alive. I wasn't on drugs — I was a kid excited by the music. People were flying all over the place, the band was all over the place, the room was hot, crowded and wild. Up until them, I'd never seen anything like Black Flag. Their sound was totally unique. The charge I got from them and early Agent Orange spoke to me. I'd seen English bands, bands in bigger places, but something about the close quarters was explosive.

STEVEN McDONALD (Red Cross): The first group we ever saw from the Hardcore movement was when we shared a rehearsal space with Black Flag at The Church in Hermosa

Beach. They decided to have a party; usually you couldn't have those because the landlord was this acid-damaged Hippie freak who hated everyone. They had this band play at the party called The Skrews from Huntington Beach who were all these people who worshipped Sid Vicious — which couldn't have been any more uncool at that moment — and sang with English accents. It was unbelievable to us. There was lots of violence. They were our age but we had little in common. There was a gang that called themselves Vicious Circle — all these Orange County teenage guys who eventually turned into TSOL.

The Church was about to evict everyone right as Dez joined Flag, so the band invited every violent goon they knew for a massive demolition party.

DEZ CADENA (Black Flag): The last show at The Church, we decided to have some fun and use Orange County as a tool. We took our mailing list, invited everyone down for a party, advertising there was a new singer of Black Flag. We did the show right on the altar, as a stage; we got like 500 people to show up and fuck shit up. We were packed up and moved out at this point. The cops came down and there was a mini-riot. We got in our van when we were done, and left on tour — on our way to San Francisco, Seattle, Portland, Vancouver. We came back a week later; there was a big piece in *The Easy Reader*: 'Hermosa Beach police kick Black Flag out of town.' We'd planned it that way. We were gonna be evicted. There was trouble from people hanging around The Church. The cops were spying on us: there'd literally be detectives going around as fake bums. To say 'Screw you!' we invited all the 'hate kill destroy' people from OC to come fuck shit up. Hey, if you can fuck cops up and get away with it, why not?

Leave me, leave me, leave me alone
Now, now, now
And please don't make fun of me
— Red Cross, "Burnout"

RED CROSS from Hawthorne excelled early on. Most HC-era outfits were young; Steve and Jeff McDonald started The Tourists in junior high in '79; the brothers changed names to avoid confusion with the New Wave act that spawned Annie Lennox. On '80's *Red Cross* EP (Posh Boy) the original lineup — vocalist/guitarist Jeff, bassist/vocalist Steve, guitarist Greg Hetson, drummer John Stelia (to be replaced by Ron Reyes, later of Black Flag) — played songs like "Annette's Got The Hits" and "Cover Band," as well as a paean to the rape of Connie Francis (which emerged in Hetson's next group, Circle Jerks, as "I Just Want Some Skank").

Steve McDonald (above) and Jeff McDonald of Red Cross, 1982
Photo by Steve Housden, from *Born Innocent* LP

DEZ CADENA (Black Flag): Ron started living at The Church, and joined Black Flag. I joined Red Cross on second guitar for about six months — it wasn't a very successful lineup but we did a couple of shows. It was this guy Johnny something on drums, me, Jeff, Steve and Chet Lehrer the guitarist from Wasted Youth. Obviously, there was a lot more people than we needed.

By 1982's *Born Innocent*, Red Cross was a "half-all-girl band": Steve and Jeff plus Tracy Marshak on guitar and Janet Housden on drums. In a highlight of their career, they appeared on the cover of *Flipside*.

JEFF McDONALD: *Born Innocent* was funny to make because we didn't realize we were making an album. Steven and I were both heavily into pot at the time, so the only way the guy could get us to do sessions was to promise us bongload after bongload. This guitarist Tracy played on half the record. She overslept the first session. The second session, when she did show up, she had these hysterical crying fits in the studio, where we had to beg her to play. It was pathetic. We were all pathetic back then.

STEVE McDONALD: The moment we split from Hardcore was the day we said weren't gonna cut our hair anymore. And that was 1982. The music wasn't interesting; socially it was just a drag. By the time we were on the *Flipside* cover, we had shoulder-length hair, and your average reader was bummed. We had two girls in the band, so Jeff and I said in the interview that we were saving up money to get sex changes so we could be an all-girl group like The Runaways. You couldn't get more alienating. Between that, the *Born Innocent* album, and us deciding not to cut our hair, sealed the deal that we were no longer part of that scene. There was no turning back. When I should've been enjoying the fruits of Hardcore, we forced people to buy thrift store records and get into Arthur Lee.

Red Cross became Redd Kross to avoid confusion with the relief service. That was '84, the year of their Trash Rock magnum opus *Teen Babes From Monsanto*, with takes on the Stones' "Citadel" and "Deuce" by Kiss, shocking covers for a HC band. With loud guitars, long hair, and tawdry vibe, Redd Kross developed a thrift-store New York Dolls vibe. (Many cite Redd Kross's '87 album *Neurotica* as the first Grunge record ... they still carry on, in greatly altered form.)

Circle Jerks, LA, 1981
Photo by Edward Colver

STEVE McDONALD: Back in '84, we were told 'Hey, you guys are into the Dolls, you should play with this band Poison.' They were doing a Dolls thing, but sounded more like Van Halen, and the singer looked like Pamela Sue Martin. Rather than hooker makeup he wore frosty Donna Mills makeup. Their fans hated us. The girls all wore lingerie and g-strings, which at the time was shocking to us. I remember Poison rented a limo for after the show, so they could party some more in the parking lot.

CIRCLE JERKS were an elite early-80s Hardcore outfit, on par with Black Flag and Dead Kennedys. They could play to 500-1000 kids in any city in America. But their luster quickly faded.
   Keith Morris, after leaving Black Flag, and Greg Hetson, formerly of Red Cross, got together to form this "supergroup." Depending on who you ask, they first played either Kahuna's Bearded Clam under the Redondo pier, or Blackie's in Hollywood with The Germs and Top Jimmy.

KEITH MORRIS: We were fed up with the bands that we were in, and the fact that in one band, they never wanted to practice, and in the other, all they wanted to do was practice.

When you're in a band, that's all fine and great: getting together with the guys, jamming and writing songs. But there's also a thing called having a life — getting drunk, scoring drugs, et cetera. We were tired of what we were doing. We didn't get along with some of the personalities. Various problems, nothing real deep.

Circle Jerks, Whiskey A-Go-Go, LA, 1981
Photo by Edward Colver

JEFF McDONALD (Red Cross): Keith quit Black Flag at the same time Greg quit our band, so they instantaneously put together a group. We went to see their first show at The Bearded Clam in Redondo Beach. Greg Ginn was also there. We were shocked to find their set consisted of songs my brother Steven and I had written, and that Ginn had written. They just stole all these Black Flag and Red Cross songs. It was weird: Greg Hetson co-wrote a few Red Cross songs — but those weren't the songs they used. Or for a song I wrote the music to and he wrote the lyrics to, he'd change the title and lyrics and keep my music. But because Greg Ginn was so good at threatening with lawsuits — even back then — the shit hit the fan and they dropped almost everything. Circle Jerks were truly 'made;' they were the first Hardcore Monkees. They were shrewd, which I respect, although we never had those career aspirations at the time. By the time they did their record they'd sifted most of their plagiarism out of the set, but there are a few little pieces which I'm still mildly irked by.

Things moved fast for Circle Jerks in LA. In 1980 came *The Decline...*, which featured the outfit prominently, a spot on the noted *Rodney On The ROQ* comp — where their raw interpretation of Garland Jeffreys' beatnik anthem "Wild In The Streets" first appeared — and *Group Sex*, their classic album on Lisa Fancher's noted label, Frontier Records.

GREG HETSON (Red Cross/Circle Jerks): The album was 18 minutes long. On the first pressing, we added four or five seconds between each song, so people didn't feel they were getting ripped off. In retrospect, it was kind of funny. Was that 14 songs in 18 minutes?

MIKE WATT: Circle Jerks: good guys and stuff, but they ripped off all the songs. Do people know that *Group Sex* was songs ripped off from each band they were in? 'Gimme Sopor' is 'World Up My Ass.' 'Annette's Got The Hits' is somethin' else. I don't wanna bury them. *Group Sex* is classic, but they took the best songs from all their bands, and Keith wrote the words.

DEZ CADENA: People will always say there was a big feud between Flag and Circle Jerks, and in a way there was. A lot of it had to do with Keith leaving Flag, and Greg feeling there was some hanky panky with the songs. It was a very incestuous thing.

Circle Jerks followed with '82's *Wild In The Streets* (Faulty Products) and '83's *Golden Shower Of Hits* (LAX). One of the most intense HC bands was the Jerks' short-lived summer '83 union of Morris, Hetson, ex-D.O.A. drummer Chuck Biscuits, and Saccharine Trust bassist Earl Liberty (that ended immediately thereafter when Liberty found God and quit the scene).

Keith was an entertaining frontman, and Circle Jerks shows were always a great place to get physical. There was a time in '84 where Morris went on tour in a body cast, after he broke his back stagediving. The problem was, their records started to suck — as if they just ran out of ideas. After the woeful Metal Crossover of *Wönderful* (Combat Core '85) and *VI* (Relativity '87), Morris and Hetson knew it was time to throw in the towel.

KEITH MORRIS: We got lazy and fell into a mid-Rock tempo. We thought it was cute, that it would irritate a few people, and that it was a different twist since everyone expected us to make another *Group Sex*. 'Killing For Jesus' and 'Making The Bombs' did not go over, to say the least. But you go for it and deal with the consequences later. It can be difficult to carry on with the parody and comedy and sarcasm. You just do what you do; you do what you have inside you. There are no rules, no set guidelines.

DESCENDENTS were the model for all "melodic" HC that followed. Three 15-year-old geeks from the Hermosa/ Manhattan Beach area — guitarist Frank Navetta, bassist Tony Lombardo, drummer Bill Stevenson — came together in late '78, and recorded their first 7", "Ride The Wild," a blend of DEVO -style New Wave and Dick Dale-like Surf.

Descendents, LA, 1982
Photo by Al Flipside, scanned from *Flipside* #37

MILO AUKERMAN: We started drinking too much coffee; 'cause of that and the addition of me, the music became very quick and all about bursts of energy. It's interesting: we started very melodic, then moved to Hardcore, but melded the two at a certain point and became melodic Hardcore.

After a failed six-month trial with Punky girl Cecilia singing, the group hooked up with vocalist Milo Aukerman, in time to record '81's Fat EP. Descendents weren't out to change the world — as song titles like "Weinerschnitzel," and "My Dad Sucks" suggest. Fat led to '82's *Milo Goes To College* — whose cheeky love songs disguised as HC blasts became the most aped formula in Rock.

BILL STEVENSON: It was so desperate; four people with no friends except the ones in their band — and they don't even get along that well themselves. It was a desperate bid to get attention — amplified logarithmically by like 400 gallons of coffee. It was great.

Descendents went on hiatus for a few years — Bill played with Black Flag and Milo wrote his doctoral thesis on the genetics of corn — not very Hardcore. He became a scientist, studying DNA. Apart from Flag, Stevenson spent his time fishing off Catalina in his small boat, *Orca*.

MILO AUKERMAN: When I decided to go to college, the guys in the band were pretty hip on it because they knew how big of a nerd I was. Like, 'What else would you expect him to do but to go off and be a nerd ?' I mean, I've got a Ph.D. in biochemistry — how uncool is that?

BILL STEVENSON: The band had time off so I spent like two years with Black Flag. I got in over my head. When I joined Flag I had every intention of doing both bands but it was physically impossible. Flag had all this stuff in progress, so I put Descendents on hold.

After Stevenson's painful '85 split with Flag, Descendents reformed with an excellent new lineup — Bill, DYS/Dag Nasty vocalist Dave Smalley, and Stephen Egerton and Karl Alvarez of Salt Lake City's Massacre Guys. By '87, they became All. (Bill maintains forms of Descendents and All.)

MILO AUKERMAN: Bill and his high school buddy Pat'd fish all night for mackerel which they'd sell to catfood companies. When they fished all night, they drank lots of coffee to stay awake. Bill would come to school the next day smelling like fish. While drinking all this coffee in the midst of catching mackerel they came up with the concept of All — doing the utmost, achieving the utmost. The more they got into it the more it turned into their own religion; it's partly humor, but it's also an outlook on how to conduct your life: to not settle for some, to always go for All.

Saccharine Trust, LA, 1980
Photo by Spot, from *Rock And The Pop Narcotic*
Courtesy of Joe Carducci

SACCHARINE TRUST were part of the scene by virtue of being down with the SST guys. Jack Brewer's Beat-poetry style lyrics and Joe Baiza's harmolodic Jazz guitar bewildered HC audiences. Some of the most incredible shows were on the Black Flag/Minutemen/Saccharine Trust tours of 1981 and '82, Strategically, it was best to get there early enough to see Saccharine Trust's weird shit, get loaded outside during the Minutemen, then return in time to rage for Flag. Saccharine's LPs for SST like *Pagan Icons* ('81) and *Surviving You, Always* ('84) were incredible. (Baiza later led the underrated Prog Jazz group Universal Congress Of.)

> *Extract the nectar, burn the tree*
> *I've gotta be damned to be free*
> — Bad Religion, "Damned To Be Free"

BAD RELIGION played with a lot of the South Bay bands but they came from the San Fernando Valley, home of the "Valley Girl" celebrated by Frank and Moon Unit Zappa. In 1980, across the entire Valley, you'd find maybe two or three Punks at any given high school. Bad Religion members attended El Camino Real High — Brett Gurewitz and Jay Bentley dropped out, Greg Graffin graduated. Bad Religion's first show was October '80 with Social D at a warehouse party in downtown Fullerton. By early '81, they played monthly The Vex, a notorious, nefarious East LA club.

The first Bad Religion record of summer '80 was a six-song 7" EP of good songs and shitty production — recorded at an old-school Rock studio out in Agoura where no one knew what the fuck they were doing. The EP — Epitaph Records' first release — sold out its first pressing of 3000 copies right away. Then came '82's classic *How Could Hell Be Any Worse?* album, driven by the powerful-yet-smooth vocals of Greg Graffin.

GREG GRAFFIN (Bad Religion): We were the epitome of the non-Rock Star. It was done more as a way to exercise these creative demons we had, something to do after school every day, but it was also fun to just be part of a scene. We only played in the western US, as far as we could travel on a weekend. We weren't that motivated. We didn't worry about the popularity repercussions. We weren't thinking of it long-term, of how to build our career. When the band started, I was 15. The first LP came out when I was 16. I was a kid. It was just somethin' to do.

Bad Religion, LA, 1981
Photo by Edward Colver

In the fall of '82, Graffin left for the University of Wisconsin, so Bad Religion basically went on hiatus. Graffin would return on holidays and long weekends to record. From those sessions came the album that destroyed their HC rep: the '83 keyboard-driven *Into The Unknown*, which sounded closer to Styx/Journey-style Arena Rock than Hardcore. When Graffin transferred to UCLA, the group jumped back to their earlier sound. With second guitarist Greg Hetson, of Red Cross/Circle Jerks fame, they recorded the aptly-named *Back To The Known*. But the damage was done.

BRETT GUREWITZ (Bad Religion): Sorry, I can't talk about that era, it's been Stalinized! Sometimes I go back and hear one or two songs I can tolerate, but all in all that album was a mistake. It's good for what it is, but we never should've put it out. We were so young: one of my Punk ethics was I did things just because I could. Greg and I made that album because we could. I don't talk about it because I don't understand how we could've done something like that. I don't like it, I won't reissue it. Have you heard that album? It's got nine-minute epics about the wilderness, songs about malcontents who kill their wives and leave home — it's sick. I was heavily into LSD, but that's no excuse. It was the Punkest thing we could do at the time. It was what everyone didn't want us to do, and we didn't care.

The Bad Religion album you'll never hear
Zine ad for *Into The Unknown*, 1983
Collection of the author

GREG GRAFFIN: Well, when you're that young, you do a lot of crazy things. We had the ability to record any kind of music we wanted, and we thought it was Punk, so we threw the entire Punk community for a loop. We were just a bunch of kids screwing around. In retrospect, the fallout was totally expected, and at the time, I figured people were just idiots. But they were right. I mean, we learned a valuable lesson about marketing and maintaining a fan base, and giving your fans what they expect. That doesn't mean catering to them, but it does mean that if you want to build a legacy for your band, you've got to remain somewhat consistent. So we made a tactical error, but we learned how not to alienate our following.

Bad Religion were second-tier, behind Black Flag, DKs and Circle Jerks, and rated no higher than third group on big five-act LA bills. They meant little nationally, only gaining legendary status well after the scene ended.

GREG GRAFFIN: It's interesting: Bad Religion was never given credit for even being part of that scene — you actually have to do your homework to realize that we were in the thick of it and were one of the handful of popular bands from back then. But that's something that's been with us since our inception. It's both a gift and a stigma.

YOUTH BRIGADE (not the like-named DC band) played a crucial role in Hardcore's rise. The Stern family, with brothers Shawn, Mark, and baby Adam, moved to LA from Toronto in 1970. Dad was a film industry hotshot. Within a few years, the elder siblings took up surfing and became total beach bums, 14- and 15-year-olds who'd ditch school to hang out at the dunes or at stoner arena shows. At 16 and 17 they formed their first band, Mess, playing Zep and Hendrix covers at parties. Discovering Punk in '78, The Sterns started The Extremes, writing original material which Shawn sang with a trite British accent. Shawn and Mark were also among the few teens who hung out at the Hollywood flophouse, The Canterbury.

Youth Brigade, LA, 1982
Photo by Al Flipside, scanned from *Flipside* #32

At the end of '79, the two elder brothers moved in with their Beverly Hills High pals Kevin Hunter (later of Wire Train and linked to Courtney Love) and Rob Reiner's younger brother Lucas (of The Johnnies) at a huge two-story party house around the corner from Hollywood High. Called "Skinhead Manor," it boasted five bedrooms downstairs and three upstairs, a **small stage in the living room, and a ten-foot fence around the property. At any given time, at least ten people lived and another ten crashed there. Black Flag, Circle Jerks, and No Crisis practiced there, and Youth Brigade formed at Skinhead Manor, in its spring '80 heyday.**

SHAWN STERN (Youth Brigade): We moved into Skinhead Manor — that house became a real meeting place. We were 19 to 20 — most of those kids were about the same. People'd drive like 100 miles for shows. The Starwood did Tuesday night shows where we'd hang, then everybody'd cruise back to our house, and drink till the early morning. Crazy stories, crazy times. When Darby Crash came back from England, he came over and hung out with us. He built a rehearsal space in the garage and practiced there with the Darby Crash Band right before he killed himself. We met the people from Oxnard, San Diego, Huntington and Long Beach, and became friends with everybody. That was the basis of Youth Brigade and BYO.

Shawn and Mark observed LA nihilism and police brutality firsthand. Seeking to make a positive statement, they formed Better Youth Organization (BYO) in late '79, a quasi-collective promoting shows and spreading humanist ideals.

SHAWN STERN: The idea for BYO hit me in summer '79 because there was a riot at an Elk's Lodge show — the first time Punks and cops got into it. The lodge had different rooms; there was a Mexican wedding going on — people from the two crowds got into it, and the cops came and started beating people. The next day at The Masque there was a press conference, and I had the idea that we should start something of our own to give out a more positive image. I wanted this idealistic commune, sorta like what they do with the squats in Europe. But it didn't really happen that way.

Youth Brigade started out in summer '80 as a six-piece Punk/Ska outfit — with less than stellar results. Then younger brother Adam joined.

ADAM STERN (Youth Brigade): We wanted to be a Punk Rock Swing band, but weren't good enough. We ran ads in the paper, auditioned horn players. We got kids from high school Jazz bands, rehearsals and got the tunes down, but when we told these really straight kids they had to shave their heads, nobody showed up for the next rehearsal. So that was that. This guy Zippy from Huntington was a good fighter — he'd lay people out with one punch. These were the types of guys who were our early singers. We settled into a lineup of six pieces: two guitars, bass, drums, two singers. It didn't really work. We played a half-dozen shows, like at The Vex with D.O.A. and Legal Weapon. It was so bad.

BETTER YOUTH ORGANIZATION
PRESENTS

SOMEONE GOT THEIR HEAD KICKED IN!

Booklet Layout & Design By MARK STERN & GLEN E. FRIEDMAN
Center-Spread Photos By GLEN E. FRIEDMAN
except Social Distortion-24 Colver / Blake-M. De Ross / Adolescents-?
BYO Logo By Brian "PUSHEAD" Schroeder
Typesetting By MARK STERN

Cover of booklet with BYO compilation
Someone Got Their Head Kicked In!,
1982
Collection of the author

Skinhead Manor fell when Darby Crash, an occasional resident, OD'd and died after stealing the rent money. When the landlord evicted everyone a few weeks later, someone torched the place.

MARK STERN: By the end of '80 that house sort of died. It was getting way too out of control, too many people crashing out. It started out that we all bought food together and shared; it got to the point where everyone locked their doors and the cupboards. The landlord wouldn't fix the place, we were on rent strike, it was complete craziness. We just said 'Fuck it' and got the hell out. It mysteriously was burned down by a small cup of gasoline and a lighter. We don't know who, but I have a pretty good idea. You ever see that guy Eugene in *Decline...?* He was like, 'If we can't have the Manor, nobody can.' Him and Moger, the singer of No Crisis.

The post-Manor Sterns directed their energies towards Youth Brigade and BYO, which really blossomed when Mark started to promote shows in early '81 at Godzilla's, an old Sun Valley supermarket. That's where Youth Brigade first played as a Hardcore outfit, New Year's Eve 1981. Godzilla's closed down in summer '82, but for a year or so, that place gave many HC bands the opportunity to play, and was the first place for violent gangs to organize.

MARK STERN: Godzilla's was just past North Hollywood, a swap meet place, a bowling alley, a skating rink, with a huge room that held 1500, and a little disco room with a bar. The whole idea was, 'We'll run the place and hire everybody.' Shawn was in charge of security. Everyone knew someone who worked there, so everyone respected the place. The idea was peer pressure: if anyone started a fight, chances are someone would know them and guilt them into feeling ashamed about fighting. Beers were a buck, the restaurant was cheap. It was five bucks to get in; if the group was from overseas, it'd be six. Then we realized we were getting ripped off by the guy there. So every night we'd walk out with like ten Hefty bags filled with money. All of us would fill our pockets and go back to our house in Hollywood. We were all working for practically nothing, anyway. We took all the money we had siphoned out and bought this school bus.

Youth Brigade and BYO got serious attention for their "Youth Movement '82" extravaganza at the Hollywood Palladium — a major success, but the Palladium held onto all the money after a drunk girl fell off the balcony and sued the venue.

SHAWN STERN: This chick came in on the guest list, fucked some guy in the bathroom, fell off the balcony, broke her hip, and then sued us, the club, and the security. It was Jenny Berry, the daughter of Ken Berry who was in *F Troop*. She was a nutcase who we knew, and she sued us — it was fucking stupid. TSOL were playing and they were blasting, and when she hit the ground, you could hear it over the music. The whole scene was nuts. Some guy jumped off the balcony, grabbed the curtain, went sliding down Zorro-style onto the stage. Some freaky guy was roller-skating through the crowd and he got beat down.

PAT DUBAR (Uniform Choice): I saw that whole incident of the guy getting his head kicked in. It was insane. We were at this gig and this guy was literally skating around on skates. He wasn't a Punker, man. This was at the point where the scene started getting really violent. All of a sudden, this group of Skinheads started chasing him. One guy got him down, and they kicked this guy in the fucking face like fifty times. He went into a coma. I don't know if he ever died or not but he was fucked up, man.

Summer '82 saw the *Someone Got Their Head Kicked In!* comp — the first BYO record, featuring suburban outfits from the Palladium gig: Adolescents, Bad Religion, Social Distortion, Battalion Of Saints, and The Joneses — with skate hero Steve Olsen on bass and future TSOL drummer Mitch Dean. So began a long-running enterprise.

Wasted Youth, LA, 1981
Photo by Edward Colver

MARK STERN: We started the label and put out that record with a thousand dollars each. It was our Bar Mitzvah money, our bond money. We scammed the bank, the guy cashed it for full value, although it had a full ten years to mature. Is that Punk Rock or what? In terms of the comps, we included a lot of bands that we didn't really like their music so much, but they were good friends that we drank with.

Youth Brigade and Social D departed on the ill-fated *Someone Got Their Head Kicked In!* tour in the Sterns' graffiti-spangled school bus — as documented in the movie *Another State Of Mind*. Battalion Of Saints and Agression planned to meet up with them in NYC for a big BYO show, which never materialized.
Youth Brigade broke up after a big summer '85 show at Fender's Ballroom, after which Adam split for art school. Shawn and Mark plodded along for a year or so as The Brigade, blending the worst of The Damned and U2. (Youth Brigade occasionally reunite, and the Sterns still run BYO.)

WASTED YOUTH (not to be confused with the UK proto-Goth act) came into being in 1977 — as a bad garage band covering Hendrix and Trower. This West LA

sensation, which featured Red Cross guitarist Chet Lehrer, sounded similar to Circle Jerks — their pals with whom they shared many bills. A lot of kids were into Wasted Youth's *Reagan's In* LP of 1981, with bratty anthems "Reagan's In," "Fuck Authority" and "Problem Child," and an intense Edward Colver cover photo of a stagediver. (They broke up in early '83, but resurfaced in '87 as a longhaired Speed Metal troupe.)

D.H. PELIGRO (Dead Kennedys): At Florentine Gardens, a bouncer put on a DKs shirt and went out with a two-by-four with nails in it, smashing people. A full blown riot went off — windows got broken up, the place got trashed. Now the place is a disco. The photo from that show's on one of the Wasted Youth records where the guy's jumping off the PA column.

Speak with passion
Tell the truth
And don't forget the angry youth
— Legal Weapon, "What's Wrong With Me"

Plenty more LA-area outfits were involved in the rise of Hardcore. One of the scene's most interesting participants was Brandon Cruz, the child actor who played Eddie in *The Courtship of Eddie's Father,* who sang for DR. KNOW (not to be confused with the Bad Brains guitarist). When Brandon delivered fiery political raps, kids would mock him, "Eddie!, Eddie!" LEGAL WEAPON, an excellent Punk/Rock hybrid led by hot vocalist Kat

Press shot of Brandon Cruz
Left: as child star of *The Courtship Of Eddie's Father*
Right: as singer of the LA Hardcore band Dr. Know
Courtesy of Taang! Records

Arthur and handsome Rock guitarist Brian Hansen were totally ignored by the HC scene to which they played (their '81 debut *No Sorrow,* also featured Patricia Morrison, later of Gun Club and Sisters Of Mercy). SIN 34 played out a lot (drummer Dave Markey, later of PAINTED WILLIE, went on to make the indie films *Desperate Teenage Lovedolls* and *1991: The Year Punk Broke*). NIP DRIVERS did a few so-so albums, like '82's *Kill Whitey* and '84's *O Blessed Freak Show.* AMERICA'S HARDCORE was a running HC joke. MAD SOCIETY were so young their babysitter Kathy Samples put them together. An Oxnard scene ("'Nard-core") centered around AGRESSION and ILL REPUTE. Groups like RED SCARE, DECRY, DETOX, THE GRIM, STALAG 13, RF7, ANTI, and BL'AST (nee M.A.D.) also circulated. And don't forget THE MENTORS, led by notorious Eldon "El Duce" Hoke, whose wretched paean to misogyny "The Four Club" incited the wrath of Tipper Gore's mid-80s PMRC witch hunts. •

ORANGE COUNTY: KIDS OF THE BLACK HOLE

I've got a strong desire
To set myself on fire
— Agent Orange, "Tearing Me Apart"

TONY CADENA (Adolescents): You know those bad retro movies like *The Stoned Age?* That was what I lived. I said, 'Why would someone wanna glorify this?' It was the beach, pot, bad music: the 70s. I got into Punk because it was a rejection of that. It blows my mind to see how Pearl Jam got so popular because they're what I ran away from in the 70s. The music back then was awful — until the first Ramones album.

Hardcore kids involved in anti-social behavior;
Grave robbing in Orange County, 1981
Photo by Edward Colver

For a counterculture to exist in law-and-order-loving Orange County seemed unthinkable in Punk's early days. By '79, scattered action began in OC as Punk-minded garage bands played high school keg parties. The first and only OC outfit to gain acceptance in Hollywood Punk circles was Santa Ana's Middle Class, with frontman Mike Patton (not the Faith No More/Mr. Bungle singer). Middle Class probably put out the first HC single, the "Out Of Vogue."

In 1980, the Hollywood vs. the beach crowd rift widened as disorderly OC kids drove up to H'wood to cause trouble at shows. No artistic hipsters, these were products of the American Dream gone awry, by way of broken families or parental apathy, with some absolute monsters among them.

RIKK AGNEW (Adolescents, Christian Death): The urban Punk explosion of New York or London was based on older people who were into it for more artistic reasons, whereas in the suburbs like Orange County, it was crazy kids who needed an excuse to go nuts, rebel, and let off steam.

TONY CADENA: Orange County was a very suburban Right Wing, White middle-class stifling environment. There was no father in my family. We were dysfunctional, a welfare family living in an upward middle-class neighborhood. My family did not fit in. Punk came along at just the right time — it gave me a chance to reject everything I couldn't have anyway. I started bringing bands into my garage to rehearse. It was exciting to tip that 'hood on its ear. It was the final fuck-you.

DEZ CADENA (Black Flag): These Orange County kids didn't have many choices: either get into Hardcore music, become a cop, or go down to San Diego and join the Marines. This guy Mike Marine in *Decline...* was one of the biggest menaces, a ringleader of trouble — nothing against football because I love the Giants, but you play the game on the field, then you go home. You don't live that lifestyle. Okay, we all feel like we're fighting a war, but here's some guy just watching a band, not fighting you — who cares if he's got long hair? When the music got more popular, you'd get people showing up with their *gang*. I could never relate to that.

Circa 1980, the only place in Orange County for Punk-style groups to play was The Cuckoo's Nest, a shithole in Costa Mesa. There one could see the likes of The Crowd, The Chiefs, Eddie And The Subtitles or Snickers. Its door faced the door of Zubie's — a cowboy bar about which The Vandals wrote a song — 20 yards away. Zubie's had an electric bull, ridden by wannabees in ten-gallon hats and Tony Llama boots. There you'd see totally outrageous late-night fights betweeen some dude with triple mohawk and bondage pants and some yahoo in a cowboy hat.

MIKE WATT (Minutemen): The Cuckoo's Nest was where the gigs were. You had to bring your own mics. I remember one gig we were doing: it was Minutemen with Red Cross, when they were still little kids,

After the lights go out:
The Cuckoo's Nest, Costa Mesa, CA, 1981
Photo by Edward Colver

before the voice change. The only mic was a tape recorder mic taped to a cymbal stand, and this was rich Orange County. It was hard to have clubs there — the pigs were really heavy. They carried around sheets with mugshots of Punks — guilty of being a Punker. If you looked funny, they'd take your picture and you went on a sheet. I felt bad for them kids.

The walls are closing in om me
I don't know what to do
Please tell me who is who
— Adolescents, "Who Is Who"

The first OC Hardcore bands — Social Distortion, Adolescents and Agent Orange — arose from a small, scene centered around Fullerton. Those groups came out of The Detours, a short-lived '78 band from Lahabra, with Casey Royer and Rikk Agnew, then called "General Hospital" or just "General." The Agnews — Rikk and younger brothers Frankie and Alfie, born of an Irish father and Mexican mother — all played in one of the aforementioned outfits at one time or another.

TONY CADENA: The Agnew family was really fun to be around. There was Rikk, an older sister, Frank — who had long hair but when he cut it he kept a really long tail that he'd bobby pin up because his father would kill him if he saw it. And there was Alfie, who was a little kid then. They were a uniquely American family. They were from Fullerton. Rikk was older, so he had the freedom to go to Hollywood to see shows.

We had to create a scene because we didn't have the transportation or financial capacity to get out of the neighborhood. We looked up to Rikk and Mike Ness; they were the first guys we knew that were making it happen. We were dorky high school kids, and these guys had that English look with bleached hair. Where we were from, it was more flannel and blue jeans.

Death and life as I've never seen before
One more trip like that and I'm in the mental ward
— *Social Distortion, "Hour Of Darkness"*

SOCIAL DISTORTION was started by Mike Ness in late '78. Born in 1962 into an alcoholic, dysfunctional welfare home in Fullerton, smack in the heart of low-rider territory, Ness was a notorious OC character always ready for a fight, in fedora hat and mascara.

Mike and a few friends recorded some songs, among them a classic: "Moral Threat." In '79, he decided to get serious. The first "real" Social D lineup had Ness on guitar with Casey Royer on drums and a fucked-up Rikk Agnew always in and out of the group. Robbie Fields at Posh Boy put out their initial 7", "Mainliner,"

Social Distortion, 1981; Mike Ness, right
Photo by Edward Colver

recorded as a three-piece with Dennis Danell playing bass and Ness on guitar. All of a sudden, hundreds of kids were at their shows. Social D's early following congregated at "The Black Hole," Ness's run-down Fullerton pad. Both Adolescents ("Kids From The Black Hole") and Social D ("Playpen") memorialized the place on record. The cops shut down The Black Hole in early '80.

Uniquely, Social D — the Rolling Stones of Hardcore — played Blues-based Rock, Punk style. Seeing what the Stones could do with two guitars, Ness added a rhythm player — the group covered the Jagger/Richards standard "Under My Thumb" as B-side to "1945," their second single.

Social D hit their peak in '83 with *Mommy's Little Monster*, an amazing album — but they'd devolved into a total mess. Their label, 13th Floor Records, basically functioned as a vehicle for this manager type to meet young chicks and score free drugs by hanging with Ness. Mike was so high on dope that he couldn't tour, aside from some one-off gigs in Arizona and Vegas. *Another State Of Mind* documented Social D's only national tour — six shows in the old school bus with Youth Brigade.

MIKE NESS: After that album came out I dove into heroin. My alcoholism peaked. It took me five hours to get drunk. I did scary things in blackouts. With $20 worth of heroin I'd feel like Marlon Brando. I felt so cool doing it; it fit in with the Keith Richards/Sid Vicious thing. I was one of the first people in Fullerton to be doing heroin. I was trying to hold a band together — but I was in and out of county jails and detoxes. I went from a teenager going to gigs to having to maintain a habit. I was running gangsters and criminals. I'd get into three fights a night.

MARK STERN (Youth Brigade): We came to New York on the *Another State Of Mind* tour and Mike Ness got the shit beat out of him — he literally shit his pants. It was at the club 2+2. I mean, of course he was drunk, and he threw a bottle and broke Roger of Agnostic Front's kneecap.

MIKE NESS: I remember that me and Mark from Youth Brigade drank a lot on that tour. That was the only thing that kept me going. The guys who made the movie missed a lot of stuff ... the huge fight we got into with these Puerto Ricans in Connecticut ... some chicks ... a roadie giving me a black eye, but I really don't remember much. I was in pretty bad shape.

Zine ad for first Social D single, 1982
Collection of the author

A good half-decade passed before Ness got his shit together. He bottomed out in '87, spending a few months in jail. He then he got straight and reformed Social D with Dennis Danell, exploring his trials and tribulations on '88's *Prison Bound*. (Ness has since moved in a C&W-flavored direction, but he and Social D — minus Dennis, who died of a brain aneurysm at age 38 — have stayed true to the game, with credibility firmly intact.)

It's a futuristic modern world
Things aren't what they seem
Someday I'm gonna wake up from this stupid fantasy
— Agent Orange, "Bloodstains"

AGENT ORANGE, from nearby Placentia, unlike blue-collar Social D, were kids of a high financial bracket with nice gear. Vocalist/guitarist Mike Palm led this pioneering power trio, that melded Punk fury with the local Surf of The Ventures, and the slick proficiency of state-of-the-art Rock. The classic "Bloodstains" — written by Palm and Rikk Agnew — became a top "Rodney On The ROQ" request in late '79. They did a few tours and made some superb records — check out '81's *Living In Darkness* (Posh Boy) — but never pursued HC as a serious career. History often overlooks them.

ADOLESCENTS, unlike many contemporaries, had well-formed musical ideas: militant attack with Pop hooks. Adolescents represented the poppier approach of The Buzzcocks, but with Black Flag's anger.

Agent Orange bassist Steve Soto teamed up with Tony "Cadena" Brandenburg at a Social D gig at a Santa Ana cantina in November '79; Soto recognized Tony as the skinny kid who dove off the stage at his shows. The group came together and was playing live in a matter of weeks, first gigging at an invitation-only party with Social D and Agent Orange. Around that time Rikk Agnew joined on guitar, with brother Frank and drummer Casey Royer.

TONY CADENA: Me and Steve talked of forming a band because he knew his Agent Orange days were numbered. Mike Palm was the leader of that band, and they disagreed over the direction they should go in. We started the band at that point. He introduced me to Frank; Steve said, 'Frank, this is Tony — he's going to be our singer.' I said 'hi,' shook his hand and then picked up a can and bit the can and tore it in half. I thought this was a great way to make a first impression.

We started rehearsing in this guy Peter Pan's garage and then at The Detours' studio, which was a chicken coop behind this lady's house. She had a hen house that she turned into a rehearsal studio. Rikk started playing drums and we were a four-piece. We'd borrow drums from people and Rikk would crack a cymbal or break a head. We learned quickly that if you borrow people's equipment, they want it back in the same condition they gave it to you in. We suggested to Rikk that he switch to guitar and that's when he introduced us to Uncle Casey. We all started playing, and the scene started to steamroll. We played a few hall shows in Hollywood and LA and then started to play at clubs like The Starwood and Hong Kong Cafe.

Adolescents cut their first demo in April 1980 — four songs for $80. Eddie Subtitle paid for the next demo, shelling out $200 for five songs. Posh Boy asked them to contribute a track to the *Rodney On The ROQ* comp; they responded with their near-hit "Amoeba."

Adolescents, 1980
Photo by Al Flipside, scanned from from *Flipside* #21

TONY CADENA: In all fairness to the Hollywood crowd, we had a lot of support from them. The Germs crowd really liked The Adolescents. Rob Ritter from The Bags was a big fan. We played one night with Black Flag and The Subhumans — the Agnew's parents came. My dad helped Rikk's dad lift a guitar amp up the stairs. Of course, half the band had to be home by 11. We had popularity with people in the Hollywood crowd 'cause we'd stand up to our audience if they got violent, and wouldn't hesitate to stop a show if there was a fight. We felt it was inappropriate for Punks to be fighting Punks. We'd come from playing parties in Orange County where longhairs and jocks would come in; the parties'd turn into brawls. It wasn't uncommon for the door to fly open, 30 people walk in, and start fighting. I was picked up and thrown across the drum kit at one party.

The classic Adolescents lineup — Tony Cadena, Steve Soto, Rikk and Frank Agnew on guitars, Casey Royer on drums — recorded their classic self-titled album in late 1980. But by the next summer — around the time of their follow-up "Welcome To Reality" single — Rikk quit. Then things fell apart.

TONY CADENA: There were big fights between me and most of the band for of my refusal to take out the word 'fuck' and change it to 'suck.' The parents of two members were upset by the profanity — this was our big chance to become junior Pop Stars; they wanted to tone it down for a wider audience. I looked at groups like Stiff Little Fingers and said, 'This is where that leads to.' They wanted to sell out; I wasn't comfortable with being anybody's role model. I was an awkward, nerdy, goofy teen — within two years I was suddenly some spokesman for the angry teenager. I wasn't anyone's spokesperson; I could barely speak for myself! Everybody hated me, then they all loved me. I didn't have enough real friends around to differentiate between what friendship was and what was a passing infatuation. It just wasn't comfortable for me.

The Adolescents reformed in '86. Rikk's '85 solo *All By Myself* and *Team Goon* by Casey's next outfit D.I. apparently contained material intended for a second Adolescents record. Cadena formed The Abandoned, who often played with Suicidal Tendencies — although their style was more Punk than Speed Metal. He

re-emerged in the late-80s with Flower Lepers, then Sister Goddamn. (He currently tours and records with the ADZ).

D.I. (Drug Ideology) included everyone who belonged to a big OC Hardcore band at any time. Penelope Spheeris saw D.I. play at the Anti-Club and put them in her 1983 film *Suburbia* — and put their banner song "Richard Hung Himself" on the soundtrack. By '85, D.I. was a virtual Adolescents reunion, with vocalist Casey Royer and guitarists Rikk and Alfie Agnew. In retrospect, D.I.'s D.I.Y. got stifled by their own D.I.

Army, Navy,
Air Force, or jail
— TSOL, "Superficial Love"

Upper-middle-class Pacific seaside communities like Huntington Beach spawned a new breed of monster. That's where violent slamdancing originated. By 1979-80, bad kids were perpetuating violence at gigs by local groups like Vicious Circle and The Crowd. It was an even more intense vibe than what spawned Social D and Adolescents.

TONY CADENA: We were from northern Orange County — the more sedate part of the scene. The beach was a more moneyed area; those bands had great equipment. Half the time, we didn't even have gear. I didn't have a PA; I didn't own anything to sing out of, so I sang out of a guitar amp and put my fingers in my ears so I could hear myself.

TSOL, 1981: Jack Grisham, center
Solarized photo by Edward Colver, from *TSOL* EP, Posh Boy
Collection of the author

BRIAN BRANNON (J.F.A.): I can't overestimate the importance of Huntington Beach to the whole thing. It's where slamdancing was invented; they originally called it The H.B. Strut. If you were from Huntington Beach, you were trouble. We played with The Crowd at The Cuckoo's Nest; I went out to the floor when The Crowd was playing and it was a pure fistfight. I got punched in the face, neck and back. I spent most of my time trying to get out of that pit.

TSOL (TRUE SOUNDS OF LIBERTY) were the ones that most violent OC kids gravitated to. TSOL's coming on the scene signaled a whole new era. No one knew what to make of four huge, athletic surfer dudes.

MIKE WATT (Minutemen): Jack [Grisham] could hold his own — a good fighter, but the sweetest guy. I remember the first time I saw him, thinking 'What the fuck're you guys doing here? You've got tans, you're good-looking, this scene is for losers.' They just liked our music, and that was like the first affirmation that this stuff might mean something; it's not just for each other.

TSOL rose from the ashes of Vicious Circle, whose gigs were infamous for carnage. VC vocalist Jack Grisham and drummer Todd Barnes, of Long Beach, teamed up in early 1980 with Huntington Beach guitarist Ron Emory and bassist Mike Roche, who'd started TSOL a few months earlier, with Rick Fritch singing. Turf wars raged at those early TSOL gigs.

JACK GRISHAM (TSOL): The Long Beach scene I was involved with was a mix of the LA and Orange County scenes. We were from the suburbs; we weren't from the city. We were more athletic, lotsa jock kids, surfers; we all wore black and were like thieves. A lot of guys in Huntington Beach who were just like us, we made friends with. My Long Beach friends were upset with Todd and I for playin' with Huntington Beach guys. No one liked us. There were Long Beach bands that didn't like us either; Super Heroines and Rhino 39 thought we were jock-ish kids. But that's what it was — a lot of those people were smaller. None of *us* got picked on at school, y'know what I'm sayin'? We were more like the pickers.

Grisham and Barnes first teamed up in late '77 with primitive projects like John Coathanger And The Abortions and SS Cult.

JACK GRISHAM: I'd been kicked out of every school district in Long Beach. This girl came up and she goes, 'I know these guys that are just like you.' So she introduced me to Todd, and it was like, 'Wow, this is my friend,' like, 'What do you wanna do tonight?' 'Let's get machetes and chop up garden hoses.' We were Punks in the literal meaning. It's funny about our first gear. The girl that introduced us, we were hanging out at her house after we'd just met; she had a guitar and an amp and we said, 'Let's take this with us when we go.' We just took it.

TSOL sticker, 1982
Collection of the author

We couldn't play for shit, no one knew anything. We had the guitar we stole from this chick and couldn't figure out how to tune it. We had busted some strings, so we just left the two top strings on and tuned those to an open E — at least they said it was an open E — I had no clue if that's what it was or not. We just played the two strings on that and then we ripped off some gear from the school and we had a big marching bass drum. We laid it on its side and beat on it with some sticks that we stole and I just screamed into the mic. That was our band. I remember Jello Biafra got mad at me one time and he said, 'Why do you do this?' I said, 'To rape, pillage, and get money!' and he got all pissed off at me. That's what it was, it was just a bunch of fuck-alls. In my neighborhood, it was all the jerks.

Vicious Circle — frontman Grisham, drummer Barnes, guitarist Steve Housden (of The Klan, who did "Cover Girls"), and bassist Laddy Terrell — lasted from summer '78 through most of '79. Though good musically, to get bookings was nearly impossible. Their gigs were magnets for mayhem.

TONY CADENA (Adolescents): A lot of the tough-guy element seen in *The Decline Of Western Civilization* came out of Vicious Circle. I saw them play one night and the whole room erupted into a brawl — a lot of knuckleheads were showing up. In all fairness, I'd seen the same kind of chaos at Germs shows and that was not a beach band. I saw the Germs at the Hong Kong and it was duck-under-a-table-because-you-had-no-idea-what-was-going-to-happen-next. Those Vicious Circle gigs were insane.

JACK GRISHAM: At the end of Vicious Circle I had to split. The violence had gotten so bad, I had shellshock. There were stabbings. We played a show — 'Frenchie's Machine Shop Massacre' — the whole night was a bad deal. A friend of mine grabbed me and I threw him; he landed on a big metal boring drill — which ripped the back of his head wide open. There was a fight between the Huntington Beach and Long Beach guys. I tried to stop it, but it just turned into multiple stabbings. Smitty from Hard As Dirt, Cheap As Nails got stabbed seven times. It was a fucking bloodbath. I had to go away to Alaska for a while because things got so fucked. I got home and asked my parents to loan me some money. They weren't too happy, but I was on the plane that morning. I came back and didn't really want to play music that much. Then Todd, Mike and Ron came over to my house one day, and said 'Hey, we'd really like you to sing for this band...' The one time I had dealings with Roche, we found forty bucks on the ground and it was two twenties. So I ripped the bills in half and gave him two halves and I took the other two halves and split. He was trying to hunt me down for months trying to find that fucker with the money.

TSOL first gigged at crazy house parties, like one in March '80 at an old Black Panther house in downtown Long Beach, near where Snoop Dogg grew up. But most parties happened at suburban rich kids' parents' homes, which would usually get looted, vandalized or otherwise destroyed.

JEFF McDONALD (Red Cross): All those Orange County people were so strung out on cocaine — the most unhip drug — they'd always go in and steal from their friends' parents' houses — and they'd always get busted and start doing time. All those kids lived in houses like *The Brady Bunch* and they'd have parties where the parents' safe would get broken into, and somebody's father's gold chain collection would be stolen. It was pretty intense at the time. It wasn't just like another broken window.

TSOL were always a step ahead of the audience. Their self-titled 1980 EP with "Abolish Government" was lauded for its political conviction. By 1981, Jack was smearing makeup on his face to affront the Surf Punks — and people called it "Goth." About that time they recorded *Dance With Me* with producer Thom Wilson with "Code Blue" and "Sounds Of Laughter."

JACK GRISHAM: People talk about how TSOL changed so much from the first EP to *Dance With Me*, from Political Punk to Gothic Punk. But we had all those songs before we did the first EP. If you look on the first EP cover, my hair's sticking straight up, I'm wearing some Frankenstein suit, and I've got black makeup all over my eyes. We knew Posh Boy was gonna burn us, but we wanted to put out a record. So it was like, 'Let's give him these — and we'll save the good stuff for later.' During *Dance With Me,* we were

Dance With Me,
TSOL LP, Frontier, 1981
Collection of the author

labeled Gothic/Horror — whatever. Yeah, we dug up some graves but we dug up graves even before the first record. All that crap, like breaking into mortuaries — we'd done that before. Look at the first TSOL record, it thanks the church PA — we'd been busting into churches and desecrating the altars. We'd steal the PA and spraypaint the altars.

Dance With Me's impact confirms SoCal Hardcore as a source of the American Goth scene. A great '82 comp *Hell Comes To Your House* (Bemisbrain) featured Social D and Red Cross along with the likes of Christian Death with Rozz Williams and Rikk Agnew, 45 Grave with the Germs' Don Bolles, and Eva O of Super Heroines.

EDWARD COLVER (photographer): Back then, we called it Death Rock. It wasn't called Goth yet. TSOL, Christian Death, 45 Grave and even Social Distortion started that whole mess. They all wore lots of pancake makeup and pissed off a lot of the Punk Rockers in the process. Those were some great bands — it was an amazing, in-your-face era. George Bellinger of the original Christian Death is now a sheriff in Missouri.

"Jack from TSOL," as he was known, found Punk Rock an ideal forum for antisocial behavior. He assumed a different name on every record — Jack Greggors, Alex Morgan, Jack Ladoga, Jack Delauge — both to fuck with audiences and to keep one step ahead of the law. Todd used the surname "Scrivener," the name of the street he lived on. For TSOL there were no calculated career moves — it was all a total joke to them.

JACK GRISHAM: You don't do that much shit and build up that kind of karma without the rubberband snapping. That fucker was stretched to the limit. The karmic scales were way unbalanced. We were piling shit up and it was bound to snap, and that's what happened. Everybody in that band got destroyed. Drugs, jail, suicide attempts. We were cursed.

By '82, their huge, sick West Coast gigs regularly sold out to thousands at rooms like the Hollywood Palladium, but traveling eastward TSOL drew far less — they were a second-tier outfit in New York, Boston and DC. I saw at least five of their East Coast shows; none drew over 150 people.

The experimental nature of '82's *Weathered Statues* 7" EP (Alternative Tentacles) bewildered some fans. But TSOL lost their hard-to-please fanbase overnight with '83's keyboard-driven *Beneath The Shadows* LP. As a wave of HC bands tried a more "mature" sound in the vein of The Damned, it made sense at the time, but constituted a suicidal career move; too bad, as *Beneath The Shadows* sounded powerful and progressive.

Final lineup of "the original TSOL"
Photo by Edward Colver
Press shot for *Beneath The Shadows*, 1983

JACK GRISHAM: We learned to play. We wanted to try more things. We're not going to pretend we're something that we're not anymore. It's funny, Mike Roche got mad at me for doing what I did, but he was the one that turned me on to Roxy Music. After hearing different singers and music I'd never heard before, you're bound to expand. The trouble with being a popular band is that all your changes are aired for the public. So yeah, we ventured and a lot of the stuff went too far. But how do you know where you are if you don't go too far? Using synthesizers wasn't popular with Hardcore — to be honest, a lot of the synth sounds at that time weren't very good, but we went for it. I've met a lot of people like you that say, 'That record was cool.' At the time, it was — for me, at least.

JACK RABID (editor, *The Big Takeover*): *"Beneath The Shadows* being rejected by the Hardcore scene was the final straw for me, after many, many straws. Here was this most fascinating outgrowth of Punk — they could've been our Damned or Siouxsie And The Banshees — retaining that original guts and drive, taking into this unique direction. The Hardcore audience rejected them, the Rock & Roll audience figured they were still Hardcore, so there was no audience for the music — they broke up. It was a very bad time. It became a rugby game with no meaning.

Like their predecessor Vicious Circle, TSOL went out on a sour note.

JACK GRISHAM: A show at SIR [Studios] was the final straw. It was a huge show that turned into a big riot. The cops came in so I said, 'Hey everybody, lay down on the floor and then they can't do anything about it.' So there's 3000 of us laying on the floor and I said, 'There's more of us than there is of them — let's get 'em,' — it turned into a huge riot on the Strip. I got threatening anonymous calls, but what really messed me up was an article that said, 'You know how well Jack controls a crowd.'

People yelled out stuff at shows after that: 'Tell us what to do, Jack' — I didn't want any part of that. I told myself, 'I'll play lounge music to get these people away from me.' I was sick of TSOL. It got out of hand. We couldn't even play a show. It was a fucking nightmare. The last show we played was for 100 people on a rainy Wednesday night under an assumed name. We couldn't play anywhere because every show we played was just thousands of people going fucking nuts.

In late '83, Grisham quit TSOL and renounced Hardcore to continue on the path of *Beneath The Shadows*. He played with the keyboard-driven Cathedral Of Tears (as Jack Lloyd), and Tender Fury, working briefly with former Bowie bandmate Hunt Sales, son of Borscht Belt comedian Soupy Sales. From such perfect platforms he further alienated his fanbase. (Jack resurfaced in the mid-90s with The Joykiller, briefly inked to Epitaph.)

With Jack and Todd out of the picture, Emory and Roche assembled a second TSOL lineup in February 1984 with two cool Rock dudes, drummer Mitch Dean and vocalist/guitarist Joe Wood. But they failed to alert their fans they were moving in an Aerosmith-style direction. Though "the new TSOL" put out a few solid mid-80s records — contrary to popular opinion, at least as good as those by Guns N' Roses — calling themselves TSOL only subjected the new incarnation to unrealistic expectations and bad vibes. In 1989 the group, having *no* original members, packed it in; the final line-up included bassist Murph Karges, later of Sugar Ray.

The "new TSOL",
Hit And Run, Enigma, 1986
Collecton of the author

In the sickest outgrowth of the "old TSOL vs. new TSOL" debacle, Jack's sister Dee wed Joe Wood. At the Grisham's Long Beach house in the late 80s, I saw Mrs. Grisham, Jack, Joe Wood and Dee, with their kid and her kid from a previous relationship with a Marine, living together, pretending nothing was wrong. Meanwhile, Joe had milked TSOL's good name — playing shitty shows to 100 poodleheads — and served legal papers on Jack, Todd, Ron and Mike to thwart a one-night reunion of "the original TSOL" (the founders had to bill themselves by their four full names).

Everyone involved with TSOL crashed and burned. Ron Emory, though a great guitarist, had a lot of personal problems; his brother OD'd on heroin, and for years Ron traveled a similar path. Mike Roche, hip and rich, had set up the first store that sold Punk clothes and Doc Martens in OC; by the 90s, he dealt dope, living in a car with his girlfriend and dog. The worst of the bunch was Todd Barnes, TSOL's truly troubled soul. In '83, I remember the gory details of he and his pals beating someone blind over a parking space. Jack told me he'd tried to play with Todd in Tender Fury in the late 80s; but Todd, in and out of jail over the decade, had trouble playing a kick drum after years of shooting speed in his leg. Only *Beneath The Shadows* keyboardist Greg Kuehn "made it," playing with the likes of Bob Dylan. ("The original TSOL" reunited circa 2000, the one "old-school" outfit to retain their power and intensity. Todd past away soon thereafter.)

Anarchy, throwing shit
Let 'em know you're sick of it
— The Vandals, "Anarchy Burger (Hold The Government)"

The Vandals, LA, 1982
Photo by Edward Colver

The Vandals, the group most closely linked to TSOL, starred frontman Stevo, a violent fucker known for busting heads and smashing toilets. The Vandals' EP *Peace Thru Vandalism* (Epitaph '83) featured killer tunes like "Legend Of Pat Brown" and "Anarchy Burger (Hold The Government)." And similar to TSOL, they'd taint their name by touring and recording with different lineups. In '85, capable Dave Quackenbush replaced Stevo.

BRIAN BRANNON: The Vandals personified the Punk Anarchy thing. They used to have a song called 'The Frog Stomp' — they'd take all these dead frogs they bought from the same place schools buy them and throw these frogs at the audience and the audience would throw them back or stomp on them till their guts exploded. It was cool.

CHINA WHITE, named for the dope that killed Darby Crash, exemplified the so-called violent Beach Punk explosion. If you asked any HC kid in '81 to name a half-dozen West Coast acts, China White would surely surface. Despite a great name and intense image — describing themselves as "a black leather band" — the music never cut it. The best thing about the well-distributed *Dangerzone* 12" (Frontier 1981) was the Ed Colver photo of a murder scene he came across after a Fear show, using the available light of a police car. They never again did anything of note.

We love America, who dropped the bomb
We love America, our nation's strong
We love America, the youth of today,
We love America, in God we prey
— Shattered Faith, "We Love America"

SHATTERED FAITH, another active OC outfit, did some cool records on Posh Boy: '81's classic "I Love America"/"Reagan Country" 7" and their self-titled '82 album. I saw Shattered Faith play Hollywood's Cathay de Grande in '83; they — especially frontman Spencer Alston — came off like a bunch of coked-out rich-kid yo-yos.

CHANNEL 3 from Cerritos, an essential outfit of the era, made the early-80s Posh Boy records *CH3* (with "Manzanar"), *Fear Of Life* (with "You Make Me Feel Cheap"), and *After The Lights Go Out* (with "I'll Take My Chances"). CH3 came across like a nastier, better-looking version of the Ramones. I set up their DC gig in '83; they did a phenomenal show and were righteous dudes. CH3 also had a Skinhead following due to the release of *I've Got A Gun* on the London-based Oi! label No Future. Like many of their OC contemporaries, CH3's "musical development" was their death knell. Vocalist Mike Magrann began to play cheeky

Cock Rock, the low point being '85's *Last Time I Drank...* (Enigma), which featured a cover of Aerosmith's "Lord Of The Thighs." Not surprisingly, that was Channel 3's final record.

SUICIDAL TENDENCIES, though from Venice Beach not Huntington Beach, were closely identified with the OC scene. Suicidal were awesome — if Hardcore with Metal riffage and wanton violence was your thing. Suicidal drew a proverbial line in the sand: Punk versus Metal, scene unity versus gang violence, and so on. There was no middle ground. *Flipside* readers voted them '82's Worst Band; they

Channel 3, CBGB, NYC, 1983
joined onstage by Doug Holland of Kraut on guitar
Photo by Karen O'Sullivan

won Best Band and Album Of The Year in '83. They were the first HC group to sell lots of discs, and the first to get regular MTV rotation, for "Institutionalized."

In late '81 a loose-knit gang with *cholo*-style bandannas, mutated into Suicidal's first lineup. The ringleader, vocalist Mike Muir, was the younger brother of DogTown icon Jim Muir. "Suicidal Mike" came to attention when he was featured in a lurid summer '82 *Penthouse* article on LA Punk violence. Suicidal were true monsters, totally vicious assholes — you'd always find Mike busting heads on the dancefloor.

The Suicidal posse took shit over at shows. That's why people truly hated them. If Suicidal was on a bill, many people wouldn't go 'cause they and their friends would fuck shit up for anyone trying to watch.

IAN MACKAYE (Minor Threat): Suicidal had two things going for them: they had Glen Friedman hyping them, and they had this gang. The whole gang aspect made them intriguing. But I don't think of them as a quintessential band. They had a moment when they were burning bright.

Suicidal teamed up with Lisa Fancher's Frontier Records, The classic '83 *Suicidal Tendencies* LP was recorded and mixed in three days for $3000. Suicidal made their first US tour in drummer Amery Smith's dad's old orange Winnebago. Moonie, a roadie who'd eat live slugs for a quarter, went along. The $100 I paid them at DC's Space II Arcade was the most money they made on that trek. Before their next gig, at NYC's CBGB, Harley Flanagan and a few Skinhead pals beat bassist Louiche Mayorga to a bloody pulp while he was taking a piss in the bathroom.

By summer of '84, Suicidal was big news. The massive success of *Suicidal Tendencies* and the blazing "Institutionalized" launched them — and HC in general — into mainstream consciousness (Black Flag and DKs never did. Suicidal sold 200,000-plus albums, while Flag sold maybe 60,000 at their peak.). Slamdancing and stagediving escaped the underground.

Suicidal pursued their Metallic imperative, never to regain the initial degree of success. The

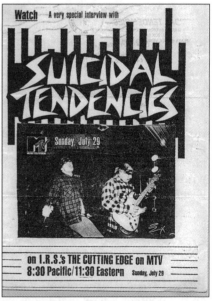

Watch A very special interview with

SUICIDAL TENDENCIES

MTV Sunday, July 29

on I.R.S.'s THE CUTTING EDGE on MTV
8:30 Pacific/11:30 Eastern Sunday, July 29

Suicidal Tendencies, the first HC MTV band
Flyer for an MTV appearance, 1984
Collection of the author

DEC 26,1981
AT THE VALLEY WEST
19657 VENTURA BLVD
IN TARZANA
TELEPHONE NO. 342-7166
AT 8:00 P.M.
WITH; RED CROSS AND
RF-7

THIS IS A
PUBLIC
SERVICE
BUY IT
NOW!!

Show flyer for Circle One,
Tarzana, CA, 1981
Collection of Laura Albert

next LP, '87's *Join The Army* (Caroline) wasn't bad, with its über-mosh beats and axe solos. (But the ensuing Epic albums left much to be desired, and lame Muir side projects like Infectious Grooves and Cyco Miko led to a late-90s Suicidal reunion, further soiling their rep.)

MIKE MUIR (Suicidal Tendencies): We didn't start out to be Rock Stars, we didn't go out to kiss people's asses. We just did our own thing, we were ourselves, and didn't listen to other people. I'm very proud of this band and everything we created. People shouldn't worry about me. They should worry about themselves.

CIRCLE ONE, like Suicidal, began as a gang-turned-band. Formed by Guitarist Michael Vallejo in November '80, the "Circle One" concept ran along the lines of "a group bound together by common interests" — "united as a whole, undivided." Frontman John Macias, a crazy Black dude, gained notoriety for leading The Family, a so-called Christian Skinhead gang. With Jesus as his savior — and Punk as his weapon — Macias formed PUNX, a communal BYO-type crew that booked shows, sheltered runaways, and spread a twisted gospel. Though few were as fucked up, they made a good album in '83's *Patterns Of Force*.

STEVE McDONALD (Red Cross): Circle One — a politically-oriented Hardcore band — went through this weird born-again phase. The problem I had with them was their macho jock mentality where they beat people up.

PAT HOED (Adam Bomb of KXLU): From having Macias on my show, I could tell you he was a real violent guy — a huge man who intimidated with his stares. He did find God, though I don't know how long that lasted.

MIKE WATT (Minutemen): I was at a police riot with DKs, D.O.A. and us at the Longshoreman Hall near Long Beach. That started because of John Macias of Circle One. The guy had a Jesus Punk gang or something; I really didn't understand it. This gig had Samoan security people who did not know Punk at all. John's big plan was for the Punks to rush the door and ruin the show but these Samoans took table legs and started beatin.' The police came in, cornered the band onstage, forced everyone out. Luckily, we got out with the kids. There was a door on the sidestage that let us out. They wanted to fucking beat our ass with nobody looking. Macias was killed a few years ago. He went crazy and was pushing people off the Santa Monica Pier, so the cops shot him to death.

UNIFORM CHOICE was the Huntington Beach group that represented the "next generation" of Hardcore. Unlike the drug-friendly TSOL or Social D, UC (originally Unity) dealt out a severe Straight Edge agenda.

PAT DUBAR (Uniform Choice): It's a great story how I became a singer. One guy had a guitar, another a bass. Pat Longry and I were high school friends, so we flipped to see who'd sing and who'd play drums. Neither of us wanted to come up with the cash for a drum set. I won, so I sang. We played a party a few days later. We had only one original called 'Neighbors Suck' because the neighbors called the cops the first time we practiced. We covered 'Belsen Was A Gas' by the Pistols. We played those two songs over and over, like ten times. We ended up in a big fight. Our drummer broke a grandfather clock in this guy's house 'cause people were throwing water on us. That was my first gigging experience.

Uniform Choice were fucked-up OC jock Punks — guitarist Victor was in Vicious Circle; Pat played baseball at Pepperdine during UC's apex.

PAT DUBAR: We were labeled as being positive, but unity wasn't really our trip. Uniform Choice was weird because we really came from a place of anger and hatred. We were never dicks to people but we didn't put up with shit. That was not our thing, at all.

Pat Dubar (Uniform Choice), LA, 1984
Courtesy of Pat Dubar

By 1986, UC's attempts at musical evolution had disillusioned their fanbase. They'd grown their hair and quit the Straight Edge raps. UC did go on to make some engaging music — but no one cared. The second album was their waterloo (Dubar went on to Mind Funk and Corporate Avenger).

PAT DUBAR: We had this idealistic view of Punk, that everyone was open-minded, and would be accepting of new directions. We couldn't have been further from the truth. Nobody had an open mind. My attraction to Punk — aside from the fact the music spoke to me — was: everyone could be who they were. If you wanted three mohawks and orange hair, you could do that and nobody cared. But when our music changed — because it was what felt good to us at the time — we were considered to be these dicks. This was '86 or '87. We put out and toured that second record — everyone laughed at us, thinking it was a big joke. Sure enough, a year or so later, everyone was doing what we had just done. Ian came to see us on that tour and told me of the new band he'd started called Fugazi.

The scene changed in the mid 80s. For those with half a brain, HC shows were no longer safe or fun, especially with gangs around. Territorial clans — the Suicidals from Venice, the HBs from Huntington Beach, FFF (Fight For Freedom) from the Valley, the LADS (LA Death Squad) from Hollywood (who'd hang out late nights at Oki Dogs or the Cathay De Grande) — these crews would fuck each other up for no reason.

SCOTTY WILKINS (Verbal Abuse): I was in the LADS, and of course Suicidals didn't like the LADS. Everybody started dressing like *cholos* — but we were still wearing leather jackets. Guns started to get involved. I remember sitting across from Perkins Palace in Pasadena, with a few dudes from FFF. They started passing out guns and I was like, 'I'll see you later.' These gangs were big, 200 or so in each one. There were only about 50 in the LADS of Hollywood. Bad Religion used to be a LADS band; the LADS would go and help bounce. It was all pretty stupid. That's why I left in '83 for San Francisco. I also got out of LA because the Olympics were coming. Every weekend the vice squad, because of the Olympics, had to 'clean up Hollywood.' We just said, 'Let's get the fuck out of here.'

All the violence and bullshit reduced crowds sizes noticeably. At Hardcore's 1981-to-'83 pinnacle, big gigs were at The Olympic, Santa Monica Civic, or

Hollywood Palladium, which hold thousands. In '84 and '85, the major shows happened in Long Beach at the 1500-capacity Fender's Ballroom, infamous for ruthless Samoan security men. It was ugly. You'd go there and see puddles of blood all over the floor. This shit was getting old.

SHAWN STERN (Youth Brigade): When all that gang shit started, that killed everything. Everybody was fighting with each other. People started carrying guns to shows. I was promoting shows at Fender's, and we'd have shootings. It sucked. I mean, kids punching each other, that's a fact of life. The fights in the early days, most of the time, were one-on-one, plus it was about something. When Suicidal copped that gangster look, it definitely helped make the gang scene come alive. It existed before for sure, but it got bad later on. That's when it was over.

Battalion Of Saints, 1982;
George Anthony second from left.
Courtesy of Taang! Records

Cops are out
I see what they're up to
They wanna create fear
A police state is clear
— Battalion Of Saints, "Cops Are Out"

San Diego, a picturesque city due south of LA and OC, was great for catching rays or scoring meth, but lousy for underground music.

By 1980, the only local Punk outfit was The Neutrons, who played a few shows with Dead Kennedys. A year later The Neutrons became **BATTALION OF SAINTS** (for the great Mormon land march of the 1860s), an important band who played some of the top LA HC bills. But history has overlooked them, largely due to their problems with the dodgy Mystic Records.

The early 80s saw a small local skater scene basically aping OC; San Diego kids called it "Slow Death." Battalion Of Saints, on the other hand, were Punk louts, into an English sound and style and wearing studs and leather — a real statement in SD's hot climate.

From their earliest days Battalion Of Saints constantly played LA at Godzilla's or the Olympic Auditorium, opening for British acts such as Discharge, Vice Squad and UK Subs. Many HC kids knew their manager, artist "Mad" Marc Rude, for his cover art on The Misfits' *Earth A.D.* album.

GEORGE ANTHONY (Battalion of Saints): Yeah, Mark tried to be our manager. He got us a few shows and drew some of the artwork but he'd tell us, 'You've got to be everybody's friends.' I'd say, 'I'm playing for them — I don't want to be their friend, I don't wanna have to talk to them.' Then our bass player Dennis fucked his chick and took off with her. Six years later, Mark came to my house and smashed my window. I have no respect for the cunt. He said, 'You stole my shit.' I said, 'I wouldn't steal your shit — I don't want it.' He got pissed off because he's a sensitive artist type. Chris [Smith] had nicked it and told him it was me.

Battalion Of Saints were great 'cause they walked the walk and talked the talk — check out the UK Subs vibe of '82's *Fighting Boys* EP and their spot on the *Rock In Peace* comp.

GEORGE ANTHONY: The original lineup was Dennis Frame bass, Chris Smith guitar, Ted Olsen drums, me singing. Dennis got thrown in jail for running over some guy so we got another bass player, Travis, but his mom told him to quit because we were bad boys. Barry played bass and started shagging Chris's girlfriend — so he got kicked out. We had James Cooper playing bass, who went on to the Meatmen. After that we had Captain Scarlet. Ted quit right before an East Coast tour and we had to get this kid, Joey, from Miami, to play drums. We were never saints by any means.

Of course, Battalion self-destructed just as things looked promising. By '85, with Enigma wanting to do a deal and Capitol showing interest, guitarist Chris Smith was too nodded-out on dope to give a fuck. Back in the day, SD losers slagged them as "Battalion Of Aints," but when they broke up, what little scene there was dried up.

GEORGE ANTHONY: This friend Michael Adriscoll used to rob banks with a Battalion Of Saints shirt on. We were hanging out at Chris' house and the doors come flying off the hinges — the FBI was there with guns to us. 'Where's Michael Adriscoll? We know you're a gang.' 'No, we're a group!' They searched everything. There was a sheet of LSD right on top of the TV — they never even saw it. Then Mike called. 'Hi Mike. The police are right here.' He says, 'Let me talk to an agent there.' He tells 'em, 'For every minute you hold those people, I'm gonna kill a cop.' They ended up catching him — he got 365 years. They brought him to New York to try him for bank robberies, and he escaped, so they never let him out again. He took the grid off the light bulb, filled up the sink, put his feet in, and put his finger in the light, thinking he'd do himself in — but just ended up blacking out the prison. There were FBI agents at our gigs once in a while because of that.

The one original member still alive is frontman George Anthony. (He resurrected Battalion Of Saints in the 90s with Terry Bones, of Discharge and Broken Bones fame.)

GEORGE ANTHONY: Nobody would get in a band with me for a long time — they thought they were gonna have a horrendous habit and OD, which was probably true at the time. I moved back to SD in '87 after a few years in DC, and everybody started dying. Chris died, Barry [Farwell] died, Donnie [Diaz] died, Dave Astor died, two roadies died. ODs, one suicide, one AIDS. It was pretty fucking tragic. •

DEAD KENNEDYS & SF: CALIFORNIA ÜBER ALLES

Zen fascists will control you
100% natural
You will jog for the master race
And always wear the happy face
Dead Kennedys, "California Über Alles"

DEZ CADENA (Black Flag): Chuck Dukowski got reprimanded for spray painting 'Black Flag' in pink, because that's the only paint he had. The cops said, 'Next time, use black.' That was in San Francisco.

Dead Kennedys, Whiskey A-Go-Go, LA, 1982; Jello Biafra, center
Photo by Edward Colver

Unlike law-and-order LA, in San Francisco — a port city settled by sailors, hookers, 49ers, Chinamen and other riff-raff — residents traditionally turned a blind eye to "alternative lifestyles." That's why the Bay Area served as a fertile breeding ground for generations of subculture and subversion.

The first American Punk scene after New York arose in San Francisco; things were going on there by early '76, at least a year before LA. SF Punk bands definitely equaled those in London or NY, they just didn't have the same infrastructure to propel them. The first SF outfits were Crime (with Frankie Fixx) and The Nuns (with a young Alejandro Escovedo).

As they did in Beatnik and Hippie days, misfits and idealists flocked to SF in the Punk years — especially after the Sex Pistols played their final show at Winterland on January 10, 1978. That influx produced some of the best American Punk: The Dils (with Chip and Tony Kinman, later of Rank And File), The Avengers (with Penelope Houston), Negative Trend (with Will Shatter and Steve Depace, later of Flipper) and Pink Section.

WINSTON SMITH (graphic artist): What I liked about the early Punk scene in San Francisco was that there wasn't a star trip. It wasn't like, 'I'm a star, meet me backstage.' It was a more casual atmosphere. It was the first time in a long time people actually tried to encourage each other. San Francisco is only seven miles wide, so it's a small community. The scene was played up in the media as violent and drug-infested but that wasn't the essence of what was happening.

Mabuhay Gardens, a small Filipino restaurant in North Beach, started to book bands on the side in late '75. The Mab was to SF what CBGB was to NY. Promoter

Dirk Dirksen and Mab owner Ness Aquino booked virtually every touring Punk and Hardcore group throughout the early 80s. Even the most marginal outfits could get a gig at The Mab.

STEVE DEPACE (Flipper): After I graduated high school, I worked the mailroom for Bank Of America. This was '77; I was dating this girl who invited me out one night. I was working swing shift, so I got off at midnight and met her at The Mabuhay Gardens. The scene blew my mind. It was situated on Broadway in San Francisco, by a bunch of strip joints and nightclubs. Anyway, a lot of the strippers went to this club. The family who owned the place was into theater and upstairs was a theater called the On Broadway, which did Punk shows later on. The Mab opened my eyes…

By '78, both LA and San Francisco had strong Punk scenes. The Whiskey in LA and The Mabuhay were where these acts played. The Mab had lots of bands coming up from LA like The Weirdos, The Screamers, UXA. We once decided to do a cultural exchange: Whiskey Night at The Mab, Mab Night at The Whiskey. Dirk Dirksen chose four of the hottest local bands to play The Whiskey: Negative Trend, The Sleepers, The Nuns and The Offs.

Other great SF Punk bands included The Mutants, VKTMS, Angst, and all-girl The Contractions; most were on the *Can You Hear Me? Live at the Deaf Club* comp.
In more a Hardcore-to-come vein, Sick Pleasure and Code Of Honor were the same line-up with different singers. The amphetamine-fueled Pop-O-Pies erupted with three LPs and a great single "Truckin'" (the Dead song done fast). The band dried up when Joe Pop-O-Pie split town over a speed deal gone bad. These combos played shitholes like The Deaf Club, Tool & Die, or The Compound — a very marginal, fucked-up scene.

Boot to the head of Biafra, LA, 1982
Photo by Edward Colver

I am the owl
I seek out the foul
— Dead Kennedys, "I Am The Owl"

DEAD KENNEDYS were the SF ensemble most responsible for making Hardcore happen nationwide. They identified a nascent movement and nurtured it. They sought out like-minded artists, and aided many unknown upstarts. In their zeal to establish a united scene, DKs set the ground rules for everything Hardcore since Day One.

DKs singer Jello Biafra — HC's biggest star — was a powerful presence whose political insurgence and rabid fandom made him the father figure of a burgeoning subculture. A most inspirational force, Jello could also be a real prick. From inside and outside the scene, Biafra was singled out for criticism. In the end, Biafra was a visionary, incendiary motherfucker.

Jello Biafra, born Eric Boucher in 1958, grew up in Boulder, Colorado. Inspired by Abbie Hoffman, Jerry Rubin and the Chicago 7, Eric went west at 18 to attend UC-Santa Cruz.

JELLO BIAFRA: Boulder was dominated by Country Rock snobs. It was great in the late-60s because in a town of 50,000, there were 20,000 Hippies in the summer. This was back when long hair was dangerous. It was a great place to grow up. By the time I'd come of age, that scene wasn't there anymore. You couldn't even get good acid by the time I was getting out of high school. Worse yet, the spirit of resistance was long gone. People were cutting their hair, putting on corduroy jackets with patches on the sleeves, opening businesses. 'This candle's made from all-natural ingredients, therefore it's fifty bucks. Don't argue with me, man, it's not cool.' Dope dealer mentality and lingo used in new ways to fuck over people drove both my anger and my serious depression before Punk happened. The terms 'New Age' and 'Yuppie' weren't invented yet, so I vented my attitude about Boulder in songs like 'Holiday In Cambodia,' 'California Über Alles,' and 'Terminal Preppie.' I got a lot of my grist for social satire from going back to Colorado. San Francisco's so damn safe. There's always shows to see, other artists to bounce ideas off of. If you're running out of ideas, take a BART train to the suburbs and see how everyone else lives. You'll remember what brought you here.

The moniker "Jello Biafra" made a caustic statement in itself: "Jello," Amerika's favorite dessert, and "Biafra," the African region noted for civil war and famine. The blasphemous nature of the DKs name spoke for itself.

Jello Biafra, LA, 1981
Photo by Edward Colver

JELLO BIAFRA: Dead Kennedys couldn't have gotten started anywhere but San Francisco. It was very hard to find places to play at first. The name alone prevented it in New York and Boston.

For their first gig, DKs opened for The Offs and Negative Trend at The Mab, July 19, '78. They created an immediate stir. In fall '79, Biafra came to national attention when he ran for mayor of SF. In an astonishingly successful campaign, he received over four percent of the vote, running fourth place out of ten candidates (with 6137 votes), and helping force a run-off election, eventually won by the wretched Diane Feinstein.

JOEY SHITHEAD (D.O.A.): I first met Biafra at Mabuhay Gardens in '78. We played a couple of successful nights there; I was hanging out with a bunch of beer I smuggled in. Security tried to take it away, so I shook one up and sprayed it in his face. Three of them strong-armed me out the door and Dirk Dirksen, promoter, said, 'You're out of here, Shithead. You're gone.' Biafra got me back in and we became friends after that.

WINSTON SMITH: I worked for a loose-knit group called Rock Against Racism, which started in Great Britain and had a chapter here. We put on Punk shows in an old synagogue downtown next door to The Fillmore, The Temple Beautiful, back in '79. A friend I worked with there looked at my artwork and said, 'You think just like this friend of mine [Jello]. You guys should meet.' My friend played me a record that'd just come out that week, Dead Kennedys' first 45, 'California Über Alles.' I said, 'That's like a musical version of my artwork' — which some people later called 'the artistic version of their music.' My friend arranged for us to meet at The Mab and we immediately hit it off. He looked at a picture of a cross made of dollar bills and he said, 'We gotta have this as our first record cover,' which later came out on the 12". We've been partners-in-crime ever since.

Biafra asked me to come up with something with 'DK' on it, since lots of bands back then used initials, and their publishing company was Decay Music. I wanted something uncomplicated, so anyone could do it. I went back the next week and met with Biafra at the now-defunct Mediterranean Café in Berkeley. As soon as he saw it, he said, 'That's it.' We went to a show that night. I went to take a leak in the bathroom and on the wall was a DK logo. I had just made it, and Biafra had scribbled it all over the place. My friend recently came back from Moscow and Eastern Europe; she saw people with that on their coats and lunchbuckets in Red Square. I heard it's even on the wall of a prison in Moscow! Unfortunately, you don't get any royalties or residuals from graffiti but it's nice to know it's been around.

The diligent DKs constantly networked, toured and recorded. They lost their shirts on their first East Coast trek (summer '79), despite stunning fans at Max's Kansas City in NYC and The Rat in Boston. A second, more-extensive fall '80 tour went much better, largely due to hype arising from the "California Über Alles" and "Holiday In Cambodia" singles' British success, and the brand-new *Fresh Fruit For Rotting Vegetables* album.

JELLO BIAFRA: I learned from the hell of our first New York tour that the reason there wasn't much going on in mid '79 was all the venues were over-21, and the fire was coming from people under 21. So we demanded all-ages shows and the music press dismissed it as a cheap gimmick. But the people who came to those shows grew into dozens of bands in the next five years. I still get letters from people who say their first exposure to Punk was Dead Kennedys at Bond's in New York — that matinee show where we played horribly. It was way too early in the day for a show but people loved it and figured, 'Hey, I can do this too. I think I will.'

Dead Kennedys, 1981
Peligro, East Bay, Biafra and Flouride
Photo by Edward Colver

Biafra first identified the suburban Hardcore phenomenon. Jello supported hot young groups in every city — when such interest by headliners was unheard of. He assembled the bills and made sure promoters dealt properly with rowdy, slamdancing crowds. Biafra understood that the bouncers were totally out of control and that, in the worst problem at shows, kids would jump onstage to share the mic and get fucking drilled by security.

JELLO BIAFRA: We learned that from our first tour. In Philadelphia, we had a Metal band with nazi armbands open for us because they were friends with the promoter. A Mafiosi band did the same in Pawtucket, Rhode Island because they provided a free P.A. — and nearly beat everyone up after the show. We didn't want that to happen again. Some people from the artier side of the underground scene were upset with me for going with Hardcore bands, especially in Boston, but I felt the vanguard was coming from those who had the most energy, pure and simple. Boston, in particular, tried to keep Hardcore people out of the venues and we tried to change that. Little did we know that some of those new people would act like the old Boston guard within two years of being able to play.

ALEC PETERS (Boston promoter): When you did a show with Jello, he owned the stage, the whole area. We'd put a guy on either side of the stage — that's how we ran the pit. Those were the only people, and all they did was keep things clean, and let the kids do their shit. Soon, Jello's band was so big that the big Rock clubs started booking them because they were a legitimate draw, but he'd spend most of his time fucking browbeating the bouncers.

JISM (Ism): Dead Kennedys started reaching younger audiences — 14- and 15-year-olds. They had a lot to do with the rise of the American Hardcore scene. They demanded all-ages gigs with all the local popular bands in the early scene. They were smart — they knew how to brainwash the youth. They knew how to make money, the correct way of doing it. I give

Jello Biafra credit, he knew what he was doing. He was a capitalist or whatever, but they were an integral part of the Hardcore scene.

An unbelievably animated frontman, Jello would act out lyrics with manic, exaggerated stage gestures. Biafra introduced most people to stage diving. He was the first guy to "crowd surf" — he'd jump into the audience, lie on his back, and get passed around. It was all quite revolutionary.

JOE CARDUCCI (SST): They were great. I saw 'em their first time in Portland. They were doing 'California Über Alles' and there was this break in the middle part. Jello was sitting on a table Indian-style chanting with his eyes closed, mocking that Jerry Brown meditation bullshit. One local girl pushed the table over, so when he got off the floor with the mic, when the lyrics kicked back in, he began using her in the dramatization of the lyrics. He was sharp. People were usually so amateurish; if you knocked someone off a table in another band, they might've started crying.

Dead Kennedys, LA, 1980
with original drummer Bruce Slesinger
Photo by Edward Colver

DKs thought they did the right thing by contracting for IRS Records to release *Fresh Fruit* in the US, but it turned out a total disaster, the LP available only on import via UK indie Cherry Red for the first year. That nightmare only hardened their resolve to stick to a staunch D.I.Y. ethos.

JELLO BIAFRA: Jim Fouratt, who in some ways I owe my entire livelihood to, played 'California Über Alles' to Bob Last of Fast Product, who released it in England. We sold maybe 1000 in the US and in one week 20,000 in England. People hadn't heard anything like us over there. We knew there were cool bands here, but English people generally didn't. The people who came to see us play kept asking, 'Why are you the only good band in the United States?' I said, 'There's so many more, you just have to hear them.' At the time, it was impossible for an underground American band to get attention, unless it was an arty one from New York who had connections. That was the original motive for *Let Them Eat Jellybeans* — to expose British Dead Kennedys fans to the big picture. But music writers and labels over there didn't want to know. We put it out on Alternative Tentacles because no label there would touch it, not even Cherry Red, who put out *Fresh Fruit*. They said they didn't want to be closely associated with Dead Kennedys. Shortly thereafter, they weren't.

At this time Biafra, helped by European manager Bill Gilliam, initiated Alternative Tentacles, a label arising from the frustration of seeing The Dils, Screamers and Negative Trend come and go without recording albums. After the first DKs singles and LP, Alternative Tentacles issued *Let Them Eat Jellybeans* in early '81. Side one of this influential compilation was "Hardcore" — Black Flag, D.O.A., Bad Brains — while side two waxed more experimental — Geza X, The Feederz and Voice Farm. *Jellybeans* opened eyes to the idea of a homegrown movement. Biafra earned a rep for liking eccentric artists, the DKs being early patrons of quirky acts such as Butthole Surfers, Half Japanese and Crucifucks.

Alternative Tentacles scored with two late-'81 DK classics: the "Too Drunk To Fuck" 7" and *In God We Trust, Inc.*, a 12" EP. Great discs by D.O.A., 7 Seconds and TSOL expanded the roster. Summer '82 saw DKs' *Plastic Surgery Disasters*.

In their heyday, Dead Kennedys and Alternative Tentacles had a cool scene and a bustling enterprise. Through manager Mike Vraney I met the AT crew: freaky African-American drummer Darren "D.H. Peligro" Henley, laid-back guitarist "East Bay" Ray Pepperel, egghead bassist Jeff "Klaus Flouride" Lyle, roadie and jack-of-all-trades Michael "Microwave" Bonano, artist Winston Smith, and soundman

Manic DKs stage action, LA, 1982
Photo by Edward Colver

Chris Grayson. One of the TSOL guys said Chris — later live mixer for the Red Hot Chili Peppers — was murdered in 1990, hacked into pieces and stuffed in a bus station locker over a bad drug deal.

One of HC's most startling case studies, Peligro as a hyperactive child from the St. Louis ghettos got turned on to Emerson, Lake & Palmer, and stole a drumset from his school to emulate these heroes. After a few years of jamming out on Aerosmith and ZZ Top numbers, he threw that ol' drumset onto a Greyhound bus bound for SF with $8 in his pocket. He spent a few weeks living on the streets, then stumbled on a warehouse filled with decadent speed-shooting homeless Punkers. There he met and started to play drums with the group SSI.

D.H. PELIGRO (Dead Kennedys): SSI was named for Supplemental Security Income. It means you're crazy. It used to be a lot easier to get. People would do speed and stay up for weeks, shove peanut butter up their ass and eat it, all sorts of other tricks to get SSI. Don't bathe. Stank. Talk incoherently. Wear gay bondage stuff — crazy whacked out — or go in there butt-naked. Take your pants off and complain it's too hot when it's cold — it's a lot cooler in San Francisco — or just sorta start undressing slowly. I guess psychiatrists were a bit more gullible back in the day.

DKs sounded incredible, like fucked-up circus music at 78 rpm: Biafra's whine driven by seasoned musicians. To compose, Biafra would hum a few bars to Klaus; he'd construct a tune, altering keys to fit Jello's voice. Ray embellished the result with his trademark surfy, noodly guitar parts. Peligro's manic energy drove the outfit live — but many of his ultra-fast drums fills failed to make it to vinyl, due to bad equipment and poor production.

Jello Biafra, LA, 1981
Photo by Edward Colver

JELLO BIAFRA: Ray and Klaus are quite a bit older, and had played in other bands. Before Dead Kennedys, Ray played in a Rockabilly band called Cruisin' which did 50s covers. Peligro'd get shit from his Black friends for liking White people's music — but White people didn't want him in their bands. Punk was a great outlet for him. I first saw him in a lost band, SSI — a drummer with a shit-eating grin who could sing like Little Richard. As for earlier members, 6025 was our second guitarist the first six months; he left to become the Captain Beefheart of Gospel — which I don't think'll ever happen. Bruce Slesinger was our first drummer, but Klaus, Ray and Peligro were the core of Dead Kennedys.

Kids shuddered at the mention of Dead Kennedys. Cops showed up at every gig, and Biafra was always defiant — only adding to the notoriety. Of course, by the mid-80s DKs turned into what they hated most: a band suburban yo-yos loved.

KEN INOUYE (Marginal Man): One of the most fucked up things — a high point and low point of Marginal Man — was opening for Dead Kennedys in Berkeley in '84, the final show at a club called The Keystone. What struck me was how many assholes liked that band. Every band that opened up for them that night got booed and had shit thrown at them. We stepped onstage; I started seeing how many ice cubes and beer cups I could dodge. When the Kennedys hit the stage, I realized that eventually this music would be huge: the very people I hated in high school were getting into it.

Alternative Tentacles logo
Art by Winston Smith

Though the top act of the HC era — a considerably larger draw than Black Flag or Circle Jerks — DKs weren't as successful as you'd think. Sure, they had earned high name recognition, but they weren't Rock Stars.

WINSTON SMITH: We still all had to pile into Klaus's station wagon: there were no limos. We had to carry our own equipment; there were no groupies backstage. You had to clean the trash and slime on instruments and hope that your car hadn't been towed away or stolen while you were at the club. There was nothing glittery about it. Many talented people were not appreciated because they were the same people who had to sweep up the mess at the end of the night, too. A lot of us had day jobs at the copy shop or making sandwiches. If we wanted to go to the movies, we'd grab our pennies and wait for the bus — literally.

By '84, internal problems developed. Well into their 30s, East Bay and Klaus grew uneasy with the young, violent audience. Always fucked up, D.H. began a downward spiral (he'd play with the Chili Peppers for a few months in '88 but was too far gone even for them). DKs split bitterly with Mike Vraney, who left to manage "the new TSOL." DKs still played great gigs, but at the end of the day, everyone got sick of Biafra's histrionics.

Biafra was caught up in his own personal hell. He married his girlfriend Theresa in '82, and it was great for awhile. Her parents gave them a shiny white BMW as a wedding gift (the last car a DK should be seen in); Jello left it covered in the backyard. In late '83, his pal Frank Discussion of the Phoenix outfit The Feederz went on the lam from the Feds after pulling an elaborate prank, circulating a letter on Arizona Board of Education stationery to local schools, offering "scholarships" for winners of an essay contest on "Why School Is A Waste Of Time." After hiding out at Biafra's house for almost a year, Frank ran off with Theresa and Jello's money. Many of Jello's pals feel he never recovered from that.

In '80 and '81, DKs toured the US sounding unique. By '86, they played the same Thrash as the kids. DKs knew it was time to throw in the towel.

D.H. PELIGRO: East Bay walked in one day and said, 'I've got a bomb to drop on you: I'm leaving the band.' We scrambled around thinking of maybe getting Ron Emory from TSOL, but in the end we came to the conclusion that that just wouldn't be Dead Kennedys anymore. So we just hung it up after that. And I was really broken. With all the havoc and all the bullshit and all the racial tension that I got, at least I had Dead Kennedys, and we were in it together. There was a part of me that still wanted to carry on, that our greatest shit was yet to come.

Personal and professional problems aside, a highly publicized obscenity suit killed the Kennedys after they included an H.R. Giger poster with their '85 LP *Frankenchrist*. Deputy LA Attorney Michael Guarino filed criminal charges against Biafra and AT for distributing harmful material to minors, after a San Fernando Valley housewife complained to authorities when her teen daughter brought home the album from a Wherehouse Records store in the Northridge Fashion Mall. The ACLU came to AT's defense, but the entire episode killed the business, which operated on a very tight margin.

If a local government had tried to sue a major-league Rock Band whose album cover offered unsetteling or obscene imagry, the music biz would've circled its wagons and dispensed armies of hot-shit lawyers. But "they" could sue some dipshit Hardcore group and win — then make that judgement stick. Luckily, justice prevailed: the court dismissed all charges. But the damage was done: the group ran out of steam. In late '86, right after their final show at UC-Davis and the release of *Bedtime For Democracy*, Biafra announced to the world that the Kennedys would be no more.

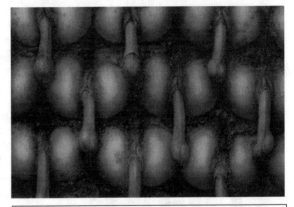

Landscape XX, ©1973 H.R. Giger
This painting was reproduced on a poster included with
DKs *Frankenchrist* LP (Alternative Tentacles, 1985)
Courtesy of Leslie Barany

JELLO BIAFRA: Yeah, that's when we broke up. I'm not sure it's over but there's no plans for some stupid-ass reunion tour. The music lives on, the words still stand, people still pick up albums in small but consistent amounts. Something like The Velvet Underground, but on a smaller scale. I would hope I and Dead Kennedys helped smash the 70s. Going after what came after it is a much harder job.

At the urging of poet Harvey Kubernik, Jello parlayed his notoriety into Spoken Word records and tours. But alienation resulting from his legal and personal woes caused him to retreat into a shell. Jello's nadir was 1994 when he took a vicious beating by some SF Skins down with *Maximum RockNRoll*. Though Biafra had originally spread the *MRR* gospel, editor Tim Yohannon and crew protected the assailants' identities. If you ever needed proof that scene unity was a crock of shit, that was it. (At press time, Ray, Klaus and D.H. [who tours and records as Peligro], won a $220,000 judgement against Biafra and Alternative Tentacles for royalties due.)

D.H. PELIGRO: There's things I can't talk about, but I really dislike having been mistreated by Alternative Tentacles, the label I felt I had a part in building and growing with. So to find out that I'd been stabbed in the back, that's just fucked, it's wack, I ain't with that. And as little trust that I already had in people, it's just little less trust that I have.

Flipper, Mudd Club, NYC, March 1982
Bruce Loose (Left) and Will Shatter
Photo by Fred Berger

Granted, Biafra did a lot of the work, but a lot of that work and exposure comes with a certain level of responsibility that you have to own up to.

The people speak as one
The cattle
The crowd
— Flipper, "Sacrafice"

FLIPPER, one of history's most in-your-face outfits, was championed by Biafra. Although not Hardcore kids, these SF Punk vets with ex-members of The Offs and Negative Trend made their name playing to HC crowds. Ted Falconi, Steve DePace, Bruce Loose and Will Shatter — a sleazy, usurious indulgent mooch of dubious character, but an incredibly talented artist and musician — could torture young audiences like no one else. With pure genius discs like "Sex Bomb" and *Generic Flipper*, Flipper was a giant "Fuck You!"

STEVE DEPACE (Flipper): Negative Trend fizzled out — Will Shatter wasn't doing anything. I was at a party one night and was approached by Ted Falconi who took me to a rehearsal studio. He was jamming with Will and the singer from The Sleepers, Ricky Sleeper, Flipper's original singer. He's the guy who named the band. He had a lot of pets at his house: a cat, a hamster, a goldfish, a bird; they were all named Flipper. He was so fucked up that it was easier for him to remember just one name. When we were kicking around names he offered Flipper as his suggestion. For lack of better ideas, we went with it. Ted came up with the fish logo.

Flipper stood out from the crowd and Jello, liking things that were different, took a liking to us. We did lots of shows at The Mab and left to become the house band at Sound Of Music, a drag queen strip joint which on weekends became a Punk venue. It was in the bowels of the Tenderloin on Turk Street, a really rough street. We helped establish the club and it helped us to build our audience. Then clubs started opening up all over the place; we started playing the Bay Area circuit: The Deaf Club, 10th Street Hall, Temple Beautiful. At this time the DKs went on their first big tour. Jello, in every interview they'd ask him 'Who's your favorite band?' and he'd say 'Flipper.' He really helped put our name in people's minds.

We had an opportunity to come to New York in 1981, right after 'Sex Bomb' came out. We got a call from somebody who wanted to fly us out and to play Danceteria — an incredible amount of money they were going to pay us. We were just playing local shows for $100; this guy wanted to pay us $2500. We did Saturday night at Danceteria but we flew out on a Thursday and played an unannounced show at The Mudd Club. Who's the openers? Hose. Rick Rubin got up and did three or four of our songs. He had a Flipper cover band. I was rapping to these kids out front

FLIPPER
ALL AGES
FRIDAY DON'T BE LATE
MARCH 5
3:00 – 6:00
AT MEDIA WORKSHOP 6TH FLOOR
367 BOYLSTON ST
along with **?**
by SSD

Show flyer for Flipper, Media Workshop,
Boston, March 1982
Collection of the author

and they were too young to get in. We had to bum rush the door to sneak them in. They were short little guys who said they had a Hardcore band called the Beastie Boys. Also around '81, the Dead Kennedys played at The Whiskey. They chose us to come down and be their opening act. I remember the audience hated us.

I think the album *Generic* was already in progress. It was recorded over the course of a year. We'd pop into a studio when we had money and time. So we go out on a national tour headlining clubs; with Jello putting the word out, all our shows were packed. Bruce and Will, Punk Rockers that they were, hated that. They'd rather have four people that hated us in the audience then 400 that loved us. There was a show in New Orleans where 100 people showed up; by the time we finished playing, there was like six people left. We just gave 'em our instruments and went to the bar. That was the first time we drove everybody out of the place. Bruce and Will took a liking to doing that. From time to time, they'd wanna be really fucked up and horrible. Our true fans loved those shows! Flipper got a rep — 'the band you love to hate.' A lot of people hated what we were doing but they'd be at the show. You never knew what was gonna happen at a Flipper event. It could've been great — or horrible — but there was always a surprise.

If you experienced Flipper's slow, dissonant drone, you'd never forget it. At one NYC gig, they were so high they played for three hours, including a painful 45-minute "I Am The Wheel." Bruce and Will, who'd switch off on bass and vocals, were drugheads who'd shoot speed to kick dope. (Will OD'd in '87). Falconi did so much speed once, he took a car engine apart and put it back together. DePace was the group's so-called straight guy.

Dave Dictor (MDC), "Rock Against Reagan", Central Park, NYC, 1984
Photo by Karen O'Sullivan

STEVE DEPACE: We always had fans that loved what we were doing and said they started bands because they heard Flipper. Interviews with Kurt Cobain said Flipper influenced him to cut his hair, buy a guitar, and start a band. In the past few years I've come to realize the broad influence we had over a generation, many of whom started bands, some of whom became huge. Every band on Earth played 'Sex Bomb' at shows or in their garages. In fact, in about '84 a radio station in Boston asked every garage band to send in a cover of 'Sex Bomb'; they got so many tapes they did a two-day marathon. It was like the 'Louie Louie' of the time.

My life in a cage
Show my outrage
— MDC, "Born To Die"

MDC (MILLIONS OF DEAD COPS) were perhaps the most politically extreme Hardcore outfit. They started in '78 in Austin, Texas as The Stains, who released the classic "John Wayne Was A Nazi" 7" (later an MDC standard). MDC's self-released *Millions Of Dead Cops* LP of '82 represented a milestone in radical music and politics. If Biafra was HC's Abbie Hoffman, MDC frontman Dave Dictor was its Chè Guevara.

KING KOFFEE (Butthole Surfers): MDC were doing rad stuff. Touring the country as a Hardcore band called Millions Of Dead Cops was an intense thing to do. 'What's the name of your band, son?' 'Millions Of Dead Cops.' That's not an easy thing to say. And crossing the border into Canada with a name like that. It took a lot of balls to be part of the Hardcore scene back then, but for MDC, every day was intense.

AL QUINT (editor, *Suburban Voice*): I got ahold of the first MDC album. I wouldn't attribute it entirely to them, but hearing anti-corporate lyrics affected my way of thinking. I was 22, somewhat impressionable, idealistic, and naive. I'd drive to work everyday blasting that MDC album. I thought, 'I don't have to work. I don't have to do this with my life if I don't want to.' So I quit my job. That did not please my parents. They said, 'Get another job because we want you to get out.'

AL BARILE (SS Decontrol): That first MDC album was amazing. I hung with them a lot; I remember driving through Cambridge trying to find them a vegetarian place. They seemed like good guys. Later, I heard a lot of weird stories about the singer, that he was a transvestite, but it wasn't apparent at the time. They were one of the hardest-working bands after Black Flag. They were determined. I gave their record to Oedipus of WBCN in Boston. I wanted him to play it on his show — of course he never did.

Dictor flourished in SF's activist Left-Wing subculture, where there were plenty of other dogmatic Marxists interested in the destruction of Amerika. Many of them were 60s holdovers, anxious to recruit young blood. That's how MDC secured the backing of the Yippies for their notorious "Rock Against Reagan Tour" of '84 (MDC, Dicks, Crucifix, DRI).

MDC IS A HARDCORE POLITICAL HUMANIST BAND FROM SAN FRANCISCO. FORMERLY the STAINS FROM AUSTIN, TEXAS, THE GROUP CHANGED ITS NAME AND ADDRESS IN MARCH OF THIS YEAR, AND RELEASED THIS RECORD 3 MONTHS LATER ON R Radical Records, THE BAND'S LABEL MILLIONS OF DEAD COPS IS THEIR FIRST ALBUM. THIS IS THE THIRD PRESSING AND WAS REMIXED FROM THE ORIGINAL TAPE BY KLAUS FLOURIDE AND EAST BAY RAY OF THE DEAD KENNEDYS, REMASTERED BY GEZA X AND ERIC WOLFE.

MDC IS CURRENTLY PLAYING EUROPE WITH the DK'S, WITHOUT BREAK FROM A HUNDRED DAY TOUR OF THE USA AND CANADA. FOR INFORMATION ON DISTRIBUTION OF THE ALBUM contact RUTH SCHWARTZ at ROUGH TRADE RECORDS / 326 6th St. /SF, C. 94103 / 1-800-272-3170 OR WRITE MDC / 2440 16th St. #103 /SF, Ca. 94103

MDC press release, 1982, in which they bill themselves as "Hardcore Political Humanist"
Collection of the author

GARY FLOYD (Dicks): Through MDC we hooked up with the Yippies out of New York. They said, 'There's this thing called the Rock Against Reagan Tour — we'd love for you to be involved.' With an old beat-up van and our new manager Debbie Gordon who quit the stock exchange to manage us — which meant making sure there was beer, and somebody gave us $15 at the end of the night — we loaded in a van with out any drums, no amplifiers, just guitar and a bass — and we went on a three month tour sponsored by the Yippies. That meant they gave us a little money for gas and once a day you could eat a big meal of turkey dogs that somehow they'd gotten. They made all the plans. They'd talk to some kid in like Cleveland or Michigan or wherever and the kid would say, 'Yeah, you can come stay with us — we'll put this show on.' So two school busses full of fuckin' weird Yippies, Hippies and other shit-adopters, and two vans full of MDC, Crucifucks, DRI, and the Dicks. We'd pull up in this yard; the parents would of course scream, 'You're not staying here!' It was complete chaos. The Yippies sponsored the chaos of the Rock Against Reagan Tour.

MDC, touring around the country in their gnarly van, presented quite a sight. You had the shaved head, piercing eyes and yammering jaw of Dave Dictor. Bassist Franc'o Mares was known for his marijuana haze and his funky odor. Drummer Al "Schvitz" Schultz served serious jail time in the 90s for his crank habit.

Ultimately, MDC's political dogma worked against them. To cool things, they varied their title: Multi-Death Corporation, Millions Of Dead Children, Male Dominated Culture, Misguided Devout Christians. But as much as MDC agitated

to spread the Hardcore gospel, they were also total killjoys. It just wasn't cool anymore. Mediocre releases, and a late 80s lineup with future Rancid bassist Matt Freeman, led to MDC's fade into obscurity.

WINSTON SMITH (graphic artist): I remember Dave from MDC had more fun than the audience did sometimes. Call it cruelty to animals!

KING KOFFEE: We played The Mab in San Francisco and I offered one of the MDC guys a burrito. But then Franc'o began this lecture on how cheese was exploiting animals. I thought it was really silly — considering we were all starving. That was way too extreme for me.

Come on fucker!
Give me a break!
You fuckin' pig
Death is your fate!
— Dicks, "Kill From The Heart"

In addition to MDC, other Texas HC outfits migrated to SF's activism and enlightenment, like THE DICKS (Austin), VERBAL ABUSE, DRI (Houston) and RHYTHM PIGS (El Paso). Most lived at The Vats, an abandoned Hamm's brewery on 4th Street at Bryant. Over the course of four years, The Vats was the focus of local squat culture, hosting 20 or so full-time residents and a regular flow of kids crashing, bands practicing, and touring acts playing. The other significant "Vats groups" were THE FUCK UPS and CONDEMNED TO DEATH. I was there once, and remember this one girl with a pet rat, her face scratched up by a rat who was a rival of her rat. The place was fucking filthy. When The Vats was condemned in late '84, the SF Hardcore scene ended. The site is now a parking lot.

The Vats, Hardcore squat, during demolition, 1984
Photo by Spike Cassidy

SPIKE CASSIDY (DRI): When DRI moved to San Francisco, we were living in our van in a parking lot outside a supermarket. The van next to ours was Verbal Abuse's. We did that a few months, until they brought us to The Vats. Bands squatted there in very unsanitary conditions. It was four floors of long hallways; off on the right and left were beer vats. Most of them had little doors you had to crawl through — the only way in and out of most of the vats. There was running water in a bathroom on the fourth floor, although no hot water. The conditions weren't great but it was a better than living in a van. It was a place to practice and keep our gear.

SCOTTY WILKINS: I used to squat in this cool place The Vats, an old brewery, the most developed squat scene I'd ever seen. People paid rent. All the bands rehearsed there for basically free. There were four floors, and four vats per floor. The first floor was all flat — and that's where MDC lived. It was our own little world: fights, everybody getting drunk, drugs everywhere of course. We were just drinkin', stinkin,' and doing no thinkin.' In LA, everybody went home to the burbs, but in San Francisco, everybody went back to The Vats.

With a scene not nearly as violent as LA's, the city most closely paralleled NYC and Philly: desperate, urban, drug-fueled.

JEFF McDONALD (Red Cross): The biggest difference between San Francisco and LA back then was that crystal meth played a huge part in San Francisco. Speed killed the Hippies, but it also fueled the Punk scene — some of the leaders were big tweakers. So you had these dangerous older people with worldly philosophies and these homeless kids with no teeth cuz they lived on speed. I think that's why San Francisco never really had a music scene: it was a much more drugged-out, so there wasn't the focus. Sure, LA was just as drugged-out but cocaine and heroin are a slower demise than speed, which can turn you into a homeless nightmare crazy person in a matter of months.

SCOTTY WILKINS (Verbal Abuse): In San Francisco, anywhere we went was a problem. If you journeyed into The Mission, the cholos were going to hassle you. If you go up to the Fillmore, all the brothers were going to get down on you. Basically, the cops were the enemy, too.

Zine ad for Crucifix "Nineteen Eighty-Four" single, 1983
Collection of Sal Canzonieri

You go on playing with people's lives
Using their minds
You want total control
Stay in line!
— Crucifix, "Annihilation"

By the mid 80s, the Berkeley-based crew at *Maximum RockNRoll* had basically taken over the Bay Area Hardcore agenda. MRR deserves credit for fostering the scene, but this pack of thirty-something Bolsheviks also manipulated kids to codify their own narrow interests. MRR Editor Tim Yohannon assembled the influential comp *Not So Quiet On The Western Front,* a terrific two-LP portrait of Northern Cali and Nevada HC, including SOCIAL UNREST, INTENSIFIED CHAOS, BAD POSTURE, CHURCH POLICE, and RIBSY. The most impressive outfit of that San Francisco scene was CRUCIFIX, led by Cambodian-born frontman Sothira. They peaked with their 1982 7" EP called *1984.*

In reaction to scene rigidity and leftist dogma came anti-*MRR* "Drunk Punks" like Metal-edged TALES OF TERROR. Not bad, but the reactionary attitude (today's "political incorrectness") went totally nowhere.

The best Berkeley HC outfit was FANG — famed for their gnarly groove on "Skinheads Smoke Dope" and "Berkeley Heathen Scum" on the noted Boner Records (Fang singer Sammy, who recently finished serving time for murdering his girlfriend while on a heroin binge, is playing out again, performing the old songs with a new lineup.).

San Jose also experienced HC action, with cool skater outfits like THE FACTION, LOS OLVIDADOS, TONGUE AVULSION, as well as the esoteric WHIPPING BOY, led by Stanford University student Eugene Robinson. The South Bay also harbored the great zine *Ripper,* which compared well with Flipside and *MRR* back in the day, and the short-lived *Skate Punk Magazine,* edited by pro skater and The Faction bassist Steve Caballero.

I can see the lights
The helicopters are coming
Down on me tonight
— Fang, "Fun With Acid"

Bay Area Hardcore fed the Punk/Metal Crossover. Berkeley was home to Ruthie's, the first Crossover club, where, around '84, SF HC fused with East Bay Metal, via Metallica (with future Megadeth star Dave Mustaine), Exodus (with future Metallica guitarist Kirk Hammett) and Possessed (with future Primus guitarist Larry Lalonde). Slayer, from LA, played some of their first shows there,

back when they wore silly makeup. Original Metallica bassist the late Cliff Burton played in high school ensembles with future Faith No More guitarist Jim Martin and drummer Mike Bordin; then Cliff turned James Hetfield and Lars Ulrich onto The Misfits and The Dictators. Faith No More, whose '85 debut LP *We Care A Lot* was the first or second release on Ruth Schwartz's Mordam Records, first synthesized the SF Punk, Hardcore and Metal experiences.

Whipping Boy, A7, NYC, 1983; Eugene Robinson, singing
Photo by Karen O'Sullivan

The so-called Riot Grrl movement also grew out of SF HC. Punk crash pad The A-Hole housed SF's coolest outfits, Frightwig and Tragic Mullato; Courtney Love even hung out for a while, ingratiating herself and first honing her chops with Faith No More and Frightwig — whose masterpiece *Faster Frightwig, Kill! Kill!* heavily influenced Lunachicks and L7.

SF's late-80s scene mimicked the early decade. Lawrence Livermore of *Lookout* fanzine and Lookout Records and *MRR* opened 924 Gilmore, the Oakland club which spawned the Ska act Operation Ivy, with future members of Rancid and Green Day. But that umpteenth-generation incarnation is another story. •

BAD BRAINS:
HOW LOW CAN A PUNK GET?

Don't care what they may say
We got that attitude
Don't care what they may do
We got that attitude
— Bad Brains, "Attitude"

Bad Brains, 1981
four Black guys in a crazy White world
(L-R) Darryl Jenifer, Earl Huson, Dr. Know, H.R.
Photo by Laura Levine, courtesy of ROIR

East Coast Hardcore begins with Bad Brains. A force of one, before them no movement existed. 1980's "Pay To Cum" 7" — easily the fastest record of its time — was an instant classic. You can debate whether Bad Brains developed their hyperspeed formula in response to or independent of simultaneous Southern Cal events, but their music defined the essence of Hardcore.

Bad Brains were vocalist Paul "H.R." Hudson, drummer Earl Hudson, guitarist Gary "Dr. Know" Miller, and bassist Darryl Jenifer. They were an oxymoron, a novel cultural hybrid: middle-class Blacks Jazz Fusion fans from suburban DC who developed their own unique response to Punk; first exposed to Rastafarianism and Reggae by Brit Punks like The Clash and The Ruts. As boxing impresario Don King says, "Only in America."

DR. KNOW (Bad Brains): We wanted to be the fastest band in the world, that's what we wanted to be known for. The Ramones were the fastest but we could improve on that. At the same time, we didn't want to be doing that same three-chord routine. Not that there's anything wrong when The Ramones do it but we had something to prove musically. That's how we've always been, wanting to keep it challenging and interesting. The gift of musicality is not to be taken for granted.

Easily HC's most technically proficient outfit, Bad Brains musically surpassed all others of the realm. Other Hardcore outfits created a blur of volume and speed — the Bad Brains hit all the notes and made it look easy. Creative ability mixed with frenetic presentation and Rasta evangelism, making for an unbelievable experience. Bad Brains should've been *huge*.

IAN MACKAYE (Minor Threat): I saw the Bad Brains for the first time in June of '79, opening for The Damned at The Bayou, this disgusting jock bar. I needed a fake ID to get in.

The Bad Brains opened, and transcended anything I'd ever seen. They were *the* band. They've managed to really fuck up their reputation, but that band had a profound impact on music. They moved me.

AL BARILE (SS Decontrol): My interpretation of Punk was that it was very guitar-driven. I went to New York one weekend when The Clash was playing Bond's and someone told us to go to this loft party where the Bad Brains were playing. The Bad Brains hit their first note and it was the most dramatic music moment in my life. It was definitely magical.

H.R. (Bad Brains), Irving Plaza, NYC, 1982
Photo by Karen O'Sullivan

JOHN JOSEPH (Cro-Mags): Seeing the Bad Brains was a spiritual experience for me because I was in the Service, and for a young person at 17, it was definitely a time of searching. I was very confused about what life was about, so when I first encountered them — H.R. especially — me and him went out back on the side of the club, and we talked for hours that night. It was amazing. I mean, I saw the early Clash gigs at Bond's, but to me, all those early Bad Brains gigs in DC were much more important.

I had a rough childhood, and I was looking for answers. Punk Rock — yeah, it was cool and it was fun and it was about getting fucked up and breaking shit up — but it didn't really offer any answers for me. The Bad Brains were someone who could provide spiritual insight to the music without being all preachy. It wasn't like preaching religion onstage; it was raw energy and power, and then you could speak to them afterwards. It was having an effect on my soul. When Bad Brains were in their heyday, they were the greatest. It inspired me to play music and everything else.

DREW STONE (The Mighty COs): When I'm on the porch with my grandkids, I'll tell them about the greatest band that ever walked the Earth: the Bad Brains. They were the most incredible live band I've ever seen. They played these shows that were just magic. They bridged the gap, man — here's four Black kids with dreads playing Hardcore and Reggae.

While the 60s British Invasion extolled (and plagiarized) the American Negro, Punk had no place for Blacks. Anti-Black by no means, the scene in fact attempted to graft Reggae onto the style: witness The Specials and the Two-Tone Ska scene. But Black-White Punk unity never happened. And though HC never achieved true racial unity either, the Bad Brains did more to achieve a Rasta/Rock fusion than anyone past, present, or future.

DARRYL JENIFER (Bad Brains): Here we were, Black homeboys checking out Rock & Roll and vice versa. It's all just music now, and that's the way it's supposed to be, all about open-mindedness. There was a lot of separatism back in the day. By people checking each other's cultures out, barriers and stereotypes are broken down. And that's what we need.

Paul and Earl Hudson started out as typical Army brats. Eventually their dad left the military and got a job in the security field; the family settled in suburban Prince George's County, Maryland, and the brothers led normal lives, going to high school in Capitol Heights with Gary "Dr. Know" Miller, Darryl Jenifer and Sid McCray. In early '78 the five started playing music together, their first efforts imitating the Jazz Fusion of Weather Report and Mahavishnu Orchestra, with lots

of crazy chord progressions. **The line-up called itself Mind Power, reflecting an interest in the nebulous self-help principles of P.M.A. (Positive Mental Attitude). By all accounts, Mind Power could've never cut it as Jazz cats. Sure they could play, but they jumped around too much — too hyper and uncool for the Fusion world.**

DR. KNOW: I remember in the ninth grade, Earl could yo-yo real good. So he would come in doing walk-the-dog, around-the-world, cat's cradle — he had it goin' on! H.R. was in a grade higher than Earl and I, and Darryl was a grade younger. Where they lived it was all apartments, so there wasn't anywhere to play music. We had this friend Alvarez who was fortunate to live in a house — he had a basement. His mother would go out to play Bingo on Tuesdays and Thursdays and we'd go down in his basement and just kick it — Return To Forever and John McLaughlin. We didn't have the chops, we just used to sit around and emulate them guys.

DARRYL JENIFER: When we was kids, it was all about music. I'd play my guitar like Ernie Isley. It wasn't about Jimi Hendrix for us back then, it was more like Funkadelic and Sly & The Family Stone. As youth, we had to kick it with our instruments. So to take it one step further back then, it's like 'I don't play Kool & The Gang, I play a little Mahavishnu.' So

H.R. (Bad Brains), teaching the youth
Irving Plaza, NYC, 1982
Photo by Karen O'Sullivan

we went off into that. I'd come to school and bring the Return To Forever album because it's about the chops and the riffs.

Our first lead singer was this dude Sid McCray, who's my bass tech. He's the one who actually brought Punk Rock music to us: 'You've been listening to that Mahavishnu but these motherfuckers is crazy. This is some bad shit.' So we got Dead Boys and Ramones albums and I got the *No New York* album with James Chance and I used to love that. What happened was, H.R. used to play guitar and sing — Sid would be the frontman singing. The cosmics at the time wasn't making it happen with Sid. He was way ahead of his time even with us. He was so esoteric, like the minute two people started clapping for Bad Brains he was like, 'This is commercial.' He stepped out of the picture and we took the band and ran with it. That's when the Brains took the musicianship of Jazz and grafted it onto the don't-give-a-fuck rough-and-ruggedness of Punk Rock.

Not as much but with such intensity
I'd like to be what they would not want me to be
— Bad Brains, "I"

After Sid sufficiently blew the minds of Paul, Earl, Doc and Darryl in late '78, the quartet renamed itself Bad Brains. Dr. Know once gave me some late-nite rap to the effect that, in Black lingo, "bad" means good, while "brains" relates to provoking thought. He said their first record's cover sported a picture of lightning striking the Capitol building as their statement against people in power. And of course, the Ramones sang "Bad Brain." Paul became "H.R."; explanations of the nickname differ. Darryl's version: "Do you notice how rich people are called by their initials? The whole concept of being 'H.R.' was as if he was a rich man." I recall it as an in-joke: "Hunting Rod," referring to his sexual prowess. Eventually H.R. used the monogram to stand for "Human Rights."

Bad Brains quickly made waves around DC.

ROB KENNEDY (The Chumps): The Chumps did a gig at Georgetown's Hall Of Nations with Cramps and Urban Verbs. We were tossed the bone of opening 'cause there was a dubious notoriety about us. We had a sizeable chip on our shoulders, so when four totally Punked-out Black guys showed up begging to sneak in we were only too happy to accommodate. That's how we got invited to party at their place in Suitland, MD, a middle-class Black suburb. I guarantee you there were only four Black Punks in Suitland at that time — in all DC for that matter. Nonetheless, they had a happenin' party there. The local Black kids looked at them as wild freaks; the savvy honkies knew they were seeing something special. Both elements were doing fine behind some serious ganja-huffing. The Chumps left there knowing we had to spread the word that the Bad Brains were for real.

Show flyer for
Bad Brains first gig,
Towson, MD, 1979
Collection of
Rob Kennedy

Soon after [early '79] we got pitched by these wack Punks from Annapolis, Judy's Fixation, to organize a show at a VFW hall in Towson, MD, which I thought was just another DC suburb but turned out to be a redneck/jarhead town way at the Beltway's edge. We put together a great bill: The Chumps, The Slickee Boys, Judy's Fixation, and the world premiere of Bad Brains. Bad Brains played to an audience of a dozen slack-jawed crackers and off-duty Marines — too stunned to know how to react — and of course the blown-away members of the other bands that were going to have to follow. The Brains ripped through a set that wasn't been more than a half-hour long. They didn't do any Jah stuff and they went fairly easy on the Mahavishnu influences. They were mind-boggling. HR was a reckless young Iggy. Doc was numbingly fast and Earl and Darryl were so on it, it was scary. Thank God Judy's Fixation played next, not us!

A riot began shortly after The Chumps hit the stage. The crackers and jarheads were well lubricated by then; there were a lot of empty cans and bottles. After a few got chocked at us we turned up the attitude. It wasn't long before fists were flying. I remember the Brains pretty much hanging back out of the fight. It petered out almost as fast as it had started, but by the next issue of the local DC culture rag it had become a race riot that the Bad Brains were in the center of. If they weren't exactly embraced by the DC clubowners before that, imagine how they did after. That was their only gig for a while, until Madam's Organ opened up and there was somebody booking bands they *hoped* would cause a riot.

Still figuring it all out, the Brains "Punked out" — wearing messy hair, sharkskin suits, and thin wraparound shades. H.R. came off like an African-American Johnny Rotten.

DARRYL JENIFER: When I first got into Punk, I'd wear leather dog collars and all that shit. We'd do evil shit like set tablecloths on fire in the club, but it was all Punk Rock to us. We'd wear ripped-up suits with mirrors taped on and safety pins and zippers everywhere, leopardskin spandex with jockey underwear on top with 'Fuck you' or something like that on the crotch. We were on the border between Punk and Funkadelic. It was Black freak Punks — like George Clinton with the diaper vibe crossed with the Sex Pistols fuck-you vibe, too.

Bad Brains were essentially a cover band in those early days, copying the songs of Eater, Sex Pistols, The Saints, and The Damned. They'd do "You Drive Me Ape" by The Dickies, "12XU" by Wire, "Screaming Fist" by Canada's The Viletones. Soon

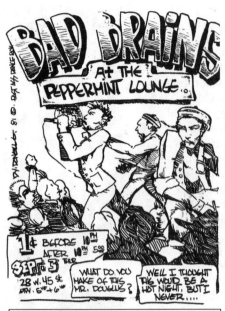

Show flyer for Bad Brains,
Peppermint Lounge, NYC, 1981
Collection of the author

they added originals: "Supertouch/Shitfit," "Pay To Cum," and "How Low Can A Punk Get?" In fall '79 came "Don't Bother Me" — their vinyl debut on the Limp Records comp *30 Seconds Over DC*, which they cut a few months earlier with Don Zientara at Inner Ear, his four-track Arlington, VA studio (the session tapes saw the light of day in 1996 as *Black Dots*). That session also initiated Zientara's association with DC Hardcore.

DR. KNOW: Don Zientara made all his own boards, his own machines and everything. I remember H.R. recording the vocals out in Don's yard because there was no isolation booth; he was out screaming in the trees! We made some great music there. He's doing very well these days, I hear.

Bad Brains wrought havoc everywhere they went. Each performance left damage, and each new DC club appearance was usually their last. The 9: 30 Club, DC Space, and the Bayou blacklisted the group, now literally "Banned In DC" (the title of one of their later songs).

Through most of '79 and '80, the only local spot to welcome the Bad Brains was a Yippie flophouse in the then-marginal Adams' Morgan neighborhood called Madam's Organ. Impressionable teens like Ian MacKaye and Henry Rollins showed up at Madame's Organ, planting the roots of DC Hardcore. The same kids would also hung out at the wild basement parties the Bad Brains threw at a house they rented in Forestville, Maryland for around six months in '79.

Show flyer for Bad Brains, CBGB, NYC, 1981
Collection of Laura Albert

DR. KNOW: All the DC bands played our parties — Black Market Baby, The Penetrators, everybody. Then from us playing fast, Teen Idles, S.O.A., and all those kids got their shit happening. You can't fight the youth!

Mo Sussman, owner of restaurant Mo & Joe's, was managing the Bad Brains in 1980 when they cut a killer demo at Omega Studios (released 18 years later as *The Omega Sessions*). Things never worked out with Mo, but he was the one who took them to see the Jamaican movie *Rockers* with Gregory Isaacs, Big Youth, and Leroy "Horsemouth" Wallace — essentially, that's what got them into Rastafari. Experiencing a Capitol Center double bill of Bob Marley and Fusion hero Stanley Clarke sealed the Bad Brains' spiritual path a few weeks later.

DARRYL JENIFER: We went to see Bob Marley with Stanley Clarke and I was smokin' dust. I'm walking in the Capitol Center, seeing crazy people with long hair. I was more like a DC brother, and I was like, 'Whassup with this?' I remember Stanley Clarke standing there before he went onstage and he had his bass on. All the White boys was going 'Stanley!' and all the niggas was going 'Clarke!' I was there and I wanted his autograph. I yelled, 'Stanley!' and he wouldn't even look at me. I used to write him letters as a teenager. I remember this White guy goes, 'Clarke, sign my money!' — he was holding a dollar. Stanley took the dollar, signed it and gave it back to him. I remember that had some meaning to me. I was like, 'Fuck this guy.'

At the same time, behind him in the backstage corridors is Bob Marley sitting down in a chair. He looked very miserable and he had a spliff ... he's got big dreads and looked heavy — not diabolical, just burdened. I had the feeling he was the main man with this African vibe. So, I went off, smoked my little dust, my little reefer, drinked my beer, and got all high and wild. Stanley Clarke came on and it wasn't even all that. Bob Marley came on and everyone paid more attention. The bass was real loud, I was complaining. I'm standing there and see the girls going; I see him getting wound up, then I started to groove on this shit. I remember leaving there feeling like I'd just seen something I didn't mean to see. No way this was those people's real hair. I remember how foolish I sounded. Life went on, but I will always remember the Bob Marley experience.

DR. KNOW: The Capitol Center gig was our turning point with Reggae. We used to play at Madame's Organ in DC, and in that location there were a lot of West Indians. We did know about Reggae through The Clash and the whole English thing, but we didn't know about Rasta. We met some Rasta brothers; they schooled us on the real deal. So, it was actually a natural progression. But that Bob Marley show changed our lives. I can remember just feeling the bass, in this room with 16,000 people. Seeing the power of him and his dreadlocks, I'll never forget it.

Harley Flanagan (Stimulators), stagediving at Bad Brains gig, Irving Plaza, NYC, 1982
Photo by Karen O'Sullivan

Bad Brains played NYC as early as '79, getting to know the cool young locals like The Stimulators (with 11-year-old drummer Harley Flanagan) a Max's Kansas City band, and The Mad (led by noted gore artist Screaming Mad George), who established themselves at CBGB. Bad Brains would crash at George's place across the street from CBs for weeks at a time, thus Bad Brains played there, too. Aiding their rapid ascent in the Downtown scene, Dave Hahn, drummer of The Mad, became their manager.

DARRYL JENIFER: We used to read this book *Think And Grow Rich* [by Napoleon Hill]. Its positive self-motivating ideas about how successful people like Andrew Carnegie recognized the power of suggestion and the power of positive thinking, things that helped them get what they wanted in the face of adversity. We were into that as young men. *Think And Grow Rich* clearly states that you've got to progress. We figured, 'If we make some noise in DC that's one thing. But if we make some noise in New York that's the next thing.' A mistake a lot of great hometown bands make is they stay home and go work for the phone company. They never go out and give their shit a shot. People gotta realize you've gotta make noise where it counts. I was down by Canal Street and I used to think Manhattan ended on St. Mark's Place. I had no idea. We stayed at Nick Marden's house, who was the bass player in Lords Of Discipline. We stayed up there for a few weeks and then went back to DC to play some shows. We came back to New York and hooked up with Screaming Mad George, so we lived there.

Banned in DC with a thousand other places to go
Gonna swim across the Atlantic
Cause that's the only place I can go
— Bad Brains, "Banned in DC"

Bad Brains got their first break in June '79, opening for The Damned at The Bayou in DC. Bad Brains were so fucking hot that night, Rat Scabies and Dave Vanian invited them to tour England with The Damned.

DR. KNOW: The Damned liked us and offered us the chance to come to England and tour with them. It was great but we didn't know we hadda have working papers, small details like that. The flight was leaving from New York, so we came up and stayed for a week before our flight. We played CBGB once, then left for England. They didn't let us in because we had no money, we didn't have nothing. We'd sold Earl's drums to buy the tickets so we had no drums. The only thing we had was our guitars; those were stolen at JFK while we got on the plane. We found out about that hustle after the fact. So we got to England, couldn't get in, and had no gear. They just put us on the next plane — we came back and stayed with our friend Screaming Mad George across the street from CBGB. So that established us in New York. We stayed for a while then went back to DC for a minute to regroup.

Show flyer for Bad Brains, Minor Threat,
9:30 Club, DC, 1982
Collection of the author

DARRYL JENIFER: As soon as we landed in England, we went through customs with ripped hair. They'd never seen no shit like this. They found a vial on the dude that was supposed to be our tech but it didn't have no coke in it. The guy took it, wet it, rubbed it; the thing changed colors. So they took our passports and detained us. They put us in a room with a TV, couch, chair, and bed, like a hotel room. They told us, 'Don't sit on the bed, don't sit on the chairs.' They made us sit on the floor. We all sprawled out, then they woke us up, put us back on the plane, gave our passports to the pilot, and told him, 'Don't give 'em back till you get to New York'. It seemed like it happened in one day. We were begging for cash to get back to Manhattan. Then we set off again — CBGB, Max's, and back to 171A.

The aborted tour left them heading home to DC with their tails between their legs, but also made them more determined than ever. Most of 1980 they spent in DC, though they recorded "Pay To Cum" — a flawless piece of Hardcore — with Jimmi Quid of The Dots in NYC. If Bad Brains were trying to play twice as fast as The Ramones, they succeeded. When you first put on that 1: 33 of fury, you had to make sure your turntable wasn't on 78 rpm.

DARRYL JENIFER: While in New York, we went to see The Dots; they was kickin' it. Their singer Jimmi Quid reminded me of Stiv Bators. He's dead now; he was a heroin addict. Dave Hahn also died of heroin. Anyway, Jimmy and The Dots was phat! They had a girl guitar player who died, too. They had a shop on St. Mark's called Trash & Vaudeville. Jimmi took us to record at the Mony building. We recorded 'Pay To Cum' and that jingle on the back, 'Stay Close To Me' — I guess that's The Clash in us. I often wonder how we got into Reggae — we had no Caribbean influences. It was strictly a Punk Rock band. That record proves it.

KEN INOUYE (Marginal Man): When I brought that single home, it was the same feeling of confusion I got from hearing the Sex Pistols. I remember listening to those two songs on the 7" over and over again, just because everything was so different about it — the sound, the way they played, the speed, the guitar tones. That just opened up a whole new door.

I make decisions with precision
Lost inside this manned collision
— Bad Brains, "Pay To Cum"

Think And Grow Rich had taught Bad Brains they had to progress, which meant figuring out a way back to NYC. The solution came when a progenitor of NYHC, Cigaretz guitarist Jerry Williams, booked the Bad Brains to play three Saturdays in May '81 at 171A, his studio/rehearsal space on Avenue A between 10th and 11th Streets. The two parties hit it off creatively, and Bad Brains thought it'd be great if they could live there, too.

JERRY WILLIAMS (producer/soundman): The Bad Brains, thanks to their manager the late Dave Hahn, came by the studio with a proposition. At that time we had gotten nervy and started putting on live showcases, a band or two a week where we'd collect money at the door. As long as we didn't sell alcohol, the fire marshals would tolerate us. Dave convinced me to have a showcase with the Bad Brains, and that I should record them on the four-track machine. We worked out a package deal; the rest is history. When the Bad Brains showed up to 171A on May 2, '81, I was not prepared for what transpired. They'd really honed their act; they were monstrously tight and musical and exhilarating and inspirational.

Bad Brains
cassette-only album, ROIR, 1982
Collection of the author

Bad Brains scored a major triumph in June '81 by opening a show on The Clash's fabled week-long stint at Bond's Casino on Times Square at 45th and B'way. The Clash got into "Pay To Cum" through The Damned. Rock writers have written and rewritten the history of the Bond's show and the lives it changed, but as someone who was there, I can tell you that the Bad Brains made little impact. The crowd came to see The Clash; they could've cared less about anything else. On other nights of that series, Grandmaster Flash, Kurtis Blow and ESG endured the booing of Clash fans throwing beer cans and yelling, "Disco Sucks!"

Bad Brains spent the rest of '81 hanging out in the East Village and recording with Williams at 171A. From those sessions came their spring '82 self-titled full-length release on ROIR (Neil Cooper's cassette-only label), arguably the most important Hardcore recording ever.

DR. KNOW: We were living in New York. We weren't necessarily the talk of the town then, but all the New York bands started coming around to 171A, a rehearsal studio. So, there was starting to be a scene in New York — there were a dozen or so bands coming to 171A. It was a place where people could rehearse and actually record — save up their $1000 and put out 1000 singles. That was really good for New York. This great friend of ours, Dave Hahn, was a drummer for The Mad. He was a kid, like 15 or 16, but he knew how the music business worked. Dave knew Neil Cooper, who had just started ROIR. The Stimulators and us were probably the third and fourth releases that he did. Jerry Williams had 171A and we were constantly recording there — we'd never go to sleep before six in the morning. Neil's thing was cassettes, so we went ahead and did it.

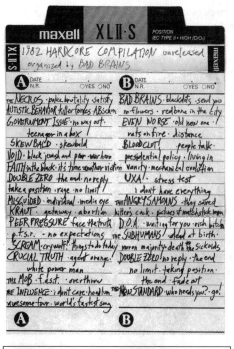

Cassette of unreleased Hardcore material
compiled by Bad Brains and Jerry Williams
at studio 171A, 1982
Collection of the author

Recording began at 171A for an East Coast answer to the DK's popular *Let Them Eat Jellybeans* comp. Williams and Bad Brains documented over a dozen groups, such as Reagan Youth, Subhumans and Scream, receiving tapes from many others, like D.O.A., Necros and Ian MacKaye's project Skewbald. Tragically, that album never saw the light of day. Alternative Tentacles in 1982 released the Bad Brains 12," culled from the ROIR tape.

Also in 171A's heyday appeared Bloodclot!, a short-lived project of Bad Brains associates: Williams on guitar, future Cro-Mag singer John Joseph, drummer Alvin Robertson, and bassist Ted Horowitz (currently thriving as Blues artist Poppa Chubby). Bloodclot! opened for Necros, Heart Attack and Bad Brains at Irving Plaza on February 27, '82, and broke up soon after.

JOHN JOSEPH: My first band, Bloodclot!, we were all roadies from the Bad Brains. When something goes wrong, Jamaicans yell 'Bloodclot!' — every time something broke onstage, Bad Brains yelled 'Bloodclot amp!' or whatever. As their roadies, we thought it was funny to call the band Bloodclot! It was not the greatest music, but it was fun.

You tell me what to say and when to say it
You tell me what to do and how to do it
— Bad Brains, "The Regulator"

By '82, Bad Brains had totally committed to Rasta, dreading their hair, speaking with *patois*, making efforts to stop eating forbidden foods, and carrying around Bibles. The Bad Brains saw themselves as victims of the African diaspora; Rastafari represented a Christian interpretation of their mindset. Tempering their precise Fusion licks with soulful Reggae grooves, they dedicated their lyrics to spreading the word of Jah. Songs like "I Love I Jah" and "The Meek Shall Inherit The Earth" reflected the evangelism that didn't connect with angst-ridden fans.

TOM BERRARD (DC scene): Bad Brains did this show at The Bayou right around the time they first started getting into Rasta. As a joke, Ian MacKaye went to Sunny Surplus and bought a dozen white knit hats. When they started playing their first Reggae song, we all put on the white hats and started skankin,' kinda making fun of Rasta tams. We were respectful — after all, they were the Bad Brains, one of the greatest bands ever — but as time went on and they became serious Rastas, we had less in common.

Unfortunately, many criticisms of Bad Brains had a basis in truth. The banddidn't exactly practice what they preached. In early '82 — at their apex, in the midst of their break-out national tour — things started to get ugly.

JERRY WILLIAMS: Bad Brains took a definite left turn March 27, '82, our last night in California after three-and-a-half weeks of gigs. They'd gained undiluted acceptance; it was a total success. We had one more gig to play in the LA suburbs, a major show at some hockey arena with Circle Jerks. Bad Brains had a members-only meeting that afternoon. After the gig, you could tell something was in the air. We got back in the van for an afternoon gig in Phoenix, and they woke me very rudely approaching the Arizona weigh-station — I had all the papers for the van. That was a first inkling something had changed. These guys could be real angels, but for the first time showed real disrespect. It seems that before that last night in LA they talked about the direction of the band; H.R. and Earl insisted they stop playing Rock, and only play Jah music: pure, Bob Marley-style Reggae, the only music acceptable for true Rastafarians. Darryl grudgingly agreed, but he clearly likes to play Rock.

Bad Brains should've become major Rock icons, but succumbed to self-inflicted damage. Burning their bridges with shocking regularity, they left a legend of bungled deals and fucked-up behavior. If you loved them, you did so in spite of themselves — you literally had to pretend not to know them or their "do what ya gotta do to survive in Babylon" vibe.

Bad Brains' homophobia ignited their most infamous episode in Austin, Texas in April 1982, on their first national tour — an ugly incident involving Big Boys and MDC that resulted in a nationwide grassroots boycott from which Bad Brains never truly recovered.

Show flyer for Bad Brains,
Ukranian Culture Center, LA, 1982
Collection of Laura Albert

DARRYL JENIFER: We toured the States, ran into MDC, had a little homophobic problem which haunted us. I'll tell you the deal with that: Early in our teenage years, early twenties, we were under the impression that being Rastafari meant we had to discriminate against certain things. That not only stems from the concepts of Rastafari but from Caribbean-based Blacks and their problems with homosexuality.

JERRY WILLIAMS: We hooked up with MDC when we got to Austin. We stayed in their and their friends' houses. They hooked up some gigs for us, one of which was with the Big Boys. I was outside loading equipment after that gig when H.R. got overexcited; he got abdominal cramps from Bibleing out members of Big Boys. He cursed them and called Jah down to have their heads for being 'bloodclot faggots.' The next day, in the front yard of the house where we were staying, Darryl got into it with the female Skinhead roadie of MDC, Tammy, saying her 'womb was barren,' that the Bible said she wasn't supposed to shave her head. Inside, evidently other Bad Brains were denouncing other faggots. It just got too deep. Doc was the only one keeping his head — he's a businessman from way back; he was actually a burger house manager in his past life. The day we left, he left an envelope with money for some weed as previously arranged; that's the last I heard of it until I talked to MDC months later: when they opened the envelope, it said, 'Thanks for the herb, too bad about the money. Fire burn all bloodclot faggots! Bye-bye!' It seems that HR came in after Doc put the envelope on the dresser, took out the money, and left his personal note.

TIM KERR (Big Boys): When Bad Brains came — and to this day they are one of the best bands you've ever seen live — we hooked them up for a show. Because they were Black, that was a big deal; all these White kids really wanted to be their friends. The Stains [later MDC] latched right onto them. Now The Stains were also the kind of people who you got real tired of hearing, they preached so damn much, the kind who would walk with you down the street and tell you the words to their new song. Whatever.

About two days before the show, I got a call from Dave, about how the Bad Brains hated homos. So they all came to the house. We'd never been around Rastafarians before — now I know better. They came with this guy Ray who was their cook. He was definitely from Jamaica and Rastafarian; you had to make him repeat himself three or four times because of the *patois*. At the house we had a test pressing of our first EP that Spot had done. They wanted to hear it, and I wasn't thinking, and the first song was 'We Got Soul.' They were amazed, and they liked all my Jazz and Reggae records, too. They hadn't yet started spouting off the Jerry Falwell stuff.

They stayed for two or three days. The house was really small, and in the bathroom was a poster Biscuit made which had shut down Raul's for two days because it offended the Texas Alcohol And Beverage Commission. Biscuit's poster had a picture of a guy from *Colt* Magazine, no clothes on, his dick hanging down, with a big cowboy hat, that said, 'Hot and Bothered Men at Raul's: The Dicks, The Inserts, Big Boys.' I remember going into the bathroom and seeing this little glob of tissue stuck over the guy's dick. I thought it was funny and took it off, it didn't hurt the poster.

The day of the show, Bad Brains didn't get to the show until after The Dicks played, which at the time I just thought was this Rock Star move. I realized later what it was — they saw Gary Floyd in that nurse's uniform, and they weren't having it. After the gig, Biscuit and H.R. got along great; we all loved each other's bands. Then all of a sudden, H.R. steps back and turns to Biscuit and goes, 'Biscuit, are you gay?' When Biscuit admitted it, H.R. was grabbing his head, screaming, 'We're in Babylon! This is holy Hell! San Francisco is Babylon! All these faggots and these bald-headed women running around!' Biscuit screamed back at him, a total brick wall. The best thing that happened was when Biscuit finally turned and looked at H.R. and went, 'Yeah, this is Babylon! And I am The Devil!' It was great.

Needless to say, things got pretty weird when they came back over to the house. So, they needed some pot, and Biscuit had some pot he was willing to sell to them very cheap, even after all this. They were supposed to pay in the morning. The next morning I went to work, and my wife was still home. I suddenly got this call from Beth who was all upset and crying, telling me I needed to get home. Beth doesn't get upset very easy, so something was definitely up. I came home and what I saw was The Stains and Bad Brains in my little front yard, standing on either side of the sidewalk screaming at each other. I thought it was all so stupid, I didn't know what to do, I was completely shaking inside. I went into the house and saw Beth crying, pleading with me to do something. The Bad Brains were yelling, 'Women oughta be home having babies' — the kind of nonsense that makes Jerry Falwell look like a saint. So I went out, totally trembling, and said, 'This is my house, if you wanna go to your house and scream, that's fine, but nothing else here.' Then Dr. Know and them pulled me aside saying,

Cover of *Damaged Goods* fanzine, 1981
Art by Donell
Collection of Sal Canzonieri

'Man, but this is the truth, you can't argue with the truth' kinda shit. I didn't wanna hear it.

It got worse. I asked them to leave, to move on for their Dallas gig. H.R. didn't have a bedroll, so I gave him an old one I had in the garage. It was a scene and it was a mess. Finally they all left, and one of them, not H.R., handed me a sealed envelope that seemed like money. In hindsight, I should've opened it. It was sealed, and it was to Biscuit. I just didn't even think, I was just so completely flustered. They left, and we unplugged the phone and didn't talk to anybody for two days — it was that traumatic.

Biscuit came over for the money, opens up the envelope, — in it was a bunch of crumpled-up paper that said, 'May you burn in Hell — Bad Brains.' At the same time all this was going on, I walked into the bathroom; there was a piece of tape stuck on the guy's dick. There was no way to get it off unless you ripped the poster, which sucked. I knew exactly who did it then. Before that, I was like 'to each his own.' But when you do shit like that — it's like there's good people and bad people; good people don't do that shit.

In the meantime, we'd already heard from Dallas. Word spread quick. People slashed their tires and I don't know if they let 'em onstage or not. That was basically it. This whole thing was the downfall of Bad Brains — because from then on, they never got back to where they were. It's a weird situation for all our friends in DC. They idolized the Bad Brains, but we're like family with the Dischord people. This story follows us to this day. I can pretty much guarantee you that was the demise of the Bad Brains.

DARRYL JENIFER: One or two of the Big Boys was gay. Literally, my man was trying to press up on H.R. It wasn't a thing where we came on like gangbusters going 'Look at this faggot.' Staying at their house, my man was acting — you know what I mean. Nowadays, people can be however they want to be. Nothing warrants condemnation. We were supposed to hook up some ganja. The weed was more the Big Boys' gripe as opposed to the trip about homosexuality. Being the type of individuals they were, they hooked up with MDC and set off on this campaign to tell the world that Bad Brains were these religious, evangelistic, homophobic, Southern Baptist bastards because we weren't receptive to the guys at that time. Even those guys could probably look back and laugh today. We got in some beef over a bag of weed, these guys tried to press up on our singer, so it's 'Fuck you, let's get the weed. We're going to Kansas.' Next thing ya know, a band's passin' out flyers about you. We're not homophobic. The gay community may think we're homophobic when we aren't. We all recognized that everyone should be loved. What I'm saying is that in our early 20s, we weren't so down with the gay vibe. Now as a grown man, I've learned to live and let live. There's heavier things going on.

Hardcore comprised a close-knit scene. When someone got screwed over, everyone else knew. And know, they did.

JERRY WILLIAMS: Things stayed healthy through most of '82, until September, when word of the Bad Brains' Austin incident got out fully. I remember seeing these newsletters circulated — one from Philly — saying Bad Brains were homophobic

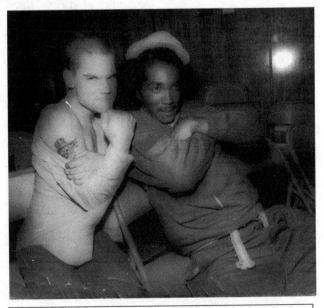

Harley Flanagan (Stimulators) shows off his first tattoo, with Darryl Jenifer backstage at Bad Brains gig,Irving Plaza, NYC, 1982
Photo by Karen O'Sullivan

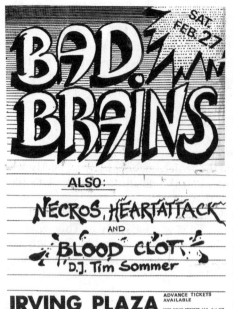

ALSO:

NECROS, HEARTATTACK
AND
BLOOD CLOT
D.J. Tim Sommer

IRVING PLAZA ADVANCE TICKETS AVAILABLE
17 IRVING PLACE at 15th St. E. $7; $7; $7

FREE BEING RECORDS 129 2nd AVE
SWEET B. FIORUCCI 135 E 80 ST
BLEECKER BOB'S MAC DOUGAL ST.

Show flyer for Bad Brains, Necros, Heart Attack,
Irving Plaza, NYC, 1982
Collection of Laura Albert

racists. The general idea was 'Don't support the Bad Brains.' I noticed people badmouthing them. The reaction had set in even in New York. But even with the bad vibes, their shows at Irving Plaza and the bigger venues continued to rack 'em in. But it was the start of a different scene altogether.

TIM KERR: The Stains, or MDC, were on their big tour, starting to get really noticed. They rode this incident to the hilt. They went everywhere talking shit about the Bad Brains beliefs, and how they fucked over these gay Punks. To me, MDC were doing the same fucking thing. Even if I may have agreed with MDC more, they were really not standing on any higher moral ground than Bad Brains. So, everywhere The Stains would go, we'd get calls and mail. I heard from kids in Detroit, where Bad Brains started playing more Reggae than Hardcore, so the kids started yelling for the Big Boys during their set. Shit like that kept coming — I don't know how many years went by — no more than three — when the Bad Brains came to Dallas. The club in Dallas called us and said, 'Hey, the Bad Brains are coming here — I'm taking that money out of their door, to pay you back.' I told him that wasn't the point; the Bad Brains needed to pay it back. So I wrote a letter, Xeroxed it off, and told them if they didn't pay, I was gonna send copies to *Flipside* and to *Maximum RockNRoll*, to decide for themselves. We got the money in the mail, no note or anything. So it's over.

> We gonna step right through that door
> Not gonna come back no more
> — Bad Brains, "Leaving Babylon"

Another tragedy resulting from the Bad Brains' deceit was the fall of 171A — home to Beastie Boys, Reagan Youth, Cro-Mags, and others. Nothing has ever replaced 171A as a rec center for underground music.

JERRY WILLIAMS: I financed this Bad Brains tour, using 171A petty cash to pay for gas, food and expenses for seven guys on the road until we could start getting gig money. By the end of the tour, we were owed over a thousand dollars, and Dr. Know was supposed to be taking a bit out of each night's receipts, sending regular installments back to NYC after every gig of an eight-week tour. In New Orleans he admitted he hadn't been sending money back at all. He hemmed and hawed with some excuse about needing to divert money back to his family, not to worry.

We were living hand-to-mouth this point in the tour, especially after days with no gigs. I felt obligated to keep the tour going because this was Bad Brains — obviously this band was headed for great things; if we could just hold it together, we'd all benefit. I held onto that belief as long as I could, even after April 10, when I called the studio — Scott Jarvis said the landlord was evicting us, they were moving everything into the basement, and that the studio's history. The shame is that it cost the East Village: it wasn't only a great, cheap rehearsal spot, 171A was a social center for a scene. The killer is that, to this day, it's a vacant building.

DR. KNOW: It was hard, man. Jerry Williams was our soundman. He was out with us, and we ran up huge phone bills trying to get from gig to gig. But we didn't make any money, so we really couldn't play him back. At that time, it wasn't really a money-making thing. Jerry has all the tapes, man, he has all the great shit.

Bad Brains, 1983
Photo by Marcia Resnick from *Rock For Light*, PVC/Jem

In May, Bad Brains forged an unlikely union with The Cars' Ric Ocasek, who produced '82's *Rock For Light* for PVC/Jem. The LP suffered not from the songs, but from Ocasek's weeny production style: the sound was tight and clean, but ultra-thin; it seems he mislaid their guts. As luck/karma would have it, Jem closed down within six months of the record's release.

DR. KNOW: We hooked up with Ric Ocasek because he'd heard the ROIR cassette. The night before we were to play Boston, we were in DC — once again, we got our equipment, our van, everything ripped off. When we got to Boston, it was a nightmare … we got there late, obviously — while I'm talking to the opening band about using their equipment, Al SS Decontrol is yelling at me, 'Ric Ocasek's here!' After I finished getting the equipment organized, Al brought me over to see him, but it didn't register in my mind at first. He started telling me he wanted to make a real album with us, not just another cassette. He took me over to his studio and gave me his guitar and amplifier, so I didn't have to use this kid's gear. A month later, we're back up in Boston cutting *Rock For Light*.

DARRYL JENIFER: We played this church in DC, and these little kids was running down the street with our road cases. We had new equipment; somehow they'd gotten in our van and taken everything. It was the fourth time that happened. This time was the most comical — we were actually trying to chase them down. At the Boston gig Ric was there because he owned the ROIR cassette; he said he listened to our stuff on tour with The Cars. He gave Doc an amp and a guitar and said, 'If you guys wanna make a real record I'll do it.' So you had a DC band teamed with this Rock Star who I used to hate — I couldn't stand The Cars. I use to go downstairs and whip this dude's ass who played The Cars. This is the irony of Bad Brains. That one scenario is how it's been for us with everything.

Working with industry hipster Ocasek brought major label interest. A lucrative early '84 offer from Elektra provoked the first of many breakups: H.R. rejected "bloodsuckers in suits" (record execs) and swore he'd never return to the Bad Brains, taking brother Earl with him. The Hudsons' next group, H.R. (Human Rights), was one of the least interesting Pop Reggae outfits of all time.

DARRYL JENIFER: This has always been a big thing with Bad Brains: eluding the labels. That was when my man H.R. started to recognize more the crucialness of Rasta and started to react more crucial — which he still does. That's all that's about, crucialness. Sometimes it's necessary in life but often it isn't.

So you say you gonna live the truth
Well have you checked out
The future of the youth?
— Bad Brains, "Rock For Light"

H.R. may go down as one of Rock's greatest frontmen, but he's also one of the biggest jerks you'd never wanna meet: a misogynistic, homophobic, racist, mentally ill loser who disappointed virtually everyone he touched. He has fucked over his own bandmates on numerous occasions.

H.R. invited me to his Adams Morgan apartment for a series of meetings in spring '84. He was involved with the dodgy Olive Tree Records, through which he sponged loot off a nasty Hippie trust-fund chick who was bangin' him and his Rasta bred'ren. Our discussions proposed to propel Olive Tree towards world domination, but accomplished little more than much ganja burned and histrionics displayed. During our third or fourth meeting, H.R. ran out the door screaming some Rasta gibberish. I never heard from him again. Weeks later, I learned H.R. had a "revelation" that I too was gay.

Despite it all, Doc and Darryl were ready to carry on without H.R. and Earl. They relocated upstate to Woodstock and "reformed" the Bad Brains with lanky singer Ras Michael Jr. and drummer Mackie Jayson from Frontline and the Cro-Mags. They wrote and practiced for a year around '85, and played a disastrous live show opening for Sun Ra at Irving Plaza.

Through the Bad Brains' friendship with DC native Henry Rollins, SST offered a deal in early '86, but attempts to record without H.R. went nowhere. With Human Rights falling flat, the factions were ready to patch things up. The four founders reunited to create *I Against I,* one of the best albums in Rock history, its impact largely due to the top-notch production of NYC Dance remixer Ron St. Germain.

DR. KNOW: That record was like changing time zones, you know what I'm saying? We were finally starting to get accepted somewhat in the mainstream, and we wanted a record that reflected that. It was definitely a turning point. Ron's background was working with people like Diana Ross, so we went to a real state-of-the-art studio. The sound was tremendous. Ron lent us money to do that because that was far beyond the recording budget for a record on SST. He made it possible for us to work at that level.

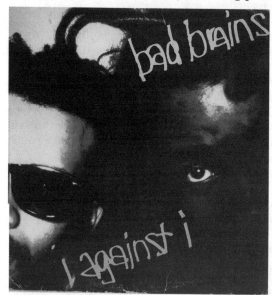

I Against I
Bad Brains LP, SST, 1986
Collection of the author

Putting *I Against I* together was no easy feat — especially after H.R. got tossed into prison. H.R. — at that point "Ras Hailu Gabriel Joseph I" — did not succumb to government harassment of True Rastaman, as his disciples claim. The same undercover cop who busted him six months earlier nailed him for selling (beat) nickel bags in DC's Malcolm X Park! H.R. recorded the vocal to "Sacred Love" over the phone from jail, a tribute to St. Germain's production acumen.

DR. KNOW: DC's so fucked up. Especially back then, every time they see dreadlocks, they'll pull you over. If they know you got a joint, they're ready to lock you up. Before we did the record, they found shit in the car. The court date came up when we were recording; Sacred Love was the only song we hadn't completed as far as lyrics. The next day, he had to go to court; we couldn't believe it when they locked him up. So Ron St. Germain figured out that if H.R. unscrewed the mouthpiece of the phone and held it away so it wouldn't feed back, they could record him over the phone from jail. The engineer rigged up some *I Spy*-looking gizmo plugged into the board. We had to get permission from the head of the jail because he was on the phone for hours. In retrospect, that really made the song.

The success of *I Against I* led to another tour. H.R. agreed to go only on the condition that a contract rider make each promoter supply them with an ounce of herb. Unsurprisingly, they mostly played long, painful Dub jams on that tour. The following year saw another failed label deal, this time with Island Records. Being very crucial again, H.R. had a beef with Chris Blackwell over his treatment of Bob Marley. So that was that. During a gig in England in fall '87 — with a packed house who thought Bad Brains were gonna sign with Island and tour with U2 — H.R. suddenly announced that it was their final show. Once again, the group crashed and burned right when it seemed they'd achieved that illusive big takeover. For 1989's *Quickness*, the group brought in H.R. at the last moment to do vocals on tracks already recorded with Mackie on drums (though Earl appeared in all cover photos).

You gotta feel sorry for Doc, Darryl and Earl. Even if they've been less than angels, they've never gotten their due — especially Earl, who's stuck by H.R. through thick and thin and has zilch to show for it. You can almost forgive Doc and Darryl for all the frontmen they've worked out: Chuck Treece (McRad, Underdog); Chuck Moseley (Faith No More, Cement); Taj; and, on '93's awful *Rise* (Epic), the best H.R. imitator of them all, Dexter "Israel Joseph I" Pinto. But without H.R. there is no Bad Brains, and he lost his spark years ago. The ugly '95 reunion on *God Of Love* (Madonna's Maverick Records), as well as their touring as Soul Brains (having lost ownership of their own name) are classic cases of too little too late.

ADAM YAUCH (Beastie Boys): I don't know what went wrong. Some of their shows were the most powerful things I've ever experienced. But something just didn't click. Somewhere, it all went terribly wrong.

AL BARILE (SS Decontrol): Bad Brains should've been the biggest crossover band of all time, but their personalities were too fucked up. They had so many White guys trying to get them on track — but they ended fucking every one of them over. •

SSS RECORDS
P.O. BOX 1, LAWNDALE, CA
90260 ● (213) 835-8977
FAX (213) 835-3522 TELEX (101) 6502965811

PAUL HUDSON
a.k.a. RAS HAILU GABRIEL JOSEPH I, (HR)

HR's SINGIN' IN THE HEART (SST 224) exhibits the rich spiritual essence of an individual whose music can connect with your soul. His vigorous, seductive form of reggae is derived from a melting pot of jazz, gospel, funk, punk and Rastafarianism. He and his younger brother, drummer Earl Hudson, are founding members of the Bad Brains.

HR's work is characterized by a variety of Eastern and Western music influences. Reggae Beat, in a review of HR's first album, VIVA AZANIA (SST 117), stated that; "HR creates his own brand of world beat and sings Jah praises with a musical range used by few dread brethren."

Singin', skankin', moshin', rockin' and rub-a-dubin' as no other Rasta, HR delivers scorching reality and sensual pleasures on SINGIN' IN THE HEART. Take a little hit of this fine, slow-burnin', fire-breathin' riddim and you'll be on a trip down "Treat Street" with HR mon. Jah Luv!

HR DISCOGRAPHY

SST 117	HR--VIVA AZANIA/HUMAN RIGHTS (LP/CA/CD)
SST 171	HR--THE HR TAPES (CA/CD--117, 179+)
SST 173	HR--NOW YOU SAY (45 RPM EP)
SST 177	HR--KEEP OUT OF REACH (45 RPM EP)
SST 179	HR--IT'S ABOUT LUV REISSUE (EP)

ALSO, HR WITH THE BAD BRAINS:

SST 065	BAD BRAINS--I AGAINST I (LP/CA/CD)
SST 160	BAD BRAINS--LIVE (LP/CA/CD)

SST press release on H.R.'s solo career
Collection of the author

MINOR THREAT & DC: FLEX YOUR HEAD

I'm gonna knock it down
Any way that I can
I'm gonna scream, I'm gonna yell
— Minor Threat, "Screaming At A Wall"

If LA spawned Hardcore, it reached fruition in DC. The term Hardcore now implies the sound, style and aesthetic coming out of early 80s Washington.

I moved to DC in late '80. I'd gone to a few Punk and New Wave shows in New York City, and expected to find a similarly vital scene in our nation's capitol. Such was not the case. DC Punk/New Wave was like a bad joke: the Pop-Surf of Slickee Boys and Insect Surfers, the Bowie-style Egoslavia (with Greg Strzempka, later of Raging Slab), art school wannabees Urban Verbs (with Roddy Frantz, brother of Talking Head Chris Frantz), and some of the stupidest acts ever, Tony Perkins And The Psychotics and Tru Fax And The Insaniacs. Goofy guys from Virginia and Maryland with wraparound shades and New Wave buttons dominated their crowd.

HENRY ROLLINS (S.O.A., Black Flag): All these places that booked 'Roots Rock' bands like The Nighthawks were now letting in 'New Wave' bands. They had 'New Wave Nights' — they'd play [The Rolling Stones'] 'Some Girls,' then [The B-52s'] 'Rock Lobster,' and everyone would get on the pseudo-Disco dancefloor with their skinny ties, 9-to-5 haircuts, and a button that said, 'Why Be Normal?' It was a bunch of suburbanites looking to get loose. That's how we learned about this stuff.

TOUCH AND GO
no. 22
$1.50

DC Hardcore's best-known products, Ian MacKaye and Henry Rollins
Cover of *Touch & Go* #22, 1983
Courtesy of Tesco Vee

DC's first Punk band was White Boy — led by the fucked-up father-son team of James and Glenn Kowalski. If you heard the 1977 "I Could Puke" single, you'd never forget it. Expect no White Boy reunion: calling it the worst case of child sex abuse in DC history, Prince Georges County (MD) prosecutors busted James Kowalski on 84 counts of child molestation and child pornography; he's currently serving a 700-year sentence.

IAN MACKAYE (Teen Idles, Minor Threat): In ninth grade at Gordon Junior High, which was 95% Black, there were these White kids from Tacoma Park; one of them had singles by a band White Boy — 'I Could Puke,' with 'Disco Elephant' and 'Sagittarius Bumper Sticker' on the B-side, on their own label, Doodly Squat. It was a father-and-son team, Mr.

Ott and Jake Whipp — James and Glenn Kowalski. His younger son Gary Kowalski, who I bought it from, was their sound guy. I loved that record. I mean 'I Could Puke,' wow! He'd take his underwear and shoeshine polish, rub it on the crotch for this song 'Rotten Crotch Disaster,' and throw it in the crowd. He was real theatrical — in his 50s, but a really great frontman.

Slickee Boys, DC's leading New Wave act, played around town once or twice a week, cultivating a local following and influencing many future Hardcore kids; lead Slickee Kim Kane gave quite a few groups their first gigs as openers. Another early "Alternative" experience, Power Pop troupe Razz came from Maryland; they would spawn woeful Indie Rock hero Tommy Keene.

Slickees happened when the few lowly regarded local Punks — such as Bad Brains, Black Market Baby, The Penetrators and The Chumps — often played Madame's Organ. Their uptempo music influenced later DC Hardcore, as did the intense English outfits like The Ruts, The Damned, Sham 69 and UK Subs.

Show flyer for The Chumps, Hall Of Nations, DC, 1980
Art by Rüki Dreyfuss
Collection of Rob Kennedy

TOM BERRARD (DC scene): The Pistols never played DC, The Damned were a DC favorite; but when UK Subs came to town, they were the people we really looked up to. They were so much older ... we were all like 18 or 19, and to us they looked 40. Charlie Harper's gotta be as old as Mick Jagger. We also loved The Ruts — by the time they came here the band was called Ruts DC, as Malcolm Owen had already died. I think they were blown away by how into them DC was. And don't forget Stiff Little Fingers.

Black Market Baby were the ultimate American blue-collar Punk group. Imposing frontman Boyd Farrell avidly supported DC Hardcore. At any given show (like their many double-bills with the Bad Brains), you'd find the BMB crew holding court by the bar. I remember a Black Market Baby gig in NYC at the Mudd Club in '82 or '83 being a big event.

JACK RABID (editor, *The Big Takeover*): Black Market Baby is one of the great forgotten bands of that time. They made great records like the 'Youth Crimes' single and the *Senseless Offerings* album. All the DC kids liked them because they were a Punk band in a Hardcore time. But in retrospect, no one cared; the scene'd become so specialized that it would no longer accept even a blistering record that wasn't all that fast.

DC's first club for to New Wave was The Atlantis at 930 F Street NW. It folded in '80, reopening as Nightclub 9: 30, a plaything for Dodi Bowers — a gift from her husband, real-estate developer John Bowers. Tommy Keene's manager Seth Hurwitz booked it, and eventually assumed control. Contrary to local lore, The 9: 30 did not support Hardcore — it banned Bad Brains and Teen Idles almost from the start. Even at the scene's height, with the packed club making loot — after reversing its no-HC policy — the management said nasty shit about bands and fans.

Instead of studying theory
We're gonna get up and go
— Teen Idles, "Get Up And Go"

Ian MacKaye of Teen Idles and Minor Threat, and founder of Dischord Records, set in motion an aesthetic that begat almost everything we call indie music. MacKaye's anti-industry, anti-star, pro-scene exhortations translated into a way of life for many. Those credos are Rock Biz clichés now. Hippies fired the first salvos in the battle for artistic independence; Punks talked a good game of D.I.Y.; Ian and DC HC codified the mindset.

Teen Idles, bus station Dallas, on way to SF & LA, 1980
Xeroxed copy insert with *Flex Your Head*, Dischord, 1982

IAN MACKAYE: In DC, we called ourselves 'Hardcore' to distinguish between us and the Sid Vicious kind. We were 'hard-core' Punks — we weren't into the fashion as much as we were into the approach and intensity and urgency. I've put a lot of thought to this — even before D.O.A.'s *Hardcore 81* record, we'd begun to make a distinction that we were more hard-core. That's how we came up with 'harDCore' — a play on the word. It was just zeitgeist or serendipity that we all felt the same way. D.O.A. came to Washington in October of 1981 and they played Madame's Organ, with Tru Fax and the Insaniacs and The Cleavers, who became Trenchmouth. We were hard-core, no doubt about it.

TEEN IDLES, the original harDCore outfit, came out of The Slinkees, a short-lived '79 Wilson High School cover band which comprised guitarist Geordie Grindel, drummer Jeff Nelson, bassist Ian MacKaye, and vocalist Mark Sullivan. At Teen Idles' formation, Nathan Strejcek replaced Sullivan. Through their limited ability, they developed a new style: buzzsaw guitar played as fast as possible, with songs two minutes long max.

KEN INOUYE (Marginal Man): The Beatles made me want to listen to music, Kiss made me want to learn how to play, the Sex Pistols made me want to perform, and the Teen Idles made me want to write. When I heard the Teen Idles record, I had to start from scratch.

BRIAN BAKER (Minor Threat): I was in the audience when the Teen Idles opened for The Cramps at the Ontario Theater, summer 1980. All of a sudden, everyone I knew started doing this strange vibrating pushing thing. I'd never seen anything like it. Teen Idles were this huge screaming wall. I was completely overwhelmed. I was instantly hooked.

After graduating from high school in '80, Teen Idles jumped on a Greyhound to play two gigs in California, in LA and SF. Pal Henry Garfield — later Henry Rollins — came along as roadie. From that "tour," a financial disaster, they returned home with glowing tales of the Beach Punks they'd hung out with and gotten into trouble with.

MIKE WATT (Minutemen): Teen Idles came to Hollywood and played the Hong Kong Cafe. I didn't see the show but I remember everyone was kind of interested about it. We were thrilled there was stuff happenin' on the other side. These kids were much younger, but seemed more earnest than Orange County bands like Adolescents, China White and TSOL. I just felt more in common with the DC bands than what was goin' on around us.

HENRY ROLLINS: I couldn't play any instrument but I could damn well carry the cabinets and amps. I was their biggest fan. Luckily, almost every show of theirs is on tape. I was the only one who'd dub that stuff. I had to rig together my stepfather's tape deck and my mother's tape deck and make these wobbly copies. That was the early days when you'd have 30 people at a show. It was a great time to be around. Towards the end of Teen Idles, Ian said, 'Here's a song I'm saving for my next band.' He played 'Straight Edge' with one hand on a piano. Seeing what that turned into was an awesome moment to be next to Ian. Many awesome moments have I had standing next to him..One of the major influences of my life is Ian.

IAN MACKAYE: My Uncle Stanley, who we stayed with in LA that Teen Idles tour, wanted us out, like 'You guys gotta go,' so he took us to the Greyhound station at 10 in the morning. We planned to go to Disneyland and put our stuff in the lockers. These two guys came over; one said, 'I didn't know the circus was in town.' We were like, 'Fuck you!' As we walked away, Jeff grabbed his ass at them — the next thing we know Jeff was handcuffed and dragged across the floor. We chased after him; he was taken into a little office — we were put in this hallway. We looked through the vent and he was being interrogated. He was held on homosexual propositioning charges 'cause he grabbed his ass. They

Show flyer for Teen Idles,
Reek's, DC, 1980
Collection of Ken Inouye

slapped the shit out of him. Henry was on his knees trying to see what was going on through the vent — another cop came in and kicked Henry so hard in the ass that it knocked him flat. They brought Jeff out and said, 'You guys have to leave now.' We said, 'Our bus isn't till seven tonight.' 'You've got to leave now.'

So we got tickets to Disneyland — took a bus there. How long does that take, two hours or something? They dropped us off and we walked a mile across a parking lot. We got up to the gate — this guy in a suit walked out and says 'Good afternoon fellas. Thanks for coming to Disneyland.' We're like, 'Yeah, sure.' He says, 'No, thank you very much,' and put his arms out in a Y, like he was collecting us. He says 'Have a nice day.' We're like 'No, we're just coming in.' He says, 'I'm sorry. You're not welcome here today.' It still hadn't dawned on us that he was rejecting us. I was like, 'Wait a minute. We can't come in?' 'Yeah.' 'Why not?' He said, 'I'm sorry, we don't allow people with ripped T-shirts.' 'Well, we'll go buy a Mickey Mouse T-shirt.' He said, 'Sorry, we don't allow dyed hair.' I said, 'Do you have any women in there right now who dye their gray hair? What are you talking about?' He pointed to Henry's mohawk — we said, 'He's a Marine.' We were trying everything. He said, 'I'm sorry. You just don't meet the dress code.' I said, 'Can I see the dress code?' He said, 'I am the dress code.' I was like, 'Just like that, huh? Then he talked into his walkie-talkie and these guys come out on little carts — and they have guns! They marched us all the way back to the street, driving their carts on both sides of us.

We were so unhappy and waited for the bus. This armored car pulled up and this side door opened; this cop was in there sitting on a chair with his rifle. He spread his legs, grabbed his nuts and said 'Punk faggots!' We're like 'Damn, this is terrible.' So we got on the bus to downtown LA. We're walking around, we have six hours with nothing to do. We walked up to a theater; some guy got stabbed right in front. We decided to go and see a Kung-Fu movie but it was dubbed in Spanish. We sat there all afternoon watching this movie over and over in Spanish. Then we got on the bus — I was so happy to get out of LA.

In San Francisco, we went to see Circle Jerks and The Mentors play The Savoy, and then we went to The Mabuhay to do our gig. We put all the Huntington Beach kids on the guest list and [SF promoter] Dirk Dirksen was there saying, 'I don't want any horizontal dancing.' We really wanted those LA kids to come. We were playing New Wave night with The Wrong Brothers, Lost Angeles — I forget the third band; there was nobody there. We were standing out front and heard an incredible scream — it was this man running down the street being chased by 15 Hardcore kids. He tripped and they beat the fuck out of him. It was frontier justice. Then we played and those kids went off and danced so hard — at one point, a fight broke out and some guy busted a bottle on this kid Greg's head. Henry got into it and everyone was fighting. We felt a connection to these kids and they thought we were the fastest band they'd ever seen. The next day, we hung out with them in the street; some guy yelled something from a car and they chased that motherfucker down. It was amazing to us — exactly what we wanted to do. We came back to DC with a lot of attitude. We knew what we wanted to be. There'd been fights before we got to LA but when we came back we went crazy and started fighting all the time.

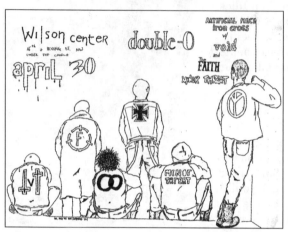

Show flyer for Minor Threat, Iron Cross, Double O, Faith, Void, Iron Cross, Artificial Peace, Wilson Center, DC, 1982
Artwork by Tomas Squip
Collection of Laura Albert

Not surprisingly, Teen Idle's West Coast odyssey influenced the harDCore look. They adopted a Beach Punk style: lotsa chains and, if not Doc Martens, then big black boots with scarves and chains wrapped around the ankles. Henry wore a chain for a belt. Buying D-rings at G Street Remnants and sewing bondage straps to one's pants was very DC.

IAN MACKAYE: People thought chains and spurs were a visual thing but for me it was a sonic thing. When you hear a bunch of kids walk in with spurs and chains, the sound will stay with you. At one point, I even pitched the idea that we all wear some shitty cologne because you'll never forget a smell. To this day, the smell of Pomade [hair gel] will always make me think of Punk Rock. I wanted to create an imprint; I wanted to a part of a gang. I wanted to be part of a group … you could identify as a tribe. I never thought of it as exclusive. I was trying to create something inclusive. I was never trying to keep people out of anything. Of course, anytime you're that focused on trying to create something it's intimidating to people on the outside. Later on people said, 'You guys were such dicks.' I thought we were nice guys. The older Punk Rockers in DC were offput because they thought we stole the scene. Damn right we did! But we didn't steal shit — we created something. We came with our own crowds. People say, 'You guys came in and took over.' Took over what? We built the motherfucker!

> *Lose control of your body*
> *Beat the shit out of somebody*
> **— Minor Threat, "Bottled Violence"**

Ian and Henry and their circle were nasty pricks always into some physical conflict — especially when they traveled as a wolfpack to NYC "to represent." The worst troublemakers in their crew were these huge mooks Billy McKenzie and Jay Garfunkel (Jay cut some kids ear off with one of his boot spurs while stagediving).

I remember a Circle Jerks show at Irving Plaza where the DC kids came to fight — not even listening to the music.

HENRY ROLLINS: At that point, we were 'hardercore' than anyone. There'd be people on the dancefloor with cigarettes, talking while a band played. We'd just hammer these people. We were definitely into the 'DC's in the house' thing. There were shows where bouncers came up and said, 'Quit it.' That's what we liked to do.

IAN MACKAYE: By 1981, it was payback. We were like, 'Fuck you!' We were gonna be the worst motherfuckers — we wanted to scare people. It was a form of intimidation backed up by the threat of unpredictableness.

TESCO VEE (Meatmen): The whole thing was rife with contradiction. There were legendary shows where Ian, Henry and Sab Grey, in whatever Skinhead phase they were in, would come to New York, cause huge brawls and say they went up and kicked New York's ass. How stupid is that?

By '81, the initial harDCore crew consisted of 50 or so kids, many attending Wilson High, over the river in Arlington, VA, or elite Georgetown Day School in the upper Northwest area. They were "Georgetown Punks" — most born of affluence — and their attitudes reflected it. They lacked the desperation of NY, SF or even LA.

TOM BERRARD (DC scene): Most of the DC Hardcore kids came from well-off families. The whole joke in the media was 'Georgetown Punks' since that was one of the richest parts of town. It was seen as hypocrisy, but you can be unhappy if you have money — it's not your money anyway. We didn't care what the media thought, we took on 'Georgetown Punks' as a rallying cry.

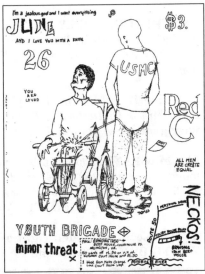

Show flyer for Minor Threat, Youth Brigade, Red C, and Necros, Arlington, VA, 1982
Artwork by Tomas Squip
Collection of the author

'Flex Your Head' comes from *The Washington Post* calling us 'muscleheads' — so we flipped it and said 'Flex your head' or 'Use your head.' We were proud of what we were and didn't apologize for the fact that our parents had money. And like most rich kids, it was very cliquish.

JAY ROBBINS (Government Issue): It's undeniable all these kids came from wealthy backgrounds. I had trouble relating to that because I come from the bottom of the middle class. My dad sells cars, so at first it gave me pause, 'Oh, the ambassador's kid's onstage screaming' but that makes the famous DC Punk Rock conscience more interesting in a way — like already being aware of the World Bank because your dad works there. DC was a notoriously cliquey scene. It's always been and it still is.

REED MULLIN (C.O.C.): We drove from Raleigh to see DC shows every weekend we could, like to all those Punk-a-thon Wilson Center shows. I remember UK Subs two nights at the 9:30 Club with Anti-Nowhere League. That was my first experience with DC's uppity exclusivity. We didn't look the part yet — we were middle-class kids from Carolina who showed up in a station wagon — we were still figuring it all out. We kept trying to talk to everybody; they all blew us off. This one dude, John Falls, was always a jerk to us. He's a well-known photographer now.

BUBBA DUPREE (Void): To this day, you can go to any Dischord show and it's full of Volvos with Fugazi stickers. That has to do with scenes like DC where the kids were not poor and their parents were ex-Hippies. My parents were Hippies, I'm right there with them, but it wasn't the same set of morals that inspired it all. It was a very violent do-gooder thing.

DC was the first Hardcore scene in which a handful of hot, bitchy girls, hung out, a welcome relief because many HC chicks — although certainly not the majority — cultivated dysgenic affectations as an art statement.

BARRY HENNSLER: We went and visited DC and were like, 'Wow! Punk Rock girls in kilts.' For girls alone, it was this Valhalla compared to where we lived. It was awesome.

CYNTHIA CONNOLLY (author, *Banned In DC):* I don't know, it wasn't that amazing. No one looked that great. There were enough women participating in DC. The ones I knew, I didn't like what they were doing. From my perspective, Hardcore discouraged women from doing things.

After Teen Idles broke up in fall '81, the first DC Hardcore record came out: their *Minor Disturbance* 7" EP — the first release on Dischord Records. While not very good, that primal disc signified things to come.

IAN MACKAYE: The Teen Idles recorded eight songs. When the band broke up, we had this money in a cigar box, money we'd saved up all year. We could've split the money up and had $150 each or we could put out a record. Everybody said to put out a record. There were four-song EPs but no eight-song EPs. We just thought 'value for money.'

The scene exploded right after Teen Idles broke up. Nathan Strejcek started YOUTH BRIGADE (not the LA outfit) with Tom Clinton, Danny Ingram and Bert

Youth Brigade, 1981
Photo by Paul Nee, xeroxed copy insert with
Flex Your Head, Dischord, 1982

Queiroz (the latter two from Alec MacKaye's group, The Untouchables). Meanwhile, Ian MacKaye and Jeff Nelson hooked up with Georgetown Day School students Lyle Presslar and Brian Baker to form MINOR THREAT. Lyle's previous combo, The Extorts (or Vile Lyle And The Extorts), played just one show, on the roof of the Georgetown New Wave clothes store Smash. The other Extorts started S.O.A. (STATE OF ALERT) with Henry Garfield on vocals. And John Stabb started Government Issue.

GDS was a real harDCore breeding ground, from there came Presslar, Baker, Hampton, Guy Picciotto, Brendan Canty, Mark Haggerty, and Chris Haskett (later of Rollins Band). Guy and Brendan of INSURRECTION were the "D.O.D. (Dance Of Death) Boys": when kids slamdanced, the two of them rolled around on the floor. If you did the D.O.D. now, you'd be killed.

BRIAN BAKER: My intro to Punk, believe it or not, was the result of peer pressure. I grew up in DC, went to GDS. It was a matter of osmosis. I was 14 and had low self-esteem; the only people I knew cut all their hair off. GDS guys were intimidated by kids from public schools. After I went to that first Teen Idles show I went to everything with a handmade flyer.

Henry Garfield scooped ice cream at a Haagen-Dazs shop in Georgetown and he sometimes took a portable record player to work. Often, a few friends would hang out until closing, at which time Henry cranked the latest Misfits or AC/DC records while cleaning up.

Henry's stint with S.O.A. lasted October '80 through summer '81. They used a few songs from their brief Extorts experience — Henry jumped in and rewrote the lyrics. I saw S.O.A. once; they were a mess, but Henry was ferocious. Their *No Policy* EP (Dischord, '81), made little impact at the time. After S.O.A.'s demise, bassist Wendell Blow formed Iron Cross with vocalist Sab Grey, while guitarist Michael Hampton and Ivor Hanson (son of Admiral Thor B. Hanson) went on to The Faith (with Alec MacKaye). Henry changed his surname to Rollins and split to LA to join Black Flag.

TOM BERRARD: Minor Threat and S.O.A. played together all the time. I loved Minor Threat but S.O.A. were much more fun. It's un-PC to admit it, but it was more violent — the slamdancing during S.O.A. was way more intense. At the shows we were all friends; we all knew each other; nobody was trying to hurt anybody. You just went at it harder during S.O.A.

JACK RABID (editor, *The Big Takeover*): To this day, I think the Teen Idles single sucks. Only because we know the people involved, we think it's important. The S.O.A. record sucks as well; it's toneless garbage. I swear to you, Steve, if Henry Garfield jumped off a bridge in '81 and there never was a Henry Rollins, no one would give a fuck about that S.O.A. single either. Whereas if Ian MacKaye jumped off a bridge in '85 and there was never a Fugazi, people'd still be buying Minor Threat records up the wazoo. That's my basis for making a clear distinction between Minor Threat and S.O.A., considering they were such close friends.

S.O.A.'s final show before Henry joined Black Flag occurred in July '81 in the blue-collar South Philly 'hood of Kensington. For months after that, you'd hear of the nasty showdown that night in which Philly cops sat back as a vicious mob of urban rednecks with baseball bats attacked unsuspecting Hardcore kids.

Henry Rollins (singing) with SOA, 1980
Xeroxed copy insert with *Flex Your Head*, Dischord, 1982

IAN MACKAYE: In Philadelphia, a Black Flag show turned into the biggest riot because we were in the wrong neighborhood to be fucking with kids. It was S.O.A.'s last show, opening for Black Flag at the Starlight Ballroom in a neighborhood called Kensington. About thirty of us drove up. It was a big gig; there were a bunch of Philly Punks, a bunch of New Jersey kids, some New York kids, and a whole bunch of us. At this point, people had gotten cocky and were trying to fight all the time. My role was to cool things down and break up fights. S.O.A. played, then when Flag were playing some kids who came in from off the street were being really weird. They were Polish or Irish-Catholic, all in white muscle-T's: crazy looking kids. I don't know how it got started. I was trying to get it to cool down but no one would listen to me so I went up to the side of the stage to watch the show. Then I saw a fight break out and the kids from the neighborhood take off with a bunch of DC kids chasing them — a pretty typical scene at shows at this time. But I thought, 'Something's weird about this.'

The stage was in the front of the building on the second floor, so I was able to go down a flight of stairs to try and head them off at the pass. I came down the flight of stairs to intercept but everyone kept running past me. At the front of the club, you're on one street looking straight down another street and those kids just went down that street and twelve to fifteen DC kids ran right after them. They got about a half a block down when all these other kids came out from two alleys with bats and sticks. I remember Sean from Void and his brother just kept running all the way around the block and everyone else tried to make their way back and run through that line. So many people got hammered; it was terrifying. Jamie Bittle got his head split open — people were fighting everywhere.

Then four or five police cars pulled up and got us separated. The DC kids were on the side of the street, and all these Kensington kids were on the other. Still, the Kensington kids would run across the street past the police cars and start punching us. The cops were very angry about this situation so they said, 'In five minutes, we're leaving. You're welcome to leave now or you can sort it out on your own.' Everyone was scrambling to their cars to get the fuck out. I got in my car, a '70 Duster, and my alternator died, so my battery was dead. I went to one of the cops and said, 'I need a jump start.' So he gave me a jump start; he was the last cop there. It was raining and the middle of the night. We made it about three blocks and I could feel the engine dying so I turned off the radio, then the wipers, then the lights. We finally broke down in the tunnel underneath Society Hill. Me and Ann and Cynthia crawled up the ladder through the street and came up a sewer and slept in the park on the ground. It was a real lesson. In one of the fights with the Philly kids, Mark busted the nose of a kid who turned out to be best friends with Alison Schenkenberger, who ran Southern Studios for a long time. She hated us for that. When Minor Threat played Philly at this BYO event, Lyle was a snoot to her and then she really hated us. We became good friends years later but she told me how much she fucking hated us. I was mortified to realize how much hatred we instilled in people. We were such assholes.

> *Pay no mind to us*
> *We're just a minor threat*
> — Minor Threat, "Minor Threat"

MINOR THREAT are the ones most interviewees herein rave about: the intensity of the shows, the breakdown of band/crowd barriers, the gravity of the lyrics. Vocalist Ian MacKaye, guitarist Lyle Presslar, bassist Brian Baker and drummer Jeff Nelson set the standard for what's now Hardcore.

Minor Threat take a rest onstage
(L-R): Lyle Presslar, Jeff Nelson, Brian Baker, Ian MacKaye
Great Gildersleeves, NYC, 1982
Photo by Karen O'Sullivan

TESCO VEE: Minor Threat in their prime was the most intense, heart-thumping Punk experience I ever had and will ever have again. Every other band paled in comparison. If kids today could only hear the passion, the ferocity and the hate ... the vitriol that flew between those guys fueled the band. It's a chemistry you can't buy. To a man, they hated each other. Ian's very dogmatic, Jeff Nelson's very private; they're all very stubborn and set in their way. Lyle Presslar we called the G. Gordon Liddy of Hardcore because he walked into a room and just like somebody's dad, commanded all the respect and hatred.

BRIAN BAKER: Minor Threat existed for Ian to write. Teen Idles were the most popular band in DC and they had a record out. It wasn't that Ian wanted to be the star of the show, he just wanted it put to his own words. Lyle and I went to school together but we weren't friends. Ian and Jeff knew they were gonna dump Teen Idles and Ian knew he wanted to sing. I don't know how Lyle met Ian, but they had a guitarist, drummer and singer, and I honestly believe I got the gig because I was the only Punker in DC that played a stringed instrument and was not currently starting another band. I was 15, Lyle 17, Ian and Jeff 18. If Minor Threat hadn't been good, it wouldn't have been a big deal. The two things were the band could play and Ian's a genius. There's something special about him.

Ian MaKaye, 1982
Insert with *Out Of Step*, Dischord, 1983

Minor Threat — at one point early on called Fifth Column — started out in November 1980. The first show, a Bad Brains-organized benefit to help Paul Cleary of Black Market Baby replace his stolen bass amp, took place Dec. 17 in the living room of a rowhouse at 1929 Calvert Street, with 100-ish people attending. S.O.A. and The Untouchables also played. Minor Threat gigged about once a month through summer '81, including at the YMCA Pow Wow House, DC Space, and two Unheard Music Festival shows.

IAN MACKAYE: The first show we played was a party, then the Unheard Music Festival, a big show for DC. From the beginning I knew this band was solid. The feeling was so much more confident than Teen Idles. There was a big show we did with the Circle Jerks; that band inspired Minor Threat a lot. The *Group Sex* album was phenomenal. I remember thinking 'I'm gonna blow them off the stage.' During soundcheck I was doing 'Screaming At A Wall' — I hit it so hard that something went snap in my throat. I lost my voice completely. So I wrote the lyrics on signs and held the signs up and the whole crowd sung. That was a great show.

KEN INOUYE (Marginal Man): That show was interesting because Ian lost his voice. They nearly canceled that gig. When they got onstage, Lyle got on the mic ... 'Ian has something he wants to say to you.' Ian stood up there with these flash cards ... 'I-have-lost-my-voice,' and with the last bit of voice he had left, screamed into the mic for 'Guilty Of Being White' — and then the crowd went bananas. Everyone had already gotten the demo, so they knew the words. Here was a band that didn't even have a record out and everyone was singing along loud enough you could hear it over the P.A.

Minor Threat's most pronounced influence, Bad Brains, represented the hypothetical ideal to which MacKaye and crew aspired. And the Brains were not shy in reciprocating the attention: when they exhausted the good will of DC practice-space owners, they turned to Ian, who hooked them up. The resulting experiences kicked Minor Threat's lilly-White asses.

BRIAN BAKER: I'd heard the lore and heard the tapes and was totally intimidated by this incredible band ... grown men who were really playing their instruments. They were real

Zine ad for early Dischord records, 1982
Collection of the author

musicians and we were kids. I had to borrow Darryl Jenifer's bass amp — I'm like five feet tall with eyeglasses and spiky brown hair: 'Excuse me sir, can I borrow your bass amp to create Punk Rock?' The whole thing I remember now is a lot of adrenaline. It was an overwhelming thing for me.

Minor Threat made two excellent 7" EPs in '81: *Minor Threat* (Dischord no. 3) with "Filler" and "Straight Edge," and *In My Eyes* (Dischord no. 5) with "In My Eyes" and "Guilty Of Being White."

The 80s saw great overindulgence and excessive intoxication. Naturally there arose an opposing mentality — largely through DC HC — promoting a "clean" mind. That mindset became known as Straight Edge.

While the movement arose around the lyrics of a Minor Threat song, they were not a Straight Edge band. Only perhaps three of their 26 songs concerned the philosophy. But their influence played out: in DC the first kids to profess a Straight Edge lifestyle appeared.

TOM BERRARD (DC scene): When I was in high school, I drank with my friends and smoked pot. But in the DC Hardcore scene the peer pressure was to not drink, so I said 'Fuck it' and stopped. It wasn't like people were giving you a real hard time; it just was not cool to be drinking. I remember being at this Black Market Baby show and someone looking down their nose at me 'cause I had a beer — and I did stop shortly thereafter. Straight Edge was 'I *choose* not to drink or smoke or get fucked up and diminish my capacities.' It wasn't like Mothers Against Drunk Driving or some morality issue — it was a personal statement of 'this is what works best for me.'

CYNTHIA CONNOLLY (author, *Banned In DC*): Straight Edge kids came to think that everybody in DC was Straight Edge and that we had a gang. Nobody called us Straight Edge. I wonder now if people even realize the term came from a Minor Threat song.

BRIAN BAKER: Ian wrote a song he was singing in the first person in 1980. It was a song, okay? The entire time I was in Minor Threat, I was straight but I wasn't knocking drinks out of people's hands. The reason I didn't drink was because I missed that period where people break into their parents' liquor cabinets. It wasn't a huge statement, I just didn't drink. I had funny hair, I was playing in bands, and at least my mom knew I wasn't getting fucked up so it was okay for me to come home at one a.m. It was just practical. It wasn't militant. I didn't start drinking until I was 21 and then it wasn't with vigor. It was never a big thing.

Just as things really got going for them, Minor Threat broke up for the first time in September '81 when Lyle Presslar went off to Northwestern University. Ian and Jeff Nelson teamed up with guitarist Eddie Janney and bassist John Falls and, in the basement of the Arlington house they named Dischord House, launched Skewbald (or Grand Union, as Jeff called it). Skewbald recorded three songs in December '81 but never played live. Also around that time came the underground tape of Roslyn Rangers, a project with Ian on piano and Nathan Strejcek on vocals along with Sab Grey and Rich Moore. Brian Baker went off to play guitar with Government Issue. But things didn't click for Lyle at college, so he came home in March '82 and returned to Minor Threat, who hit the road that summer.

BRIAN BAKER: Government Issue is what I did when we had our first breakup, after 'In My Eyes.' The breakup was contingent on Lyle going to college and that DC ethic of 'if you lose a member, you can't replace them.' I'm not sure where we were at personality-wise, but it was always Ian and Jeff against me, then me and Ian against Jeff and Lyle. There was all this weird personal stuff going on which had a lot to do with the fact that we were so young to be in a professional working situation. Ian and Jeff were gonna start something with Eddie and John Falls, so I joined the DC band I liked the best who needed somebody — Government Issue. They were a great band, especially early on. I wanted to play, but I wasn't invited to join Ian and Jeff. I was in Government Issue and I'd gone to New York and played a few times, done a record, and Skewbald never got off the ground. One day, I got a call from Ian that Lyle was back from college. The question was if we should try and do this again; I of course said yes. By this time, the Minor Threat myth had started to build; we were bigger after we had broken up than we ever were together. Instantly, we were the biggest band in DC, bigger than Bad Brains. I wanted to be the biggest band in the world. I called Government Issue, 'Sorry, but if you were me you'd do this too.' It was amicable after [G.I. singer] John Stabb calmed down but everyone else understood and didn't have a problem.

Minor Threat set list, 1982
Collection of the author

IAN MACKAYE: The summer of '81, we were doing really good gigs. We had to go on tour so we went out with [DC] Youth Brigade. So, we got Tommy Clinton's mom's van, my Duster, Brian Baker's mom's Volvo, and took off. We had shows all the way across the country with 16-year-old kids riding with us. Tom Berrard, my brother, Anna Connolly, Giovanna, Mary Skinhead — all these kids…First we went to Lansing and hooked up with The Necros. Then we made it to Chicago, did a show at O'Banion's, did a gig in Madison, and then we got a call from Tommy Clinton's mom: 'Bring the van back or you're not going to college.' We had shows all the way across the country but they had to go back. So they took the equipment with them — we stayed with the Volvo and the Duster. We played shows in Detroit and Windsor, Canada, then we came home. We were discouraged we didn't make it to the West Coast. We had shows booked in San Diego, San Francisco, Los Angeles and Reno that didn't happen. We wanted to meet these people. We were all writing to each other and talking on the phone.

We came back and did a show: Minor Threat, Scream, Youth Brigade maybe, and The Faith probably. It was a 9:30 Club show and the line was down the block. That was the show where everyone was like, 'Whoah! This shit's large.' So we played a few more shows; our last show in September '81 was at this party at Jeanelle's house. Then Lyle went off to school. We weren't mad at each other; he just went to college. So he was gone and I tried to do Skewbald with Jeff and it was not working out. Keep in mind that was a real busy time for Dischord. We were on our fifth single and still working on the *Flex Your Head* album. We moved into Dischord House, which was a big deal too. That was the first group house and that set a whole new tone. Before, all the kids involved with Punk Rock lived at home with their parents. Dischord House changed everything.

In early 1982, I remember seeing the Bad Brains after they'd gone across the country on tour and I was talking to H.R. I said, 'How was it? He said, 'Oh man, it was great. So many kids everywhere. People want to see Minor Threat.' I said, 'That band's done with.' He said, 'You just sing about Straight Edge and leave it at that. You've got to go out there and play. You started something, you've got to finish it.' Coming from H.R., it was a big deal to me. It so happened that Lyle came home at Christmas and said, 'I really miss the band.' It turned out his roommate at Northwestern was Kato from the horrible piece-of-shit band Urge

Show flyer for Minor Threat, Necros,
SS Decontrol, The F.U.'s, Boston, 1982
Collection of Hank Peirce

Overkill. So I was talking to Lyle and said, 'Let's re-form.' Lyle quit school, came home at Easter and we started to play again. The first show was April 29, 1982 — Bad Brains and Minor Threat, two shows at the 9:30 Club. We opened with the infamous Cashing In song and threw money at the crowd. When we told our friends we were going to re-form, people were furious at us. It really upset me how mad everybody was at us for reforming. Even my brother said, 'You're selling out.' Then we did a Wilson Center show the next night which was the night I started going out with Cynthia Connolly.

In summer '82, the reunited Minor Threat finally played the West Coast, returned to DC, and decided to expand their sound by adopting a two-guitar attack. With Baker moving to second guitar and Steve Hansgen joining on bass, they recorded the *Out Of Step* 12" EP of '83. For those who wanted Threat to remain the same, this signaled the beginning of the end.

BRIAN BAKER: I don't know if Marginal Man beat us, but we were one of the first five-piece Hardcore bands in DC. Initially, it was an incredible success ... because we were massive. Steve was a better bass player than I was, Lyle had become a great guitar player, and I was as good as he was.

IAN MACKAYE: Around May '82, Brian started to get up in arms about how he didn't want to play bass anymore. Brian was a guitar player first and foremost. Brian played with

Show flyer for BYO show with Minor Threat,
Chatsworth, CA, 1982
Collection of Laura Albert

Santana when he was twelve ... He was a hot-shot guitar player from Grosse Point [Michigan], and his friend's father owned a restaurant. Santana came to eat there and invited them to see the gig that night. They went down early for soundcheck; Brian jammed some Blues with Carlos, who said, 'You've got to come out for the encore.' So at Cobo Hall in Detroit, Brian played with Santana on stage. Brian was a very good guitar player. The only reason he was in Minor Threat as a bass player was we'd met Lyle who said, 'I know this kid Brian who has a bass amp.' We all knew Brian was a snotty little kid. Lyle said he was a great guitar player but I wanted Lyle to play guitar. So Brian came over and said, 'I would kill my mother to play in your band.' Brian was a great bass player but he wanted to play guitar. I was filling in for ten days for John Stabb at Olsson's Records & Tapes and Brian came by and said, 'I just met this guy Steve and I think he should play bass.' The next practice, Brian's like, 'Either I'm going to play guitar or I'm going to quit.' I was like, 'Okay, I guess we'll try this out.' Brian brought him in and he played every song perfectly. We did a summer '82 tour, and it was when we came back from tour that all this went down. Hangsen's first show was in Baltimore in October '82 ... he sang every song while he was playing and I thought, 'That's what I want.' Then we did the PiL show … a big show for us. I met so many people who said they first saw us opening for PiL. I was totally against that gig but the rest of the band wanted to. All I said was 'Deli tray and Cokes.' We get there and the security guys had eaten the deli tray, and a case of Kragmonts. I was so mad.

BRIAN BAKER: After the PiL show, we did the *Out Of Step* record. On that tour, instead of $35, there was $300. We were still driving uninsured vans and sleeping in The Vats in Frisco with MDC and splitting up a loaf of bread. In major cities where there were big scenes, we'd do well but we still had to get across the country, so we'd play in Dallas to 100 people. The touring scope had developed to where you knew where your big cities were and you plotted how to get from one to the other, stopping wherever there was sort of a scene. That's how we wound up in little places on a Tuesday night making $50, but you had to do it. In Minor Threat, we never lived off the band. The first band I did that with was Dag Nasty. The first Minor Threat tour was a summer tour and the next one was after we'd broken up and gotten back together. If you're going to go do this thing, you had to go do it and fuck everything else and clean up the mess when you come. Yeah, everybody would go back to work the minute they came home.

Hangsen was good but his presence changed the chemistry. As Minor Threat's biggest problem was constant personality conflicts, another guy in the crowded van didn't exactly ease the situation.

BRIAN BAKER: Steve Hangsen left because Ian said he either leaves or we break up. I'm sure it was a consensus. After we spent a lot of time with this Steve, it was evident that because he didn't have the luxury of growing up with us hip DC Hardcore kids, he did some things that were grating on us. The breakup was Jeff, Lyle and I rehearsing every day in the basement of Dischord and writing songs and Ian being in the same house and not even coming down to rehearse. He wasn't interested in singing. As he put it — and we've talked about it since then — we started to write our own music. Ian was the primary writer always. By *Out Of Step,* I had a few songs and Ian had a few songs, but Ian was still the main guy. When we started to write where Ian wasn't participating, that was the beginning of the end. We were writing this music that at the time was even more progressive; Ian didn't feel he could sing to it and he didn't feel like he could write lyrics to the music we had written. It doesn't seem that much different but it was to him.

Zine ad for Minor Threat, *Out Of Step,* 1983
Collection of the author

The aesthetic Ian espoused caused many of the financial problems that ultimately sank Minor Threat. They wanted to play gigs "for the kids," meaning cheap admission, so they struggled to stay afloat on the road. *Out Of Step* was the biggest Dischord record up to that time, but they were selling it so cheap to distributors that the label lost money on every copy.

KEN INOUYE (Marginal Man): I applaud the values but I also applaud pragmatism. For instance, *Out Of Step* — they lost a fortune, once you included shipping costs, production, this and that, they were losing at least 20 cents a record … they wanted the record to sell for

Show flyer for one of the last Minor Threat shows,
with The Faith and Marginal Man
Niightclub 9:30, Washington, DC, 1983
Collection of Ken Inouye

x amount … In a sense, that's very cool and ideologically pure but you're not keeping in mind how much you're putting out to get it out. I was like, 'Hey man, I'm as Punk Rock as the next guy but I'm not in this to pay money so someone else can hear me. I want at the very least to break even.'

BRIAN BAKER: There was always inter-band squabbles. We got tired of it and it would be impossible to be a proper Dischord band if you didn't break up at the height of your popularity. It was Ian's thing and he wasn't into it anymore. Rather than try and convince him otherwise, Minor Threat was big enough that Lyle and I thought we could form our own band and continue to do something progressive. We understood why Minor Threat was important but didn't do all the math. We didn't see how unique it was. We called up Glenn Danzig and he said he'd play with us. We thought we had the plan of the century.

After the final breakup of Minor Threat, Ian did Embrace ('84-'85) with Michael Hampton, Chris Bald and Ivor Hanson of The Faith. Ian also did a 7" as Egg Hunt with Jeff Nelson, then teamed up with Guy Picciotto, Joe Lally, and Brendan Canty for Fugazi. Presslar and Baker hooked up with Danzig to form a "supergroup" that became Samhain. Baker went on to Meatmen, Dag Nasty and Junkyard before joining Bad Religion. Nelson played in Senator Flux, a late-80s Alternative outfit, before settling down to a normal life. Presslar went on to become a mid-level major label exec.

BRIAN BAKER: I've been following my guitar where it takes me. I've been doing everything I could do to get to play guitar for a couple more years. I'm no Ian MacKaye, I'm a guy with a guitar.

The Faith, Detroit, 1983
Alec MacKaye singing
Photo by Tim Caldwell

*We are the new breed
And we will have our day*
—Iron Cross, "New Breed"

Ian MacKaye's and his younger brother Alec were close, and Ian always hooked up his brother's bands — The Untouchables, and then The Faith. The Untouchables played many shows and contributed cuts to the essential DC Hardcore comp *Flex Your Head* (Dischord no. 7).

THE FAITH records — '82's Faith/Void split LP (Dischord no. 8) and '83's *Subject To Change* (no. 11) — got attention. Their final show, in '83 at the Space II Arcade, was a big DC event. But Alec's work, compared to Teen Idles and Minor Threat, was strictly second-tier. Alec busted his spleen in a bad motorcycle accident in the late 80s, which cut short his career. Recovery was slower than expected.

GOVERNMENT ISSUE (or "GI," as in the Germs' album title) vied with Minor Threat as the top harDCore band in 1981-82. G.I.'s classic first record, '81's *Legless Bull* EP (Dischord no. 4), best exemplified smartass suburban HC. Their original lineup — frontman John Stabb, drummer Marc Alberstadt, bassist John Barry and guitarist Brian Gay (later of the Chicago group Savage Beliefs) — was incredible.

DAVE SMALLEY (DYS, Dag Nasty): Government Issue was one of the best bands in the history of American Hardcore. For one reason or another, they were jinxed. Their van'd break down; they'd do tours and have ten people at the show because of no publicity — everything bad that could happen to a band happened to them. But they were amazing.

In '82 Government Issue improved further by adding guitarist Brian Baker (of the temporarily defunct Minor Threat) and bassist Tom Lyle (a dental assistant by day, he served as the unofficial archivist of DC HC soundboard tapes). G.I. developed a heavy Rock feel, unlike straight-ahead Hardcore. I remember a great show of theirs in '82 at The Chancery with SS Decontrol. But once Baker returned to Minor Threat, G.I. quickly faded.

Zine ad for Government Issue record, 1983
Collection of Sal Canzonieri

BRIAN BAKER: I wasn't a bass player and Government Issue was a chance to play guitar. They were better with John Barry on guitar but they were biggest when I was in the band. Their whole sound was his insane guitar playing, which I played nothing like. I played like Ace Frehley.

In '85, G.I. reinvented itself again. Tom moved to guitar. New drummer Pete Moffitt, a squeaky-clean kid, turned into a gnarly tattooed Rock dude overnight. Jay Robbins, who played in Punchline, a Tacoma Park Thrash troupe, joined on bass; he was so nervous at his first show, at The Electric Banana in Pittsburgh in summer '85, he played with his eyes shut.

Unfortunately, most who went to see G.I. through the 80s still expected to hear Hardcore reminiscent of the first EP. The groupt was moving into a softer, R.E.M. direction, and none of their fans gave a shit about such profound maturity. (After the fall of G.I., Robbins formed Jawbox.)

JAY ROBBINS: The end of G.I. was in summer '89. After looking at the situation objectively, having done monster tours of the US and Europe, and after a terrible van accident in England where Pete shattered his ankle, we felt we were beating our heads against the wall. It was clear that all four of us had different ideas of what we wanted to do. I think those guys just got tired of working with each other. We booked one last show at 9:30 Club, which was massive, ridiculous and fun. That was it.

IRON CROSS, probably the first American Skinhead band, developed a "Fuck you, we drink, we're into Punk, we don't care what you think" vibe, which was a welcome relief from the rigid DC mindset. Imposing frontman Sab "Grey" Prausnitz and ex-S.O.A. bassist Wendell Blow would always get in some kind of trouble. If a fight occurred at a show, chances are one was involved — though with often more bluff and blunder than bloodshed. One time Wendell walked into a biker bar and stood on top of the bar screaming 'Fuck you, longhaired

mutherfuckers!' — at which point they beat him up and dragged him out. I remember flinging copies of their '83 *Hated & Proud* EP off our roof like frisbees with Sab's green-haired girlfriend Maria.

Many in DC laughed off Iron Cross as quasi-nazi buffoons. In retrospect, Iron Cross were important. Their song, "Crucified For Your Sins," later became an Agnostic Front standard.

TOM BERRARD: Sab came from Baltimore with that Skinhead vibe. He talked about Iron Cross not being racist but I never quite got that. He had Black friends and all, but you just wondered, 'What the hell's the point of the iron cross?' It's not something I'd be into but I liked some of the English music he emulated — I have Skrewdriver records. Sab was just into the English thing, and the English thing was wearing Doc Martens and cuffing your jeans. That's how it all started.

TESCO VEE: The media can make things larger than life. There was only like a dozen Skinheads in Detroit; in DC there was Sab and Wendell Blow. When I first visited DC, Sab was a Punk. Then when I moved there, he was a total Oi! boy — boots, braces, the haircut. But he'd vacillate between these things. A lot of Detroit kids use to think Sab was God. Then they came to DC. He'd happen to be in one of his purple hair phases, lookin' like Sid Vicious, and they'd all be so disillusioned.

SCREAM was one of the most impressive outfits of the HC era. Unlike many of their contemporaries, Scream had a singer who could actually sing, and the band could actually play. They were also relatively good-looking guys who attracted the opposite sex — very rare back then.

Scream, DC, 1982
Insert with *Still Screaming*, Dischord 1982
Photo by Mimi Baumann
Collection of the author

PAT DUBAR (Uniform Choice): Scream were my favorite band, ever. To give you an idea of how I felt, Nirvana was a fucking great band, but when I saw Nirvana play early on, I watched Dave Grohl, thinking 'Scream would've blown away every fuckin' band on the stage tonight.' They were that good. The Stahl brothers are great songwriters. What they do still continues to move me.

In '79, guitarist Franz Stahl, bassist Skeeter Thompson and drummer Kent Stax were just about the only Punks in the Alexandria/Falls Church, Virginia area. In fact, Skeeter was probably the only Black kid in the state into that music. They'd jam on everything from Sex Pistols to Hendrix to Parliament. When Franz's younger brother Pete joined as vocalist in early '81, the four became Scream. Their first shows were keg parties with Southern Rock bands and nearby gigs with bad Virginia New Wave acts like The Laymen or The Distractors.

PETE STAHL (Scream): The first gig we played with people from the DC scene was at Woodlawn High — most people walked out because they thought we were poseurs. D.O.A. came with Jello Biafra while we were playing; people wanted us off so D.O.A. could go on. We were angry about it, but Biafra came up and gave us words of encouragement, which really meant a lot then. It wasn't until Ian started checking us out that others began to think it was cool, too.

Although they hadn't yet cut a record, in summer '82 they toured the US by virtue of being from DC. As a highlight of that trek Scream, earning $300 at The Metropolis in Seattle, did a show noted for the attendance of future Mudhoney, Soundgarden and Nirvana members. The success of that tour led to late-'82's classic *Still Screaming* (Dischord no.9), produced by Ian with Eddie Janney; completed it in three days.

This Side Up, their next record, didn't come out for two years. Dischord was broke and had no distribution, so Scream saved up to record. Dr. Know of the Bad Brains produced Side One. By the time they worked on Side Two, Robert Lee "Harley" Davidson joined on second guitar.

As was the trend circa '83, Scream attempted to fill out their sound with a second guitarist. Harley, a stereotypical Metal dude from the VA burbs, played in a cover band called Tyrant. Pete and Franz knew him because he dated their sister. They turned Harley on to The Damned, and they'd all jam together. When Harley stepped onstage with Scream with his long hair, feather earring, eye makeup, and leather gloves, he threw Hardcore kids for a loop. It was as if he was more Punk than the Punkers.

PETE STAHL: It was cool because for the time it was a real mindfuck ... This guy outta some Metal band playing with us was definitely fucking with people. At the same time, our music changed with him and Franz writing. He's a great guy, very intelligent, and we got along well.

Though an excellent drummer, Kent Stax quit after *Bang The Drum* in '87 because he was married and had a kid to support. Dave Grohl from Dain Bramage replaced Kent. Grohl's entry was seamless — he was one of those great talents that could hear something and play it by ear.

FRANZ STAHL (Scream): My first impressions of Dave was that he was gonna be a fuckin' star. In a Foo Fighters bio he said I came over and said, 'OK, what do ya wanna play, some AC/DC or Black Sabbath?' I don't remember that shit. I remember he came over and we blew through every song on *Still Screaming.* He was much more powerful than Kent. I knew that he was immediately in. It took awhile for him to become accepted, since he was 17 and we were in our late 20s. The first show we did with him was at the Hall Of Nations. His mother and father came down, and it was an awesome show. That was the peak of the band, us with Harley. Dave made us even that much better. His drumming carried the band even more.

Scream set list, 1983
Collection of Laura Albert

In the end, what sunk Scream was Skeeter's drug habit. Everybody in the band was doing blow, but by the mid-80s Skeeter was smokin' the shit and acting erratically. He once split during their '87 European tour, but after rejoining in '89, he pawned their gear for drug money. Ben Pate took his place until Rick Rubin enticed him to join supergroup-that-never-was The Four Horsemen. G.I.'s Jay Robbins replaced Pate for a moment, till Skeeter returned — only to bail again, this time in LA. With all this crap, Grohl split to Seattle to join Nirvana. (In the 90s, the Stahls recorded two albums as Wool. Franz replaced ex-Germ Pat Smear for a spell in Grohl's post-Nirvana sensation Foo Fighters. Pete, tour manager of Foo Fighters and Queens Of The Stoneage, went on to earthlings? and Goatsnake.)

VOID, probably the first Metal Crossover outfit, made incredibly fast, disturbingly noisy guitar-heavy music. There was no middle ground: you either loved 'em or hated 'em. Half-Black, half-Filipino guitar prodigy Bubba DuPree was legendary in certain circles. Their tracks on the split LP *Faith/Void* and *Flex Your Head* prove they were far ahead of their time.

Void came from Columbia, MD, a sterile "planned community" halfway between Baltimore and DC. Like Scream, Void didn't possess the DC scene pedigree — so their sound was unique in local Hardcore. And, unlike their Straight Edge friends in Georgetown, the Columbia kids took lots of LSD.

Void graphics
Xeroxed copy insert with *Flex Your Head*,
Dischord, 1982

JOHN BRANNON (Negative Approach): Bubba was one of the great guitar players of the scene. Void shit was totally out of control. They were underground but that album, it's a total classic of the time.

KEN INOUYE (Marginal Man): There was this great debate: whether or not you thought Void was good — which to me is the first sign of any really great band. If you've made enough of an impact on people where they actually debate whether you're good, you must be doing something right. The fact that you had to defend yourself for liking this band made you like them even more. I seriously believe that they are at least partially the root of the latter-day Speed Metal sound and style.

MARIA MA (Raleigh scene): Void's the band I'd play for Metal kids at my high school. I'd say, 'You think Judas Priest or Iron Maiden are heavy, listen to this.' They couldn't believe it, at least the ones who would get it. Void were one of my all-time favorite bands. When Bubba would show up at shows wearing a bullet belt, lipstick and a Mötley Crüe T-shirt, it was so radical for the time. His band after Void broke up was called Lipstick.

BUBBA DuPREE (Void): Void, we were the outcast rednecks. To this day I don't understand why we were accepted in the DC Hardcore scene. We were so blatantly not a part of it. By the time we started to get big, we didn't consider ourselves Hardcore. We thought we were playing Rock.

Void were down with DC Hardcore because their drummer Sean Finnegan befriended Ian and Henry. At first Void played often in DC but by '83 they seemed disinterested and only gigged about once a year. Their only NYC gig, a much-anticipated CBGB Sunday Matinee in '83, ended after the first song, "Unchained," when singer John Wiffenbach broke his leg during the stagediving mayhem and got carried out on a stretcher.

Touch & Go planned to issue a Void LP in '83, but never did — apparently it was "too Metal," according to some close to the project. That killed Void. (DuPree and Graham McCulloch years later made a major-label record as Earth 18, a futuristic Glam band. Bubba last appeared onstage playing backup guitar on the final Soundgarden tour.)

Quite a few DC Hardcore kids came from the sterile suburb of Rockville, MD, home to Yesterday & Today, the area's top indie record shop. Store owner and friend to the scene Skip Groff financed Minor Threat's *In My Eyes* single — Skip and Y&T employed Ian for years.

ARTIFICIAL PEACE were the first notable Rockville outfit related to DC Hardcore. They played a lot in '82, put out an EP called *Exiled,* and contributed a few cuts to *Flex Your Head.* I saw them once or twice, and they were very good.

Artificial Peace, 1982
Xeroxed insert with *Flex Your Head,* Dischord, 1982
Collection of the author

BRIAN BAKER: Artificial Peace: absolutely a great forgotten band of that time. G.I.'s played with Artificial Peace. We did a Rockville party at some rich girl's house, so we went out to the burbs and got to see what was up. That's the only band that sticks out as something really great.

MARGINAL MAN rose from the ashes of Artificial Peace. "Marginal Man" — a sociological term denoting one on the fringe of two or more cultures, assimilated into neither — describes these guys to a tee. The group included Whites, Asian-Americans, and Ken Inouye, son of powerful Hawaii Senator Daniel Inouye. That a Senator's son played in a HC band during the Reagan era would seem significant, but no one gave a shit — Ken was just another kid on the scene. Marginal Man's records, '84's *Identity* and '85's *Double Exposure,* stand the test of time. At their March '88 farewell gig at The 9: 30, Shudder To Think opened, in one of their first shows.

KEN INOUYE: I'll never forget that first tour we did — every city we went to, it was, 'Are you Straight Edge? Do you skate? Do you know Ian MacKaye?' Those were the three questions they'd ask in every single city.

Double O, later known as DOVE or ENB (Eric's New Band), played many seminal shows. The quartet — vocalist Eric Lagdemeo, guitarist Jason Carmer, bassist Bert Queiroz and drummer Rich Moore — rocked DC with 82's *Double O* EP, featuring "Death Of A Friend." Eric L was one of the coolest, best-dressed on the scene, with spiked hair, black cape, and walking stick. He never pursued music with urgency — like many in DC's scene — going on to work for his well-to-do family.

Zine ad for Double O, 1982
Collection of the author

JAY ROBBINS: Double O was amazing; their 7" EP was outstanding. I remember all my friends being really impressed with their singer Eric as the ultimate Hardcore icon, specifically because of some swan dive that he did off the stage of Wilson Center. That picture is in the book, *Banned In DC*. Later, Eric got into this Glam Rock trip where he was doing these very polished demos. He wanted to do more commercial-sounding Rock, so he took singing lessons — and my friends were very disappointed. I always felt that was the ultimate Punk Rock statement.

There were others. **RED C** — Eric L, Tomas Squip and the late Toni Young (who died on pneumonia in the late 80s) — did cuts on *Flex Your Head*. **SECOND WIND** — Bert Queiroz and Rich Moore from Double O plus Steve Hangsen — was a Minor Threat clone, down to covering Wire (Minor Threat covered "12XU" on Flex Your Head, Second Wind did "Mr. Suit" on '83's Second Wind). **PEER PRESSURE** — with Danny Ingram, of Teen Idles and Youth Brigade, and Tom Berrard — opened for Anti-Pasti at The 9: 30. **THE FOUR HUNDRED** — Brian Baker, Graham McCulloch, and Ray Hare of Deadline — made a shitty tape and broke up. **UNITED MUTATION**, **HATE FROM IGNORANCE**, **SOCIAL SUICIDE**, **NUCLEAR CRAYONS** and **GRAND MAL** were so unremarkable they defy comment.

Meatmen [see "IQ 32 (Midwest Fuck You)" chapter] frontman Tesco Vee relocated to DC's "HC paradise" in early '83. Within weeks he was delivering papers

dutch hercules ep

at 4 a.m. and working afternoons as bag-checker at Olsson's Books & Records in Georgetown. Minor Threat's Lyle Presslar and Brian Baker did a few outrageous shows with Meatmen in '83 and '84, and Ian MacKaye had a guest spot on the '83 *Tesco Vee And The Meatcrew — Dutch Hercules* 12" (Touch & Go). "Dutch Hercules" was Tesco as caveman, decked out in fur, boots and tight cotton briefs. In Meatmen's finest hour, Tesco took the stage Judas Priest-style at a fall '83 Wilson Center gig with The Misfits.

Dutch Hercules
Tesco Vee (Meatmen), Touch & Go, 1983
Collection of the author

TESCO VEE: Wilson Center, 1983. People still talk about that. I came out on a moped trying to do my Rob Halford spoof. I had a Prussian military helmet with chains hanging down the side, a spike on top, and gold metal pants. Back then we used a real dry ice machine, a 50-gallon drum with these giant hoses that went across stage. I remember going backstage between songs — Glenn Danzig's back there with his gloves, shoveling buckets of ice into this drum. It looked like The Devil at work stoking the furnaces of hell. It was a show for the ages.

GRAHAM McCULLOCH: Tesco rode out on a moped and gunned the engine. There was smoke going off. Then in our second show, we did a fake Glam Rock thing where everyone was dressed in drag. I had the Rock & Roll nurse miniskirt with a silver glitter wig and lipstick. Before we went on, Tesco wrestled Fred Smith of Beefeater — both dressed as cavemen. We were trying to do comedy Stadium Rock.

THE OBSESSED's singer Scott "Wino" Weinrich, a long-haired Maryland redneck with a switchblade in his pocket — and a heart of gold, stumbled onto the primitive DC scene. Of course Wino stood out like a sore thumb at shows. Few would fuck with his unsettling presence. The Obsessed played Black Sabbath-style Metal but got Hardcore gigs, often as a joke. They put out an indie 7" in '81 and had a cut on *Metal Massacre 6* in '84. They opened for 45 Grave at Wilson Center, and played monthly in '83 at Charmichael's, a cheesy New Wave disco near Dupont Circle where Straight Edgers were known to sneak drinks (Many professed Straight Edge types did intoxicants when the opportunity presented itself.).

By '84, once Speed Metal took over, The Obsessed were washed-up. Wino split for LA in '85 to replace Scott Reager as vocalist for SST Metal godz Saint Vitus. Wino and Vitus made beautiful music: the EP *Thirsty And Miserable* (a reworking of the Black Flag song) and *Born Too Late*.

Wino was always doin' tons of meth; I remember around the time of Vitus' legendary summer '86 tour with The Mentors, his switchblade was entirely corroded through by the shit. A few years later he assembled a new outfit — also called The Obsessed — who did a CD for Columbia in the 90s.

Obsessed, 1982
The Metal godz of DC Hardcore
Courtesy of Wino

WINO (The Obsessed): I was associated with the DC scene through friendships. Basically I was the longhaired freak at these shows to see my favorite bands like Faith and Void. I kinda liked Minor Threat, but always had a lot of respect for those guys. I knew John Stabb from G.I. and Sab Grey of Iron Cross. That early scene was very moving. The Obsessed was all about real music, and that's how I thought about that Hardcore scene. I'd catch a little heat here and there, although nobody had the balls to fuck with me. As I got to know people and they'd hear our music, they'd wanna put us on their bills, kinda as a goof. Basically, the way we could play was at Hardcore shows. We had really fast songs and a Hardcore attitude. The kids recognized that.

Some DC bands didn't quite fit the harDCore vibe — chief among them was NO TREND. I hooked up with No Trend's Jeff Mentges in fall '82. Jeff knew I was promoting the PiL/Minor Threat show at Ritchie Coliseum and called me every day for like two months to get on the bill. Of course that never happened, but his group's confrontational approach absorbed me. They hated everyone and everything; their grinding Flipper/PiL onslaught constituted a complete fuck-you to DC scene conformity. When I met 'em, they were shoving flyers that read "No Trend, No Scene, No Movement" up all the Georgetown Coke machines frequented by Straight Edge types.

For two years, I immersed myself in No Trend. With no experience, I put out four of their records: '83's "Teen Love" 7" and the *Teen Love* 12" EP, '84's *Too Many Humans* and 85's *A Dozen Dead Roses* with Lydia Lunch. In early '83, I came across a retired-but-functional '76 Ford ambulance for $600. With that I organized and endured three national No Trend tours, including one with DKs. We did some fine shows: with Big Boys (Austin) and Butthole Surfers (San Antonio), supporting Hüsker Dü for a weekend (Chicago, Minneapolis, Madison), headlining over Soundgarden (Seattle) and Flaming Lips (Norman, OK). We played in over 40 cities — amazing given the cultural terrain then. We were lucky to make $50 a show, and we lived on $5 a day, which we made selling records from the back of the van.

Everybody always went at each other's throats. And Jeff wasn't exactly a nice guy. In those two years No Trend went through at least 10 members. I finally bailed when Jeff accused me of ripping them off. No Trend was a losing proposition — records, tours and publicity sucked up the money I made promoting shows. No Trend were great and attained a cult following, but weren't exactly a hot property.

Too Many Humans
No Trend, 1984
Collection of the author

I was lucky to get out only two grand in the hole. After I left DC in '85, No Trend did one last album before breaking up: *Tritonian Nash — Vegas Polyester Complex* (Touch & Go, '86).

KING KOFFEE (Butthole Surfers): I felt an affinity for No Trend, 'Teen Love' was such a great single. Bands like No Trend, Flipper and ourselves were part of a reaction to Hardcore. Even though we were all Hardcore bands, we were all reacting against how limited it was defining itself. We all thought it was so silly how everyone was playing faster and faster. It got so fucking stupid. We all confused a lot of people, but people who liked us had an understanding of what it should've been all about.

JACK RABID (editor, *The Big Takeover*): 'Mass Sterilization Caused By Venereal Disease by No Trend: that's the way anybody with any brains'd approach it if they still wanted to make really loud hard music in 1983. You had to do a Big Black or a Hose or a No Trend. You had to turn the music inside out, to the point where Hardcore kids were gonna hate it, so hopefully you'd find smarter people who still liked the dictates of aggressive music but weren't Hardcore.

JELLO BIAFRA (Dead Kennedys): No Trend — the anti-DC DC band, to a fault. Their sound had more in common with Flipper than anything from the East Coast. They probably picked that just to annoy people. I first met Jeff and Frank when they came up to me at Yesterday & Today — 'Do you hate John Stabb?' 'Well, no, not really.' 'Do you hate Ian MacKaye?' Just real grim, negative stuff. I said, 'Stay in touch and send a tape.' The tape had more humor to it, but a much more fatalistic view than most bands. Frank told me everybody in the world should stop having kids as a solution to overpopulation. I've heard Frank killed himself. He saw the big picture too clearly but wasn't able to get pleasure out of fighting it.

> *I thought we all wanted something new*
> *How did it end up the same?*
> **— Youth Brigade, "It's About Time That We Had A Change"**

Unlike most other cities, DC allowed bars to admit minors as long as they didn't serve 'em alcohol. If you were underage, they'd put an "X" on your hand. Hardcore kids later adapted that "X" as a badge of honor.

Through early '82, most shows took place at alcohol-driven clubs like The 9: 30 or The Bayou in Georgetown. I saw a few shows at The Chancery, a Capitol Hill dive — Teen Idles played one of their several "final" shows there, as did SS Decontrol, with Iron Cross and G.I.

The coolest shows were house parties and basement gigs; a few took place at a downtown loft known as Hard Art. Janelle Brooks threw parties in her parent's Rockville basement, a spot called The Shithole. Woodlawn High even saw a few shows, most notably D.O.A. on the *Hardcore 81* tour.

Flyers — wheatpasted on walls and lampposts around Georgetown — and telephones spread the word for Hardcore shows. The network of radio and record stores was minimal. WHFS was the only left-of-center radio; they played the day's alternative music, from Leo Kottke to The Clash, but zero Hardcore. In college radio, there was nothing. WGTB at Georgetown University played New Wave in the late 70s, but "liberal" Jesuit administrators closed them down in 1980 because some of the station's programming was not in keeping with the zeitgeist of the Roman Catholic student body. There were a couple of carrier-current stations (not true broadcast radio, they operate only in a network of campus buildings) at George Washington University (WRGW) and American University (WAMU) as well as the low-wattage WMUC at University of Maryland. You could also find out about shows at the few somewhat-hip record stores like Olsson's in Georgetown, Record & Tape Exchange (RTX) of Arlington, Yesterday & Today in Rockville, Joe's Record Paradise in Silver Spring, and Howie's Music Machine, out by Baltimore in Pikesville. That was it.

My first three years attending GWU, I was involved with the carrier-current WRGW. In '81 I started as DJ; a highlight was having Ian MacKaye on my show, where for two hours we spun Minor Threat, Youth Brigade, Necros, et cetera — the first time most of those records played on radio.

In the summer of '82, I assumed the position of station music director. A few weeks later, at a TSOL show at Hitsville in Passaic, New Jersey, I hooked up with Mike Vraney, who managed TSOL as well as Dead Kennedys. He approached me about setting up a DKs show at my college. I teamed up with fellow WRGW DJ Dave Rubin and got to work. Vraney showed us how to produce and promote from start to finish. Plenty of problems arose — especially when the GWU switchboard (four blocks from the White House) lit up over calls for "Dead Kennedys." That July event united DKs, Faith, Void, Double O, and 1500 other kids in the GWU Marvin Center lunchroom. From early '82 through summer '84, I put on over 20 HC shows, the largest I was involved with being the "Punk Funk Spectacular" with Trouble Funk, Minor Threat and Big Boys at Lansburgh Cultural Center, and PiL/Minor Threat at Ritchie Coliseum.

My favorite show was when 250 HC kids and curious onlookers packed GWU's "Rathskellar" for TSOL and No Trend. After, I learned that during the gig all the Theater Department's costumes got ripped off. The only ones with access to the floor were TSOL. I haggled with administrators for days over the incident, finally convincing them TSOL had nothing to do with it.

JACK GRISHAM (TSOL): We got some good shit that night. We ripped that place off blind. I'd gotten into the costume department and took everything. I had these Herman boots with 18-inch heels, and so I'm 6'3 with 18 inches on the heels. I had a big Napoleon hat. It was great riding in the van down the highway in Seventeenth Century garb.

Some of the better shows happened at the Space II Arcade, an unusual arcade I ran across: near Union Station with PacMan and pinball machines where one could purchase food and even liquor. The place had a 475-capacity room with a stage that opened out into a gated parking lot. I put on about a dozen shows there, the highlights being Circle Jerks (the legendary lineup with Chuck Biscuits and Earl Liberty), GBH's first American date, The Faith's final show, CH3 from LA with The FUs from Boston, and Suicidal Tendencies on their first tour.

TOM BERRARD: Space II Arcade was so great, it's a shame somebody with money didn't make it into a full-time club. It was perfect — in this total industrial neighborhood, no neighbors to be bothered at night, in

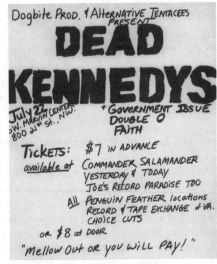

Show flyer for Dead Kennedys, GWU, 1981
Art by Claire Burke
Collection of the author

The D. C.
FUNK-PUNK SPECTACULAR
LANSBURGH'S CULTURAL CENTER
420 7th ST., N.W. (IN THE HEART OF THE DOWNTOWN DISTRICT)
FRI. SEPT. 23   9:00 P.M. 'til 2:30 A.M.
TROUBLE FUNK
"DROP THE BOMB" * "PUMP IT UP"
"TROUBLE FUNK EXPRESS"
MINOR THREAT
"STRAIGHT EDGE"
BIG BOYS
"FUNK PUNK AUSTIN, TEXAS"
★ SPECIAL SCRATCH-RAP TEAM
"NEW YORK and the STATIC DISRUPTOR"
ALL NIGHT DISCO BY SOUND TECH PRODUCTIONS
BEER & WINE AVAILABLE ALL NIGHT!
ADMISSION $5.00
Tickets on sale at: KEMP MILL RECORDS · YESTERDAY & TODAY (Rockville) · RTX (Arlington)
JOE'S RECORD PARADISE TOO (Wheaton) · COMMANDER SALAMANDER (Georgetown)
A DOGBITE PRODUCTION & BLUSH PRODUCTION

Show poster for "Funk-Punk Spectacular"
Lansburgh Center, DC, 1983
Collection of the author

a weird part of town, away from the hip clubs, but you had a devoted following who'd go there. My friend used to call it the Punk cocktail party because you could just hang out — it was totally casual. It was a good-sized room with a big side door — vans could load in easily. They sold pizza and Cokes and had pinball machines; it wasn't like you were at the 9:30 Club — it was an amazing place to see a show.

The summer '83 Circle Jerks show had many problems. The crowd was much larger than expected, the Jerks' road manager was an old-school Rock Biz asshole, and the fire marshalls showed up, just like they did at every show of mine. I ran back to the office for a minute, to take a break from the bedlam. Sitting there was J.C. Jackson — son of the owner, Mrs. Gloria Jackson — and his sister. They told me to chill, and offered me a hit of what they were smoking. I'd never done freebase before — they told me to inhale slowly and blow it out my nose. When you smoke cocaine, you enter an intense personal realm. The last thing you want is to deal with "reality." The next thing I knew, a fierce pounding assaulted the door. The fire marshall had returned with more questions and complaints. He demanded I tell him why he shouldn't shut the whole damn show down. All I could think about was not puking on his shoes. I spoke in slow, measured answers until he split.

By the end of '84 I had had it with the whole scene. I was totally fried and couldn't wait to get away from all the snooty DC twinkies. Most of the local music sucked by that point but I wasn't even listening to HC anymore. If I wasn't with No Trend, I was driving around the DC ghettos in the red Firebird of Dave Rubin, who'd become a top promoter in the hot Go-Go Funk scene (Trouble Funk, Chuck Brown and the Soul Searchers, Experience Unlimited). That summer, after setting up one final show with Black Flag, Meat Puppets and Nig-Heist, I hit the road with No Trend in the ambulance for six weeks — and never returned.

Outer confrontations are meaningless
It's the inner struggles that make the change
— Youth Brigade, "Point Of View"

DC Hardcore was basically over. Attitudes had changed.

IAN MACKAYE: 1983 was a tough year for DC bands: Minor Threat broke up; The Faith broke up; things started to fall apart. I had this philosophy: 'Bruise the ego, not the body' — even though I fought a lot, I never sent people to hospitals. My thing was to show people I wasn't scared of them, but I wasn't out to maim. We fought for our community. What I didn't take into account is that I'm not everybody; plenty of other people wanted to fuck people up. By '84, DC was in a depressing situation. There was intense friction within the Dischord scene, the shows sucked and violence was so prevalent. The kids were all nationalists: 'Oh, you're a Communist, we'll beat you up.' There were 'Drunk Punks' and gay-bashing — suddenly it was all stupid. It drove us crazy — we'd talk about what we were going to do.

Some people were like, 'Fuck this. I'm out.' But for a lot of us, this was all we had; we decided that October '84 was gonna be 'Good Food October,' which meant we were all gonna form new bands in October and create our own scene. Instead of trying to take back the scene, we were just gonna let them go on, form a new community and start again.

Then we redesignated a time frame: Revolution Summer. We actually pulled it off. By the beginning of '85 the bands were happening; we started to play shows. The first thing we found out was all these other kids hated us because we were 'pussies.' We'd confront them on every level. We'd make kids sit on the floor, to fuck with them. I had a big argument with [local Black female Skin] Lefty at a Rites Of Spring/Embrace/Beefeater show in Baltimore. There'd been a tremendous fight during the show; it spilled onto the street. I was talking to her and said, 'What's your fucking deal? Why do you fight?' 'Because you used to defend the scene but now you don't fight anymore. Now we're doing it.' That's when I thought, 'I'm not fighting no more — ever.' Also, H.R. said something like that. I was at a Bad Brains gig with him; we were watching the opening band and there was a kid who was being crazy dumb. I turned to H.R. and said, 'This is ridiculous.' He said, 'You created it.' That hurt.

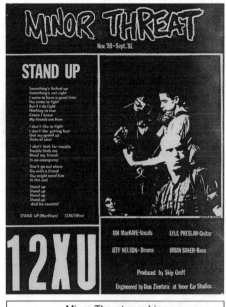

Minor Threat graphics
Xeroxed insert with *Flex Your Head*, Dischord
Collection of the author

During the "Revolution Summer" of '85 many harDCore types reinvented themselves. "Emo," for emotional post-Hardcore , described the move to softer, more emotive music, embodied in Ian's project Embrace, Brian Baker's Dag Nasty, Tomas Squip's Beefeater, Kingface with Mark Sullivan, Bobby Sullivan's Lunchmeat, and Rites of Spring with Guy Picciotto and Eddie Janney.

IAN MACKAYE: Revolution Summer was to reinvolve everybody and remove the parade of macho behavior. So by 1985, we became really politicized. At the beginning of our scene, we were very anti-political and in fact ridiculed people who were into politics. But for some reason in '85, art and politics suddenly made sense to us and we ran with it. Apartheid, women's issues, and the homeless were really galvanizing issues. Tomas from Beefeater was a pied piper for us in that sense.

JAY ROBBINS: There was an amazing gig at Hall Of Nations with Embrace, Dag Nasty, Beefeater and Rites Of Spring. There was a Skinhead problem in DC at that point, and I remember Fred from Beefeater did this little acoustic song about how Skinhead guys really turn him on. He went and sung it outside, in full view of these brawny and scrawny Skinhead types. It was hilarious, and very disarming.

GRAHAM McCULLOCH (Meatmen, Negative Approach): Some of those later shows, it was unbearable. Rich girls would cry and throw flowers at the stage. It became Emotional-Core.

DAG NASTY — the big DC band of that era — was the model for much of the Alternative Rock to follow. Minor Threat's demise so disillusioned Brian Baker he attended GWU for awhile. But all the new action in town inspired him to form Dag Nasty in '85. Original vocalist Shawn Brown sang for their early shows, but Dave Smalley of Boston's DYS replaced him for the '86 debut *Can I Say*. For a moment flashed one of those rare sparks.

DAVE SMALLEY: *"Can I Say*, we knew it was something special. It was unique and exciting. Ian produced it and I remember I was doing vocals for one of the songs and it was just him and Don Zientara in the control room. Ian was shaking his head and looking down at the console and I thought, 'I fucked up, I was off-key — he must not like our band.' I walked in and said, 'Ian, what's the matter?' He said, 'It's a fucking great record.' It was like he wished he'd been doing it.

Unfortunately, Smalley's participation was short-lived; he accepted a graduate studies scholarship through NYU's Middle Eastern Studies Center in '86 that took him overseas. Dag Nasty made two LPs without him ('87's *Wig Out At Denko's* and '88's *Field Day* with vocalist Pete Cortner), but things were never the same.

BRIAN BAKER: Smalley's in the band; we've recorded our first record but it's not out. I don't know how long we've been a band with Smalley but we've done enough legwork where we're going to New York, getting killer shows at Irving Plaza like opening for GBH. We're selling out the 9:30 Club and Smalley all of a sudden decides he's going to Israel to go to school. I'm like, 'That's great. The first album's coming out and you're going to Israel.' It was insanity to me, like 'Why didn't you tell me this before?' I was like, 'Fuck you!' That was it — immediate rift.

DAVE SMALLEY: I found out I got that scholarship to Israel and I just took it. I was in Israel for a year and then I was in Egypt and Turkey for a few months. Mike Gitter sent me the second Dag Nasty album in the mail. *Wig Out* was great; I remember hearing it and crying. It was midnight and I listened to it on my little boombox. I remember saying, 'God, if I'd done that record, I'd've done it better.' I cried as if it was my group. I could've stayed over there and gotten my MA. So I told Gitter, 'I wanna be in a band again.' The next thing you know I got a call from Bill Stevenson in Los Angeles. We spoke many days in a row for hours — his phone bill was like $1000. 'I'm starting this new group called All named after the last Descendents album.' He sent me that album and I loved it, so I flew back, stayed with a friend in New Jersey for a few days, and got on a plane to Los Angeles. There they were in the van. We went to Alfredo's and went to practice on the first day.

Fugazi, 1986
Ian MacKaye's band after Minor Threat,
Photo by Adam Cohen
from *Fugazi*, Dischord, 1988
Collection of the author

Revolution Summer led to a new generation: proto-Indie Rock like Swiz and Soulside, the brattish Nation Of Ulysses, and Shudder To Think. Not bad, but compared to what took place earlier, a real letdown. There was still Ian at Dischord House, with Fugazi, but the terrain had changed.

TOM BERRARD: The end of DC Hardcore was the dilution of the audience; you went to a show and didn't know everybody anymore. We definitely felt that small was better. I'd've never considered seeing a show in an arena back then. Now I'll only go with a backstage pass and see it up close. •

BOSTON NOT LA:
THE KIDS WILL HAVE THEIR SAY

Now it's time to let go
My boiling point's about to show
— SS Decontrol, "Boiling Point"

DAVE SMALLEY (DYS): To us in the Boston scene, California bands were the enemy. They were drinkers. Darby Crash died of a drug overdose. That was an opposite value system from what we were trying to do.

Boston nurtured one of the most intense Hardcore scenes. Everyone apparently saw what was going on in DC — and hammered it home. It didn't necessarily produce the best music, but everything about it was fierce. The militant attitude of a few Boston bands left a lasting legacy.

Boston Punk/New Wave circa 1980 was dominated by inebriated 60s-style Garage Rock troupes like The Neighborhoods, Del Fuegos, Lyres, and Blackjacks — none of whom had that HC vibe. A few young acts who played with a dated sound came close, like Boy's Life and The Outlets — both on a 1981 split-EP — but shit was never cool.

SS Decontrol, A7, NYC, 1982
Springa singing, Al Barile on guitar
Photo by Karen O'Sullivan

AL BARILE (SS Decontrol): The Boston Punk scene was a congregation of drugged-out losers. They had this elitist attitude. I could not get with it at all. It was an older thing. The Neighborhoods and Mission Of Burma were the established bands but they had no connection to me: the guitars weren't heavy. I remember I went to a Neighborhoods show in 1980 or '81. There was this Punk there, Bob White, and he was the first victim of some kind of ritual slam thing with me. The other guy I was with got arrested because we slammed this Punk around so hard.

Alan Barile, a beer-drinkin' hockey jock from blue-collar Lynn, MA, transformed in '81 after seeing Minor Threat at New York's Irving Plaza. Barile originated what became Boston Hardcore, and almost everyone involved fell in line with his hard-line vibe. With shaved head, Straight Edge militancy, and take-no-prisoners physicality, Barile exemplified modern HC stereotypes. He was the Pavarotti of shots to the body.

DAVE SMALLEY: Don't confuse education with intelligence because Al is extremely intelligent. I've gone to school all my life — I know there's a billion people way smarter than I am. Al's a unique character. He's not the kind of guy who'll open up to you, but he has a strong set of morals that he still follows to this day.

SS DECONTROL was put together by Barile in summer 1981. Originally "Society System Decontrol," they soon shortened the name — and would later shorten it again to SSD. For a year or so, SSD was awesome. Powered by a potent rhythm section — bassist Jaime Sciarappa and drummer Chris Foley — they became legendary for Al's brutal guitar riffage and virulent Straight Edge lyrics, delivered by the roaring throat of one of Hardcore's great frontmen, Phil "Springa" Springs. Springa, a former Outlets roadie, was a scrappy fucker who could slamdance and stagedive with the best of 'em. SS Decontrol's debut album, '82's *The Kids Will Have Their Say* (the first release on Al's label, X-Claim!), certifies as a classic.

Show flyer for SS Decontrol
Gallery East, Boston, 1981
Collection of Hank Peirce

DAVE SMALLEY: SSD were *the* guys. Without SSD, there wouldn't've been a Boston Crew, there wouldn't've been a Hardcore scene or a Straight Edge scene. Give credit where it's due.

CHRIS DOHERTY (Gang Green): SSD were the focal point of the scene because they were the first band that would go out and rent a P.A., find a hall and do shit on their own. That's when everyone else realized they could also do it, instead of trying to play regular clubs, and deal with all the nonsense. They were a band, and they were promoters, too. You were lucky if you got to play with SSD.

DREW STONE (Mighty COs): I can't emphasize how many people believed in SS Decontrol. Their hopes and dreams were on this band. They were talking the talk and walking the walk. It's not like it is now where you have a blueprint to go by. SS Decontrol, Minor Threat and especially Black Flag created the blueprint.

MIKE GITTER (editor, *XXX*): Obviously, Al was very influenced by what was going on in Washington, DC. Him being a complete extremist just took it to the next step, which is why SSD sounded a lot fiercer than Minor Threat. It was very extreme music for the time.

The local HC scene came together at early SSD shows. They first gigged at the Gallery East in September '81; second on Cape Cod at the Mill Hill Club in Yarmouth, MA; third back in Boston at Street's, a lame Rock Disco.

DAVE SMALLEY: SSD played early on at The Rat, the first time a real Hardcore band ever played there. The Rat had circular tables all the way up to the stage … there's ten of us there. Springa came on: 'We're SS Decontrol and we're not fucking nazis!' They started playing — the ten of us started slamming. Two tables instantly got knocked over. I felt this big hand grab my neck and toss me through the air. It was a bouncer, so I punched him. He grabbed my head and slammed it against the wall twice; I still have a big scar on my head from that. Jamie Sciarappa saw it, threw his bass down, charged and punched him; a little riot ensued. I got thrown out the back door; I was lying on the ground, my head bleeding. Another kid, J.T., got thrown out, his eye badly cut. It was like the movies. We looked at each other on the ground, bloody and defeated. Then, this great woman on the scene, Katie The

Cleaning Lady, rescued us. She took me to the hospital, waited while I got my stitches, then took me back to her apartment. She had two rats, Sid and Darby. Trouble seemed to always find us back then.

While Al Barile came from a Brooklyn-tough North Shore town, most Boston HC kids came from nice South Shore towns like Braintree and Quincy — Gang Green, Jerry's Kids and Springa — and upscale Marblehead — Jake Phelps, Andy Strahan of DYS, and Last Rites' Tony Peretz.

Boston Hardcore's rise tied in with skateboarding. Crazy-ass skaters with kamikaze DogTown attitude made up a large segment of the scene. They caused trouble at Cambridge skate parks like Zero Gravity or Z-Bowl.

The first regular Boston Hardcore shows took place in late '81 at Media Workshop and Gallery East, two small (150-capacity) art galleries. Kevin Porter operated Media Workshop out of a shoddy old Boylston Street office building with no elevator; bands lugged gear up long flights of stairs. At one memorable gig, Flipper on a Tuesday afternoon, the building's business people flipped out over the crazy scene. A mini-riot erupted two songs in; Porter was seen running out the back, a briefcase of cash under his arm.

Al Barile made Gallery East shows major Boston HC events. He set up all the bills, which usually featuring SSD. Al ran an orderly show, and treated everyone fairly. In summer '82 Gallery East presented Minor Threat/SSD/The FU's/The Proletariat, and Meatmen/Necros/Negative Approach (the "Process Of Elimination" tour) with DYS and Gang Green, as well as MDC/SSD/Deep Wound.

Show flyer for SS Decontrol,
Media Workshop, Boston, 1982
Collection of Hank Peirce

AL BARILE: I became tight friends with the guy who owned Gallery East. To that point he just did the occasional arty show. He saw us and got caught up in the whole thing. I met him when I was still drinking. I went to one of these shows, put my hand through the wall of his gallery and told him I'd come back and fix it the next day. I don't think he believed me but I came back the next day and fixed it. I said, 'Someday I want my band to play here.' He was like, 'Yeah, yeah.' Later I came back and played there. I was soon promoting shows there — MDC came through, all the DC bands — but Circle Jerks and DKs still played the New Wave clubs; they didn't play these do-it-yourself shows. That said a lot to me at the time.

CHRIS DOHERTY: In the early days, 30 or 40 kids at a show in Boston was a big deal. Every Sunday at the Gallery East, it was like going to the playground in elementary school. It was the same vibe — no egos and a lot of fun. If there was no matinee, you were bummed because you had nothing to do; 1981-82, that was a cool period of time.

When Dead Kennedys first came to town they'd hook up with Alec Peters, who organized bills at the 1500-capacity Bradford Hotel, the 1000-capacity Fensgate Ballroom — in an Emerson College dorm on Beacon Street — and the 250-capacity club Maverick's: Hüsker Dü played there, as did Beastie Boys; Flipper played there the night John Belushi died.

Bad Brains played a legendary Boston show at Maverick's in May '82. The club had to shut down by 2 a.m. — the Brains showed up at 1: 30. With no sound check, they went up and played 20 minutes of jaw-dropping Hardcore.

ALEC PETERS (Boston promoter): It was 12:45, and there's a 2:00 liquor license law, and the band hasn't shown up yet, and the other bands had been off for a while. The place was absolutely sold out — I didn't want to give people back their money. Lo and behold they came, at like 1:30. The guy behind the bar said, 'It's cool, I'll keep sellin' beer.' So all the regulars from the pit ran out in procession and grabbed something from their van, and had the band set up inside of five minutes. They plugged in, and the fucking place exploded. It was unbelievable. They had it.

D.O.A. was playing Cantone's late '82 when the ceiling caved in, causing a toxic asbestos hazard. The Misfits played a church in Cambridge where fans so scuffed its floor, it never held another show. Bloody fights marred an infamous Watertown VFW show with Minor Threat, Meatmen, Necros, DYS and Negative FX. That free-wheeling era ended when lame New Wave clubs like The Channel and The Paradise decided they could make a few bucks promoting Hardcore shows.

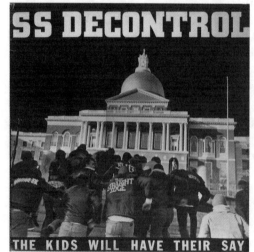

THE KIDS WILL HAVE THEIR SAY

The Kids Will Have Their Say
SS Decontrol, X-Claim!, 1981
Collection of Sal Canzonieri

Who cares what we do
Cause we are Boston Crew
— SS Decontrol, "Boston Crew"

The clique that formed around Al Barile and SS Decontrol was 20 or so belligerent Straight Edge kids known as Boston Crew. They shaved their heads, both as a Hardcore statement and to differentiate themselves from New Wavers with stupid angular haircuts. Boston Crew are running up the capitol stairs on the cover of the first SS Decontrol album. Crew bands included SSD, DYS and Negative FX. Other important Boston Hardcore groups like The FU's, Gang Green and Jerry's Kids smoked weed or drank beer, thus excluding themselves from the Straight Edge pack.

DAVE SMALLEY: When I say 'Boston Crew' I'm talking about Straight Edge. That's why so many kids identified with DYS and SSD — everyone has a friend who's been an alcoholic or a heroin addict. That kind of experience makes you not want to live that way.

AL BARILE: Boston Crew was the fundamental makeup of the Boston Hardcore scene. It started with a few skateboarders from Marblehead. Jake Phelps from *Thrasher* was part of the Crew, as was Jon Anastas and Dave Smalley of DYS, and Choke of Negative FX. We'd pile in my van, 15 or 16 people; we'd make an impact wherever we went. When SSD was playing, I felt like Boston Crew was playing. I've always been extremely physical; I take a lot of pride in cleaning house. In New York, I'd go to clubs like A7 — a drugged-out crowd doing the party thing. We used to kick their ass. We weren't trying to hurt anybody, we were just bringing that youthful enthusiasm. All those old people were totally petrified.

SHRED (DJ): Boston Crew was an intimidating force. Militant, exclusive; I didn't find myself part of it. I was Straight Edge but my hair wasn't short enough. Al was an asshole.

Boston has earned its rep as a tough town and life in the HC scene implied brawling. For instance, when Youth Brigade came to Boston, literal riots broke out between kids and bouncers. At the first gig, The Channel hired dickhead football jocks as security; the ensuing melee spilled into the streets, producing police, ambulances and broken bones. HC kids in conservative Boston generally invited conflict just by how they looked.

DAVE SMALLEY: Anytime you were sitting outside waiting for the trolley, cars would drive by: 'Punk faggot!,' 'Fuck dayglo!' No understanding of Hardcore or anything. We'd hang out in Kenmore Square, right by Fenway Park. Any night after a baseball game got out, the townies would have these foot-long souvenir Red Sox bats. If they saw us, they'd chase us, and if they got us, we'd get beaten with bats.

ALEC PETERS: In the late 70s, the Disco guys used to come over and beat up the Punk fags at The Rat all the time — it was the guys from the North Shore coming down in their fucking Camaros to kick butt on the Punk fags. Disco was macho. When Hardcore came along, the kids were mean and physical, and if ever those Disco guys made the mistake of picking on these young Hardcore kids, they'd get their asses handed to 'em in a big, big way.

With all those physically-minded kids, Boston HC shows constituted the most violent East Coast experiences. You'd see a lot of Al Barile clones trying to fuck someone up — under the guise of "unity," of course.

Kids in the pit literally piled on each other in "pig-piles." This distinct local pastime — like the scene itself — often turned into a scary mess. At some point they'd throw some poor kid's ass onstage and pigpile him right there. There'd be as many as 25 kids — stacked up so high they'd touch the lights — crushing those on the bottom.

Show flyer for "DC Hardcore Comes To Boston," Gallery East, 1982
Collection of Laura Albert

AL BARILE: It's a Boston thing. I think I was the first person to push someone down and start the pile. This D.O.A. show at The Underground was the first pigpile I remember. It got so crazy the drummer trashed his kit and jumped on top of the pile. We then brought it to DC; this is one of the stupid things we did: took some DC kid, threw him on the ground to start the pile and jumped on top. Ian and those guys didn't know what to do. They didn't do anything but I think they were mad. I injured my knees jumping off the stage at the Peppermint Lounge [NYC] and Choke got hurt, but we never tried to hurt anyone else. The Boston style was more punch-driven.

"STRAIGHT EDGE" HANK PEIRCE (Boston scene): Boston was much more violent than slamming I'd seen anywhere else. We described it as 'punching penguins.' It had a name — 'The Boston Thrash.' New York had that big circle-storm thing. DC wasn't as organized — more chaotic with more diving. LA was the king of running in circles with no sense of rhythm to it. When you watched *The Decline Of Western Civilization* you said, 'That's slamdancing!' But Boston really changed things.

Headed Straight
Get it Away
Glue
V.A
Nothing Done
Screw
Police Beat
Boiling Point
Under the Influence
Fight them
Fun to You
X-Claim
How Much Art
Forced down Y.T.
Who's to Judge
No Reply
The End

SS Decontrol set list
A7, NYC, 1982
Collection of Laura Albert

Dancefloor action could turn savage but wasn't about shots above the shoulders or blatantly hitting a face. There were lots of bloody noses, but after knocking someone down, you'd bend over and pick them up.

ALEC PETERS: At Hardcore shows back then, there was sanctimony in the pit. You didn't fuck around, you didn't do the wrong thing. Those kids slamdanced, they did The H.B. Strut and all that shit. They had formalized methods of slamdancing, like they'd do the circle dance, and if a kid didn't know what he was doing, he could hurt someone or he could get hurt bad.

Boston was the birthplace of holier-than-thou Straight Edge enforcers. For the first time in Rock history, some asshole would come up and knock the beer out of your hand — that stupidity began in Boston Hardcore.

BRIAN BAKER (Minor Threat): You're right, Boston people who came to DC would knock drinks out of people's hands. They'd stepped up the militant non-drinking thing. They were way into the Straight Edge thing — they made that their flag.

AL BARILE: That's some folklore. There might be some truth — I don't remember targeting people drinking. During the course of a show maybe something like that happened, but I don't think it's as calculated as people say. It definitely happened, but we weren't fascistic truth-seekers.

But let's not get misty-eyed with Straight Edge nostalgia here — plenty of kids got totally wasted at these shows.

DEBBIE SOUTHWOOD-SMITH (The Channel): A lot of bands were doing coke in Boston then. I partied with those bands. I partied with The Misfits when they came to town; they were definitely not Straight Edge.

Of course, you've got to view Boston Hardcore in terms of its Yankee roots: that insular "liberal" Kennedy/Democrat heritage of academia, old money, and some of the most volatile race relations in American history.

"STRAIGHT EDGE" HANK PEIRCE: The Boston scene is pretty closed off and people are hesitant to welcome you in. You need to prove yourself, which is very much an East Coast thing. I'd met people who had similar backgrounds: liberal parents, well-educated, and a lot of us had gone to private schools. Then you started meeting kids who were from the working class suburbs of Boston. It was interesting to see what attracted them to it. For most of us, we were outsiders — that's why we came to Hardcore.

Why were the Boston Hardcore kids so militant? Why did some embrace Right-Wing politics? Why did many move on to conservative forms like Heavy Metal?

TAD KEPLEY (Anarchist activist): If there was such a thing as Right-Wing Hardcore, or more conservative Hardcore, it came from Boston. I loved The FU's but their politics could be called reactionary. I never went for that Boston Straight Edge stuff, and they all showed their true colors by what they did later on — DYS and SSD more or less went Metal. The kids in the Boston scene weren't particularly cool.

IAN MACKAYE (Minor Threat): Al Barile once said 'You say you care about the kids. Let me ask you this: how come you don't give 'em pictures with your name on it? Cheap Trick throws out pictures with their names.' He was dead serious. That explained a lot to me about the Boston scene.

Al Barile rocks out, Boston, 1983
Photo by Phil N Phlash
Courtesy of Taang! Records

> *No, you won't tell me what to think*
> *No, you won't tell me what to do*
> *Government, religion, drugs*
> *— Negative FX, "Mind Control"*

SS Decontrol's music and message unrelentingly avowed Straight Edge and Hardcore militancy. It paralleled martial music in some ways. Fiery songs such as "Get It Away" — as in "Get your drugs away from me!" — and "Headed Straight" displayed strong soldiery underpinnings.

"STRAIGHT EDGE" HANK PEIRCE: The Straight Edge chant, which was recorded on a Slapshot album, Choke wrote for a show in New York when SSD and Minor Threat played together. Ian said, 'Those guys in Boston take Straight Edge way too far. They're militant about it,' and Choke was like, 'Yeah, I'm militant about it.' Choke wrote a military marching thing which they did at Irving Plaza before SSD played. Then, everyone there from Boston charged off the stage and squashed everyone in the crowd.

History often overlooks SSD because it was always a secondary pursuit for Al. In the end Barile, as committed as he was to HC, committed more to his day job for GE Aircraft Engines in Lynn (where he still works).

AL BARILE: Bands like MDC, Circle Jerks, Black Flag, Dead Kennedys, worked their asses off. Not that I'm saying we were of their stature, but we didn't tour the country. We didn't try to sell records — I'd press 3000, then it wasn't available anymore. The second record, I only pressed 4000. It wasn't like we tried to be popular. But when we did play, we tried to make it a big event. We made one trip to the West Coast — it was a typical Al crazy trip: drove non-stop to the West Coast, didn't play anywhere in-between — totally stupid. We hung out for a week and played seven or eight shows in California with GBH and Kraut, then drove straight home ... our one and only tour. We played DC four or five times, NY eight or ten times, Detroit once, Philly three times, Canada once; that was it. Then we flew to California twice and played two shows. Black Flag touched every small town, I see how they were influential. We just never worked it that hard.

DYS borrowed their name from the Massachusetts Department Of Youth Services, the state bureaucracy in charge of juvenile lockups. In the early 80s, high-profile media reports exposed the Boston facility for wretched conditions: girls entering the system got raped, guys got killed. Naming a Hardcore group after such a phenomenon made sense. Many called DYS obnoxious Straight Edge jocks — which is probably true.

Negative FX, Boston, 1982
Courtesy of Taang! Records

SHRED: DYS instilled fear into people. They had leadership quality. People listened to what they had to say. DYS was a very important band.

Jon Anastas and Dave Smalley were smart-ass college kids who met in '81 while working at Newbury Comics; back then a little dump selling New Wave import singles and comic books. The lineup on the first DYS LP, *Brotherhood* (X-Claim!, '83) — vocalist Smalley, bassist Anastas, guitarist Andy Strahan, drummer Dave Collins — quickly became an essential scene element. For a moment, these guys really had it going on.

DAVE SMALLEY: The best thing about DYS is it started out as a lie. Newbury Comics had a little bulletin board, and on it, it said: 'Drummer with full equipment and bass player with full equipment looking to start a Punk band, need singer and guitar player.' So I called up and said, 'Yeah, I've got my own mic.' Of course, I didn't. So we all got together and it was awful. We sucked so bad — everybody was terrible at their instruments.

Hüsker Dü were in Boston for a few days while DYS was recording their LP at Radiobeat Studios, so they sang a few lines on "Wolfpack" — a DYS standard. Unlike Springa of SSD, Smalley (who'd performed in high school plays) could actually sing.

DAVE SMALLEY: I don't want to be like Paul Weller and spit on my past. Weller was at his best in The Jam — in his interviews, he talks down on it. Having said that, DYS was not a great band. We were four little kids. It was our first real band that played shows. We fought all the time and by the end we were playing Metal. I don't think we were the best band — but the reason we were 'legendary' is because we were very true to our value system — one of the first bands to articulate that. Minor Threat had the song 'Straight Edge' but DYS and SSD lived it and said 'Fuck you!' to anyone who didn't believe in our system. Whether that's fascistic is a debatable.

Last Rites, 1983
Photo bt Edward K. Casey
Courtesy of Taang! Records

NEGATIVE FX, though mythical in Boston Hardcore lore, played less than a half-dozen shows. Frontman Jack "Choke" Kelly could be even more of a Straight Edge zealot than Al Barile. Choke was the kind of prick who'd eat steak and then preach about the evils of red meat. If a fucked-up gang-mentality incident hit a show, you could bet the Skinheaded Choke was in the middle. But nonetheless '82's *Negative FX* album was damn impressive.
LAST RITES was Choke's next group in '83. They played one show, and put out a posthumous 7" in '84, infamous for its very-matter-of-fact Adolf Hitler cover art. In '86, he returned with Slapshot, the most ardent Straight Edgers of the late 80s (if not of all

time). **The rise of Slapshot paralleled the rise of hordes of fascist Skinheads within the Boston scene.**

MIKE GITTER: That last Negative FX show was all of two or three songs, maybe three minutes long. The show was held in this ballroom and I don't think they ever had a Hardcore show there before. Security jumped up and started getting real heavy, so Choke said, 'Fuck this.' There were cymbals flying, it was great. It's was fast, chaotic and over. It was a cool way to go out. I remember being young and thinking, 'This is potentially violent —' Last Rites was like that, too. They practiced for ten or eleven months and played one show with Deep Wound. It was short, sweet and over. It's funny, a lot of Boston bands did not play consecutive shows — they'd play a few shows and call it a day. I think the Last Rites tape is one of the best.

GANG GREEN were big in the Boston scene, but they were definitely not Straight Edge. They began in '80 with guitarist/vocalist Chris Doherty, a 15-year-old brat from Braintree who delivered pizzas on his skateboard and played Ramones covers in his basement. Springa from SSD was one of their first fans. From their earliest days, Doherty and his revolving pack drank tons of beer and did stupid amounts of blow. With their Metal riffs and party-hearty lyrics, Gang Green were quite entertaining for a while.

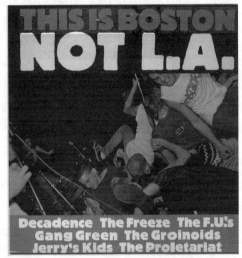

MIKE GITTER: Gang Green weren't Hardcore. They were fun-lovin' Metal guys — conservative, Ozzy-loving, beer-swilling, slightly-offensive Rock guys. If the Boston bands lacked a sense of social commitment, Gang Green never even considered it.

Gang Green first recorded for the *This Is Boston Not LA* ('81) and *Unsafe At Any Speed* ('82) comps on Newbury Comics label Modern Method. Local kids would bitch and moan about *This Is Boston...* as a blatant stab at exploitation. Ironically, such debate inspired many to do it themselves.

This Is Boston Not LA,
Boston HC compilation,
Modern Method, 1981
Collection of the author

CHRIS DOHERTY: There weren't many bands around doing what we were, so it wasn't like they had to weed out bands for the compilation. Why do you think Gang Green have so many songs on that album? That record did well. I wonder where all the money went?

Gang Green first broke up after '83's "Sold Out" 7" — the first release on prolific Taang! Records. Doherty joined Jerry's Kids for eight months, played with the Stranglehold three or four months, then did a short stint with Cheapskates (with future Mighty Mighty Bosstones members).

Gang Green re-emerged in '85 with a new lineup and new vigor, issuing "Alcohol," the ultimate anti-Straight Edge anthem: a high-speed AC/DC-style romp later covered by the likes of Metallica and Meatmen.

JERRY'S KIDS, named for the beneficiaries of the Jerry Lewis telethon, featured guitarist Bob Censi, one of the cooler guys on the scene. Jerry's Kids, like Gang Green (with whom they shared members over the era), had cuts on *This Is Boston Not LA* and *Unsafe At Any Speed*. Right after *This Is Boston...*, 15-year-old vocalist Bryan Jones broke his leg in an onstage scrum — so his parents made him

Jerry's Kids, CBGB, NYC, 1983
Photo by Karen O'Sullivan

quit. Older brother and bassist Rick Jones took over vocal duties for the recording of *Is This My World* (X-Claim!), with Chris Doherty guesting on second guitar.

THE FU'S, working-class kids from Dorchester, made rude records like '82's *Kill For Christ* EP (X-Claim! #2) and '83's *My America* (X-Claim! #5). Drummer Bob Furapples wrote most of the songs. I booked The FU's — with Channel 3 at DC's Space II Arcade — after *My America* came out; guitarist Steve Grimes and singer John "Sox" Stockings were cool guys, and their live set kicked ass.

The FU's so-called flag-waving album *My America* ignited serious underground debate in '83. Zines like *Maximum RockNRoll* predictably blasted the group as fascists but The FU's were just being contrarian. People took it the wrong way — which is kinda what they wanted.

> Take it or leave it
> Buy it or fly it
> Love it or leave it
> Like it or lump it
> — The FU's, "My America"

In '85, The FU's decided to "get serious" about a Rock career. Changing the name to Straw Dogs, they expanded their sound and signed to Restless/ Enigma — which is why you never heard more from them.

THE FREEZE weren't taken very seriously, probably because they were townies from Cape Cod. "I Hate Tourists," off their 1980 7", was their big Punk statement. The Freeze and their friends weren't old enough to drive to Boston, so singer Cliff Hangar set up all-ages gigs at The Mill Hill Club in Yarmouth and the Compass Lounge in Orleans, where a few Boston HC outfits played with The Freeze. Recordings such as '82's *Guilty Face* EP and '83's *Land Of The Lost* LP (both on Modern Method) generated a buzz — off which they did a few well-received national tours.

The FUs, Boston, 1982
Photo by Drew Stone

SHRED: The Freeze weren't given credit for anything but there's a lot of bands these days that owe so much to The Freeze. They had their own melodic style that draws more from Punk Rock than Hardcore. The Freeze were a total drug band. They never fit into Straight Edge.

ALEC PETERS: Cliff Hangar from The Freeze's a real character. He's a crank dealer who's known to stay up a week at a time. He supports himself by being a professional shoplifter, stealing CDs from Strawberry's. He made huge contributions to the scene.

THE PROLETARIAT played vicious HC fused with a jagged Gang Of Four/Killing

Joke edge. Frontman Richard Brown wrote poetically oblique lyrics with a distinct Marxist bent — part Burroughs, part Mao. *Soma Holiday*, their '83 LP, was way ahead of its time. But as soon as they built some momentum, Brown quit, and The Proletariat fell apart in '84 — though they limped on for awhile without him.

SHRED: The Proletariat were a Hardcore band that had a backbeat you could dance to, the most slam-danceable — they had that serious marching beat down. They were given the Hardcore tag because they wrote short songs and kinda fit in.

THE LOUD ONES was a notorious local outfit that featured prominent South Shore skaters Fred Smith and Sean McLain. They never made a record but their gigs were incredible spectacles, where skaters would "go off" onstage, and pull rad moves off the P.A. **THE GROINOIDS** — heard on *This Is Boston, Not LA* — would re-form as Kilslug, one of the sickest outfits ever. DXA played a few shows, but were nothing to write home about. Ditto for **THE MIGHTY COS**; singer Drew Stone moved to NYC to front Antidote. **SORRY**'s '84 *Imaginary Friend* (Radiobeat) got good ink. **THE NOT** toured the US before most other local acts but no one took them seriously. Also in '84 came **IMPACT UNIT**, with young Dicky Barrett (later of The Mighty Mighty Bosstones) on vocals. FUs roadie Sam — the only Black kid in the entire Boston scene — played in that band.

Show flyer for The Freeze and Jerry's Kids
Media Workshop, Boston, 1983
Collection of the author

> *Your right to freedom of expression*
> *Depends on what you have to say*
> — The Proletariat, "Purge"

Boston served as an epicenter of college radio. In the early 80s, WERS (Emerson), WMBR (MIT), WZBC (Boston College), and WMWM (Salem State U.) all supported Hardcore. For instance, WERS always had a show devoted to HC; Choke appeared a while when he was a Fine Arts major at Emerson. In 1984-85, Shred DJ'ed the half-hour-long "The Faster Than You Show," on WERS: the object was to play the fastest, shortest songs possible.

Quite a few college women populated Boston's scene, most functioning as DJs, photographers, or friends. Katie "The Cleaning Lady" Jacobs, whose flophouse hosted many touring outfits, and Angie Sciarappa, wife of SSD's Jaime Sciarappa, was a regular at shows, as was future TV starlet Christine McCarthy.

DEBBIE SOUTHWOOD-SMITH (The Channel): The strongest female presence in the Boston scene at that time was limited to like ten people. It was me, Sheena and Spencer — they were The Mystery Girls on WMBR — Katie The Cleaning Lady, Julie Farman. We all had some power, either had a zine, a radio show or booked a club. I feel we made a difference.

Boston was home to the nascent zine culture. In 1980 came a New Wave rag run by Newbury Comics called *Boston Rock*, as well as Michael Koenig's mag *Take It*, which introduced Hardcore to many, with flexidiscs of Angry Samoans and DKs.

FORCED EXPOSURE

NUMBER 3
$1.00

GANG
GREEN

Gang Green, cover of Boston's premiere
Hardcore zine, *Forced Exposure* #3, 1983
Collection of Sal Canzonieri

But Jimmy Johnson, with Katie "The Cleaning Lady," started the first exclusively Boston HC zine, *Forced Exposure*.

IAN MACKAYE (Minor Threat): When Minor Threat broke up for a six-month period, I went to Boston to see Government Issue play. Jimmy Johnson interviewed me for the first issue of *Forced Exposure*. I was definitely talking crazy shit. I was throwing down. When we played with Bad Brains in New York in May of '82, the Boston kids came down for the gig. I was goofing around onstage — Jimmy hated my guts for that because Boston guys were so mean and macho. *Forced Exposure* was the advent of the bitter old man magazines, like *Your Flesh*.

The impact of *Forced Exposure* launched a flood of other zines — among the best: Al Quint's *Suburban Punk* (later *Suburban Voice*); *Smash*, which covered HC from a Left-Wing angle; and Mike Gitter's *XXX*, which was crucial to mid-80s Hardcore/Metal fusion.

MIKE GITTER: There were the older Punk zines like *Take It*, where Byron Coley came from. There was *Boston Rock*. As the arty scene formed with bands like Mission Of Burma and labels like Propeller, you'd see mags go from *Take It*, which led to *Forced Exposure*, which led to *Suburban Voice*, which was called *Suburban Punk* for the first six or seven issues. *XXX* was totally *Suburban Voice*-inspired.

AL QUINT: I started out reviewing records and shows for *Concentration X*, a Xeroxed cut-and-paste local zine, which put out two issues. Then I started to jot down record reviews and live reviews and put out *Suburban Punk*. Four plain pages of one-column typewritten text with a scrawled logo across the top, no graphics. I gave it to my dad and he ran off 50 copies where he worked. I sold it for a quarter at shows, and the response was good. My first issues were incredibly primitive.

Fuck those rules
And show your might
— SS Decontrol, "Wasted Youth"

By '85, SSD, DYS and Gang Green had decided to go Metal, but none were very good at it — especially considering they grew up on that style. They went straight from solid Hardcore to quasi-Metal. The experiment failed — with disastrous results.

MIKE GITTER: Al Barile [of SSD] fucking worshipped Def Leppard. John Anastas of DYS wore Venom T-shirts to gigs. Twisted Sister or Girlschool would come to town, and those guys would be there to see it. SSD couldn't get away from Rock culture. I'm sorry, that's Joe Perry's guitar sound. The standard was Marshalls, not some beat-up Fender amps. It was total boys' club. My amp/dick is bigger than yours.

CHRIS DOHERTY: What I liked about Boston was that you could do what you wanted and like what you wanted — people didn't really give you a hard time about anything. If you were in a Hardcore band and listened to AC/DC, it wasn't a big deal. When I saw AC/DC, I said,

'Wow, that's the best Hardcore band I've ever seen!' And they were.

Escalating friction between Barile and Springa posed another problem for SSD. They always got in each other's faces, threatening each other. The rift grew out of Barile's frustration — Springa, an engaging frontman who could incite the crowd, couldn't sing a lick. Adding a hot second guitarist in François Levesque only exacerbated the problem, as heard on the slick, Metal-driven final two LP, '84's *How We Rock* and '85's *Break It Up*.

And of course the hypocrisy of Springa preaching Straight Edge while gettin' high worsened over time.

Zine ad for SSD *Get It Away*, 1983
Collection of the author

DAVE SMALLEY: Springa got abuse from a lot of people because he was loud, obnoxious, and always wanted to be the center of attention. But he was the singer for SS Decontrol and everybody knew him. The cool thing about Springa was that he was Punk Rock. I mean, Sid Vicious didn't win any popularity contests. But yeah, I heard that Springa used to smoke pot after practice. They practiced in Al's basement, and Springa would apparently go smoke pot in the yard while they were all downstairs.

AL BARILE: I can only speak for myself. I know what I am, but I never could answer for the other guys. I hope that shit wasn't happening. Those were *my* lyrics. Unfortunately Springa had to sing 'em. It's tough when you write songs and have another singer sing your ideas. The reason I wrote those lyrics was because his writing was embarrassing. It's really tough to find four or five people that have the same ideals. If you've found it, you better be happy — you've got something special. I said I was Straight Edge and those guys knew how I felt, but I never asked them, 'Are you getting high?' I wasn't their parent. You can't clone yourself.

Many maligned *How We Rock* and *Break It Up* as "bullshit AC/DC wank." The intense fallout had SSD breaking up within a year, officially splitting in '86 having done their last show April '85. But in truth SSD had stopped playing Hardcore. Ironically, most so-called Hardcore today incorporates the SSD-style two-guitar Metal "crunch" Barile and Levesque developed.

AL BARILE: We were well-liked on the West Coast, well-liked in New York and other East Coast meccas, but by the end they were spitting at us. Back in those years there were clear boundaries of what was Metal and what was Hardcore, there was no crossover. The only thing we were trying to do was to get better as a band. We weren't trying to be Metal and I don't think our records sound Metal. Clearly, we were on the downswing. Rather than be a hanger-on like Gang Green, we called it a day. I sold all my equipment and bought a jet-ski.

Even clumsier in their Metal transition, by the end DYS were actually writing power ballads. They'd discarded most of their old songs for a set that included "Everybody Wants Some" by Van Halen. In '85, on the verge of signing with Elektra, the new DYS broke up over the decision.

DAVE SMALLEY: The end of DYS was when we started playing Heavy Metal like The FU's and SSD. The reason the Boston kids starting playing that was because we got good enough at our instruments to do it. It was, 'Oh my god, I know how to play a lead — I can write a song with a bridge and two choruses.' It was getting pretty Rock but I was still a Punk. Elektra wanted to sign us but they said, 'You have to make the decision whether you're going to be Punks or Rockers.' All the other guys were like, 'Yeah, let's sign!' — but I didn't want to be that. I graduated college and headed back to Virginia. That was the end of it.

I'm desperate let me out
I'm desperate get me out
— Jerry's Kids, "Desperate"

Many people still talk about Jerry's Kids' "final" show at The Paradise in 1984. Springa jumped onstage and said in his thick Boston accent, "This is the end of Hardcore. We started it and we're ending it here today." It sounds cliché but it's true: it was the end of an era. (Jerry's Kids reformed in '89, and many times thereafter; drummer Brian Betzger went on to join Chris Doherty in the reformed Gang Green. As of this writing, Rick Jones works as a medical X-ray technician).

MIKE GITTER: The last true Boston Hardcore show was in the winter of '84 with Jerry's Kids, The FU's, DYS, Terminally Ill — half of which became Slapshot a few years later — and Post Mortem. There was a fuckin' blizzard out; it was cold as hell. I remember all those bands playing as Hardcore bands for the last time. The FU's became Straw Dogs, added a second guitar player, Steve Martin, and went bad Rock. It was the last show of those bands remaining true to what they were. They all changed their sound after that. It was totally over.

The ensuing years saw the rise of Alternative Rock with Volcano Suns, Salem 66, and Christmas. Though smug and dull, those acts came off no worse than what the Hardcore bands had turned into.

Gang Green winning the WBCN "Rock & Roll Rumble" in 1986 drove the proverbial final nail into the coffin of Boston Hardcore. The entrenched Rock scene which dominated The Rumble completely dismissed Hardcore. The Rumble's big success story was future MTV poodleheads Extreme. When Gang Green won The Rumble, HC had finally become socially acceptable.

Jerry's Kids set list,
"Final" show, Boston, 1984
Collection of Laura Albert

ALEC PETERS: Gang Green got to The Rumble because they had good songs and rocked the fuck out. It was a total rush. Three hundred people standing on their chairs going mental — it was awesome, the biggest rush I ever got from doing Rock & Roll. They won, got a whole pile of money and did nothing but coke every day after that.

BRIAN BETZGER (Gang Green, Jerry's Kids): There are kids today who call us from the old Hardcore days sellouts and whatnot. The only way kids'll really find out is when they grow up and see that things in life have to change. Face it, you can't be in a Hardcore band all your life. People involved in the scene have a real life, a real job. You can't do both. •

NEW YORK THRASH

We're gonna say it loud
We're gonna live it fast
Let's try it my way
— Stimulators, "Loud Fast Rules!"

As a suburban cultural movement, the antithesis of the urbane, Hardcore reacted to the pretension that is New York. And just as New York differs from any other place in America, NYHC differs from all other regional experiences.

JACK RABID (editor, *The Big Takeover*): New York was different from LA and other places because the classic Hardcore convention of being from the suburbs wasn't true here. It was a bunch of poor kids: bands from Queens like Reagan Youth from Rego Park, Kraut from Astoria. Beastie Boys came from a lot of money; it's so funny to see them always portrayed as Street Punks. But I think we in New York were authentic.

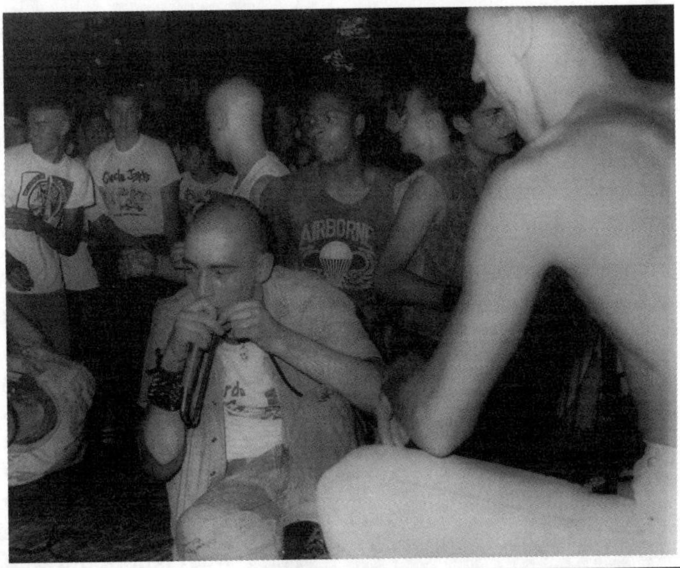

JESSE MALIN (Heart Attack): New York had a much more urban, dirty vibe to it, more connected to Punk. Being In New York, I don't think we could ever escape the Ramones or Johnny Thunders. When Hardcore went through Heavy Metal Queens, you could definitely hear Black Sabbath in the guitar sound.

Jimmy Gestapo (Murphy's Law), CBGB, NYC, 1983
Photo by Karen O'Sullivan

NYHC saw two distinct eras. In '81, Punk's possibilities empowered a small free-for-all of open-minded bad kids. Bands like Kraut, Reagan Youth and Heart Attack, compared with those elsewhere, were not particularly impressive. In the more violent second period, which began by 1985, participants more likely embraced seemingly Right-Wing philosophies — overrun with Skinhead gangs and Straight Edge zealots. People now hail "classic NYHC" — Cro-Mags, Murphy's Law, Agnostic Front, Youth Of Today — all from that second wave.

Hardcore developed at a slower pace in New York than in other cities. In fact, DC and Boston scenesters were into West Coast-style slamdancing and stagediving at least a year before those behaviors hit NY.

JOHN JOSEPH (Cro-Mags): When I was a DC kid, we'd get in the fucking cars, go to New York, and wreak havoc. In New York, people didn't even know how to stagedive. There was only like two people slamdancing in the audience, then there was us. When we stagedived, it was on top of people who didn't know anything about the scene — they didn't know what the fuck to expect. Everyone in the crowd was standing back watching us do what we were doing out on the floor. I mean, people were still pogoing in New York when we came up.

ADAM YAUCH (Beastie Boys): Ian MacKaye always talks about the huge tension between NY and DC — he was always on the verge of fighting with everybody. It's weird, because somehow I missed that. I remember when Black Flag played New York — before Henry joined — all the DC kids came up because it was the first time Black Flag played here. That was the first time I ever saw kids stagedive and really slam. Before that we'd pogo, and then the DC kids came up and would be jumping off the balcony.

A few outfits stretched parameters but weren't playing what would be Hardcore. Such "transitional" bands included The Stimulators, The Mad, The Fast, The Whorelords, The Blessed and Th' Influence, a Black Punk act predating Bad Brains. These played Max's Kansas City and CBGB. CBs drew that low-rent Ramones-type crowd; Max's, with its history of Andy Warhol Factory characters, was a seedy cabaret with a restaurant downstairs.

HARLEY FLANAGAN (Stimulators, Cro-Mags): I was hanging out in Max's back when it was a Hell's Angels hangout; there were very few Punk Rockers. New York Dolls played regularly; I used to see Deborah Harry working as a waitress when I was ten years old! I caught all the historic stuff. My mother was as down with the Dolls and The Velvet Underground as I was with Hardcore. I come from a long line of Rock & Roll people — a

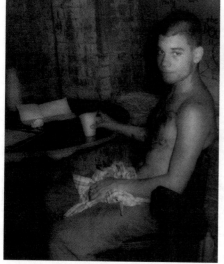

Harley Flanagan (Stimulators, Cro-Mags), NYC, 1982
Photo by Karen O'Sullivan

family of freaks. I was fortunate to witness it all from the beginning.

BOBBY STEELE (Misfits, Undead): I don't think I ever bought a drink back then. You'd hang out at the bar; when somebody would put down their drink and look away, you'd take their drink and move on to the next person. You could get away with that back then. People were at a Punk club and expected people to act like Punks. I got arrested for slashing this guy at Max's — the first thing the judge asked the prosecutor was 'Where did this happen?' The prosecutor said, 'Max's Kansas City,' and the judge said, 'What do you expect?' He wanted to dismiss it right there.

At a 1980 STIMULATORS gig, maybe 30 kids would show. But that was the roots of New York Hardcore — most of those kids started bands. Although the Stims' music predated HC, their shows served as a meeting ground because they were the only good young Punk group around.

JACK RABID: I don't think I gave it much thought; I just immediately understood the appeal of a local scene — the idea of being like a select club that met on a regular basis where you all got to know the same people. I'm sure a lot of them were like me — they enjoyed the band and thought they were good, but mostly they were going because it was this club, where no one ever took membership and there was no barrier to entry. The fact of your being there meant you were accepted.

JERRY WILLIAMS (producer/soundman): Early in '81, Dave Parsons took me to Max's to see The Stimulators. Max's had tables all the way up to the stage — as soon as the curtain rose, the audience stormed the floor, threw aside the first 30 feet of tables and chairs, and trampled 'em. It was a melee, a total free-for-all. The Stimulators were real and had an earthy, up-to-date East Village image. Their music was Power Pop. They had the look, they had talent; they were important.

The Stimulators — drummer Harley Flanagan, vocalist Patrick Mack, guitarist Denise Mercedes and bassist Anne Gustavson — worked out of the same East Village apartment building that housed Richard Hell and Allen Ginsberg. That old chickenhawk Ginsberg became the mentor and patron of Flanagan, publishing and writing the introduction for a book of poetry by Harley . Eleven-year old Harley played drums in a seedy Punk group alongside decadent twenty-something types 'cause Denise Mercedes, The Stims' chief decision-maker, was his aunt. After the 1980 release of their first 7", "Loud Fast Rules" — not to be confused with their 1982 ROIR tape of the same name — Nick Marden came in to play bass.

JACK RABID: Nick Marden was the ringleader of our scene. He had the place where everyone met. If there wasn't a gig, everybody knew to hang out at Nick's, this unkempt tenement with records everywhere. He'd play us the new Albert Y Los Trios Paranoias or the Stranglers or Damned; that's was how we spent days in the city. Nick was heavy into Bad Brains straight away. We went the first time they came up here, at these stupid-ass gigs run by the Yippies at Studio 9, across the street from CBGB. I have to give him credit: he knew everything; he introduced me to so many obscure bands it's not funny. He had all the West Coast stuff. The first time I heard 'Dangerhouse Records' came from his lips, I'm convinced.

The Stimulators befriended Bad Brains and brought them to NYC — really lighting a fire under everyone's ass. Unfortunately, the universally immediate realization of Bad Brains as the wave of the future led to a rift between the two groups. The DC'ers became instant gods of the NY scene.

Loud Fast Rules
Stimulators, cassette, ROIR, 1981
Collection of the author

JERRY WILLIAMS: When Bad Brains came around, everybody's heads turned. They used to stay at Stimulators headquarters on East 12th Street. But a feud ensued — jealousies really exploded. I don't wanna get too deep into the intrigue, but Bad Brains, before they moved up to New York, stayed at a house with this big, kinda slow dude, Bob, who owned a lot of audio equipment. One day Bob disappeared, so the Brains took his equipment up to New York. Late that summer ['81] Bob showed up — somehow he started going out with Denise Mercedes. The next thing I knew, Bob, through The Stims' manager, asked for his equipment. Needless to say, a lot of the gear had disappeared en route to New York. There'd been jealousies before; this really poured oil on the fire. The bands didn't want to be identified with each other anymore. The Stims got uptight if any members of Bad Brains were around. The Stims accused Bad Brains of being rip-offs; the Bad Brains accused them of being homosexuals. All of a sudden, the singer's gayness became an issue. That was a real sour note in an otherwise great year for Hardcore music in New York.

JACK RABID: Bad Brains were so fucking hot, they instantly latched into The Mad and The Stimulators scene. Then The Stimulators went more Metal and got more cocksure as they were drawing big crowds and started thinking they were a big deal. They got pissed when their appeal waned. It's not as simple as saying Bad Brains came in and took over — it was that the pendulum had shifted naturally from the kind of music The Stimulators made towards the sort of music Bad Brains made. That, and the fact that Bad Brains had that attitude of inclusion, while The Stimulators were getting more distant and suspicious and paranoid. The crowd was changing — kids wanted to hear things fast and loud — the first sign that the Stims would be left behind. By '81 I could see their popularity declining. They couldn't figure out why kids didn't want the music they were playing. The singer died of AIDS in '83, long after nobody cared about them anymore.

Hardcore first hit New York in summer '81 and things started to change. DKs played at Bond's, and Circle Jerks and Misfits at Irving Plaza.

JIMMY GESTAPO (Murphy's Law): You're right — that was when it really evolved from Punk Rock. I went from pogoing to jumping off the stage and creepy crawling. Within three years, all hell broke loose. I was jumping off of P.A.s, smoking dust, taking acid — I was out of my fucking mind and letting loose, with no inhibitions. I'm glad I survived it.

In 1981 and '82, New York University's radio station WNYU weekly aired *Noise The Show,* **a lifeline for the burgeoning New York Hardcore scene. Students Tim Sommers and Jack Rabid spun the newest discs and gave info on upcoming gigs. Ed Bahlman at 99 Records supplied vinyl. At its height,** *Noise The Show* **inspired over 150 letters a week from turned-on kids. In summer '81, Sommers contributed the "New York Nooze" column to** *Trouser Press* **and** *Sounds* **— the first major press for NYHC (years later, Sommers was the A&R man who signed Hootie And The Blowfish).**

No more than a few hundred metro area kids were into Hardcore. For instance, the fall '81 Misfits/Heart Attack bill at The Ritz didn't close to sell out.

MICHAEL ALAGO (music biz exec): In those days — '80 to '83 — a place like The Ritz, with a capacity of 1500, didn't want to take chances with Hardcore because they didn't know how to handle the kids. It always ended in a bloody mess and everyone went home disappointed. That's why clubs like A7 came about. They were smaller, the people who ran 'em were more adventurous and besides, what kind of damage could really get done? They were just four walls where kids could go in and play.

Show flyer Bad Brains, NYC, 1982
Collection of the Laura Albert

> *I hate music*
> *You hate music*
> *We hate music*
> **— The Mad, "I Hate Music"**

The East Village and Lower East Side of the early 80s didn't resemble the twinkie tourist zone of today. Few White people ventured east of Second Avenue — it was just too fucking dangerous. Avenue B was an open drug mart and Tompkins Square Park (a.k.a. "Needle Park") was home turf to vicious, knife-wielding Puerto Rican gangs.

RAYBEEZ (Agnostic Front, Warzone): Some of the cops in the Ninth Precinct were cool. That precinct on 5th Street was really corrupt, they didn't give a shit about nothin'. We use to buy 'em beer. The Lower East Side was so fucked up — and no one gave a shit. Puerto

Rican gangs, hitmen on Avenue C — it was no joke. That Irish gang from Hell's Kitchen used to run down there once in a while. There were so much drugs the cops didn't wanna deal with it. I remember a few times robbin' stores or stealin' cars — they'd chase us, and when they'd catch us, they'd go, 'Get outta here.'

New York Hardcore made its spiritual home at A7, an East Village shithole at 7th Street and Avenue A. In total perhaps 200 square feet, the room had two small P.A. speakers hanging from a low ceiling above a small L-shaped stage maybe eight inches high and five feet deep, wedged into a corner. A few beat-up couches lined the wall opposite the stage. The bathrooms, with no locks on the doors, lay directly facing the entrance — so you'd catch someone squattin' on the pot several times a night. A7 shows were face-to-face situations. You'd consider the club packed if 75 people showed; it's insane how many people they'd cram in for the Bad Brains or Circle Jerks or Black Flag. On the best nights, Raybeez worked the door, Doug Holland bartended, and Jimmy Gestapo spun records.

Jack Rabid (*Noise The Show, The Big Takeover*)
Photo by Karen O'Sulivan

ROGER MIRET (Agnostic Front): You'd walk into A7; it was so tiny. All our friends would come and play. I remember getting my little brother Freddie in — he was seven years old. A7 was an after-hours club. No shows started till one or two in the morning and went right to six or seven. Back then the neighborhood was bad. I remember people trying to stab me. There were lots of gangs. It was a very Hispanic 'hood. I'm Hispanic, so I was the in-between man talking to these people.

PARRIS MITCHELL MAYHEW (Cro-Mags): There'd be ten bands a night for three bucks. There'd be a sheet of loose-leaf paper with the band names. You'd knock on the door and enter this little world where there was 70 or 100 kids. You'd go across the street; there'd be 150 kids hanging out in the park. It was so tight. You look at Avenue A now and see galleries and restaurants. The only thing on Avenue A back then was A7, the bodega and Ray's Pizza. Everything else was burnt out.

JESSE MALIN: A7 on a Friday or Saturday, they'd have the equipment built into the stage. If you were a band, you'd grab your guitars and put your name on the list. Bands would play until seven in the morning. I'd have to walk into the sunlight, and take two trains and a bus back home.

DREW STONE (Antidote): For a Hardcore band, playing A7 in '81 was like playing Madison Square Garden. If you played a good song, people'd yell for you to play it again. I remember playing one of our songs four times.

Up the street from A7 was The Park Inn, a seedy bar which like most places in town, turned a blind eye to underage drinking. It was a key NYHC meeting ground where everyone got loaded. The jukebox, the place's best feature, spewed Motown hits as well as Bad Brains' "Pay To Cum."

HARLEY FLANAGAN: It wasn't a club but was connected to the scene — a spot for the beer-drinkers where we got stupid drunk. You'd be drinking and some shit would go down and it was a matter of half a second before the entire bar turned upside down. Whoever started shit got pounded to a pulp by everybody in the bar. The neighborhood was very different back then, and the kids who migrated to hang out adapted that same tough ethic.

Jerry Williams ran another important NYHC spot: 171A, on Avenue A off 11th Street. Opened in fall 1980, in full swing by early '81, this recording studio/practice space/illegal club served everyone from Richard Hell to the upstart HC groups.

Black Flag, Circle Jerks, UXA, Angry Samoans, Canada's The Subhumans and many more jammed at 171A when coming through town; Bad Brains and Beastie Boys cut records there.

JERRY WILLIAMS: The spot was an abandoned glass store filled with raw wood and office furniture and panes of glass. It took months to throw everything out and build a stage. We moved there September 1980 and by November started having gigs. This was all totally illegal; the landlord had no idea what was going on. It all came to a head at the gala New Year's Eve party; the fire department closed us down. After that, I decided to carry on as a rehearsal studio and started doing 'showcases.' I figured if we just stayed on the first floor and didn't sell liquor, we could get away with it. We charged six to eight bucks per hour to practice. Musicians loved it — here was this large space with an actual concert-sized P.A.. The crowds weren't huge, but were very enthusiastic: you had to be brave to come to that neighborhood at night to see a gig. They numbered a hundred at most — but the hundred most committed Hardcore fans in existence!

Johnny Feedback (Kraut),
171A, NYC, 1983
Photo by Karen O'Sullivan

HARLEY FLANAGAN: 171A was very important. It was like a social club for bands; it was a studio; the Bad Brains lived there. I hung out there every day when I was playing hooky. Had it not been for that place, the Bad Brains wouldn't've had a way to exist in New York. They lived there pretty much for free. Back then, there was a support system built into the 'hood. We were all vegetarians — we knew people who worked at different health food stores; they'd sneak us food out the back. We were all hustlin', nobody had a job, nobody had a life but there was 171A. Everybody rehearsed there on weekends. There'd be shows there; sometimes Performance Art. They once showed the movie *Shellshock Rock*, about the Irish Punk Rock scene. When Rat Scabies was in town, I jammed at 171A with him. It was a place you could go work out your chops for little money. That's where Black Flag auditioned Henry for a week. Three or four blocks down you had A7.

JOHN JOSEPH: I lived in 171A, where all the bands used to come from out of town. Everybody played there. We had the upstairs apartments. Then there was a fire, which left just the downstairs. But that's where Henry Rollins auditioned for Black Flag, where the Bad Brains recorded the ROIR cassette; that place was historical. That was Jerry Williams' space — an important place for the Lower East Side, the whole New York music scene. Everybody rehearsed there — even bands that weren't Hardcore, like Konk. Every weekend was gigs. It was a great place to hang out, a great meeting place. The Beastie Boys hung out there in the early days. I was at the Beasties' first gig. They opened up for Bad Brains.

JIMMY GESTAPO: I loved 171A — they showed cool movies there, too. They showed *Shellshock Rock* and *Self Conscious Over You* and The Stimulators played in the middle of the two movies. One of the favorite songs of my whole life — the lyrics make me cry because they're about me — was In The Front Line by The Stimulators. Harley jumped over the drum kit without knocking over anything, grabbed the mic, and did the song. I think they charged three dollars to get in.

RAYBEEZ: 171A was our meeting point. That was our place to go, and the people that ran it were totally into what we were doing. Avenue A was where we met. When that was a studio, it was so cool. It's where I first met Dave Insurgent from Reagan Youth. He knew what was going on — he was a true Punk. Back then it was so true, so street. You'd get music from Rat Cage; you couldn't even imagine going to a Tower Records.

In the 171A basement, Dave Parsons opened his Rat Cage record store, then started his label Rat Cage Records, which put out some of the first NYHC records, like the first efforts by Beastie Boys (1982's *Polly Wog Stew* EP) and Agnostic Front (1983's *United Blood* EP).

JERRY WILLIAMS: Rat Cage was an esoteric record store dealing in imports and independent labels. Dave got so far into it, he developed his own label. Originally he put out *Mouth Of The Rat* fanzine; that went about to Issue 20, then it became a record store. 'Mouth of the Rat' is the literal English translation of his hometown's Spanish name: Boca Raton, Florida.

Flyer for Rat Cage, NYC, 1982
Collection of the author

JESSE MALIN: We'd all hang out at Rat Cage, Dave Parsons' store at 171A. You'd come in, play any record you'd want, and sit there all day and smoke pot. Nick Marden would sell buttons he made of all different bands. I remember always having a quart of beer in my hand. It was essential — until Straight Edge happened!

Aside from Bad Brains — from DC — no NYHC groups clicked nationally. There were a few early records but most of them were very good. The ROIR compilation cassette *New York Thrash* was a major landmark; but most of the bands on it were not very good. Another problem was that few kids in the NYHC scene had money — unlike their rich suburban counterparts from OC, DC or Boston.

JESSE MALIN: Even the shittiest bands from the West Coast would have records out for every move they made, full-length albums right away. For us to even get that single out was such a big deal. So a lot of New York bands went undocumented before it became too late. Like the Reagan Youth album should have come out years earlier. They put out a half-assed record past their prime, no representation of how great they were. The same with Heart Attack: we always waited too long to record and we didn't get to put out albums. We didn't have enough money to buy guitar strings and pay for the rehearsal, let alone pay to press records. We had to talk people into paying for it, and it took a while to find a sucker.

JACK RABID: None of us had money — we were all in a marginal urban scene; there were certainly no record labels interested. Not only was Punk dead, but this new quasi-Hardcore outbreak was even more threatening. It was hard to even get a booking, hard to get any respect. There wasn't much indie distribution, there weren't many indie labels, and those labels were certainly not interested in kids yelling and screaming, in a Punk movement that was supposedly dead five years ago.

JIMMY GESTAPO: We're the people that work in the factory. We're the people that work in a record store, that drive cabs, that are bouncers in clubs. We're the people that pay taxes. We're the people that get shit on the most. We're the people from middle-class families and see our parents get shit on. That's what New York Hardcore represents. We weren't rich kids. We were busy doing instead of documenting.

Many people in DC truly hated New York and NYHC. They frowned on the blue-collar vibe and the primitive sound — with that typical whitebread DC elitism and inferiority complex towards the Big Apple.

New York Thrash
NYHC compilation tape, ROIR, 1982
Collection of the author

JACK RABID: DC's scene was a little smarter than New York's scene. I think DC had their leaders in the Dischord people, and they set that tone. To use a highway analogy, the New York kids were always following the slowest car, while DC kids were following the fastest car.

JESSE MALIN: Unity was between suburban scenes that could relate, like Boston and DC. The early DC scene was generally more intelligent and richer and they didn't dig New York. It was too dirty and ugly and stupid to them. I think they were just intimidated by New York.

BILL DOLAN (NYHC scene): First time I saw Minor Threat, Ian came out and said, 'People say I've been talkin' shit about New York. Anyone who believes that, come up and take a swing at me,' pointing at his chin.

You gotta go backwards
To go onward
— Kraut, "Onward"

By summer 1982, a coherent New York scene started to coalesce.
THE UNDEAD, Bobby Steele's group after he left The Misfits, was one of the first high-profile NYHC outfits. A leather-jacket-clad loudmouth with a limp (from a foot deformity), Steele was a total character — and The Undead were excellent for a year or two. By the time of '82's *Nine Toes Later* EP, The Undead had grown as big if not bigger than The Misfits.

BOBBY STEELE (The Undead): The Undead started out as The Scabs. We'd done one or two shows before I joined The Misfits, and while I was in The Misfits we'd get together on Sunday afternoons when nothing else was going on — just hang out, get stoned and jam. When I got kicked out of The Misfits I got The Scabs back together but the drummer wasn't into it; he was into Heavy Metal. We got rid of him, picked up Patrick Blank, and changed the name. The first gig was January of '81 at A7.

DANNY SAGE (Heart Attack): The Undead — that lineup of Jack Natz, Patrick Blank, Bobby Steele — was amazing. By the time they made albums, they were a whole other thing.

For me Undead were over by '81. I wanted to be in The Undead, I used to call up Bobby all day, I still have a live tape of them that's so great. No one now knows how amazing they really were.

BOBBY STEELE: When the Hardcore scene was starting out and The Undead were the top band in New York, I was sticking up for little bands. If they got screwed over by a club, I would call and say, 'We're not showing up until Jesse [Malin] calls and says they got what was promised to them. Then we'll do the gig.' I tried to start a union. I wanted to see bands get treated fairly and get paid — that helped get me in bad with club owners. They didn't want bands to be sticking together and fighting for each other.

I was selling 'ludes to Keith Richards, John Cale — a lot of big names were coming to me. I was constantly fucked up. I was once so fucked up I got on the phone, called all these clubs in the Midwest, and booked a tour without realizing I'd done it. From just after I left The Misfits up 'til '83, I don't think there was a day I was straight. I was always into trouble — getting thrown out of clubs. They wouldn't let me in the Pep Lounge

Davy Gunner (Kraut)
Mudd Club, NYC, 1982
Photo by Fred Berger

when the Heartbreakers played because they didn't want any drug problems. Just before we'd go onstage I'd take a 'lude. Just about every show we did I was so fuckin' out of it. I remember The Mudd Club — you'd see some girl, grab her, go in the bathroom and fuck her. You wouldn't even ask her name.

Steele split for LA in '83, trying to reform The Undead with Olga of The Lewd and Robo from Black Flag — after Robo quit The Misfits — but things never panned out. Steele returned to NYC, reconstructing The Undead with his Jersey pals Brian Payne and Steve Zing. In early '84 they recorded the material which eventually became *Act Your Rage* — but by then, Steele's music had dated and they'd lost their Hardcore reputation.

BOBBY STEELE: The Hardcore crowd was getting into the political thing with MDC and Dead Kennedys. Since we weren't singing about politics we were no longer relevant. I just decided to drop out at that point. I was disgusted with the New York scene and I decided to move out to California and commit suicide. That was my initial goal.

KRAUT were the most recognized early NYHC outfit — especially after 1981's "Kill For Cash" 7" and their opening slot for The Clash at Bond's — came from Astoria, Queens, a blue-collar 'hood just across the East River from Manhattan. The NY scene's closest thing to a solid Rock group, Kraut cut the anthem "Onward" — something like a cranked-up version of Alice Cooper — for '83's fine *An Adjustment To Society*. Unfortunately Kraut's sound also dated quickly; after their weak '84 album *Whetting The Scythe*, they threw in the towel. In '85, guitarist Doug Holland joined Cro-Mags.

REAGAN YOUTH, led by Dave "Insurgent" Rubenstein of Rego Park, Queens, was the most intense outfit on the scene. The election of fascistic Ronald Reagan, spurred this fiercely anti-establishment outfit to action. The only problem was, you had to experience Reagan Youth live: their only disc, a seven-song 12" in '84, was too little, too late. Probably because they were so fucking scrungy, a lot of dirtbag "Peace Punks" into Brit Punk and anarchist-style politics took to them.

Dave Insurgent (Reagan Youth) singing
A7, NYC, 1983
Photo by Karen O'Sullivan

Reagan Youth carried on for eight years — through the entire Reagan era — after which a band so-named was no longer relevant. The late 80s and early 90s saw the depths of Dave's junkie hell, which hit rock bottom in 1993 when cops on Long Island found the body of his hooker girlfriend Tiffany decomposing in the back of serial killer Joel Rifkin's truck (Oddly, Harley and Dave both dated streetwalkers whom Rifkin murdered.). Then his mom died in a car wreck. A few months later, Dave took his own life.

NICKY GARRETT (UK Subs): Dave Insurgent was one of the great American Punks. Not only was Reagan Youth great, they really stood for something. In the days of Reagan, it was really important for there to be a band who expressed all the pain, anguish and alienation kids were feeling. You're writing a book on Hardcore; Dave Insurgent was one of the most important people of that scene. He and his music should not be forgotten.

HEART ATTACK were crucial to the NYHC outbreak. Started by frontman Jesse Malin in late '80 — right after his cover band Rocker won a Queens high school talent show — they auditioned at CBGB, made demos, and did a few gigs, like with The Mob at Max's. After experiencing the fury of the Bad Brains, Heart Attack sped up their sound. That's about the time they recorded their '81 *God Is Dead* 7" EP — most likely NYHC's first single (only 300 copies pressed).

Heart Attack's next records — '83's *Keep Your Distance* and '84's *Subliminal Seduction* (Rat Cage) — were recieved positively by kids around the country. They were also the first NYHC outfit to tour; an '84 trek saw them open for GBH in LA, to 4000 at the Olympic and 2000 at Perkins Palace. They played DC twice, at the 9:30 with Scream and Insurrection, and Space II Arcade with The FU's and CH3. Like Reagan Youth, kids called Heart Attack a "Peace Punk" band. In 1985, after a few dumb fights, they broke up. (Years later, Malin and guitarist Danny "Sage" Stuart would play in D Generation).

Jesse Malin (Heart Attack) singing
Rock Against Reagan, Central Park, NYC, 1983
Photo by Karen O'Sullivan

JESSE MALIN: When we ended Heart Attack, we felt everything was such a cliché and a formula — the whole scene was so predictable and so boring and so dead — all the initial bands had broken up. The end of Heart Attack was '84, I just didn't want to do that type of music anymore. The scene felt completely different, there just seemed to be no point in it.

THE MOB, in the Bad Brains vein — although not very good at it — played a lot of the first NYHC shows. Leader/guitarist Jack Flanagan ran their label, Mob Style Records, which put out one of the absolute best NYHC records, Urban Waste's *Big Deal* eight-song 7" EP of '83.

JERRY WILLIAMS: The Mob were the first pure New York Hardcore band that I remember. I did two EPs and an album with them. They liked me and were willing to pay me — and believe me, there wasn't a lot of money in working for Hardcore bands, especially in the beginning. I liked The Mob, but there were certainly better bands.

EVEN WORSE was started by "Noise The Show" hosts Pete "Jack Rabid" Corradi and Tim Sommers. They played 25 shows and released two 7"s — '82's "Mouse Or Rat" and '83's "Leaving" — during their active two-year history, but just were not significant. When frontman John Purdis quit — actually he just never showed up for a gig at the Tompkins Square Park bandshell — they picked out the coolest-looking kid in the crowd to sing — future Beastie Boys founding member John Berry. The ubiquitous Ken "Tantrum" Templeson replaced Berry on vocals, then Thurston Moore from Connecticut joined on second guitar. Jack went on to put out the legendary zine *The Big Takeover*, named for a Bad Brains song.

FALSE PROPHETS, a militant Left Wing troupe, did many early NYHC gigs. If you saw 'em, you'd never forget their crusty squatter frontman Stephan Ielpi for his Hitler moustache, long dirty fingernails, and shrill "Fuck the system" stage rants. False Prophets had their fans — such as Jello Biafra, who brought them to Alternative Tentacles — but were not very good.

Jesse Malin (Heart Attack) singing
CBGB, NYC, 1984
Photo by Karen O'Sullivan

JIM FOSTER (Adrenalin OD): When they came onstage, people would be like, 'Let's go out and get a beer at a bodega' to avoid all the preaching. I remember the Vancouver Five benefit for the guy from the Subhumans — Stephan from the False Prophets goes, 'After all, all he did was bomb this structure' and I thought that was so vague and stupid.

THE MISGUIDED, another musically-challenged NYHC outfit, was the brainchild of drummer Lyle Hysen, an NYU student from tony Great Neck. Hysen's claim to fame is that he brought fellow NYU kid Rick Rubin to the scene. The Misguided's brawny frontman John Rizzo couldn't hit a note if you paid him. What I most remember of their set opening for UK Subs at CBs was the worst-ever rendition of Sham 69's "Borstal Breakout." Hysen also put out *Damaged Goods* fanzine, and issued a Heart Attack 7" on his Damaged Goods imprint. One show was the *Damaged Goods* benefit at 171A with Heart Attack, The Mob, False Prophets and Th' Influence in '81. Lyle and Misguided guitarist Alex Tutino went on to form SST Records' proto-Grunge act Das Damen.

DANNY SAGE: I was friends with The Misguided, and honestly, no one really liked them. You'd go to their gigs, and it was a really bad scene. There's nothing else to say about them.

BEASTIE BOYS arrived early on the scene. Unlike the multi-Platinum act they became, the original brat pack was a second-rate Hardcore group no one took seriously. Only later — applying HC attitude to Hip Hop — did they make a splash.

The Beasties arose from The Young Aborigines, a PiL/Siouxsie-style outfit with Mike Diamond and Kate Schellenbach on drums, John Berry on guitar and Jeremy Shatton on bass, plus various singers. Adam Yauch hung out at rehearsals, sometimes jamming with them afterwards.

Mike D (singing) and John Berry
Beastie Boys, A7, NYC, 1982
Photo by Karen O'Sullivan

ADAM YAUCH: I wanted to start a Hardcore band but Hardcore hadn't really come to New York. We knew there was Hardcore in DC — we thought, 'Let's start a New York Hardcore band.' So we tried to write some faster Punk songs. It was kind of a goof but then we talked Mike into singing and Kate into playing drums. We played on my 17th birthday. Dave Parsons saw us play and said, 'You guys have got to make a record for my label.' So we went into the studio [171A] with Scott Jarvis, recorded those songs, then the band broke up. The record came out and kids were actually listening to it. We got offers to do shows so we got back together and figured out how to play the songs again. We did some shows and became a band. Before the record came out, we did one show at A7 and one at The Playroom opening for Even Worse. H.R. was at that show and he really liked us and asked us to open for them at Max's. It all went from there.

Yauch, the coolest Beastie, was a longhaired skater down with the small but dedicated skate scene hanging out in the West Village. He was also the world's biggest fan of local New Wave act The Speedies and their "Let Me Take Your Photo" 7".

SEAN TAGGART (artist): I liked Adam a lot. The others were complete spoiled bastards. I hated the whole crew. They were these effete little shits — a very snotty, elitist bunch … the ultimate wise-asses.

Future Beastie Adam Horovitz (son of playwright Israel Horovitz), came out of THE YOUNG AND THE USELESS, who'd play HC versions of "Grease" and "Billy, Don't Be A Hero." I saw them open for Fear at the Mudd Club in '82, and they were fucking awful. When I was booking shows in DC, PiL's manager called me on a few occasions, trying to con me into booking The Young And The Useless for $1000 — a total joke.

The Beasties' debut *Polly Wog Stew* 7" EP (Rat Cage, '82) with "Egg Raid On Mojo," didn't impress. But no one had ever heard anything like the subsequent 12", "Cookie Puss"/"Beastie Revolution" (Rat Cage, '83) — the first White attempt at Uptown Hip Hop. On the A-side, the Beasties placed a crank call to a Carvel ice cream shop (makers of "Cookie Puss" cakes) over primitive beats and scratches; the B-side was a cheeky stab at Bad Brains-style Dub.

There'd be no Beastie Boys as we know them today had not Rick Rubin stepped in — first as their DJ, then as their producer/boss at Def Jam Records. A chubby NYU student from Long Island wearing tight leather pants and bullet belts, Rick was quick to throw dad's money around. His first Rock Biz foray — an uptown/downtown fusion gig with Heart Attack, Liquid Liquid and Treacherous Three at the Hotel Diplomat — was a total flop. Before he got involved with the Beasties,

Show flyer, Beastie Boys, TR3, NYC, 1981
Collection of the author

Rubin played in THE PRICKS and in HOSE — a funny
Flipper-style act who'd do ultra-slow versions of Rick
James' "Superfreak" and Black Sabbath's "Sweet Leaf" —

Rubin and Run DMC manager Russell Simmons
became partners, working out a deal for Def Jam with
Columbia. The Beasties' Rubin-produced *Licensed To Ill*
became the surprise mega-hit of 1986. Of course Rick
signed the 20-year-olds to a dick-'em-down deal — and
they got the shaft.

Yauch also played in Brooklyn, a short-lived '87
project with Bad Brains' Darryl Jennifer, Murphy's Law
drummer Doug E. Beans, and guitarist Tom Cushman.
That made news: both Beastie Boys and Bad Brains had
just released big albums — *Licensed To Ill* and *I Against I.*
The Brooklyn demo tape was good but the Beasties
obviously took priority.

HOLY THURS
SAMPSON
EGG RAID
BUCKET OF CH.
NEW SONG
HOLY SNAP.
CHEESE + TRIM
FUN + BURGER
SUBCULTURE
JOKE

Beastie Boys setlist, A7, 1982
Collection of Laura Albert

ADAM YAUCH: In '87 after finishing the *Licensed To Ill* tour,
we were fed up with everything, with each other, with Def Jam. I
always looked up to Darryl as my idol, the greatest bass player in the world. It seemed like a
great idea to form a band. Darryl felt strongly they should be recorded in a good studio. We
spent the little money I had from touring, twenty grand or something, thinking I was going
to get repaid from Def Jam shortly. The tape came, recorded tight and clean, sounding stupid
because I can't sing. I sent it to a few labels but I'm glad it never came out. Then Def Jam
didn't pay us. Russell [Simmons] put pressure on us to go back in the studio with Rick. I
didn't want to go in the fuckin' studio with Rick. I thought he ripped us off and I didn't get
along with him that well.

The Beasties Boys proceeded to fame and fortune. In some ways, they
transcended the Rock Star establishment; in other ways, they were totally
business-as-usual. The more things change, the more they stay the same.

ISM — another humorous NYHC act in the same vein as the Beasties — was
started by Joe "Jism" Ismach of Bayside, Queens — a classically trained pianist
and Julliard student. Ism (the first letters of Ismach) began in 1981 as Elvis
Costello-style New Wavers; Joey sang and played Farfisa organ. But when HC hit,
friend/manager Bob Sallese showed Joey a new direction. The group fused upbeat
assault and Partridge Family shlock.

Though not East Village regulars —
they were a "studio Hardcore band" —
Ism loomed large in the Metro Area.
WLIR, Long Island's major New Wave
station, gave rotation in '82 to both
"John Hinckley" and their "I Think I
Love You" cover, and Ism headlined
over The Stimulators at My Father's
Place in Long Island. "A7," the B-side
of "I Think I Love You," was actually
quite funny. But as a joke band, the
joke was eventually on them.

JISM (Ism): Everything we did was a
gimmick. Most of the ideas came late at
night when we were very drunk. To tell you

Brooklyn demo, short-lived project with
Adam Yauch (Beastie Boys) and Darryl Jenifer (Bad Brains)
Collection of the author

PUBLICITY

Press Release No. 1

Dateline: Manhattan (the most dangerous island
in the world!)

Here it is! The new Def-Jam release: "Mobo", "Girls" and
"Going to the Zoo" by everyone's faves, HOSE. HOSE is a hot
four-human combo featuring Michael Espindle (vcls), Rick
"wrong speed" Rubin (gtr), Autumn Goft (drms) and Warren Bell
(bs). Rising out of the ashes of hardcore godfathers THE
PRICKS, HOSE have been giging continuously for years. The
world can't get enough of their tightly arranged mood/concept
pieces. Three of the most exemplary tunes are revealed
here in vinyl for the first time. "Girls" is a punk anthem
that has almost single-handedly spurred the current O1
revival in this country. "Mobo" is an elusive concept piece
about a chic French disco, and "Going to the Zoo" is a fine
example of drawing on past experiences for inspiration. All
are suitable for play on airwave transmissions as well as at
social functions. We had a lot of fun recording this record
but due to the unique etching that is the label it was a real
bitch getting it pressed up. A short tour of the more
susceptible parts of the country is on the planning table,
as well as a massive tour of Japan. So be on the lookout
for HOSE gigs near you.

Tell all your loved ones!

HOSE / DEF-JAM RECORDINGS

99 Records, 99 MacDougal Street,
New York City, New York, U.S.A. 10012
(212) 777-4610

The first Def Jam Records press release
for Hose "Mobo" single, 1983
Collection of the author

the truth, I took Ism as far as it could go. Musically what else could you do? I got bored with it. Maybe that's how everybody else felt, I don't know.

THE NIHILISTICS, scowling, menacing Skinhead-types from the blight of Long Island's sprawling suburbs, drew a violent crowd. In some respects they were more intense than many of the city bands. They hated the burbs, making them in that regard the ultimate Hardcore outfit. The virulent machismo of latter-day NYHC first surfaced in physical frontman Ron Rancid. Their self-titled LP of '83 was chock fulla hate, but in the end they never got their just due.

We're gonna have to fight
To prove that we're right
— Murphy's Law, "Skinhead Rebel"

By '84 New York Hardcore changed, shifting from a somewhat Left-Wing scene to a violent Skinhead stance led by Cro-Mags, Murphy's Law, Agnostic Front, and Cause For Alarm. Slick promoter Chris Williamson arrived to book huge shows at Rock Hotel on Jane Street and at The Ritz on East 11th Street. It was as if all the smart people were being driven out — definitely ending the first wave. Most remember NYHC for Skinheads, a product of the second wave. You'd hear insane stories of crazy retribution runs, attacks on kids — not a whole lot of fun.

SEAN TAGGART: One guy who's the key to the whole swing to the Right in New York Hardcore, Paul Dordal — an incredibly charismatic guy, pretty bright and totally crazy. Paul

Hanging out — Steve Poss (left) and Paul Dordal, NYC, 1982
Photo by Karen O'Sullivan

dropped out of high school, went to California, hung out at the Black Flag church, was there when Henry joined. He did the whole LA Hardcore thing and came back as a Skinhead, before Skinheads were this regimented neo-nazi thing. He showed up at my high school, I guess '81 — he had these big boots spray- painted black, bandanna around the knee, and said, 'This is what real Punk is about, everyone else is a poser. Anyone with a leather jacket and funny-colored hair is a circus clown.' He tried to get a band together with Harley; it didn't work out. He wrote the Murphy's Law song 'California Pipeline.' He was the first Punk to say, 'What's wrong with being a Republican?' He was very influential.

He was good friends with Harley, they went out and committed crimes together. There was a weird conservative slant all of a sudden, not a big shocker as you had all these conservative Catholic guys from Queens. Paul argued with girls that abortion was immoral; meanwhile, he was fucking every one of them, and I'm sure he wasn't using a rubber.

RAYBEEZ: Harley was the first NYC Skin I know of, the little Charles Manson of New York at like ten years old. Then came Jimmy Gestapo, James Contra, and others, but everyone was Punk, too — we didn't just shave our heads one day and say, 'We're Skinheads.' We got into the movement, not the fashion. Me and Vinnie Stigma used to have mohawks, then shaved our heads at the same time. Gradually we all turned into Skinheads.

HARLEY FLANAGAN: The Lower East Side was different. In front of Trash And Vaudeville on St. Mark's Place's was where the scene used to hang out 'cause all them White kids didn't wanna go to Avenue A. The cops would keep chasing us down the block over the years until there was nowhere to go except to Tompkins Square Park. There'd be fights there all the time — the neighborhood Spanish kids would be like, 'What the fuck's up with all these White boys coming in the neighborhood?' All my buddies from the scene back then all had the good fortune of being able to go home at the end of the night after we'd have fights with the neighborhood gangs. I'd still have to go to school and deal with these same motherfuckers the next day. The scene for some people was just a place to come and hang out. For me, it was a place I had to fight for and catch a lot of beatings for. It's part of the reason my reputation escalated to such an out-of-proportion level over the years. There'd be a lot of true stories and then a lot of exaggerations and false stories that'd arise out of that.

Joe Bruno and Vinnie Stigma, 1984
Photo by Karen O'Sullivan

LAURA ALBERT (NYHC scene):
Harley was a fucking hooligan, a real bully. He was a vicious little fucker. People were scared of him, and rightly so. If Harley and those people didn't like you, if you were a little out-of-town Punker, you were primed to get a beating. Harley and his pals were really fucked up; few people would admit that because they wanted his acceptance. If he had a problem with you, life was hell. They were so fucked up all the time they didn't know half the shit they did.

HARLEY FLANAGAN: The crew I hung out with were like the Little Rascals on the scene. We were inseparable — we used to get more shit than anyone on the scene. We used to get more pussy and kick more ass and do more drugs than anybody and we were barely teenagers. That was a reason for our infamy. It was like, 'Who are these delinquent kids?'

JIMMY GESTAPO: We were crazy back then: high on music, high on pot, high on life. There's a lot of people with broken noses and wired jaws and bloody faces who didn't expect to get smacked around by a bunch of kids with eightballs in socks. They never talked shit about us again.

Many NYHC Skins lived in East Village and Lower East Side squats. Many runaways and abused kids on the tough streets found a home in Hardcore.

JIMMY GESTAPO: A lot of New York Hardcore kids were from troubled families. My alcoholic father abused my mother and beat me up. A lot of the kids I grew up around were abused. Some of them didn't have fathers. I remember my father kicking the shit out of me, then me leaving home and going to Norfolk Street. It was called Apartment X; everybody lived there.

RAYBEEZ: We were on Avenue A. There were a few hundred kids, and shows all the time. We'd go to a show then go spare-changing on the street and get up enough money for food, then go have a big family meal, 30 or 40 of us. It was tight — the same people at all the shows. As it grew, we just took everyone under our wing. We'd sleep together 10 people in a room like brothers and sisters. The sense of loyalty was so intense. Back then, we all knew each other. Even when we disagreed, we knew we were coming from the same place. It was Punks and Skins together, a total gang, and the girls were as crazy as the guys. It wasn't a gang selling drugs, it was a gang in the sense of territory and family. Guys and girls who became brothers and sisters and loved each other enough to die — and a couple of us did die. The true meaning of a street gang is looking out for each other in your neighborhood. We were really united, man. It was a fuckin' family, no joke. Over the years, I've seen bands start not for the sincerity of the movement but because they said, Let me put myself on a pedestal. Back then, no one thought Agnostic Front, Murphy's Law, Cro-Mags and Warzone would turn into what they turned into. We were just speaking our minds.

Major Conflict, CBGB, NYC, 1983
James Contra (bottom center)
Photo by Karen O'Sullivan

ROGER MIRET: Angel dust was *the* drug. And glue. We were on drugs every day. You had to be. I remember being on acid and watching someone's head explode. That big roller thing went down the street; somebody jumped in front and their head popped like a pimple. We were anti-Straight Edge. We were street kids. Kids from DC and Boston didn't understand because they were living in suburbia with their mother and father. You can't come home bombed all the time when you're livin' at home. We were livin' in the street and were totally whacked. You hafta be drugged to be livin' in the streets.

Until then, tattooing was not cool. Henry Rollins may have introduced "ink" to HC, but really everyone copied Harley Flanagan's Skinhead style.

PARRIS MITCHELL MAYHEW: When Harley showed up with his first tattoo, everybody was like, 'Tattoos are for jocks' — when Harley walked up to them, all of a sudden all those people saying 'Tattoos are for jocks' shut up. He had half the tattoos — and his chest tattooed — by the time I was 16 years old. This is back when nobody had tattoos. Roger Miret saw this and was like, 'Wow, that's cool' and got his body tattooed.

ROGER MIRET: The people who brought tattooing to New York Hardcore were Vinnie Stigma, me and Harley. We'd get together and go to Mikey's Tattoos. We went all-out. It was more out of the Oi! tradition. Our first tattoos were 'Strength Through Oi,' 'Crucified Skins,' et cetera.

Talk about unity
Talk about conformity
You're the one that tells em what to say
Why don't you get the fuck away from me?
— **Agnostic Front, "United Blood"**

John Joseph (singing) with Harley Flanagan on drums
in the short-lived M.O.I., CBGB, NYC, 1983
Photo by Karen O'Sullivan

CRO-MAGS set out to be the heaviest band on the planet. For a moment, they certainly were. Only Cro-Mags and Bad Brains — the two biggest Hardcore groups out of NYC — could headline a big room like The Ritz.

Cro-Mags — named by Black Flag roadie Mugger — built slowly. Bassist Harley Flanagan and former Bad Brains roadie John Joseph McGeown had the short-lived band M.O.I before they started Cro-Mags in January 1982, with Parris Mitchell Mayhew, an Uptown guitarist into Rush and the Dixie Dregs, and then-Bad Brains manager Dave Hahn.

John Joseph was the first Hardcore kid to get turned onto Hare Krishna consciousness. He distributed leaflets which called for vegetarianism, anti-materialism and pacifism. He'd also go off on long temple retreats to Hawaii. So for a year or two, Harley and Parris enlisted Eric Casanova to sing.

PARRIS MITCHELL MAYHEW: Our first discussion about the band was in a bar. I was 15, he was 13. Sitting in a booth, drinking beer, looking at each other talking about this band. We were so serious. And we were just little kids sitting at a bar.

HARLEY FLANAGAN: Parris heard of a mugging I'd been involved in and he looked at me going, 'I can't be in a band with him, he mugs people!'

By the time of spring '85's *Age Of Quarrel* demo — recorded by brothers Jerry and Tim Williams — John Joseph was back, and Cro-Mags included Mackie Jayson from Frontline on drums. Within a few months, Kraut's Doug Holland entered the fold on second guitar. That '85 tape captured the group's intensity far better than '86's noted debut LP of the same name (on Chris Williamson's Rock Hotel imprint released through Profile Records).

Cro-Mags were the first band to attract both Skinheads and Metalheads audiences; their music the point where Hardcore nihilism met Metal power. Harley, a gnarly street rat influenced by Lemmy of Motorhead and Black Sabbath's Geezer Butler, played a hollow-body bass, with a chain for a strap.

Show flyer for Cro-Mags, CBGB, NYC, 1984
Collection of Laura Albert

HARLEY FLANAGAN: We evolved parallel to the scene but our music was so strong, people on the scene had to step back and acknowledge us as the real deal — they knew we were the shit. There'd never been a Hardcore band strong enough to attract metalheads. Most Hardcore bands back then, even though they may have had a lot of energy, were musically just four bar chords played at hyperspeed. Aside from the Bad Brains, there was nothing else that had a real drive musically.

Ultimately, Cro-Mags proved their own worst enemies. In their major dichotomy, Cro-Mags juxtaposed Krishna spirituality on a brutally violent vibe. After the *Age Of Quarrel*, John Joseph left on very bad terms (Harley sang on '89's *Best Wishes* and '92's *Alpha-Omega*). As epitomes of Hardcore attitude, their only logical conclusion was self-destruction. (The bad vibes continued in 1997 as the Navy arrested John Joseph, AWOL since 1981, allegedly on a tip to police by former bandmembers. For four months he was in a naval brig, from where I interviewed him for this book. (Harley and John made their peace, and to play with Doug and Mackie, and with Rocky George from Suicidal replacing Parris).

MICHAEL ALAGO (music biz exec): Harley Flanagan — here was a person who was so incredibly charismatic, but he always needed money. I would feed him and give him money to live on during the week. There were always people helping him but this is a person that never knew how to rise above all the self-pity bullshit — he was always chasing his tail. Here we are today, but where is he? This was someone with a real star quality about him, and just doesn't know what to do with it.

MURPHY'S LAW, whose shows became legendary for drunken, drugged, physical stage action, started as a side project of NYHC's youngest, most nightmarish delinquents — Cro-Mag Harley and Jimmy "Gestapo" Drescher of Astoria. Eventually, Harley left and Murphy's Law took off.
Jimmy's tie to the scene began when he was 13 years old in 1980. That's when he met Doug Holland, in his pre-Kraut outfit, the Apprehended.

JIMMY GESTAPO: I met Dougie talking on the CB radio. He would do what's called 'splashing' — he'd play the Pistols over the CB. We roadied for this gig — I fell in love with

the whole scene. I started gettin' into it, and went to Max's and saw The Stimulators and Th' Influence, the Black Punk Rock band before Bad Brains. I could only go out once a month — I'd get punished for staying out late. I spiked my hair, got beat up, started to hate everyone. I got beat up daily up for bein' different. And that was Punk Rock — as soon as you choose to be a different individual, society turns on you.

Jimmy Gestapo (Murphy's Law) ready to kick ass
Mudd Club, NYC, 1982
Photo by Fred Berger

Murphy's Law's first played New Year's Eve '83 with Reagan Youth and MDC at Giorgio Gomelsky's "Green Door" loft on 24th Street. After a series of crazy-ass gigs, their milestone *Bong Blast* tape of '84 earned them lots of attention and led to

their signing with **Rock Hotel/Profile**. The buzz off the '86 Murphy's Law LP led to an opening spot on the *Licensed To Ill* tour with Beastie Boys and Fishbone. They played to mainstream crowds, going to Dubuque, Iowa and rocking 20,000 out-of-the-loop fans — it was the first instance of arena slamdancing and stagediving. Sadly, label problems prevented any benefit from such opportunities. (Thankfully, Jimmy never gave up: Murphy's Law continues as a popular underground phenomenon.)

Crucial Truth, A7, NYC, 1983
Photo by Karen O'Sullivan

JIMMY GESTAPO: You're right, by the time our first album came out, it was a different crowd. Murphy's Law started out when we were kids in the early New York Hardcore scene, and I've lived through all phases of the shit. We didn't blow up when we should've, but those problems inspired us to never give up. And I've never given up. Never fuckin' will. What I'm doing is my fucking life, this is what I live and I have the scars to prove it.

AGNOSTIC FRONT included some of the most notorious Skinheads of the era. Singer John Watson, guitarist Vinnie Stigma, drummer Rob Cryptcrash — later of Cause For Alarm — and bassist Diego started playing together in '82 as The Zoo Crew. Ray "Raybeez" Barbieri replaced Cryptcrash by the end of the year, by virtue of the fact that he was fucking Crazy Emily, who lived in the Eldridge Street storefront where the group, re-christened **Agnostic Front**, rehearsed.

RAYBEEZ: I came from Washington Heights, which was the Lower East Side of Uptown. The A train went from where we lived to West 4th Street; that's how we got down here. I know kids who lived in Brooklyn and Queens who never came to Manhattan because it was a big trip. For me, it was ten minutes on the A train. If we stole a car or something, we'd get on Harlem River Drive and be here in five minutes. I was familiar with different neighborhoods in the city where crazy stuff was going on.

Raybeez couldn't play to begin with, and he wouldn't go onstage until he snorted some lines, smoked a dusted joint, and drank a few 40s. I saw AF's first out-of-town show — with MDC and Minor Threat at Terminal 406 in Baltimore — and remember how the DC kids goofed on AF and their knucklehead fans with freshly-shaved heads, who slamdanced in a unified circular motion. After that show, Watson left. A few singers later came Roger Miret, a gnarly Cuban kid from Union, NJ who sang in Jersey Punk acts like The Psychos and Distorted Youth, and got into Oi! through tattoo artist Elio. Early '83 saw the new AF hook up with producer Don Fury to record their classsic *United Blood* EP — put out by Rat Cage later that year.

ROGER MIRET: Once I shaved my head, I was totally accepted. I was at a Great Gildersleeves show and Raybeez approached me and said, 'Do you want to sing for Agnostic Front?' I saw AF and they were terrible.

United Blood was weak. When I joined, that stuff was already written. The music was cool but the lyrics made no sense. I never liked it but I did it anyway. I added two Psychos songs to *United Blood*: 'Discriminate Me' and 'Fight.' We'd do shows and I'd just yell anything.

Vinnie came up with the name; he did a fanzine called *Agnostic Front*. We never wanted to be just a band, we wanted to be a movement like BYO. Anywhere we went, we showed

NYC Skins, outside CBGB, NYC, 1984
Photo by Karen O'Sullivan

people our New York Hardcore style. When people thought of New York, they automatically thought of Agnostic Front. We were crazy but nice guys. People would be intimidated when they first saw us but when they spoke to us, they saw we were down-to-Earth.

Raybeez left Agnostic Front in summer 1984. A few weeks later, he joined Warzone — whose 1986 debut 7" EP was the first release of the prolific Revelation Records (started in Connecticut by Jordan Cooper and Youth Of Today's Ray Cappo). But Warzone were more of a late-80s outfit.

RAYBEEZ: Everybody was partyin' a lot … trippin' and doin' all kinds of shit. We were so fucked up on acid and dust. In summertime of '84, I went away for like six weeks. I was dating this girl; her family had a blueberry farm in Maine, so I went there to chill out and pick berries. I was trippin' like crazy — I just couldn't be in Agnostic Front anymore. They got another drummer, so at the end of summer I joined Warzone on drums. AF and Warzone were like family: everyone hung out together. I played drums in Warzone for two years, then went on to sing. Back then, everyone shared musicians, everyone shared lives.

ROGER MIRET: If it wasn't for Ray, there'd be no Agnostic Front, but he was holding us back. He wanted to play drums but he couldn't do it. I ended up telling Ray he'd be better off doing vocals. I was a moving in a Punkier, Discharge/Crucifix style. We had to let go of Ray.

Victim In Pain (Rat Cage "84), although sonically inept, is an incredible disc. Many have derided Vinnie Stigma's guitar talents, or the lack thereof (today, he "plays" live onstage with his amp unplugged!), but he's the only guitarist on those classic first two records.

ROGER MIRET: Vinnie's a true Punk. He used to hang out with Sid. When I joined Agnostic Front, Vinnie was already 26. He comes from straight-up old-school Punk Rock. He's got pictures of himself with spiked hair and a mustache. One of our songs, 'The Eliminator,' came from his band before AF, The Eliminators. What got me upset was he didn't want a second guitarist. His playing on *United Blood* and *Victim In Pain* was great; it was out of time, but who cares, it's Hardcore. We fought for a second guitar because Vinnie wasn't really right. We added Alex from Cause For Alarm because I thought it'd be cool to cross CFA with Agnostic Front. It turned out to be a mistake because Alex was doing too much Metal. Vinnie got lazy from that point on. Once we added a second guitarist, he decided he didn't want to actually play anymore. He's an entertainer, a real ham. Vinnie's the only person that could get away with that.

AF's next LP, though controversial, made them famous. Some say 1986's *Cause For Alarm* (Combat Core) brought Hardcore and Metal together. Roger and Vinnie hired Pete Steele of the Brooklyn Metal band Carnivore (and later of Type O Negative) to write material — because they were too lazy, fucked-up and devoid of ideas. *Cause For Alarm* was their biggest-selling record, but AF lost most of their original fans — some due to the Metal direction, others over Steele's objectionable lyrics, such as his unfriendly view of welfare recipients in "Public Assistance." *Maximum RockNRoll* branded AF the musical voice of The Fourth Reich. During a

Murphy's Law show at Rock Hotel on Jane Street, Harley came out in a longhair wig and an AF shirt — implying that AF was a cheesy Metal act. (AF carried on through the 80s, until Miret was jailed on drug charges, leading him to quit music for a while to become a motorcycle repairman; until the group's mid-90s reunion.)

ROGER MIRET: Pete Steele and I were managed by the same person at one point, Connie Barrett. Carnivore was the ultimate 'Road Warrior' Metal band — we were the ultimate Hardcore band. Then they started doing more Hardcore and we started doing more Metal. We were best of friends — then things fell apart. Vinnie loved Carnivore. We ended up playing a benefit for CBGB where we did a Hardcore show in the afternoon and at night we played with Metal bands. I think Carnivore was one, Manowar the other. We did shows with Exodus and Slayer. What I couldn't stand about Metal was the lyrics. Some of the music was okay but most of it was too fast.

Look, what happened was a mistake. I was never for it. In fact, I quit the band. I just wasn't into the songs. They had another singer for awhile, Carl from The Icemen, who was gonna play a show with them. At the last minute, Vinnie called me to come back. But as much as I'd say it was a mistake, *Cause For Alarm* sold the best of all our early albums. We were one of the first New York bands to 'cross over.' I had a friend search the Internet and it says we were the first big Crossover band.

PETE STEELE (Carnivore): They were on a critical time frame so they asked me for my help. I didn't want to diverge from their style, so I did what they asked and wrote within it. It was a good album for its time. They still owe me money — but whatever. There were certain people that

NYHC fashion, 1984
Courtesy of Steve Poss and Jimmy Gestapo

didn't like the lyrics I came up with. I have two things to say about that: first is that I was told what these songs were to be about; I was to write based on the subject matter. Second, I would not have written these songs if I did not agree with what I was saying. I had no problem with what they asked me to write about.

> *Trace our steps and see what we've done*
> *It's time for us to go back to square one*
> — Cro-Mags, "Seekers Of The Truth"

The ragged legacy of New York Hardcore inexorably linked with the Bad Brains's troubled history: when they were fresh and hot, so was NYHC. And an application of their fluidity and guitar crunch would become "Mosh" — a sound popularized at all-ages Sunday matinees at CBGB.

HOWIE ABRAMS (NYHC scene): Mosh style was slower, very tribal — like a Reggae beat adapted to Hardcore. Back then, Mosh was a very specific thing; you were either doing it correctly or you weren't. It was an outbreak of dancing with a mid-tempo beat driven by floor tom and snare. C.O.C. were a huge phenomenon in NYC. Their early dirge-y, Sabbath style was close enough to the Mosh vibe that people could deal with it, and you could see this strong reaction to that band. They'd bring other bands from North Carolina with them, and nobody liked the other bands, which proved to me C.O.C. had that dance beat.

The next wave came by 1985, mixing Bad Brains/Cro-Mags power with Minor Threat "austerity." The best outfits were Gilligan's Revenge, Token Entry, and Gorilla Biscuits from Queens, Crumbsuckers from Long Island, and Youth Of Today — from Connecticut, but players of NYHC.

ROGER MIRET: I never liked people that acted like they were there — prime example: Youth Of Today. They were never a New York Hardcore band, they were from Connecticut. They're my friends, they're good people, but why pull this 'New York Hardcore band' stuff?

HOWIE ABRAHMS: It took bands from out of town to get the whole Straight Edge thing started here. Youth Of Today were the biggest catalyst for the change in NY to a Straight Edge scene. Ray Cappo told me about the first time they were playing CBs, and Johnny Stiff was trying to convince him that there would never ever be a Straight Edge scene in New York. Ray said that was one of the most inspirational things for him, in terms of making sure that it did happen. No easy feat.

"Crossover" reached full effect by '85. Basically two types of Hardcore diverged: one Punk-based and one Metal-based. The Brooklyn Metal club L'Amour booked a few HC bands to play with their poodlehead acts, while CBGB matinees started to book longhairs who ripped dueling axe solos. It was a whole 'nother world from '81.

PETE STEELE: There weren't that many problems. I can't say there was total interaction. It was cliquish but everybody seemed to get along. The scene started to attract so much attention that the Hardcore kids got of it and bowed out. You'd have kids showing up that looked like Skinheads but weren't really Skinheads — it was just a style. I feel sorry for the founding members of the Hardcore scene — it got exploited and became commercial. That's what happens in this country.

IAN MACKAYE (Minor Threat): In New York, the Bad Brains created a monster. This mosh thing caused problems for the rest of us. Cro-Mags, Agnostic Front and all of them were typical New York street thugs. I'm not saying that in a derogatory way — not tryin' to say they were shitty; they were quintessential New York bands. The blue-collar macho thing

became attractive to kids throughout the Northeast: '85, that took root. Meanwhile in Washington we all turned into a bunch of art fags or whatever. •

Bad Brains, Rock Hotel, NYC, 1985
Photo from *I Against I*, SST, 1986
Collection of the author

THE MISFITS: HITS FROM HELL

This street we walk upon
This corner full of piss and fear
— The Misfits, "Cough/Cool"

The Misfits — Lodi, New Jersey's answer to the Ramones — though crucial to the rise of Hardcore, were in fact in a league of their own. Named after Marilyn Monroe's final film, The Misfits delivered a hyper-yet-melodic assault based in 50/60s-style Rock, taking the Buddy Holly/Gene Vincent foundation and making it nuclear.

They arrived in the late 70s but were not major players in the New York Punk scene. Many HC fans rabidly collected Misfits singles, but it was only well after '82's *Walk Among Us* album that they achieved legendary status. In the low-tech, low-brow Hardcore world, The Misfits came off as larger than life. Dressed like mutant sci-fi/comic-book Kiss-style characters, these blue-collar ginzos took the stage and utterly awed their audiences.

Misfits founder and frontman Glenn Danzig was the Elvis/Jim Morrison of

Press photo of Misfits, 1982, from Misfits Fiend Club mailing
Glenn Danzig, Arthur Googy, Doyle, Jerry Only
Collection of the author

American Hardcore. As a teen, he trained as a graphic artist and sang in a few Sabbath-style bands. He graduated high school in '73, wrote the three-verse poem "Bullet" in '74, and presided over The Misfits' forgotten early lineups as far back as mid-1976. At first Glenn couldn't find a compatible guitarist so he played keyboards through a fuzz box.

GLENN DANZIG (Misfits): I grew up in Boston, Lodi and — in my later teen years — in Manhattan. They're all pretty rough areas. I guess I had a wild childhood, expelled from public schools and shit like that. Eventually I was able to find outlets to express anger and frustration. I was a drum roadie, but eventually tried out as a singer for a band and got the gig. Over time, I started writing my own songs. I had piano lessons for six months but I couldn't play guitar at all. When I was a kid, I also played clarinet. It all went from there. I went to art school after high school and photography school at New York Institute Of Photography. My favorite photographers are Man Ray and Helmut Newton. In the beginning of New York Punk, art was a very big part of it — and art is still important to me.

The first practical Misfits lineup appeared in March '77: Glenn on vocals and electric piano, bassist Jerry "Only" Caiafa, and Manny, a 30-year-old drummer from the 'hood. They first gigged at a CB's audition night in April. Glenn and Jerry — not your typical scrawny fuckheads — were athletic Italian-Americans: Glenn a

Jerry Only and Glenn Danzig
getting ready for gig, Irving Plaza, NYC, 1981
(note cat in in right background)
Photo by Karen O'Sullivan

proficient wrestler, Jerry a football player. The three recorded the "Cough/Cool" 7" that summer, releasing it on their own Blank Records imprint. That band was quite different from what would come.

JERRY ONLY (Misfits): When we formed our band, Glenn looked like he always looked and I had the short Punk hair dyed fluorescent blue. We'd wear pointy shoes from England. You could say we dressed like British Punks. It took us a while to figure it all out, to do our own thing.

GLENN DANZIG: Basically we'd shock people, open mouths dripping. I remember this one show at CBGB. It was Jerry's first gig and he showed up in Glam clothes — like shoes with platforms and open toes — and I was like, 'I'm *not* going onstage with you.' It was really hard getting people to understand what it was about, especially back then.

Mercury Records also used the Blank Records name, a fake indie label front for their Pere Ubu album *The Modern Dance*. Mercury exec and future Metallica manager Cliff Burnstein made a deal where The Misfits gave up the Blank moniker in return for 30 hours of recording time at Mercury-associated C.I. Recordings Studios. The Misfits renamed their label Plan 9 Records, in tribute to Ed Wood Jr.'s cult film *Plan 9 From Outer Space*.

By January '78, Glenn and Jerry had enlisted fellow Lodi townies Frank "Franché Coma" LiCata, guitar, and James "Mr. Jim" Catania, drums. They recorded the *Static Age* album, arguably The Misfits' highest-quality work — which wouldn't see release for 20 years (Caroline, '97). Labels showed zero interest, though Glenn shopped the tape to every major and indie in the biz. From the *Static Age* sessions arose future Misfits records such as the four-song 7" *Bullet* EP, and a slew of compilation cuts and B-sides.

Most Hardcore groups never had the money to properly produce and distribute independent records, and a recurring theme of financial issues sully The Misfits history. Glenn told me that financing their earliest discs forced him to sell off large chunks of his comic book collection. And Jerry underwrote many Misfits' ventures.

JERRY ONLY: My Dad started a company — Pro Edge, an X-acto-knife-type of line. During the 70s it was doin' really well; that's when I began to work there. When we teamed up with Glenn, we'd take our paycheck, go to the music store, dump it into equipment, then go out that weekend and smash everything we worked for. The Misfits was a money pit; my dad never took it seriously — which lead to problems when the band broke up. We didn't copyright and publish things, which left us for the pickings when we broke up with Glenn. He did deals behind our backs and made lots of money. We had to chase him for a long time. Early on, he was a humble individual. I know a lot of people can't grasp that, but he was a really nice guy to work with — a hard worker. The way we viewed The Misfits was, I'd finance the band by working at the machine shop every day then we'd team up at night and work on material. During the day, Glenn'd silkscreen shirts, answer fan mail, book gigs. He'd be the business manager during the day while I earned the money to finance the project. We worked well together for seven years. The only fight we had was the last day of the band.

A lot of people think that me and him were bitter enemies and always at each other's throat but that was never the case.

The Misfits first drew attention at Eddie's Lounge in Teaneck, a seedy blue-collar cover-band bar which once a month or so booked NYC acts like Sic Fucs or The Cramps. Playing every Tuesday for most of '78, The Misfits gained a following across the northernmost reaches of Jersey.

By November '78, Mr. Jim lost interest, while Frank freaked out during a weekend gig in Toronto where they played with Joey Shithead's pre-D.O.A. unit, The Skulls.

Misfits, Irving Plaza, NYC, 1982
(L-R): Jerry, Doyle, Glenn (singing)
Photo by Karen O'Sullivan

The next Misfits lineup featured guitarist Bobby Steele, who had played in the Whorelords, and drummer Joey Image.

BOBBY STEELE (Misfits, Undead): I was looking to get in a serious band. I came home one night — there was a message from this guy Glenn of The Misfits. All I knew of them was 'Cough/Cool,' so I wasn't even gonna call them back — I thought it was a horrible-sounding record, no guitar, just keyboards through a distortion pedal. I wasn't interested but I figured what the hell, I went down and went through five or six songs with them. We were playing in Jerry's garage; you couldn't hear anything. They played the *Static Age* sessions for me; that's when I got interested. When I got home that night I told my friend Bobby Snotz, 'I tried out for this band that wanted me to play guitar.' He told me, 'Do it, man. This band's starting to move.' That's how it started. A week later I did my first show with 'em.

The first thing that struck me about Glenn was he had an earring in his right ear — which back then meant you were gay, so I didn't wanna get too close to him. I was the musician of the bunch. They were all into football and shit like that, so I wasn't involved in those conversations. But we all got along well in the beginning. We'd put up posters all over New York, and go back to Jerry's house and make these huge ice cream sundaes. Jerry was a rich kid. His father had a few manufacturing businesses, one being the company that competes with X-acto in the art knife biz. He also had two or three racehorse-breeding farms. They must've owned half of Vernon, New Jersey. It was a lot of fun working with those guys. We got into a lot of mischief, we got into a lot of trouble. We were there for music and fun.

During the Bobby Steele era, '79 and '80, The Misfits played every few months at Max's, expanding their Manhattan notoriety. Two days after the Jonestown Massacre, the new lineup first gigged there opening for Trixie Sly — they threw buckets of grape Kool-Aid on an unsuspecting audience.

The Misfits' outrageous performances quickly gained them a reputation. They'd drape huge sheets of seamless paper across the front of the stage and project reels of trashy 50s horror-flick trailers while setting up. The very last trailer would have something to do with one of their sci-fi song titles, and right as it ended, they'd hit the first chord and dive through the screen. Then at one Max's gig, Steele threw a glass into the audience that smashed on a table and took out a girl's eye. Needless to say, The Misfits never played there again. That episode led to the demise of Max's, as their insurance rates shot up dramatically.

BOBBY STEELE: It was real violent. We'd get pieces of tables thrown at us — we'd throw shit back at the audience. It got dangerous. One show, I got arrested for slashing a guy. I threw a glass into the audience; it broke and went into this guy's arm. Somebody threw a chair at Jerry — he kicked the chair off the ceiling, it came down and busted a girl's jaw. There were a lot of bloodbaths, those old shows. They useta keep an ambulance parked outside Max's when we played. But we knew what we were getting into.

> *I don't wanna be here in your London dungeon*
> *I don't wanna be here in your British hell*
> **— The Misfits, "London Dungeon"**

An ill-fated UK tour with The Damned in fall '79 lasted all of one show. Glenn and Jerry booked it through the musician's union, receiving contracts from The Damned's manager outlining the pay for each gig. They got zip for that first date, allegedly because Jerry never signed the papers. They probably could've worked it out, but inner turmoil erupted. Joey Image left.

BOBBY STEELE: Joey quit the band while we were in London. He got up one morning and went home. We were supposed to play with The Damned at Rainbow Theater — Joey just got

Jerry Only (Misfits)
Irving Plaza, NYC, 1982
Photo by Karen O'Sullivan

fed up and left, so we couldn't. We tried to pick up a drummer there 'cause there was a chance we might get on a Clash tour. I don't know much about Joey. A friend of mine who grew up with him told me when they were very young they were playing around the cliffs in Weehawken — Joey's brother fell. and a buncha rocks came down and crushed him. That probably explains why Joey had a really bad heroin problem. After his split with The Misfits, we got into a real nasty fight on St. Mark's Place.

JERRY ONLY: Joey had a drug problem. Here's another example of guys who wanted to be in the band 'cause it was cool, and to get into places for free. Joey was really good, and then got really bad. I had trouble with him tryin' to pinch stuff from my house. The last time we played with him was in England, when were talking to a guy at CBS about putting us on a world tour with The Clash. Joey got on a plane and split before we could do the audition, which was another turning point in the band. I wasn't trying to straighten him out, I just wanted to get rid of him.

BOBBY STEELE: We could've done things a lot better. The way I looked at it, we shouldn't have walked off The Damned tour. Glenn and Jerry were like 'Fuck this!' I said to Glenn, 'Let's do the tour. We have the union behind us. Jerry's got the money to subsidize us.' But they just blew it off after the one show at the Rainbow Theater. If we'd stuck it out, we would have made a big impression in England. *Beware* was coming out and would have sold phenomenally. We would have been a lot bigger band.

JERRY ONLY: When The Damned's manager refused to pay us a hundred bucks a night, I told him to forget it. He said, 'What are you guys — nuts? Anybody would give their right arm to open for The Damned.' I said, 'Fuck you. I fly my whole band here and you can't give me a hundred a night?' We were being exploited. They were turnin' the P.A. down, they wouldn't let us use their equipment, and they rented us real shit gear. They were trying to make us look like jerks so they looked better. I felt that keeping face and walking off the tour was more important than exposure.

The night after The Misfits' only London performance, Glenn and Bobby got arrested and spent two nights in jail — one in ancient Brixton Prison — leading to their powerful song "London Dungeon."

BOBBY STEELE: Hanging out in a pub across from the Rainbow, Glenn for some reason thought these Skinheads were conspiring to beat us up. I was hungry; I went down the street to a fish-and-chips shop. When I came back, he was standing in front of The Rainbow sharpening a piece of glass; and a couple of security guys came and dragged him in. I ran after him and I threw my chips at the guards so they grabbed me. They held us down until one of the guards recognized me from The Damned show the night before and said, 'He's cool, let him go,' but they held Glenn for the police. They let me go but Glenn had all our money, and I had no place to go. I went back to the police station but they wouldn't let Glenn give me any money. I phoned the US embassy collect, and they wouldn't take the call.

I was pretty fucked up — I'd been drinking and taking Mandrax. I had to piss so I was like 'I'll go back to the station and ask to use the bathroom. If they say no I'll piss right there and get myself arrested.' When I got to the police station, the head of security from the Rainbow was coming out the door and started screaming at me. I didn't know what he was going on about. He kept mouthin' off — I finally turned and spit at him. I didn't know that in England spitting is a bigger offense than rape. All of a sudden, all these cops came flying out and dragged me in. I always thought the best defense if the cops're roughin' you up is to fall down and play unconscious. I laid there totally limp — they grabbed me by my feet and dragged me into a room. They threw water on me and shook my head. There were all these cops sitting around me. One cop looked like Peter Noone — kinda gay. I was wearing skintight leather pants and a leather jacket and he says, 'Are you gay?' so I said, 'Why do *you* want to know?' Then they went, 'You're a Yank aren't you? Nixon's a crook.' I said, 'So what? The Queen's a fuckin' whore' — they beat the shit out of me after that. Then they said, 'Are you gonna walk to your cell or do we have to drag you?' I was like, 'I'll take the ride.' They dragged me through the station and threw me in a cell. They took me to get my picture taken but the camera was broken. I refused to give them my name, so I was listed as 'John Doe, Yank.'

Doyle (Misfits)
Irving Plaza, NYC, 1982
Photo by Karen O'Sullivan

Next morning they took me to the courthouse. You know these British TV shows where the solicitors and judges are wearing wigs? I was hoping for that but nobody was wearing one. I was thinkin' 'This is a burn. I wanna see some wigs on these people.' It was a total trip. We pleaded not guilty; they put us back in the holding cell, then took us down to Brixton and held us there for the night. This guy Derek, who was interested in managing the band at the time, bailed us out and took us to the Hard Rock Café. It was the night of The Who concert in Cincinnati when people got trampled — I was eating when it came on the news. Jerry wasn't there at the time, he was with Sid Vicious' mother in Kent. Derek hired a lawyer for us, we pled guilty and he paid the fine for us. I had a good time.

Far more Punk than the Lodi guys, Bobby never got along with the rest of The Misfits. He and his girlfriend would pick each others' noses and eat it in public, and such behavior didn't exactly enamor him to his bandmates. And while Steele was a very good guitarist, he just didn't present a heavy sound — and The Misfits were definitely getting heavier.

Sticker for Misfits "Die Die My Darling" 7", 1982
Collection of the author

By '80, the scene had changed; in that transition to up-tempo Hardcore, Steele didn't make the cut. Jerry yearned for serious muscle on guitar, so he created a twin tower attack with his younger brother, guitarist Paul — later known as Doyle. At 16, Doyle perfectly fit the bill — over six feet tall, big and muscular, he could stand up there and bash out the songs. Bobby experienced a classic I quit/you're fired scenario.

BOBBY STEELE: We were at rehearsal discussing an upcoming show — they wanted to open the set by coming out of coffins. My idea was to fill the coffins with rats. It was right after that film *Nosferatu* had came out; visually, it would've been great, but they were bummed. I said, 'The crowd is gonna stomp most of them to death. We'll give them all strychnine and whichever ones get past the crowd will die from the poison.' That was the last time I ever heard from them. A guy called me around '86, '87 and told me that was the reason Jerry gave for kicking me out. I've heard so many different reasons. At the time, Glenn didn't wanna tell me why. He told me to call Jerry; he told me it was because I sucked on guitar, that Doyle was better. I told him on the spot, 'You know I'm a far better guitarist.' 'Well, Doyle looks better.' That's what it was. I've always suspected that Jerry wanted his brother in the band so Jerry could have more influence. When I was in the band, Glenn was the leader — what he said went. As you can see, Jerry has taken control of The Misfits and is doing his own thing with it.

JERRY ONLY: The reason we picked Bobby to take Frank's spot was: one, Bobby was from Jersey; two, Bobby was covering Sex Pistols songs and had an idea about what we were doing. The problem was that Bobby's problems were bigger then the band problems. If Bobby had something to do, then the band came second. It always seemed Bobby would show up and not have a guitar so he'd have to use Doyle's. Then he'd break all of Doyle's strings and Doyle would come to me and say, 'Why do you let this guy use my guitar?' I said, 'Until you're ready, we've got to do this. You've got to hang in there.' We eventually replaced Bobby with Doyle — and the rest is history. Doyle is a phenomenon as far as guitar players go.

GLENN DANZIG: Jerry didn't want Bobby anymore. Originally, I didn't want Bobby in the band *at all*. They wanted Bobby out and Doyle in. I said, 'Look, I don't really care, but don't lead Bobby on anymore.' I was teaching Doyle stuff on guitar and it wasn't working — his hands were just too big. Eventually, they didn't tell Bobby, so I did. They wanted him to come down to the show and not know he was out — or something, which was not cool.

Steele would form The Undead, the short-lived kings of early NYHC — at least as popular, if not more, than The Misfits in '81 and '82. The final US release by the noted Stiff label was '82's underrated *Nine Toes Later* EP.

BOBBY STEELE: In the beginning of The Undead we all got along well. Glenn put up the money for The Undead to go in the studio and record *Nine Toes Later*. He was originally gonna put it out on Plan Nine, until the shit hit the fan. An article in *Sounds* said The Undead accomplished more in six months than the Misfits had in several years. That was a real blow to their pride. It started to get dirty between us and them. I don't wanna go too deeply into it — there's still lawsuits going on. Things have been settled between Glenn and Jerry, and Jerry got a lot of money from Caroline. Part of that's supposed to go to me but he won't give that to me. I just wanna see things settled and get paid for what I did.

Even this early on, Danzig was growing uneasy with his bandmates — a situation only made worse with two Caiafas in the fold. Glenn was always in search of "artistic creativity," while Jerry and Doyle weren't always thinking in those terms, if ya know what I mean. That rift provided the rationale behind Glenn's 1980 solo single on Plan 9, "Who Killed Marilyn?"

GLENN DANZIG: I was into the *Mad Max* movies, trying to get the guys to see 'em. I wasn't happy. I didn't like the way my songs were coming out and what was going on with the band. I mean, Doyle couldn't play guitar — Jerry didn't practice at all. I was disillusioned. I recall [Arthur] Googy and I telling them that if we didn't play more, we were leaving. That's around the time I did 'Who Killed Marilyn?' Creatively, I had no other choice.

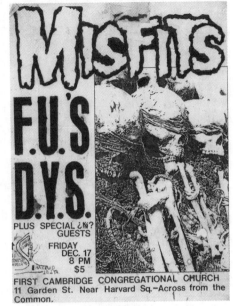

Show flyer for Misfits, The FU's, DYS
Cambridge Congregational Church,
Boston, 1982
Collection of Hank Peirce

New pide-blonde drummer "Googy" had never played in a band prior to his stint with The Misfits. The first gig with Googy and Doyle was with Screamin' Jay Hawkins at Irving Plaza, Halloween 1980, an amazing show. Sure, they were sloppy — but they had such attitude. Glenn suckerpunched audience members with his spiked leather gloves. This foursome recorded *Three Hits From Hell*, with "London Dungeon," "Horror Hotel" and "Ghoul's Night Out." On a roll, The Misfits were attracting a noticeable following.

JIM FOSTER (Adrenalin O.D.): The Misfits were smart. They were a self-contained entity. You'd only see Jerry and Doyle at the biggest shows; they weren't supporters of the scene. Glenn came out to many small shows at A7 and whatnot — he just liked to check things out. They didn't consider themselves part of the Jersey scene, and we never tried to make them part of the Jersey scene either. The Necros from Ohio were actually the ones who introduced us to The Misfits.

You gotta see this big reaction
No resistance
— The Misfits, "Children In Heat"

By the time Hardcore hit, The Misfits had played a few times in Detroit — as early as summer '78 in their Mr. Jim/Franché Coma days — and made a big impact. A bunch of Detroit kids loved them, proselytizing endlessly about the "eerie" outfit. The resulting alliance was largely responsible for the transformation of The Misfits into true HC icons. They meant little on a national level before Detroit kids came to their defense.

BARRY HENNSLER (Necros): The Misfits were an oldschool New York guido thing. I remember coming to New York and saying, 'I like The Misfits' — and everyone was like, 'You're obviously a Midwest bumpkin if you like em.' Us kids from Detroit said, 'Fuck you, they're great.'

Show flyer for Misfits, Necros
The Big Room, Akron, 1982
Collection of Laura Albert

TESCO VEE (Meatmen): We were in awe of The Misfits. I mean, we followed it from the beginning. The *Bullet* EP was one of the first records I saw Chris D review in *Slash* — he was droppin' loads about how great it was. We went out and got it, and Glenn Danzig became this cryptic figure to us, like 'I wonder what he's like!' We just thought they were the coolest thing. When they played in DC, people *hated* them. They didn't fit in. People didn't understand. There were people like Barry Hennsler and me who thought they were great, but everybody else made fun of us.

ANDY WENDLER (Necros): We went to see The Misfits at Bookie's in 1981 — they were considered a dead band at this point. Hardcore was so real and these guys had this ghoulish imagery. We went to see them — and ended up hanging out and just totally got along. That sparked two years of playin' gigs and hangin' out together all the time. We thought they were really good and had some great ideas, and vice versa. I think we really opened them up to Hardcore — you could hear it on the records. It went from Ramones-type stuff, to nine months later, when they put out records that were so fast it's unreal.

The ultimate cult band, Misfits commanded attention with their style and stage show. Adorning themselves in spikes and leather, they invented a unique image somewhere between movie monster and pro wrestler. Their trademark "devilock" hairdos resembled pompadours pulled down to the chin. The Misfits looked incredible onstage but their spraypainted, skull-covered gear would always cause problems.

Show flyer for Misfits, Necros
Detroit, 1983
Collection of Andy Wendler

TESCO VEE: Well, live — they were a fuckin' nightmare 'cause they'd buy these really cheap guitars and then cover them in black goo, so they'd go out of tune real easy. It just never came together. But they were really cool guys. Their whole image was awesome.

JERRY ONLY: Once I came up with the hairdo and Doyle joined, we wound up being like The Ramones. As you know, Doyle is my little brother; we got the devilock thing going down. Glenn touched on it but didn't take the same hairdo. He wanted a little bit the fatter thing with the side part, kind of like what he's got now. Googy stuck out like a sore thumb because he looked like Billy Idol. He had bleached-blond hair on the *Walk Among Us* album. We kept tellin' him, 'C'mon Googy, you gotta do something.' He kept trying to talk us into doing Rap like the Beastie Boys.

GRAHAM McCULLOCH (Negative Approach, Meatmen): We stayed at Jerry and Doyle's parents house during the *Process Of Elimination* tour. His parents owned X-acto's biggest competitor — that's where they got all the spikes. Doyle's room was a basement, with cut stones to look like a castle dungeon. They had manacles and chains hanging, black carpeting, and over the windows was coffin lining. They built the bathroom doorway up to look like a turret. The shelves were cut out like bat wings, the edges were painted blood red. They had all these Japanese toys — and a big pet iguana. Five steps out the door was a heated pool. It was the weirdest thing. 'The Halloween Room,' where they kept their secret projects: nobody could look in. It was rumored they were working on a bat-shaped guitar for Doyle. We never got to see it but that's the thing I remember the most.

In 1981, The Misfits released the "Halloween" single, and headlined The Ritz in NYC — where they recorded the live version of "Mommy, Can I Go Out And Kill Tonight," which would appear on their epic *Walk Among Us* LP of '82. The Misfits' best and best-selling album, they recorded it for three grand at Mix-O-Lydian Studios in Boonton, NJ, for Ruby Records, a subsidiary of the LA-based Slash label.

Despite the success of their first national tour, in support of *Walk Among Us*, the friction among four guys in a van led to huge spats, particularly between Glenn and Googy — leading to Googy's departure upon returning home. The two argued over the stupidest things. They once had a fistfight over cheeseburgers: Googy wanted two; Glenn would only get him one. Many will tell you that working with Glenn could be very unrewarding.

JERRY ONLY: I liked Googy, he was really dedicated. When we did *Walk Among Us,* he was spot-on. He worked in Manhattan, lived in Queens, would take a bus from Port Authority to Hasbrouck Heights to Lodi, and we'd pick him up. He'd show up three, four times a week, sometimes five. He'd do his job; I'll never say anything about him during that *Walk Among Us* period. That's why that album is the real calling card for our band.

Ad for Misfits Fiend Club, 1982
Collection of the author

This ain't no love-in
This ain't no happening
— The Misfits, "Night Of The Living Dead"

An unbelievably violent episode at SF's Elite Club during the tour with Googy greatly accelerated The Misfits' notoriety. For years thereafter, scenesters decried Misfits violence — only adding to their legend.

GLENN DANZIG: All night people were getting hit with bottles and beer cans. These kids singled out Doyle and were hitting him with full beer cans. Finally, Googy jumped in the audience mid-song, started a huge fight with one of the guys throwing shit. Googy started getting his ass kicked. Doyle saw one guy throwing beer, so he hit him in the head with his guitar. It went crazy after that — a big riot basically. When *Maximum RockNRoll* did their story, it was one-sided, saying that everybody wanted The Misfits gone but that's bullshit because a lot of people had come there to see us. It was typical yellow journalism from *Maximum RockNRoll.*

JERRY ONLY: That show was very mismanaged, run by a guy who had very bad security. He had a bunch of Black guys doing security, a bunch of White teenagers he was serving drinks to. I'm not saying there were racial problems, but you had eight Blacks, 2000 kids. When we take the stage that's exactly what we do: we take the stage. Doyle was defending himself — it got out of hand. It shouldn't've happened. I feel bad about it.

The Misfits and Black Flag became close over the years. Henry Rollins, a huge fan, sported a prominent Misfits "crimson ghost" tattoo. In early '83, Flag drummer Robo moved to Jersey to replace Googy. When their summer tour hit LA, Glenn, Jerry, Doyle and Robo went into the studio with SST engineer Spot to cut *Earth A.D.* — which turned out to be their final recording. The Misfits' strengths as a Hardcore group lay in non-HC attributes — melodic songs and larger-than-life aura — but by the time of *Earth A.D.* Glenn was writing hyperspeed blasts that sounded very standard. Though many now consider the LP a masterpiece, at the time it was poorly received, its best feature being the gnarly cover art of "Mad" Marc Rude.

Newspaper ad for *Walk Among Us*, 1982
Collection of the author

JERRY ONLY: It got to a point that Glenn was trying to form the band into a commodity that lent itself to what was hip at the time. I didn't see any sense in "Demonomania." "We Bite" — I liked the song but not the title — it's a queer joke or something. I think Glenn was tapped. He was taking a band doing songs like "Halloween" and "Vampira," making them do songs of lesser quality. He was a real hard-ass about it, too.

GRAHAM McCULLOCH: When Misfits played fast, they lost what they had that was special. They wrote really good Punk Pop singles. It was a big part of your record shopping trip to find those singles. They looked cool and sounded cool. But quite honestly *Earth A.D.* was a total piece of shit.

GLENN DANZIG: I didn't like *Earth A.D.* at all. The songs were played too fast. Certain songs like "Earth A.D." were meant to be played fast, but others like "Devilock" weren't meant to be like that — and the album ended up sounding like one long song. That's because the guys in the band couldn't play. I just couldn't get them to slow down. I mean, a lot of people swear by that album — it's like their bible — but I prefer our other material.

JERRY ONLY: If Glenn will give me the two-inch tape, I'll let you hear what that record *really* sounds like. Glenn slept through it. We'd done a gig at the Santa Monica Civic Center with Black Flag; after the show they took us to this studio. We recorded from midnight to nine the next morning. My amps faced one way, Doyle's faced the other way — Robo sat between the two stacks. We recorded it while Glenn slept. The only time Glenn got up was when we did 'Mommy, Can I Go Out And Kill Tonight?' You can hear him lay it down so we could start the song — then he went back to bed. We had 24 tracks and we did tracks where we'd just let our guitars feed back. That's why you hear all that squealing at the start of 'Earth A.D.' Glenn doesn't even know what's on that tape 'cause he wasn't awake when we did it. I know the way he mixes; he tries to save money, and do it in these rinky-dinky places. I am sure he didn't sit down and listen to each of the tracks, and that's what needed to be done. I gave what he did a D — it could have been an A-plus. The whole concept behind *Earth A.D.* was Motorhead meets The Misfits —it should've been *Walk Among Us* and the cream of the crop of Thrash. That would have been the right move but Glenn didn't want to hear that. People consider it the Thrash Metal Bible; to a certain extent it is, but it broke up the band. He just wanted to be like everybody else.

Robo worked at Pro-Edge and moved to the Caiafa farm in Vernon after they sold their Lodi house. Once Robo wore out his welcome, he got shipped to Glenn's house — which didn't work out either. Glenn couldn't stand Robo and apparently let him know it. He especially couldn't stand that Robo was into the Jerry/Doyle blue-collar lifestyle: now three macho dudes with hot cars would jam on Van Halen songs all night long. This type of shit drove Glenn crazy and sent him further from the fold.

BILL STEVENSON (Baltimore promoter): I booked The Misfits in Baltimore towards the end of their career — they were a trip. We'd moved the show to this high school party at a rec center after we'd had problems with the owner of the place we usually booked. It was a weird sight: Robo trying to get blowjobs from 15-year-old girls and Jerry and Doyle not far behind him. Glenn was not amused.

GLENN DANZIG: I hated the whole Heavy Metal attitude. Those guys were happy working for their dad, making lots of money. They liked Judas Priest and Van Halen — I couldn't stand that shit. I liked loud music but I liked Motorhead more. There's a big difference between Judas Priest and Motorhead — Motorhead were a loud, heavy Punk band with double kickdrum. I never liked Priest and I still hate Van Halen. I'd spent a lot of time doing The Misfits but I wasn't happy anymore. It was time to move on.

Bickering between Glenn and Robo precipitated Robo's departure. During The Misfits' final show, in Detroit on Halloween '83, his replacement, ex-Genocide drummer Brian Damage, got too nervous/drunk after a song or two — so they pressed their friend Todd Swalla of the Necros into duty.

Show flyer for Misfits *Earth A.D.* tour, LA, 1983
Collection of the author

GLENN DANZIG: Robo never got his own place. He was working off the books for Jerry's family and I was like, 'You've lived here for a year now, it's time to pay some bills.' He said, 'I'm moving out then.' The other guys wouldn't put him up even though they had more room, and he left the band. After that, we used Todd from The Necros for a New York show, then used this guy — I think his name was Brian — he got totally trashed and couldn't play, so we had to have Todd come up again and play drums for the last show. That was it. The Misfits had a ton of drummers.

JERRY ONLY: We picked up Robo and he was another hard worker. He'd repair our van. Then Robo and Glenn got into a fight — another reason we broke up. We had a Halloween show and were supposed to tour Germany on *Earth A.D.* Robo was living with Glenn and coming to work with me since nobody had any money. My mom did a lot for the band and she put up Black Flag and many other bands at my place. When Robo came in, my mother was like, 'Listen boys, you've got like Chè Guevara living in my house.' We told Glenn, 'You've got to put up Robo, my mom's not hip on him.' Glenn started being mean to him so Robo said in October, 'I'm outta here.' Robo was older and he didn't want to deal with that shit. He split and we had no drummer. The only way we could've done the Halloween show and the European tour in November was to get a drummer who already knew the songs. I promised my dad that I'd do enough work during October to cover me for the month I was gone. I didn't have time to teach anybody. Glenn refused to play with Googy — he picked a kid based on the way he looked. It seemed Glenn's ego was too big for the band. I gave him the benefit of the doubt. I had seven years of time and so much money in the band — for me to walk away would have been stupid. I said, 'Find a drummer; if we pull off Halloween and the kid's good, I'll go to Germany.' We opened with "20 Eyes"; the kid didn't get one beat in the right spot.

Doyle walked over, tapped him on the shoulder and said, 'Get outta here.' So the drummer from The Necros jumped up — he knew all our shit. Glenn could have told me, 'We'll take the guy from The Necros to Germany. I'm sorry, you were right.' But he didn't say that; I told everybody that night, 'This is our last night. I'm not going to Germany.'

Show flyer for one of the last Misfits shows
with Necros, Detroit, 1983
Collection of Andy Wendler

> *I can't believe what you said to me*
> *You got some attitude*
> **— The Misfits, "Attitude"**

The Misfits behind him, Glenn began his next project: Samhain — a pagan word for Halloween. His fusion of the ghoulish might of his past work with the best Goth and Metal elements made Samhain influential.

GLENN DANZIG: Basically I disbanded the band. I could've kept calling the band The Misfits after we split but didn't think that would be right. We were gonna call it Danzig but we called it Samhain. It was what I wanted to do all along — a blending of what people call Goth with some slower grooves and tribal drums; mid-tempo, dirgey, and more progressive, for sure. Punk was getting boring. I started listening to March Violets, Sex Gang Children, Foetus, Bauhaus, Alien Sex Fiend. I like music with the original Punk ethic — change it as soon as it gets boring. Music's always been revolutionary for me. Samhain was more a real approach. It's what *Earth A.D.* was supposed to be. The other guys made it cartoon-y.

Samhain started out as a Hardcore supergroup — Glenn, with guitarists Brian Baker and Lyle Presslar of Minor Threat, and either Al Pike of Reagan Youth or ex-Negative Approach Graham McCulloch on bass. But things never panned out, so Glenn hooked up with two rabid Misfits fans he knew from Jersey, bassist Eerie Von of Rosemary's Baby and drummer Steve Zing from Mourning Noise (Baltimore native London May later replaced Zing).

BRIAN BAKER (Minor Threat): That band was short-lived. It came as Minor Threat was breaking up — it seemed like we were moving up. We thought, 'We're gonna get with the best singer in Hardcore.' At that point, Glenn Danzig was an absolute god. The fact that he'd play with Lyle and I was amazing. We had a new thing to pursue — which of course fell through. That's because Glenn is a self-sufficient person. He writes the music and plays as many instruments as he can on every record. Things didn't work out with Lyle, I and he because we all wanted to write songs. Obviously, image is a huge thing with Glenn, and Lyle and I aren't big image people — I never wanted to be in a horror movie. At a point I wasn't in Samhain any more but Lyle still was. Lyle played on Samhain's first record but wasn't actually in the band. Glenn saw Samhain in his head and tried to plug us into it, but we didn't fit. We weren't visually what he wanted; we didn't play stylistically what he wanted. Also, by this time we were good musicians, certainly better guitar players than Glenn Danzig was.

GLENN DANZIG: I went to work with Lyle and Brian — they wanted to do a new band, work with a real singer — Ian's a great frontman but he couldn't sing. I was interested because I always liked Minor Threat. I went down there; they wanted to do something similar to what I wanted, but there were too many ideas, none of the songs gelled properly. We tried to work it out with just Lyle but he ended up just doing one show at Rock Hotel. We knew it wasn't gonna work.

Samhain made great records like *November-Coming Fire* (1986, Plan 9), but never received their due. Glenn teamed up with Rick Rubin and Def Jam in summer '86, embarking on his prolific Metal career as Danzig.

GLENN DANZIG: Samhain played to way more people than The Misfits ever did. People think Misfits was a big band but it wasn't. We could have big shows in NY or LA, but anywhere else, except Detroit, you were looking at 50 to 500 people. The money was much better in Samhain and the band was able to play five nights a week, as opposed to Misfits, where the guys wanted to fly in, do three

Show flyer for first Samhain show,
Rock Hotel, NYC, 1984
Collection of Laura Albert

nights, and fly out to be back at work. Of course, that became two nights, and then one night. They wanted me and Robo to sleep in the van while they'd fly in for the shows. They were total prima donnas. When I first saw *Spinal Tap*, I was like, 'Hey, this is my old band.'

Samhain's first show in LA was at the Stardust Ballroom across from a big Metal bill at The Palladium. We did over 1500 paid while Motorhead had only 300. Actually Green River opened the show. We had direction and were moving. That's the band Rick Rubin saw at the New Music Seminar. We represented the US in a show with Celtic Frost, D.O.A., and MDC. Rubin signed Slayer at the Seminar the year before. He came backstage; I didn't even know who he was. Here's this guy with a long ZZ Top beard going crazy backstage — I'm like 'Who the fuck is this guy?' He's telling me people he knows, people who know me. He said, 'Call Glen and he'll tell you who I am.' Samhain was getting to be too much for me to handle. I was looking for a label, and we had interest from Elektra, Epic, and of course Rubin's label, which was Def Jam at the time. I decided Rubin's label would be the best to go with. That became a whole other nightmare, but he did get the band out there.

Jerry and Doyle lived a very different life, working 12 hours a day in the machine shop, then lifting weights an hour and a half. The Caiafas didn't really pick up their instruments again until '87, when they formed Kryst The Conqueror, one of the worst Metal acts conceivable, with poodlehead-for-hire Jeff Scott Soto on lead vocals. Their self-produced *Deliver Us From Evil* EP is among history's funniest records — only Jerry and Doyle weren't in on the joke. Lucky for you, the family biz was booming and Kryst The Conqueror went the way of the dinosaur.

JERRY ONLY: I was fed up — the thing with Glenn aggravated me. I had to go back to work the day after the Halloween show. We owed my old man money. I had to look in the mirror and say, 'You might end up working here the rest of your life.' It was a scary realization. If you listen to Kryst The Conqueror, it's got a lot of riffs. It sounded very Metal — that's what we were trying to do at the time. Kryst The Conqueror was the test music we wrote while we were building equipment. You build a guitar, you want to see if it will work.

We listened to other bands and loved the way Jeff Scott Soto sounded on Yngwie Malmsteen's *Marching Out* album. We paid him a couple grand and he did the job. He was into Top 40 music and never wanted to play. So Kryst The Conqueror ended up being a dead end.

> *There's some kinda love*
> *And there's some kinda hate*
> **— The Misfits, "Some Kinda Hate"**

Glenn and Jerry never fully resolved their differences — they still don't talk. In response to Metallica covering their songs, Jerry resuscitated The Misfits in '95 to keep the legend alive, bringing all the acrimony between Glenn and him back to the surface. In all fairness, Danzig wasn't being a dick: he didn't wanna drag the name through the mud. In order to have The Misfits without Glenn, Jerry and Doyle agreed to cede virtually all future publishing royalties to him. Indeed, money changes everything.

GLENN DANZIG: I'm not gonna badmouth The Misfits. There was a time when The Misfits did live up to their legacy — probably the greatest band around. That we were sloppy live wasn't my fault — which I proved with Samhain and Danzig, where there was less bullshit, less cartoon-y shit, and more of the real thing. It didn't matter how tough or wild I was onstage, I had two comic book characters beside me and it had to end. The band you see now as The Misfits is not The Misfits. It's one guy trying to relive something and make some money because Punk is fashionable again. Everyone who's seen them and called me said, 'What the fuck is this?' •

Doyle and Glenn, in happier times
Irving Plaza, NYC, 1981
Photo by Karen O'Sullivan

IQ 32 (MIDWEST FUCK YOU)

Too many buildings
Not enough people
Left to go around
— The Effigies, "Haunted Town"

Midwest cities like Detroit and Chicago, built by heavy industry, come off very blue-collar and conservative. The mindset anchors in reality: no heads in the clouds, like in LA or SF, no one right off the Mayflower, like in Boston or DC. Meat-and-potatoes America echoed in Midwestern Hardcore.

PAUL MAHERN (Zero Boys): Midwest music, especially Pop and Rock, is grounded in total Rock. If ya grew up there in the 70s your only option was Rock Radio. Most Midwest Hardcore bands had a real Detroit Rock edge. DC bands were more about hooks and Pop elements; that's the big difference.

ANDY WENDLER (Necros): The thing with early Midwest Hardcore — it was all the good points of Midwestern Hard Rock without the bullshit, without the ballads, and without the hair and silly rants.

JOHN KEZDY (The Effigies): It's a very straightforward Midwestern sense of reality. We were totally low-key. We picked up on the aspect of Punk Rock that was — in a word — *understatement*. We didn't dress up. We thought it was okay for us to go up there and play in t-shirts because it drew attention to the music and what we were trying to say.

John Brannon (Negative Approach) center
Courtesy of Tesco Vee

All genres produce initiators of ideas and those who pick up the ideas and run with them. In art and industry, for instance, Los Angeles and New York develop concepts; the Midwest builds things. Indeed, cooler, savvier outfits from the coasts created Hardcore, but the Midwest bands saw it through.

The most noteworthy included: Necros, Meatmen, and Negative Approach (Detroit); Hüsker Dü (Minneapolis); The Effigies, Naked Raygun and Articles Of Faith (Chicago); Die Kreuzen (Milwaukee); Toxic Reasons (Dayton); Tar Babies (Madison); and Zero Boys (Indianapolis).

DETROIT

Many people say Detroit had the first Punk scene, led by highly influential, heavy-ass urban artists like Iggy Pop and The Stooges and The MC5. The Stooges incited physical conflict with their crowds — highly unusual in the post-Hippie daze of 1970.

RON ASHETON (The Stooges): We weren't accomplished musicians, so out of frustration we had to do more because we couldn't express our feelings with our instruments. We hated

Hippies and were freaked out by the racial situation going on around us. We were pissed, and maladjusted. It was so much fun to watch Iggy terrorize people in the early days.

MEATMEN

Tesco Vee (Meatmen), center
from *Process Of Elimination*, Touch & Go, 1981
Collection of the author

A decade of simmering race war, White Flight, urban decay and drug abuse left few survivors. Circa 1980, the Detroit New Wave scene was small and not particularly good. The big local success story was The Romantics, with the hit single/beer jingle "What I Like About You." Most interesting of that era were Destroy All Monsters — with The Stooges' Ron Asheton, femme fatale painter Niagara, and conceptual artists Mike Kelly and Jim Shaw — and the late Fred "Sonic" Smith's Sonic Rendezvous Band, who kept that way-out Archie Shepp/Albert Ayler side of The MC5 alive.

Detroit New Wave revolved around Bookie's, a converted bowling alley which put on the first area gigs of The Police and Echo & The Bunnymen — and that's where Black Flag first played town in July '81. There was also Nunzio's, a small room with a bar and DJ, that held around 100 people.

The Hardcore scene, which came together in '81, centered on downtown with a few native bands, but thrived on suburbanites who visited the city on weekends. From the local crew came Negative Approach and L7 (Detroit) and, spread across Detroit's suburban sprawl, the Meatmen and Crucifucks (Lansing), Violent Apathy (Kalamazoo), and Necros (in nearby Maumee, OH). Many of those misfit got together either buying records at Schoolkids in Ann Arbor or grinding wheels at a skateboard park in Roseville.

JOHN BRANNON (Negative Approach): The early Detroit Hardcore scene was about 20 guys, and a few chicks taking photos. There was an early Punk scene but it was more about fashion, and the bands sucked. So they finally started letting our bands play the clubs in '80. They were really frightened at first, before they gradually caught on.

MEATMEN frontman Tesco Vee — large (6'6"), rude and intimidating — became the prime motivator of Detroit's Hardcore legions. Tesco fucked with anybody and everybody with his *Touch & Go* fanzine, and released the first Midwest HC records on his Touch & Go label. He was at least six or seven years older than most of his partners-in-crime (a serious age gap in a very teenage scene), but he remained immature enough to be right at home. Prior to his Punk baptism, Tesco was the ultimate 70s rocker, sporting a huge afro and a Budgie "In For The Kill" jacket — later covered with a Meatmen cloth.

TESCO VEE (Meatmen): My dad was school superintendent — I really fuckin' bummed him out. I'll never forget the night we moved to Lansing. It was my senior year — all the fuckin' preppy cheerleaders came over to the house at 11 P.M. to welcome the superintendent's son to the neighborhood. I answered the door in cutoffs and this giant hair — they looked at me like I came from Mars. It was so great. They all came in; it was uncomfortable conversation for ten minutes, then they left. Of course, I immediately hooked

up with all the biggest burnouts in school — the guys that
drove hearses and inhaled ether from the science lab and
guzzled cans of Old Milwaukee at 9 A.M. I managed to
graduate from college so I'm living proof that you can party
and get the job done!

**The unbearable burbs of East Lansing and Okemos
spawned other bad apples like the notorious Ramsey
brothers — Rich on bass and younger brother Greg on
guitar — of Meatmen, as well as members of Crucifucks.**

DAVID WEST (artist): I remember the original Meatmen.
The older Ramsey brother went to the Navy, where he became
a loan shark. He joined to spite his parents, who were
academics. There he got exposed to a lot of early Punk, and
reveled in what he found. Bob Vermuellen — or Tesco Vee —
was the leader of an insurrection at our very political high
school. He had his own underground paper called *The Iguana*,
which was seminal. This was a druggy scene. It was a
criminal sect, but a very smart one.

TESCO VEE: I went to the same high school that spawned
Rich Ramsey, who I must credit with part of the motivational
insanity for the early Meatmen. He looked like a normal guy.
He'd bring a bowling bag to any bar he went to; in the bag he
had a bottle of liquor with the mixers and ice and plastic cups.
Right there I said, 'This guy's cool!' He'd cover his jacket with
the most graphic *Hustler* beaver shots — safety pin 'em on. He

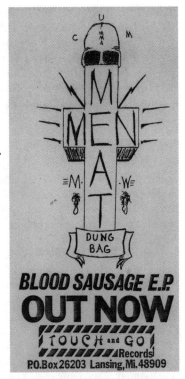

did really mean pranks to people; we just hit it off. Rich was
in the Navy. As a matter of fact, at one time he was the caterer for Frank Zappa — there's a
trivia tidbit for ya. Years later, after I moved to DC, when we did *Dutch Hercules*, he moved
all his shit into my apartment and tried to get a lame job for a week; when it didn't happen,
he went back to Michigan and didn't tell me. So I put all his shit in the basement, and all the
Salvadorans in my apartment building were walking around in MDC t-shirts: they stole all
his shit! He had big fishbowls full of change and books and 7"s, and I just stuck it in the
basement. Needless to say, we've never been friends since.

**After high school, Tesco majored in English at Michigan State. Inspired by
caustic *Slash* mag critics Chris Dejardines (of The Flesheaters) and the late Claude
Bessey (a k a Kickboy Face), he began writing about Punk. His first zine was The
999 Times, a short-lived four-page xerox hero-worship of the group 999. Then came
Touch & Go, a top HC rag. "Touch & Go" was the title of an early 7" by Magazine.
Bob V. adopted "Tesco Vee" after seeing a photo of Throbbing Gristle posed in front
of Tesco, the British dimestore.**

TESCO VEE: 'Meatmen' came from B.F., the other half of *Touch & Go* Magazine — another
former good friend who I've left strewn behind me on the trash pile of life. I'd pick him up —
he was living with his folks; every time he'd let out a big belch, I could guess what meat he
had for dinner. So I said, 'You are the meat man!' That's why I called the band the Meatmen.

**The Meatmen spewed infantile music with sophomoric lyrics. Their late 1979
taping of the intro to "Tooling For Anus" on a reel-to-reel in the Ramsey parents'
bedroom sounded like kids recording their farts and finding it riotously funny —
unfortunately, these were college students. The first two Meatmen 7" EPs, '81's**

Blood Sausage (with "Tooling For Anus" and "I'm Glad I'm Not A Girl") and '82's *Crippled Children Suck*, infamous for its tasteless cover rendering of a handicapped child, were packaged as '83's breakthrough album *We're The Meatmen ... And You Suck* — over 100,000 copies sold to date.

By that '83 heyday, Tesco's life had become a strange sociological juxtaposition: out of college and (through his dad's pull) working daytimes as an elementary school teacher — then wearin' leather chaps and stickin' microphones up his butt by night.

BARRY HENNSLER (Necros): Tesco was this decadent, drug-taking, scammer, smoking-jacket-slick motherfucker banging all these broads. He was king funny-guy and supreme bachelor — then morning comes and he's off to teach fourth-graders how to string sentences together. We were in high school, living with our parents, and it was a great excuse to go crazy whenever we'd go hang out with him. We'd get completely fucked up, run around Lansing and fuck with people — and he'd encourage it. To this day, I have the world's worst reputation in that town. We'd go to parties and no one fucked with us because we were so much younger than everybody. We'd fuck people's houses up, steal shit, and go crazy and not care. We could get away with anything, fuck with everybody. We had a great time with him. He was this older brother none of us ever had. He was hedonistic but it was tempered with cool cultural things. He turned us onto good books and records. Most importantly, he pushed us and made us stay a band.

TIM CALDWELL (Detroit scene): My favorite time seeing Tesco was when the Meatmen played The Freezer Theater, in a slimy area down by the funeral home where Houdini was embalmed. Tesco spraypainted a pair of hot pink leather pants with jackboots, and as this was the *Blood Sausage* tour, he pulled out this giant kielbasa and started swinging it around like it's his shlong, and he knocked out this Wayne State University professor cold. I could never quite look at that guy the same after witnessing that.

Whippin' my wood to the girlie mags
Provin' to myself I'm not a fag
— Meatmen, "Orgy Of One"

A major event in developing an American HC network occurred in April '81 when Teen Idles sent their 7" EP to *Touch & Go*. By June, Tesco and his friends from the Necros were making road trips to DC. Right about that time, Tesco helped Minor Threat get a booking in the Detroit area — they held a record-release party

Show flyer for Necros, Detroit, 1981
Collection of Tesco Vee

at the Coronation Tavern over the border in Windsor, Ontario. That was the start of a so-called alliance between the formative Detroit and DC scenes.

BARRY HENNSLER: Our alliance with DC was very tenuous. Our sense of humor really differed from those people. They were very preppy, kids of people in government. There was just always this weird gap. On a musical level we related well but on a personal level ... we didn't give a shit where anyone was from; the DC people wouldn't even talk to the New York people. With us, if someone was friendly, we were friendly back ... just a Midwest thing. I got into Punk to get away from snobs — not to become a snob. They were rich DC kids and we were Midwestern bumpkins who didn't summer in Martha's Vineyard. I thought that if you aligned yourself with this specific lifestyle, it meant dropping all the bullshit from the lifestyle you left.

NECROS from Maumee, Ohio — a suburb of Toledo, which is a far suburb of Detroit — were also important to the rise of a national scene. Chubby vocalist Barry Hennsler and guitarist Andy Wendler, and wiry classmate Todd Swalla, were smart-ass upper-middle-class Nugent fans who started a Punk group as high school juniors. Then the ferocity of Black Flag's first EP turned their world upside down.

NECROS

BARRY HENNSLER (Necros): What I thought the Necros were always trying to do was to have the Nugent Rock vibe. One of the last Rock records I bought was *Double Live Gonzo* by Ted Nugent. I remember thinking, 'If this was ten times faster, I'd really like it.'

Barry Hennsler (Necros) singing from *Process Of Elimination*, Touch & Go, 1981
Collection of the author

Hennsler put out *Smegma*, a zine with the tag line "Absolutely no *Rocky Horror Picture Show* or AC/DC." He wrote to Tesco at *Touch & Go* — and a bond developed instantly: *Smegma* and *Touch & Go* just spewed all that snotty mean-spiritedness now *de rigeur* in zine culture.

TESCO VEE: I can still remember Barry, he was a fuckin' Punk. He was a snobby kid with an attitude 'cause his parents broke up. He'd spit loogies through windows. If some girl at McDonald's parking lot gave him shit, he'd hock a loogie 30 feet in the air — and land it right on her face. I thought he was cool. But we were just rebelling all around. We were Punk, but we were children of privilege; living in America it's hard not to be.

Necros first played in January 1980 at an Ann Arbor basement party, opening for Cult Heroes, an ensemble of old Stooges roadies. Barry and crew realized how bad they played that night, so they practiced and improved. On March 15, 1981 they opened for Flipper at the Second Chance to a crowd of over 400.
   The first release on Tesco's Touch & Go Records was the ultra-rare (200 copies pressed) Necros four-song 7" with "Police Brutality," in early '81. Late that year came a Necros nine-song 7" EP with "IQ 32" and "Past Comes Back To Haunt Me" — future Touch & Go Records owner Corey Rusk played bass on that one. Rusk was in the band for over a year, until he broke his leg on tour. His replacement Ron Sakowski played on '83's noted *Conquest For Death* album.

BARRY HENNSLER: Corey and I went to school together, at Maumee Valley Country Day, then at Maumee High School. We hung out and ended up being in a band together. Any misgivings I have about him — which I don't really — as time passes you realize what's petty. We just didn't click — a lot of people in our little crowd held that against him. There was a certain savviness that he lacked. But he fuckin' worked his ass off. He loaded wood onto trucks at his old man's company — he didn't have some slick job cuz he was the boss's kid. He had a shit job, worked eight hours a day, and *Touch & Go* became his. It may have been Tesco's zine; while it was half my dad's money and half Tesco's money for the first Necros single, Touch & Go #1, it wasn't a real label until Corey took over. He built it up, he earned it, it's his thing. It wasn't like he took it. When it comes to business, he inherited an amazing aptitude from his dad. His family owns Freeman Industries who make building

NEGATIVE APPROACH

John Brannon (Negative Approach) singing
from *Process Of Elimination*, Touch & Go, 1981
Collection of the author

supplies and wood products, have offices in Japan, and shit like that. You've got to hand it to him, he's the success story of our clan.

NEGATIVE APPROACH was one of the era's most intense outfits. Frontman John Brannon was an imposing motherfucker with shaved head, scowling demeanor and brutal vocal delivery — which served as a prototype for all American Skins to come.

OTTO BUJ (editor, *Sold Out*): Negative Approach was the definitive Hardcore band — them and S.O.A. made the best Hardcore singles. John Brannon's presence was so intense. He started that whole hardass stance. There's no precedent for what they did. All other Hardcore and Metal bands that followed — all these Pantera guys — are doin' the Negative Approach vibe essentially.

BARRY HENNSLER: Brannon was a burnout kid. They used to print up fake acid; he would go down to Cobo Arena and sell fake hits for five bucks a pop and split with 500 bucks. I recall seeing him at a club with all this money and he goes, 'Sammy Hagar played here tonight. I ripped off all these burnouts.' Negative Approach were great. I don't think their records were any good but live they were heavy-duty.

No-bullshit Brannon lived in Detroit but grew up in upscale St. Claire Shores, son of an Episcopalian minister. His first band, the Iggy/Dead Boys-style Static, made an excellent demo tape.

JOHN BRANNON: Growing up in the 70s, we were listening to music before Black Flag. We were into shit like Stooges, T Rex, Cooper, the Dolls. All my favorite bands had dudes who dressed up like chicks. My first show was when Kiss did that album *Kiss Alive*. I was in eighth grade — a bunch of my friends are in that picture on the back cover.

Brannon started Negative Approach after checking out the Necros. NA's first gig was in Necros drummer Todd Swalla's mom's basement in Maumee. Their two Touch & Go records ('82's 7" EP and '83's *Tied Down* LP), though good, didn't come close to their live performances, in which they did amazing covers of The Stooges' "Raw Power," and "Never Surrender" by Blitz. But despite their legend, NA soon faded. (After their summer 1983 breakup, Brannon went on to front proto-Alternative junkie band Laughing Hyenas. He was characteristically dopesick during our interview for this book).

JOHN BRANNON: It blows my mind that people still get excited about Negative Approach. I guess we were this legendary band because there were only 3000 45s and 3000 albums ever printed. It's all so mysterious because nobody saw the gigs. And it was all a lifetime ago.

Negative Approach roadie Laura Lee was a key figure in Detroit's scene — a scary-looking Black lesbian with a shaved head and tattoos, part-groovy Earth Mama, part-nasty street urchin. Years later, she took her own life.

JOHN BRANNON: It all died around '83 for me. All the original bands either broke up or died out. The whole thing started repeating itself, and getting uninteresting. There's only so much you could do with that fucking beat. I mean, we had a lot to do with inventing that whole style. We took it as far as we could, then said no more. With Negative Approach, it all just fizzled out. The end was on the road, in the middle of the *Tied Down* tour — our last show was in Memphis. The guys freaked out on the road. They were young and couldn't deal with all the hassles. Fucking pussies.

Show flyer for Necros, Negative Approach
Coronation Tavern, Windsor, Ont., 1982
Collection of Andy Wendler

L7 (not the all-girl 90s act), though fans of and friends with the Hardcore set, didn't quite qualify as a Hardcore band; they were too damn arty.

Tesco offered to put out an L7 record on Touch & Go; but the bandmembers thought themselves too left-of-center for the HC label. That's how their *Insanity* EP came out in '82 on "Touch & Go/Special Forces." L7's only tour, in support of that record, was four Midwest dates with The Gun Club.

The coolest member of L7 was their biker chick guitarist Larissa Strickland. Drummer Korey Clarke became notorious as a target of Tesco's caustic gay-baiting humor — hear the "Korey Clarke Dude Ranch" rap on the first Meatmen record. (Clarke moved to NYC to form the Metal band Warrior Soul. With ex-Necros Todd Swalla and Ron Sakowski, Larissa joined John Brannon in Laughing Hyenas.)

KEN WAAGNER (Detroit promoter): Korey Clarke was the closest thing I knew to a Kurt Cobain-type person. It was scary to see how much Cobain was like Korey before he turned into the Metal god of Warrior Soul. When I first met Korey, he was 18 with spiky blond hair, looked just like Billy Idol, had been completely ostracized in school. Everybody thought he was a freak; nobody liked him — except girls, who thought he was cute.

BARRY HENNSLER: Korey was a New Wave gay boy, then he became a Rock & Roller; that's the bottom line. I mean, how he's *not* a star boggles my mind — he's had the world's best management, best labels, and amazing budgets. Maybe the kids know what's up. He's one of those dudes that annoyed me enough when I was 16 to smack him and years later it was the mortal wound of his life. I hadn't thought twice about Korey Clarke until I read in magazines that he talked shit about me. The funny thing is, people who read it were going, 'Who's Barry Hennsler?'

CRUCIFUCKS' vulgar name and discordant assault lumped them in with Hardcore, but they were an entity unto themselves. Nefarious guitarist Gus Varner was known around Lansing to sell "Super Dope," an ethyl-alcohol wash of stems and shake from bad pot. Vocalist Doc Dart had one of the most distressingly shrill vocal styles imaginable. The name Crucifucks really pissed people off — and songs like "Cops For Fertilizer" poured fuel on the fire. Loud, blasphemous, hilarious to watch, their two Alternative Tentacles were absolutely unlistenable (Drummer Steve Shelley joined Sonic Youth in '87).

THE FIX (not twee New Wavers The Fixx), featured a big-haired, bandanna-wrapped Black guitarist and a singer who'd come onstage with his feet wrapped in bandages. Tesco loved them and put out their '81 single "Vengeance"/"In This Town" (Touch & Go #5, only 200 copies made) and the '82 EP *Jan's Room* — named for a Lansing boarding house notorious for its vicious rapes and murders. The Fix went through a "Germs" phase, then a "Discharge" phase, but their records capture neither vibe.

VIOLENT APATHY from Kalamazoo were musically nondescript. Their singer who'd lost a hand, would recklessly flail away with the stump — which could be very entertaining during their interpretation of "La Bamba." Elliott Rachman of the original Meatmen drummed.

BLIGHT was Tesco's brief art-noise project. They once opened for DKs, where they took the stage with 48" black lights and broken TV sets, and Tesco writhed on the floor covered in fluorescent paint. The ultra-rare *Blight* 7" EP of '81, which Touch & Go has threatened to reissue for years Blight was just another way for Tesco to say, "Fuck You!"

Elsewhere around Detroit, Andy Wendler of the Necros had a dumb joke group, **MCDONALDS**. Some cite **BORED YOUTH** but they never put out records (a bootleg 7" surfaced years later). **YOUTH PATROL** was based around NA's rhythm section. **SUBURBAN THREAT, FATE UNKNOWN** and **ZERO DEFECTS** (from Canton, OH) also circulated.

The best Detroit outfits appeared on the *Process Of Elimination* EP (T&G#2, 1981), the premiere Midwest Hardcore compilation.

GRAHAM McCULLOCH (Negative Approach): *Process Of Elimination* was recorded in the home studio of these Detroit Hippies. Everyone showed up one morning and hung out in the driveway. You'd take turns going in and you'd get two cracks at it. People remember all of the bands as being a lot better than they were. Early Dischord and Touch & Go stuff is the worst-recorded shit in the world — like the Negative Approach *Total Recall* CD: fifteen tracks recorded on a boom box at a live show. What's that doing on a CD? It sounds better when you hear the cracks on a record.

Show flyer for *Process Of Elimination* tour
Gallery East, Boston, 1981
Collection of Andy Wendler

Summer '81 saw the *Process Of Elimination* Tour — Meatmen, Necros, Negative Approach. Many interviewed herein cited the gigs as influential events.

TESCO VEE: We played DC — us, Red C, Iron Cross, Negative Approach and Necros. Then we played the Mudd Club in New York, the now-legendary show captured on tape. Beastie Boys were pesky kids back then going, 'Yo yo, Meatmen, Necros — get us in free.' We were like, 'Fuck you, get away.' Then we played Boston at Gallery East — it was fuckin' intense: a big room with vaulted ceilings, full-frontal windows and plants. It was a happening. Early Meatmen in Boston — I don't know why — but something about that clicked. The *Blood Sausage* EP was high on the *Boston Rock* Reader's Poll. And those were the only three shows on the *Process Of Elimination* tour!

By late '81, The Freezer Theater, a bare-bones storefront with a stage, was packing in a couple hundred kids for bills that might feature Necros, Meatmen, Negative Approach, and whatever out-of-towners that were around. The Freezer was the Detroit Hardcore meeting ground.

KEN WAAGNER: We lived, hung out, rehearsed, shopped, did everything in that neighborhood when we were 19 and drunk, high — whatever. Three hundred kids driving in from the suburbs, parking their cars there, coming to shows — it was the only place we could get away with it.

After The Freezer shut in '82, John Brannon ran a similar venue nearby — The Clubhouse, at Cass and Willis, four blocks from the projects, in the worst slums in town. Also a dilapidated storefront, it'd have five or six groups play every Friday and Saturday, always to the same 50 kids. Black Flag jammed here with Rollins on their way back to LA, before he officially joined; Youth Brigade and Social D gigged here on the *Another State Of Mind* tour.

TODD SWALLA (Necros): There were a lot of gigs then. It was a lot more intense; there was lot of violence. But we encouraged that violence, too. It was a unique time: you'd go to The Freezer or The Clubhouse and see Meatmen, Necros, L7, Negative Approach, The Allied, Bored Youth, all for two bucks, and people bitched when the shows became five bucks.

Necros played the last show at Detroit's top New Wave club, Bookie's, in late '81 and totally trashed the joint. Its owner launched Clutch Cargos in early '82. After a highly-publicized grand opening, the cops shut 'em down because they had no liquor license. The venue reopened a few months later, enjoying a solid year-long run, but pulled out when their landlord started pulling crazy shit. They moved to St. Andrew's Hall in late '82: Black Flag in '83 and Circle Jerks in '84 each played there to over 1000 kids. In late '84, the club relocated to Congress Street to accomodate increased business.

Necros manager Ken Waagner booked Clutch Cargos and Paycheck's, a Polish immigrant bar. He'd put on his first show — Misfits/Big Boys/Radical Left — at the Henry Ford College lunchroom. By '84 came competition from ex-con Scary Cary who booked The Hungry Brain, and from Corey Rusk, at The Greystone.

Show flyer for Necros, Meatmen
Freezer Theater, Detroit, 1982
Collection of Andy Wendler

KEN WAAGNER: If every person who said they were at a show was actually there, I'd be a millionaire. That's one huge misconception — that it was a raging scene. There was a total of about 20 core people: the Negative Approach guys, Necros, L7, and some people in smaller bands just trying to help out. It was not a big deal. If I would've been a shrewd businessmen, I could've made money taking advantage of people. But I'm more geared towards nurturing and baby-sitting. That was why I got into doing what I did in the first place — it needed to be done. Once in a while I'd have a show that I'd make 500 bucks, but next week I'd lose 300. I never signed a contract with anybody, ever.

Detroit developed a rep for "Right Wing" Hardcore; certainly a lot of violent Skinhead types came to shows to smash heads. Perhaps that mindset sprang from the rage of blue-collar Midwestern kids alienated by their obsolescence in the post-Industrial 80s. Maybe not. Negative Approach were a magnet for Skinhead behavior due to their White thug vibe, but never wrote racialist lyrics. By 1983 came THE ALLIED, an intimidating outfit hellbent on becoming America's answer to Skrewdriver, started by NA's original bass player.

JOHN BRANNON: Detroit was very violent in the early 80s. There was a really big

First Touch & Go Records press shot
Necros, 1983
Collection of Andy Wendler

Skinhead scene going on. I felt bad because I thought Negative Approach was the soundtrack to these kids beating the fuck out of each other. We turned all these kids onto Oi! shit, and it came back to haunt us.

TESCO VEE: A lot of nazi boys from the Detroit Hardcore days have gone on to be full-time White supremacists. They used to all come out for Negative Approach.

BARRY HENNSLER: All these stupid dudes who ended up as White supremacist loser pieces of shit — we turned all of them onto early Oi! singles like The 4 Skins, The Last Resort and Blitz, and that whole clan quickly became nazi Skinheads. They started their own zines and always dissed the Necros — even though the Necros turned them on to everything they were raving about. We weren't bleeding-heart liberals going, 'Hey, don't be a racist.' The thing with Hardcore was it was our thing. It was reflective of us without any airs put on other than trying to act tough, and here were these Skinheads walking around with English accents.

JOHN KEZDY (The Effigies): A big Skinhead scene started in Detroit. The Allied were pioneers of that whole thing. When we played Detroit, people loved us up there. Those guys in Michigan, they were gung-ho, man.

The fall of Detroit HC paralleled the erosion of relations between Corey Rusk, and his ex-friends, Tesco and the Necros. From '83, after *Conquest For Death*, through most of '85, the Necros didn't even know if they were still on the label, because of the passive-aggressive power struggle.

By '87, the Necros had grown their hair, slowed their music, and taken a full step into Metal. First came the "Tangled Up" 7" on Psycho-Mania — the label of Detroit poodleheads Seduce — then the *Tangled Up* album through Restless/Enigma — replete with Ed "Big Daddy" Roth's "Rat Fink" artwork and a version of Pink Floyd's "The Nile Song." Touring with both Megadeth and Circle Jerks that year was pretty much the end of the Necros.

To this day, relations between Rusk and the Necros are strained to the point where those early Necros records have never seen reissue. (Hennsler went on to sing for Big Chief before relocating to Chicago. Andy, with a degree in Pop Culture from Bowling Green U., runs a printing business. Corey still heads the prolific Touch & Go label. Tesco moved to DC in '83, where he still fronts Meatmen lineups.)

KEN WAAGNER: Corey took a lot of things personally when he left the Necros and there were weird feelings going on. He retained the rights to *Conquest For Death* but quit putting it out. I felt it cost the Necros a lot of momentum because that record had gotten so much great press — it was truly great. But he just put it out of print. He, Barry, and Andy supposedly had conversations about re-releasing it but things never materialized. It's fucked up. The least he could do is let them have the rights back to it.

JOHN BRANNON: Tesco had his magazine; the label evolved out of the zine. Tesco documented us to the world — he let everyone know about this great Midwest scene we had going. But he had his own other secret life, so he gradually let Corey take the reigns on the label. And that was that.

TESCO VEE: The second Necros EP came out. Corey Rusk paid for it but at that point it all shifted — I think the record had both our addresses on it. His dad was rich — he owned all these lumberyards around Ohio — so he asked me if he could take the label over. I really had no desire to run a record label, so I said, 'Sure.' Of course in retrospect I should have kept ten percent but I didn't. But I'm not gonna talk about him. Fuck him.

CHICAGO

Chicago — as compared to other major US cities — has contributed relatively little to Rock history. Prior to 1980, the only notable exports were Styx, Chicago, Cheap Trick from Rockford, The Shoes from Zion, and a few Jewish kids like Michael Bloomfield, Randy California of Spirit, and Jerry Goodman of Mahavishnu Orchestra — not a very impressive resume for a major American metropolis with a strong ethnic and Black music tradition.

As elsewhere across the country, gay bars and New Wave clubs were the first cultural outposts into marginal neighborhoods. The first club devoted to Punk culture was La Mer Viper (The Sea Snake), a dump located among the Blues bars near DePaul University. The neighbors despised La Mer so much that the club mysteriously burned to the ground in late '78.

O'Banion's, a sleazy gay bar whose scene revolved around DJs and New Wave dancing, filled the void left by La Mer. Arty acts like Special Effect (with Al Jourgensen, later of Ministry, and Frankie Nardiello, later of My Life With The Thrill Kill Kult), Epicycle, Ono, The Dadistics, and Immune System played the back room but you could hang at the front bar and ignore 'em

John Kezdy (The Effigies) singing
Chicago, 1981
Courtesy of John Kezdy

if you wanted. Chicago's notorious for bad drugs and at O'Banion's you could get your hands on cheap MDA and coke and ditchweed. A small crew of loud, drunk, pimply-faced boys congregated in the corners, bugging DJ Monica Lynch to play some Damned or Sham 69. Thus began Chicago Hardcore.

JOHN KEZDY (The Effigies): The early Chicago scene was basically art schoolers and poseurs, very much the posturing crowd — they didn't do much in the way of making music. They latched onto a scene mostly fed by music from England. They were very much against a lot of California Punk but were into the New York stuff. It didn't really produce anything; there was a very small cliquish group of people who just monopolized a few bars in Chicago: La Mer and O'Banion's.

Local HC reacted fiercely to the flash and phoniness promoted under the Punk umbrella and to the first whiffs of gentrification, which New Wavers and their comrades, the Yuppies, spearheaded. Chicago never underwent the ruinous race riots of Detroit, yet by the late 60s came the "niggerization" of the entire South Side. Hardcore made sense for a few relatively smart, disenfranchised kids during oppressive times and a need to vent called to action.

A life of restraint
Doesn't make you a saint
— The Effigies, "Hi-Lo"

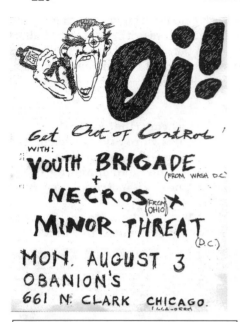

Show flyer for Minor Threat, Necros, Youth Brigade
— O'Banion's, Chicago, 1981
Collection of Laura Albert

Oz, another New Wave club based on a gay clientele, opened in '80. Occupying numerous locations, as cops repeatedly shut it down — probably cuz they didn't pay off their alderman — Oz was home to the original local HC scene. Dem, the guy who ran Oz, became The Effigies' manager, and put together the essential Chicago comp, *Busted At Oz* (Autumn Records).

The Chicago HC bands were The Effigies, Strike Under, Big Black and Naked Raygun, who all worked together, played together, and watched each other's backs, in a self-contained universe. At least that was the plan.

Though none of these outfits played in a Hardcore style, they were HC by virtue of their intense fucking attitude. Chicago HC groups had a rep as "intellectuals," and though most of the participants were educated kids from the burbs looking to blow off serious steam, few were what you'd call rocket scientists. And liquor-loving, blue-collar Chicagoans definitely did not embrace fervent Straight Edge — when I was there in '83, I remember a bunch of crewcut bulldog types in combat boots and suspenders, reeking of beer and whiskey.

TOM BERRARD (DC scene): I went on tour with Minor Threat as kind of the roadie. In Chicago we played and it wasn't all-ages. We had a big discussion with the club to figure out a way to make it okay. Ian said, 'Put an 'X' on somebody's hand, they won't drink. We don't wanna drink. Alcohol is nothing to us. We just wanna see the show.' We came across like aliens 'cause Chicago is a hard-drinking town. They just didn't understand.

THE EFFIGIES, from the northern suburb of Evanston, ranked with the best national outfits, fusing the Brit-flavored melodic sense of The Ruts and The Stranglers with stripped-down high-energy Hardcore onslaught.

JACK RABID (editor, *The Big Takeover*): The group that did it for me were The Effigies. They were the perfect Hardcore-ish Punk band — super chops, massive edge, and some of the most erudite lyrics around on social issues. They stood against the prevailing 'Boo Reagan' vibe, with stuff like *We're Da Machine*. They emerged from the pack because they were great. They went on tour, they made several albums. They mattered.

DAVE SMALLEY (DYS, Dag Nasty): The Effigies — great band. John Kezdy was really articulate and intent on not being a scumbag. Kids gave him shit 'cause the records sounded good. They stayed at DYS's house when they played Boston, and he told me, 'Where is it written in the Punk Rock Rulebook that our album has to sound like shit? We produced it with the same amount of money as these other bands, we just did it right.'

JOHN KEZDY (The Effigies): We tended to be real Chicago-based ... a lot of people took that to mean a real parochial, narrow music, but it wasn't — we wanted to set ourselves apart from other bands around the country. There was an LA scene and New York scene but we definitely had our own ideas about what Chicago represented. So we naturally let that define us.

Frontman John Kezdy fucked off at The University Of Wisconsin for a year, but got homesick and returned to Evanston in June '80 to form The Effigies with best friend and neighbor, drummer Steve Economou. Like many HC types, beefy Kezdy came off as a pushy peacemaker, always looking to tell someone what to do. But he made things happen around Chicago.

Naysayers attacked The Effigies as vicious Skinheads, but their "boots and braces" look derived from Brit Punk style rather than racialist dogma. And their bohunk roots definitely meshed with that "working-class-bloke" ethos of Sham 69 and Angelic Upstarts.

Show flyer for Effigies
Cubby Bear, Chicago, 1983
Collection of John Kezdy

JOHN KEZDY: Within Hardcore was a political split, Left and Right Wing. You see Skins on *Oprah* today — a lot of fuckheads who've been co-opted by the Ultra-Right. That's not what we were. We were into spare living, similar to the Straight Edge vibe in DC except we weren't religious about it. We were drinkers, but had a get-your-shit-together attitude, too. We had our own way of doing things. Henry Rollins embodies that — and nobody's gonna call him a Skinhead. You know how the Skinhead thing gets muddled: like in England — some were apolitical, and many were football hooligans. Angelic Upstarts and UK Subs were decent blokes, nice guys — more in line with the people I was used to dealing with in Chicago.

Kezdy entered nearby Northwestern U. in fall '80. He got a letter a few months later from Steve Albini, offering to work for free for The Effigies. He never did, but largely based on a shared distrust of the music biz, the two became fast friends. They'd endlessly discuss the need of all "real Chicago bands" to pool resources, help each other book gigs, create artwork, and network. Kezdy and Albini took their idea to Jeff Pezzati of Naked Raygun, initiating long, heartfelt problem-solving sessions. Those encounters bred the Ruthless Records co-op; it put out the first discs by The Effigies, Albini's Big Black and Naked Raygun.

JOHN KEZDY: Ruthless, at one point, Steve Albini kinda took over, though it really was just a co-op; everyone pitched in. As much as I hate to admit it, it a totally communistic experiment. It worked for a while then fell apart. The guy from Rifle Sport eventually picked up the label and moved to Minneapolis. At that point it had nothing to do with us anymore.

Events justified Effigies's contempt for record labels. Autumn Records, the shady operation behind *Busted At Oz*, arranged to release the Effigies' debut *Haunted Town*, a six-song 12" EP recorded and mixed in one Sunday afternoon. Autumn head George Kapulis hoped to take over the music biz, with The Effigies spearheading his schemes. But right after pressing the vinyl, George got married and split town. Only after a nightmare ordeal did The Effigies get the disc back. (Haunted Town reappeared in '84 as part of The Effigies, the outfit's best-seller.)

In view of early enthusiasm, the Ruthless kibbutz vibe quickly faded. Despite noble ideas, no one knew what the fuck they were doing. Abysmal record sales proved that this trial by fire was a money pit. In '83, The Effigies moved to so-called indie Enigma Records for *We're Da Machine* — the title referring to the corrupt Chicago Democratic political machine. After '84's *For Ever Grounded* (the initials spelling "effigy") they ditched their machine-gun HC for a more serious sound, signing with the Fever label, best known for novelty band Dead Milkmen. Depending who you ask, their Fever albums, *Fly On A Wire* ('85) and *Ink* ('86), rated either as post-HC gems or shoddy garbage. Like every Effigies record, few copies sold.

JAY ROBBINS (Government Issue): I immediately fell for Effigies, especially since nobody I knew cared about them. People used to say they were this Right Wing Skinhead band, something I always found really hard to swallow in Hardcore, but I never saw that or got that from their records. I just thought: here's a band with real intelligent lyrics, trying to express their rage in a constructive way, musically kick-ass and adventurous. Even those last records, *Ink* and *Fly On The Wire*, were awesome.

Show flyer for Naked Raygun
O'Banion's, Chicago, 1982
Collection of the author

The Effigies worked too hard for little reward: after six years banging their heads against the wall, they broke up in 1986. As fate would have it, Metallica offered The Effigies a tour just afterwards. They did reform in '87 for a year or so, and still reunite for occasional one-off gigs. Ever the enforcer, Kezdy continued his education, earning a law degree. He now runs a prosecutor's office, dishing out a different set of rules and regulations.

JOHN KEZDY: I'm a prosecutor in Kankakee, IL. Of course, people point to that — the *[Chicago] Reader* wrote real nasty, catty comments. I don't spend my time busting kids for smoking pot — that's not an offense we go after. The people we go after, believe me, are bad. I've always felt I was on the side of good — and I know this sounds Pollyanna-ish — I think I'm still idealistic about what I do. I don't know about where you live but the criminals here are motherfuckers who will kill you at the drop of a dime. These people to me are my enemy — just like the cops who bust kids over the head for no reason. I don't stand for that shit, it's illegal. Not all police are assholes — that's too simplified a world view; that's kid talk.

Big Black didn't play Hardcore but projected the same fuck-you stance — hear 1983's *Lungs* EP and 1984's *Racer X* (both Ruthless). The Industrial grade assault of singer/guitarist Steve Albini, guitarist Santiago Durango, and bassist David Riley, aided by a drum machine, effectively provided an angst-ridden response to the rigid English post-Punk of Gang Of Four or Psychic TV. Big Black played a lot of HC bills early on — Albini got deep into the scene through his smarmy *Maximum RockNRoll* rants and his work with Ruthless. (Durango, like John Kezdy, became an attorney; Albini, later of Rapeman and Shellac, produced *In Utero*, Nirvana's final studio album.)

NAKED RAYGUN, like Big Black, were trailblazers of Alternative Rock. They had all the right credentials — they played many seminal HC bills, and their first records, the "Flammable Solids" 7" and the *Basement Screams* 12", came out through Ruthless — but HC fans never grasped the oblique lyrics and stark post-Punk melodies. Raygun seemed lost when action in the pit turned violent. Jeff Pezzatti and crew remained a mid-80s wonder.
STRIKE UNDER also had a gruff Effigies-style working class sound. Though they had few fans, their '81 debut 12" EP gained fame as the first release by the

prolific Wax Trax! label. They broke up in late '83; striking frontman Steve Björklund formed Breaking Circus (who later relocated to Minneapolis) with brother Chris on guitar and John Kezdy's younger brother Pierre (who played in Naked Raygun, Bloodsport and Pegboy) on bass.

By '83 came Chicago Hardcore's next wave, more tuned to the national scene. Suddenly, "unity" and standardized HC mattered, in antithesis to the first wave. Leftist activists Articles Of Faith and frivolous party combo Rights Of The Accused led the way — both whom negated the austere blue-collar vibe of Effigies or Naked Raygun. From the nearby burbs came the Garage Rock of The Suburban Nightmare, who did an album for Midnight Records — they relocated to San Francisco to become the vile Dwarves.

ARTICLES OF FAITH was fronted by vigilant politico Vic Bondi, a Jello Biafra type who acted as the conscience of the mid-80s Midwest scene. People truly

Articles Of Faith, 1983
Xeroxed photo by Marie Kanger, origin unknown
Collection of Laura Albert

listened to him. Bob Mould of Hüsker Dü produced their first record, '84's *Give Thanks*, and '87's *In This Life*. Most of AOF's extensive history occurred after 1986, falling outside this book's scope. (Bondi put out a solo LP in '87, formed Jones Very, and became a college professor.)

AL QUINT (editor, *Suburban Voice*): Articles Of Faith, great band, great guys. Vic was very smart and articulate and could express viewpoints much better than I could. I thought this music could change the world.

JOHN KEZDY: Vic Bondi went to DC and came back after seeing Minor Threat with his head shaved — an instant transformation that I was very suspicious of. There was a rift between The Effigies and Articles Of Faith. Vic's first band, Direct Drive, did Springsteen covers. They had a Left Wing agenda and were Clash clones in the political sense. I disagreed with that, but I really didn't like the fact they were already copping somebody else's position; it was so secondhand by that point. He became this big icon for what can be termed the second wave of Chicago Hardcore, which as you said were Articles Of Faith, Rights Of The Accused. By that point, the bands cloned each other. They sounded homogeneous — I stopped being able to discern between bands. They started becoming less melodic, and if you ever hear anybody talk about the Chicago style what they really mean is Hardcore with melody. It was less thrash and more tunesmithing.

What ultimately killed Hardcore in Chicago killed all local art and music: lack of support. No one in the media wrote about it, covered it, or took it seriously. Hitting a dead end, most participants figured they'd be better off quitting or moving — although a few persevered and prospered.

Chicago writhed in the throes of the mid-80s Wax Trax! "Industrial Revolution." Unlike the sadistic Noise of Throbbing Gristle and SPK, the nascent Industrial scene grew out of "Jack Your Body" House à la Frankie Knuckles, which came out of gay dance culture and high-bpm DJs. Medusa's hosted many early House and Acid parties — and on off-nights Sean Duffy booked HC shows. Pailhead, an '88 partnership of Ministry's Al Jourgensen and Ian MacKaye, symbolized the Industrial/HC crossover.

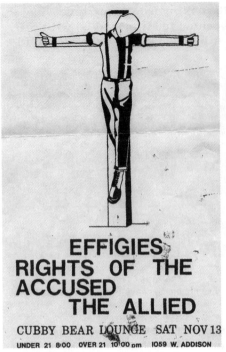

EFFIGIES
RIGHTS OF THE
ACCUSED
    THE ALLIED

CUBBY BEAR LOUNGE SAT NOV 13
UNDER 21 8:00   OVER 21 10:00 pm   1059 W. ADDISON

Show flyer for Effigies, Rights Of The Accused
Cubby Bear, Chicago, 1983
Collection of John Kezdy

JOE CARDUCCI (SST): I really wish Chicago had more to offer. I do like it as a place to live and work but it's a blue-collar town that doesn't generate a bohemia that is fearless. It generates a real tight-ass negative type who's not open-ended, so they have no impact and leave no trace in town. I kept waiting for things to happen. The Effigies had the sound to make things happen there but no Chicago band wanted to go out and play the burbs. Lately, a lot of people have moved to Chicago, so there's more Alternative stuff going on. Smashing Pumpkins came from the burbs, and now there's a scene in the burbs, so it's a bit hipper than it ever was.

MINNEAPOLIS

Prior to Punk, Minneapolis provided little fodder for the music industry. No Rock & Roll tradition existed. Maybe there was nothing to rebel against.

Life in friendly places tends to make kids crazy and rebellious. Thus, Mpls cultivated it's own brand of alienation and self-loathing.

The first Punk club was J.'s Longhorn Bar. The scene grew slowly, but eventually bands arose, most notably Suicide Commandos — and their classic *Emission Control* 7" — and The Suburbs, whose self-titled EP was the first release on the noted Twin/Tone label.

HÜSKER DÜ (Swedish for "Do you remember?" and the name of a popular strategy board game), a young outfit whom the J.'s Longhorn scene inspired, played a pivotal role in Hardcore's do-it-yourself explosion. The trio of vocalist/guitarist Bob Mould, drummer Grant Hart, and bassist Greg Norton in turn inspired many kids to pick up instruments.

Hart and Norton worked at Cheapo Records, St. Paul's only Punk store. Regular customer Mould — a flannel-shirted Macalester College student from upstate New York — worshipped Suicide Commandos, and took lessons from their guitarist Chris Osgood. Hart played drums and keyboards in South St. Paul garage ensembles. Bassist Norton (sporting a Rollie Fingers-style waxed handlebar mustache) learned fast.

Hüsker Dü first gigged in June '79, filling in for a cancellation at Ron's Randolph Inn, a St. Paul dive. They next performed at Macalester parties. Like other HC pioneers, Hüsker Dü weren't accepted in local circles.

GRANT HART (Hüsker Dü): The overall reaction from the local Punk and New Wave scene: the speed our songs were played at was dismissed. Also, we were only 17 and 18 — very young for the scene. They were like, 'Who are these uncultured people who play too fast? Don't they know the first Ramones album came out two years ago?'

Hüsker Dü's debut 7", "Statues," came out on Terry Katzman's Reflex label in January 1981. The dissonant high-speed Hardcore of their early days starkly contrasts with the proto-Alternative sound for which they'd become legendary.

GRANT HART: Katzman was the mercantile end of things. He worked at cool record stores, and we associated with him as closely as possible. Though he was a friend, I admit there were ulterior motives. We compared the way people were doing things — especially the Crass scene in the UK, which emphasized more communal aspects. People realized, 'We could treat this as an unsuccessful business or outstandingly successful commune.' Many bands profited from being able to mix their capitalism with their socialism. That's where we were coming from.

Hüsker Dü first hit the road playing Chicago late '80 and early '81. Greg Ginn and Chuck Dukowski of Black Flag caught one gig; totally blown away, they initiated SST Records' long relationship with the trio. They hoped to do a Hüsker LP, but no one had any cash. The next discs — '81's *Land Speed Record* **(live in Chicago) and '82 's brilliant "In A Free Land" single — instead came out on New Alliance, the imprint of Flag's pals, the Minutemen.**

Hüsker Dü, 1984
(L-R): Greg Norton, Grant Hart, Bob Mould
from *The Blasting Concept Vol. II*, SST, 1985
Collection of the author

JOE CARDUCCI (SST): Without SST, Hüsker Dü — if you've heard their first 7" — may not have survived that hipster attitude you describe. The general attitude was 'Punk Rock is over.' I remember Bob Mould telling me they went through a bad time. He didn't elaborate but I know what that bad time was: they doubted their own vision and let it distract them a while. Bob kept a bit of that sheen on his guitar but they dropped that thing fast. They saw Black Flag in Chicago on Flag's first tour. It either changed them or confirmed that they'd been right in the first place, and they just dropped whatever the fuck else they were doing.

A call to Mould could usually guarantee a traveling HC outfit a Twin Cities date, and one of the Hüskers'd always put up out-of-town vanloads for the night. When I went with No Trend for a string of '83 Midwest dates with Hüsker Dü — Chicago, Madison, Mpls — the Huskers were cool enough to split the take three ways with us and the local openers, $120 per band at best.

The trio were all gay men hung out with outcast teenage boys. Everyone who knew them says their predations were discreet — and they basically were. But one creepy Hüsker memory persists of an overweight, barefoot and drugged-out Grant Hart, on the prowl for young meat after a show.

By '83, Hüsker Dü's sound was evolving. Beatlesque hooks and reflective lyrics came to the forefront, as Mould tempered his over-the-top axe assault. This new direction accompanied their official move to SST with '83's *Metal Circus* **and '84's noted double-album** *Zen Arcade***. Like-minded '85 works** *New Day Rising* **and** *Flip Your Wig* **connected with a relatively wide audience — thanks to SST's excellent distribution. For the first time, some form of Hardcore percolated to the upper realms of the Rock media.**

Dü's sonic maturation was probably a good thing, because they were an unsuccessful HC group. Other Midwest bands with whom they associated — Effigies, Naked Raygun, Die Kreuzen, Tar Babies — had similar problems.

JOHN KEZDY (The Effigies): There came such factionalization. People only wanted Hardcore, they weren't interested in bands like Hüsker Dü or The Effigies. We played with 'em the night they recorded *Land Speed Record* — and no one was there. Bob Mould's a great guy, and talk about networking — he put us up a few times. They'd do their HC set whenever necessary, depending on the crowd. They were elder statesmen who could offer more than just Thrash. But most Hardcore fans were never into 'em.

Show flyer for Hüsker Dü
North Base Armory, Norman, OK, 1983
xeroxed from *Maximum RockNRoll* #4
Collection of Sal Canzonieri

Hardcore happened in Mpls primarily due to Hüsker Dü's hard work, particularly in setting up all-ages Sunday matinees at First Avenue and Goofy's Upper Deck. The Hüskers obviously influenced up-and-coming artists who played those gigs: The Replacements, Loud Fast Rules (later Soul Asylum), Man Sized Action and Rifle Sport.

THE REPLACEMENTS, Paul Westerberg's group, were originally Hardcore, though they'd ultimately earn more mainstream acclaim. I saw 'em in '82 at DC's 9: 30 Club, touring for their second record, *The Replacements Stink*, where guitarist Bob Stinson, wearing a dress and dripping mascara, drunk to the point of crying, repulsed the sparse crowd of Straight-Edge types.

LOUD FAST RULES were a ragtag HC outfit of 15-year-olds. They became SOUL ASYLUM, at which point Bob Mould produced their '84 debut *Say What You Will* (Twin/Tone). (Dave Pirner and crew flirted with stardom — undone the day then-President Clinton declared them his favorite band).

MAN SIZED ACTION would probably not be remembered had not Mould produced 1983's *Claustrophobia* (Reflex). Others on the scene included the Hüsker-inspired RIFLE SPORT, BREAKING CIRCUS, OTTO'S CHEMICAL LOUNGE (a White Funk combo that mutated into the Twin/Tone band Blue Hippos), and FINAL CONFLICT — the only local Thrash outfit.

Minneapolis's budding mid-80s Rock scene gravitated to the building at 2541 Nicollet Avenue, home of Twin/Tone Records. Hüsker Dü and The Replacements rented office space there, and both The Replacements and Soul Asylum recorded at Nicollet Studios in the basement. (In '88 Grant Hart put out the solo EP *2541*, a thinly-veiled jab at that scene.)

By '85, the Hüskers' kinship with SST reached a climax, in a dispute more rooted in artistic than economic concerns. They particularly felt limited by SST studio guru Spot's eccentric, "anti-production" values. Mould, Hart and Norton got so worked up that, to ensure artistic control, they allowed no one outside the group (not even trusted soundman and producer Lou Giordano) in the studio during their sessions.

Hüsker Dü left SST and inked to Warner Bros., the first Hardcore outfit to jump to a major. Indier-than-thou types ragged on their '86 big league debut *Candy Apple Grey*, but the only distinction between it and previous efforts was improved production quality. The Dü threw in the towel in '87 after manager and best friend David Savoy killed himself — although Hart's very-ugly drug woes surely pushed the situation over the edge.

(Bassist Greg Norton later played in a minor outfit called Grey Matter, and now lives in Red Wing, MN and works as a chef. Hart stepped out from behind the drums with solo records and with Nova Mob. Mould realized significant success as a solo artist and with his combo Sugar).

INDIANAPOLIS

Indianapolis saw surprisingly good Punk and New Wave activity, probably due to ubiquitous boredom and dissatisfaction in that conservative-Christian second-rate city. Dow Jones And The Industrials, a DEVO-type flop, and Latex Novelties, in the Vibrators vein, toiled on the local circuit. But the best shit came from an hour south, in Bloomington, Indiana: The Gizmos, Midwest rockers with a revved-up sound, short haircuts, and bad attitude.

ZERO BOYS, a powerful outfit similar to (and as important as) Hüsker Dü or The Effigies, were influenced by The Gizmos (1976-1980) and their four 7" EPs. Indianapolis HC began and ended with Zero Boys' short reign.

Zero Boys vocalist/guitarist Paul Mahern discovered Punk in '78, as a scrawny, zit-faced 14-year-old. Immediately inspired to play along with Ramones and Pistols records in his bedroom, he joined with like-minded school chums to play a party in January '79 which other future Zero Boys members, all at least five years older, attended. Sharing an uncommon interest, they bonded.

Show flyer for Zero Boys, Repellents
Heads Or Tails, Indianapolis, 1982
Collection of Laura Albert

PAUL MAHERN (Zero Boys): I cut my hair spiky and wore a black leather jacket. To Black kids I was Fonzie, to White kids I was just some fag. Punks were the ultimate outcasts, far below nerds on the popularity chain. Also, here in the Midwest, the general populace is a bit behind the times, so they didn't understand what my deal was. I had a small group of four or five friends that also listened to and explored similar music.

Zero Boys — dressed Ramones-style in leather jackets, ripped jeans, and high-top sneakers — first played April '79, opening for Latex Novelties at Crazy Al's, Indy's CBGB; they covered "Sonic Reducer" (Dead Boys), "Faster and Louder" (Dictators), "Search and Destroy" (Stooges). Zero Boys started to play once or twice a month to the same handful of misfit kids. They released their own 7" EP in January '80, *Living In The 80s*, but they were not yet playing Hardcore. That came in '81 — after they started to make regular pilgrimages to Chicago to see the Bad Brains and DKs. Two influential LA groups also made it to Indy back then — X on their second album tour in early '81, and Black Flag in early '82.

PAUL MAHERN: A key event was seeing Dead Kennedys in Chicago. I remember having someone stagedive on my head and bust my nose in two different places! That was a formative moment. It was one thing to be in the pit all the time — that was always fun — but having your nose busted definitely took it to the top! And it wasn't even a boot, it was an elbow. The crowd was so sick, this guy dove on top of the crowd and he couldn't get down, he couldn't get to the floor, so he rolled on the top of people's heads and he just whipped around with his elbow. At that moment, I was kind of paranoid because I was in the middle of this mass of people that were all pushing, and as soon as my nose was broken, it parted like the Red Sea, and I was tossing people out of the way.

Experiencing the intensity of Hardcore instantly transformed Zero Boys. They played out-of-town, and tried to nurture a local scene. In spring '81, they played with The Effigies in Chicago and with Toxic Reasons in Dayton — then the buzz

Acceptance
Mecht Mensch, Bone Air, 1981
Collection of Sal Canzonieri

started. HC style was peaking as they cut the great album *Vicious Circle*. Alternative Tentacles showed some interest but nothing happened, so in early '82 local imprint Nimrod released it. Around that time, Mahern set up Indy's first all-ages HC shows, trying to hook up TSOL, Articles Of Faith and Die Kreuzen. Unfortunately, he lost his shirt on those gigs — he was lucky if 30 kids came.

Mahern borrowed loot from his parents in '82 to start a label he planned to be Indy's SST or Dischord. Affirmation Records put out some collectable records over the next two years: the two *Master Tape* comps, and 7"s from Articles Of Faith and locals Killing Children. *The Master Tape, Volume 1* was incredible: good recordings, great performances, that you can put up against *Flex Your Head* or *This Is Boston Not LA*. Unfortunately, Affirmation folded in late '83, for basically the same reason many other labels did — they couldn't survive the deep financial rut resulting from the collapse of the independent record distribution network. With virtually no money to be made in the first place, they fell deeply in debt.

Like any Hardcore legend, Zero Boys ended up disillusioned, burned-out and broke. Coming from Indianapolis, they could turn to literally no one for support. Zero Boys toured the East Coast once, playing four Boston shows and one in New York. They hit the West Coast and drove up through Canada. In late '82, they threw in the towel, though Mahern would become a noted Alternative Rock producer. There hasn't been a great Indy band since.

MADISON

Madison, like DC or Austin, a college town (site of The University Of Wisconsin) with a liberal tradition, didn't deal with much desperation; most kids were the offspring of educators and bureaucrats. Madison's first HC outfit MECHT MENSCH played their first parties in early '81. These jerky DogTown–style skater kids — using a silly rendering of an alligator as a symbol — were known for their cult song, "Arf, Arf, It's A Dog's World." Mecht Mensch spawned TAR BABIES, whose guitarist Bucky Pope was the guy to call if you wanted to play Wisconsin's capital. Bucky also ran the local label Bone Air. He and about 75 other scraggly kids treated No Trend well when we played a VFW with Hüsker Dü in '83.

In the mid-80s Tar Babies inexplicably dumped Hardcore to emulate the pulsating, rhythmic groove of DC Go-Go Funk à la Trouble Funk, Experience Unlimited and Chuck Brown. These sly Wisconsin boyz obviously could play all the notes adeptly — check out their LPs for SST: '87's *Fried Milk*, '88's *No Contest*, '89's *Honey Bubble* — but they could never truly "freak the funk" — an average White band, indeed!

Zine ad for Clitboys, 1983
Collection of the author

Indie Rock pioneers Killdozer, the most notable by-product of Madison HC, recorded their first LP, '84's *Intellectuals Are The Shoeshine Boys Of The Ruling Elite*, for Bone Air.

MILWAUKEE

Another Midwestern industrial hub, Milwaukee is to Chicago as the Moon is to the Earth — nearby, lifeless and ultimately inhospitable.

Around '80, Milwaukee's "Punk Nights" revolved around seemingly gay clubs down by the recently-gentrified waterfront. Two notable New Wave acts circulated: Couch Flambeau made a few arty records, and The Stellas, a teen outfit in the Psychedelic Furs vein. The Stellas graduated to the fury of Hardcore in '82, changing their name to the tougher-sounding "DIE KREUZEN" — German for "the crosses."

Die Kreuzen's '82 7" EP, *Cows & Beer* — saluting their state's agrarian-Teutonic heritage — was a Midwest HC classic. I saw Die Kreuzen four or five times during that era — I was on tour with No Trend, and both groups opened for DKs — and they were amazing. After awhile, I'd hang around early just to watch their soundcheck.

CLITBOYS, a short-lived outfit, were the only other locals to play the few poorly-attended shows circa 1982-84. They put out *We Don't Play The Game*, a surprisingly good 7" EP in '83. But if you lived in Milwaukee and wanted to see a good HC show, you went to Chicago.

Zine ad for Die Kreuzen
Collection of Sal Canzonieri

The mid-80s Die Kreuzen, like many other HC outfits, grew its hair and got in touch with its Metal roots. The psychotic Speed Rock of guitarist Brian Egeness, bassist Keith Brammer, and drummer Eric Tunison blasting over Dan Kubinski's screeching vocals created an exciting crossover. The sound and vibe of their early Touch & Go records ('84's *Die Kreuzen*, '86's *October File*, '88's *Century Days*) influenced Soundgarden and Voivod).

OHIO

Cleveland and Akron spawned many Punk icons — DEVO, Dead Boys, Pere Ubu, Pagans, Chrissie Hynde, Rachel Sweet — but Hardcore told a different tale. Some shows happened here and there, but nothing you'd call a scene. Except for a few SST outfits, tours didn't usually hit Ohio's industrial belt or college towns like Dayton or Columbus. Numerous out-of-towners played the Euclid Tavern in Cleveland, Bogart's in Cincinnati, or across the river in Newport, Kentucky, at the famed Jockey Club, where Elvis and Jerry Lee Lewis once rocked.

TOXIC REASONS, founded by frontman Ed Pittman and guitarist Bruce Stucky in Dayton in October '79, toured their asses off throughout the HC era. Quite influential — considering they never drew more than 50 people per gig — Toxic R made two solid albums: '82's *Independence* and '83's *Bullets For You*. Like much Midwest HC, they blended melodic Brit Punk with harsh assault. After a few lineup changes, such as adding Zero Boys guitarist Tufty, they promoted the members' three nationalities — American, Canadian, British — but things never panned out. (They're still around in some form and retain a sizable German following.)

KING KOFFEE (Butthole Surfers): Toxic Reasons were horrible beyond belief — this anthemic shit. They were billed as having members from three nations; I thought they

sucked three times as hard. They played this clone D.O.A.-type of music. It's no surprise that people aren't still talking about them today.

THE HEARTLAND

St. Louis, despite its rich Jazz and Blues history, had zero Rock. How bad was it? The local FM station KSHE-95 was the birthplace of AOR (Album-Oriented Rock), the format of Styx, Journey, Kansas, et cetera.

Punk and Hardcore in St. Louis matched such mediocrity. By 1980, a few New Wave acts had surfaced: Zany Misfits, Trained Animals, The Strikers, The Ooze Kicks. In '81, during that brief era when Chuck Biscuits drummed, Black Flag were relegated to playing Mr. A's Discotheque, a dive bar across the river in Belleville, Illinois.

That Belleville gig influenced BLIND IDIOT GOD. Speed was a critical HC issue, so Blind Idiot Gods' first tunes never exceeded 50 seconds: they'd do a 10-song set in 15 minutes. Their first show, a September '83 basement party, lasted one song, a Reggae version of "Hava Nagila," then cops shut it down for noise complaints. SST bands toured the heartland relentlessly, so Blind Idiot God ended up on SST in '85 (sounding very different by then, with a heavy Dub and Free Jazz bent).

Maximum RocknRoll's devoted early readers knew of WHITE PRIDE, the St. Louis area's so-called White Power group. It seemed every other *MRR* issue featured some long diatribe about these alleged White Supremacists, who sang off-color tunes like "Hoosiers Are Niggers Turned Inside Out," and "Put Up A Fence, Close Down The Border" (to the Frito Bandito theme).

GABE KATZ (Blind Idiot God): White Pride achieved cult status, and wanted people to think they were serious — they'd start rumors about how they killed Black people. There was a older guy, Bob Leech, this fucked-up one-sixteenth-Chinese guy into homemade porno, guns, and selling stolen equipment. He always wore sunglasses, even at night. The rap on the band was that two of them were card-carrying racists. The bassist Mike Teppi worked at the Budweiser brewing plant. Mike apologized years later after he married a nice Jewish girl: 'We were just kidding about that shit.'

Columbia, MO, home of The University of Missouri, had a small role in the Hardcore scene for the "Thrash Bash," an annual event at or near the campus. I witnessed the first Thrash Bash in the summer of '83 with Die Kreuzen, CAUSES OF TRAGEDY and THE CROPPY BOYS, and the most interesting thing about it was all the students and yokels gawking at the spectacle. You've probably never heard of Columbia HC, and for good reason: small shows, lousy bands, and redneck cops looking for trouble.

Kansas City, MO, and Topeka and Lawrence, Kansas — about a 30-minute drive apart — can be considered a single scene. They generated a Midwest Hardcore subculture similar in size to Minneapolis' or Austin's.

KC's a rough city and notorious drug hub, and there was lotsa LSD and heroin available when I passed through with No Trend to play with DKs, Die Kreuzen and NOTA at a VFW hall in '83. HC locals were ORANGE DOUGHNUTS (The ODs),

TUNNEL DOGS, THE SLABS, NEAR DEATH EXPERIENCE, and EXPLODING RODENTS. (ODs singer Harvey Bennett Stafford moved to San Francisco, becoming an illustrator best known for his cover artwork for The Melvins' Kiss-style solo records.)

ANDY HAWKINS (Blind Idiot God): The first time we played Kansas City, we went into a 7-11 and I was immediately surrounded by 12 Black transvestite prostitutes. None of them could have been over 16. 'Ooh honey, I'm gonna get one of these lollipops because I look good when I suck it.' We'd never seen or heard anything like that.

N.O.T.A., 1984
From *None Of The Above,* Rabid Cat, 1985
Photo by John Spath
Collection of the author

Many of the region's most innovative minds gravitate to the liberal oasis of Lawrence, home of The University Of Kansas. Lawrence provided touring outfits an excellent stop with a supportive scene — you could always expect 100 or so kids to show up, without gangs or violence, and no crackers out to kill you. Lawrence boasted a cool indie record store, Exile Records, and University Of Kansas radio station KJHK, one of the first to regularly play Hardcore (the school shut it down in the late 80s). Four miles outside of town in a cornfield, The Outhouse, a cinder-block garage, put on shows around '85.

The few amazing local outfits all fell victim to inadequate exposure. Bill Rich of Fresh Sounds and the zine *Talk Talk* put out seminal recordings by THE EMBARRASSMENT and MORTAL MICRONOTZ (later The Micronotz).

TAD KEPLEY (Anarchist activist): The Micronotz from Lawrence were one of the original American Hardcore bands. They started playing in 1980, and broke up in '86 after an album on Homestead. They never got the recognition they deserved. They were along the lines of The Replacements — and were equally as popular in the Midwest. They played Minneapolis all the time at First Ave/Seventh Street Entry, and they played Oz in Chicago. The first Micronotz record and EP could easily fall under Hardcore — the other bands back then certainly considered them to be Hardcore.

Oklahoma, home to vicious cowboys and drunk injuns, had shows by '82, and most Texas Hardcore groups played there at one time or another. The HC sensation in them parts, Tulsa's NOTA (NONE OF THE ABOVE), played all across the Dust Bowl. Their *Live At The Crystal Pistol* demo tape and their *Toy Soldiers* 7" EP (on Austin's Rabid Cat label) were damn good.

SPIKE CASSIDY (DRI): We went there once or twice back then. I'd get a call. 'Do you guys want to play Oklahoma in three weeks? We can give you 50 bucks.' You'd go, 'Okay. Great.' We'd get up halfway and run out of gas and siphon some gas out of someone's car, get to Oklahoma, and start looking around for other shows. We played two or three times a week, and the rest of the time was trying to survive on a dollar a day for pizza.

Norman, OK, site of The University Of Oklahoma, had shows at VFW-type halls. I visited there twice with No Trend in '83 and '84; the second time, we drew 50 people. The opening group that night performed Pink Floyd's *Dark Side Of The Moon* from start to finish. They were Flaming Lips. •

TEX-ASS

It's hard for me to take a stand
When everyone has got the plans to push the button
And the bomb it's just a game and I'm the pawn
— Big Boys, "Apolitical"

The Great Nation Of Texas bred unique Hardcore. Unlike NY or LA, whose Hardcore evolved under a hypercritical lens, Texas produced crazier and more adventerous artists. Austin, Houston, San Antonio, Dallas, even the West Texas town of El Paso spawned some of the era's best, like Big Boys and Dicks (Austin), Really Red (Houston) and Butthole Surfers (San Antonio). There were all part of the same explosion, yet none of them sounded alike.

Gary Floyd (Dicks) singing
From *Kill From The Heart,* SST, 1983
Photo by either Suzanne or Carlos
Courtesy of Gary Floyd

KING KOFFEE (Butthole Surfers): Texas Punk bands, for whatever reasons, tend to be more theatrical than bands from the rest of the nation. There's a sense of isolation — Texans feel we're our own nation. We were more influenced by our direct peers. The bands, especially live, influence each other a lot, perhaps a reason for this precedent of weird Texas bands. The Dicks and Big Boys, the two big Austin bands, would play together all the time, both extremely theatrical with costumes and singers in drag for like every performance. They were fucking great. I think *[Dicks frontman]* Gary Floyd is the best Blues singer Texas has produced since Janis Joplin.

SPOT (producer/soundman): Texas bands were a bit more low-key and humble. A lot of it's 'cause there was no music industry — as far as I'm concerned, there still isn't, and maybe that's the way it should stay. A lot of these bands were out of the loop 'cause they weren't in a place with big media culture like LA or NY, or even SF. Ultimately, I think that might be all to the good 'cause the media has all but destroyed what existed.

AUSTIN

Austin, state capital and home of the University of Texas, has always comprised the region's liberal mecca, legendary for its rich, diverse music culture. Prior to Punk, it churned out "cosmic cowboys" à la Asleep At The Wheel and Jerry Jeff Walker. Local icon Willie Nelson sponsored the major bash every July 4, "Willie's Picnic." Austin HC arose reacting to such stuff.

TIM KERR (Big Boys): We were living through the hangovers of that whole 'cosmic cowboy' trip — I didn't wanna see another fucking armadillo drawn. We weren't dealing with the LA Hippie vibe Black Flag talked about; it was that whole Jerry Jeff Walker/Michael Murphy/Doug Sahm scene that Austin is best known for. We were tired of that. As Texas Punks, we were saying, 'No, we don't all wear cowboy hats.'

Austin played a huge role in spreading New Wave to the heartland. Local FM stations broke The Police's commercial Punk; the town loved Jonathan Richman; The Clash and Elvis Costello made major splashes at the 1700-seat Armadillo World Headquarters — famed for Texas hospitality, a fine PA, and good, cheap drugs. Austin's more-sophisticated audiences encouraged the diversity, and musicians enjoyed the intimate venues.

A small clique of UT students comprised the late 70s Austin Punk/New Wave scene. The Huns made headlines first: *Rolling Stone* in '79 ran a shot of frontman Phil Tolstead being led from a club in handcuffs after kissing a cop (On televangelical programs he'd later renounce his past). The Re*chords played all over town on a flatbed truck, and once got arrested for setting up and playing in the capitol rotunda. The Skunks, a rude bar band, scored with "Cheap Girl." Lo-fi groups like Standing Waves, The Next, The Textones and Terminal Mind were cool. The Violators, D-Day, The Delinquents and Delta also stayed active. The Tex-Mex New Wave of Joe "King" Carrasco and the Crowns was the chief export. By 1980, Punk had become an establishment of its own.

Show poster for the Big Boys-organized "Texas Love-In", A.L.A. Club, Austin, 1984
Collection of the author

RICHARD LUCKETT (Austin Punk scene): The underlying factor to the early Austin Punk scene was rampant White Trash drug abuse — especially crystal meth. On the back porch at Raul's on any given night, the big thing was to do a whole bunch of lines of crank and dance in this sweaty closed-in space. Then we'd find someone with an air-conditioned house and go there afterwards. We were all college kids getting *wasted*.

In response arose a crop of louder, more aggressive groups not content with what was going on around town. As elsewhere across America, Austin Punk scenesters didn't take to these new arrivals. Things came to a head in 1980 with a literal schism: the so-called "intellectual" bands like Terminal Mind, The Re*chords, Standing Waves — "the ones with songs" — versus gnarly young HC bands like The Dicks, Big Boys, The Stains (later MDC) and Sharon Tate's Baby.

TIM KERR: The Stains played this 'Hardcore versus New Wave' rift to the hilt, which up until Black Flag came to town wasn't even in the picture — Punk was all-encompassing: Sex Pistols and Joy Division were the same thing. The Stains put up posters around town: 'Are you Hardcore or are you New Wave?' They listed bands that were Hardcore and that were New Wave — of course the New Wave bands sucked 'cause they were arty types. Bands like us, The Offenders, The Inserts were put into the category of HC, bands like Terminal Mind were thought of as New Wave. The Stains instigated it all. Our song 'Fun, Fun, Fun' addressed that issue; people really took sides.

Back cover art of Big Boys *Fun, Fun, Fun,* 1982
Collection of the author

GARY FLOYD (Dicks): We felt the New Wave people were capitulating to the big record companies. I remember one night Elvis Costello came to Raul's and everyone was acting like there was this big star in the club and he wasn't talking to anybody. It was ridiculous. Then Black Flag, who to us were big stars, would come and were all chitty-chatty — and they put us on their label. We were lucky we were able to play with bands like that.

The rise of Austin Hardcore hooked in with skateboarding. The 70s skatepark construction boom across Texas spawned a small crew of *Skateboarder Magazine*-reading, DogTown-inspired shredders. Many started bands.

BIG BOYS — all literally big boys — were the gnarliest local skaters. They first gigged October '78 in an old fur vault with four songs, including super-fast covers of "The Twist" and "Hello, I Love You." For the next five-plus years, Big Boys were the kings of Austin Hardcore.

Others may have done Punky Funk (Rick James) or funky Punk (PiL), but Big Boys were the first true Punk-Funk group, blasting out a previously-unseen blend of speed-driven HC, rump-shakin' groove, and shock theater. 250-pound homosexual frontman Randy "Biscuit" Turner wore tattered dresses onstage — which wasn't just unhip, it was downright distressing. Big Boys' motto, "Go start your own band!" inspired many kids to action.

SPOT: The first time, Big Boys just knocked me out. At Raul's, might have been at soundcheck, these big funny-lookin' guys with a silly name got up and played something totally unique — it just kicked butt.

Big Boys' sets mixed inspirational empowerment and mindless anthems of mayhem. Austin HC's heyday paralleled their reign.

KEN INOUYE (Marginal Man): My earliest Big Boys memory was the first time Marginal Man went on tour. It was booked by Lyle Presslar — he put together this little tour book, giving us background info on each date. When it got to the Texas dates, it said, 'You're playing with the Big Boys, you guys are gonna have a lot of fun. Under no circumstances do you allow them to talk you into headlining and having them open for you — that's a very big mistake.' After I saw them play, I could see why. On their home turf, it was just something to see — people went absolutely bananas.

Big Boys comprised of vocalist Biscuit, guitarist Tim Kerr, bassist Chris Gates, and a procession of drummers. Steve Collier was the first one, but his mom made him quit (he'd later form Doctor's Mob). Greg Murray, the twin brother of Terminal Mind's Doug, played drums on *Where's My Towel?* and *Live At Raul's*. Fred Schultz played on *Fun, Fun, Fun*. When he quit, Big Boys brought in Sharon Tate's Baby drummer Rey Washam (who went on to Scratch Acid and Rapeman).

The first Big Boys record, 1980's "Frat Cars" 7", required two studio attempts — the first time the engineer didn't know what the fuck to do with them. For subsequent records, Kerr ran his guitar through a Marshall stack turned all the way up to "11" — then things got interesting. The cover of their 1981 record featured three pictures of a baby holding a hatchet. Depending on who you ask, it's called either *Where's My Towel?* or *Industry Standard* — quoting responses by their label, Wasted Talent, about a dubious clause in their contract: "Oh, that's just an industry standard."

Most of this book's interviewees cite Big Boys as legendary — amazing, as they rarely toured and their records came out on small labels. I saw both of their DC shows, in '82 at The Psychedeli — a deli with a back room — then in '83 when I had them play "The Funk-Punk Spectacular" with Trouble Funk and Minor Threat (in what turned out to be Minor Threat's last show). Big Boys opened and tore the roof off the sucka.

Sadly, Big Boys just frittered away. Ironically for a group so positive, and uplifting, petty jealousies and rivalries caused their demise. Due to the weird psycho-sexual tension between Chris and Biscuit, everyone was always threatening to quit — all poor communicators in that wonderfully passive-aggressive Texas manner. Verging on national acclaim, they fell off with two crappy LPs: *Lullabies Make The Brain Grow* and *No Matter How Long The Line Is At The Cafeteria, There's Always a Seat!* (both Enigma), the latter, a half-assed effort for which Biscuit didn't even write.

Zine ad for Big Boys *Fun, Fun, Fun,* 1982
Collection of Sal Canzonieri

Tim Kerr carried on in Funk-style Bad Mutha Goose and Monkeywrench (with Mudhoney's Mark Arm and Steve Turner), but remains best-known for Poison 13, vital to the development of Grunge.

TIM KERR: People fucking hated Poison 13: they were not into our shit at all — I mean, 30 people would come to our shows. You had those who thought we were trying to be the Big Boys; they weren't even gonna listen. You had those that heard what we were up to and since it wasn't Hardcore, things got ugly. While I totally stand behind what the Big Boys were saying and doing, we got put on a pedestal: people would follow every line of our songs. Poison 13 tried *not* to say anything, just writing about driving cars, graveyards, and girls — nothing anyone could follow, was the premise. To guys in Seattle bands, Poison 13 and Tales Of Terror started that Grunge shit; to this day I can't convince them that nobody liked us. Poison 13 was a long way off from the Big Boys.

Chris Gates relocated to LA, trying his hand at Sunset Strip Cock Rock with Junkyard, his bad-ass Metal act that did two poorly received late-80s albums for Geffen — one lineup of which featured Minor Threat's Brian Baker. When Junkyard would play an Austin venue, Biscuit would litter the parking lot with fliers reading: "Chris Gates is a big fat pig."

TIM KERR: Biscuit definitely has problems. He's gotten a whole hell of a lot worse as time's gone by. Really bitter. What happened between Chris and Biscuit was, Biscuit knew Chris when he was a kid — they lived in the same neighborhood. I don't think it was so much sexual, it was just more, That's my little brother... Then when you think your little brother has fucked you around and hasn't at least apologized in the way that you want him to, that's kinda what happened. He's one of those people, and we all have friends like this, they put all their eggs in one basket. For some reason he's real bitter his band broke up. There's definitely a lot of people who think people owe them a lot of money now. I thought everybody was more like how I am about it, then I realized there were a lot more people who felt the other way. I can only speak for myself. We all put everything we had into it, but a lot of people, that was their life, period. It's like they didn't realize that there's all kinds of other stuff going on.

THE DICKS always gigged with Big Boys, and Austin HC evolved around those two groups. The Dicks were led by Gary Floyd, fat gay singer dressed in weird drag, who'd take enema bags filled with liver and condoms filled with mayonnaise and hurl them at the crowd.

The classic Dicks — frontman Floyd with mean-ass members bassist Glen Taylor, guitarist Buxf Parrot, drummer Pat Deason — started as a "poster band," the posters promoting imaginary shows at fictitious clubs, saying things like "First ten people with guns drink for free." Their first gig was May 1980, at "The Punk Prom" at Armadillo World Headquarters.

Gary Floyd, whose powerful Johnny Winter-style Texas Blues howl made him one of the era's great vocalists, was a virulent Marxist who delivered incendiary anthems like "Dicks Hate Police," the title of their first single (self-released in '80 on Radical Records, not to be confused with R Radical Records, later MDC's label) and "Anti Klan." In '83 *Maximum RockNRoll* put the Dicks on the cover: a picture of Gary in a mohawk and a mu-mu with the title: "The Dicks A Commie Faggot Band."

GARY FLOYD (Dicks): Communism was such a shocking word. A guy dressed up like a nurse with chocolate frosting in his pants singing about Communism, that's weird. Even now, that's a little weird. Most of those attitudes pervasive in those songs had root in meaning, but a lot of them are put out publicly in a shocking manner that was Hardcore in the 80s...

Maybe I wasn't the only gay within the band but it's not for me to say. I would say it was about half and half but I was really out and always had been. Those guys were very supportive of me — since I was doing the lyrics it sorta set the mode for what the band was. I don't think a lot of people would've put up with all the bullshit that I was talking, but somehow they did and I love them for it.

Millions Of Dead Cops,
Millions Of Dead Cops LP, R Radical, 1982
Collection of the author

HC circles best knew The Dicks for *Kill From The Heart*, their arresting '83 SST album. By then, Floyd had convinced the band to relocate to San Francisco — a great place to be gay and leftist in the early 80s — in fact leading the wave of Texas bands who moved there, with MDC, DRI, Verbal Abuse. Unfortunately, the other guys got homesick. Floyd tried a few SF lineups of the Dicks, which included drummer Lynn Perko. They made an excellent album on Alternative Tentacles in '85, *These People* — but no one seemed to give a shit. (After The Dicks' '86 demise Floyd and Perko formed Sister Double Happiness; Perko later moved on to Imperial Teen).

THE STAINS — later MILLIONS OF DEAD COPS (MDC) — another intense Austin outfit, started out shortly after the Dicks, and a few months after the Big Boys.

Dave Dictor, from Glen Cove, Long Island, was a gay Hippie with Leftist tendencies who dropped out of Boston U. in the mid-70s to focus on playing Bluegrass fests with his Folk group Solar Pigs. After disappearing to Montana for a year or so to live out his "Rocky Mountain High" trip, Dave relocated to Austin, home of his hero, Willie Nelson. In '78, seeing the band Female Trouble forever altered his path. For this 60s throwback, Punk and insurgent politics fit like a glove. The Stains came together in '79, and in early '81 issued their first single, "John Wayne Was A Nazi."

Dave Dictor (MDC) singing
Rock Against Reagan, Central Park, NYC, 1983
Photo by Karen O'Sullivan

Dictor knew to send one of the 300 copies of the 7" to Tim Yohannon at *Maximum RockNRoll*. Yohannon hooked him up with Jello Biafra; Jello set up an SF gig for The Stains and The Dicks in June '81. Dictor also befriended Black Flag when they played Austin earlier that year; Flag arranged a show — Henry's first with Flag — at The Cuckoo's Nest in Orange County with both the LA Stains and the Austin Stains opening.

To end name confusion — and after witnessing police violence at the OC show — Austin's Stains, on the suggestion of Dicks guitarist Buxf Parrott, rechristened themselves Millions Of Dead Cops — MDC. The first copies of the "John Wayne" 7" displayed the awkward "MDC-Stains" tag. In '82, they split for the activist utopia of San Francisco. [see SF chapter]

> *Distrust and mistrust are all I can see*
> *You're always trying to put something over on me*
> — Big Boys, "Nervous"

Some of the coolest shit was goin' on in Austin. Struggling touring outfits could play a well-attended gig that was friendly yet out-of-control — and later get invited to one of those wondrous Sunday BBQs. Seedy clubs Club Foot and Voltaire's Basement were always good for intimate shows, while Liberty Lunch and The Ritz hosted larger ones. Austin had excellent record stores, plus dirt-cheap thrift shops, Mexican restaurants, and rents. Most important, Austin HC kids didn't usually have to worry about rednecks hassling them — a few drunken fratboys notwithstanding.

Mid-80s Austin was a very different terrain. Big Boys broke up. The Dicks and MDC were long gone. Newer sounds included the gnarly Garage Rock of Poison 13, the brutal Metal-edged attack of The Offenders (after an early stint as a Clash-style outfit), the noisy art assault of Scratch Acid, and the twisted tongue-in-buttocks Country & Western romp of the Hickoids. They all sounded great, but it just wasn't Hardcore anymore.

SAN ANTONIO

San Antonio, only an hour south, is very different from Austin. San Antonio maintains the heritage of a conservative outpost town, proud of its Tex-Mex culture and Heavy Metal. Punk made zero impact — even though the Pistols played the local redneck joint Randy's Rodeo in January '78. Hardcore also had little effect, although it did produce a small scene of 75 or so ratty kids, a few shows, and an important musical contribution: BUTTHOLE SURFERS.

The Buttholes — started by Trinity College students vocalist Gibson "Gibby" Haynes, guitarist Paul Leary, and the Matthews brothers Quinn on bass and Scott on drums — were a weird-ass band with a name that freaked people out. Gibby, whose dad is Mr. Peppermint, a respected Captain Kangaroo-style kid's TV personality in Texas, was an all-American kid: a 6'7" beanpole who went to Trinity in '78 on a hoops scholarship, and won '81's Accounting Student Of The Year award. Success led to a stint at Peter Marwick, one of America's most prestigious

Paul Leary and Gibby Haynes (Butthole Surfers) singing
Uncredited photo from *Maximum RockNRoll* #4, 1983
Collection of Sal Canzonieri

accounting firms. But right after graduation, he abandoned a promising CPA career, for drugs and music. Within months, Gibby and Paul, the group's dysgenic Lennon and McCartney, were dropping acid every day and washing dishes for a living.

The Buttholes embarked on a disastrous California tour in '82: no money, car trouble, bad gigs playing to dumb kids who didn't get it; so the Matthews bros returned home. Luckily, Jello Biafra had seen them in SF, and took Gibby and Paul under his wing. He brought the Buttholes' mindfuck to Alternative Tentacles, and in every interview, hailed their stinky name.

Paul "King Koffee" Coffey, drummer of the Dallas-area HC outfit Hugh Beaumont Experience — named after the actor who played Dad on *Leave It To Beaver* — joined the Buttholes in '83, and played on "Wichita Cathedral" and "Bar-B-Q Pope" from the *Butthole Surfers* EP (a k a *Brown Reason To Live*). Live, King stood, playing just two drums, a floor tom and a snare.

KING KOFFEE (Butthole Surfers): I was in high school when I first saw the Buttholes. Here's a singer in boxer shorts, clothespins in his hair, with a sax, doing one of the cheesiest songs ever, 'D.O.A.' by Bloodrock — which I couldn't believe 'cause Bloodrock were from my hometown, Fort Worth. It was so uncool it was great, unlike any Punk I'd ever heard. I immediately related.

The Buttholes recorded their follow-ups for AT — '84's *Live PCPEP* and '85's *Psychic...Powerless...Another Man's Sac* — at local studio The Boss. It was there Gibby and Paul assembled the definitive Texas HC comp *Cottage Cheese From The Lips Of Death* (on The Boss' label Ward 9, 1983), which featured shit from the likes of Big Boys, Dicks, Really Red and Buttholes. The most intense cut was "Meltdown," by the Austin proto-Speed Metal outfit Watchtower (whose singer Jason McMaster went on to front multi-Platinum poodleheads Dangerous Toys). MARCHING PLAGUE contributed the hilarious "Rock & Roll Asshole" — their singer Keith Rumbo was the "Anus Presley" in the Buttholes' "The Revenge Of Anus Presley," and drummer Brad Perkins played on the first Buttholes EP. PRENATAL LUST, a Marching Plague side project, also appeared on *Cottage Cheese*.

On No Trend's '83 tour, we played San Antonio with the Buttholes, and they arranged that we crash at The Boss. But we all got tossed out at 9AM, right before the day's first recording sessions. So we killed time for a few hours at Taco Cabana, downing 49-cent tacos and 25-cent Big Reds.

A year or so after King joined, the Buttholes added Theresa, a scrawny acid casualty who often drummed topless — the pair delivered an awesome double-kit assault à la Grateful Dead and Allman Brothers.

The Buttholes lived communally on the road for years, crashing in the van (with their dog Mark Farner, named for the Grand Funk guitarist) or on people's floors in SF, NYC, Athens and Atlanta, before relocating to Austin to become underground icons. (Haynes'd later become so infamous in crack-smoking circles, Mexican dealers on Austin's east side refer to their extra large baggies as "gibbies.")

DALLAS

In the law-and-order town of Dallas, being Punk just asked for trouble. Sex Pistols played Longhorn Ballroom (formerly the strip club owned by Lee Harvey Oswald assassin Jack Ruby), and there were some gigs at The Hot Club, that was it. By '80 came Zero's, a small Fort Worth club.

As for Hardcore, Dallas was home to two groups, STICKMEN WITH RAYGUNS and THE HUGH BEAUMONT EXPERIENCE.

KING KOFFEE: I played for The Hugh Beaumont Experience, a teenage band, really into the Pistols ... our singer sang with a British accent; a lot of Dallas bands did. We all listened to British Punk so we were aping our heroes. Once Hardcore happened, we started playing faster, aping what was happening in DC and LA.

The only other Dallas band was Stickmen With Rayguns, one of the best I've ever seen. They were fronted by Bobby Sox, a manic Buddy Holly-type, scary motherfucker who'd pick fights with the audience. He shoved the mic up his butt during a show and the Buttholes had to play after that, so Gibby sang with the mic from the kick drum. Bobby sang with earlier Dallas Punk bands, like The Vomit Pigs and The Scuds. Stickmen With Raygun had such intensity about them.

In '81 Hugh Beaumont Experience recorded *The Cone Johnson EP*, a four-song 7". The guy who put it out only sold half the 500-copy run — so he got fed up and quit the business, and destroyed the remainder. Also around that time, King Koffee issued a small HC zine, *Throbbing Cattle* — five issues, 500 copies each, all given away free.

Show flyer for Hüsker Dü, Hugh Beaumont Expereince, Studio D, Dallas, 1982
Collecton of Laura Albert

Quite a few touring outfits played Studio D, a bombed-out warehouse just blocks from a police station. Cops would hassle the kids, ticketing them for shit like wearing studded bracelets — deadly weapons, y'know. In '83 I was in the crowded Studio D parking lot when the police pulled in. Everyone braced for trouble, then the cops barked over their loudspeakers, "Hey, you kids shouldn't be listening to music like that. You should be listening to music like this —" at which point they cranked some George Jones. They burned rubber out to the street, laughing all the way out.

Studio D closed in '84, and nothing went on in D-FW for a while. Hugh Beaumont Experience split for Austin. Then half the guys got involved in a check-

Show flyer for Butthole Surfers,
Stickmen With Rayguns, Mydolls
The Island, Houston, 1982
Collection of the author

writing scam and had to flee the state. King knew the Buttholes — in '83 HBE gigged with DKs, Buttholes, MDC and Stickmen With Rayguns at Studio D — and he was perfect fit, another hallucinogen-takin' HC freak.

KING KOFFEE: Being a Punk in an oppressively Southern Baptist state was a bit much. The people in a liberal college town like Austin made it easier, but walking down the street with a mohawk in Fort Worth was self-imperilment — just wearing a Dead Kennedys t-shirt in public was enough to get punched out. But then again, here I was with a mohawk in Dallas, Texas in 1983 — what did I expect? That's why I went to Austin.

HOUSTON

The sprawling metropolis of Houston mimics LA — a small downtown amid boundless burbs — but without the beaches or the culture. A population explosion propelled by a short-lived late-70s oil boom, led to the incorporation of a patchwork of placid cowtowns with constables into Greater Houston.

Houston's infamous police force — who make the LAPD seem laid-back — hampered the rise of Hardcore. In the early 80s I went to H-town a few times and always saw shocking news accounts of cops murdering or torturing locals. Lawmen used "throw-down guns" — untraceable weapons: they'd shoot minorities, then toss a gun next to the body to "prove" the victims shot first. So Houston had the most violent Texas scene — the kids were products of their redneck environment.

TIM KERR: Houston police were really bad, even worse than LA. That was bad, scary news. Dallas wasn't usually so bad: typical Texas cops. In Austin, the cops wore Earth Shoes; they were no threat. For us, the biggest problem was fucking idiot frat boys and sorority girls who would yell and scream out the cars and throw shit. Houston had far bigger problems.

If you wanna lead a better standard of life
You better learn how to kiss behind
— Really Red, "Nobody Rules"

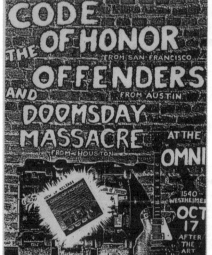

Show flyer for Code Of Honor, Offenders,
Doomsday Massacre,
The Omni, Houston, 1983
Collection of Laura Albert

A small scene did evolve out of the powerful shows and records of Houston's premiere HC-era band, REALLY RED — started in '79 by fiery frontman Ronnie Bond; a.k.a. U-Ron Bondage. On their own CIA imprint they issued some amazing vinyl, like '81's LP *Teaching You The Fear* and '82's EP *New Strings For Old Puppets*. Really Red's spot on *Let Them Eat Jellybeans* led many to compare Bond to Jello Biafra — though Ronnie could caustically question authority without whining.

GARY FLOYD (Dicks): Really Red were really overlooked — I don't know how people don't seem to know about them. Their albums were great, they were produced well. All in all, they were fucking incredible.

KING KOFFEE: Talk about overlooked bands — Really Red left behind some great records, but the memory of their live show is still vivid. Had they only toured more, they'd be considered legendary. They took a strong political stance yet were able to pull it off. Unlike MDC, who were overly preachy, Really Red had amazing anthems — Ronnie Bond'd just scream for all he was worth. It wasn't typical Left Wing propaganda. Seeing Really Red in Houston, where they were really popular, was very moving, powerful stuff. They were great — they made sense to me.

MYDOLLS, an excellent all-girl outfit, opened for Really Red and did two records for CIA. LEGIONAIRE'S DISEASE, THE DEGENERATES and THE HATES also circulated. Noise terrorists CULTURCIDE were the brainchild of Perry Webb, who reinvented himself later as the conceptual artist Mark Flood.

Original lineup of D.R.I., Houston, 1982
Courtesy of Spike Cassidy

Many local kids were inspired by seminal thrashers VERBAL ABUSE — led by Nikki Sikki, who moved from Houston to San Francisco to front Sick Pleasure (and returned to Houston to do Afterbirth, then Humungous). DOOMSDAY MASSACRE played out a lot and put out a cool single. By 1984-85 came new names like STARK RAVING MAD, PISSED YOUTH, ORGASM, and DRESDEN 45.

DRI, the most influential band outta Houston, played even faster than Bad Brains. They took the HC formula and left everyone else in the dust. DRI's driving force, guitarist Spike Cassidy, was a Long Island rocker who moved to Houston in early '81. Originally called USDRI — Us Dirty Rotten Imbeciles — they first gigged July '82 at Joe Starr's Omni with The Degenerates.

SPIKE CASSIDY (DRI): I had a roommate, also a guitarist, who was looking for a band. I wasn't. I was doing maintenance for apartments. My roommate put the word out — somebody called to see if he wanted to jam and start a band. When the guy called, my roommate had moved back to New York, so we wound up talking. I started jamming with some of those guys, and we started DRI.

TIM KERR: I thought DRI were cool 'cause they were really young kids. Their set list would have like 160 songs — they'd roll up the list, tape it to the wall, and roll the paper down the wall, across the stage, and onto the dance floor. I thought that was pretty fucking great.

DRI played every week or so for about a year, until everybody got totally sick of them. So they started touring throughout the state and the Midwest. Their willingness to lay it all on the line led to some of the most brutal low-budget van tours ever: they'd play night after night for nothing. In '84, following in the footsteps of many of their peers, they moved to SF.

SPIKE CASSIDY: MDC were a band with similar political values, from Austin, two hours away, but always played Houston. They were one of our favorite bands; we opened for them a lot and got to know 'em. They picked up and moved to San Francisco; then The Dicks did, and Verbal Abuse moved out. We were in Houston almost two years playin' the same places, opening for bands coming through. We were reading *Maximum RockNRoll* and seeing scenes all over the place. So we jumped on the bandwagon and moved to San Francisco. We got there and two weeks later we played a show. A few weeks later, we were off on our first tour, Rock Against Reagan — us, MDC, Dicks, Crucifucks, and a few bands we picked up here and there. That was a whole US tour. We went to soup kitchens, gave blood when we had to get gas money, just roughed it for the whole tour. Since most of it was free shows at colleges, we didn't get any money. Once in a while, we'd take up a collection and get people to drop quarters in a hat.

Zine ad for first D.R.I. record
with 22 songs on a 7"
Collection of the author

Hardcore bands could play a few local dives: Rock Island (a.k.a. Paradise Island, or The Island), booked by Phil Hix; The Axiom, booked by Doomsday Massacre's JR Delgado; Cabaret Voltaire, booked by Ronnie Gaitz; Joe Starr's Omni; plus a cool, short-lived industrial space, Apocalypse Monster Club, and Lawndale Art Annex, a community center. Ronnie Bond booked many bills, as did Chuck Roast, who did a radio program on Pacifica station KPFT. But most indie action ground to a halt when Really Red broke up in '84, (Ronnie Bond relocated to the wilds of Washington state).

EL PASO
If you were from El Paso and were into alternative culture, you'd leave. Case in point: the Tex-Mex-flavored The Plugz, who emigrated to LA in '78 to take their place in Punk history.

Most local Hardcore scenes arose due to the drive of one or two individuals — in El Paso, RHYTHM PIGS bassist/vocalist Ed Ivey did his best to ignite some viable action for a year or two.

ED IVEY (Rhythm Pigs): I was a shrimp little bastard; I always got beat up. Hardcore was a way to level the playing field. Shave your head, get your teeth busted out in the pit, all of a sudden people don't wanna fuck with you anymore. My friend Greg Adams said, 'Ever heard Punk Rock?' I said, 'You mean like Oingo Boingo?' He said, 'No man, come to my sister's warehouse tonight. You'll see.' I showed up — he had a ghetto blaster listening to Black Flag with three guys; they were all slamdancing. That was my introduction to it — I fell in love with the whole energy.

Inspired to action, Ed started Rhythm Pigs; since nothing was going on in El Paso or nearby, he realized they had to create a scene. MDC, the only HC outfit to visit town, played to 50 people in late '82. So starting in '83, Ivey set up all-ages shows at The Koke House, an old Coca-Cola bottling plant — Black Flag, DKs, D.O.A., and Minutemen all gigged there. Over 100 skater types showed up for No Trend in '83; Ed paid us fairly — about 100 bucks — and a kid laid a sack of cheap-but-decent herb on me as I walked out.

Jello Biafra suggested that his friend Roger Morgan of Unclean Records out of Sand Spring, Oklahoma put out a Rhythm Pigs record; their six-song 7" *An American Activity*, was recorded in one afternoon for $85.

Despite all their hard work, Rhythm Pigs, like those before them, saw the need to get outta town. Inspired by tales of HC glory, they moved to SF in '84. Jello hooked them up with Ruth Schwartz and her new Mordam Records, who issued two LPs: '84's *Rhythm Pigs* and '86's *Choke On This.*

ED IVEY: Our drummer had a girlfriend who was very connected to the San Francisco scene. She went out there to find a job. I woke up one morning — there was a note on the kitchen table that said, 'I moved to SF.' That's why we moved out — there was no other drummers in El Paso. We knew if we wanted to continue, we were gonna have to move. We moved in early '84, and by late '84 our first LP was out.

Show flyer for J.F.A.
Kokehouse, El Paso, 1983
Collection of Laura Albert

Between the making of *Rhythm Pigs* **and** *Choke On This*, they appeared on a compilation of which Ivey says: "Mordam got us on a comp which helped buy bullets for the African National Congress so they could kill people." Rhythm Pigs soon fell out with the Bay Area HC elite over such political bullshit.

ED IVEY: We got written up in a *MRR* editorial decrying participation in a Bill Graham concert. We played with The Damned at The Fillmore and *Maximum RockNRoll* wrote that we'd sold out 'cause the tickets were $12. We got in a tiff and wrote a song about it, "Little Brother" which came out on *Choke On This*. Ruth Schwartz was also a big cheese over at *Maximum RockNRoll*, and when she heard the song, she immediately said, 'I'm not gonna put the record out.' We had to say, 'It's Punk Rock — can't we say what we want?' She called up Biafra, who'd been our torch-carrier, and asked him what she should do. Keep in mind that two months before that the Feds kicked in his door and seized his personal property. Biafra told her, 'Don't put the record out.' We had to go back to Ruth and say, 'He's doing to us what they did to him.' To her credit she said, 'Okay, you made your point. I'll put the record out.' But it damaged our relationship with Ruth to the point where she didn't talk to me anymore. *MRR* never wrote about us again. Of course, Biafra still brings it up every time I see him. •

AMERICA'S HARDCORE

Future generations will fuck up again
At least we can try and change the one we're in
— Deep Wound, "Deep Wound"

EAST COAST

In 1980, over-with small cities and run-down ghost town mill towns dotted the Northeast US. Kids had nothing to do. Punk of any kind earned a cultural death sentence in the land of stiff upper-lipped Yankees. That cultural isolation was the impetus for a few local Hardcore scenes.

WESTERN MASSACHUSETTS, for one, had a fairly active scene of 100 or so kids circa 1982-84. The Western Mass bands — Deep Wound, The Outpatients, Pajama Slave Dancers, All White Jury, Cancerous Growth, Brain Injured Unit — and their fans didn't match the intensity of those two hours away in Boston.

LOU BARLOW (Deep Wound): Before Western Mass was a Hardcore scene, it was a weird musical collective of fringe bands. There were New Wave bands playing, us — the young Hardcore band — and all different shades of mid-tempo Punk bands. There was still this New Wave glow happening but we destroyed it completely. We took the musical diversity of New Wave and curated it into this marching electric guitar music.

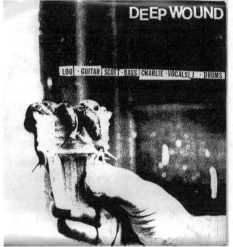

Deep Wound
Deep Wound 7" EP, Radiobeat, 1983
Collection of Sal Canzonieri

AL QUINT (editor, *Suburban Voice*): I went to Western Mass since those shows were mellower and friendlier than Boston. Deep Wound were raw Hardcore, but you had The Outpatients, Brain Injured Unit, and All White Jury with Murph from Dinosaur Jr. I'd roadtrip there a lot, a two-and-a-half hour drive. It was the excitement of seeing bands, meeting people, trading zines, and interviewing people.

DEEP WOUND were the top Western Mass HC outfit, though that's not saying much. They started in Westfield in early '82 with two 14-year-olds — guitarist Lou Barlow and bassist Scott Helland — and two 16-year-olds — singer Charlie Nakajima and drummer J. Mascis. Deep Wound put out a 7" EP in '83 and contributed two songs to an '84 comp. They looked like nerds, and their future work bore that out. (In late '84, Mascis and Barlow, with Murph from All White Jury, formed Dinosaur Jr., laying the foundations of Indie Rock. Barlow went on to Sebadoh and Folk Implosion.)

LOU BARLOW: Mascis was from Amherst, like 17 miles from us, so his dad had to drive him with his drums to practice. By the time we were doing gigs, J. had his driver's license. We did our first show at an Amherst youth center. Scott Helland's brother Eric's band Mace played — who became The Outpatients. Our first Boston show was with DYS, The Mighty COs and The FU's. It was very intense for us. We were so intimidated.

The Outpatients were Deep Wound bassist Scott Helland with his older brother, guitarist/vocalist Eric "Vis" Helland from Mace, a 1980-82 Metal troupe that covered Motorhead but also dug Black Flag — a rare blend of influences back then. The Outpatients were musically competent, as displayed on '83's *Basement Tape*.

The first Western Mass gigs were set up by Todd Cote and J Mascis at The Guilded Star Grange Hall in bucolic Greenfield, 20 minutes from the Vermont border. Shows also happened at Pulaski Hall in Easthampton and a few at halls in Northampton. The legendary Rock Against Reagan tour with MDC, Dicks, Crucifix and DRI hit UMass-Amherst in summer '83.

By '85 came a new generation, led by more-physical types like SEIGE, whose tape (released years later on CD by Relapse) influenced the late 80s "Grindcore" sound of Napalm Death and Godflesh. Other like-minded groups — CATHARSIS, NO PRESERVATIVES, BLACK X-MASS — were also on the scene.

VERMONT had a handful of HC kids who'd travel to Western Mass and Boston for shows. Burlington's THE WARDS played a few Western Mass bills around '84, and put out two weak 7"s, while Montpelier's PUBLIC DISTURBANCE were known to play with Deep Wound and The Outpatients.

NEW HAMPSHIRE — the Northeast's White Trash capital — had no HC culture to speak of. Early 80s NH kids most likely favored Metal. A band of mohawked lunkheads, THE ABORTION SQUAD, known for their retarded anthem "No Authority, No Rules," played Boston occasionally. THE QUEERS were around in some form but did not tour until years later. The singer of Portsmouth's DVA, went on to White Power band The Bruisers. NH's greatest export was not quite HC — the late GG ALLIN of Manchester, who abused audiences like no one else before or since.

GG ALLIN: I was the first fuckin' Punk in my town. Nobody knew what to make of me. I'd fuck with everybody — shower 'em with blood and guts and Rock & Roll. I hated the shitheads I grew up with. I was on a mission to destroy them. Then to destroy the world.

AL QUINT: I saw GG in Boston at The Rat in '81; his stageshow was still kinda tame. He'd go to Punk shows in Boston every so often, smelling like he hadn't bathed in years. I recall seeing him pull out his schlong in the middle of The Channel parking lot. GG was on the scene periphery but rarely played around 'cause he got banned everywhere.

The World Ain't Pretty And Neither Are We
The Wards 7" EP, No Thanks, 1980
Collection of Sal Canzonieri

MAINE, always lame, lagged especially in the HC years. The one exception was Portland's THE STAINS (later Ice Age), who did a cool marble-colored 7" in '80. Portland misfits made the trek to Boston for shows and record shopping.

Hit Squad For God
Vatican Commandos 7" EP, Pregnant Nun, 1983
featuring a young Moby on guitar
Collection of Sal Canzonieri

RHODE ISLAND's scene revolved around The Living Room in Providence, a great club for touring acts. Owner Randy Hein treated musicians well — and his mom cooked 'em big meals like turkey dinners. Paradoxically, HC circles knew the club best as the meeting ground for New York and Boston bands, with feuds and brawls the norm. Locals VICIOUS CIRCLE, one of at least three so-named nationwide, made the biggest splash; in their wake came RASH OF STABBINGS, IDLE RICH and POSITIVE OUTLOOK. The problem in Providence before and after shows was avoiding getting fucked with by local ginzos.

CONNECTICUT saw some action. In New Wave days, you'd go to Pogo's in run-down Bridgeport. For Hardcore, The Anthrax — first in Stamford, then Norwalk — was the Nutmeg State's answer to CBGB. The first "CTHC" outfit, New Haven's CIA, put out *Gods, Guts, Guns*, a decent '83 EP. Later came VATICAN COMMANDOS — with a young Moby on guitar, credited as "M.H." on '83's *Hit Squad For God EP*, 76% UNCERTAIN — with ex-CIA members, and New Haven homeboys, LOST GENERATION. REFLEX FROM PAIN did '83's *Black & White* EP; WHITE PIGS issued a 7" in '84. In '85 came the most famous local band: YOUTH OF TODAY, who billed themselves as NYHC.

NEW JERSEY circa 1980 was overrun with truly awful Springsteen-style party bands. For example, Sayreville teen John Bongiovi — later Jon Bon Jovi — emulated said style at Jersey Shore "shooter bars" and proms.

SUNDAY
at the Living Room

HARDCORE
ALL AGES
17 Bands!

PSYCHO VICIOUS CIRCLE VERBAL ASSAULT
BONEMEN OF BARUMBA NEUTRAL NATION
CANCEROUS GROWTH *THE* CIVIL DEATH
TERMINALLY ILL NOT OUTPATIENTS
IDLE RICH POSITIVE OUTLOOK SIEGE
WHITE PIGS POST MORTEM KILSLUG

and special guests THE **V**IBRATORS

Sunday, Feb. 19
SHOW STARTS AT NOON
ALL AGES

All This for Only
$5.00
521–2520
273 Promenade St. Providence, RI

Show flyer for 17 bands for $5
The Living Room, Providence, RI, 1985
Collection of Laura Albert

BOBBY STEELE (Misfits, Undead): I grew up an outcast in the burbs of New Millford, New Jersey where everybody listened to Allman Brothers and Grateful Dead. When I got outta high school I played in cover bands, the only time I've made money doing music. We were called Stars. We did school dances, making two grand a night. It was fun but I wanted to do originals. Then I read about the Pistols and Ramones, which woke things up. I put together a band called Paradox, and instead of coming to New York where it was safe to play Punk, we'd book ourselves at high school dances and whatnot. The Adrenalin OD guys were at one of those dances. We played biker bars and Country & Western bars, and picked up a following. We played the Lodi Boy's Club in 1977 and during one of our breaks this kid came up to me. He said his friends had a band called The Misfits. This kid was Steve Zing. He was in eighth grade at the time.

Hip Jersey kids end up in NY or LA. NYHC types from the garbage-strewn Garden State included former Misfit Bobby Steele and Jack Natz of The Undead

(Natz later of Virus and Cop Shoot Cop), Jack Rabid, The Psychos with Roger Miret (later of Agnostic Front) and Billy Milano (later of SOD), and the Cause For Alarm guys.

Early-80s Hardcore shows in Jersey were scarce. Hitsville in Passaic booked the rare TSOL show; shitholes like Club Mod in Garfield, Aldo's Hideaway in Lynhurst, Maxwell's in Hoboken and The Dirt Club near Union also tolerated some HC. Great shows included Kraut, at Patrix in New Brunswick, and MDC, at The Jetty on the Jersey Shore.

ADRENALIN OD were the only Jerseyites on the popular NYHC comp New York Thrash, and to receive regular airplay on WNYU's *Noise The Show*.

JIM FOSTER (Adrenalin OD): AOD wouldn't have gotten any breaks if not for *Noise The Show*. We got a lot of shit for being from Jersey — the kids from Queens or wherever did not wanna take us seriously. We brought tapes to Tim [Sommers] and Jack [Rabid] and they supported us. Because of those guys we went from playing nowhere to within six months opening shows at Irving Plaza, City Gardens or Peppermint Lounge.

AOD were the kings of Jersey HC. Vocalist Paul Richards and bassist Jack Steeples came out of a Dead Boys-style cover band called East Patterson Boys Choir. AOD's debut 7" EP, '83's *Let's Barbecue With Adrenalin OD*, was hilarious, and their shows could be powerful, but they were soon stuck in the rut of trying to write comical songs. The band broke up in disgust in '86, as their music started to appeal to the same Jersey Metal yo-yos they lampooned.

By '84, Hardcore hit New Jersey. ROSEMARY'S BABY, weak Misfits wannabees, starred bassist Eerie Von, later of Danzig. MOURNING NOIZE resembled Misfits sped up to 45 rpm. BEDLAM's guys ran Buy Our Records, the top NJHC label and home of AOD. MENTAL ABUSE played a few CBGB matinees. Also-rans included PLEASED YOUTH, NO DEMOCRACY, CHILDREN IN ADULT JAILS, BODIES IN PANIC, SAND IN THE FACE, SACRED DENIAL, SUBURBICIDE, MY 3 SONS, STETZ, BORSCHT, CYANAMID AND AUTISTIC BEHAVIOR. NJ shows usually sucked because of lousy music — and the kids were knuckleheads.

Paul Richards (Adrenalin OD) center
Uncredited photo from AOD promo sticker
Collection of the author

GENOCIDE, NJ's most notorious outfit, were led by wretched Bobby Ebz, a huge influence on GG Allin. Genocide's days paralleled HC's, and they did a split LP, *Last Rites For Genocide And MIA*, with the OC-style outfit MIA. For a short time, Genocide featured future Hair Metal hero Rachel Bolan of Skid Row. One of Genocide's biggest fans was Inger Lorre, later of the Nymphs.

New Brunswick, home of Rutgers U., was a cool place in the early 80s. Though it had no Hardcore, "The Hub City," halfway between NY and Philly, supported a New Wave scene rivaling Manhattan in decadence. At the Melody Bar, Matt Pinfield spun New Wave import 12"s — and all the blow, booze and ecstasy made it sound amazing. Touring groups never played town before I hooked up gigs in 1984-85 at the Court Tavern, with Butthole Surfers, Faith No More, TSOL, Dinosaur Jr., Mentors with Saint Vitus, and Tex And The Horseheads. Now, "Brunfuss" is a regular tour stop.

I saw Black Flag — the first HC band to regularly play Jersey — at least five times there, three during the brief Emil-on-drums era. By '84, Flag's NJ landings included a Metal bar in South River and a Freehold roller rink. One cannot overstate the impact of those suburban invasions.

WFMU's Pat Duncan championed Hardcore on the radio, publicizing any event between Philly and NYC. WRSU (Rutgers) and WPRB (Princeton) aired underground music, though oblivious to HC. The Misfits and AOD appeared on UHF TV's *The Uncle Floyd Show*. A few smart-alecks put out zines like *Jersey Beat, Flesh And Bones* and *Hard Times*. Most Jersey kids met at record stores like Pellett Records in Morristown, Sal Canzonieri's Rebel Rouser in Irvington, and Looney Tunes on Route 23, run by the Dramarama guys.

Zine ad for Philly Hardcore Records, 1983
Collection of the author

By '86, a next wave of Jersey groups were playing to maybe 75 kids. A scene thrived down by the Shore in Toms River, but all-ages shows at Brighton Bar, the label Mutha Records, and CHRONIC DISTURBANCE were nothing special.

PHILADELPHIA — home of *Rocky*, "Broad Street Bullies," and some of America's most racially stratified 'hoods — ain't no "City Of Brotherly Love." The rich R&B of Gamble & Huff — Teddy Pendergrass, The O'Jays, Harold Melvin — had zero impact on local suburban White kids.

Philly produced no great Punk either, contributing at best New Wave flops like The A's, The Vels, Executive Slacks, and Bunnydrums. The best, Regressive Aid, from nearby Trenton, NJ, featured bassist Andrew Weiss and drummer Simeon Cain — they'd later join Greg Ginn's Gone, and co-found Rollins Band.

Everyone seeming so fuckin' unsatisfied made Philly ideal for Hardcore. They lived in the stylistic shadows of NY to the north and DC to the south. If you were a Philly HC kid, Whites hated you, Blacks hated you, and cops were ready to kill you. Just as in NY or SF, many Philly kids were crusty, methed-out types living in urban squalor; many of them violent, sleazy criminal types.

D.H. PELIGRO (Dead Kennedys): In Philly someone booked a gig in an Irish ghetto — Irish people didn't want anybody in their 'hood that didn't live there or be Irish at least. There were thugs with bats trying to beat down the door and get into the club. And the police, they're down with the people. Some cats drove by with plastic dynamite, threw it into the crowd, and blew a kid's leg up. The cops came by with a dog, and the dog jumped on the car with Hardcore kids trying to get in — another anarchic night.

SADISTIC EXPLOITS, Philly's premiere HC band, concentrated more on inciting stage action than playing songs — though their '81 "Freedom" 7" was quite good. Manager Nancy Exploit (who later married SSD's Al Barile) put out the zine *Savage Pink* with Allison Schenkenberger (who'd later run Southern Studios in the UK). Other Philly products included: MCRAD — with pro skater Chuck Treece, AUTISTIC BEHAVIOR, ELECTRIC LOVE MUFFIN, YDI, CIRCLE OF SHIT, FLAG OF DEMOCRACY, INFORMED SOURCES, and RUIN, professed Buddhists who dressed in white and burned candles on stage.

Some of the era's best shows took place in Philly, of which fans drove hundreds of miles to attend. Most of these occurred in '82-'83 at Love Hall, booked by postal-worker-cum-tattoo-artist "Fat" Howard Saunders. A short-lived local BYO chapter also put on some gigs. But when Love Hall shows stopped, the scene died. Most touring outfits ended up playing New Wave discos like East Side Club and, later, the Trocadero. By '86, Philly's finest were ZEN GUERILLA, MORE FIENDS, and SERIAL KILLERS, but DEAD MILKMEN gained the most success, with the pathetic novelty hit "Bitchin' Camaro." By then, most people I knew split town or, deep into heroin, didn't give a shit.

HARRISBURG, in the heart of the law-and-order Keystone State, saw a few shows, at old Duncan Hall, and Li'l Joe's, a gnarly biker bar. Mike Rage (one of a few from H-burg who'd make pilgrimages to Philly and DC) set up shows; his group

THE OUTRAGE or WASTED TALENT opened every one of 'em. Suicidal Tendencies rocked Li'l Joe's on their first tour with No Labels and COC. Crucifix played there, as did The Freeze. In '83 Scream played the first HC gig in the nearby Amish Country of Lancaster.

PITTSBURGH's The Electric Banana, a rattrap in the heart of the dead Steel City, held some poorly-attended shows. The only local HC act was REAL ENEMY. Black Flag and Circle Jerks played there a few times, always with problems. In '84, I was with No Trend and the club promised the band 60 percent of a $5 door. We drew 75 kids easy, on a rainy Thursday night, but the box office strong-armed us into leaving with $18, rather than the $200-ish earned. So I grabbed a bottle of Alka-Seltzer tablets from the van, found the club owner's car, and poured 'em down his gas tank.

Show flyer for Necros
Li'l Joe's, Harrisburg, PA, 1983
Collection of Andy Wendler

PAT DUBAR (Uniform Choice): We played Pittsburgh at The Electric Banana, trapped with no money, in the hottest fucking summer I can recall, taking a bath in the fountain at Three Rivers 'cause we had no money. We slept on top of the van, and played the Electric Banana four days into the tour. It was the second show — the promoter Johnny Danger pulled a gun on me that night after telling me how he shot at Keith Morris of the Circle Jerks for trying to rip off a mic.

BALTIMORE circa 1980 was a tough-but-strange blue-collar ghetto, resembling its portrayals in John Waters films. Screwballs such as "The Egg Lady" Edith Massey and Half Japanese hail from there. It always followed the stylistic lead of DC. Though a mere 35 miles apart, the cities maintain little connection. But that didn't prevent some decent Hardcore action.

TOM BERRARD (DC scene): We never minded going to Baltimore for a gig. The problem was that we were never able to know about it. There was Marble Bar; later on there was The Loft. Black Flag were amazed there wasn't a better connection 'cause in LA driving 40 miles was considered an in-town gig. I went to see D.O.A. in Baltimore, and the stage collapsed; a hole actually formed in the center of it. This was right around the time that Florida had sinkholes. But Baltimore and DC were not alike. In fact, there's no place quite like Baltimore, I'm quite sure of it.

LAW & ORDER (not the late-80s Hair Metal outfit) were the only locals who fit in with the DC Hardcore style. They played with Bad Brains and S.O.A. in late '80 at the Oddfellow's Hall, home of the first indie HC shows.

Law & Order's William, Pete and Joe Dagher, all in engineering school or med school, in summer '82 fomed BOLLOCKS with redneck kid Bill Stevenson — not the Black Flag/Descendents drummer — from nearby Waverly. The brothers were panicking to find a singer so they could open for DKs; in 10 days Bill had to learn 20 songs. Law & Order's 7" EP and the first Bollocks 7" came out in fall '82; a second 7", *Mediteran*, came out in '83.

FEAR OF GOD (initially Jerry's Kids), White Trash kids from Arbutice into esoteric shit such as Zappa, DEVO and Tangerine Dream, were very HC in spirit. They were best band in town but sadly never made a record.

Marble Bar, Baltimore's primary "alternative" venue, usually booked shitty local New Wave acts like Null Set and Ebeneezer And The Bludgeons — but sometimes did touring bands, like Psychedelic Furs, Dead Boys, and Bauhaus.

Meditteran
Bollocks 7" EP, Fetal, 1983
Collection of Sal Canzonieri

When D.O.A. played there on the Hardcore 81 tour, admission was a buck. DKs played there in '81 and '82 for $7.

Bill Stevenson booked HC gigs at Terminal 406 at 406 North Eutaw, a small room with balcony and high ceiling, first presenting Black Flag on June 5, '82. That summer he did Meatmen/Negative Approach/Necros, Code Of Honor, and MDC/Minor Threat/Agnostic Front. I wouldn't get to see Minor Threat or MDC 'cause I spent the night in City Jail after a police parking lot sweep: guilty as charged with public consumption. (Locked down during a Million Of Dead Cops gig — Dave Dictor would've been proud!)

BILL STEVENSON (Baltimore promoter): That night, Agnostic Front/Minor Threat/MDC, was crazy. Al from SSD in Boston came — people as far south as Florida came up. The soundman freaked out over the scene — everybody just sang a cappella, without the PA. Eventually I convinced the soundman to give some mics back — something was said about taking his PA home with us.

Bill later booked "Jules' Loft" or "The Loft," an illegal club on the corner of Eutaw and Mulberry circa 1983-84. That was the apex of the Baltimore scene. Any HC band could come up and play — if money and sound quality were no issue. Crucifix, Fang, and COC were amongst those to hit The Loft.

Lousy turnouts crippled Baltimore shows. Code Of Honor drew about 40 kids. DKs could draw 400 max. Bad Brains rarely went there because they expected at least $500 — way too high to even consider.

Maryland's strict liquor laws also made all-ages events impossible. The rare shows — at Typographer's Hall on Calvert, or Sgt. Pepper's on Eutaw — never justified the hassles. In a hard drinkin' town, the last thing some blue-collar bar owner wanted to hear about was underage Hardcore gigs.

Concurrent with the '85 rise of "Emo" in DC came a few like-minded Baltimore outfits. The best was REPTILE HOUSE; Dischord released the MacKaye-produced *Reptile House*. And the singer of GREY MARCH had a real hard-on for Ian Curtis of Joy Division. But Hardcore in Baltimore — as everywhere else — was over with.

THE SOUTH

You never knew what to expect with Hardcore south of the Mason-Dixon line. Few Southern scenes developed. If touring bands ever experienced ill will, it was probably in The South. Though smaller and less sophisticated than elsewhere, crowds generally appreciated anyone who played their town. The problems began once you stepped outside the venue ...

RICHMOND, former capital of the Confederacy, was the first major city south of DC on I-95 — but no one there gave a fuck about Hardcore. WHITE CROSS, gnarly dudes with bad attitudes, were the big guys in town. They put out a few records and opened for virtually everyone that came through. DEATH PIGGY, a weird group, spawned the even-weirder Gwar. THE PREVARICATORS put out the cool "Ode To Mr. Ed," 7" EP in '83. GRAVEN IMAGE did a tape split with HONOR ROLE; a few guys in Honor Roll originated in Indiana, where they played in Battered Youth. The owners of Richmond's only indie music store, Plan 9 Records, ran the local HC label Zero Degree. Most of those groups broke up by '84 — and no one replaced them.

NORFOLK, a huge naval-base town, holds a spot in Hardcore history. An affinity grew between HC and military types: they cut their hair the same, and both were ready to fight. But a Hardcore Punk in the service made for the ultimate fucked-up character; Hardcore, first and foremost anti-establishment, clashed with the Navy's job: to protect the status quo.

Ray "Raybeez" Barbieri — later of Agnostic Front and Warzone — and future Cro-Mags frontman John Joseph McGeown didn't join the US Navy out of a sense of patriotism, but as the result of a judge's order. Before becoming NYHC stalwarts, they both served aboard the U.S.S. *Yellowstone*, the first American military vessel with women sailors. A pack of Navy chicks into Punk got high with Raybeez and John Joseph in the storerooms.

Zine ad for Richmond Hardcore,
Plan 9 Records (a store and label), 1984
Collection of the author

The Hardcore and Navy sets met a few times at The Taj Mahal, Norfolk's lone New Wave club. Many DC groups first played out-of-town shows there.

JERRY WILLIAMS (producer/soundman): The Taj Mahal was where Bad Brains played when they came to town. I saw The Untouchables and Teen Idles in summer '80. They were very entertaining. It was a small club in terms of production values — once they started playing, the sound was a blur. Don Fleming told me of these great DC bands to check out, even more extreme than the Punk bands I was seeing, which was fine with me. One of my impressions, besides not being able to hear, was seeing one especially enthusiastic stagediving roadie named Henry. I liked them all right away.

IAN MACKAYE (Teen Idles/Minor Threat): The Untouchables and Teen Idles had a show in Norfolk in 1980 at this place, The Taj Mahal. We got down there and the DJ was playing The B-52s and The Vapors and that shit. There was eight or ten of us and we all went onto the dancefloor and jumped up and down in unison to make the record skip. Then we played the gig and people just sat there — it was weird. We went to King's Dominion on the way back and got into a huge scrap, being that we were 1980 Punk Rockers in an amusement park. That was a fun trip.

The **RALEIGH-DURHAM-CHAPEL HILL area, with its major universities, offers a bit of a reprieve from the prevalent Jesse Helms-mindset surrounding it. But it was still Carolina, and Punk — in any way, shape or form — was an unacceptable form of behavior.**

Raleigh's first Punk group, Th' Cigaretz, played Rock with that fuck-you vibe. The group — with drummer Scott Jarvis (tour manager and DJ on Beastie Boys' breakout '85 tour with Madonna), guitarist Jerry Williams (future Bad Brains producer), and soundman Tim Williams (later engineer for Cro-Mags) — relocated to NYC in late '79.

By 1980, a few clubs, like The Pier in Raleigh, Cat's Cradle in Chapel Hill, and Friday's in Greensboro, started to book New Wave. Some Raleigh kids too young to attend created their own scene, setting up shows with their own Hardcore music — **CORROSION OF CONFORMITY (COC), NO LABELS, COLCOR, ORAL FIXATION, and STILLBORN CHRISTIANS.**

No Labels/C.O.C. cassette tape, 1983
Collection of the author

Chew tobacco, spit it out
Find some punks, fight it out
— COC, "Redneckkk"

REED MULLIN (COC): The Pier was underneath this parking lot in a shopping mall, Cameron Village. There were all-ages shows … they weren't incredibly successful. Double O played there to a hundred people including all our parents who came to get us in. The Mob played. So did DKs — one of the few times we played there. Jello specified us, No Labels and Stillborn Christians. We all grew up around this mall — the video arcade was where we hung out. If we were lucky enough to scam our way into the club, we would. If we couldn't, we'd hang out and play Space Invaders.

In a scene this small, as long as you weren't a frat jerk or redneck, you could participate. It all started around parties at the North Street home of original COC frontman Benji Shelton, and Turner Street, where second COC singer Eric Eycke lived. Lee Johnson, who played in **BLACK GIRL** and put out the zine *Southern Lifestyles*, also organized a few parties.

MARIA MA (Raleigh scene): The first Raleigh show I saw was Youth Brigade at someone's backyard party in '83. A Mongolian BBQ Restaurant also had shows, where they'd take out all the booths and COC would play, people diving off the counters and shit. There were shows in parking lots. I remember people cutting the shit out of themselves on the gravel; they would bring out chairs so they could dive off them. There was 50 or 60 people at these shows. The bigger shows would attract Marines from Fort Bragg, like when DKs played. The Raleigh scene was very close-knit.

COC was Raleigh's great export. After the original lineup — drummer Reed Mullin, bassist Mike Dean, guitarist Woody Weatherman, and vocalist Benji Shelton — they burned through numerous singers over the years: Eric Eycke, Simon Bob, Mike Dean, Karl Agell, Pepper Keenan. A confusing ensemble, COC mutated from fiery Leftists touring Amerika in a beat-up van to muscle-car-driving musos into Sabbath-powered chops. But COC had their moments, making blistering records like 1983's *Eye For An Eye* and '85's *Animosity*. One of HC's hardest-working outfits, their music and attitude was largely responsible for the "Crossover" that followed.

Reed and Woody also played in No Labels — basically a cover band doing Black Flag, Discharge and GBH songs in Reed's bedroom. Stillborn Christians played sickeningly fast, with a Free Jazz flavor.

Reed's No Core label put out the only NCHC comps: the *No Core* tape with No Labels, COC (with Benji) and Colcor, and the *Why Are We Here* 7" with COC, No Labels, Stillborn Christians and BLOODMOBILE, from the state's western mountains area.

By '84, Raleigh saw at least one show a month, a stopover for groups going between DC and Atlanta. As in most towns, the enthusiasm of one or two kids propelled the entire scene. When the COC guys — alienated and burned out — threw in the towel for a year or so in late '85, the small Raleigh scene crumbled.

REED MULLIN: Working-class folk in Carolina did not understand us kids at all. We represented evil — they'd pull guns and shoot at us in the parking lot. We thought the cops were on our side until the day we finally rumbled — me, Woody, this guy named Joe, and four rednecks. They started it, and they had a baseball bat. And we finished it. Of course we got arrested and taken downtown. My van had graffiti, everybody in Raleigh knew it — it was an eyesore. With all the stress, I dropped out of high school. I was becoming homicidal. I got my G.E.D. and started working for the folks.

NO CORE compilation cassette
46-minute cassette (Maxell)
41-song hardcore compilation cassette from North Carolina
featuring: COL COR
         NO ROCK STARS
         NO LABELS
         CORROSION OF CONFORMITY
w/lyric booklet
$4.00 postpaid//overseas $5.00

Zine ad for *No Core,* North Carolina HC compilation
Collection of the author

CHARLOTTE's small scene revolved around The Milestone club. Black Flag — seemingly the only reason HC hit "The Queen City" — played there twice on the *Damaged* tour. HC's call to action inspired 30 or so kids, resulting in two local outfits: NO ROCK STARS (on *No Core*) and ANTISCENE (still active). COC's Mike Dean lived in Charlotte for awhile; Benji of COC came from there.

Other Hardcore activity scattered over the languid Mid-Atlantic. The ROANOKE area limited itself to a few hip Virginia Tech students in Blacksburg involved with college station WUVT, a lone bastion of cultural freedom in the Shenandoah Valley Bible Belt. A few kids would drive to Raleigh and DC for shows. One group came outta Blacksburg: MIR (Russian for "peace"). MORGANTOWN (Univ. Of West Virginia's home) had TH' INBRED, and the club The Underground Railroad booked Flag and a few others that passed through.

ATLANTA was where you'd find gaudy New Wavers in gold lamé pants at Hardcore gigs. More than a few touring outfits suffered through wretched local openers like DDT and NEON CHRIST at the 688 Club. In 1984, marijuana activist Paul Cornwell opened The Metroplex, a cooler spot where many major names performed. Nearby college town ATHENS (U. Of Georgia), caught up in REM-style proto-Alternative hysteria, took zero notice of Hardcore.

While most shows in The South were "outlaw," the most outlaw of all took place in FLORIDA. The Sunshine State, infamous for youth culture repression, simply did not tolerate skateboarding or any other countercultural activity. Hardcore shows happened at cowboy bars, Hippie acid parties, in garages and parking lots,

even out in cowfields. A case of Black Label usually supplied the ambience. Fifty
kids made for a good gig.

Florida 1980 was overrun with horrific Lynyrd Skynyrd/Molly Hatchet
Southern Rock cover bands. Florida's first HC outfit was ROACH MOTEL from
GAINESVILLE (U. Of Florida), who did songs like "I Hate The Sunshine State" and
"My Dog's Into Anarchy." A scene started to coalesce after the 1981 Black
Flag/Roach Motel(!) tour of the state.

GEORGE TABB (Roach Motel): Black Flag shows up at my Gainesville apartment; it's all
these guys that look like Hippies. I'm like, 'Who the fuck are these longhairs?' Then they all
jumped into my building complex pool dressed. That got me thrown out of my fuckin'
apartment, which pissed me off — but okay. Then we drove down to our first show in Tampa
at The New Rose, to about 200 people. It was so violent, we had to get outta there quick. One
guy stagedove and missed, hit the side of the stage, and broke his jaw in three places — there
was blood everywhere, but he kept slammin', with his jaw hanging down like a fleshy piece of
meat. The next night we played in Fort Lauderdale at Finder's, a hotel bar on the beach. And
of course there were complete and utter riots, kids trying to kill both bands. Then we went to
play the $20,000 Club in Daytona, and there were only like 30 kids there, but it was so loud
that everyone walked out deaf.

Roach Motel hung with RAT CAFETERIA, sick fuckers from TAMPA. Jimmy Barf
ate cockroaches, cigarette butts, even other's snot and spit. A scene existed briefly
in TALLAHASSEE, at Smitty's, a shack on cinder blocks. Old redneck fisherman
Smitty let HC bands come in and fuck up the place. SECTOR 4 and HATED YOUTH
played there. CRUCIAL TRUTH moved from Pompano Beach to NYC, where they
shook up Skinhead circles. MIAMI had MORBID OPERA. The Destroy Records 7"
comp *We Can't Help It If We're From Florida* featured most of these outfits.

Shellshock
Shellshock 7" EP, Vinyl Solution, 1981
Graphics by Tracey Hammill
Collection of Sal Canzonieri

Only a few touring acts hit Miami —
it was too off the beaten path to play for
no money. The bigger ones played The
Cameo Theater, others hit Flynn's, a
decrepit hotel/club. And once there, they
usually didn't like what they saw.

GEORGE TABB: I left Florida 'cause
nazis starting moving in on the whole thing. A
lot of people coming to our shows were really
into wearing swastikas, then the Klan start
moving in. The worst shit was Cuban kids,
anti-Castro Skinheads — totally fucked. It
went from '80, no scene, to '84, some of the
worst idiots you've ever seen.

TESCO VEE (Meatmen): The most
notorious Meatmen gig was in 1986 in Miami.
There was this Black guy, who for whatever
reason didn't like me. He hassled me all night.
I held up a picture of a girl pissing on a guy in
a gorilla mask. This guy ran across the stage
and grabbed the picture out of my hand, so I
grabbed him by the hair. Now this was a big show, like 800 kids in a movie theater. I went
crashing to the floor, then I leapt up and we started really going at it. When the kids realized
I was fighting this guy, they went off on him. Then I got dropped to the ground again in the
crush, and my guitar player got on the mic and said, 'Somebody get that shit-skin! Kill the

nigger!' I was on the ground, crushed by humanity, thinking I was gonna die. If we weren't in the most racist state in the United States, we would've either had the plug pulled or got kicked out or got our asses beat. So this guy continued to try to get me the rest of the night. The last I saw of him, he climbed onstage, and the kids saw he was coming for me again, so they grabbed him by the legs, yanked him off, and he dropped six feet right on the back of his head on the concrete floor. After the show, he waited for me outside, so they tapped us a keg and told us to stay and party in the club. I remember that as one of the most bogus experiences of my life.

NASHVILLE, the Country Music capital, did not embrace Hardcore. Black Flag and Circle Jerks rocked it for 100 kids at Cantrell's for $200, but there was no scene. Nashville's only HC band COMMITTEE FOR PUBLIC SAFETY opened for The Faith's final show at Space II Arcade in DC. KNOXVILLE had STD, who toured the region a bit. In MEMPHIS, another black hole, grimy vanloads would feel lucky to earn 50 bucks playing at The Antenna Club.

REED MULLIN (COC): The first show of our tour was Memphis, put on by this guy Skankman at The Antenna Club.There were four people there: two guys were from the Navy, one was Tom Hazlemyer, later of Amphetamine Reptile Records. Skankman didn't have any money, so he tried to lose us. He got in his car and drove away — so we chased him all the way back to his house and made him let us stay the night. It was ugly.

NEW ORLEANS, another celebrated music town, was not into Hardcore either. A few touring outfits played the famous French Quarter nightspot Tipitina's — they'd be treated okay but crowds were small. Gigs at an old whorehouse called Storyville were small and the acts rarely got paid.
Circa '80, N.O. boasted a few unsung Punk groups like THE SLUTS and THE NORMALS (not Daniel Miller's The Normal of "Warm Leatherette" fame).

JOE CARDUCCI (SST): There was a great single by The Normals in '77-78. I've no idea what became of them, although I could guess. The only other New Orleans band I knew of was The Sluts. Their singer was the guy who might've joined Black Flag instead of Henry. They were both in New York auditioning while Dez was still in the band.

RED ROCKERS opened for every HC group that first came through town — until late '82, when they moved to SF, and inked with Howie Klein's ill-fated New Wave label 415, home of Romeo Void and Wire Train. There Red Rockers transformed into a junior Clash — replete with slicked-back hair and matching leather jackets — and lost all their HC cred. (Bassist Darren Hill resurfaced in Boston with Chris Doherty of Gang Green in mid-90s major-label flops, Klover.)

DARREN HILL (Red Rockers): In New Orleans, the music we played was too much for people there to handle, so we had to leave. We migrated out West when we recorded for 415. We did shows with Black Flag, and toured with D.O.A., TSOL, The Adolescents. Jimmy Reilly of Stiff Little Fingers played drums for a while. But we got a lot of bad career advice. It was scary how it all ended up.

Shellshock, 1981
Photo by Fish from *Shellshock*
Collection of Sal Canzonieri

Red Rockers influenced SHELLSHOCK — who put out a 7" EP in '81, and played a handful of shows in Texas. After breaking up due to lack of interest, they somehow remained inspirational, as kids who'd attended Shellshock gigs included future Pantera frontman Phil Anselmo and COC's Pepper Keenan.

Starting out northeastward from New Orleans, little HC action happened until one hit Atlanta. In BIRMINGHAM in the summer of '84, No Trend played The Pit, literally four concrete walls off the interstate. Inside, it was hotter than hell — I remember someone throwing up from the heat. There were tales of fucked-up gigs in Louisiana redneck bars, in BATON ROUGE and SHREVEPORT, where bands had their lives threatened. In the Deep South, rednecks and jocks comprised an omnipresent enemy.

Joey Shithead (D.O.A.) second from left, 1982
Photo by Edward Colver

NORTHWEST

There was little reason for Hardcore outfits to go to the Pacific Northwest. It was way off the beaten track, and there wasn't much going on.

It rains there all the time, and there's nothing for kids to do but cruise in their cars, listen to music, drink beer after beer and smoke joint after joint. Northwest HC came out of that incredible ennui — a reaction to redneck loggers/truckers, hard-ass cops, and drunken frat boys.

VANCOUVER was the only Canadian city to embrace Hardcore, partly due to its proximity to Portland and Seattle. But D.O.A.'s tours and records propelled the scene across the Northwest — and the rest of North America.

Nobody wants you
Nobody needs you
Nobody's gonna live for you
— DOA, "Liar For Hire"

The D.O.A. story begins in Burnaby, British Columbia, ten miles from downtown Vancouver. In 1976 came a high-powered combo of rowdy Burnaby North High grads, Stone Crazy — known as The Stoned Crazies for all the herb they smoked. Hearing The Ramones, of course, changed everything. Within weeks, Joey "Shithead" Keighley, Ken "Dimwit" Montgomery, Gerry "Useless" Hannah, and Brad "Kunt" Kent had added a cover of "Beat On The Brat" to their repertoire of bonehead Rock, like "Rock 'N' Me" by Steve Miller Band or Led Zep's "Rock & Roll." They played shitty bars in the logging town of Merritt until early 1977, when one club fired 'em for brawling with drunken rednecks.

JOEY SHITHEAD (D.O.A.): Interesting times — Dimwit had long hair. We were all really straight at our school and this guy was a pseudo-Hippie. He introduced us to the world of Black Sabbath and pot smoking. His little brother Chuck, this rugrat, used to listen to us practice. Chuck had learned to drum, so we got him in D.O.A. — he was 15 years old. Another Montgomery brother, Bob, roadied for D.O.A. for a long time.

With the bar gig over, Shithead and Dimwit hooked up with Burnaby pals Brian

"Wimpy Roy" Goble and Simon Werner to form The Skulls — who along with The Dishrags, The Modernettes and The Furies fueled a small-but-active Punk scene who hung out at Vancouver's version of CBGB, The Smiling Buddha.

In late '77, The Skulls moved east to Toronto, Canada's music biz capital. They made a big impression during their four-month stay, blowing away The Viletones at The Crash And Burn Club, and trashing a hip soiree thrown for local New Wave stars The Diodes — an incident D.O.A. wrote "Let's Wreck The Party" about. In Toronto The Skulls recorded three songs: "Fucked Up Baby" — later reworked by D.O.A. as the anti-Reagan "Fucked Up Ronnie"; "Waiting For You" — which resurfaced on D.O.A.'s *Hardcore 81* album; and "No Escape."

With Toronto conquered, The Skulls moved to London, England, but Shithead and Dimwit went home in February '78. Within weeks, Wimpy was back at his parents' house, broke and humiliated. Werner remained in London, teaming with Jim Walker of early PiL fame to achieve minor New Wave acclaim as The Pack. Meanwhile, back in BC, Dimwit, Wimpy, Gerry Useless and Mike Graham formed SUBHUMANS (not the Brit group of the same name).

Shithead began his rival outfit D.O.A. in summer '78 with Dimwit's younger sibling drummer Charles "Chuck Biscuits" Montgomery and peroxide-blond bassist Randy "Rampage" Archibald, and Brad Kent, who later moved to SF to join the Avengers' final lineup. By '79's end, D.O.A. added second guitar Dave Gregg (of Private School), completing the cast on 1980's epic *Something Better Change* LP.

The Skulls' London debacle and subsequent breakup ignited a legendary rivalry between Subhumans and D.O.A. Hating each other only made for a more competitive environment.

Early D.O.A. was incredible. A brawny hockey-player type, Joey Shithead (what a great stage name!) would spit beer and urinate on the crowd. He was an engaging singer and guitarist, who'd snarl and growl his

D.O.A., 1981
Joey Shithead, Randy Rampage, Chuck Biscuits, Dave Gregg
Photo by Edward Colver

way through D.O.A.'s rapid-fire, Clash-on-meth assault. Not just the best drummer of the HC era, Biscuits was a consummate showman, twirlin' sticks and makin' silly faces. Although not a great bassist, Rampage had true star quality. Dave Gregg had an ultra-cool vibe. Too bad those guys never got along.

DUFF McKAGAN (The Fartz): D.O.A. were so amazing. I wanted to be Randy Rampage — he was a huge influence on me. The first time I met Joey Shithead in 1980, I was totally shaking. They should not be overlooked.

D.O.A.'s excelled at politically-minded Hardcore. Like other such artists — MC5, The Clash, Stiff Little Fingers — a third party carefully orchestrated their revolutionary fervor, in this case, anarchist activist manager Ken Lester, a close Dead Kennedys associate.

JOEY SHITHEAD: Ken helped us focus on politics. He helped us with song titles. He was a newspaper editor when we hired him. He saw us as a [MC5 manager] John Sinclair-type situation. He told us that Sinclair said, 'The problem with The MC5 is they only wanted to be as big as The Beatles, but I could've made them as big as Mao.' Ken was our mentor. There was a funny rivalry between The Subhumans and D.O.A. Both had anarchist managers: we had Ken Lester, they had David Spanner. There was trouble between the two because Ken had gone out with David's sister, and Ken opened a yogurt shop, so David thought Ken had become a capitalist. We'd call him an anarcho-capitalist.

Groundbreaking early tours took the quartet to SF by '78, and to Portland and Seattle the following year. D.O.A., the first HC band to hit most Midwest and East Coast markets by '80, were pioneers on par with Black Flag or DKs.

The first D.O.A. records came out on obscure Canadian indies, so most people's first exposure came when Jello Biafra signed them to Alternative Tentacles in late '81. That year D.O.A. redid their first single — '78's "Disco Sucks" (on Joey's own

Zine ad for D.O.A. *War On 45*, 1982
Collection of the author

Sudden Death imprint) — for AT as "New Wave Sucks" on *Positively D.O.A.* Their '82 LP for AT *Bloodied But Unbowed* combined tracks from the Canadian discs: the "World War III" and "The Prisoner" 7"s and cuts off *Something Better Change* and *Hardcore 81*.

D.O.A. made a tactical error in relying on others to release their music — and they suffered for it. One constant prevails in their career: a bad run of luck with labels — Friends, Quintessence, CD Presents, Faulty Products, Rock Hotel, et cetera. Finding their shit remains difficult today.

JOEY SHITHEAD: Sudden Death was my label. Nobody had put out an independent record in Vancouver or even had an idea how to. I just went to pressing plants and checked out prices. My first wife's unemployment checks came in all at once — she had over 1000 dollars. I said, 'I have a plan for your money...' We printed the records and were so eager when we packed 'em up that there were thumbprints on the first copies 'cause the ink was so fresh. That was the "Disco Sucks" single. Then a record shop called Quintessence put out the "13" single and distributed the "World War III" single. They ripped us off, so we got even by going into the store and stealing 800 albums. They couldn't call the cops — the phone'd already been cut off. We sold the 800 records to our second label, Friends Records, for 1300 bucks. A lot of things made no sense about these deals. Quintessence was run by Ted "The Nose'" Thomas and Friends by Roy 'The Bigger Nose' Atkinson — all the money they made went into cocaine.

Vancouver, as earlier noted, segued into the American continuum — unlike the rest of Canada. Even the most ambitious US acts had trouble touring those vast expanses. Gnarly HC outfits trying to cross the border in shoddy vans full of cheap gear with no working papers were targets for harassment. More often than not, Americans bailed at the last moment on their Canadian dates.

D.O.A. steadily toured the Canadian heartland, inspiring a generation of Canuck outfits — all who had little success in the Lower 48: SNFU (Edmonton), PERSONALITY CRISIS (Calgary), YOUTH YOUTH YOUTH (Toronto), FLESH COLUMNS (Windsor), THE NILS (Montreal), STRETCH MARKS (Winnipeg), and NOMEANSNO and THE NEOS (Victoria). Most appeared on BYO's '84 comp, *Something To Believe In.*

Subhumans were very active, but far less successful than D.O.A. "Slave To My Dick" on *Let Them Eat Jellybeans* spread Subhumans' name, and they toured a lot for *Incorrect Thoughts* (Friends, '80) and *No Wishes, No Prayers* (SST, '83) — but no one seemed to gave a damn.

Gerry Useless quit the band in '80. Girlfriend Julie Belmas introduced him to her anarchist friends in nearby Squamish, BC. That gang, a guerrilla-style cadre of aspiring revolutionaries, become known as The Vancouver Five after being busted in '83 for firebombing video stores, a hydroelectric plant, and a Litton Systems facility. In the latter, 80 pounds of dynamite maimed five employees, three cops, and two passing motorists, and caused $3,000,000 damage. According to *The Vancouver Sun* of May 24, 1984, police wiretaps revealed plans of "sabotaging the defense department building in Ottawa, blowing up CF-18A fighter jets at the Canadian Forces Base at Cold Lake, Alberta, and dynamiting the icebreaker Terry Fox, under construction at a North Vancouver shipyard."

D.O.A. turned out to be the only true friends of The Vancouver Five in their time of need — recording a benefit EP and sponsoring several "Free The Five" concerts, including one with DKs. But The Five were found guilty — Useless got six years, Belmas got ten, comrades Brent Taylor, Ann Hanson and Doug Stewart each got twenty. Fortunately, all received early release; Belmas did the least time, testifying against the others before turning to religion.

JOEY SHITHEAD: Brian and I knew Gerry Useless since we were six years old. We were in Detroit when I got this call from Ken Lester saying, 'Gerry's been arrested with a huge cache of weapons…' They'd done a bombing, and whether you agree with it or not, they were unfairly vilified in the press. It wouldn't be far from the sensationalism of the Oklahoma City bombing. I knew one of the other guys really well — Brent Taylor, who got twenty years. Brent's uncle's one of the richest men in Canada — a fact covered up by the Canadian press. They blew up Litton Systems, which produced the guidance system for cruise missiles. They also firebombed two porn-video stores and blew up a power station under construction. Nobody died, fortunately."

VANCOUVER   FIVE   UPDATE

Jailed couple traded punk rock for terror

The Sun THURS., MAY 24, 1984 ★★★

By JES ODAM and TERRY GLAVIN

The anger of punk rock was not enough for Julie Belmas.

So she laid down her guitar, picked up a gun and started reading books with titles such as How Terrorists Kill.

She practised shooting at targets with human figures drawn on them, talked about how it would be "great action" to blow up military planes and "real heat" to blow up the icebreaker named after cancer victim Terry Fox, rehearsed lobbing an armored-car guard and was the voice that warned that a van load of explosives was due to go off at the Litton plant in Toronto.

In the words of a Crown prosecutor, she became an urban guerrilla soldier.

And a judge, saying it was necessary for him to deter others from practising anarchy and terrorism," has given her a 20-year jail term.

Belmas, just 21 years old, is appealing its length.

The boyfriend she took with her from the world of punk to the world known as "Direct Action" has also been jailed.

Gerry Hannah, 27, bass player and writer of lyrics such as "—— You" for a band known as the Subhumans — once banned from the Commodore in Vancouver because of its "obnoxious" fans — was sentenced to 10 years by the same judge.

During their trial in B.C. Supreme Court in New Westminster both had changed their pleas to guilty from not guilty on a number of charges.

As well as the Litton bombing, Belmas admitted conspiring to rob the guard in order to finance other activities — as well as the attempted arson of a video store, possession of weapons and explosives, possession of a stolen truck, a stolen two-way radio and other equipment and thefts of three cars.

Hannah admitted the attempted arson, robbery conspiracy, the vehicle charges and possession of stolen guns and the other equipment.

Both got 10 years for the robbery conspiracy, which the Crown said was not carried out because the two were arrested just days before it was to be committed, with lesser concurrent sentences for the other B.C. offences.

Belmas got a second, consecutive, 10-year term for her part in the attack with 250 kilograms of dynamite on the Litton plant, where the guidance system for the U.S. cruise missile is manufactured.

Five employees were injured in the bombing, as were three police officers and two passing motorists. Damage was estimated at $3.87 million.

Before sentence was passed, Belmas apologized for the injuries, which have caused permanent injury to five of the victims.

As friends looked on from the gallery, she read a prepared statement that said in part: "I meant no harm to any people. I was acting against a war machine, not against the people held within it."

Her lawyer, John Conroy, asked for a term of no more than 10 years and characterised her as a woman who was passionately committed to the ecology and anti-nuclear movements as well as an animal lover and ardent feminist.

The judge rejected her apology, saying it was of little solace to the injured.

And he said that other Canadians share the concerns of Belmas and Hannah, but do not resort to the same violent means to reach a political objective.

The court had been told earlier that a police planted electronic bug picked up a conversation in which Belmas agreed with a friend more than a year ago that she was proud of her role in the bombing.

The bug also relayed to a listening post in the Coordinated Law Enforcement Unit headquarters talk by Belmas in December, 1982, and January, 1983, about sabotaging the defence department building in Ottawa, blowing up a number of CF-18A fighter jets at the Canadian Forces Base at Cold Lake, Alberta, and dynamiting the icebreaker Terry Fox, then under construction at a North Vancouver shipyard, the judge was told.

Senior prosecutor Jim Jardine said Belmas concluded she preferred the Cold Lake proposal to the Ottawa one and said blowing up 40 CF-18As "would be a great action."

Belmas was heard also to say she thought blowing up the icebreaker, to be used in oil-well operations in the Beaufort Sea, "was real neat" because it showed strength and conveyed the public image of a group fighting for northern native peoples and against environmental damage.

How did Belmas, who once worked with mentally-handicapped children, and Hannah, described by his mother as one of the kindest people in the world, get involved in acts of political terrorism?

Belmas, born in New Westminster into a large, Roman Catholic family, later grew up in Port Coquitlam and North Vancouver.

She canoed, hiked, studied guitar and coached softball. Then she got a job at Woodlands school, working the night shift to look after the handicapped patients while taking an ethics course at Douglas College during the day.

But her life was changing. From helping organise benefit concerts by punk bands, she went into a magazine calling for radical activism, the feminist movement and El Salvador protests.

She met Hannah through the Subhumans and gradually both became disillusioned with what they were to later call the punk movement's lack of commitment to "real radical change."

In 1981, the pair left Vancouver for Jasper. She worked as a highways flagman, he on maintenance at a nearby ski resort — later the scene of the theft of a number of radios

and other equipment that were eventually found at a home the pair shared in New Westminster.

While in Jasper, Belmas filed a grievance against her supervisor on the road crew, charging him with sexual harassment. The man later committed suicide.

One lawyer who later acted for Belmas said the situation had a great deal of emotional impact on her.

Hannah was born and raised in Burnaby, the youngest of five children.

His mother, Lois, says he grew up loving the environment but watching the world around him change for the worse. As a boy he would come home with stories of turtles splashing in ponds near his home, in an area now covered by a shopping mall.

His frustration led him first to the angry music of the punk movement and fellow Burnaby North high school student Rick Zimmerman remembers he always "had some band or other going."

After dropping out of school in Grade 11, in 1974, he worked at various jobs. Then he chose the name Gerry Useless and joined the Subhumans, playing bass and writing lyrics such as one that goes:

"You call us weirdos, call us crazy.
"Say we're evil, say we're lazy.
"Say we're just the violent type.
"Kind of dumb, not too bright.
"We don't care what you say,
"—— you."

With Belmas, whom he called his wife-to-be, he became active in environmental, feminist and native-rights campaigns.

BELMAS

Press coverage of The Vancouver 5
From a "Free The Five" flyer; reprint of May 24, 1984 article in *The Vancouver Sun*
Collection of the author

D.O.A. press shot, 1984
Collection of Joe Keithley

The mid-80s saw D.O.A.'s decline as a viable entity. Though respected scene vets, their music lost its edge — starting with 1984's Bachman Turner Overdrive-style *Let's Wreck The Party* — signaling the beginning of the end. As no young local groups arose to pick up the slack, the scene withered away.

Biscuits went on to Circle Jerks, Danzig and Social Distortion. Dimwit replaced Chuck in D.O.A. for a while, joined Rick Rubin's ill-fated The Four Horseman project, then OD'd in 1994. Rampage reappeared as the falsetto-Metal frontman of Annihilator, who had a minor late 80s MTV hit, "Alice In Hell." Dave Gregg became a Rock merchandising honcho. Joey Keighley, changing his last name to Keithley, continues with ever-changing D.O.A. lineups.

KEN INOUYE (Marginal Man): D.O.A.'s overlooked 'cause of the way they kinda faded away towards the end. Latter-day D.O.A. is just not all that good, whereas *Hardcore 81* is brilliant. They toured constantly. They were fucking incredible.

SEATTLE Hardcore, though not the biggest or most amazing scene, made history for what it spawned: the late-80s Grunge of Nirvana, Soundgarden, Mudhoney et al. The HC vibe and ethic of inspired those Sub Pop bands.

Rock history in Seattle prior to HC offered little. Ze Whiz Kids, a 70s gay glam theater troupe that dished out confrontational performance, represented the only local subculture. Whiz Kid David "Tomata DuPlenti" Harrigan moved to NYC with boyfriend Michael "Gorilla Rose" Farris, and became key Downtown figures. According to rumor, Tomata outfitted and named The New York Dolls.

The two returned to Seattle in '76 to play the first-ever Punk shows in the region as The Tupperwares, dressing like Brian Jones and performing Iggy covers and Ramones-fueled originals. By early '77, Tomato and Gorilla split for LA, where they took their place in history as The Screamers.

In their wake came The Enemy, The Lewd, The Mentors, and the crappy New Wave of The Mice, Chitas Comidas, and X-15. The best — The Telepaths, later The Blackouts — spawned Paul Barker and Bill Rieflin of Ministry. The scene congregated at a tiny dive, The Bird.

Most everyone from Seattle who was serious about artistic expression moved away, usually to California. Expatriates included Penelope Houston of The Avengers, Eldon "El Duce" Hoke of The Mentors, Mötley Crüe's Nikki Sixx, Fartz bassist Duff McKagan (later of Guns N' Roses), and The Lewd.

ART CHANTRY (Seattle artist): Penelope Houston from Bellingham was in one of my art classes at Western Washington U. One night her and some friends were watching this show *Weekend* with a segment on English Punk — America's first exposure to the Sex Pistols. Many who saw that show dropped out, moved to San Francisco, and formed a Punk band. That was Penelope's trip: she just said fuck it and formed The Avengers.

By '81, Seattle had a Hardcore scene of 200 or so fucked-up kids; many went to Roosevelt High in the city's north end, but most came from the burbs. As elsewhere across the US, the entrenched crowd dismissed HC as the realm of dumb teens with skateboards.

TOM PRICE (U-Men): A lot of kids in Seattle's scene were children of Hippie biker types — a lot of piss-poor people, Canadians who'd gotten in trouble in other places. There were also kids in the scene who were genuinely mentally defective — actual mentally handicapped types and hospital escapees. There's a few token retards still up here.

The Showbox, a run-down theater from the 30s where Jazz greats like Cab Calloway played, ruled the scene — until it got shut down. In the New Wave days, it'd host DEVO or PiL, and most LA Hardcore bands first played town there. The Metropolis did HC shows for a year or two — where local outfits hung out, watched each other play, and handed out crappy flyers to each other. Other shitholes included Behind The Gray Door, Graven Image and The Meat Locker. But all-ages shows led to insurance problems, and club owners quickly realized these kids not only weren't there to shake their booty; they were probably gonna trash the bathroom. So came a wave of VFW-hall type gigs, but cops shut down half of 'em — 15 squad cars'd show up over a crowd of 75 kids.
    SOLGER were probably the first of that ragtag scene.

TOM PRICE: The first Seattle band in the Hardcore vein — Anarchist lyrics and high-speed music, all low-tech and noisy — was Solger. They put out a four-song 7" recorded on a ghetto blaster, and made 500 copies. They were influential 'cause their singer Kyle Nixon was the first 'man with a message' in the scene. He later became a successful chef. See, the only jobs anybody could get back then was working in restaurants, so a lot of guys, like The Fartz's Steve Hoffman and Kyle of Solger, are now famous veteran chefs.

PAUL SOLGER (Solger): I quit school and met this guy Kyle and we started Solger. I'd just turned 15 and was working at The Showbox cleaning up after shows. They gave us a place to practice. The band started in '80 and made it to '81. Our first show was opening for Black Flag at The Showbox and we only had five songs. After that I played in another weird band. Then somehow I got in The Fartz.

THE FARTZ were the big guys of Seattle HC. They toured the West Coast with DKs and Black Flag, put out intense records like *World Full Of Hate* and *Because This Fuckin' World Stinks*, and covered Black Sabbath's "Children Of The Grave" well before the Metal Crossover. Future Guns N' Roses bassist Duff McKagan — previously in The Cheaters, The Veins, Missing Links, and The Fastbacks — drummed for a spell.

TOM PRICE: The Fartz were the main guys. They were serious junkie dudes, but their singer Blaine [Cook], later of The Accused, was this incredibly shy, weird little troll. He'd be up there singing; a few older bonehead Punks really down on Hardcore would taunt him, 'You're just copying the Germs...' and the guy'd literally hide behind the drum riser and start crying. He was very young and it took him awhile to develop confidence. The Fartz got a lotta shit but eventually became very popular.

Zine ad for Fartz *Survival Of The Fittest*, 1983
Collection of the author

The Fartz fell apart in late '82 over personality clashes and drug abuse, and because *World Full Of Hate* came out just as its label Alternative Tentacles' distributors went belly-up. Duff, Blaine, and Paul Solger formed the oft-cited Ten Minute Warning (though no Ten Minute Warning records showed up until their late-90s reunion on Sub Pop).

ART CHANTRY: The Fartz were from Federal Way, one of our outlying suburbs. When they came to town, they were outsiders. Members came and went — very gang-like and tribal. The Fartz were another Seattle band nobody paid attention to until way after they broke up. Ten Minute Warning are now considered godhead — they played with everybody, and during their history probably went through 50 members. I intentionally missed many of those shows because it was just a bunch of stupid kids jumpin' around.

Zine ad for Rejectos/Accused split album, 1983
Collection of Sal Canzonieri

THE REJECTORS, suburban kids in hockey shirts, were regarded as Fartz protégés. People often confused them with THE REFUZORS, badass junkie types in tattered leather jackets who sounded like Kiss and ignited flash-powder-filled coffee cans on stage. Their drummer Wedge, through those years was (and still today, is) a fireplace salesman, working in a showroom. RPA (REBELLIOUS PEASANT AMERICANS), whose singer Doug Rockness played bass in Solger, were a Motorhead-style act with a cool 45, "Shoot The Pope." THE DTs — Duff McKagan, Paul Solger, Mike Refuzor and Jane Brownson of The Fags — were fueled by a love of black tar heroin. Other names included FEAST, TRUTH DECAY, ROOM NINE and H HOUR, with future Grunge icon Tad.

A lot of White Power types lived in the Seattle area, making shaving heads and beating each other up popular pastimes. Seattle Skins were mostly poor kids who took lotsa drugs, stole food, and lived in filthy group houses. EXTREME HATE carried that banner, along with FIRING SQUAD and THE BOOT BOYS (later THE SUFFOCATED). CANNIBAL, a spin-off of The Refuzors, put out "David," a 7" about the singer of Extreme Hate. Shitty self-production defined those few Seattle Skin recordings — no one could afford much better.

TOM PRICE: There's a lotta nasty White people up here; White Supremacist groups headquartered in Eastern Washington or in Idaho. The first time I traveled to New York, Chicago and San Francisco, I couldn't believe it — Black people involved in the scene. There were maybe two Indians, and a Chinese kid in Seattle. It was a very White scene.

THE FASTBACKS, though not Hardcore, drew scene attention. Guitarists Kurt Bloch and Lulu Gargiulo and bassist Kim Warnick recorded their first 7" — '81's "It's Your Birthday" — with a young Duff on drums. Kim revealed to me her HC claim to fame: she once dated Ron Emory of TSOL, "but didn't go all the way."

KIM WARNICK: Please keep in mind that during this time, we weren't the most well-received band. We weren't Punk or Hardcore, we were a total anomaly. We played on bills with Black Flag and D.O.A. — those bands'd draw like 500 people and here was me and Lulu, these two dorky girls playing real fast. I always felt our music was too happy for that scene. We went to all the shows, knew all the people, and played on the bills. We were in the community.

McKagan's tenure assured The Fastbacks a place in Heavy Metal history. In late '84 Duff wound up in LA, joining the group Road Crew, which became Hollywood Rose and then Guns N' Roses. In '85, Duff called up his former bandmates to help set up a Seattle gig, at which the G N'R name was first used. Duff always stood out from his tight-trousered, poodlehaired compatriots.

DUFF McKAGAN: Me and Izzy [Stradlin] started writing, Axl came over and we got Tracii Guns. I booked a tour for us starting in Seattle, coming through Portland, Eugene, Sacramento, SF, playing all to Hardcore kids. Tracii and Rob the drummer were scared to leave LA, so I said, 'Why don't we get Slash and Stevie [Adler] in the band? They'll go.' Our first gig was opening for The Fastbacks in Seattle. We hitchhiked a thousand miles — our van broke down. I called Kim and said, 'Can we use your equipment?'

Circa '84, Gorilla Gardens, an old two-screen Chinese theater, with two separate rooms: any given night would see simultaneous Hardcore and Metal shows. Before that existed absolutely no Crossover — if a bunch of Fartz fans and a flock of poodleheads into local Metal like Queensrÿche or Metal Church met on the street, a violent confrontation would often result. Gorilla Gardens bridged that gap.

ART CHANTRY: Both crowds'd pull into the lobby at halftime. They started talking instead of killing each other, and found they had everything in common but the haircuts. When you think about it, Grunge hair was the perfect mix of Metal and Punk hair.

Mark McLaughlin, from affluent Bellevue, allegedly coined "Grunge" as a musical term. McLaughlin, known as Mark Arm, rose to local infamy for MR. EPP AND THE CALCULATIONS, a joke band who postered around for months before buying gear. Like Flipper, Mr. Epp aimed to abuse HC types. Their "Mohawk Man" — off *Of Course I'm Happy, Why?* — was an '84 hit on *Rodney On The ROQ*. Steve Turner, who led LIMP RICHERDS, joined Mr. Epp as it ended. (Turner and Arm went on to Green River, Mudhoney, and Monkeywrench.)

Zine ad for Deranged Diction
with Jeff Ament, later of Pearl Jam
Collection of the author

TOM PRICE: Mr. Epp played with all the Hardcore bands, and were the most hated Seattle band. The dudes in spiky leather jackets would try and beat 'em up; Mr. Epp'd totally bait these guys. 'Mohawk Man' — a lot of the Hardcore types didn't take too kindly to that. Rarely would they make it through a set — it'd usually take three or four songs before somebody got on stage, grabbed their guitars and broke 'em in half.

By '85 came a wave of hard-drinkin' Seattle kids growing long(er) hair, and emulating the testicular Rock of Johnny Thunders and The Stooges. Debate erupted in national zines on the validity of these new outfits.

THE U-MEN — named for a Pere Ubu bootleg — blended MC5-ish riffage and manic HC action. Their '85 self-titled EP came out on future Sub Pop founder Bruce Pavitt's Bombshelter imprint (the song "Gila" later showing up on Sub Pop's first release, *Sub Pop 100*). For '86's *Stop Spinning* EP, Pavitt hooked them up with the Homestead label. The U-Men, while influential, were not successful. Their first tour, three months long, consisted of five shows: four in Austin, one at the local Woodshock festival. Their second and final tour in '86 didn't fare much better. (Price went on to Gashuffer and Monkeywrench.)

TOM PRICE: The U-Men were a bunch of fuck-ups, high-school dropouts living in a squat. The recession was really bad in the Northwest during the early 80s — it was sometimes impossible to even find a dishwashing job. The logging industry basically collapsed; all these people were moving to Seattle. Every shit job you could think of was snapped up by a family man with a wife and two kids. We were together as a band like three and a half years before we got a record out. We had no money and made no money.

GREEN RIVER, the prototype for Grunge, began when Mark Arm and Steve Turner and their friend Stone Gossard, teamed with Jeff Ament, who'd just moved from Missoula, Montana with DERANGED DICTION, his politically charged Bay Area-style HC combo. After three records — starting with 1985's *Come On Down* EP — Green River's fall resulted from conflicting visions: two members wanted to be The Stooges, the other two wanted to be Bad Company. So you ended up with two very different future projects: Grunge icons Mudhoney, and Glitter-flavored Mother Love Bone (whose demise led to Temple Of The Dog and Pearl Jam).

Tom Hazelmyer, a Marine based on Oak Harbor Island, started the label Amphetamine Reptile. "Haze" hung with Blaine Cook and Tommy Niemeyer of The Accused (a mid-80s Crossover act on Sir Mix-A-Lot's Nastymix label). One of the first AmRep releases was by The Thrown Ups, with Arm and Turner. At that time, The Melvins, from the logging town of Montessano, near Aberdeen, started to make some noise. In early '86, the Aberdeen act Nirvana started. A new era was dawning.

DUFF McKAGAN: There was great bands in Seattle. But we didn't have a Frontier Records, a Slash, or an Alternative Tentacles — we didn't have anything. Homestead did The U-Men record after I left town. I left because there was nowhere to go and heroin was saturating the scene. Paul Solger was shooting smack, my roommate started doing smack, my girlfriend was doing smack — it seemed like I couldn't get away from it.

Prior to Sub Pop's '85 onset, few indie labels operated locally. Engram Records put out the *Seattle Syndrome* comps and Blackouts records. Kurt Bloch of The Fastbacks' label No Threes issued the first Fastbacks 7" and 12", and a single by The Accident from Bellingham.

Poison Idea
Photo by T. Hockabee, from *Maximum RockNRoll* #4, 1983
Collection of Sal Canzonieri

TOM PRICE: Up until '86 or so, when Grunge started, there was no Seattle music business for the underground. It was rare a band even had a manager; there were no labels other than the bands themselves scraping money together, no booking agents. This one company called Modern Productions dominated the larger concerts. There were no PR people, no A&R people; there was nothing. For many bands, especially Mudhoney and Soundgarden, it took a long time to get over being suspicious of industry types.

KIM WARNICK: Things were horrible here before Sub Pop happened. People think it's cool to say that the scene was way better before, but it wasn't. It was depressing — there was nowhere to play. Now you can afford to be choosy. Thank God for Sub Pop.

Bruce Pavitt named his KCMU radio show "Sub Pop," prior to his similarly minded column in *The Rocket*. Imitating his pal Calvin Johnson at K Cassettes in Olympia, Pavitt started to release tapes. His first, *Sub Pop 100,* and subsequent milestone 7"s, raised Sub Pop to an independent music empire.

ART CHANTRY: When Pavitt and Jonathan Ponemann started to hype Sub Pop coverin' this big Seattle scene, there was no scene. It was a fraud. But when the media declared there was a scene all of a sudden it erupted.

PORTLAND had a Hardcore scene as big as what was going on in Seattle at the time, and Poison Idea were the best-known Northwest band after D.O.A. — but Portland never got much respect on a national level. What was most most surprising was there was virtually no interaction between Portland and Seattle. Both scenes were off in their own little worlds.

JOEY SHITHEAD (D.O.A.): We came down to Portland quite a few times early on, and we picked up a pretty decent following. I don't know what to say about it other than it was 100 or so nasty, no-bullshit kids. There were always some rowdy behavior at shows.

Portland's big contribution to Punk history was Greg Sage's power trio The Wipers, who began in '78 (and still exist in some form). A Nirvana predecessor if ever there was one, The Wipers spewed blistering fury with strong harmonic development, as heard on '79's classic *Is This Real?*

GREG SAGE (The Wipers): Portland never had much of a Rock scene, and definitely not much of a history. The Wipers came out of nothing. We wore flannel shirts because that's what we'd be wearing anyway. If you wanna know how much we thought about Portland and its underground music scene, look how quickly we split for New York.

By 1980-81, a small crew of maladjusted White kids gravitated around Black Flag and D.O.A. shows in Portland. These kids weren't what you'd call "intellectual" or "sophisticated." You just got a bunch of lumberjacks-gone-wrong — drunken louts ready to fight.

Dead Friends
Lockjaw 7" EP, 1983
Collection of Sal Canzonieri

JERRY A. (Poison Idea): I never gave a shit about the scene or unity or whatever. We made our own fuckin' music and hung with our friends. There were some great Hardcore bands and some really shitty ones. But I didn't hang out on the scene. I thought it all got very stupid very fast.

Most Hardcore types who played Portland first played the local club The Met (booked by Bill Hicks), and then at The Satyricon. Black Flag recorded their live *Who's Got The 10 1/2?* album at The Starry Night in August '85. You could always count on at least 75 kids to show up for any given gig.

Portland HC produced a few notorious bands. SADO NATION was started by guitarist David Corboy and vocalist John Shirley — who went on to be a top Sci-Fi author (with works like *Dracula in Love*). Shirley was replaced by one Mish Bondage, a foul-mouthed bitch who definitely fit the HC mindset. Their '82 album *We're Not Equal* was fucking great. Sado Nation and their friends LOCKJAW had terrible reps in *Maximum RockNRoll* circles for alleged neo-fascism (not entirely an incorrect assumption). Lockjaw put out two decent 7" EPs, '82's *Shock Value* and '83's *Dear Friends*. Others on the scene included FINAL WARNING and THE RATS (who became Dead Moon).

POISON IDEA was Portland Hardcore's most notorious export. Fat frontman Jerry A. and guitarist Tom "Pig Champion" Roberts made incredible records during the HC era — '83's *Pick Your King*, '84's *Record Collectors Are Pretentious Assholes*, '86's *Kings Of Punk* — but made most of their impact years later. Poison Idea were immense White Trash heroes who offered no Straight Edge, no fashion or style — just pure, unadulterated HC assault.

Show flyer for D.R.I., Poison Idea, Lockjaw
Satyricon, Portland, 1984
Collection of Spike Cassiday

JERRY A: I know you want me to offer up all this flowery bullshit about how great things were in Portland in the old days, but I've got nothing to contribute. I could truly care less about all that. Go ask someone else about that shit.

Portland, like Seattle a scene of bad apples, ended up nowhere. The difference was that Seattle had a new generation inspired to action. Most of the Portland Hardcore kids just sat at home and got fucked up.

SKEENO AND BEYOND

If you toured in a van west of Texas or Minneapolis (but east of the Left Coast), you played for gas money at best. In the Far West's vast expanse, gigs were few and far between. Historically, its rugged small cities arose as oases for cowboys, prospectors, and other noncosmopolitans traversing dry, unforgiving terrain. That old-time vibe persisted into the Hardcore days.

RENO produced the best HC action in that part of the US. Relative poverty or wealth drove other scenes; Reno's sprouted from boredom. Most scenes evolved around one band or individual; in the case of Reno's, it developed around 7 SECONDS and frontman Kevin Seconds. There was nothing going on prior to or after Kevin.

KEVIN SECONDS (7 Seconds): Living in a place as fucked-up as Reno encouraged us to do more and more. In Reno anything youth-oriented was simply not encouraged. The state of

Nevada's based on gambling and making money, and helping kids is the last thing on their minds. We all had fairly cool parents; we weren't rebelling against them. We were rebelling against the environment; it was so redneck, if you walked down the street with short hair you could be beaten up — and were at times. There was one Black family in our neighborhood, and no one talked to them. As a kid I remember thinking that was very strange.

Kevin fostered a Reno HC scene based upon what he'd seen and read about elsewhere. Emphasizing "community" and Straight Edge, an East Coast-style scene developed. Calling it "Skeeno" — for Reno-Sparks-Lake Tahoe — about 100 friends, siblings and lovers came together for shows. They even created their own HC look, a tribal marking: charcoal under the eyes, like athletes or Indians. Shaving one's head HC-style was an affront to the cowboy-hat-and-pickup-truck set, and any HC gathering meant drunken yahoos waited across the street with baseball bats.

KEVIN SECONDS: 'Skeeno' was our nickname for Reno. It started as a joke. All these towns had nicknames for their scenes: San Diego — Slow Death, Huntington Beach — H.B. We went of town a lot to see shows, as hardly any bands came to Reno. When we'd go to San Francisco and a band like Circle Jerks were playing, they'd bring kids from LA. So we figured, 'When we go there, we're gonna let 'em know we're from Reno,' which is silly when ya think about it. That's where the whole black-under-the-eyes started. And long overcoats with engineer boots. Anything we could grab onto, we did. We thought Skeeno sounded serious and weird — a few of us even got 'Skeeno HC' tattoos. The funny thing is, over the years, I've seen kids with 'Skeeno HC' tattoos from places like Ohio.

"7 Seconds" was a nuclear-armageddon term adopted from Frederick Forsyth's bestseller *Day Of The Jackal*. Kevin Seconds and brother Steve Youth, athletic and handsome outcasts, started 7 Seconds in December '79.

Guitarist/vocalist Kevin, brother Steve Youth on bass, and drummer Tom Borghino shook up HC fans with a series of self-released tapes. They recorded the first, '81's 14-song *Socially Fucked-Up*, straight to a boombox at Tom's mom's house.
To make the vocal audible, they propped up the ghetto blaster and Kevin sang into the tiny condenser mic. They cut the next tape, *Three Chord Politics*, on a friend's two-track, releasing it later that year.

Kevin Seconds (7 Seconds) left
as "Teen Pin Up" in *Touch & Go* Magazine, 1983
Collection of Tesco Vee

KEVIN SECONDS: We practiced with our friend Tom, who never played drums but picked it up quick. We'd jam wherever we could, our house, his mom's — six or so hours every day. It was insane. I sang with an English accent, trying to mimic Joe Strummer. Our first gig was March 2, 1980 at a biker bar that did Country and Top 40 bands, The Townhouse, to 30 people — and 20 hated us. Our friend Cliff, who was letting us practice for free in his basement, somehow talked the guy into letting him do a Monday 'New Wave' night. He had to call it 'New Wave' — at the time, you could not call it Hardcore. The following week he invited us back; we opened up for The Zeros, one of our favorite bands of the time. That kicked it off hard; after that, we were totally hooked.

Zine ad for 7 Seconds
Committed For Life 7" EP, 1983
Collection of the author

7 Seconds' vinyl debut, '82's *Skins, Brains & Guts* EP, came out on Alternative Tentacles. When AT's distributors went bust in '83, their next effort *United We Stand* was shelved (released in '91 as *Old School*). Drummer Troy Mowatt joined in late '83, in time for the *Committed For Life* EP, seven songs recorded and mixed in three hours — and sounding like it, too.

> *If we can walk together*
> *Why can't we rock together?*
> — 7 Seconds, "Walk Together, Rock Together"

In '84, they went on tour, and while in DC, spent a night recording with Ian MacKaye and Don Zientara at Inner Ear Studios. The ensuing *Walk Together, Rock Together* put 7 Seconds on the map — and best embodied its aesthetics: anthemic Minor Threat-ish HC with Pop hooks. Kevin wrote personal songs of emotional conflict, scene politics, and Straight Edge. The strife between "straight and alert" Kevin and his zonked-out brother further fueled the music.

Elsewhere around Skeeno, Tom Borghino's brother Dim, whose mug graced the *Skins, Brains & Guts* cover, had SECTION 8, who put out a tape and were on the *MaximumRockNRoll* comp *Not So Quiet On The Western Front*; Joey from D.O.A. tried to help 'em do a single but nothing came of it. THE WRECKS, one of the only all-girl HC outfits, were way ahead of their time. They had a tape in '83 and did a track on the *MRR* comp (bassist Jone Stebbins resurfaced years later in Alt-Rock act Imperial Teen). Steve Youth briefly played in JACKSHIT with guys from The Atheists out of Salt Lake City. THRUSTING SQUIRTERS was a quasi-Rockabilly joke.

LAKE TAHOE, 30 miles from Reno, came URBAN ASSAULT, who spawned Troy Mowatt and future 7 Seconds guitarist Dan Pozniak. The next closest city, an hour-plus away, was SACRAMENTO, home of REBEL TRUTH, who did a great 7" EP in '83, and SQUARE COOLS; both had cuts on the *MRR* record.

In late '82, Kevin began a BYO-style collective to book shows, release records, and promote causes — first called Rockers Active, then United Front, and finally Positive Force. You'd hear of Positive Force gigs with Social D or Black Flag in some garage on the Paiute Indian Reservation. Positive Force ran a warehouse space for a while where they built a stage and charged $2 to see the likes of Suicidal Tendencies, Scream and Necros. Kevin also booked a few shows in Sacramento — a less-than-stellar enterprise.

KEVIN SECONDS: Everything went well for about two years. We kept harassing bands — 'Hey, don't skip Reno...' Then we started hearing from others, saying they'd like to form a Positive Force. There were a few — Positive Force Las Vegas, Positive Force Chicago, one in Oregon. Mark Anderson still does Positive Force DC. That's cool, but I didn't see it as anything other than something we were doing in Reno. After that, a lot of people in the Reno scene started to move apart — the usual thing, people disagreeing on how things should be done — and it became less and less fun. Everyone was over it.

The first Positive Force record was *Nuke Your Dink*, a 7" comp of Nevada groups with an initial pressing of 300. That led to a flurry of releases — five by 7 Seconds. But the label's probably best known for Youth Of Today's debut 7" EP, '85's *Can't Close My Eyes*. 7 Seconds, an icon in NYHC circles, clearly inspired the fervent Straight Edge ethos of Youth Of Today.

KEVIN SECONDS: I liked Youth Of Today. They sent me a tape they'd recorded with Don Fury that was great — better than the record they made. They wanted me to produce the record but it never actually happened. They'd printed the covers themselves because they knew someone who could print them really cheap. On the back it said 'Produced by Kevin Seconds' — but by the time I got the tape, it was late and they had a tour planned, so we got the record pressed as was. So in actuality, I had nothing to do with it. By the time we realized it was gonna sell like crazy, there was lots of weird personal things going down, so I just gave them the tapes back, and told them to do whatever they wanted with it. I realized I wasn't up to the challenge of being Record Label Dude. It was a lot of work.

Zine ad for Kevin Seconds-produced shows in Sacramento, 1983
Collection of the author

For years after HC's demise, 7 Seconds carried on, moving toward Alternative Rock — thus losing most of their core audience. Somewhere along the way, Kevin ditched his zealous indie-only ideal (as evidenced by their brief 1997 deal with Epic. The group continues in some form today.).

LAS VEGAS was not a Hardcore spot. Aside from the rare Social D or TSOL show, this desert metropolis had no one who kindled a collective vision as Kevin Seconds did in Reno.

Vegas' closest thing to 7 Seconds was MIA, started by Mike Conley in '79, but relocated to Newport Beach, CA in early '82, where they made a few solid OC-style records. An MIA demo tape never intended for release came out on the split LP *Last Rites For Genocide And MIA* (Smoke Seven). When Mike spent eight months in jail in '83 on a drug charge, MIA lost momentum — and never really recovered. Upon prison release, Conley and a few Shattered Faith ex-members recorded '84's politically-minded *Murder In A Foreign Place* (AT). Their Damned-flavored *Notes From The Underground* ('85) and Killing Joke-style *After The Fact* ('87) both stand the test of time.

PHOENIX — another sun-drenched city — saw some underrated activity. Its scene arose circa '80 around derelicts that hung at college flophouse The Hate House. That scene spawned minor acts The Deeds, Charlie Monoxide and The Very Idea Of Fucking Hitler. The big guys were THE FEEDERZ, led by infamous Frank Discussion, a rude pranksters who'd tie dead cats to his guitar and fire M-16s full of blanks at audiences. Their "Jesus Entering Through The Rear," on *Let Them Eat Jellybeans*, was at once distressing and genius.

MEAT PUPPETS — brothers Curt and Cris Kirkwood, and Derrick Bostrom — were the most peculiar outfit from that neck of the woods; way off on their own psycho-delic Neil Young-on-speed trip. World Imitation, the label of the Van Nuys, CA outfit Monitor, put out the Puppets' mind-boggling debut 7" EP *In A Car* ('81), in exchange for their performance on Monitor's version of *Hair*. That Cali connection led the trio to Black Flag, and a stint with SST that generated seven albums essential to the roots of Alt Rock.

KING KOFFEE (Butthole Surfers): Meat Puppets were so bizarre when they came out — they were so fast, it was an art form. They made no sense whatsoever. Their version of 'Tumblin' Tumbleweeds' was fucking great. Then when I saw them, here were these Hippies. I put them up at my house when I was a kid — my dad was cool about it. Afterwards we went out to eat and, hanging out in their van, I was amazed they *really* liked Neil Young. It was all so confusing to me that I loved it. I was so baffled by the Meat Puppets. I love bands that do that to me.

BRIAN BRANNON (J.F.A.): Meat Puppets were so way out, they bummed people out. The Kirkwoods came from the west side of Phoenix, and they'd smoke a lotta bohoofus and draw crazy pictures and practice all day long. It was so fuckin' hot outside, you had to stay inside. They had nothing else to do but read comic books, do bong hits and play music."

Surf Punks we're not, skateboard we do
We have the fun, we're the new crew
— J.F.A., "Beach Blanket Bong-Out"

J.F.A. (JODY FOSTER'S ARMY) were Phoenix's HC heavyweights; smart-aleck skaters who named themselves in honor of Jody Foster-obsessed, would-be Reagan

Brian Brannon (J.F.A.) singing
From back cover of *Blatant Localism* 7" EP, 1981
Collecton of Sal Canzonieri

assassin John Hinckley. In early '81 lead delinquent Brian Brannon and drummer Bam Bam assembled the group (originally The Breakers) with guys they knew who skated at "The Ramp." Legendary as an early "Skatecore" band — you had to skate to be in J.F.A. — they first gigged at New Wave clubs, where everybody pogoed while J.F.A. and their friends did The HB Strut. No HC collection would be complete without a copy of *Blatant Localism*, their '81 debut 7" EP with "Beach Blanket Bong-Out."

BRIAN BRANNON: Our first gig — as The Breakers — was with The Crowd from Huntington Beach in March or April '81. All of our skater friends wore big engineer boots with bandannas wrapped around them. Before we found out we had to change the name, our drummer Mike Sversvold made some green bandannas out of an old sheet and put 'J.F.A.' on them. Jody Foster's Army was what we called the kids at our shows. Of course, this was right after John Hinckley shot Reagan. When we found out we had to change our name, we became Jody Foster's Army.

Phoenix HC shows took place at the aptly named Madison Square Gardens, a pro wrestling venue, where gnarly bands played in the ring while thrashers bounced off the ropes and onto the mat. The low-rent zine *Phenis* documented local activity; an indie label, Placebo, put out J.F.A., SUN CITY GIRLS, MIGHTY SPHINCTER and THE ZANY GUYS.

BRIAN BRANNON: Placebo Records was Tony Victor and his buddy Greg Hines, the Mighty Sphincter drummer. Mighty Sphincter were an early shock band. The singer Ron Reckless, a fat guy with a pink mohawk, would fuck himself with a dildo and a fake pussy he had strapped on, and later in the show he'd have a baby. Anyway, the Placebo guys also promoted a lot of shows in Phoenix. They ran Mad Gardens and The Salty Dog, a dinky-ass club with a six-foot ceiling that people'd cram into to see Social D and Wasted Youth. We played there once and it was packed so I started to light off bottle rockets and roman candles. People got pissed at me that night, but it looked cool watching them bounce off people's heads.

Flyer for Septic Death, Boise, 1984
Artwork by Pushead
Collection of Laura Albert

TUCSON, largely due to early roadwork by SST, regularly hosted tours by the mid-80s. Downtown Performance Center (DTPC) and Hotel Congress had a few decent shows. But not much happened there — the endless miles of rusted-out B-52s on the edge of town certainly summed up the area's zeitgeist.

ALBUQUERQUE — gateway to atomic test sites and alien spacecraft — saw a few gigs, and considered El Paso a sister scene. I was in Albuquerque twice with No Trend; you could count on 50 or so delinquent skaters to show up (but not pay to get in). In '83, we played a house party; in '84, we did "B&M Lock," an old locksmith's shop in a dangerous homeboy part of town — the kids called it "Bash And Mash." I don't recall anything about local HC groups: BENT, KOR-PHU, HELLCATS, THE MABES and JERRY'S KIDS.

BOISE — in the middle of nowhere — saw Brian "Pushead" Schroeder set up a few American Legion Hall gigs; usually 50 skater types would show up. His band SEPTIC DEATH opened for everyone who played town; his *Cleanse The Bacteria* comp was crucial to Metal Crossover. In spite of other local outfits like BLIND ACCEPTANCE, DISSIDENT MILITIA and COMMON SENSE, this scene ended when Pushead split in '84 for a *Thrasher* editorial job in San Francisco.

SALT LAKE CITY also had little going on. In fact, the very notion of Salt Lake HC is an oxymoron on par with the NBA's Utah Jazz. Everything was so nice and clean and mentally ill in that Mormon evangelical way.

Show flyer for TSOL, Massacre Guys
Maxim's, Salt Lake City, 1983
Collection of the author

Zine ad for Frantix cassette, 1983
Collection of the author

Brad Collins (son of DJ Jazzbo Collins) was the guy to call to get an SLC show. Brad did a radio show and ran Raunch Records, the only hip record store. The Minutemen played town a few times, drawing at least 100 kids.

Circa 1980, the only local Punk outfits were Spittin' Teeth (on a Posh Boy comp *The Siren*) and The Atheists (a heavy name in SLC). They inspired the one HC band, MASSACRE GUYS, with future Descendents/All members Karl Alvarez and Stephen Egerton. In '83 No Trend played a Sunday-night party in the basement of a Massacre Guys' friend. We made $34 passing around the hat; I got a really lousy blowjob from a really pretty blonde chick in the bathroom. Later, a Massacre Guy gave me their Black Flag-style *Devil's Slide* tape (which still sounds good).

STEPHEN EGERTON (Massacre Guys/Descendents): We were total Germs freaks, the only three of us in our high school who liked that stuff in Salt Lake. Everyone else wanted to either beat us up or make fun of us or throw food at us and not go on dates with us. Whether it be DEVO or the Minutemen, it was all the same to us. If it didn't sound like Zeppelin, we listened to it, whether it was New Wave or Hardcore.

Few touring outfits fared well in DENVER. Hüsker Dü drew 12 people on the *Everything Falls Apart* tour, their smallest-ever crowd. The DKs did well everywhere, but Jello coming from nearby Boulder made Denver an important gig for them. The LA-brutal police were the biggest threat to a local scene. During an infamous '82 police riot, Denver cops stormed a DKs show; Jello saw the raid start, so the band launched into the anti-authority "Police Truck." Of No Trend's '83 gig at some shithole in a bad Mexican 'hood, I most recall the pigs returning two or three times to hassle young kids for no reason.

A local HC label Local Anesthetic put out six or so records, the best being '83's "My Dad's A Fuckin' Alcoholic," a gonzo Flipper-style 7" by FRANTIX (with future members of Grunge heroes The Fluid). Unmemorable acts like YOUR FUNERAL, WHITE TRASH, HAPPY WORLD and BUM-CON also came outta Denver.

In many smaller towns, one or two people propelled a whole scene, as previously pointed out. When those movers and shakers quit or moved on or burned out, nobody on that same totally driven level replaced them. Those scenes may have had the requisite anger or boredom, but not the same political/philosophical motivations larger cities provided. In other words, they had to work within the milieu Black Flag, Dead Kennedys, Bad Brains et al established. •

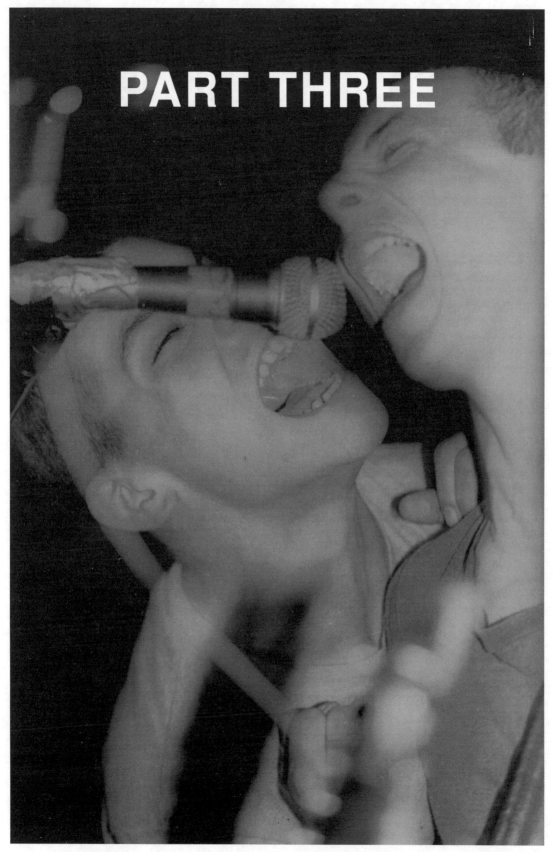

PART THREE

Harley Flanagan and Doug Holland (Cro-Mags), CBGB, NYC 1984. Photo by Karen O'Sullivan

PLAN 9

POSITIVE FORCE

ALTERNATIVE TENTACLES

DISCHORD

X CLAIM!

TOUCH AND GO

RATcage

FORCED EXPOSURE

FLIP SIDE

PHILA. B.Y.O.
Strength & Unity

SPACE II ARCADE

TAANG!

MAXIMUMROCKNROLL

RABID CAT
RECORDS

"KOKEHOUSE"

D.I.Y.

If I had a voice
I'd ask for a change in the marketplace
— The Proletariat, "Marketplace"

MARK STERN (Youth Brigade): We were about doing it yourself, thinking for yourself, believing that no matter how fucked up the world is and how fucked up the situation around you, that you can make a difference and can affect change and inspire people.

Punk gave lip service to "Do It Yourself" (D.I.Y.) and democratization of the Rock scene, but Hardcore transcended all commercial and corporate concerns. Today's indie network began with kids who put on their own shows, released their own records, and set up their own tours.

If you played Hardcore, you couldn't have possibly been in it for the money, although you might've gone for the glory. If you aimed to achieve stardom through HC, you were bound for disappointment.

SHAWN STERN (Youth Brigade): It was never, 'Should we sign to a major?' There was never even a consideration. They didn't want to know about us. They just wanted us to die; they couldn't kill us and we wouldn't go away; the scene kept getting bigger and they just scratched their heads and didn't understand it. We were just having a great time.

D.I.Y. in action: Minor Threat, Philly BYO, 1982
scanned from *Maximum RockNRoll* #4
Collection of the author

Hardcore established a new definition of musical success: in non-economic terms. Sociologists might see this as an example of "tribal syndicalism": unlike money-oriented economies, Hardcore was an objective-oriented, community-based culture — like a commune or an armed fortress.

JACK RABID (editor, *The Big Takeover*): I was expected to get involved. It wasn't a matter of 'Come smoke pot and hang out and watch' — everybody I met was doing something. Not all of it was music, a point that is often missed. The scene inspired and attracted talented musicians, but what it really did was inspire and attract talented people of all stripes. It was such a fresh scene that anybody who stumbled upon it was encouraged to use their talents. Even those who were somewhat talentless were inspired to develop one. I hadn't written a scrap. That was the sort of scene it was — that I'd be destined to publish a fanzine when I'd never even heard of one. It wasn't like I was a pioneer, I just had the same idea everybody else had — to find a Xerox machine in my town, write up things, and give it away at gigs.

Hardcore was one of the few forms on which major labels were unwilling or unable to capitalize. Coke-snorting A&R types refused to take the shit seriously. Bands didn't work through typical channels.

With Hardcore outfits coming from such a self-destructive underground, who

were labels gonna sign? Four belligerent kids who'd most likely wind up in a mental hospital or in jail? Practitioners of a form based upon the brazen manifesto that it would be short-lived? How do you generate profitable returns from such artists?

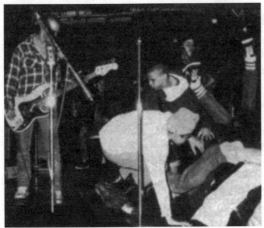

Mecht Mensch, Madison, WI, 1981
Example of a self-produced, self-promoted show
Photo by Steve Linsenmeyer
Collection of Sal Canzonieri

RAY FARRELL (SST): The first conversation I had with David Geffen was him asking me, 'So, are the Meat Puppets still fucked-up?' When I asked him to explain he said, 'Well, I talked to them years ago, and in so many words they told me to fuck off and die because they didn't wanna be on a major label.' It wasn't so much 'David Geffen, you're an asshole' it was more, 'We don't wanna be a part of that world.' Of course, he couldn't understand that, but it had more to do with a mistrust of the business. And that's a well-founded mistrust that still needs to be monitored.

Hardcore was more about reclaiming American values than undermining them. Its self-reliant, anti-corporate individuals became the entrepreneurs booking shows, starting labels and running zines.

KEN WAAGNER (Detroit promoter): "The whole entrepreneurial spirit was amazing. The networking was amazing. If a promoter was bad, word traveled fast. If a club was bad, word traveled. If someone needed a show or a place to stay, that whole network was unbelievable. You could always count on Boston, New York, DC, Detroit, Chicago, LA, San Francisco, Austin — different places where there were good people and you could count on a certain amount of support."

Fifty people at a show was the norm, 200 a success. There were no more than a few thousand kids in the entire scene, with a few hundred active participants.

Gigs took place at unlikely venues. Aside from a few shows at New Wave clubs, they went down at marginal sites in low-rent 'hoods — usually a VFW hall, church basement, or dilapidated warehouse. Those rooms generally had poor sightlines, lousy sound quality, and no stage production to speak of. If the bathroom had a door, you were off to a good start.

AL BARILE (SS Decontrol): Punk didn't have that grass-roots 'anybody can do it' thing — it was still part of the industry. Back then, we chose not to involve ourselves with any establishment. I wanted to kick out the old arty people and bring in a new breed. That's how the scene was built. No one who represents the establishment should talk anything of those years, because they didn't experience it at all.

PETE STAHL (Scream): Most of the shows were in a shitty part of town. Bands would see what was really happening in each city, and kids from the burbs were being exposed to the realities of the world at an early age. It created awareness.

Venues like A7 and 171A in NYC or Wilson Center in DC weren't established rooms on the Rock circuit. Promoters were usually kids — same as the musicians and the fans. When I was a 19-year-old setting up shows in DC, it was all very primitive: no liability insurance, liquor permits, bonded security, or anything like that. If a kid cracked his skull or OD'd, it was just too fucking bad. When someone inevitably trashed the bathroom or tore out the plumbing, it was time to find a new hall.

ALEC PETERS (Boston promoter): When you paid your money, it was more of a contribution — like paying dues. Ticket prices were regulated by the bands, so being a promoter of it was something you did just because you wanted to.

KEN WAAGNER: What I did just needed to be done — never with a thought of the bottom line. Every once in a while I'd have a show I'd make 500 bucks on, but the next week I'd lose 300. I never signed a contract with anybody — ever.

BILL STEVENSON (Baltimore promoter): I'd get phone calls every week from kids I didn't know, who got my number from somebody else and just wanted their band to have a place to play. From that I met a lot of people I respect to this day and I've lost some people along the way, too. But I can't think of anything that changed my life the way Hardcore did. I'd be a completely different person had I not fallen into this.

Kid with broken leg before Wasted Youth gig
Example of the Hardcore demographic
The Whiskey, LA, 1981
Photo by Edward Colver

Black Flag, Dead Kennedys and D.O.A. carved out territory through the trust they'd place in kids who set up their shows. That spirit made HC happen nationwide, and that was the roots of the indie touring network.

JOEY SHITHEAD (D.O.A.): It usually took one or two motivators in each town to get something going. The places would last as long as the police permitted them, so usually you played someplace different every time you went back. We'd go to places where there were no Hardcore bands — and the next year there'd be a few. We opened up places but there were places we closed down, too. The Subhumans did a tour following us and there were about three places we and our fans managed to wreck along the way, so the Subhumans got canceled."

JELLO BIAFRA (Dead Kennedys): We were all sharing information. Whenever somebody cracked open a new town, the other two bands found out about it. Black Flag were the most likely to act on that and in the long run, they cracked open more towns than anybody else.

TIM KERR (Big Boys): The first big Black Flag trek opened it up all through America. It was happening in cities that had a strong metropolitan art scene. Houston and Dallas kinda had a scene, but anyplace else, even in the suburbs of those cities — forget it. When Black Flag came through and started hitting every little town, that's what did it. That's when all these kids started picking up instruments and starting bands.

JEFF McDONALD (Red Cross): Black Flag were the first underground band to put together a touring network. They just went out there and started finding these clubs and little promoters. Now people take it for granted — every little band puts out a single and starts touring. Then it was not possible. Flag were pioneers.

Show flyer for The Faith with Negative Approach,
Paychecks, outside Detroit, 1982
Example of an independent production
Collection of Laura Albert

Hardcore offered ragtag outfits the chance to pull off that coveted tour. Sales of 1000 records adequately exposed you to tour the nation. Gang Green played 60 dates across America on a 7". No Trend did three national tours off an album and an EP. Regardless of less-than-ideal conditions, bands were usually thankful just to get the gig.

MIKE WATT: It was the exact opposite of the big leagues — we didn't tour to promote records, we put out records to promote tours. Records were like your flyers; you always hadda be fresh. Every six months we'd make records, whether it was a double-album, a 7" or whatever the fuck. That was healthy. We didn't have managers around telling us bullshit, we just went for it. We were doin' Pearl Harbors in every town — we got in and out without anyone knowing about it. If you did hear about it, it was only through this underground. And it did get bigger, stronger and closer-knit. When we played clubs, you had to worry about stuff like, 'Oh man, are they gonna put us on after or before the disco when it's still light outside?' I mean it was hairy. So we all became very self-sufficient.

DR. KNOW (Bad Brains): In those days, if you made 50 bucks for a gig, you were real happy. Record deals were the last thing you were thinking of. You had to put out your own records; scrounge up some money somewhere. The gigs rarely paid for the van and the gas. You slept on somebody's floor or in the van. You just did what you had to do.

PAT DUBAR (Uniform Choice): Our record came out so we embarked on our first national tour, which was booked by a guy named Johnny Stiff in New York. The name alone says it all. It was a miserable situation, five of us in a van going from city to city. Everyone at the time was like, 'Do it for the scene.' We could do it for the scene but when you get on the road, there are all these other costs you're taking on. You show up to a gig at some fucking laundromat — you're supposed to get 100 bucks and the guy only has 30 — it's like, 'Look man, I'm sorry but how the fuck are we gonna go 500 miles on 30 bucks when we don't have a fuckin' penny?' Those were our woes. It was still a great experience.

KEVIN SECONDS (7 Seconds): Our first big US tour was in a '58 VW bus. We slept on all the equipment. We ended up changing the engine twice; we weren't making shit. I mean, if we got paid 100 dollars, that was awesome. There was no such thing as a per diem or a contract — you were on your own. That's ignoring the fact that if someone got sick or broke a bone you were screwed. On that tour — from Reno to Salt Lake — we had 30 dollars; it was like, 'This is it, we gotta make it happen, otherwise we're fucked.'

BRIAN BAKER (Minor Threat): These tours were a combination of the Underground Railroad and the Kesey Acid Tests. You're in this van you wouldn't drive to the grocery store. You're existing 'cause you're stopping at every enclave of this little subculture. We'd drive six hours south to the Carolinas, play for 22 people in some burnt-out shack, and stay with the guys in the opening band, who happened to be C.O.C. in this case. It was totally dependent on things like that. I distinctly recall situations — we were thousands of miles from home, thirty bucks in the kitty and half a tank of gas, and saying, 'This is cool. We have enough money to get where we're going *and* get bread and peanut butter.' It was very underground.

The only opportunities to make any loot were LA gigs at the Hollywood Palladium and Olympic Auditorium produced by Gary Tovar of Goldenvoice — who'd tip musicians with fine Cali herb. NYC saw no similar shows until around '85, with events at Rock Hotel on Jane Street and at The Ritz.

In the semi-communal scene it was common knowledge where touring groups could crash for the night in a given town. Usually like-minded kids provided a bed, couch, or floor — but sometimes you had to be creative.

ED IVEY (Rhythm Pigs): We were touring in my Ford pickup with a camper shell. It got 10 miles to the gallon — we were making 20 bucks a night. We had a scam where we'd go to a 7-11: I'd sit there with the clerk and say, 'Hey, where's this highway?' and keep the guy occupied while our roadie stuck donuts, Cokes and whatever he could grab into his jacket. I come from a landed family so to be on the road with four ugly guys needing a bath and having to steal food was a real experience for me.

Show flyer for The F.U.'s, Gang Green, Jerry's Kids
Cantone's, Boston, 1981
Example of an independent production
Collection of the author

CHRIS DOHERTY (Gang Green): Times have definitely changed. I think about how we used to tour in a cargo van sleeping on top of the gear, pull up to a supermarket and say, 'Okay, you steal the cheese, you steal the bologna, you buy the bread.' To afford the gas was enough alone. There was always a few people you could stay with in any town.

"STRAIGHT EDGE" HANK PEIRCE (Boston scene): I recall coming home from school one day and these Canadians were hanging out watching TV. I said, 'Who are you?' 'We're the Stretch Marks from Winnipeg.' I was like, 'That's cool. Is anyone else here?' 'No, no one else is here.' 'Did you guys get our number from somebody?' 'Oh yeah, we ran into 7 Seconds and they gave us directions to your house.' 'Wait, I'm the first person from the house you've spoken to?' 'Yeah, the door was open so we just came in.' I guess it was cool for them to hang out."

Some HC kids knew how to obtain stolen telephone credit card numbers. Certainly, many tours wouldn't have taken place if not for "free" phone time.

MARK STERN (Youth Brigade): In those days, any phone number had a credit card code and there was a way to figure out the four-digit PIN number. You could randomly pick a number in the phone book, figure out the code, and boom, you were off. It got the point where people'd call you up from like Montreal and say, 'Hey, I've got a new number!' and two minutes later, you were on the phone with someone from Seattle giving it to them — and they

ATTENTION (YO): PHILLY SHREDS!

The Philly BYO had just opened their own hall, but Phila. Mayor Greene personally closed it down. Fear not, BYO will continue doing gigs in conjunction with other people, and urge interested bands to contact Robbie at (215) 232-9959 for more information.

BETTER YOUTH ORGANIZATION
P.O. Box 40193
Phila, PA 19106

Zine ad for Philly BYO
Example of an independent organization
Collection of Sal Canzonieri

sometimes already had that number. My girlfriend got sent away to school in Switzerland, and boy, somebody paid for hundreds of hours of phone calls.

ED IVEY: My phone would ring many times a day. All these bands started calling me and they always said, 'Hey, need a free number?' That's how we booked our tours. MCI and those fuckheads didn't have a good security system, and I booked two tours. Dude, we scammed thousands of dollars of long distance on fake or stolen credit card numbers. Later, some guy in a band from Buffalo — it might have been Capitol Punishment — pulled a blue box out of his pocket and said, 'Watch this!' — and it made the sound of a quarter hitting the back of the phone. So we started using those.

With no adult supervision, Hardcore echoed the stranded, adolescent-led society of William Golding's *Lord Of The Flies*.

LAURA ALBERT (NYHC scene): When you're a kid, you think very black-and-white. In Hardcore, a lot of those setting rules were little kids. In one sense, that was great because it's so free — on the other hand, those rules were unyielding and impractical. It's a psychological 'ism' that children from permissive parents often invent rigid rules around themselves. I didn't know anyone in the scene who didn't have a certain amount of rage — basically trading one dysfunctional family for another. We invented rules to live by, so there were safe parameters, to know who you were and how to identify others.

RAY FARRELL: There's a certain attachment — and it's more a part of the male psyche — wanting to be in some type of militaristic environment. I know this isn't particularly politically correct, but it wasn't so long ago that war wasn't such a bad idea; there were good wars, according to our parents. Wartime is always exciting to people; I think, in a way, some of this filled that need. For example, some of these kids went on to be cops.

The D.I.Y. or "anti-corporate" stand is easy when your parents have money.

HARLEY FLANAGAN (Cro-Mags): I assumed that most of the kids in the scene were poor but as I got older I realized I was one of the few that was. A lot of them were from suburban middle-class families who'd go to shows and act poor for the weekend. But there was a die-hard group of kids who were living the lifestyle, not just perpetrating.

BARRY HENNSLER (Necros): "What spawned the whole indie-versus-major stigma was 16-year-olds living at home who don't have to worry about paying the rent and where they're going to eat next."

Old dreams in the way
Don't listen to what they say
— D.O.A., "2+2"

An incredibly marginal subculture, Hardcore barely made any impact in Middle America. At record stores you had to wallow through endless "Punk" or "New Wave" bins to find any of a very few HC records.

JELLO BIAFRA: Not every store even had that. It was a battle to get a bin like that and it didn't help when nobody wanted to buy the records. You couldn't put a bin of cool music right by the cash register; ELO fans would jump for day at the thought of seeing a Weirdos single. The same went for us with Dead Kennedys.

IAN MACKAYE (Teen Idles, Minor Threat): When we put our records out, we got in our car and drove up and down the East Coast. I remember going to Bleecker Bob's [record store] in New York with five singles, a buck each. I said, 'Wanna buy a record? There's eight songs on each.' They said, 'We'll take five on consignment.' I was like, 'They're a dollar each, man. Give me five bucks for these records.' We sold tons of records at our shows. On tour, Minor Threat sold Teen Idles singles. The first Minor Threat tour, we'd just done our second pressing — [Teen Idles] frontman Nathan [Strajcek] was in charge of the stuff. He drove the van and had the singles sitting on top of the hot engine cover and melted 150 Teen Idles singles.

SST, Alternative Tentacles, Dischord, BYO and Touch & Go — all centered around one or two bands — became the first labels. It took awhile to establish themselves; they started at zero — no investment capital, no marketing structure, no sales staff or radio guy. Yet they persevered. They made records on the cheap — usually four- or eight-track recordings done for the lowest studio rates imaginable. Most records sounded awful due to poor performances and second-rate production.

TONY CADENA (Adolescents): It's amazing there were any good recordings. What's also amazing is that we managed to get an accurate sound because there'd be somebody who wanted to 'fix' us. I remember the first time we were in a studio, I started to sing and the guy turned off the tape machine and started yelling, 'You're popping your p's and you've got to watch your s's.' We got to a point where we said, 'We're going to do it *this* way. Just turn the machine on.' They couldn't comprehend raw Rock & Rolll.

REED MULLIN (Corrosion Of Conformity): We had to learn about where to get a record pressed and what mastering was and how to put a cover together. On *Eye For An Eye*, the cover was black and white — even one color was out of the question — and me and Woody did the album cover on my dad's office floor. My dad had a big shaggy dog and on the cover you can actually see some dog hairs that were attached to the glue.

RAY FARRELL: If you were to play a Hardcore record to a kid today you'd have to explain why it was good. It was the lowest fidelity recording at the time. There's a beauty in saying, 'We're gonna do this. We don't even know what we're doing, but we're gonna make a record.'

In those zealous footsteps came a torrent of independent Hardcore 7"s.

PAUL MAHERN (Zero Boys): As part of the Hardcore ethic, what'd you do after you formed a band? You played a gig. Then you'd released a record. So, we went into a friend's basement, recorded a record, and put it out ourselves. That's the roots of the Zero Boys, and many others like us.

My Dad's A Fuckin' Alcoholic
Frantix 7" EP, Local Anethetic, 1983
Example of independently released record
Collection of Sal Canzonieri

LOU BARLOW (Deep Wound): We were really committed when we first started, so we started to play as fast as possible. 'Okay, we gotta do a demo.' 'Cool.' 'We've got a show coming up with The FU's and DYS.' 'That's cool.' 'Make a record.' 'Cool.' There was a lot of commitment and discipline behind it. It's hard for me to imagine being that way now.

JIM FOSTER (Adrenalin OD): We didn't know what the hell we were doing. It was, 'Isn't it time we put a single out? Where's a pressing plant? Here's the Yellow Pages. Call the plant and print up a thousand.' You called up a few distributors, they took it, and you were done. You made no money. For 19-year-olds to do that was great.

Starting in '81, a few indie distributors formed to meet the demands of a rising scene. If you put out a HC record back then, you'd call Rough Trade and Systematic in SF, Greenworld in LA, and Faulty Products, Bonaparte, Important and Dutch East India in NYC. They'd each take like 200 copies on consignment. The bestsellers of the era were Dead Kennedys, Black Flag, Bad Brains, Circle Jerks, and D.O.A.

Unfortunately, that budding distribution system collapsed; Faulty Products, Greenworld and Systematic all went out of business by '84. In a market of limited demand, fierce competition left zero margin for error. So just as Hardcore took off, the critical system it relied on undermined it. When those distributors went belly-up, they owed huge amounts of money. Most labels couldn't handle the blow.

MIKE WATT: You don't know the hate I've got for some of those people, man, 'cause we really were doing it for love, and they'd go out of their way to fuck us over. Nobody knows about that. When you hear about SST not havin' the money to pay people, nobody says, 'Hey, they were ripped off by their distributors big time.'

Exacerbating Hardcore's problems, old-school Music Biz scumbags tried to rip off young musicians. Guys like Robbie Fields from Posh Boy Records and Doug Moody from Mystic Records earned total scorn from their signees.

SHAWN STERN (Youth Brigade): We recorded some of our first stuff at Mystic. We unfortunately introduced Doug Moody to the scene. He said he'd recorded the first Led Zepplin record, but we couldn't believe anything he said 'cause he's so full of shit. But we learned a lot. He hooked us up with manufacturers. He also screwed us. He did the first pressing of *Someone Got Their Head Kicked In* and we never got paid. All the cuts were recorded with him except Social D — the best Mike Ness could come up with was a cassette tape — and Bad Religion, who we took right off a record. The Adolescents gave us a quarter-inch tape of an old recording from before their first record.

GEORGE ANTHONY (Battalion Of Saints): I got ripped off so many times by Mystic — we got totally fucked. That guy [Moody] made thousands off *Rock In Peace* and all those singles. I didn't see a penny; I didn't even get a copy. His big claim to fame was that he recorded a snare drum in an elevator shaft on the first Zep record. He had a little studio in Hollywood and kept getting all these bands in; he'd run off with the tapes. Before you knew what was going on, you had a single out. That guy was slipperier than an eel. He's got a lot of good stuff in his catalog that a lot of people want. But he knows if he sells, everybody's going to sue whoever buys it."

A lot of well-intentioned kids swept up in the D.I.Y. zeal got themselves into trouble. From top to bottom, no one knew what the hell they were doing — and financial concerns always got in the way of "trying to do the right thing."

AL BARILE (SS Decontrol): I was always going to school or working so I never had the luxury of time. The label, the band, the crew, the scene — what do I do? I'm not a schmoozer; I don't like talking to people on the phone; I don't like begging for money. I just want to be treated fairly, and this business isn't like that. So I got rid of the label [X-Claim!] and gave my third and fourth records away. When I made those records, I got no sense of gratification when they came out. I had no sense of accomplishment, and that's why I got into this to begin with — I wanted to have an impact. Maybe I avoided financial disaster by giving those records away, but it was an empty experience.

FU82
Fuck-Ups 7" EP, Fowl, 1982
Example of independently released record
Collection of Sal Canzonieri

PAT DUBAR: I learned from running a label that artists have an inflated imagination for the number of records they sell. We set out, on our labels Wishing Well and Massive Sound, to give bands a chance for their music to be heard. That's all we wanted. All the other shit got in the way: royalties, mechanicals, publishing — things we had no fucking idea about. We weren't businessmen — we were just kids. We offered to do all these things for bands we liked and to use our own money. They wanted to get paid, but we lost money doing it. So, I quickly learned how the music business works.

RAY FARRELL: I was very content to work for independents, but I soon realized you can have an incredibly false sense of community working for labels like that. You feel like you're working toward a goal, but you don't own the label, and business decisions are made by whoever owns it — whether it's right or wrong, whether it's right for the scene or not. I realized there were no saints, independent or major. I went to a major — I realized there were a lot of people who knew nothing about music, coulda been selling refrigerators — and a lot of those people hated me. There's insincerity everywhere. •

MEDIA BLITZ

We've got nothing better to do
Than watch TV and have a couple of brews
— Black Flag, "T.V. Party"

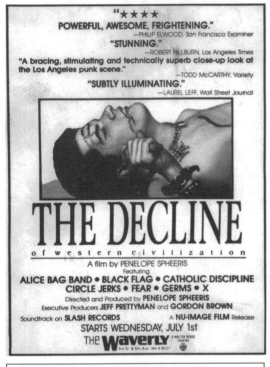

"★★★★
POWERFUL, AWESOME, FRIGHTENING."
—PHILIP ELWOOD, San Francisco Examiner

"STUNNING."
—ROBERT HILLBURN, Los Angeles Times

"A bracing, stimulating and technically superb close-up look at the Los Angeles punk scene."
—TODD McCARTHY, Variety

"SUBTLY ILLUMINATING."
—LAUREL LEFF, Wall Street Journal

THE DECLINE
of western civilization

A film by PENELOPE SPHEERIS
Featuring
**ALICE BAG BAND • BLACK FLAG • CATHOLIC DISCIPLINE
CIRCLE JERKS • FEAR • GERMS • X**
Directed and Produced by **PENELOPE SPHEERIS**
Executive Producers **JEFF PRETTYMAN** and **GORDON BROWN**
Soundtrack on **SLASH RECORDS**   A **NU-IMAGE FILM** Release
STARTS WEDNESDAY, JULY 1st
THE **Waverly** A WALTER READE THEATRE
3rd St. & 6th Ave. · WA 9 8037

Film poster for *The Decline Of Western Civilization*
Penelope Spheeris, director; Nu-Image Films, 1980
Collection of Laura Albert

The mass media had no clue as to what was going on with Hardcore, though reporters and producers soon realized it made for great copy. They treated it as a troubling cultural epidemic, airing nightmare parodies on TV sitcoms and dramas. News accounts warned of dangerous teens displaying anti-social behavior. Naturally such alarms concerned parents, inspired law enforcement — and intrigued kids.

A 1982 episode of Jack Klugman's cop-medic series *Quincy* sent shockwaves across America with its images of murderous Hardcore types roaming the streets. In a club scene, the group "Mayhem" (modeled after Fear) did a song called "Next Stop Nowhere, I Wanna Get Off." Of course, the show ended with Dr. Quincy's tough love redeeming the "troubled teens." In an episode of *CHiPs*, hunky actor Erik Estrada turns wayward HC kids on to cool Disco music. *Simon & Simon* and *After School Special* had stories about drug-addled HC youths trying to figure it all out.

GREG GRAFFIN (Bad Religion): All the stupid TV shows like *CHiPs* and *Quincy*, and their portrayal of Punkers, was so absurd from my point of view — but so accurate from their point of view. When it was happening, I just pooh-poohed the whole thing. In retrospect, I realize it was accurate from the perspective of the average American citizen.

LAURA ALBERT (NYHC scene): No one knew what Hardcore was, and the media showed stereotypically horrible things about it. A girl in combat boots was enough to be called a nazi. That *Quincy* — my friend's parents sent him to a hospital after that. It was classic 50s-style hysteria. Nobody understood, or cared to understand.

KEN INOUYE (Marginal Man): I will never forget after that *Quincy* episode my dad sitting me down — trying to figure out what the hell was going on. There was some scene in that show where the kid was cutting himself up or something. I guess the thing that put both my mom's and my dad's minds at ease was realizing that a lot of what made me gravitate towards Hardcore was the values that I was brought up with.

Paradoxically, it was through such shrill coverage that many kids first heard about Hardcore. A TV show featured some shocking story on it; the next week thousands of kids would dress like what they saw on the tube.

Broadcast news reports fanned the fires. Camera crews regularly captured "Hardcore violence." Televangelists like Ernest Angley riled their flocks by quoting Circle Jerks and DKs lyrics. A highly publicized Fundamentalist outfit, "Parents Against Punks," specialized in "Punk deprogramming."

GREG HETSON (Red Cross, Circle Jerks): The Religious Right would say, 'Look what these kids are listening to' — holding up records of ours, reciting lyrics of Circle Jerks and Flag, talking everyone's going to Hell, that the nation's moral fiber was in jeopardy. That's what was going on.

TONY CADENA (Adolescents): Sometimes we were depicted that way by popular media. I was standing in front of The Starwood one night — Mike Ness was being interviewed by *2 On the Town,* a local LA show. They were talking about Hardcore violence; Mike was saying the media creates it. As he said that, a guy walks from behind, takes out a razor and slashes Mike's arm open. It was insane.

Film poster for *Suburbia*
Penelope Spheeris, director; New World Pictures, 1983
Collection of Laura Albert

Fear's November '81 appearance on *Saturday Night Live* constituted a major milestone in Hardcore's rise. The show made national headlines after a horde of HC kids invited by John Belushi trashed the studio (for years that was the only episode NBC never re-aired). Belushi hung around with Fear frontman Lee Ving and attended many of Fear's shows, and his last notable act was hooking up that event — he OD'd a few weeks later at LA's Chateau Marmont.

LEE VING (Fear): Our appearance on *Saturday Night Live* took place because John Belushi was a big fan and good friend to the band. The people in charge of the show thought they wanted some sort of crazy shit on the air. Judging by what went down, I don't think they knew what they were getting themselves involved in. The rest is history. So you've got to give credit to Belushi for helping put this music on the map.

IAN MACKAYE (Minor Threat): Penelope Spheeris told John Belushi about us, that's how we ended up being on *Saturday Night Live*. Belushi had left the show but *Saturday Night Live* asked him to do a cameo. He said he'd come if they'd let Fear be the band. Then he was talking to Penelope and said 'I want to have people dancing' and she said, 'The only real Punks I ever met outside of LA are from DC' — so he got my number. [Producer] Lorne Michaels called me and put John Belushi on the phone. He said 'I want you to come and show these people what it's all about.' So 30 kids from Washington came up. We weren't even big fans of Fear — they were kind of a joke band — but the idea of it was so funny. We just thought 'We'll fuck shit up.' We were into representing, but it was met with complete hatred.

JOHN JOSEPH (Cro-Mags): Lee Ving was buddies with Belushi, and hooked up all the DC kids. They kept us in this room for the first set, then on the second set we went down. At the first note, I was like the first one to dive off the stage. We just wrecked all the equipment. This big fight broke out between us from New York and the DC kids, which I didn't wanna get involved with because those guys were my friends, too. Also, it was funny — it was Halloween and everyone had pumpkins — so we all started throwing pumpkins at the NBC officials, who then called the cops on us and cleared us out. Ian MacKaye said on the mic, 'New York sucks' — that's when they cut it off the air. There was something in the newspaper about $250,000 worth of studio equipment got destroyed, cameras and all kinds of shit. I mean, we went crazy. And it was funny because at the end of the show, both the DC and New York crews ran out laughing together.

Under the makeup.
Over the edge.
An incredible
journey through
the underground.

Coastline Films
Presents
A Stuart/Small
Production

ANOTHER STATE OF MIND

Featuring
SOCIAL DISTORTION
YOUTH BRIGADE • MINOR THREAT
and a 10,000 mile, 25 city adventure
Written, Produced and Directed by Adam Small and Peter Stuart.

Film poster for *Another State Of Mind*
Adam Small and Peter Stuart, directors;
Coastline Films, 1983
Collection of the author

BARRY HENNSLER (Necros): Michael O'Donahue called Ian MacKaye: 'I want you to bring a bunch of your neo-nazi friends up to New York.' So we went to see Fear on *Saturday Night Live* and fucked up a camera. We were all escorted out of the building; the next day the *New York Post* said we did $100,000 of damage. The funniest thing was someone gave John Brannon a mohawk, so there was all this hair all over the Green Room. We were walking to the NBC Studios and we found a huge bag of 45s in the garbage. There were spaces between the tiles of the ceiling in the Green Room, so we covered the entire ceiling with these records. The TV people were really freaked out. The woman came in and looked, got really wide-eyed and ran out. The hair was cleaned up, the records were pulled down and when she came back with her boss, it was all clean and we were drinking Pepsis. Then we went and slamdanced. The 'damage' ended up being a three-buck wiring job because someone knocked a camera over. Ian said 'New York sucks!' on the mic; Brannon said 'Negative Approach is going to fuck you up!' and it got on the air. It was cool.

TOM BERRARD (DC scene): The password to get in NBC Studios was 'Ian MacKaye.' They put us in the Green Room, which overlooked the stage. The show started; we went down and started to slamdance — it got out of hand. Our friend Billy McKenzie grabbed a huge Halloween pumpkin and smashed it onstage — all sorts of shit. In the next day's paper were headlines of $100,000 damage, which was misleading — what it meant was a $100,000 camera almost got broken.

   A few movies dealt with Hardcore, foremost director Penelope Spheeris' 1980 *The Decline Of Western Civilization* — a defining media moment. Through interviews and performances by Black Flag, Circle Jerks, Fear and others, *The Decline...* examined the collapse of the American Dream and the alienated kids left strewn in its path. Anyone who followed Hardcore saw *The Decline...* at one point or another, and anyone associated with the flick immediately gained elite membership in the movement.

LEE VING: That movie speaks for itself. There were some reasonably candid interviews with people on the scene. No one was told what to do. They just started filming when we played — nothing was planned. It was a real documentary. That was an accurate portrayal of the time and the issues people were speaking about.

TONY CADENA (Adolescents): I was at a few shows they filmed; it was close to what was happening. I don't think those people got Fear — they took them more seriously than Fear intended. A lot of people put on a show because the cameras were there, too.

KEITH MORRIS (Circle Jerks): *Decline* is still a great film. I feel it's a must-see for kids nowadays so they can see where the bands that they're locked into right now came from, where they copped all their riffs. Then they can go back even further and see all the bands from the late 50s and early 60s, to see where we stole all of our stuff from.

In 1983, Penelope Spheeris made another movie, *Suburbia*, about desperate Hardcore types living in squalor and doing bad things. The film had its moments, but it's basically a bad exploitation flick.

Then in '84 came *Repo Man,* a Sci-fi-style flick about a HC kid (Emilio Estevez) working as an auto reposessor, and his square mentor (Harry Dean Stanton). The movie features a great cameo by Circle Jerks as a lounge band. The soundtrack, with Circle Jerks, Black Flag, Fear, Suicidal Tendencies and The Plugz, sold well.

On more of an indie level, Adam Small and Peter Stuart's *Another State Of Mind* documented the summer '82 BYO tour with Youth Brigade and Social D. Like the tour itself, the film was stark, choppy and had its share of problems.

MIKE WATT (Minutemen): They made this stupid movie — *Another State Of Mind* — you don't know how we laughed! Everybody was actin' like they were on the big tour. We'd already done a tour in a little van, not an old school bus and then flyin' home after five gigs like these guys. I don't want these bands to think I'm down on 'em. I mean, we played with 'em a lot and they're good guys as peers — but we were snobbish on their scene because they didn't live as hard as us. We lived like fuckin' knuckleheads.

The mainstream Rock Press generally didn't support Hardcore. It was outsider music, from the realm of stupid kids.

TONY CADENA: They totally ignored Hardcore. *Slash* was good but the reading was higher than where I was at. The first mag that ever spoke to me was *Flipside* — it was aimed at my scene. I liked the comfortable atmosphere that came across with Al and Hud at *Flipside*. *Rolling Stone?* Please. *BAM?* I saw *BAM* a few years ago with all the Epitaph bands on the cover and laughed because they finally had to admit times had changed.

MIKE WATT: In *Rolling Stone,* I remember them writing about us and a Hüsker Dü record and mixing us up. They didn't know who the fuck we were and they didn't wanna know. They truly wanted to kill that music.

MTV started in 1981, and for the first few years they played zero Hardcore. The music just did not fit the MTV mindset. It wasn't until late '84, at the tail end of the scene, that Suicidal Tendencies' $5000 video for "Institutionalized" went into heavy rotation — as kind of a novelty song. But that was about it.

MIKE WATT: The Minutemen made a video for MTV in '84 — 'This Ain't No Picnic' — for 400 bucks. They nominated it for best video, but we lost to Kajagoogoo. •

HOW MUCH ART CAN YOU TAKE?

How much art can you take?
How much art can you take?
— SS Decontrol, "How Much Art Can You Take?"

The term "Hardcore art" is an oxymoron. HC types fancied themselves dismissive of art. Theirs was an essentially undecorated, unadorned world. Yet the term will be useful herein.

Hardcore communicated through graphics that read as art. Appropriated fragments of advertising and photojournalism comprised stark stylistic hodge-podges announcing shows and records. Those graphics, like the music itself, confronted brain-dead consumers, Reagan's government, and evil corporations.

Flyer for Wasted Youth album *Reagan's In,* ICI, 1981
Example of Hardcore era art
Collection of the author

WINSTON SMITH (artist): There was a drive to get away from fine, finished-looking work that looked like it came out of a record company art department. Instead of creating overblown work that makes the individual feel smaller, Hardcore made the individual feel included. It was not a glamor trip; the artwork was chaotic and spontaneous.

HC kids considered art a stupid bourgeois indulgence that was nothing but bullshit. Of course enough of it seeped into the mix to incite a recognizable HC graphic style. Collage, illustration and typography predominated, almost always in affordable black-and-white. A tribal iconography manifested itself in distinctive album covers and show flyers, their intensity proclaiming, "This is hard-core."

GLENN DANZIG (Misfits): It had a definite look and style — there's an art to brutality. That's why certain boxers are better than others — there's an art.

True to Hardcore's anti-art philosophy, the scene's creative types corrupted words and images lifted from books and magazines, or drew outrageous, offensive pictures. No subject was sacred or taboo. At that point in history a large supply of deteriorating Vietnam-era mags offered plenty of war photos, which when mixed with porno, celebrities, mushroom clouds and cut-out type made for arresting presentations. President Reagan's photo loomed as an iconographic metaphor for repression. Angry political themes merged with B-movie imagery. Abortions, assassinations, atrocities, auto wrecks — it was all there, degraded by countless generations of xeroxing.

Hardcore kids claimed to hate anything with an "art school" vibe. Pretentious, pseudo-intellectual "arty" types lacked primal intensity. The word "art" itself aroused ill will, implying snobbery. SS Decontrol's "How Much Art Can You Take?" shot to prominence in the scene as a statement of HC's schism with the art world.

DAVE SMALLEY (DYS, Dag Nasty): There was a big gap between us and the art fags. They thought we were jocks, basically.

Hardcore artists emulated the immediacy of the music with quick, sloppy, angry creations. Central to their artistic impulse was the proliferation of the marker pen, or "magic marker." Also, an ever-growing number of xerox copiers allowed them to easily make hundreds of show flyers. The eight-and-a-half by eleven letter-size paper used in copiers became a standard format. Xeroxed flyers were the primary source of information in local undergrounds.

Cover illustration from MDC, *Multi-Death Corporation,*
R Radical, 1983
Art by Vince Ransid
Collection of Sal Canzonieri

ART CHANTRY (Seattle artist): The flyer was the primary source of communication. You could tell by its rotten, crappy, scrappy style that it was either what you didn't want to go to, or what you wanted to go to. A couple of dozen flyers could pack a joint because everyone saw it and word of mouth passed. It was another way of talking to each other.

WINSTON SMITH: Flyers just require a flat surface; you didn't have to pay anyone to advertise. It's totally illegal to wheatpaste on walls, but unless you got caught right under someone's nose, there was nothing they could do about it. It was always satisfying to see that someone had tried to rip them down. You couldn't tell if they were offended by it or they thought it was really cool and wanted to take it home.

TIM KERR (Big Boys): Flyers were as big as the bands themselves in Austin. Down here we were just doing flyers to piss people off, mostly the frats and stuff. We'd take pictures from the local paper of a hazing incident, promptly cut out that picture, and make flyers with a line like, 'I'm a big dumb-ass,' and hang 'em everywhere. But nobody could figure out who was behind it. It was about being involved and trying to make a change — or just trying to get a reaction. That's where we were at.

Spraypaint also provided an effective means of communication. One could spread tons of info. Black Flag became LA's most notorious band by spraying their name and logo on virtually every highway overpass and abandoned building. NYHC kids got known for their graffiti "tagging."

> *Bunch of of used parts*
> *From garbage pails everywhere*
> **— Dead Kennedys, "Your Emotions"**

As throughout Rock history, artists formed alliances with bands: Winston Smith with Dead Kennedys, Raymond Pettibon with Black Flag, Shawn Kerrie with Circle Jerks, Brian "Pushead" Schroeder with his group Septic Death, Mad Marc Rude with Battalion Of Saints and Sean Taggart with a few NYHC groups.
　　The collaboration between DK's Jello Biafra and Winston Smith — who'd been a roadie for Santana, Journey and CS&N — worked well: the artist's relatively

Cover illustration from Dead Kennedys,
In God We Trust, Inc.
Alternative Tentacles, 1981
Art by Winston Smith

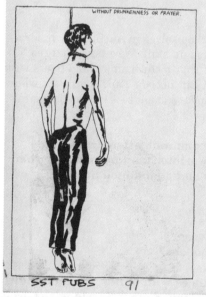

Booklet cover illustration from Raymond
Pettibon's *Just Happy To Be Working,*
SST, 1983
Collection of the author

refined political collage art effectively translated
Biafra's satiric images.

WINSTON SMITH: Collage is an expression of angst
— it's quick, fast and easy. It graphically came out
looking chaotic and disorganized. It was like, 'Listen to
me!' — which is also what the music was all about. It's
not any easier than painting or sculpture, but was a
quick way for people to render an image without having
to learn how to draw like Raphael. They could just pick
out a picture and put something next to it. Collage had
this vandal appeal. You were destroying something that
someone else had made, then you were substituting
your own slant on it.

**Through work that was used by Black Flag
and SST Records, Raymond Pettibon established
perhaps the most recognizable style of the era.
His stark, vicious ink drawings with depressing
captions echoed the overall mindset: hateful,
bored, and listless. Arcane knowledge acquired in
pursuit of his economics degree imbued
Pettibon's work with irony and pathos.**

RAYMOND PETTIBON: I haven't spoken to SST in
ten years-plus — I'm written out of their history. I don't
want to get into all this 'cause it just continues
something that I don't want to be a part of now and
didn't really want to be a part of then. The first and
last time I ever advertised anything, it was my
brother's [Greg Ginn] idea. It was advertised in *Slash*
magazine — I sold one copy. I have nothing in print and
none of it ever's going to go back in print. If anyone
wanted it, they could have gotten it then. Face it, I
have a very tenuous relationship with the music. Who
gives a fuck about cover art? Those people who do
couldn't name one important real artist if their life
depended on it.

"Rock & Roll is such a powerful medium — your
work can be in museums and galleries around the
world and it all comes back to a record album. It just
gets annoying after awhile. I didn't consider myself an
illustrator, cartoonist, or poster artist. That stuff just
happened to end up on those posters or record covers
because I knew people in bands who wanted to put it
there. I never did them on commission. They'd choose
the ones that were the most violent and offensive. I
didn't draw them for an art director. At the time, I was
getting a little sick of it because they'd always choose
my worst stuff. It was never what I meant to do. If I
could do it all over, I'd say, 'Let me do it as cover art,
something that makes sense within the form.' None
were done as cover art. These bands wanted really
nasty artwork."

Pushead was best known for his death-imagery drawing style. He single-handedly put his hometown of Boise, Idaho on the map, promoting shows and networking. He flourished as a *Thrasher* columnist, and as the magazine's music editor. His endless renditions of skulls, all seemingly alive, transcended his HC roots; he went on to do Metallica covers.

WINSTON SMITH: Pushead was important in that scene because his work superseded the mundane skull-and-crossbones. His execution was finely done. The work that was done well like that legitimized the scene. If someone's good at what they're doing, the message gets across.

Sean Taggart came to prominence for his NYHC show flyers, as well as for the cover art for Agnostic Front and Cro-Mags.

SEAN TAGGART: I was a cartoonist. Because I was involved in the scene, I was constantly drawing fictional Hardcore characters. Kevin [Parris] was a cartoonist and we started doing Hardcore comics. When he got into the Cro-Mags, he dismissed his art talent. He made a conscious decision to be a musician and asked me to do flyers for them. That's what got me known as the East Coast Hardcore artist, doing all these Cro-Mags flyers. I knew Roger from Agnostic Front; I did a cover for them, then I was doing art for everybody. I was only 19 and people really appreciated what I did. I was a little wimpy kid but all these tough guys kept me around because I was a cartoonist — and when I got drunk I was really insane; they enjoyed that.

Art movements predicate themselves upon the notion of an ever-evolving aesthetic: after today's style comes tomorrow's, which will be an improvement. Art movements nourish striving, growth and improvement. Hardcore art, on the other hand, celebrated not being hip and happening. Like the scene itself, it was totally primal. Such an energetic confluence of social currents and youthful angst will never again occur. •

Show flyer for Fuck Ups, DRI, Verbal Abuse
Tool And Die, SF, 1983
Example of Hardcore era graphics
Collection of Spike Cassiday

Show flyer for Necros, Dove, Hose
Space II Arcade, DC, 1983
Art by Steven Blush
Collection of the author

BIG BOYS

BLACK FLAG

SOCIAL DISTORTION

FLIPPER

DRI

NEGATIVE FX

THE STAINS

MDC

HÜSKER DÜ

VERBAL ABUSE

WHITE CROSS

WASTED TALENT

ARTIFICIAL PEACE

BATTALION OF SAINTS

NOTA

THE FAITH

ARTICLES OF FAITH

TOXIC REASONS

CIRCLE ONE

WASTED YOUTH

THE EFFIGIES

DEAD KENNEDYS

BAD RELIGION

URBAN WASTE

7 SECONDS

US DRI

DXA

VOID

TSOL

REBEL TRUTH

PART FOUR

Photo by Edward Colver

EVERYTHING FALLS APART

What did I do to deserve this?
I've painted myself into a corner
— Circle Jerks, "Trapped"

By 1986 Hardcore was over. The participants died, failed, lost interest, moved on, OD'ed, got girlfriends pregnant, whatever — but there was more. The scene itself committed suicide.

Several things marked '86 as the end. Black Flag, DKs and The Misfits had all fallen apart. Minutemen's D Boon died in a December '85 car crash. Hüsker Dü signed to mainstream Warner Bros. Minor Threat evolved into the less-visceral Fugazi. Circle Jerks and TSOL were "going Metal."

Heavy Metal, long despised by Hardcore types, eventually ate its way onto the scene, marking the rebellion's end. By '86 the freshest shit was coming from HC-influenced metalheads like Metallica and Slayer, ushering in the age of Hardcore/Metal Crossover music. Also that year, the first shoe-gazing took place; Alternative Rock and Indie-Rock were born; Grunge was in the air. A new generation arose, with new mindsets, new experiences — and new problems.

PAT DUBAR (Uniform Choice): Around '86, everything died. It was weird because things were so strong, then suddenly there was nothing — no substance. Hardcore had become fashionable. To me, the risk was that breath of fire in the beginning — and it was gone.

MILO AUKERMAN (Descendents): In the mid-80s, there was a big difference in the scene. It went from being incredibly obscure and dangerous in 1980, to 1986, where there was a more popular scene of very safe characters.

Hardcore ended for numerous reasons:

• **BUILT-IN OBSOLESCENCE:** Short-lived by its own definition, it included many self-destruct mechanisms — anger, nihilism, constant confrontation and reactionary politics. No one planned for the future. The musicians needed to grow and change, an impossible goal if they remained true to the original vision.

• **CONTRADICTIONS ABOUNDED:** It paid lip service to freedom of expression, yet in its ranks dogma prevailed. The bands professed they weren't in it for money, yet most broke up due to lack of profit and market impact. Those moving on to other forms were chastised as sellouts; those staying behind fell victim to entropy.

• **DUMBING-DOWN:** The scene devolved so much it parodied itself.

The new crop of kids weren't replacing the scene's intelligentsia — Jello Biafra, Gregg Ginn, Henry Rollins, Ian MacKaye et al. The kids who followed contentedly lived out an idealized, narrow view of HC, becoming lunkheads with a look. From a potential revolutionary force Hardcore in six years mutated into just another social caste — codified and conventional — becoming more intolerant than the narrow-mindedness against which it claimed to rebel.

JELLO BIAFRA (Dead Kennedys): You know me — there's nothing I like less than intolerant people, especially conservative Punks. Originally, every band sounded totally different. Nowadays it's been put into all these narrow parameters. A band picks a style, plays in nothing but that style, and puts the intelligent members of their audience to sleep.

be in terms of independence and freedom quickly became such a formula and book of rules — how to dress, to sound, to act — it wasn't fun anymore. It was over and it was time to do something new.

• **RESTRICTIONS OF MUSICAL FORM: Hardcore was the province of young, green musicians. Once they improved, they weren't content to just play HC; they wanted to utilize their chops. The angry simplicity of the early 80s didn't furnish a solid enough base for a career. The smarter guys wanted to move on.**

JAKE WISELEY (editor, *Uncle Fester):* As these bands learned how to play, they started to do solos. They wanted to do something more than the three chords; they wanted to be a little bit faster, and frankly, Metal was getting bigger and it was, in general, getting heavier.

• **UP-AND-COMING BANDS SUCKED: The scene's original musicians were not exactly virtuosos, but they were totally driven. Working out their sound became a matter of abilities catching up with ideas. Greg Ginn's Jazz improv vibe manifested a spectrum of inspirations; DKs guitarist East Bay Ray obviously knew all types of music. But later players taking their first musical steps emulated the alarming simplicity of Hardcore — and little else.**

PAT DUBAR: As a 12-year-old Punk, it was really hard for any other music to get in. That was in some ways good and some ways bad. That was it — Hardcore was my music. It worked perfectly for me 'cause it had a lot of anger and I already had a lot of hatred growing inside of me, which I didn't really come to grips with or understand until just recently. It spoke to me. Musically speaking, we were born of Hardcore."

> *I wanna be the bullet*
> *That goes ripping through your skull*
> — Black Flag, "In My Head"

• **CROSSOVER: Early on, Hardcore and Metal never interacted — the two camps, polar opposites, hated each other. But when Metal dudes finally started showing up at Hardcore gigs, HC changed forever.**
   Original Hardcore revolted against mainstream music like Metal, so the tendency of musicians to "re-discover their Metal roots" signaled a political shift. No longer anti-establishment, latter-day HC outfits embraced the once-spurned sound of suburban materialism. They became the people they set out never to be.

MIKE WATT (Minutemen): You mean like, 'Hey, I'm gonna live and die for the fuckin' [Motley] Crüe'? That's how I met [Black Flag roadie] Mugger: he was beatin' up a longhair who'd beat up some shorthair. There were gangs of guys who beat each other up for hair! That was the climate of the day.

STEVE HARRIS (Iron Maiden): In the early days of Iron Maiden there was a few things written about us saying we had this Punk attitude, which was bullshit. We hated Punks. We hated their attitude. Some of them were supposedly working-class street crud but most of them were middle-class kids with weird haircuts. They weren't that real at all. We felt at least we were honest about what were doing.

   An obvious distinction between HC and Metal was lyrical: the fantasy and romance of Metal versus Hardcore's socio-political or nihilistic rants.
   The spirit also totally differed. Metal acts weren't necessarily "doing it for the kids." They sought the elusive Rock & Roll dream of fame, fortune and females — and those endless guitar solos.

Hardcore players didn't have their rivals' gear, and their sound suffered. Metal displayed an expensive-equipment vibe, while four groups on a HC bill would all play through the same shitty amp.

Invariably the musics began to merge. "Crossover" outfits such as Verbal Abuse, DRI, COC and Suicidal Tendencies retained essential HC elements — only employing Metal for chunky riffage or the occasional Sabbath-style intro. It sounded like Metal without all the bullshit.

HC-inspired long-haired suburbanites — Metallica, Megadeth, Slayer — defined Crossover from a Metal standpoint. They made musical, not cultural, statements.

JAMES HETFIELD (Metallica): I recall going to school wearing a Scorpions shirt and Punk sunglasses and getting shit from both sides — 'Well, fuck you man, I like 'em both.' That's the feeling behind the early Metallica songs. There was aggression, but there's got to be more than just banging on one chord, you know? So yeah, slowly they meshed together.

MIKE WATT: In Slayer and Metallica, I really did see the baton handed down. Those bands added a technical edge that might've made it even more powerful even though they ended up just diluting it. Those bands wanted to build on the Flag vibe and mix it with their technical vibe. Slayer — that *South Of Heaven* album is the most massive fucking thing. Maybe that could never have existed without [Black Flag's] "Rise Above" or "Wasted" or *Damaged*.

But don't kid yourself — Metallica were not part of the Hardcore scene. They began as a tight-pants-wearing Metal band.

GEORGE ANTHONY (Battalion Of Saints): We played our last Battalion Of Saints gig ever in San Francisco. We'd been driving all night, drinking hard. These long-haired guys walked in our dressing room — we said, 'Get these fucking Hippies out of our room.' We played — and these guys came walking back in. We're going, 'What the fuck?' and one of 'em said, 'Before you kick us out again, we're the guys in Metallica.'

JIM FOSTER (Adrenalin O.D.): Lars Ulrich and James Hetfield came to see Black Flag in Jersey. I introduced myself because I was in A.O.D. — they kept coming up to me asking, 'Is this Black Flag? Is this Black Flag?' because they'd never seen this shit before. Flag weren't doing the Thrash beat anymore, so Lars kept yelling, 'Double-time, play faster!' and I kept elbowing him going, 'Shut up, they're not like that!'

• The politics imploded: Hardcore started a revolution — and nobody came.

REED MULLIN (Corrosion Of Conformity): We were hopeful this was going to be a bigger thing in raising consciousness — the idea that we're not just preaching to the converted, we're going to be talking about social and political issues to a new crowd. It wasn't necessarily going to be armed revolution — there was going to be a new generation to help change shit around. It's obvious what happened — kids learned about stagediving and playing fast, and that was about it. That bummed us out a lot.

WINSTON SMITH (graphic artist): It did feel rather futile to keep preaching to the converted. You'd never find anyone to disagree. It was a temptation to get approval by safely keeping within the bounds of things you know your public will approve. We always think that those who share our opinions are the most intelligent people. It was more of a challenge for me to try and get things out to the part of the public not already converted. Most people don't want to think too hard.

PAUL MAHERN (Zero Boys): Early Hardcore and Punk was a positive experience, but at some point in the mid-80s, I felt like it had attracted a negative element so I removed myself from it. The whole Metal influence I didn't get at all, because to me Hardcore was so not about Metal, there could be no symbiotic relationship between the two camps at all.

MIKE WATT: One bad thing Crossover brought was all these stupid people, so it wasn't an idea thing anymore. You know, when music reaches the masses, you don't wanna be part of it to be different — it's to belong, and that's what changes things. That's why those Metal guys only had an impact on our scene for so long — and they did, big time, for like three or four years. Motorhead wanted Flag on tour, but they wanted to charge 'em 27 grand to rent the lights and P.A! This was the old Rock & Roll scam shit. Motorhead had an old school manager and Flag said, 'Fuck you!'

 • **THE PARTICIPANTS MOVED ON: By 1986, everyone was trying to shed the "Hardcore" label. No one from the original scene was into it. Most early players ultimately denied their roles in the movement. Psychologically, they turned their backs and walked away.**

TESCO VEE (Meatmen): Hardcore spawned so many people that've gone on but never really talked about it. Once they cross that threshold, they don't go back and relive those moments. Those weren't magic days, or the halcyon salad days — they are now, because those people are big Rock stars. I mean all the Bob Moulds and the people that were there. Whatever. It's forgotten. It's like the lost art. I'd like to think I'll be playing 'Tooling For Anus' at the Holiday Inn lounge when I'm 65.

> *My luck ran out a short time ago*
> *I've lost myself and there's nowhere to go*
> — Marginal Man, "Marginal Man"

 No-one can overlook the creativity of the original Hardcore pioneers. **Everything from zines to mosh pits to the indie music network resulted from a few kids' incredible vision.**
 Considering how small and marginalized it was, Hardcore casts a vast shadow on what happens today. At the time of this writing, every up-and-coming rocker claims some convoluted Hardcore lineage.
 Like any renegade form, Hardcore had its share of self-righteous zealots to codify it and popularize it — and ruin it. •

INTO THE UNKNOWN

JACK GRISHAM (TSOL): One of the things I think people get wrong is they try to classify Hardcore as one big social movement. The majority of the kids were dropouts and they had no plans. It was just a bunch of jerks. We were for anarchy because anarchy was fun.

MILO AUKERMAN (Descendents): Kids have this inflated view of how it was because the music's been passed down and still stands out. We'd play to 12 people in Norman, Oklahoma or wherever. Sure, those people dug us, but it wasn't like, 'Rock on, Norman, Oklahoma!'

GREG GRAFFIN (Bad Religion): Kids think the old school was some magical era. They don't realize how frightening it was to live in a world where people were violently opposed to you.I was in one of the biggest cities in America, LA, where you'd think there'd be tolerance. But people wanted to kill us for the way we looked. Today that doesn't seem possible.

TAD KEPLEY (Anarchist activist): You don't have the imminent threat of a riot now, worrying about the cops coming in, fucking kicking your ass. Things are very in control. You go see what passes for a Hardcore band, and there are bouncers, barricades and high ticket prices — everything we always used to hate.

PAT DUBAR (Uniform Choice): Hardcore's now considered glamorous, but it originated from the angst and anger of all these fucked-up kids. If you go to a show now, you don't have to worry about 40 cops coming in and macing and beating the shit out of you. It was not hip; it was so unhip, you were taking a chance. Being very few and far between, we were a target for trouble. I'd be fucking hassled constantly. Anyone who was there does not need to stake a claim: you were there 'cause you had to be. I don't think people got into the business of Hardcore to be rich 'cause it just didn't happen.

KEVIN SECONDS (7 Seconds): You dealt with being chased down the streets with baseball bats. I talk to kids who assume that all the bands were tight, and loved each other, supported each other, and there were these armies of bands touring around the country and dealing with each other. It really was the opposite. There were people who connected, and everybody knew somebody else, but as far as the scenes around the country, there was little contact.

MIKE WATT (Minutemen): Another myth — that Punk Rockers were all stupid. It was just misfit people. Gregg Turner of Angry Samoans teaches calculus at Claremont and he wrote songs like 'They Saved Hitler's Cock.' It was just disenfranchised people coming together in a situation where they could let anything fly and you didn't know what was coming next.

STEVEN McDONALD (Red Cross): The Hardcore movement did spawn interesting things. There's certain things that it helped to create, but the original first movement was horrifying. I'm so grateful that it's gone, and I can't understand why anyone would care. It was painful when we were part of it at the time.

JELLO BIAFRA (Dead Kennedys): The saddest part of the perception that there's a Golden Age of Hardcore is the people who believe it — especially the ones who were there and should know better — are falling into the same glassy-eyed nostalgia that gave us *Happy Days*. Going backwards is ridiculous. To me, retro is poison.

DARRYL JENIFER (Bad Brains): I haven't talked to no young fellas nowadays about those days. I have my son and he don't have no interest in this type of stuff. There was this girl at his school and I said, 'Jesse, why don't you go talk to her?' He goes, 'Nah, she's stuck up. She hangs around these skateboard guys that listen to your band.'

PAUL MAHERN (Zero Boys): I was a part of a movement that was way more important than the 60s Hippie thing on a lot of levels. It was a movement based much more in reality — something that you could do right there. The Hippie movement was about trying to change the world, while Hardcore was about changing your mind, your attitude — and do something: make a record, a fanzine. I mean, saving the world is a great concept but you've gotta start by actually doing something, and that was very much a part of Hardcore for me.

KING KOFFEE (Butthole Surfers): Hardcore affected me in a way the Hippies were affected and the Beat Generation were affected. I'll carry this with me always. I'll always filter things through Hardcore glasses. A lot of those ideals and my own experiences from the time still mean a lot to me. We all went through some very unique American history. We're feeling the repercussions on a big scale, on the Pop music level, but the actual music was only experienced by a few thousand people. It was a true subculture, and we were all part of it.

MIKE NESS (Social Distortion): It's a part of my personality that's never gonna go away. Whether it's right or wrong, it's how I see things. If you can be yourself, that's Hardcore. There's times I wish I could have no tattoos. When you walk in a room and everyone's got a chain wallet and greased hair, it's like — 'I originally did this to be different.' People think they invented this stuff — I take it personally. I took beatings so you could dye your hair blue. Whatever. The 17-year-old kids have every right to do what I did, but tell them what they're doing is nothing new.

WINSTON SMITH (artist): The recycling of imagery's lost its punch. It watered down the meaning of the initial impact. If every word you wrote had an exclamation mark behind it, an exclamation point behind a sentence wouldn't mean anything. MTV went a long way to destroy and homogenize the scene. MTV never embraced Hardcore — it was too ugly and commercially unviable. Now a watered-down, formulaic version's regarded as 'Alternative music.' I feel the same I did in the late 70s — we're overdue for some changes.

GLENN DANZIG (Misfits): The idiots are running the show again. With happy Pop-Punk, record companies finally found a way to make millions off it. There's nothing angry about it. It's doing nothing but putting money in their pockets. It has the sound but not the attitude.

BILL STEVENSON (Baltimore promoter): As trite or contrived as it may seem, the Hardcore movement completely changed my life, I figured out there was a world outside my neighborhood, and there was a whole lot more to life than just being a little redneck. I'm more resilient because of Hardcore, and I know a lot more vocabularies had I not experienced this thing. I feel I can walk in more worlds than one now.

TAD KEPLEY: Those days were a formative experience, and I'm never gonna abandon the ideals I picked up. I'm wrecked for life because I could never lead a straight life. There's no way I could psychologically buy into it. Like so many others who grew up in that scene, I'm essentially a non-person, without a fixed address. I've never filed a tax return. I mean — I do not exist. I am so completely outside what operates around me, why bother introducing myself into it now? The people who haven't managed to find a way to incorporate the ideals give up and become cops or prosecutors.

JOHN KEZDY (The Effigies): I have an attitude that's been formed through the Hardcore years; my experiences will affect the way I live the rest of my life. For instance, money is important only as a instrument. It only buys you things like freedom or the ability to do things which ultimately bring you happiness. Money itself cannot buy you happiness. You have to be true to yourself. If you have an impulse to do something you believe in, you got to do it. The other side of that is, if you have something you really believe in, you have to stick by it, no matter what anybody else says. You just have to do what your heart tells you to do.

HARLEY FLANAGAN (Cro-Mags): Anybody's who's got any value has got to realize it's over. It's history. Hopefully, through your writing, we're gonna hear the real history instead of some horseshit story about events that didn't happen. For instance, there's this band Judge with a song about a certain brawl that happened at A7 when the Boston dudes came down. I was at that fight — none of the cats from that band were around. It's all retro. It's like wanting to be a 60s Hippie all over again. You can go to the mall and get your nose ring and green-hair dye. It's time for a new kick in the ass. Hardcore was about being an outcast by society's standards, and still having a place you could be accepted. You were a freak. You didn't have to fit into the world's codes; there was this group you could lose your mind with. They wouldn't judge you because they were just as judged as you.

MIKE WATT (Minutemen): Hardcore was all about playin' for keeps, no bullshit. You read these interviews where bands blame the major labels — I don't think Hardcore was about that. It was 'Fuck you, we're doing it our way.' It's about responsibility. I think the Hardcore guys took it upon themselves to do it — and we did it. •

AHC DISCOGRAPHY

Here is a discography of American Hardcore. It's culled from my record collection and my piles of fanzines and flyers, and from the archives and memories of a few other individuals who were close to the scene. I've attempted to make it as thorough as possible.

Assembling this was a difficult task because most Hardcore "record companies" consisted of kids with little business acumen. The cheap records they cranked out were often poorly labeled and frought with typos, mistakes and misinformation. Also, Hardcore was a scene in which dumb pseudonyms abounded, often making it difficult to ascertain exactly who was who.

Please note that this is a vinyl-only discography (except for a few entries issued only on cassette tape)— compact discs and the so-called digital age had nothing to do with Hardcore. Having said that, there are a handful of records that never saw the light of day until the CD era, so they are listed, too. There's also a few bands herein that lasted well beyond the American Hardcore era (1980-86) — only their relevent work is included here.

Every piece of information I've seen posted on the Internet regarding American Hardcore is wrong, so I've chosen to totally ignore it.

Please inform the publisher of any corrections or additions for future editions.

Steven Blush

7 SECONDS (Reno)

1981 *Socially Fucked Up* 13-song cassette (Vicious Scam)
1981 *3 Chord Politics* 15-song cassette (Vicious Scam)
1982 "Fuck Your America" on *Not So Quiet On The Western Front* comp LP (Alternative Tentacles, VIRUS 14)
1982 *Skins, Brains & Guts* 7" EP (Alternative Tentacles; Faulty, VIRUS 15) "Skins, Brains & Guts; No Authority; Redneck Society; Baby Games; Racism Sucks; This Is My Life; Anti-Klan; I Hate Sports; We're Gonna Fight"   *Kevin Seconds - guitar; vocals • Steve Youth - bass; vocals • Bix Bigler - drums; vocals*
1983 *United We Stand* (issued in 1991 as *Old School* on Headhunter) "You Lose; What If There's War In America?; Here's Your Warning; Heavy Metal Jocks; These Boots Are Made For Walking; Boss; Young 'Til I Die; War In The Head; No Class, No Way!; Definite Choice; I Have A Dream; Wasted Life (Ain't No Crime); #1 Rule; Out Of Touch; Red And Black; Diehard; Clenched Fists, Black Eyes"   **1983** *Committed For Life* 7-song 7" EP (Squirtdown) "5 Years Of Lies; Drug Control; Bottomless Pit; Fight Your Own Fight; Committed For Life; This Is The Angry; Aggro"   *Kevin Seconds - guitar; vocals • Steve Youth - bass • Troy Mowatt - drums*   **1983** on *Party Or Go Home* comp LP (Mystic)
1984 *The Crew* (BYO, 005)   *Kevin Seconds - vocals • Dan Pozniak - guitar • Steve Youth- bass • Troy Mowatt - drums*   **1985** on *Nuke Your Dink* comp 7" EP (Positive Force, PF - 1)   **1985** on *Cleanse The Bacteria* comp LP (Pusmort)   **1985** *Walk Together Rock Together* (Positive Force; BYO, PF - 2; BYO 010) "In Your Face; Spread; 99 Red Balloons; Remains To Be Seen; Walk Together, Rock Together; How Do You Think You'd Feel?; Strength"   **1985** *Blasts From The Past* 4-song 7" EP (Positive Force, PF - 3)
1986 *New Wind* (Positive Force; BYO, PF - 8; BYO 014) "The Night Away; New Wind; Somebody Help Me Scream; Tied Up In Rhythm; Grown Apart; Man Enough To Care; Opinion Of Feelings; The Inside; Calendar; Expect To Change; Still Believe; Put These Words Into Music; Just One Day; Colour Blind Jam"   *Kevin Seconds - vocals; guitar • Steve Youth -guitar • Joseph Bansuelo - bass • Troy Mowatt - drums*

76% UNCERTAIN (CT)

1984 *Estimated Monkey Time* (Shmegma)

THE ABUSED (NY)

1983 *Loud And Clear* 7" EP (Abused Music) "Loud And Clear; War Games; Just Another Fool; No End In Sight; Nuclear Threat; Watch Out; Blow Your Brains Out; Drug Free Youth"   *Kevin Crowley - vocals • Raf Astor - guitar • Dave Colon - bass • Brian Dundon - drums*

ADOLESCENTS (LA/ Orange County)

1980 "Amoeba" one-sided 7" (Posh Boy, PBS - 6)
1980 "Amoeba" on *Rodney On The ROQ* comp LP (Posh Boy, PBS-106)   **1981** *Adolescents* (Frontier, FLP 1003) "I Hate Children; Who Is Who; Wrecking Crew; L.A. Girl; Self Destruct; Kids Of The Black Hole; No Way; Amoeba; Word Attack; Rip It Up; Democracy; No Friends; Creatures"   *Tony Cadena-vocals • Rikk Agnew - guitar • Frank Agnew - guitar • Steve Soto - bass • Casey Royer - drums*   **1981** "Welcome To Reality" b/w "Losing Battle" and "Things Start Moving" 7" (Frontier, FRT 101)   **1982** "Losing Battle" on *American Youth Report* comp LP (Invasion)   **1982** "Who Is Who" and "Wrecking Crew" on *Someone Got Their Head Kicked In!* comp LP (BYO 001)   **1986** *Brats In Battalions* (S.O.S.)   *Tony Montana (Cadena) - vocals • Rikk Agnew - guitar • Alfie Agnew - guitar • Steve Soto - bass*

ADRENALIN O.D. (NY/ NJ)

1982 "New Year's Eve" and "Paul's Not Home" on *New York Thrash* comp CS (ROIR)   **1983** *Let's Barbeque With Adrenalin O.D.* six-song 7" EP (Buy Our Records) "Suburbia; Old People Talk Loud; House Husband; Mischief Night; Status Symbol"   *Paul Richards - vocals • Jim Foster - guitar • Jack Steeples - bass • Dave Scott - drums*   **1984** *The Wacky Hi-Jinks of Adrenalin O.D.* (Buy Our Records, BOR-12-002) "A.O.D. vs. Godzilla; White Hassle; New Years Eve; Small Talk; Going To A Funeral; Corporate Disneyland; Trans Am (The Saga Continues); Sighteeing; Middle-aged Whore; World War IV; Clean and Jerk; Sleep; Rah-Jah!; Rock & Roll Gas Station; Paul's Not Home"   **1985** *Caught In The Act* split 7" EP w/ Bedlam (Buy Our) "Masterpiece; We Will Rock U;Traffic Jam;Creepy Fuckin Hitchcock; Lost In Space; Live AIDS"   **1985** "Love Song" on *One Big Crowd* comp (Big City, BCR7)   **1985** "Crowd Control" and "Infiltrate" on *New Jerseys' Got It?* comp (Buy Our Records)   **1986** "A Nice Song In The Key Of 'D'" b/w "Return To Beneath The Planet Of Adrenalin O.D. vs. Godzilla Strikes Again. In 3-D" (Buy Our Records, BOR-7-005)   **1986** *Humungousfungusamongus* (Buy Our Records, BOR-12-008) "A.O.D. vs. Son Of Godzilla; Office Buildings; Yuppie; Answer; Pope On A Rope; Fishin' Musician; Pizza-N-Beer; Bugs; Youth Blimp; Commercial Cuts; Survive; Masterpiece; Crowd Control; Velvet Elvis; Fuck The Neighbors; Surfin Jew; Bruce's Lament; The Nice Song"   *Paul Richard - guitar; vocals • Jack Steeples - bass; vocals • Bruce Wingate - guitar; vocals • Dave Scott - drums; vocals*   **1986** Anarchy In The U.S.A. on *Another Shot For Bracken* comp LP (Positive Force)

AGENT 86 (Arcata, CA)

1984 *Scary Action* EP (Mystic)

AGENT ORANGE (LA/ OC)

1980 "Bloodstains" on *Rodney On The ROQ* comp LP (Posh Boy, PBS-106)   **1981** "Everything Turns Grey" b/w "Pipeline" 7" (Posh Boy, PBS12)   **1981** *Living In Darkness* (Posh Boy, PBS - 122) "Too Young To Die; Everything Turns Grey; Miserlou; The Last Goodbye; No Such Thing; A Cry For Help In A World Gone Mad; Bloodstains; Living In Darkness"   **1981** "Mr. Moto" on *Rodney On The ROQ Vol. 2* comp LP (Posh Boy, PBS - 123)
1982 *Bitchin' Summer* 12" EP (Posh Boy) "Miserlou; Breakdown; Mr. Moto; Pipeline (extended version)"   **1983** "Everything Turns Grey" on *Posh Hits Vol .1* comp (Posh Boy)   **1984** "Secret Agent Man" b/w "Shakin' All Over" 7" (Enigma)   **1984** *When You Least Expect It ...* 12" EP (Enigma, E1047) "It's Up To Me And You; Bite The Hand That Feeds (Part 2); Somebody To Love; Out Of Limits"   **1986** *This Is The Voice* (Enigma, ST - 73209) "Voices (In The Night); It's In Your Head; Say It Isn't True; Fire In The Rain; In Your Dreams Tonight; Tearing Me Apart; ...So Strange; Bite The Hand That Feeds (Part 1); I Kill Spies; This Is Not The End"   *Mike Palm - guitar; vocals • James - bass • Scott - drums*

AGNOSTIC FRONT (NY)

1983 *United Blood* 7" EP (Rat Cage) "No One Rules; Final War; Last Warning; Traitor; Friend Or Foe; United Blood; Fight; Discriminate Me; In Control; Crucial Changes"   *Roger Miret-vocals • Vinnie Stigma-guitar • Adam Moochie-bass • Raybeez - drums*   **1984** *Victim In Pain* (Rat Cage) "Victim In Pain; Remind Them; Blind Justice; Last Warning; United & Strong; Power; Hiding Inside; Fascist Attitudes; Society Sucker;Your Mistake; With Time"   *Roger Miret - vocals • Vinnie Stigma - guitar • Alex Kinon - lead guitar • Rob Kabula - bass*   **1986** *Cause For Alarm* (Combat Core) "The Eliminator; Existence of Hate; Time Will Come; Growing Concern; Your Mistake; Out for Blood; Toxic Shock; Bomber Zee; Public Assistance; Shoot His Load"

AGRESSION (Oxnard, CA)

1982 "Intense Energy," "Dear John Letter," "Rat Race" on *Someone Got Their Head Kicked In!* comp LP (BYO, 001) **1983** "Slamming At The Club" on *Copulation* comp LP (Mystic, MLP33128) **1983** *Don't Be Mistaken* (BYO, 003) "It Can Happen; Brain Bondage; Non Person; Body Count; Money Machine; No Mercy; Don't Be Mistaken; Intense Energy; S.A.T.C.; Locals Only; Insomnia; Secret Sex; Stop The Clock; Cat Killer" *Mark Hickey - vocals • Henry Knowles - guitar • Bob Clark-bass• Mark Aber- drums* **1984** *Live 7* (Mystic) **1985** *Bootleg* (Bootleg, B; T1)

RIKK AGNEW (LA/ OC)

1982 *All By Myself* (Frontier, FLP1009)

AK 47 (TX)

1980 *The Badge Means You Suck* 7" (Pineapple)

AKA (LA)

1981 "Tommorrow's Theme," "Liza Jane" on *Who Cares* comp (American Standard)

GG ALLIN (NH)

1980 *Always Was, Is, and Always Shall Be* (Orange) **1982** *Public Animal #1* EP (Orange) **1982** *You Hate Me and I Hate You* EP (Orange) **1983** *No Rules* EP (Orange) **1984** *Eat My Fuc* (Blood) **1984** *Hard Candy Cock* 7" EP (Blood, 306015) "Hard Candy Cock; Out For Blood; I Don't Give A Shit; Drink, Fight & Fuck; Convulsions" **1984** on *You'll Hate This Record* comp LP (Seidboard) **1985** *I Wanna Fuck Your Brains Out* (Blood) **1985** GG Allin and the Scumfucs; Artless (Holy War)

AMERICA'S HARDCORE (LA)

1983 "Cops Are Criminals" on *Copulation* comp LP (Mystic)

ANGRY RED PLANET (Detroit)

1983 *Angry Red Planet* 7 EP (Angry Red) "Apathy; Mummy From Hollywood; Going Nowhere Slow; You're One Too" *Tim Pakledinaz - guitar • John Pak - bass • Ve De - drums*

ANGRY SAMOANS (LA)

1980 *Inside My Brain* EP (Bad Trip) "Right Side Of My Brain; Gimme Sopor; Hot Cars; Inside My Brain; You Stupid Asshole; Get Off The Air" **1981** "Steak Knife" (censored) flexi 7 (*Take It* magazine) **1982** *Back From Samoa* (Bad Trip, BT 501) "Steak Knife; Haizman's Brain Is Calling; Tuna Taco; Coffin Case ; You Stupid Jerk ; Ballad Of Jerry Curlan; Not Of This Earth; Gas Chamber; The Todd Killings ; Lights Out; My Old Man's A Fatso; Time Has Come Today; They Saved Hitler's Cock; Homosexual" *Metal Mike Saunders-vocals; guitar• Gregg Turner- vocals; guitar • Todd Homer-bass • P.J. Galligan-guitar • Bill Vockeroth - drums* **1981** *Queer Pills* 7" EP (Homophobic) "Stupid Jerk; Time To Fuck; The Todd Killings; They Saved Hitler's Cock" **1983** on *Annoy Your Neighbor With This Tape* comp cassette (Chainsaw)

ANGST (SF)

1982 "Worker Bee" on *Not So Quiet On The Western Front* comp LP (Alternative Tentacles, VIRUS14) **1983** *Angst* EP (Happy Squid, reissued as SST 064) **1985** *LiteLife* (SST 054) **1986** *Mending Wall* (SST 074) "Some Things (I Can't Get Used To); Standing Here Alone; All Of A Sudden; The Burning Light; 127 Years; I Oblige; Richard Cory; Close The Door; I'd Rather Sleep; You Never; All Day Long; One By One" **1986** "Just Me" on *The Blasting Concept Volume 2* comp LP (SST 043) **1987** *Mystery Spot* (SST 111) "Outside My Window; Back In January; It's Mine; What's The Difference; Looking For A Reason; Colors Of The Day; Mind Average; One Life; Wazze Street; I Remember; Ah, Morning; Red Wing" *Joseph Pope - bass; vocals • Jon E. Risk - guitar; vocals • Michael Hursey - drums*

ANTI (LA)

1981 "Up At Four" on *Life Is Beautiful...* comp LP (New Underground) **1982** "Fight War Not Wars, I Don't Wanna Die" on *Life Is Ugly...* comp LP (New Underground) **1982** *I Don't Want To Die In Your War* (New Underground) "I'm Going Insane; The Cycle; Streets; What Do You Do; Fight War Not Wars; Acid Test; I Don't Want To Die In Your War; New Underground; Pushed Around; I Hate You; Poseur" **1983** "Without Love We Will Die" on *Life Is Boring...* comp LP (New Underground) **1984** *Defy The System* (New Underground) "I Try; Lies; Your Government Calling You; Working In A Factory; Map Of The Star's Home; Your Problems; Fivo Downtown; Nothing New; Club Me Like A Baby Seal; Backfire Bomber; Be Free; Overthrow The Government; Parents of Punks; Repressed Aggression" *Bert- vocals • Gary Kail-guitar • Danny Phillip -bass • Joe McCarthy- drums*

ANTIDOTE (NY)

1983 *Thou Shalt Not Kill* 7" EP (Antidote) "Life As One; Nazi Youth; Real Deal; Foreign Joblot; Zero Mentality; Got Me On The Line; Die At War; Something Must Be Done" *Louie - vocals • Nunz - guitar • Brian - bass • Bliss - drums*

ARMED CITIZENS (NY)

1983 "Thrill Of It All" on *Big City Ain't So Pretty* comp 7" (Big City) **1983** *Make Sense* 7 EP (Big City) "Make Sense; Toxic Waste; On My Own; We Want Money; Power; Not Afraid; The Thrill Of It All; Unconscious" *Chris Colon - vocals • Richie Malice - guitar • Pierre Vudrog - bass • Guz - drums*

ARTICLES OF FAITH (Chicago)

1982 *What We Want Is Free* 7" EP (Version Sound, 1) "Everyday; My Father's Dreams; Bad Attitude; What We Want Is Free" **1982** "Buried Alive" and "False Security" on *The Master Tape* comp LP (Affirmation, AFF - 01) **1982** *Father's Dream* 12" EP (Reflex) **1983** "I've Got Mine" b/w "Wait," "Buy This War" 7" EP (Affirmation/Wasteland) *Vic Bondi - vocals; guitar • J. Scuderi - guitar • D. Shield - bass • Virus X - drums* **1984** *Give Thanks* 7 EP (Reflex) **1985** "Up Against A Wall" on *P.E.A.C.E.* comp LP (R Radical)

ARTIFICIAL PEACE (DC)

1982 "Artificial Peace," "Outside Looking In," "Suburban Wasteland" on *Flex Your Head* comp LP (Dischord, no. 7) **1982** *Exiled* EP (Fountain of Youth) "World Of Hate; Against The Grain; The Future; Think For Yourself; Someone Cares" *Steve Polcari - vocals • Peter Murray - guitar • Rob Moss - bass •Mike Manos - drums*

ARTLESS ENTANGLEMENTS (LA)

1980 "How's The Blood Taste? Pt. 2" on *Cracks In The Sidewalk* comp (New Alliance) **1981** Dildos, Bondage & Toys on *Chunks* comp (New Alliance) **1984** *No Auditions* LP (Nyet, 7471)

ARYAN DISGRACE (LA)

1983 "L.A.P.D." on *Copulation* comp LP (Mystic, MLP33128) **1983** "Faggot In The Family" b/w "Teenage S&M" 7" (Mystic)

AUTHORITIES (Stockton, CA)

1982 *Soundtrack For Trouble* 7" EP (Selectra) "Achtung; I Hate Cops; Radiationmasturbation; Shot in the Head" **1983** "I Hate Cops" on *Copulation* comp LP (Mystic, MLP33128)

THE AUTISTICS (LA)

1982 *Turn Up The Volts* 7" EP (Broken) "What A Way To Go; Turn Up The Volts; Get A Job; Dr. Nick; Fifteen Minutes" *John Lesko - vocals • Craig Watt - guitar • Mark Silva - bass • Donny Rodriguez - drums*

The Wacky Hi-Jinks of.... ADRENALIN O.D.

AUTISTIC BEHAVIOR (NJ)

1983 "T.V. Messiah" and "Powerhead" on *Get Off My Back* comp (Red, PAC- 004)

BAD BRAINS (DC/NY)

1980 "Pay To Cum" b/w "Stay Close To Me" 7" (Bad Brains, BB001) **1980** "Don't Bother Me" on *30 Seconds Over DC* comp (Limp) **1981** "Pay To Cum" on *Let The Eat Jellybeans* comp LP (Alternative Tentacles,VIRUS 4) **1982** "Regulator (Version)," "Big Take Over (Version)" on *New York Thrash* comp CS (ROIR) **1982** *Bad Brains* (ROIR, A106) "Sailin' On; Don't Need It; Attitude; The Regulator; Banned In D.C.; Jah Calling; Supertouch; Shitfit; Leaving Babylon; Fearless Vampire Killers; I; Big Take Over; Pay To Cum; Right Brigade; I Luv I Jah; Intro" **1982** *Bad Brains* 12" EP (Alternative Tentacles, VIRUS 13) "I Love I Jah; I; Sailin' On; Big Take Over" **1982** "How Low Can A Punk Get?" on *Rat Music For Rat People* comp LP (Go! 003) **1982** "I and I Survive; Destroy Babylon EP (Important) Destroy Babylon; Coptic Times; Joshua's Song; I And I Survive" **1983** *Rock For Light* (PVC, 8917) "Coptic Times; Attitude; We Will Not; Sailin' On ; Rally Round Jah Throne; Right Brigade; F.V.K.; Riot Squad; The Meek Shall Inherit The Earth" **1986** *I Against I* (SST 065) "Intro; I Against I; House Of Suffering; Re - Ignition; Secret 77; Let Me Help; She's Calling You; Sacred Love; Hired Gun ; Return To Heaven" **1996** *Black Dots* (1979 demos) (Caroline) "Don't Need It, At The Atlantis, Pay To Cum, Supertouch; Shitfit, Regulator, You're A Migraine. Banned In DC, Why'd You Have To Go?, The Man Won't Annoy Ya, Redbone In The City, Black Dots, How Low Can A Punk Get?, Just Another Damn Song, Attitude, Send You No Flowers" **1997** *Omega Sessions* (1979 demos) (Victory) "I Against I, Stay Close To Me, I Luv I Jah, At The Movies, Attitude" *Paul "H.R." Hudson - vocals • Gary "Dr. Know" Miller - guitar • Darryl Jennifer - bass • Earl Hudson - drums*

BAD POSTURE (SF/NY)

1982 "G.D.M.F.S.O.B." on *Not So Quiet On The Western Front* comp (Alternative Tentacles, VIRUS 14) **1983** *Bad Posture* LP

BAD RELIGION (LA)

1980 *Bad Religion* 7" EP (Epitaph, BREP - 1) "Bad Religion; Politics; Sensory Overload; Slaves; Drastic Action; World War III" *Brett Gurewitz - guitar • Greg Graffin - vocals • Jay Bentley - bass • Jay Ziskrout - drums* **1981** "Bad Religion," "Slaves," "Drastic Action" on *Public Service* comp LP (Smoke Seven) **1982** "Only Gonna Die" on *American Youth Report* comp LP (Invasion) **1982** "In The Night" on *Someone Got Their Head Kicked In!* comp LP (BYO, 001) **1982** *How Could Hell Be Any Worse?* (Epitaph, E - 86407 - 1) "We're Only Gonna Die; Latch Key Kids; Part III; Faith In God; Fuck Armageddon … This Is Hell; Pity; In The Night; Damned To Be Free; White Trash (2nd Generation); American Dream; Eat Your Dog; Voice Of God Is Government; Oligarchy; Doin' Time" *Brett - guitar • Greg Graffin - vocals • Jay Bentley - bass • Pete Fienstone - drums* **1983** "Waiting For The Fire" and "Every Day" on *The Sound Of Hollywood 2* comp LP (Mystic, MLP 33124) **1983** on *Destroy LA* comp LP (Mystic) **1983** *Into The Unknown* (Epitaph) "It's Only Over When; Chasing The Wild Goose; Billy Gnosis; Time and Disregard; The Dichotomy; Million Days; Losing Generation; You Give Up" **1984** *Back To The Known* EP (Epitaph)

BANG GANG (Austin)

1983 "Dickhead" on *Cottage Cheese From The Lips Of Death* comp LP (Ward 9) **1983** *She Ran* 7" EP (Matako Mazun) "Dickhead; Stupid People; 4x the Fun; Charlie Lives In Our Heart" *Mofungo - vocals • Brad Parks - guitar • Frinchie Dick - bass • Birdass Fartner - drums*

BATTALION OF SAINTS (San Diego)

1982 *Fighting Boys* EP (Nutrons) "I'm Gonna Make You Scream; E ; B; Modern Day Heroes; Fighting Boys" *George Anthony - vocals • Chris Smith - guitar • Dennis Frame - bass • Ted Olson - drums* **1982** "Beefmasters," "No More Lies," "Cops Are Out" on *Someone Got Their Head Kicked In!* comp LP (BYO, 001) **1983** "Fighting Boys" on *Live At The Eastern Front 2* comp LP (Enigma, E - 1015) **1983** Sweaty Little Girlson *The Sound Of Hollywood 2* comp LP (Mystic,MLP 33124) **1983** *Second Coming* LP (Mystic) *George Anthony - vocals • Chris Smith - guitar • Barry Farwell - bass • Ted Olsen - drums* **1983** "Second Coming," "Intercourse," "Solitary Is Fun" 7" (Superseven, SS7EP128) **1983** "Sweaty Little Girls," "Right or Wrong," "Modern Day Heroes" 7" (Superseven, SS7EP218)

BEAST OF BEAST

1983 *Sex, Drugs and Noise* EP (My Ass) "Hands Off; She's Wasted; White Boys Don't Lie; Icy Eyes; Destructive Heroes; Without A Right" *Virginia Mac-vocals • Roy Felig -guitar • Brian Rat- bass • Billy Vockeroth - drums*

BEASTIE BOYS (NY)

1982 *Polly Wog Stew* 7" EP (Rat Cage, MOTR21) "Beastie Boys; Transit Cop; Jimi; Holy Snappers; Riot Fight; Ode To… ; Michelle's Farm; Egg Raid On Mojo" *Kate Schellenbach - drums; vocals • Adam Yauch - bass; vocals • Michael Diamond - vocals • John Berry - guitar* **1982** "Riot Fight," "Beastie" on *New York Thrash* comp CS (ROIR) **1983** *Cookie Puss* 12" (Rat Cage, MOTR26) "Cooky Puss; Bonus Batter; Beastie Revolution; Cooky Puss (censored)" *Adam MCA Yauch • Michael Mike D Diamond • Adam Ad Rock Horovitz • Rick Rubin* **1985** *Rock Hard* 12" (Def Jam, DJ002) "Rock Hard; Party's Gettin' Rough; Beastie Groove; Beastie Groove Instrumental" **1985** *MCA and Burzootie* 12" (Def Jam, DJ004) "Drum Machine; Mini Jerk Edit; Psycho Dust Version" **1985** *She's On It* 12" (Def Jam; Columbia, 44 - 05292) "She's On It" b/w "Slow And Low"

BEAVER (DC)

1981 *Beaver* 7" EP (Choice Cuts) "Trendy; Georgetown Sucks; Video Disease; Punch Him In The Head; Limited Nuclear War; Life Is A Joke; Vladamir; Boing; KKK - FM; No Messages" *Tom Cleaver - vocals; guitar • U - Dub - bass • Cy Fi - drums*

BENT NAILS (SF)

1982 "No More Riots" on *Not So Quiet On The Western Front* comp LP (Alternative Tentacles, VIRUS 14)

BIG BOYS (Austin)

1980 *Frat Cars* EP "Frat Cars; Heartbeat; Movies; Mutant Rock" *Randy Biscuit Turner - vocals • Tim Kerr - guitar • Chris Gates - bass • Steve Collier - drums* **1980** *Big Boys; Dicks - Live At Raul's Club* (Rat Race) *Randy Biscuit Turner - vocals • Tim Kerr - guitar • Chris Gates - bass • Greg Murray - drums* **1981** *Where's My Towel* or *Industry Standard* (Wasted Talent) **1982** *Fun, Fun, Fun …* 12" EP (Moment, BB - 001) "Nervous; Apolitical; Hollywood Swinging; Prison; We Got Soul; Fun Fun Fun" *Randy Biscuit Turner - vocals • Tim Kerr - guitar • Chris Gates - bass • Fred Schultz - drums* **1983** "The Big Picture" on *Cottage Cheese From The Lips Of Death* comp LP (Ward 9) **1983** *Lullabies Help The Brain Grow* (Moment/Enigma) *Randy Biscuit Turner - vocals • Tim Kerr - guitar • Chris Gates - bass • Rey Washam - drums* **1984** *No Matter How Long The Line Is At The Cafeteria, There's Always A Seat!* (Enigma)

BLACK HUMOR (SF)

1982 *Love God, Love One Another* (Fowl, 002)

BLACK FLAG (LA)

1978 *Nervous Breakdown* 7" EP (SST 001) "Nervous Breakdown; Fix Me; I've Had It; Wasted" *Keith Morris - vocals • Greg Ginn - guitar • Chuck Dukowski - bass • Brian Migdol - drums* **1980** *Jealous Again* 7" EP (SST 003) "Jealous Again; Revenge; White Minority; No Values; You Bet We've Got Something Personal Against You!" *Chavo Pederast (Ron Reyes) - vocals • Greg Ginn - guitar • Chuck Dukowski - bass • Robo - drums* **1980** "White Minority," "Depression," "Revenge" on *The Decline Of Western Civilization* soundtrack LP (Slash) **1980** "No Values" on *Rodney On The ROQ* comp LP (Posh Boy, PBS - 106) **1980** "Clocked In" on *Cracks In The Sidewalk* comp LP (New Alliance, NAR-001) **1980** on *Chunks* comp LP (New Alliance, NAR - 002) **1980** *Six Pack* 7" EP (SST 005) "Six Pack" b/w "I've Heard It Before," "American Waste" **1981** "Louie Louie" b/w "Damaged I" 7" (Posh Boy, PBS 13) **1981** "Police Story" on *Let Them Eat Jellybeans* comp (Alternative Tentacles) *Dez Cadena - vocals • Greg Ginn - guitar • Chuck Dukowski - bass • Robo - drums* **1981** "Rise Above" on *Rodney On The ROQ Vol. 2* comp LP (Posh Boy, PBS123) **1981** *Damaged* (SST 007; Unicorn 9502) "Rise Above; Spray Paint The Walls; Six Pack; What I See; TV Party; Thirsty & Miserable; Police Story; Gimmie Gimmie Gimmie; Depression; Room 13; Damaged II; No More; Padded Cell; Life Of Pain; Damaged I" *Henry Rollins - vocals • Dez Cadena - guitar; vocals • Greg Ginn - guitar • Chuck Dukowski - bass • Robo - drums* **1982** *TV Party* 7" (SST 012; Unicorn 95006) "TV Party"* b/w "I've Got To Run"**; "My Rules"** *Henry Rollins - vocals • Dez Cadena - guitar • Greg Ginn - guitar • Chuck Dukowski - bass • *Emil - drums • **Bill Stevenson - drums* **1982** Black Flag Interview With Frazier Smith of KLOS (SST Unicorn promo, UNIC - 95007DJ) **1982** "Scream" on *Rat Music For Rat People* (Go!, GO-003) **1983** "Nervous Breakdown," "Jealous Again," "I've Heard It Before" on *The Blasting Concept* (SST 013) **1983** *Everything Went Black* (SST 015) "Gimmie Gimmie Gimmie; I Don't Care; White Minority; No Values; Revenge; Depression; Clocked In; Police Story; Wasted; Gimmie Gimmie Gimmie; Depression; Police Story; Clocked In; My Rules; Jealous Again; Police Story; Damaged I; Louie Louie; No More; Room 13; Depression; Damaged II; Padded Cell; Gimmie Gimmie Gimmie; Crass Commercialism" *Johnny Bob Goldstein, Chavo Pederast, Dez Cadena - vocals • Greg Ginn - guitar • Chuck Dukowski - bass • Robo - drums* **1983** "Police Story" on *Copulation* comp LP (Mystic, MLP33128) **1983** *Unheard Demos* (issued as 7" EP bootleg) "What Can You Believe," "Modern Man," "Slip It In" *Henry Rollins - vocals • Greg Ginn - guitar • Dez Cadena - guitar • Chuck Dukowski - bass • Chuck Biscuits - drums* **1984** "TV Party" on *Repo Man* soundtrack (San Andreas/ MCA - SAR39019) **1984** *The First Four Years* (SST 021) "Nervous Breakdown; Fix Me; I've Had It; Wasted; Jealous Again; Revenge; White Minority; No Values; You Bet We've Got Something Personal Against You!; Clocked In; Six

Pack; I've Heard It Before; American Waste; Machine; Louie Louie; Damaged I" *Keith Morris, Chavo Pederast (Ron Reyes) guitar • Dez Cadena - vocals; guitar • Greg Ginn - guitar • Chuck Dukowski - bass • Brian Migdol, Robo - drums* **1984** *My War* (SST 023) "My War; Can't Decide; Beat My Head Against The Wall; I Love You; The Swinging Man; Forever Time; Nothing Left Inside ; Three Nights; Scream" *Henry Rollins - vocals • Greg Ginn - guitar • Dale Nixon - bass • Bill Stevenson - drums* **1984** *Slip It In* (SST 029) "Slip It In; Black Coffee; Wound Up; Rat's

Eye ; Obliteration; The Bars; My Ghetto; You're Not Evil" *Henry Rollins - vocals • Greg Ginn - guitar • Kira - bass • Bill Stevenson - drums* **1984** *Family Man* (SST 026) "Family Man; Salt On A Slug; Hollywood Diary; Let Your Fingers Do The Walking; Shed Redding (Rattus Norvegitus); No Deposit No Return; Armaggedeon Man; Long Lost Dog Of It; I Won't Stick Any Of You, Unless I Can Stick All Of You" **1984** *Keep It In The Family* 12" EP (SST UK, 12001) "Slip It In; Family Man; I Won't Stick Any Of You, Unless I Can Stick All Of You" **1984** *Live 84* CS (SST 030) "Process Of Weeding Out; My Ghetto; Jealous Again; I Love You; Swinging Man; Three Nights; Nothing Left Inside; Black Coffee" **1985** *Loose Nut* (SST 035) "Loose Nut; Bastard In Love; Annihilate This Week; Best One Yet; Modern Man; This Is Good ; I'm The One; Sinking; Now She's Black" *Henry Rollins - vocals • Greg Ginn - guitar • Kira - bass • Bill Stevenson - drums* **1985** *The Process Of Weeding Out* 12" EP (SST 037) "Your Last Affront; Screw The Law; The Process Of Weeding Out ; Southern Rise" *Greg Ginn - guitar • Kira - bass • Bill Stevenson - drums* **1985** *In My Head* (SST 045) "Paralyzed; Crazy Girl; Black Love; White Hot; In My Head; Drinking And Driving; Retired At 21; Society's Tease; It's All Up To You" **1986** "I Can See You" on *The Blasting Concept Volume II* (SST 043) **1986** *Who's Got The 10 1/2?* (SST 060) "Loose Nut; I'm The One; Bastard In Love; Modern Man; This Is Good; In My Head ; My War; Slip It In; Gimmie Gimmie Gimmie; Drinking And Driving" *Henry Rollins - vocals • Greg Ginn - guitar • Kira - bass • Anthony Martinez - drums* **1986** *Annihilate This Week* 12" (SST 081) "Annihilate This Week; Best One Yet; Sinking" *Henry Rollins - vocals • Greg Ginn - guitar • Kira - bass • Anthony Martinez - drums* **1987** *Wasted ... Again* (SST 166) "Wasted; T.V. Party; Six Pack; I Don't Care; I've Had It; Jealous Again; Slip It In ; Annihilate This Week ; Loose Nut; Gimmie Gimmie Gimmie; Louie Louie; Drinking And Driving" **1989** *I Can See You* EP (SST 226) "I Can See You; Kickin' And Stickin'; Out Of This World; You Let Me Down" **1989** *Annihilation* live '85 bootleg (Alley Kat, AK 063) "I'm The One; Annihilate This Week; Wasted; Bastard In Love; Black Coffee; Modern Man; Forever Time; Slip It In; Gimme Gimme Gimme; Wound Up; This Is Good; In My Head; Sinking; I've Had It; Best One Yet; My War; Drinking And Driving" **1989** *Last Show* live '86 bootleg (Hawk, HAWK065) "Retired At 21; Annihilate This Week; Bastard In Love; Drinking And Driving; Paralyzed; In My Head; White Hot; Black Love; Kickin' And Stickin'; Society's Tease; This Is Good; I Can See You; Nothing Left Inside; Gimme Gimme Gimme; Louie Louie"

BLACK MARKET BABY

(DC)

1981 "Potential Suicide" b/w "Youth Crimes" 7" (Limp) *Boyd Farrell - vocals • Keith Campbell - guitar • Myk Dulfi - bass • Tommy Carr - drums* **1981** "World At War" 7" (Yesterday & Today, Y&T2) **1983** *Senseless Offerings* (Fountain Of Youth, FOY3) "Downward Christian Soldiers; White Boy Funeral; Killing Time; Senseless Offerings; This Year's Prophet; Gunpoint Affection; I See - You See; Joe Nobody; Body Count; Strike First; America's Youth; World At War" *Boyd Farrell - vocals • Scott Logan - guitar • Myk Dulfi - bass • Tommy Carr - drums* **1986** "Drunk & Disorderly" b/w "Just Like All The Others" 7" (Yesterday&Today, Y&T5)

BLADES (LA)

1982 "Had Enough" on *Someone Got Their Head Kicked In!* comp

BLIGHT (Detroit)

1983 *Blight* 7" EP (Touch & Go, T&G10) "The Dream Was Dead, Real World, Be Stupid, Seven Winds Over The Gobi Desert, Prophet Of Doom"

BLOODMOBILE (NC)

1983 track on *Why Are We Here* comp 7" EP (No Core)

BOLLOCKS (Baltimore)

1982 *All Rock Stars Should Be Drafted* 7" EP (Fetal) "Another City; Blow Up The Bayou; R.I.P. Vicious; Never Mind The Bollocks; Peer Pressure; Business Man; Invasion of the Plastics; War on Drugs; All Rock Stars Should Be Drafted; Song For Baltimore" *Bill Stevenson - vocals • Willie Dagher - guitar • Joe Dagher - bass • Azar Dagher - drums • Rick Beath - synth*
1983 *Mediteranean* 7" EP (Fetal) "City Life; Meditteranean; Riot on the Rockers; It's Your Choice, But ; Your Time Is Up; Extended Truth; Inner Beirut Violence; Bo Bo"

BOMB SQUAD (Dallas)

1982 *Tomorrow the World Ends* 7" EP (Bouncing Baby) "Riot, Riot; U.S.P.S.; Warhead; Looking Out For #1" **1984** *Children Of War* EP (Bouncing Betty)

BUTTHOLE SURFERS (San Antonio/ Austin)

1982 ten-song cassette "Dub; Hey; Dub; Dub; B-B-Q Pope; Matchstick; Sinister Crayon; D.O.A.; I Love You Peggy Sue; Untitled; I Fuck Your Wife" **1983** "I Hate My Job" on *Cottage Cheese From The Lips Of Death* comp LP (Ward 9) **1983** *Butthole Surfers* EP (Alternative Tentacles, VIRUS 32) "The Shah Sleeps In Lee Harvey's Grave; Hey; Something; Bar-B-Q Pope; Wichita Cathedral; Suicide; The Revenge Of Anus Presley" **1984** *Live PCPPEP* (Alternative Tentacles, VIRUS 39) "Cowboy Bob; Bar-B-Q Pope; Dance Of The Cobras; The Shah Sleeps In Lee Harvey's Grave; Wichita Cathedral; Hey; Something" **1984** "Butthole Surfers' Theme Song" on *Rat Music For Rat People Vol. 2* comp LP (CD Presents) **1984** "100 Million People Dead" on *P.E.A.C.E.* comp LP (R Radical) **1985** *Psychic... Powerless... Another Man's Sac* (Touch and Go, T&G5) "Concubine; Eye Of The Chicken; Dum Dum; Woly Boly; Negro Observer; Butthole Surfer; Lady Sniff; Cherub; Mexican Caravan; Cowboy Bob; Gary Floyd" **1985** *Cream Corn from the Socket of Davis EP (*Touch and Go, T&G14) "Moving To Florida; Comb; Tornadoes; To Parter" **1986** *Rembrandt Pussyhorse* (Touch and Go, T&GLP#8) Creep In The Cellar; Sea Ferring; American Woman; Waiting For Jimmy"

CANCEROUS GROWTH (Western Mass.)

1985 *Late For The Grave* (Ax/ction)

CANNIBAL (Seattle)

1984 "David" 7" (Cannibal)

CAPITOL PUNISHMENT (Fresno)

1982 "El Salvador" on *Not So Quiet On The Western Front* comp LP (Alternative Tentacles, VIRUS14) ...
1983 *Capitol Punishment* EP (Stage Dive, SD1) "Two-Party System; Wrong Direction; Killer Cop; Jody Is My Bloody Love"

CATCH-22 (LA)

1982 "Stop The Cycle" b/w "Long Way Down" 7" (Posh Boy, PBS-33)

CAUSE FOR ALARM (NY)

1983 *Cause For Alarm* 7" EP "Parasite; Second Chance; Time To Try; United Races; In Search Of; Poison in the Machine; True Colors; Stand As One; Time Will Tell" **1984** "Time Will Tell" on *P.E.A.C.E.* comp LP (R Radical) **1984** *Time Will Tell* 7" EP (R Radical, CT-001) *Keith - vocals • Alex - guitar • Kabula - bass • Rob - drums*

CHANNEL 3 (LA/ OC)

1981 *CH3* 12 EP (Posh Boy, PBS 1018) "Manzanar; I Got A Gun; Waiting; Mannequin" **1981** "Catholic Boy" on *American Youth Report* comp LP (Invasion; Thunderbolt) **1981** "You Lie" on *Rodney On The ROQ Vol. 2* comp LP (Posh Boy) *Mike Magrann - vocals; guitar • Kimm Gardener - guitar; vocals • Larry Kelly - bass • Mike Burton - drums* **1982** *Fear Of Life* (Posh Boy, PBS 128) "Out Of Control; Accident; You Make Me Feel Cheap; Catholic Boy; Wetspots; Fear Of Life; Life Goes On; Manzanar; Strength In Numbers; Double Standard Boys; You Lie; I Wanna Know Why" **1982** *I've Got A Gun* EP (No Future, Oi! 11) "I've Got A Gun," "Manzanar," "Mannequin" **1983** "I'll Take My Chances" b/w "How Come?" 7" (Posh Boy, PBS - 17) **1983** *After the Lights Go Out* (Posh Boy) "What About Me?;Stupid Girl;Seperate Peace; No Love; After The Lights Go Out; Truth And Trust; I'll Take My Chances; All My Dreams; Can't Afford It; I Didn't Know" *Mike Magrann - vocals; guitar • Kimm Gardener - guitar; vocals • Larry Kelly - bass • Jack Debaur - drums* **1984** *Airborne* EP (Enigma) **1985** *Last Time I Drank...* (Enigma) *Mike Magrann - vocals; guitar • Kimm Gardener - guitar; vocals • Larry Kelly - bass • Jack Debaur - drums*

CHILDREN IN ADULT JAILS (NJ) **1985** "Fishing For Compliments," "Dog Day" on *New Jersey's Got It...* comp LP (Buy Our Records, BOR - 003) **1985** *Man Overcome By Waffle Iron* (Buy Our Records, BOR-004) "Fishing For Compiments; Sam Miami; Displacement Blues; Reptiles On Parade; Phere Of Heights; Man Overcome ...; Justice; House O' Weenies; Brick House" *Sue Braun - guitar; vocals • Chris Clark - guitar; vocals • Laurie Es - bass; vocals • Diane Farris - drums; vocals*

CHINA WHITE (LA)

1981 *Dangerzone* (Frontier, FLP - 005) "Dangerzone; Live In Your Eyes; Addiction; Daddy's Little Queen; Anthem; Nightlife" *Mark Martin - vocals • Frank Raffino - guitar • James Rodriguez - bass • Joey Raffino - drums*

CHRONIC DISORDER (CT) **1983** *Chronic Disorder* EP "Blood & Honor; Starting Over; The Final Line; A Job, A Car, A Wife; Untitled" *Spit Respectable - vocals; guitar • Rich - bass • Chuck Division - drums*

CHURCH POLICE (SF)

1982 track on *Valley Fever* comp CS (Iconoclast) **1982** *Church Police* demo CS **1982** "The Oven Is My Friend" on *Not So Quiet On The Western Front* comp (Alternative Tentacles, VIRUS14)

C.I.A. (CT)

1983 *God, Guts, Guns* 7" EP (Schmegma) "Who Cares?; Death; Hazard; Commie Control; Love & War; No Thrills" *Bones - vocals • Mark - guitar • Kenny - guitar • E.J. - bass • Bill (from Reflex From Pain) - drums*

CIRCLE JERKS (LA)

1980 *Group Sex* (Frontier, FLP1002) "Deny Everything; I Just Want Some Skank; Beverly Hills; Operation; Back Against The Wall; Wasted; Behind The Door; World Up My Ass; Paid Vacation; Don't Care; Live Fast Die Young; What's Your Problem; Group Sex; Red Tape" *Keith Morris - vocals • Greg Hetson - guitar • Roger Rogerson - bass • Lucky Lehrer - drums* **1980** "Wild In The Streets" on *Rodney On The ROQ* comp LP (Posh Boy) **1980** "Red Tape, Back Against The Wall, I Just Want Some

Skank, Beverly Hills" on *The Decline…Of Western Civilization* soundtrack LP (Slash) **1981** "Paid Vacation" on *Let Them Eat Jellybeans* comp (Alternative Tentacles, VIRUS 4) **1982** "Live Fast, Die Young" on *Rat Music For Rat People* comp LP (Go!) **1982** *Wild In The Streets* (Faulty Products) "Wild In The Streets; Leave Me Alone; Stars And Stripes; 86'd (Good As Gone); Meet The Press; Trapped; Murder The Disturbed; Letter Bomb; Question Authority; Defamation Innuendo; Moral Majority; Forced Labor; Just Like Me; Put A Little Love In Your Heart" **1983** "Wild In The Streets" on *Posh Hits Volume 1* (Posh Boy) **1983** *Golden Shower Of Hits* (LAX, 1051) "In Your Eyes; Parade Of The Horribles; Under The Gun; When

The Shit Hits The Fan; Bad Words; Red Blanket Room; High Price On Our Heads; Coup d' etat; Product Of My Environment; Rats Of Reality;Junk Mail; Golden Shower Of Hits (Jerks On 45)" **1984** "Coup D'Etat," "When The Shit Hits The Fan" on *Repo Man* soundtrack (San Andreas/MCA, SAR390019) **1985** *Wönderful* (Combat Core, CC 8048) "Wonderful; Firebaugh; Making The Bombs; Mrs. Jones; Dude; American Heavy Metal Weekend: I, I & I: The Crowd; Killing For Jesus; Karma Stew; 15 Minutes; Rock House; Another Broken Heart For Snake" *Keith Morris - vocals • Greg Hetson - guitar • Zander Schloss - bass • Keith Clark - drums* **1985** "American Heavy Metal Weekend" b/w "Wonderful" 12" (Combat Core)

CIRCLE ONE (LA)

1981 "G.I. Combat," "High School Society," "F.O.," "Destroy Exxon" on *Public Service* comp (Smoke 7) **1983** "Hate, Lust, Filth & Greed" on *The Sound Of Hollywood 2* comp LP (Mystic) **1983** *Patterns Of Force* (Upstart) "Social Climbing Leaches; Beware; The Gospel; Survive; Fading; Destroy Exxon; Patterns Of Force; Plastic Life; Rapture; Vietnam Vets; Pride; Our Sword; Unity" *John Macias - vocals • Michael Vallejo - guitar • Danny Dormen - bass • D.J. Hill - drums*

CIVIL DISOBEDIENCE

(LA) **1981** "Too Drunk Last Night," "Campaign Promises," "Confused" on *Who Cares* comp (American Standard)

CLITBOYS (Milwaukee)

1983 *We Don't Play The Game* 7" EP (Feedback) "No Such Thing; Have Faith; Sheep; Gay's Okay; Slogan Boy; So Funny; We Don't Play The Game" *Michael K - vocals; bass • Mike - guitar; vocals • Donny - drums*

COLCOR (NC)

1983 on *No Core* comp CS (No Core)

CODE OF HONOR (SF)

1982 *Fight Or Die* (Subterranean, Sub27) "Code Of Honor; Fight Or Die; Attempted Control; People's Revolution; Death To You; Stolen Faith; Be Fighting Still; New Era; And We Fight" *Johnithin Christ - vocals • Michael Fox - guitar • David Chavez - bass • Sal Paradise - drums* **1982** "What Price Would You Pay?" on *Not So Quiet On The Western Front* comp (Alternative Tentacles) **1983** "This Side; What Are We Gonna Do?; What Price Would You Pay?" 12" EP (Subterranean 36) **1984** *Beware The Savage Jaw* (Subterranean, SUB 43)

CONDEMNED TO DEATH (SF)

1984 "Gartlands Pit" on *P.E.A.C.E.* comp (R Radical) **1984** 7"

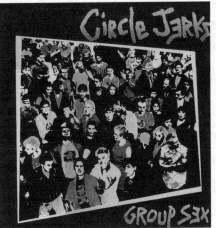

EP (R Radical, C2D) **1984** *Diary Of A Love Monster* (Landmine)

CONSERVATIVES (OC)

1982 "Suburban Bitch," "Just Cuz," "Nervous" on *Hell Comes To Your House* comp (Bemisbrain) **1982** "Confusion," "Nuclear Madness" on *You Can't Argue With Success* comp (Mystic)

CONVICTED (LA)

1983 EP (CVT, RR8301) "Can't Stand Me," "Kidnapped," "Mental Crime," "Sex is Evil" *Baiky - vocals • Rick Verbael - guitar • Brad Jackman - bass • Paul - drums*

CORROSION OF CONFORMITY (NC)

1982 *No Labels/C.O.C.* cassette (No Core) **1983** on *No Core* comp cassette (No Core) **1983** "Poison Planet," "Indifferent," "Too Cool" on *Why Are We Here?* comp 7" EP (No Core) **1983** *Eye For An Eye* (No Core) "Tell Me; Minds Are Controlled; Indifferent; Broken Will; Rabid Dogs; L.S.; Redneckkk; Coexist; Excluded; Dark Thoughts; Poison Planet; What?; Negative Outlook; Positive Outlook; No Drunk; College Town; Not Safe; Eye For An Eye; Nothing's Gonna Change; Green Manalishi" *Eric Eycke - vocals • Woody Weatherman - guitar • Mike Dean - bass; vocals • Reed Mullin - drums* **1985** *Animosity* (Enigma, 72037 - 1) **1985** *Six Songs With Mike Singing* (issued in 1988 on Caroline) " Eye For An Eye; Center Of The World; Citizen; Not For Me; What (?); Negative Outlook" *Mike Dean - bass; vocals • Woody Weatherman - guitar • Reed Mullin - drums*

CRIB DEATH (Philly)

1982 *Spoil Your Party* cassette EP

CRO-MAGS (NY) **1984** *Age Of Quarrel* demo cassette

"Signs Of The Time; Don't Tread On Me; Face The Facts; It's The Limit; Suvival (Of The Streets); Everybody's Gonna Die; World Peace; By Myself; Show You No Mercy; Malfunction; Hard Times; Dub" **1986** *The Age Of Quarrel* (Rock Hotel/Profile) "We Gotta Know; World Peace; Show You No Mercy; Malfunction; Street Justice; Survival Of The Streets; Seekers Of The Truth; It's The Limit; Hard Times; By Myself; Don't Tread On Me; Face The Facts; Do Unto Others; Life Of My Own; Signs Of The Times" *John Joseph - vocals • Harley Flanagan - bass • Doug Holland - guitar • Parris Mitchel Mayhew - guitar • Mackie - drums*

CRUCIAL TRUTH

(Florida/NY) **1982** *Darkened Days* 7" EP "Darkened Days; Agent Orange; Male Domination; In The Night" *Gary Mitchell - vocal • Mario Sorrentino - guitar • Derek Graham - bass • Mike Marer - drums*

CRUCIFIX (SF)

1981 *Ron - 2* EP (Universal) "Capitulation; You're Too Old; Religion Kills; Permanently Damaged; Brazen Hell" *Sothira - vocals • Matt - guitar • Bryce - bass • Chris - drums* **1982** "Annihilation" on *Not So Quiet On The Western Front* comp LP (Alternative Tentacles) **1982** "Steel Case Enclosure" on *Rat Music For Rat People* comp LP (Go!) **1983** *Nineteen Eighty-Four* 7" EP (Freak, E-1) "Steel Case Enclosure; Rise and Fall; Prejudice *Sothira - vocals • James - guitar • Matt - bass • Chris - drums* **1984** *Dehumanization* (Corpus Christi)

CRUCIFUCKS (Lansing, MI)
1985 *The Crucifucks* (Alternative Tentacles)
1986 *Wisconsin* (Alternative Tentacles)

CULTURCIDE (Houston)
1983 *Year One* cassette (CIA 007)
1986 *Tacky Souvenirs Of Pre - Revolutionary America* "Star -
Spangled Banner; Bruce; E&I; Michael; Let's Prance; Love Is A
Cattle - Prod; The Heart Of R'N'R (Is The Profit); They Aren't
The World; Houston Lawman; Act Like The Rich; Fake Dancing;
Industrial Band; California Punks;
Color My World With Pigs"

CYANAMID (NJ)
1985 "N.J. Is A Mall,' "Suppor"t on
New Jersey's Got It... comp (Buy
Our Records, BOR12 - 003)
1986 *Stop The World* 7" EP

DA (Chicago)
1981 "Fish Shit," "The Killer" on
Busted At Oz comp (Autumn, AU-2)

DEAD HIPPIE (LA)
1983 *Living Dead* (Pulse)

DEADLINE (DC)
1982 "Stolen Youth," "Hear The Cry,"
"Aftermath" on *Flex Your Head* comp
LP (Dischord, no. 7)

DEADLY REIGN (SF)
1982 "System Sucks" on *Not So
Quiet On The Western Front* comp LP (Alternative Tentacles,
VIRUS14)

DEAD KENNEDYS (SF)
1979 "California Uber Alles" b/w "Man With The Dogs" 7"
(Optional Music) **1980** "Police Truck," "Short Songs," "Straight
A's" on *Can You Hear Me? Live From The Deaf Club* comp LP
(Walking Dead) **1980** "Holiday In Cambodia" b/w "Police
Truck'" 7" (Optional) **1980** "Kill The Poor" b/w "In-Sight" 7"
(Cherry Red) **1980** *Fresh Fruit For Rotting Vegetables* (IRS,
9016) "Kill The Poor; Forward To Death; When Ya Get Drafted;
Let's Lynch The Landlord; Drug Me; Your Emotions; Chemical
Warfare; California Uber Alles; I Kill Children; Stealing Peoples'
Mail; Funland at the Beach; Ill In The Head; Holiday In Cambodia;
Viva Las Vegas" *Jello Biafra - vocals • East Bay Ray - guitar •
Klaus Flouride - bass • Ted - drums* **1981** "Too Drunk To Fuck"
b/w "The Prey" 7" (Cherry Red, UK) **1981** "Nazi Punks Fuck
Off" on *Let Them Eat Jellybeans* comp LP (Alternative Tentacles,
VIRUS 4) **1981** *In God We Trust, Inc.* (Alternative Tentacles/
Faulty Products, VIRUS 5) "Religious Vomit; Moral Majority;
Hyperactive Child; Kepone Factory; Dog Bite; Nazi Punks Fuck
Off; We've Got A Bigger Problem Now; Rawhide" *Jello Biafra -
vocals • East Bay Ray - guitar • Klaus Flouride - bass • D.H.
Peligro - drums* **1982** "A Child And His Lawnmower" on *Not So
Quiet On The Western Front* comp LP (Alternative Tentacles,
VIRUS14) **1982** "Bleed For Me" b/w "Life Sentence" 7"
(Alternative Tentacles, VIRUS 23) **1982** *Plastic Surgery
Disasters* (Alternative Tentacles, VIRUS 27) "Government Flu;
Terminal Preppie; Trust Your Mechanic; Well Paid Scientist;
Buzzbomb; Forest Fire; Halloween; Winnebago Warrior; Riot;
Bleed For Me; I Am The Owl; Dead End; Moon Over Marin
1982 "Halloween" b/w "Saturday Night Holocaust" 7"
(Alternative Tentacles,VIRUS 28) **1982** "Nazi Punks Fuck Off"
b/w "Moral Majority" 7" (Subterranean SUB 24, VIRUS 6) **1985**
Frankenchrist (Alternative Tentacles) **1986** *Bedtime For
Democracy* (Alternative Tentacles, VIRUS50) "Take This Job And
Shove It; Hop With The Jet Set; Dear Abby; Rambozo The Clown;
Fleshdunce; The Great Wall; Shrink; Triumph Of The Swill;
Macho Insecurity; I Spy; Cesspools In Eden; One - Way Ticket To
Pluto; Do The Slag; A Commercial; Gone With My Wind;
Anarchy For Sale; Chickenshit Conformist; Where Do Ya Draw
The Line; Potshot Heard Round The World; D.M.S.O.; Lie

Detector" **1987** *Give Me Convenience Or Give Me Death*
(Alternative Tentacles) w/ "Night Of The Living Rednecks" flexi

DEAD VIRGINS (NY)
1983 7" EP (Rat Woman) "Rape Capitol Hill; No Cause For
Concern; WW III; Emotional Strain" *Patrick - The Voice •
Michael - The Guitar • Stephen - The Bass • Peter - The Drums*

DECADENCE (Boston)
1981 "Slam" on *This Is Boston Not LA* comp (Modern Method)

DECRY (LA)
1983 *Falling*
1984 *Japanese*

DEEP WOUND (West. Mass)
1983 *Deep Wound* 7" EP (Radiobeat)
"I Saw It; Sisters In My Room; Don't
Need; Lou's Anxiety Song; Video
Prick; Sick Of Fun; Deep Wound;
Dead Babies" *Nakajima- vocals • Lou
Barlow -guitar • Scott Helland-bass •
J Mascis- drums* **1984** "You're False,"
"Time To Stand" on *Bands That
Would Be God* comp

DEGENERATES (Houston)
1982 *Fallout* EP (Hit & Run)

DEMENTED YOUTH
(SF) **1982** "Assasination Attempt" on
Not So Quiet On The Western Front
comp (Alternative Tentacles, VIRUS14)

DERANGED DICTION (Montana/ Seattle)
1983 *No Art No Cowboys No Rules* 18-song EP

DESCENDENTS (LA)
1980 "Ride The Wild" b/w "It's A Hectic World" 7" (Orca, I-
1056) **1981** "I'm Not A Loser" on *American Youth Report* comp
LP (Invasion) **1981** *Fat* EP (New Alliance) "I Like Food; Hey
Hey; Mr. Bass; Weinerschnitzel; My Dad Sucks" *Milo - vocals •
Frank Navetta - guitar • Tony Lombardo - bass • Bill Stevenson -
drums* **1982** *Milo Goes To College* (New Alliance) "My Age; I
Wanna Be A Bear; I'm Not A Loser; Parents; Tonyage; M16; I'm
Not A Punk; Catalina's Suburban Home; Statue Of Liberty;
Kabuki Girl; Marriage; Hope; Bikeage; Sean Is Dead"
1985 *I Don't Want To Grow Up* (New Alliance) **1985** *Bonus Fat*
12" EP (New Alliance) **1986** *Enjoy!* (New Alliance/Restless)

DETENTION (NJ)
1983 "Dead Rock & Rollers" b/w "El Salvador" (Vintage Vinyl)
*Rodney Matejik - guitar • Paul Shields - bass • Kevin Shields -
bass • Daniel Shields - drums*

D.I. (LA/OC)
1981 *Team Goon* (Reject) **1983** "Richard Hung Himself" on
Suburbia soundtrack LP **1983** *D.I.* EP (Revenge) "Richard Hung
Himself; Guns; Venus De Milo; Reagan Der Fuhrer; Purgatory"
*Casey Royer - voice • Tim Maag - guitar • Frederick Taccone -
bass • Derek O' Brien - drums* **1984** *Ancient Artifacts*(Reject)
1985 *Horse Bites Dog Cries* (Reject)

DICKS (Austin/SF)
1980 "Dicks Hate The Police" 7" (Radical)
1980 *Dicks/Big Boys - Recorded Live at Raul's Club* (Rat Race)
1983 *Kill From The Heart* (SST 017) "Anti - Klan (Part One);
Rich Daddy; No Nazi's Friend; Marilyn Buck; Kill From The
Heart; Little Boys' Feet; Pigs Run Wild; Bourgeois Fascist Pig;
Anti - Klan (Part Two); Purple Haze; Right Wing; White Ring;
Dicks Can't Swim: I. Cock Jam, II. Razor Blade Dance"
*Gary - vocals • Glen - guitar • Buxf - bass; vocals • Pat - drums;
vocals* **1983** "Gilbeau'" on *Cottage Cheese From The Lips Of
Death* comp LP (Ward 9) **1984** "Hope You Get Drafted" on
P.E.A.C.E. comp LP (R Radical) **1984** "Legacy" on *Rat Music
For Rat People Vol. II* comp LP (CD Presents) **1985** *These
People* (Alternative Tentacles)

DIE KREUZEN
(Milwaukee) **1982** *Sick People* CS
1982 *Cows and Beer* 7" EP (Version
Sound) "In School; Think For Me;
Hate Me; Pain; Don't Say Please;
Enemies" **1984** *Die Kreuzen*
(Touch and Go) **1986** *October File*
(Touch and Go, T&GLP#7) Cool
Breeze; Uncontrolled Passion;
Conditioned; Its Been So Long;
Imagine A Light; Man In The Trees;
There's A Place; Red To Green;
Hide And Seek; Counting Cracks;
Hear And Feel; Among The Ruins;
Open Lines; Melt *Dan Kubinski -
vocals• Brian Egeness-guitar • Keith
Brammer-bass • Eric Tunison-drums*

DISABILITY (LA)
1981 "Battling Against The Police,"
"White As A Ghost," "Rejection" on *Public Service* comp LP
(Smoke 7)

D.O.A. (Vancouver)
1978 *Disco Sucks* 7" EP (Sudden Death) "Royal Police; Woke Up
Screaming; Nazi Training Camp; Disco Sucks" *Joey Shithead -
guitar; vocals • Randy Rampage - bass • Chuck Biscuits - drums*
1979 "Prisoner b/w 13 7 (Sudden Death) **1979** "Kill Kill This Is
Pop" on *Vancouver Complication* comp LP **1979** "World War 3"
b/w "Whatcha Gonna Do?" 7" (Sudden Death) **1979** *Triumph Of
The Ignoroids* live EP (Friends) **1980** *Something Better Change*
(Friends) "New Age; The Enemy; 2+2; Get Out Of My Life; Woke
Up Screaming; Last Night; Thirteen; Great White Hope; The
Prisoner; Rich Bitch; Take A Chance; Whatcha Gonna Do?; World
War 3; New Wave Sucks" *Joey Shithead - guitar; vocals • Dave
Gregg - guitar • Randy Rampage - bass • Chuck Biscuits - drums*
1981 *Hardcore 81* (Friends) **1981** "The Prisoner" on *Let Them
Eat Jellybeans* comp (Alternative
Tentacles) **1981** *Positively D.O.A.*
EP (Alternative Tentacles) "Fucked
Up Ronnie; World War Three; The
Enemy; My Old Man's A Bum; New
Wave Sucks" *Joey Shithead - guitar;
vocals • Dave Gregg - guitar • Randy
Rampage - bass • Chuck Biscuits -
drums* **1982** *War On 45* 12" EP
(Alternative Tentacles, VIRUS 24)
"Liar For Hire; I'm Right, You're
Wrong; America The Beautiful; Let's
Fuck; War; I Hate You; War In The
East; Class War" *Joey Shithead - gui-
tar; vocals • Dave Gregg - guitar;
vocals • Wimpy Roy - bass; vocal •
Dimwit - drums; vocals* **1982**
"America The Beautiful" on *Rat
Music For Rat People* comp LP (Go!)
1982 "Unknown" on *Live At The
Eastern Front* comp (ICI/Sandblast)
1982 *Right To Be Wild* 7" (CD Presents) "Burn It Down" b/w
"Fuck You" *Joey Shithead - guitar; vocals • Dave Gregg - guitar •
Brian Goble - bass • Dimwit - drums* **1984** *Bloodied But
Unbowed* (CD Presents) "New Age; The Prisoner; Unknown;
Smash The State; Rich Bitch; Slumlord; Fuck You; I Don't Give A
Shit; Waiting For You; Whatcha Gonna Do?; World War 3 ; 2+2 ;
The Enemy; Fucked Up Ronnie; Woke Up Screaming; 001 Loser's
Club; 13 ; Get Out Of My Life; D.O.A." **1984** "America The
Beautiful" on *P.E.A.C.E.* comp (R Radical) **1984** "Tits On The
Beach" on *Something To Believe In* comp LP (BYO, 004) **1985**
Don't Turn Yer Back 7" EP (on Desperate Times) (Alternative
Tentacles) "General Strike; Race Riot ; A Season In Hell; Burn It
Down" *Joey Shithead Keighley - guitar; vocals • Dave Gregg -
guitar • Brian Sunny Boy Roy Goble - bass; vocals • Greg James -
drums* **1985** *Let's Wreck The Party* (Alternative Tentacles)

DOMINO THEORY (SF)
1982 "Scare" on *Not So Quiet On The
Western Front* comp LP (Alternative
Tentacles, VIRUS14)

DOOMSDAY MASSACRE
(Houston) **1983** *Wake Up Or Melt
Down* 7" EP (CIA, 0111) "R -U-Ready;
Attack; Pissed; Annihilation; Last Day"
*Sklunch - vocals • John A - vocals •
General Electric - guitar • J.R. - bass •
Sam - drums*

DOUBLE CROSS (Sonoma,
CA) **1982** *Here To Stay* cassette EP

DOUBLE-O (DC)
1983 *Double-O* 7" EP (Dischord/ R&B)
"You've Lost; Is It Better; Grey To
Black; Death Of A Friend; There's No
Reasoning" *Eric L -vocals • Jason
Carmer-guitar •Bert Queiroz-bass • Rich Moore-drums*

D.R.I. (Houston/SF)
1983 "Runnin Around" on *Cottage Cheese From The Lips Of
Death* comp LP (Ward 9) **1983** *Dirty Rotten* 7" EP (Dirty Rotten)
"Sad To Be; War Crimes; Busted; Draft Me; F.R.D.C.; Capitalist
Suck; Misery Loves Company; No Sense; 'Blockhead; I Don't
Need Society; Commuter Man; Plastique; Why; Balance Of
Terror; My Fate To Hate; Who Am I; Money Stinks; Human
Waste; Yes, Ma'am; Dennis's Problem; Closet Punk;
Reaganomics" *Kurt - vocals • Spike - guitar • Dennis - bass •
Eric - drums* **1983** *Dirty Rotten* LP (R Radical) (same record as a
12") **1984** *Violent Pacification* 7" EP (R Radical)"Violent
Pacification; Couch Slouch; Running Around; To Open Closed
Doors" **1985** "Snap" on *P.E.A.C.E.* comp LP (R Radical) **1985**
"Yes Mamma," "Soup Kitchen" on *Live At The Western Front 2*
comp LP (Restless) **1985** *Dealing With It!* (Death/Metal
Blade/Enigma) **1986** *Crossover* (Metal Blade/Enigma)

THE DULL (LA)
1983 "She's A Nuclear Bomb" b/w
"Reach Out and Grab" 7" (Budget
Ranch, BRR-002)

D.Y.S. (Boston)
1983 *Brotherhood* (X-Claim!, #4)
"Open Up; More Than Fashion; Circle
Storm; City To City; Girl's Got Limits;
Brotherhood; Yellow; Stand Proud;
Insurance Risk; Escape" *Dave Smalley
- vocals • Andy Strahan - guitar •
Jonathan Anastas - bass • Dave Collins
- drums* **1986** *D.Y.S.* (Modern
Method) "Late Night; Echoes; The
Loner; Closer Still; Which Side Am I;
No Pain, No Gain; Held Back; Graffitti;
Wolfpack" *Dave Smalley - vocals •
Andrew Strahan - guitar • Jonathan
Anastas - bass • Ross Luongo - drums*

EFFIGIES (Chicago)
1981 "Quota," "Guns Or Ballots" on *Busted At Oz* comp(Autumn)
1981 *Haunted Town* EP (Autumn) "Below The Drop; Strongbox;
Haunted Town; Mob Clash; We'll Be Here Tomorrow" *John
Kezdy - vocals • Earl Oil Letiecq - guitar • Paul Zamost - bass •
Steve Economou - drums*
1981 "Security" b/w "Bodybag" 7" (Ruthless) **1983** *We're Da
Machine* (Ruthless; Enigma, E1003) "We're Da Machine; Quota;
Technos Gone" **1984** "Security" remix on *WNUR Middle Of
America* comp LP (H.I.D.) **1984** *The Effigies* EP (Ruthless/
Enigma) **1984** *For Ever Grounded* (Enigma, E1056) "Smile; A
Tight and Blue Cut; Silent Burn; Patternless; What's The Beat;
Infiltrator; Hand Signs; Rather See None; Coarse In Vein; Mob
Clash; Something That…" **1985** "Blue Funk" on *Enigma
Variations* comp (Enigma) **1985** *Fly on a Wire* (Fever/Enigma)

"Forever, I Know; Fly On A Wire; West; Machine Brent;
Pushin'Pullin'; No Love Lost; Blue Funk; Bright Ice; All Told;
The Eights; Here's To It" *John Kezdy - vocals • Robert O'Connor
- guitar • Paul Zamost - bass • Steve Economou - drums*
1986 *Ink* (Fever/Restless) "Cheater; The Sound That Moves; I,
Fugitive; The Flock; Yes!; Riddle Hit; In From The Cold;With
Open Eyes;The River"

EJECTORS (Dallas)

1982 "Hydro-Head" b/w "Little Johnny" 7 (VVV)   **1983** "Fade
With The Summer" on *VVV - Live At
The Hot Club* comp (VVV, 06)

EMPTY RITUALS (Mass.)

1983 "Dressed To Kill" b/w "Hardcore"
(Metal Assault) *David Singer - vocals
• Eric Melcher - guitar • Monte
Levinson - bass • Grant Smith - drums
• Steven Rybicki - keyboards*

THE END

1983 "Holocaust Hop" b/w
"Communist," "California" (Black
Market) *Debbie Jurek - guitar; vocals
• Rick Muelder - bass • Luis Baro -
drums; vocals*

END RESULT (Chicago)

1983 "Slash" on *The Master Tape
Volume II* comp (Affirmation, Aff-02)
1983 *End Result* demo CS

MR. EPP AND THE
CALCULATIONS (Seattle)   **1983** *Of Course I'm
Happy, Why?* (Pravda)

EVEN WORSE (NY)

1982 "Illusion Won Again," "Emptying The Madhouse" on *New
York Thrash* comp CS (ROIR) *Rebecca Korbet - vocals • Bobby
Weeks - guitar • Eric Keil - bass • Jack Rabid - drums*
1982 "Mouse Or Rat" b/w "1984" (Worse Than You, Worst- 0001)
*Ken Tantrum - vocals • Steve Waxman - guitar • Thurston Moore -
guitar • Tim Sommer - bass • Jack Rabid - drums* **1982** "Contaminated
Waste," "We Suck" on *You Can't Argue With Suckcess* comp
(Mystic)   **1983** "Leaving" b/w "One Night Stand" (Autonomy)
*Ken Templeson - vocals • Thurston Moore - guitar • Tim Sommer-
bass • Jack Rabid- drums*

F (Florida)

1983 *You Are An EP* 12" EP

THE FACTION (SF)

1983 *Yesterday Is Gone* 7" EP (IM)
"Room 101; Eternal Plan; Black
Balled; Yesterday Is Gone; Bullets
Are Faster" *Gavin O'Brien - vocals
•Adam Segal-guitar • Steve Caballero
- bass • Keith Rendon - drums*
1984 *No Hidden Messages* (IM)
1985 *Dark Room* 12" EP (IM)
1985 *Epitaph* 12" EP (IM)

THE FAITH (DC)

1982 *Faith/Void* split LP (Dischord,
No.8) "It's Time; Face To Face; Trapped;
In Control; Another Victim; What's
Wrong With Me?; What You Think;
Confusion; You're X'd; Nightmare;
Don't Tell Me; In The Black"
1983 *Subject To Change* (Dischord, No. 11) "Aware; Say No
More; Limitations; No Choice; Untitled; Subject To Change; More
Of The Same; Slowdown" *Alec MacKaye - vocals • Mike
Hampton - guitar • Eddie Janney - guitar • Chris Bald - bass •
Ivor Hansen - drums*

FALSE PROPHETS (NY)

1981 "Overkill" b/w "Royal Slime," "Blind Obedience"

*Stephan Ielpi - vocals • Peter Campbell - guitar • Steve Wishnia -
bass • Matty Superty - drums* **1982** "Taxidermist," "Scorched
Earth" on *New York Thrash* comp CS (ROIR)   **1982** "Good
Clean Fun," "The Functional Song" 7" (Worn Out Brothers)
1986 *False Prophets* (Alternative Tentacles)

FANG (SF)

1982 "Fun With Acid" on *Not So Quiet On The Western Front*
comp (Alternative Tentacles,VIRUS14)   **1983** *Landshark* 12" EP
(Boner) "The Money Will Roll Right In; Land Shark; Law &
Order; Diary Of A Mad Werrwoulf;
Destroy The Handicapped; Drunk &
Crazy; An Invitation; Skinheads
Smoke Dope" *Slammie - vocals • Tom
- guitar • Chris - bass • Joel - drums*
1984 *Where The Wild Things Are*
(Boner) "I Got The Disease; Suck &
Fuck; With Friends Like You; G.I Sex;
Road Kills; You're Cracked; I Wanna
Be On TV; Everybody Makes Me
Barph; Junky Dare; Berkeley Heathen
Scum" *Sammytown - vocals • Tom
Flynn - guitar • Chris - bass • Tom
Stiletto - drums* **1985** track on *Them
Boners Be Poppin'* comp (Boner)
1985 "Send Me To Hell C.O.D." on
Rat Music For Rat People II comp
LP (CD Presents)

THE FARTZ (Seattle)

1981 *Because This Fuckin' World
Stinks* 7" EP (Fartz) "How Long; No Wordz; Campaign Speech;
Waste No Time; Congame; Idiot's Rule; War; F.A.L.F." *Blaine -
vocals • Tom - guitar • Steve - bass • Loud - drums* **1982** *World
Full Of Hate* EP (Alternative Tentacles, VIRUS 17) "People
United; Heros, When Will It End; Rights; Don't Want No Gun;
Questions & Answers; Viet-vet; Battle Hymn Of Ronnie Reagan;
World Full Of Hate; Bible Stories; What's Wrong?; Happy
Apathy; Know-It-Alls; Freight Train; Take A Stand; Children Of
The Grave" *Blaine Cook - vocals • Paul Solger - guitar • Steve
Fart - bass • Duff McKagan— drums* **1983** "Buried Alive" on *Live
At The Western Front 2* comp (Enigma)

FEAR (LA)

1978 "I Love Livin In The City" b/w "Now You're Dead" 7"
(Criminal)   **1980** "I Don't Care
About You," "I Love Livin In The
City," "Fear Anthem" on *The
Decline…Of Western Civilization*
soundtrack LP (Slash)   **1982** *The
Record* (Slash) "Let's Have A War;
Beef Boloney; Camarillo; I Don't
Care About You; New York's Alright
If You Like Saxophones; Gimme
Some Action; Foreign Policy; We
Destroy The Family; I Love Livin' In
The City; Disconnected; We Got To
Get Out Of This Place; Fresh Flesh;
Getting The Brush; No More Nothing"
*Lee Ving - vocals/guitar • Philo
Cramer - guitar/vocals • Derf Scratch -
bass/sax • Spit Stix - drums*   **1982**
"Fuck Christmas" b/w "Beep
Christmas" 7" (Slash) **1985** *More Beer*
LP (Restless) **1986** "Hank Williams
Was Queer" b/w "Fear Anthem"

FEEDERZ (Phoenix/ SF)

1980 "Jesus," "Stop You're Killing Me" b/w "Avon Lady,"
"Terrorist" 7" (Anxiety)   **1981** "Jesus Entering Through The
Rear" on *Let Them Eat Jellybeans* comp (Alternative Tentacles,
VIRUS 4)   **1984** *Ever Feel Like Killing Your Boss?* (Flaming
Banker)   **1985** *Teachers In Space* (Flaming Banker)

FIENDZ (NY)
1982 "Cry Now," "Asian White" on *New York Thrash* comp (ROIR)

FIFTH COLUMN (SF)
1982 "Don't Conform" on *Not So Quiet On The Western Front* comp LP (Alternative Tentacles, VIRUS14)

THE FIX (Detroit)
1981 "Vengeance" b/w "In This Town" 7" (Touch & Go, T&G2) **1981** "No Idols" on *Process Of Elimination* comp 7" EP (Touch & Go, T&G2) **1982** *Jan's Room* 7" EP (Touch & Go, T&G5) "Cos the Elite; Truth Right Now; Signal; Off To War"

FLAG OF DEMOCRACY (Philly) **1983** "Murder Castle," "Suburban Cowboy" on *Get Off My Back* comp (Red, 004) **1986** *Shatter Your Day* (Buy Our Records- 009)

FLIPPER (SF)
1980 "Love Canal" b/w "Ha Ha Ha" 7" (Subterranean/Thermidor) **1981** "Ha Ha Ha" on *Let Them Eat Jellybeans* comp LP (Alternative Tentacles) **1981** "Sex Bomb" b/w "Brainwash" 7" (Subterranean) **1982** *Album - Generic Flipper* (Subterranean) Ever; Life Is Cheap; Shed No Tears; I Saw You Shine; Way of the World; *vocals/bass • Ted Falconi - guitar • Steve DePace - drums* **1982** "Get Away" b/w "The Old Lady That Swallowed The Fly" (Subterranean, SUB 35) **1982** "Ever" on *Live At The Eastern Front* (ICI/Sandblast) **1982** "Sacrifice" on *Not So Quiet On The Western Front* comp (Alternative Tentacles) **1984** *Blow'n Chunks* CS (ROIR) **1984** *Gone Fishin'* (Subterranean) "The Light, The Sound; First The Heart; In Life My Friends; Survivors Of the Plague; Sacrifice; Talk's Cheap; You Nought Me; One By One" **1986** *Public Flipper Limited* (Subterranean)

FRANTIX (Denver)
1982 "Face Reality," "Cat Mouse," "Sharin Sharon," "New Questions" 7" EP (Local Anesthetic) **1983** "My Dad's A Fucking Alcoholic; Car; You're Ill; My Dad's Dead" 7" EP (Local Anesthetic) *Ronnie Jr. - vocals • Ricky - guitar • M.M.A.A.T.T. - bass • Barstow - drums*

FREE BEER (SF)
1982 "Premature Enlistment" on *Not So Quiet On The Western Front* comp (Alternatve Tentacles)

THE FREEZE (Boston)
1980 "Don't Forget Me Tommy" b/w "I Hate Tourists" 7" (Rebel 809 - 24) *Clif Hanger - vocals • Rob DeCradle - guitar • Papa Verje - lead guitar • Rick Andrews - bass • Kevin - drums • Scotter Woodless - synth* **1981** "Broken Bones, Idiots At Happy Hour, Now Or Never, Boston Not LA" on *This Is Boston Not LA* (Modern Method) **1982** "Refrigerator Heaven" on *Unsafe At Any Speed* comp (Modern Method) **1982** *Guilty Face* 7" EP (Modern Method) "Violent Arrest (1:36); Voices From My Window (1:32); Halloween Night; Guilty Face (also on 10" w/ "American Town; Broken Bones; Trouble If You Hide" (Ax/ction, ACT 12) *Clif Hanger - vocals • Bill Close - guitar • Rick Andrews - bass • Lou Cataldo - drums* **1983** *Land Of The Lost* (Modern Method) "American Town; Gardener and the Maid; No Exposure; Food Lava; Days of Desperation; Go Team Go; Nazi Fun; Won't Come Back Alive; Duh Family; So Long Ago; The Megawaki Cult; Sickly Sweet; Pig Hunt **1985** *Rabid Reaction* (Modern Method)

FRIGHTWIG (SF)
1984 *Cat Farm Faboo* (Subterranean) **1986** *Faster, Frightwig, Kill! Kill!* (Caroline) "Beverly; Crazy World; Big Bang; Punk Rock Jailbait; Manifest Destiny; The Prize; American XPress; I Am Here Alone; Freedom *Deanna Ashley - bass, vocals •*

Rebecca Tucker - guitar, vocals • Susan Miller - guitar, vocals • Cecilia Koon - drums, vocals

FUCK-UPS (SF)
1982 *FU 82* (Fowl) "White Boy; I Think You're Shit; Negative Reaction; I Hate You; Once I Had A Brother; Get Out" *Bob Noxious - vocals • Joe Dirt - guitar • Sean Tuchy - bass • Craig - drums*

FUNERAL (LA)
1981 12" EP (Azra) "Ant Trap; Will To Live; Outer Edge; Darkness On Your Doorstep; Bloody Hands" *Mike Martt - vocals; guitar • Matt Dorsett - guitar • John Neff - bass • D. Thum- drums*

THE FU'S (Boston)
1981 "Preschool Dropout," "Radio UNIX USA," "Green Beret," "Time Is Money" on *This Is Boston Not LA* comp LP (Modern Method, MM012) **1982** "CETA Suckers" on *Unsafe At Any Speed* comp 7" (Modern Method, MM014) **1982** *Kill For Christ* 12" EP (XClaim!, #2) "Civil Defense; Me Generation; Daisy Chain; Peer Police; Rock and Roll Mutha; T Sox; T.N.H.; Die For God; F.U." **1983** *My America* (XClaim!, #5) "What You Pay For; Outcast; Poor, Poor, Pitiful You; The Grinder; Unite Or Lose; This Is Your Life; My America; Choir Boy; Boston's Finest; Rifle" *John Sox - vocals • Steve Grimes - guitar • Wayne Maestri - bass • Bob Furapples - drums* **1984** *Do We Really Want To Hurt You?* (Enigma, E - 1109)

GANG GREEN (Boston)
1981 "Snob," "Lie Lie," "I Don't Care," "Rabies," "Narrow Mind," "Kill A Commie," "Have Fun" on *This Is Boston Not LA* comp LP (Modern Method, MM012) **1982** "Selfish" on *Unsafe At Any Speed* comp (Modern Method, MM014) **1983** "Sold Out" b/w "Terrorize," "Taang Dub" 7" (Taang!, T-1) *Chris Doherty - guitar; vocals • Bill Manley - bass • Mike Dean - drums* **1985** "Alcohol" b/w "Skate To Hell" 7" (Taang!, T-6)*Chris Doherty - guitar; vocals • Chuck Stilphen - guitar • Glen Stilphen-bass • Walter Gustafson - drums* **1986** *Drunk and Disorderly, Boston MA* (Deluxe)10" EP **1986** *Another Wasted Night* (Taang!, T-13) "19th Hole; Alcohol; Another Wasted Night; Voices Carry; Protect And Serve; Eight Ball; Evil; Last Chance; Fuck In A; Tonight We Rock; Have Fun; Hate; Skate To Hell"

GENOCIDE (NJ)
1982 *Last Rites For Genocide And M.I.A.* split LP (Smoke 7) "Teenage Girls; Manson Youth; Bad Name; Peggy's Got A Problem; Gonna Fight; Overthrow The Government; GTO; Syphillis Strain #5; Period; And; Endless Party"

GEZA X (LA)
1979 "Rx Rock & Roll" b/w "Pony Ride" (Final Gear) **1981** "Isotope Soap" on *Let Them Eat Jellybeans* comp (Alternative Tentacles, VIRUS X) **1981** "We Need More Power" on *Rodney On The ROQ Vol. 2* comp (Posh Boy) **1981** *You Goddam Kids* (Final Gear, YGK A - B) Rio Grande Hotel; Hungarian; We Need More Power; Isotope Soap; Paranoids;Pony Ride;Funky Monsters; Practicing Mice; I Hate Punks; Mean Mr. Mommy Man"

GHOST DANCE (SF)
1982 "Shrunken Heads" on *Not So Quiet On The Western Front* comp LP (Alternative Tentacles, VIRUS14)

GODHEAD (LA)
1981 "Hitman's Waltz" b/w "Food," "New Lottery" (Bemisbrain) *John Schaaf • Steve Hastings • Paul Reilly • Bill Courter*

GOVERNMENT ISSUE (DC)
1981 *Legless Bull* 7" EP (Dischord, no. 4) "Religious Ripoff; Fashionite; Rock & Roll Bullshit; Anarchy is Dead; Sheer Terror;

Asshole; Bored To Death; No Rights; I'm James Dean"
*John Stabb - vocals • John Barry - guitar • Brian Gay - bass •
Mark Alberstadt - drums* 1982 "Hey Ronnie," "Lie, Cheat &
Steal" on *Flex Your Head* comp LP (Dischord, no.7) 1982 *Make
an Effort* 7" EP (Fountain of Youth) "Teenager In A Box; No Way
Out; Twisted Views; Sheer Terror" *John Stabb - vocals • Brian
Baker - guitar • Tom Lyle - bass • Mark Alberstadt - drums*
1983 *Boycott Stabb* (Dischord/Fountain Of Youth) "Hall Of Fame;
Hour Of 1; G.I.; Puppet On A String; Sheer Terror; Happy People;
Lost In Limbo; Plain To See; Partyline; Here's The Rope;
Insomniac" *John Stabb - vocals • Tom Lyle - guitar • Mitch
Parker - bass • Marc Alberstadt - drums* 1983 "No Rights" on
Copulation comp (Mystic) 1983 track on *Bouncing Babies*
comp 1983 track on *Flipside Vinyl Fanzine Vol. 1* (Flipside)
1984 *Joyride* (Fountain Of Youth) *John Stabb - vocals • Tom Lyle
- guitar • Michael Fellows - bass •
Marc Alberstadt - drums* 1985 *The
Fun Just Never Ends* (Fountain of
Youth) "Fun And Games; Written
Word; Mad At Myself; The Next
Time; Bored To Death; Vanity Fare;
World Caved In; Massacre; Trapped"
*John Stabb -vocals • Tom Lyle -guitar
• John Leonard- bass • Marc Alberstadt
- drums* 1985 *Give Us Stabb or Give
Us Death* EP (Mystic) 1985 *Live!*
(Mystic) 1986 *Government Issue*
(Fountain of Youth/Giant) "Visions
And ?; They Know; Locked Inside;
Even When You're Here; Everybody's
Victim; Memories Past; Hear The
Scream; Say Something; On The
Screen; It Begins Now; Last Forever"

GRAND MAL (DC)

1984 *Binge & Purge* EP (Fountain
Of Youth)

GROINOIDS (Boston)

1981 "Angel" on *This Is Boston Not LA* comp (Modern Method)
1982 "Empty Skull" on *Unsafe At Any Speed* comp (Modern
Method)

GYNECOLOGISTS

(Indiana) 1983 "Infant Doe" on
The Master Tape Vol. II
(Affirmation, Aff- 02) 1983
"Feces & Psycopaths" 7"

HATE THROUGH
IGNORANCE (DC)

1982 "Instrumental," "Through
Posterity," "What Do You Say" on
Mixed Nuts Don't Crack (Outside)

HATES (Houston)

1979 7" EP (Faceless) "No Talk in
the 80's; New Spartans; All The
Whites Are Going Negro; Lost
Hymn" 1980 7" EP (Faceless) "Do
The Caryl Chessman; Soldier;
Bored With The Boys; City On Ice"
*Christian Arnheiter - guitar; vocals
• Robert Kainer - bass; vocals • Glenn Sorvisto - drums*

HEART ATTACK (NY)

1981 *God Is Dead* 7" EP (Damaged Goods) "You; Shotgun; God
Is Dead" *Jesse Malin - vocals; guitar • John Frawley - bass •
Javier - drums* 1982 "Shotgun," "God Is Dead" on *New York
Thrash* comp CS (ROIR) 1983 *Keep Your Distance* EP (Serious
Clown, SC 001) "Society; English Cunts; Trendies; From What I
See; Victim's Inquisition; The Last War" *Jesse Malin - vocals;
guitar • Danny Stuart - guitar • Paul Praver - bass • Javier -
drums* 1984 *Subliminal Seduction* 12" EP (Rat Cage, MOTR 27)
"Man's World; Wheels Over Indian Trails; Toxic Lullaby; Self

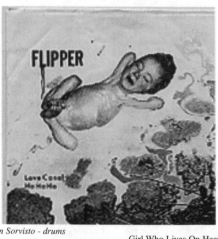

Control" *Jesse Malin - vocals; guitar • Paul Praver - bass •
Javier - drums*

HOSE (NY)

1982 *Mobo* 7" (Def Jam, DEF-SP-1) "Mobo; Girls; Going to the
Zoo" *Michael Espindle - vocals • Rick Rubin - guitar • Warren
Bell - bass • Autumn Goft - drums* 1983 *Hose* (Def Jam, DEF
SLP 1) Only The Astronaut Knows The Truth; Dope Fiend; Super
Freak; Fire; You Sexy Thang" *Rik Rosen - vocals • Rick Rubin -
guitar • Warren Bell - bass • Joel Horne - drums*

HUGH BEAUMONT EXPERIENCE (Dallas)

1981 *The Cone Johnson* EP (Cygnus, 001) "Zyklon B; Where
Did You Go, Sid?; Charity; Money Means So Much To Me"
1983 "Moo" on *Cottage Cheese From The Lips Of Death* comp
(Ward 9) 1983 "Let's Go Join The Army" on *VVV - Live At The
Hot Club* (VVV) *Bradley Stiles •
Tommy Porter • David McCreath •
King Vitamin*

HÜSKER DÜ (Mpls.)

1980 "Statues" b/w "Amusement" 7
(Reflex) *Bob Mould - guitar; vocals •
Greg Norton - bass; vocals • Grant
Hart - drums; vocals* 1981 *Land
Speed Record* (New Alliance) "All
Tensed Up; Don't Try To Call; I'm Not
Interested; Guns At My School; Push
The Button; Gilligan's Island; MTC;
Don't Have A Life; Bricklayer; Tired
Of Doing Things; You're Naive;
Strange Week; Do The Bee; Big Sky;
Ultracore; Let's Go Die; Data Control"
1982 *In A Free Land* 7" EP (New
Alliance) "In A Free Land," "What Do
I Want?" "M.I.C." 1982 on *Kitten
Kompilation* comp CS (Reflex)
1983 on *Charred Remains* comp CS (Noise) 1983 *Everything
Falls Apart* (Reflex) "From The Gut; Blah, Blah, Blah; Punch
Drunk; Bricklayer; Afraid Of Being Wrong; Sunshine Superman;
Signals From Above; Everything Falls Apart; Wheels; Target;
Obnoxious; Gravity" 1983 *Metal Circus* (Reflex/SST) "Real
World; Deadly Skies; It's Not Funny
Anymore; First Of The Last Calls;Life
Line;Diane;Out On A Limb" 1984
"Eight Miles High" b/w "Masochism
World" 7" (SST) 1984 *Zen Arcade*
(SST) "Something I Learned Today;
Broken Homes, Broken Heart; Never
Talking To You Again; Chartered Trips;
Dreams Reoccuring; Indecision Time;
Hare Krishna; Beyond The Threshold;
Pride; I'll Never Forget You; The Biggest
Lie; What's Going On; Masochism
World; Standing By The Sea;
Somewhere; One Step At A Time; Pink
Turns To Blue; Newest Industry;
Monday'll Never Be The Same;
Whatever; Tooth Fairy And The Princess;
Turn On The News; Reoccuring Dreams"
1985 "Celebrated Summer" b/w "New
Day Rising" 7" (SST) 1985 *New Day
Rising* (SST 031) "New Day Rising;
Girl Who Lives On Heaven Hill; I Apologize; Folk Lore; If I Told
You; Celebrated Summer; Perfect Example; Terms Of Psychic
Warfare; 59 Times The Pain; Powerline; Books About UFOs; I
Don't Know What You're Talking About; How To Skin A Cat;
Whatcha Drinkin; Plans I Make" 1985 "Makes No Sense At All"
b/w "Love Is All Around" (SST) 1985 *Flip Your Wig* (SST) "Flip
Your Wig; Every Everything; Makes No Sense At All; Hate Paper
Doll; Green Eyes; Divide And Conquer; Games; Find Me; The
Baby Song; Flexible Flyer; Private Plane; Keep Hanging On; The
Wit & The Wisdom; Don't Know Yet" 1986 "Erase Today" on
The Blasting Concept Volume II comp (SST) 1986 "Ticket To

Ride" on 7" comp EP (NME) **1986** *Candy Apple Grey* (Warner Bros.) "Crystal; Don't Want To Know If You Are Lonely; I Don't Know For Sure; Sorry Somehow; Too Far Down; Hardly Getting Over It; Dead Set On Destruction; Eiffel Tower High; No Promise Have I Made; All This I've Done For You"

HYPNOTICS (LA)

1981 "Weird People" on *American Youth Report* comp LP (Invasion/Thunderbolt) **1981** *Indoor Fiends* (Enigma)

ICONOCLAST (LA)

1984 *In These Times* four-song 7" EP (Flipside, #004)

ILL REPUTE (Oxnard, CA)

1982 "Clean Cut American Kid" on *Rodney On The ROQ Vol. 3* (Posh Boy, PBS - 103) **1983** "Lust Bust" on *Copulation* comp LP (Mystic, MLP33128) **1983** *Oxnard - Land Of No Toilets* EP (Mystic, M33129) "Fuck With My Head; In Society; Who Cares; Bad Rep; Greed; We'll Get Back At Them; Sleepwalking; I Won't Kill For You" **1985** *Omelette* (Mystic, MLP33139)

(IMPATIENT) YOUTH

(SF) **1982** "Praise The Lord And Pass The Ammunition" on *Not So Quiet On The Western Front* comp LP (Alternative Tentacles, VIRUS14) 1986 *Youth Don't Listen* (Lost & Found, Germany)

INTENSIFIED CHAOS

(SF) **1982** "Intensified Chaos" on *Not So Quiet On The Western Front* comp LP (Alternative Tentacles, VIRUS14) **1982** 10-song CS

IRON CROSS (DC)

1982 "War Games," "New Breed," "Live For Now" on *Flex Your Head* comp LP (Dischord, no.7) **1982** *Skinhead Glory* 7" EP (Dischord/Skinflint) "Crucified For Our Sins; Psycho Skin; Fight Em All; Shadows In The Night" **1983** *Hated and Proud* 7" EP (Skinflint, #2) "You're A Rebel," "Grey Morning," "Wolf Pack" *Sab Grey - vocals • Mark Haggerty - guitar • Paul Cleary - bass • Dante Ferrando - drums*

ISM (NY)

1982 "Attack (For Beginners Only)" b/w "Queen J.A.P." (S.I.N., #1) **1982** "John Hinckley Jr.," "Nixon Now More Than Eve}r on *Big Apple Rotten To The Core* comp (S.I.N., #2) **1983** "I Think I Love You" b/w "A7" (S.I.N., #3) *Jism - vocals • Mark Renes - guitar • Steve Sclarabo - bass • Larry Ray - drums* **1983** *A Diet For The Worms* (S.I.N., SJ04) "Auto Theft In NYC; White Castle At 3AM; White, Straight & Male; Herpes Simplex II; Man; Boy Love Sickie; John Hinckley Jr.; I Think I Love You; Life Ain't No Bowl Of Brady Bunch; Dance Club Meat Market; Medley: Vegetarian At A Barbeque; Shit List; Drunk Driving; Proud To Be Guilty; Moon The Moonies; Put On Your Warpaint" **1984** *Constantinople* 12" EP (Broken, BR - 001) "Constantinople; Bedpan Hunting; Get Real Loose; C.I.A. Man" *Jism - vocals • Mark Renes - guitar • Steve Sclarabo - bass • Greg D'Angelo - drums*

JACKSHIT (Reno)

1983 7" EP (s/r)

JERRY'S KIDS (Boston)

1981 "Straight Jacket," "Uncontrollable," "Wired," "Desperate," "Pressure," "I Don't Wanna" on *This Is Boston Not LA* comp LP (Modern Method) **1982** "Machine Gun" on *Unsafe At Any Speed* comp 7" (Modern Method) **1983** *Is This My World* (X - Claim!) "I Don't Belong; Cracks In The Wall; Tear It Up; Crucify Me; Break The Mold; Raise The Curtain; Vietnam Syndrome; Build Me A Bomb; New World; Lost; No Time" *Rick Jones - vocals; bass • Bob Censi - guitar • Chris Doherty - guitar • Brian Betzger - drums*

JFA (Phoenix)

1981 *Blatant Localism* 7" EP (Placebo) "Out Of School; Count; JFA; Beach Blanket Bong-Out; Do The Harrigan; Cokes & Snickers" **1982** "Low Rider," "American Buttfuckers" on *Sudden Death* comp LP (Smoke 7) **1983** "Low Rider" on *Live At The Eastern Front 2* comp LP (Enigma) **1983** track on *Annoy Your Neighbor With This Tape* comp CS (Chainsaw) **1983** "Bouncer" on *Amuck* comp LP (Placebo) **1983** *Surfin' JFA* (Version Sound) **1983** *Valley of the Yakes* (Placebo) **1984** *JFA* (Placebo) **1984** *Mad Garden* EP (Placebo) **1985** Julie's Song on *More Coffee For The Politicians* comp (Placebo) **1985** *Live* (Placebo) **1985** *My Movie* three-song 7" (Placebo)

THE JONESES (LA)

1982 "Jonestown" b/w "Criminals In My Car" 7" **1982** "Graveyard Rock" on *Someone Got Their Head Kicked In!* comp (BYO) **1983** *Criminals* EP (American Standard) "Criminals; Bed Rock; Fix Me; White And Pretty; Crocodile Rock; Ms. 714" **1983** "I'm Bad," "She's So Filthy" on *Hell Coms To Your House* comp (Bemisbrain/Enigma) *Jeff Drake - vocals; guitar • Steve Houston - guitar; vocals • Steven Fleming Olsen - bass; vocals • Mitch Deaner - drums*

JUVENILE JUSTICE (SF) **1982** "S&M Nightmare"

on *Not So Quiet On The Western Front* comp LP (Alternative Tentacles, VIRUS14)

KAOS (LA)

1980 *Product Of A Sick Mind* 7" EP (What) "Alcoholiday," "Top Secret," "Iron Dream" *Stingray - vocals; guitar • Lisa Adams - guitar • Amy Tracy Wichmann - bass • P.W. Curry - drums*

KARNAGE (SF)

1982 "The Few, The Proud, The Dead" on *Not So Quiet On The Western Front* comp LP (Alternative Tentacles, VIRUS14)

KILLING CHILDREN

(Indianapolis) **1983** *Certain Death* 7" EP (Gravelvoice) "Killing Children; Majority; Boring; 3 - Track Mind; Crazy; Happy Mutants; Certain Death" **1983** "Happy Mutants" on *The Master Tape Volume II* comp LP (Affirmation) *T.C. Killer - vocals • Eric Hess - guitar • John Swift - bass • Trent Nyffeler - drums*

KILLROY (LA)

1983 EP (Mystic/Ghetto-way) "99 Bottles; D-Generation; 66 Big Build Up; Gas Mask; West End Kids"

KILSLUG (Boston)

1984 7" EP **1986** *Answer The Call* (Taang!) "Into A Hole;

Henderson's Rag; Death Squad; Of Course; Demon Blues; Tart Cart; Red Devil; Make It Rain; Easter Time; Bring Back The Dead; Bad Karma"   *Larry Lifeless - vocals • Rico Petroleum - guitar • Mongoloid - guitar • Cheez - bass • Big Daddy - drums*

KINDLED IMAGINATION (LA)

1980 "Cowboy & Indian Scene" on *Cracks In The Sidewalk* comp LP (New Alliance)

KRAUT (NY)

1981 *Kill For Cash* 7" EP (Cabbage) "Kill For Cash; True Colour; Just Cabbage"   **1982** "Getaway" "Last Chance" on *New York Thrash* comp CS (ROIR)   **1982** *Unemployed* 7" EP (Cabbage) "Unemployed; Last Chance; Matinee"   **1983** *An Adjustment To Society* (Cabbage) All Twisted; Mishap; Unemployed; Onward; Don't Believe; Abortion; Bogus; Arming The World; Doomed Youth; Last Chance; Sell Out; Army Sport; Society's Victim; Kill For Cash"   **1984** *Whetting The Scythe* (Cabbage/Enigma) "Slow Down; See It Clear; Strongest Man; Pyramids; Juvenile Justice; N.G.R.I.; New Law; Flossing With An 'E' String; Backstabber"   *Davy Gunner - vocals • Doug Holland - guitar • Don Cowan - bass • Johnny Feedback - drums*

LAST RITES (Boston)

1984 "Chunks" b/w "So Ends Our Night" 7" (Taang!)   *Choke - vocals • Tony Peretz - guitar • Twisted William - bass • James - drums*

LATIN DOGS (LA)

1984 *Warning* 7" EP "Killed In Jail; World Powers; What's Wrong; Road Kills; Death To Tyrants; Go To The Window"   *Rank Confusion-vocals • Alan - guitar • Jon (The Moose) Engle - bass • Joseph Zidaravich - drums*

LAW & ORDER (Baltimore)

1982 *Anything But The Critic's Choice* 7" EP (Fetal) "Punks Like Us Get Nothing; I Hate Military Road; Teleside; Soldier Of Fortune; Adolescent Aggression; Power; Anything But The Critic's Choice; Self Destruction; I.R.A.; Caught In The Act; Violent Waltz;Law & Order"

LEGAL WEAPON (LA)

1981 *No Sorrow* 12" EP (Arsenal) "No One Listens; Live Mr. War; No Sorrow; Pow Pow; Hostility"   *Kat - voice • Brian Hansen - guitar • Patricia Morrison - bass • Charlie Vartanian - drums*   **1981** "Pow Wow" on *American Youth Report* comp LP (Invasion/ Thunderbolt)   **1982** "Daddy's Gone Mad" on *Hell Comes To Your House* comp LP (Bemisbrain)   **1982** *Death Of Innocence* (Arsenal) "Future Heat; Waiting In Line; Death Of Innocence; Out Of Control; User; Don't Pretend; War Babies; No Sorrow; Wanna Be; Daddy's Gone Mad"   *Kat - voice • Brian Hansen - guitar • Frank Agnew - guitar • Steve Soto - bass • Charlie Vartanian - drums*   **1982** *Your Weapon* (Arsenal) "What A Scene; The Stare; What's Wrong With Me; Equalizer; Bleeders; Only Lost For Today; Ice Age; Hand To Mouth; Caught In The Reign"   *Kat Arthur - vocals • Brian Hansen - guitar • Eddie Wayne - bass; vocals • Adam Maples - drums*   **1985** *Interior Hearts* (Arsenal) "Interior Hearts; Tears Of Steel; Too High; Ain't That A Lot Of Love; Over The Edge; Collisional Love; Except For You; No Direction; Charades; Damaged Memories; Don't Wreck My World"   *Kat Arthur - vocals • Brian Hansen - guitar • Eddie Dwayne - bass • Adam Maples - drums*

LEGIONNAIRES DISEASE (Houston)

1984 "I'd Rather See You Dead" 7" (Lunar)

LENNONBURGER (SF)

1982 "Reagum" on *Not So Quiet On The Western Front* comp LP (Alternative Tentacles, VIRUS14)

LEPERS (Boulder, CO)

1983 "Evil Music" b/w "So We Can Talk" (Unclean)   **1983** *God's Inhumane* 7" EP "Genius As Thief; Rock In Sick; Bitch & Moan; Christmas In Reverse"   *Alan Smith - guitar; vocals • Laz Beeken - bass; vocals • Roger Morgan - guitar; bass • Brad Carton - drums*

THE LEWD (Seattle; SF)

1978 "Kill Yourself" b/w "Pay Or Die," "Trash Can Baby" 7"   **1982** *American Wino* (ICI) "American Wino; Justice; Liberty; I'm Not Pretty; Climate Of Fear; Magnetic Heart; Suburban Prodigy; Beyond Moderation; Polluted Brain; Fight; Mobile Home; Cold & Numb; Dressed In Black"   **1983** M17 on *Live At The Eastern Front 2* comp LP (Enigma)   *J. Cats Beret - vocals • Bob Clic - guitar • Olga De Volga - bass • Christopher Clark Reece - drums*

LOCKJAW (Portland)

1982 *Shock Value* 7" EP "Prison Cell; Death To Cops; No Fun; Devil; Pop Your Head; Nazi Dentist; Go Back; Cut Up"   **1983** *Dead Friends* 7" EP "No A; Portland; Dead Friends; We Won't Go Down; Full Of Hate; She's A Slut; Need A Gun"   *Tony Arcudi - vocals • Del Murry - guitar • Rob Parker - bass • Eric Couch - drums*

LOS OLVIDADOS (SF)

1982 "Pay Salvation" on *Not So Quiet On The Western Front* comp LP (Alternative Tentacles, VIRUS14)

LOST CAUSE (LA)

1981 "Born Dead" on *American Youth Report* comp (Invasion)   **1981** *Born Dead* EP (High Velocity) "Born Dead; No Justice; American Hero; Senior Citizen"   *Johnny Ernst - vocals • Steve Young - guitar • Scott Mitchell - guitar • Helmut Willi Zarth - bass • Danny Oberbick - drums*   **1982** *Forgotten Corners* (High Velocity) "No Intro; Can't Find Myself; Misfit; Living In Hell; Don't Take A Chance; Airport Religion; Firing Line; Constipated Rage"   *Ron McCamey - vocals • Steve Young - guitar • Scott Mitchell - guitar • Helmut Willi Zarth - bass • Danny Oberbick - drums*

LOST GENERATION (CT)

1982 *Never Work* 7" EP (Incas)

L7 (Detroit)

1982 *Insanity* EP (T&G Special Forces)

THE LUST (NY)

1982 7" EP (Cork The Dog) "Dread In N.Y.; I'm Annoyed; 1000 More; Gimme More Distortion; Take Advantage"   *Janice Lynx - vocals • Ray Blood - guitar • Sandy Lynx - bass • Mat Finish - drums*

THE MAD (NY)

1981 "I Hate Music" b/w "Eyeball" 7" (Mad)   **1982** "The Hell" b/w "Disgusting," "Fried Egg" 7" (Mad)   **1982** "I Hate Music," "The Hell" on *New York Thrash* comp CS (ROIR)

M.A.D. (SF)

1982 "Holocaust" on *Not So Quiet On The Western Front* comp LP (Alternative Tentacles, VIRUS14)

MAD PARADE (LA)

1986 *Right Is Right* 7" (Toxic Shock, TOX - 007) "Right Is Right; This Is Life; Mother's Little Helper"   *Billy Ledges - vocals • Joey Kelly - guitar; vocals • Michael Lawrence - bass; vocals • Mike Sosa - drums*

MAD SOCIETY (LA)

1981 7" EP (Hit & Run) "Riot Squad; Skitz; Napalm; Terminally; Little Devil"   **1982** Riot Squad, Napalm, Little Devil on *You Can't Argue With Suckess* comp LP (Mystic, MLP33102)

MANIAX (Fresno)

1982 "Off To War" on *Not So Quiet On The Western Front* comp LP (Alternative Tentacles, VIRUS14)

MARCHING PLAGUE (San Antonio)

1983 "Rock'n'Roll Asshole" on *Cottage Cheese From The Lips Of Death* comp LP (Ward 9) **1983** *Rock'n'Roll Asshole* EP (CIA) "Rock'n'Roll Asshole; World War 4; Mom and Dad; When I Die; Oh No!" *Keith Rumbo - vocals • Adam Brogley - guitar • Flynn Mauthe - bass • Brad Perkins - drums*

MARGINAL MAN (DC)

1984 *Identity* EP (Dischord, no. 13) **1985** *Double Image* (Gasatanka/ Enigma) "Turn The Tables; Friend; Linger In The Past; Strange Feeling; Mainstream; Chocolate Pudding; Tell Me; Shades Of Reason; Someone Cares; Forever Gone; Double Image" *Steve Polcari - vocals; guitar • Kenny Inouye - guitar • Peter Murray - guitar • Andre Lee - bass • Mike Manos - drums*

MASSACRE GUYS (Salt Lake City)

1982 *Devil's Slide* CS

McDONALDS (Detroit)

1981 "Miniature Golf" on *Process Of Elimination* comp 7" EP (Touch & Go) **1982** "Untitled" on *Reagan Regime Review* comp (Selfless)

McRAD (Philly)

1983 "Inflation Dub," "Ejected" on *Get Off My Back* comp LP (Red) **1986** *Absence Of Sanity* (Beware)

MDC (Austin/SF)

1980 "John Wayne (Was A Nazi)" b/w Born To Die 7" (R Radical) (first 300 copies as The Stains, next 300 as MDC-Stains) **1982** *Millions Of Dead Cops* (R Radical) "Business On Parade; Dead Cops; Born To Die; Corporate Deathburger; Violent Redneck; I Remember; John Wayne Was A Nazi; Dick For Brains; I Hate Work; My Family Is; A Little Weird; Greedy & Pathetic; Church & State; Kill The Light; American Achievements" *David - vocals • Ron - guitar • Franc'o - bass • Alschvitz - drums* **1982** "The Only Good Cop…" on *Not So Quiet On The Western Front* comp LP (Alternative Tentacles) **1983** *Multi-Death Corporation* EP (R Radical) "Multi - Death Corporation; Selfish Shit; Radioactive Chocolate; Place To Piss" **1984** *Chicken Squawk/Millions Of Dead Children* EP (R Radical) **1985** "Missle Destroyed Civilization" on *P.E.A.C.E.* comp (R Radical) **1985** "Revolution In Rock" on *Rat Music For Rat People Vol. II* (CD Presents) **1986** *Smoke Signals* (R Radical, MDC4)

MEATMEN (Detroit/DC)

1981 *Blood Sausage* 7" EP (Touch & Go, T&G3) "Tooling For Anus; One Down Three To Go; Snuff 'Em; Becoming A Man; I've Got A Problem; I'm Glad I'm Not A Girl; Dumping Ground" *Tesco Vee - vocals • Greg Ramsay - guitar • Rich Ramsey - bass • Mr. X-drums* **1981** "Meatmen Stomp" on *Process Of Elimination* comp 7" EP (Touch & Go, T&G4) **1982** *Crippled Children Suck* 7" EP (Touch & Go, T&G8) "Blow Me Jah; Mr. Tapeworm; Orgy Of One; I Sin For A Living; Crippled Children Suque; Spread Scat Boogie #2; Meat Crimes" *Tesco Vee - vocals • Rich Ramsay - guitar • Mike Achtenberg - bass • Todd Swalla - drums* **1983** *We're The Meatmen…And You Suck!* (Touch & Go, TGRLP001) "The Rap; Tooling For Anus; One Down Three To Go; Snuff 'Em; Becoming A Man; Freud Was Wrong; I'm Glad I'm Not A Girl; Dumping Ground; Mr. Tapeworm; Meatmen Stomp; Orgy Of One; One Down Three To Go; I Sin For A Living; Crippled Children Suck; Meat Crimes; Buttocks; Mystery Track; Middle Aged Youth" *Tesco Vee - vocals • Rich Ramsay - guitar • Greg Ramsay - bass • Todd Swalla - drums* **1984** *Tesco Vee And The Meatcrew - Dutch Hercules* 12" EP (Touch & Go, T&G12) "Lesbian Death Dirge; God's Bullies; Wine, Wenches and Wheels; Dance To The Music; Crapper's Delight" *Tesco Vee - vocals • Brian Baker - lead guitar • Lyle Preslar - guitar • Bert Quieroz - bass • Rich Moore - drums*

1985 *War Of The Superbikes* (Homestead, HMS009) "War of the Superbikes; Abba, God and Me; Pillar of Sodom; What's This Shit Called Love; Punker-ama; Razamanazz; Kisses in the Sunset; Cadaver Class; Pain Principal" *Tesco Vee - vocals • Brian Baker - lead guitar • Lyle Preslar - guitar • Graham McCulloch - bass • Eric Zelsdor - drums* **1985** "War Of The Superbikes" 7" flexi (Homestead) **1986** "Rock'n'Roll Juggernaut" 7" flexi (Caroline)

MEAT PUPPETS (Phoenix) **1981** *In A Car* 7" EP

(World Imitation) "In A Car; Big House; Dolphin Field; Out In The Garden; Foreign Lawns" **1982** *Meat Puppets* (Thermidor/ SST) "Reward; Love Offering; Blue - Green God; Walking Boss; Melons Rising; Saturday Morning; Our Friends; Tumblin' Tumbleweeds; Milo, Sorghum, and Maize; Meat Puppets; Playing Dead; Litterbox; Electromud; The Gold Mine" **1983** "Unpleasant" on *Amuck* comp (Placebo) **1983** "Tumblin' Tumbleweeds" on *The Blasting Concept* comp (SST) **1984** *Meat Puppets II* (SST) "Split Myself In Two; Magic Toy Missing; Lost; Plateau; Aurora Borealis; We're Here; Climbing; New Gods; Oh, Me; Lake Of Fire; I'm A Mindless Idiot; The Whistling Song" **1985** *Up On The Sun* (SST) Up On The Sun; Maiden's Milk; Away; Animal Kingdom; Hot Pink; Swimming Ground; Buckethead; Too Real; Enchanted Pork Fist; Seal Whales; Two Rivers; Creator" **1986"** I Just Want To Make Love To You" on *The Blasting Concept Volume II* comp LP (SST) **1986** *Out My Way* 12" EP (SST) "She's Hot; Out My Way; Other Kinds Of Love; Not Swimming Ground; Mountain Line; Good Golly Miss Molly" *Curt Kirkwood - guitar; vocals • Cris Kirkwood - bass; vocals • Derrick Bostrom - drums*

MECHT MENSCH (Madison, WI)

1982 *Mecht Mensch/Tar Babies* cassette (Bone Air) **1982** *Acceptance* 7" EP (Bone Air) "Acceptance; Grinder; Land Of The Brave; Zombie; What's Right" **1983** "Killer Klown" on *The Master Tape Volume II* comp LP (Affirmation) *Marc - vocals • Dan - guitar • Jeremy - bass • Raes - drums*

MENTAL DECAY (NJ)

1984 *Mental Decay* EP (Buy Our Records, BOR -7-003)

MENTORS (LA)

1982 *Mentors* 12" EP (Mystic, M12453) "Going Thru Your Purse; Get Up And Die; Peepin' Tom; Woman From Sodom" **1983** "Police Hotel" on *Copulation* comp LP (Mystic MLP33128) *El Duce - vocals; drums • Sickie - guitar • Heathen Skum - bass* **1985** *You Axed For It!* (Death; Enigma, DEATH 001) "Sandwich Of Love; Shocked And Grossed; Four F Club; Herpes 2; Judgement Day; Sleeping Bandits; Free Fix; Golden Showers; Clap Queen; My Erection Is Over" **1986** *Up The Dose* (Death/Enigma, 72172 - 4) "Heterosexuals Have The Right To Rock; Rock 'Em Sock 'Em; White Trash Woman; Adultery; On The Rag; Kick It Down; Secretary Hump; Couch Test Casting; S.F.C.C.; Up The Dose" *El Duce - drums; vocals • Sickie Wifebeater - guitar • Dr. Heathen Scum - bass*

M.I.A. (Las Vegas/OC)

1981 "Tell Me Why" on *American Youth Report* comp LP (Invasion/Thunderbolt) **1982** "New Left" on *Not So Quiet On The Western Front* comp LP (Alternative Tentacles, VIRUS14) **1982** *Last Rites for M.I.A. and Genocide* split LP (Smoke 7) "Tell Me Why; Gas Crisis; Cold Sweat; I Hate Hippies; Angry Youth; All The President's Skin; Fucking Zones; No More" *Mike - vocals • Nick - guitar • Paul - bass • Moon - drums* **1984** *Murder in a Foreign Place* (Alternative Tentacles) **1985** *Notes From The Underground* (National Trust) "Shadows Of My Life; Voices In The Dark; Never Again; Show Me The

Way; Scotty Rew; Write Myself A Letter; Light Of Yesterday; Haven't You Heard; Make A Choice; Another Day" *Michael Conley - vocals • Nick Adams - guitar • Pablo Schwartz - bass • Larz Pearson - drums* 1987 *After the Fact* (Flipside) "Edge Of Forever; What I See; Whisper In The Wind; Beautiful World; California Dreamin; When It's Over; Time To Change; It Follows Me; Whatever Happened; It's Hard To Say You're Wrong; Broken; Out Of Control" *Mike Conley - vocals • Mark Arnold - guitar • Fraser James Daly - bass • C.Gordon Moon - drums*

MIDDLE CLASS (LA/OC)

1978 7" EP (Joke) "Out Of Vogue; You Belong; Situations; Insurgence" *Jeff A - vocals • Mike A - guitar • Mike Patton-bass • Bruce Atta - drums*

MINOR THREAT (DC)

1981 *Minor Threat* 7" EP (Dischord, no. 3) "Filler; I Don't Wanna Hear It; Seeing Red; Straight Edge; Small Man, Big Mouth; Screaming at a Wall; Bottled Violence; Minor Threat" *Ian MacKaye - vocals • Lyle Preslar - guitar • Brian Baker - bass • Jeff Nelson - drums* 1981 *In My Eyes* 7" EP (Dischord, no. 5) "In My Eyes; Out Of Step (with the world); Guilty Of Being White; Stepping Stone" 1982 "Stand Up," "12XU" on *Flex Your Head* comp LP (Dischord, no. 7) 1983 *Out Of Step* 12" EP (Dischord, no. 10) "Betray; It Follows; Think Again; Look Back And Laugh; Sob Story; No Reason; Little Friend; Out Of Step" *Ian MacKaye - vocals • Brian Baker - guitar • Lyle Preslar - guitar • Steve Hansgen - bass • Jeff Nelson - drums* 1984 *Salad Days* 7" EP (Dischord, no. 15) "Salad Days," "Stumped," "Good Guys"

MINUTEMEN (LA)

1980 *Paranoid Time* EP (SST 002) "Validation; The Maze; Definitions; Sickles & Hammers; Fascist; Joe McCarthy's Ghost; Paranoid Chant 1980 "9:30 May 2" on *Cracks In The Sidewalk* comp (New Alliance, NAR- 001) 1981 "Working Men Are Pissed" on *American Youth Report* comp(Invasion/ Thunderbolt) 1981 "Prelude" on *Life Is Beautiful - So Why Not Eat Health Food?* comp LP (New Underground) 1981 "Search" on *Rodney On The ROQ Vol. 2* comp LP (Posh Boy, PBS-123) 1981 *The Punch Line* (SST 004) "Search; Tension; Games; Boiling; Disguises; The Struggle; Monuments; Ruins; Issued; The Punch Line; Song For El Salvador; History Lesson; Fanatics; No Parade; Straight Jacket; Gravity; Warfare; Static" 1981 *Joy* 7" EP (New Alliance, NAR-004) "Joy; Black Sheep; More Joy" 1982 "Shit You Hear At Parties" on *Life Is Ugly - So Why Not Kill Yourself* (New Underground, NU-11) 1982 *Bean-Spill* 7" EP (Thermidor, T8) "Afternoons; Futurism Restated; Split Red; If Reagan Played Disco; Case Closed" 1983 "Corona" on *Hell Comes To Your House II* (Bemisbrain; Enigma) 1983 "Paranoid Chant," "The Maze," "Boiling," "Games" on *The Blasting Concept* comp (SST 013) 1983 "Base King" on *Life Is Boring - So Why Not Steal This Record?* comp LP (New Underground, NU-55) 1983 *What Makes A Man Start Fires?* (SST 014) "Bob Dylan Wrote Propaganda Songs; One Chapter In The Book; Fake Contest;

Beacon Sighted Through Fog; Mutiny In Jonestown; East Wind; Faith; Pure Joy; 99; The Anchor; Sell Or Be Sold; The Only Minority; Split Red; Colors; Plight; The Tin Roof; Life Is A Rehearsal; This Road; Polarity" 1983 *Buzz Or Howl Under The Influence Of Heat* (SST 016) "Self- Referenced; Cut; Dream Told By Moto; Dreams Are Free, Motherfucker!; The Toe Jam; I Felt Like A Gringo; The Product; Little Man With A Gun In His Hand" 1984 *Double Nickels On The Dime* (SST 028) "Anxious Mo-fo; Theatre Is The Life Of You; Viet - nam; Cohesion; It's Expected; #1 Hit Song; Two Beads At The End; Do You Want New Wave Or Do You Want The Truth; Don't Look Now; Shit From An Old Notebook; Nature Without Man; One Reporter's Opinion; Political Song For Michael Jackson To Sing; Maybe Partying Will Help; Toadies; Retreat; The Big Foist; God Bows To Math; Corona; The Glory Of Man; Take 5; My Heart & The Real World; History Lesson-Part 2; You Need The Glory; The Roar Of The Masses Could Be Farts; Mr. Robot's Holy Orders; West Germany; The Politics Of Time; Themselves; Please Don't Be Gentle With Me; Nothing Indeed; No Exchange; There Ain't No Shit On TV Tonight; This Ain't No Picnic; Spillage; Untitled Song For Latin America; Jesus And Tequila; June 16th; Storm In My House; Martin's Story; Ain't Talkin' 'Bout Love; Doctor Wu; Little Man With A Gun In His Hand; Love Dance" 1984 *The Politics Of Time* (New Alliance/SST 277) Base King; Working Men Are Pissed; I Shook Hands; Below The Belt; Shit You Hear At Parties; Big Lounge Scene; Maternal Rite; Tune For Wind God; Party With Me Punker; The Process; Joy Jam; Tony Gets Wasted In Pedro; Swing To The Right; ¡Raza Si!; Times; Badges; Fodder; Futurism Restated; Hollering; Subhuman Dialectic; Contained; On Trial; Spraycan Wars; My Part; Fanatics; Ack, Ack, Ack; The Big Blast For Youth" 1985 *Minuteflag* 12" EP (with Black Flag) (SST 050) Fetch The Water; Power Failure; Friends; Candy Rush 1985 *Tour-Spiel* EP (Reflex) 1985 *...Just A Minute* (Virgin Vinyl) 1985 *My First Bells* 1980 - 1983 CS (SST 032) 1985 *Project: Mersh* EP (SST 034)

1985 *3 - Way Tie (For Last)* (SST 058) The Price of Paradise; Lost; The Big Stick; Political Nightmare; Courage; Have You Ever Seen The Rain?; Red and the Black; Spoken Word Piece; No One; Stories ; What Is It?; Ack Ack Ack; Just Another Soldier; Situations At Hand; Bermuda" 1986 "Ain't Talkin 'Bout Love" on *The Blasting Concept Volume II* (SST 043) *D. Boon -guitar; vocals • Mike Watt - bass; vocals • George Hurley - drums*

MISFITS (NJ)

1977 "Cough Cool" b/w "She" (Blank) *Glenn Danzig - electric piano • Jerry Only - bass • Manny - drums* 1978 *Bullet* 7" EP (Plan 9, PL1001) "Bullet; We Are 138; Attitude; Hollywood Babylon" *Glenn Danzig - vocals • Franché Coma - guitar • Jerry Only - bass • Mr. Jim - drums* 1979 *Horror Business* 7" EP (Plan 9) "Horror Business; Teenagers From Mars; Children In Heat" *Glenn Danzig - vocals • Bobby Steele - guitar • Jerry Only - bass • Joey Image - drums* 1979 *Beware* EP (Cherry Disc, UK, PCP9) "We Are 138; Bullet; Hollywood Babylon; Attitude; Horror Business; Teenagers From Mars; Last Caress" 1980 *N.O.T.L.D.* 7 EP (Plan 9, PL1011) "Where Eagles Dare; Night of the Living Dead; Ratfink" 1980 *3 Hits From Hell 7* (Plan 9,PL1013)

"London Dungeon; Horror Hotel; Ghouls Night Out" *Glenn Danzig - vocals • Bobby Steele - guitar • Doyle - guitar • Jerry Only - bass • Arthur Googy - drums* **1980** "Who Killed Marilyn" b/w "Spook City U.S.A." (Glenn Danzig 7") (Plan 9, PL1015) **1981** "Halloween I" b/w "Halloween II" (Plan 9, PL1017) **1982** *Evilive* 7" EP (Plan 9, PL1019) "20 Eyes; Night Of The Living Dead; Astro Zombies; Horror Business; London Dungeon; All Hell Breaks Loose; We Are 138" **1982** *Walk Among Us* (Ruby/Slash, 25756-1) "20 Eyes; I Turned Into A Martian; All Hell Breaks Loose; Vampira; Nike A Go Go; Hate Breeders; Mommy, Can I Go Out And Kill Tonight; Night Of The Living Dead; Skulls; Violent World; Devils Whorehouse; Astro Zombies; Braineaters" *Glenn Danzig - vocals • Doyle - guitar • Jerry Only - bass • Arthur Googy -drums* **1983** *Wolfsblood* EP (Aggresive Rock, 0034) **1983** *Earth A.D.* (Plan 9, PL9-02) "Earth A.D.; Queen Wasp; Devilock; Death Comes Ripping; Green Hell; Wolfs Blood; Demonomania; Hellhound" *Glenn Danzig-vocals • Doyle-guitar • Jerry Only - bass • Robo - drums* **1984** *Die Die My Darling* (Plan 9, PL9 - 03) "Die Die My Darling; We Bite; Mommy, Can I Go Out And Kill Tonight?" **1985** *Legacy Of Brutality* (Plan 9; Caroline, PL9 - 06) "Angelfuck; Who Killed Marilyn; Where Eagles Dare; She; Halloween; American Nightmare; Static Age; TV Casualty; Hybrid Moments; Spinal Remains; Come Back; Some Kinda Hate; Theme For A Jackal"

MISGUIDED (NY)

1982 *Bringing It Down* 7" EP (Reality) You Bore Me; State Of War; C.C.T.V. **1982** track on *Charred Remains* comp cassette (Noise) **1983** *Options* 7" EP (Reality) "Defy Standards; Blacklist; They Take Your Money; Individual" *John Rizzo - vocals • Alex Tutino - guitar • John Karco - bass • Lyle Hysen - drums*

MISSION FOR CHRIST (DC) **1984** "Pennies From Hell" b/w "Pennies From Hell" (Dub) (No Trend, NT004) *Tex Borneo -vocals • Kenny Dread -guitar • JC -bass • Wag -drums*

THE MOB (NY)

1982 "Common Criminal," "101" on *Big Apple Rotten To The Core* comp LP (S.I.N., #2) **1982** *Upset The System* EP (Mob Style) "Crucial Point; We Can; NY Slam; Dr. Butcher; Pinstripe Suit; Label It; 101; Common Criminal; Fight For Right" *Ralph Gebbia -vocals • Jack Flanagan - guitar • Jose Gonzalez - bass •Jamie Shanahan- drums* **1983** *Step Forward* 7" EP (Mob Style) "Step Forward; Revolution; Unity Lives On **1986** *We Come To Crush* (Mob Style)

MODERN INDUSTRY

(LA) **1983** *Man In Black* 7" EP (Toxic Shock) "Man In Black; No Change; The Egyptian; Living In The Shadows"

MODERN WARFARE (OC)

1980 7" EP (Bemisbrain) "Dayglo; In The Shadows; Delivered **1981** 7" EP (Bemisbrain) "Nothing Left; No Passion; Suburban Death Row" *Jimmy Bemis - vocals; guitar • Ron Gowdy - guitar • Steve Sinclair - bass • Randy Scott - drums* **1981** "One For All" on *American Youth Report* comp (Invasion/ Thunderbolt) **1982** "Out Of My Head," "Street Fightin' Man" on *Hell Comes To Your House* comp (Bemisbrain, BB 123/124) **1983** "Moral Majority"

on *Life Is Boring - So Why Not Steal This Record* comp (New Underground, NU-55)

MORTAL MICRONOTZ (Lawrence, KS) **1982**

Mortal Micronotz (Fresh Sounds, FS201) "It's Not Alright; Day After Day; You Don't Say; Not Too Sure; Take 2; Don't Pull Me Under; Old Lady Sloan; They've Got It All; Shopping Spree; Daydream; The Police Song; Song 16; Blonde - Haired Ghost; Let It Out" *Dave Lubensky - vocals • John Harper - guitar • David Dale -bass • Steve Eddy -drums* **1983** *Smash* (Fresh Sounds, FS206) "Procrastination; Smash; Lately; Bob; Feels Like; Cut It Off; Over; I Got A Right" **1986** *Micronotz - 40 Fingers* (Homestead)

MOURNING NOISE (NJ)

1982 7" EP (Night Latche) "Dawn of the Dead; Fighting Chance; Laser Lights; Demon Eyes; Addiction" *Mike - vocals • Tom - guitar • Jon - guitar • Chris Draphobia - bass • Steve Zing - drums*

MURPHY'S LAW (NY)

1985 *Bong Blast* cassette (Spliff) **1986** *Murphy's Law* (Rock Hotel/Profile) "Murphy's Law; California Pipeline; Sit Home And Rot; Fun; Beer; Wahoo Dad; Crucial Bar-B-Q; A Day In The Life; Care Bear; Ilsa; Skinhead Rebel; I've Got A Right *Jimmy Gestapo - vocals • Alex Morris - guitar • Pete Martinez - bass • Petey Hines - drums; vocals*

MYDOLLS (Houston)

1981 *Mydolls* 7" (CIA 005) **1982** "Imposter" b/w "Exorcism" (CIA 008) *Linda Bond - guitar; vocals • Trish Herrera -guitar; vocals • Dianna Ray -bass • Jorge Reyes -drums* **1983** "Soldiers Of A Pure War" on *Cottage Cheese From The Lips Of Death* comp (Ward 9)

MY THREE SONS (NJ)

1984 My Three Sons 7" EP (BOR- 002) **1985** "People Who Bleed," "Untitled 13" on *New Jerseys' Got It* comp (BOR12 -003)

NAKED LADY WRESTLERS (SF)

1982 "Dan With The Yellow Hair" on *Not So Quiet On The Western Front* comp (Alternative Tentacles)

NAKED RAYGUN

(Chicago) **1981** "Bomb Shelter," "When The Screaming Stops," "Paranoia," "Libido" on *Busted At Oz* comp (Autumn) **1983** *Flammable Solid* 7" (Ruthless) "Surf Combat," "Gear Libido" **1983** *Basement Screams* 12" EP (Ruthless) **1984** "I Don't Know," "Stupid" on *Middle Of America* comp (H.I.D.) **1984** *Throb Throb* (Homestead) **1985** *All Rise* (Homestead)**1986** "Bananacuda" on *Sub Pop 100* comp CS (Sub Pop)

NBJ (SF)

1982 "Dead Porker" on *Not So Quiet On The Western Front* comp LP

NECROS (Detroit)

1980 4- song 7" EP (Touch and Go, T&G1) "Sex Drive; Police Brutality; Better Never Than Late; Caste System" **1981** "Bad Dream" on *Process Of Elimination* comp 7" EP (Touch & Go, T&G4) **1982** 9-song 7" EP (Touch and Go/Dischord, T&G3; Dischord no. 4 1/2) "IQ 32; Youth Camp; Peer Pressure; Race Riot; Wargame; I Hate My School; Past Comes Back To Haunt Me; Reject; Public High School" *Barry Hennsler - vocals • Brian Pollock - guitar • Corey Rusk - bass • Todd Swalla - drums* **1983** *Conquest For Death* (Touch and Go, T&GLP#3) "Search For Fame; Tarnished Words; No One; Satisfy; Bad Dream; Police Brutality; A.S.F.B.; Conquest For Death; Change; Count Me Out; Crying Form; Face Forward; Friend To All" *Barry Hennsler - vocals • Andy Wendler - guitar • Corey Rusk - bass • Todd Swalla - drums* **1983** "Conquest For Death" b/w "Take Em Up" (Touch & Go) **1985** *Jail Jello* split EP with White Flag (Gasatanka) **1985** "Tangled Up" b/w "Nile Song" (Gasatanka) **1985** *Tangled Up* (Restless, 7220 -1) "Gun; Blizzard Of Glass; Big Chief; Open Wound; Tangled Up; Power Of Fear; Black Water; Noise; 500 Years, A Pack Of Kools; Nile Song; A House Full Of Drunks *Barry Hennsler -vocals • Andy Wendler - guitar • Ron Sakowski -bass • Todd Swalla - drums*

NEGATIVE APPROACH (Detroit)

1981 "Lost Cause" on *Process Of Elimination* comp 7" EP (Touch & Go, T&G4) **1982** "Can't Tell No One" on *Reagan Regime Review* (Selfless) **1982** *Negative Approach* aka *Touch & Go* 7" EP (Touch & Go, T&G7) "Can't Tell No One; Sick Of Talk; Pressure; Why Be Something That You're Not; Nothing; Fair Warning; Ready To Fight; Lead Song; Whatever I Do; Negative Approach" **1983** *Tied Down* (Touch & Go, T&GLP#3) "Hypocrite; Evacuate; Said & Done; Nothing; Your Mistake; Live Your Life; Friend Or Foe; Dead Stop; I'll Survive"

NEGATIVE ELEMENT

(Midwest) **1982** 8-song 7" EP (Version Sound)

NEGATIVE FX (Boston)

1982 *Negative FX* (Taang!, #5) "Feel Like A Man; Together; Protestor; Mind Control; I Know Better; Citizen's Arrest; Negative FX; The Few, The Proud; Punch In The Face; Primary Attack; Hazardous Waste; Turn Your Back; Nightstick Justice; I Doubt; Modern Problems; Nuclear Fear; VFW; Repeat" *Choke - vocals • Pat -guitar • Rich -bass • Dave -drums*

NIG-HEIST (LA)

1982 "Walkin' Down The Street" one-song 7" (Thermidor, T10) **1984** *Snort My Load* (Thermidor, T16) "Life In General; Love In Your Mouth; T.L.P.; If She Ever Comes; Hot Muff; Balls Of Fire; Woman Drivah; Big Wheels; Surfbroad; Slurp A Delic"

NIHILISTICS (NY)

1982 "Here And Now," "Love And Kisses" on *New York Thrash* comp CS (ROIR) **1982** *After Death* EP (Visionary) After Death; You're To Blame; No Friends; Live & Learn; Kill Yourself *Ron Rancid - vocals • Chris T - guitar • Michael - bass • Troy - drums* **1983** *Nihilistics* (Brain Eater, Eater1) "Appreciation; Death & Taxes; You're To Blame; Low Life; Here And Now; Misanthrope; I'm A Patriot; My Creed; No Friends; Kill Yourself; Combat Stance; Murderer In Blue; Welfare For The Rich; Badge Of Shame; Pal O'Mine; The Truth; My Life; Black Sheep; After Death; Life's Process"

THE NILS (Montreal)

1985 *Sell Out Young* (Psyche Industry, Canada) "In Betweens; Fountains; Day Light; Freedom" *Alex Soria - vocals • Carlos Soria - guitar • Guy Caron - bass; vocals • Eloi Bertholet - drums*

NIP DRIVERS (LA)

1984 *Destroy Whitey* (New Alliance, NAR-018) **1985** *Oh Blessed Freak Show* (Bemisbrain/ Enigma)

NO ALTERNATIVE (SF)

1981 7" EP (Subterranean) "Make Guns Not Love, Metro Police Theme, Rockabilly Rumble" **1982** "Dead Men Tell No Lies" on *Not So Quiet On The Western Front* comp LP (Alternative Tentacles)

NO CRISIS (LA)

1982 "She's Into The Scene" on *Rodney On The ROQ Volume 3* comp (Posh Boy, PBS-103) **1982** *She's Into The Scene* (Ultra-Mega) "She's Into The Scene; Take It; About Face; Change Your Name; Damnation; On Your Head" *Kirk Mosher - vocals • Vid Sutherland - guitar • Mark Erwin Arnold - guitar • Johnny Snot -bass • Ron Blast - drums*

NO LABELS (NC)

1983 *No Labels/C.O.C.* split CS (No Core) **1983** on *No Core* comp CS (No Core) **1983** "Tortured Thought," "Society's Problems" on *The Master Tape Volume II* comp (Affirmation, Aff-02) **1983"** Changes," "Compromise" on *Why Are We Here?* comp 7" (No Core)

NO ROCK STARS (NC)

1983 track on *No Core* comp CS

N.O.T.A. (Tulsa) **1983** *Toy Soldiers* 7" EP (Rabid Cat)

1985 *None Of The Above* (Rabid Cat, RAB NOTA006) Ultra Violent; Den Of Thieves; I Should Kill You; Reckless; Takin' Away Your Rights; On The Pavement; Keeping You Out; Sick Society; Frustration; Self Destruct; Police Front; War On Wankers; Nightstick Justice; Propaganda Control; Redneck Mentality; Identity Crisis; Drugs And Sex; Cut The Shit; Summer Of 82 *Jeff - vocals; guitar • Russell - guitar • Bruce - bass • Bob - drums*

NOT FOR SALE (TX)

1984 *For A Few Dollars More* 7" EP (Rabid Cat) **1985** *A Taste Of Honey* 7" (Rabid Cat) **1985** Not For Sale (Rabid Cat)

NO THANKS (NY)

1983 *Are You Ready To Die* 7" EP (Dead Space) "Are You Ready To Die; Office Jerk; Rat Cheese; Fuck Everything; Poseur" *Donna - vocals • Johnny - guitar • Jamie - bass • Seth - drums*

NO TREND (DC)

1982 *Teen Love* 7" EP (No Trend, NT 001) "Teen Love, Mass Sterilization Caused By Venereal Disease, Cancer" *Jeff - vocals • Frank - guitar • Bob - bass • Mike - drums* **1983** *Teen Love* 12" EP (No Trend, NT 002) **1983** *Too Many Humans* (No Trend, NT 003) "Family Style; Blow Dry; Reality Breakdown; Kiss Ass To Your Peer Group; Fashion Tips For The 80s; Do As You're Told; Too Many Humans; For The Fun Of It All; Mindless Little Insects; Happiness Is…" **1984** *A Dozen Dead Roses* (No Trend, NT 005) "Karma Nights; Your Love; Tear You Apart; Never Again; All of Nothing; Good Day Mrs. Hamm; For The Fun Of It All; The Curse; Heartache; Who's To Say" **1985** *Heart Of Darkness* 12" EP (Widowspeak) **1986** *When Death Won't Solve Your Problems* (Widowspeak) **1986** *Tritonian Nash - Vegas*

Polyster Complex (Touch and Go, T&GLP) "One Under Par; Copperhead; Without Me; Fred Reality; Space Disco; Cry Of The Dirtballs; Angel Angel Down We Go; Overweight Baby Boom Critter; Choc-O- Jet; Freak; Bel - Pre Rising"

THE NOT (Boston)

1985 *Kids Survive* EP (Not, NR002) "We Are The Ones; Lonely Afternoon; I Know That You Can; Kids Survive; (Why The) Fighting; I Won't Run Away" *Tommy Lamont - guitar/vocals • Peter Patino - bass • Rob Wallace - drums*

NUCLEAR CRAYONS

(DC) **1982** *Nameless* EP (Outside, #1) "Outsider; Teenage Suicide; Political Punk" **1982** Nuclear Crayons, Catwalk, Blitz Beauty, Man In The Big Hat on *Mixed Nuts Don't Crack* comp (Outside) *Lynch Lavoison - vocals • Darin Drake - guitar • Justin Luchter - bass • Kendall Church - drums*

OFFENDERS (Austin)

1981 "Lost Causes" b/w "Rockin The Town" (Suffering Sounds) **1983** "Fight Back" on *Cottage Cheese From The Lips Of Death* comp LP (Ward 9) **1983** *We Must Rebel* (Rabid Cat)

OUTLETS (Boston)

1981 "Knock Me Down" on *Outlets/Boy's Life* split 7 (Modern Method) **1982** *Best Friend* 7" (Modern Method)

OUTPATIENTS (Western Mass.)

1983 *Basement Tapes* cassette (Free Association) **1985** track on *Flipside Vinyl Fanzine Vol* 2 comp LP (Gasatanka)

OVERKILL (LA)

1982 *Hell's Getting Hotter* EP (SST 008) "Hell's Getting Hotter; Our War; Burn The School; Don't Wanna Be Told" *Merrill Ward - vocals • Jeff Dimmick - guitar • Ron Cordy - bass • Kurt Markham - drums* **1983** "Hell's Getting Hotter" on *The Blasting Concept* comp LP (SST 013) **1986** "Over The Edge" on *The Blasting Concept Volume II* comp LP (SST 043)

PANICS (LA)

1980 7" EP (Gulcher, 201) " I Wanna Kill My Mom; Best Band; Tie Me Up, Baby!" *John Barge - vocals • Ian Brewer - guitar; vocals • Yara - bass; vocals • Mike Ost - drums; vocals*

PARIAH (SF)

1982 "Learning Process" on *Not So Quiet On The Western Front* comp LP (Alternative Tentacles) **1982** "Up To Us" b/w "Reputation" (Posh Boy, PBS 18) *Tony Cox -vocals • Mike Smith - guitar • Ray Lujan - bass • Greg Tavers-drums* **1983** *Youths Of Age* (Posh Boy, PBS 147) "Youth Of Age; Inside Looking Out; Blind Resistance; Faith In Mercy; White Line; All The King's Men; Passion & Pride; Running For Cover; Striking Back"

PEACE CORPSE (LA)

1983 *Quincy's Lament* 7" EP (Toxic Shock) "Quincy's Lament; Presidente Camouflage; Small Talk Death; Dead In A Pile Of Chains; One Way; Jocko Macho (Quincy Punks)"

PLEASED YOUTH (NJ)

1985 "I'd Rather Be An Asshole," "Obedience School" on *New Jersey's Got It* comp (Buy Our Records) **1986** *Dangerous Choo -Choo* (Buy Our Records)

POISON IDEA (Portland)

1983 *Pick Your King* 7" EP (Fatal Erection) "Cult Band; Last One; Pure Hate; Castration; I Hate Reggae; Give It Up; Think Fast; Think Twice; It's An Action; This Thing Called Progress; In My Headache; Underage; Self Abuse" *Jerry A. - vocals • Tom Roberts - guitar • Chris Tense - bass • Dean Johnson - drums* **1984** "Discontent" b/w "Jailhouse Stomp" 7" **1984** *Record Collectors Are Pretentious Assholes* (Taang! 46) "A.A.; Legalize Freedom; Cold Comfort; Typical; Thorn In My Side; Laughing Boy; Rubber Husband; Right?; Rich Get Richer; Don't Like It Here; Die On Your Knees; Time To Go" *Jerry A. - vocals • Tom Pig Champion Roberts - guitar • Chris Tense - bass • Dean Johnson - drums* **1985** *Kings Of Punk* (Taang! 47) "Lifestyles; Short Fuse; God Not God; Ugly American; Subtract; Cop An Attitude; Death Wish Kids; Made To Be Broken; Tormented Imp; One By One; Out Of The Picture"

POLITICAL CRAP (LA)

1981 "On Our Own," "Slow Death," "Rejected" on *Who Cares* comp LP (American Standard)

POP-O-PIES (SF)

1981 "Truckin'" b/w "Truckin' (Rap)" **1982** *The White EP* **1984** *Joe's Second Record* (Subterranean) **1985** *Joe's Third Album* (Subterranean) "I Am The Walrus; Bummed Out Guy; World-O-Morons; The Words Of Jamal, Part II (The Rainbow Bridge Version); Sugar Magnolia; Ripped Off & Promoted Lame; The Frisco Inn; Shut Up and Listen" *Joe Pop-O -Pie - vocals • Kirk Heydt - guitar • Mike King - bass • Johnny Gilliland - drums*

THE PREVARICATORS (Richmond)

1983 *No Kidding* EP (Zero Degree, ZD005) "Ode To Mr. Ed; Hanky Panky; Livin' In Khaki; I'm So Cool" *Steve Hunter - vocals • Tom Rodriguez - guitar • David Stover - guitar • Craig Thompson - bass • Hal Imburg - drums*

THE PROLETARIAT (Boston) **1983** *Soma Holiday*

(Non-U/Radiobeat) "Decoration; Splendid Wars; Famine; Embraced; Events; Repeat; Another Banner Raised; Hollow Victory; Condition; Avoidance; Pictures; Bread And Circus; Blind; Subsidized; Torn Curtain; Purge; Scars; Decide On Change; No Lesser Of Evils" *Richard Brown - vocals • Frank Michaels - guitar; vocals • Peter Bevilacqua - bass; vocals • Tom McKnight - drums* **1985** "An Uneasy Peace" on *P.E.A.C.E.* comp LP (R Radical) **1985** "Marketplace" b/w "Death of A Hedon" (Homestead) *Richard Brown - vocals • Laurel Bowman - vocals • Frank Michaels - guitar • Peter Bevilacqua - bass • Tom McKnight - drums* **1985** *Indifference* (Homestead) "Indifference; Pride; Better Man; Homeland; Columns; Sins; An Uneasy Peace; Recollections; Instinct; Trail Of Tears; The Guns Are Winning; No Real Hope; Prelude; No Real Hope; Piecework; Marketplace"

PSYCHO (Boston)

1983 *Psycho* 12" EP (Ax/ction) "Psycho; Destruction; Dark Side Of The Human Mind; Elimination Process; Contempt; Kids Are For Tricks; National Clock Society"

RASZEBRAE (LA)

1985 *Cheap Happiness or Lofty Suffering* (Unseen Hand, UHT727) Range Riders; Psychedelic Cyclaid; To Be Excessive; Stray People; Youth Song; Sweet Suicide; Raise Your Flag; Bad Moves; Hit Or Miss (Ode to Jimi);Purity; Bastardization (of Jean-Paul Sartre") *Debbie Patino - vocals • Ingrid Baumgart - guitar; vocals • Janet Housden - drums • Katie Childe - bass*

REAGAN YOUTH (NY)

1984 7-song 12" EP **1985** "Reagan Youth" on *P.E.A.C.E.* comp LP (R Radical) *Dave Insurgent - vocals • Paul Joey Turk Cripple-guitar • Pusi Korrahts bass • Johnny Aztec*

REALLY RED (Houston)

1979 "Crowd Control" 7" (CIA 001) **1980** *Modern Needs* 7" EP (CIA 002) "White Lies," "Modern Needs" **1980** *Despise Moral Majority* 7" EP (CIA 003) "Entertainment; Starvation Dance; Nico; A Reminder" **1981** "Prostitution" on *Let Them Eat Jellybeans* comp (Alternative Tentacles, VIRUS 4) **1981** *Teaching You The Fear* (CIA 006) "Too Political?; Bored With Apathy; Teaching You The Fear; Decay; Run 'Em Out; No Art; Bar-B-Que; White Lies; Nico; Starvation Dance;Prostitution;Aim Tastes Good; Entertainment; Pigboy; Ain't No Time; Lockjaw; Reminder" **1982** *New Strings For Old Puppets* EP (CIA 009) "I Refuse To Sing; No More Art; Suburban Disease; I Was A Teenage Fuck Up; Ode To Kurtis Kren" **1983** "Nobody Rules" on *Cottage Cheese From The Lips Of Death* comp LP (Ward 9) *U-Ron Bondage - vocals • John Paul Yuma - bass • Kelly Green - guitar • Robert N.M.N. Weber - drums*

REBELS AND INFIDELS (SF)

1982 *Corporate Picnic* (Fowl)

REBEL TRUTH (Sacramento)

1982 "All I Know" on *Not So Quiet On The Western Front* comp (Alternative Tentacles, VIRUS14) **1983** 7" EP (Version Sound, Dub004) "The Request; Try; In The Red; Trickle Down; Child Hosts The Parasite; Moneyman; Where The Heart Is; The Good Life; Unscene Effort"

RED CROSS, REDD KROSS (LA)

1980 "Cover Band," "I Hate My School," "Standing In Front Of Poseurs," "Annette's Got The Hits," "Clorox Girls," "S&M Partyon" *The Siren* comp (Posh Boy) *Jeff McDonald - vocals • Greg Hetson - guitar • Steve McDonald - bass; vocals • Ron Reyes - drums* **1980** *Red Cross* EP (Posh Boy) **1981** "Notes & Chords," "Mean Nothing To Me" on *American Youth Report* comp (Invasion/Thunderbolt) **1981** "Burn Out" on *Rodney On The ROQ Vol. 2* comp (Posh Boy) **1981** "Cease To Exist," "Everyday There's Something New," "Kill Someone You Hate" on *Public Service* comp (Smoke 7) **1982** "Puss 'N' Boots" on *Hell Comes To Your House* comp (Bemisbrain) **1982** "Tatum O'Neil And The Fried Vegetables" on *Sudden Death* comp (Smoke Seven) **1982** "Rich Brat" on *Life Is Ugly - So Why Not Kill Yourself* comp (New Underground) **1982** *Born Innocent* (Smoke Seven) "Linda Blair; White Trash; Every Day There's Something New; Solid Gold; Burnout; Charlie; Self-Respect; Pseudo Intellectual; Kill Someone You Hate; Look On Up At The Bottom; Cellulite City; I'm Alright" **1983** "Out Of Focus" on *Life Is Boring - So Why Not Steal This Record* comp (New Underground) **1984** *Teen Babes From Monsanto* (Gasatanka) "Deuce; Citadel; Heaven Only Knows; Ann; Savior Machine; Blow You A Kiss In The Wind; Linda Blair 1984" *Jeff McDonald - vocals; guitar • Steve McDonald - bass; vocals • Dave Peterson - drums; piano*

RED ROCKERS (New Orleans)

1981 "Dead Heroes" on *Rodney On The ROQ Vol. 2* comp LP

(Posh Boy, PBS) **1982** *Condition Red* (415/ Columbia) **1983** *Good As Gold* (415/ Columbia) "China; Good As Gold; Dreams Fade Away; Change The World Around; Answers To The Questions; 'Till It All Falls Down; Running Away From You; Fanfare For Metropolis; My House; Home Is Where The War Is" *John Griffith - vocals/guitar • James Singletary-guitar • Darren Hill - bass • Jim Reilly - drums* **1984** *Schizophrenic Circus* (415/ Columbia) "Just Like You; Blood From A Stone; Shades Of '45; Another Day; Freedom Row; Good Thing I Know Her; Eve Of Destruction? 'Both Hands In The Fire; Burning Bridges" *John Griffith- vocals/ guitar • Shawn Paddock - guitar/vocals • Darren Hill - bass; vocals • Jim Reilly - drums*

RED SCARE (LA)

1982 "Street Life" b/w "Street Life (demo)" (Posh Boy) **1983** track on *Destroy LA* comp (Mystic) **1983** "Keep America Beautiful" on *The Sound Of Hollywood 2* comp (Mystic)

REFLEX FROM PAIN

(CT) **1983** *Black & White* 7" EP (Death Threat) "Rednecks; Generic Life; Hangover; Media Control; Chemical; Holy Pictures" *Greg-vocals• Andrew-guitar • Dave-bass • Bill-drums*

REJECTORS (Seattle)

1982 *Thoughts Of War* EP (Fartz) "High Command; Rejection; Mercy Killing; Fight Establishment; Thoughts Of War; Life With Liberty; Slaves; How Do You Know; Go Die" *Bruce - vocals • Dave - guitar • Gerry - bass • Scott - drums*

RF7 (LA)

1981 "Jesus Loves You" on *American Youth Report* comp LP (Invasion/ Thunderbolt) **1981** "World Of Hate," "Scientific Race," "Long Live The Queen," "Perfect World" on *Public Service* comp (Smoke 7) **1982** *Fall In* (Smoke 7) "Viet Vets; Fall In; 666 Head; What I'm Trying To Say; Revolutionary Worker; Vampire Lady; 57 Million People; Fuck Money" **1982** *Weight Of The World* (Smoke 7) "Kiss Ass; Violence; Government Science Fiction; God Of God; Time Bomb; Scientific Race - Perfect World; Mission Of Mercy; Satan's Son; Low Class Girl; Weight Of The World; World Of Hate; Jesus Loves You" *Felix Alanis - vocals • Nick Lamagna - guitar; vocals • Robert Armstrong - bass; vocals • Walt Phelan - drums; vocals*

RHINO 39 (LA)

1979 *Xerox* 7" EP (Dangerhouse) "Xerox; No Compromise; Prolixin Stomp" *Dave Dacron - vocals • Larry Parrott - guitar • Mark Malone - bass • Tim Carhart - drums* **1981** "J. Alfred" on *American Youth Report* comp LP (Invasion/Thunderbolt)

RHYTHM PIGS (El Paso/TX)

1983 *An American Activity* 7" EP (Unclean) **1984** *Rhythm Pigs* (Mordam) "Conditional Love; Dr. Harley; Break New Ground; Human Drama; Six; Machines Are In; Peanuts; Break Or We'll Break Your Face; Taxi Cab; Searchin' For Myself; Conscience Song; Electric World; Road Machine" *Ed Ivey - vocals; bass • Greg Adams - guitar; vocals • Jay Smith - drums* **1985** flexi disc (Thrasher) **1986** *Choke On This* (Mordam) "Censorshit; Can't Change The World; Feedback; Elegy; Good For Life; Little Brother; Arkansas; Arkansas (Slight Return); Choke On This; Marlboro Man; Too High; Bad Reactor; Hooligan Bitch; Fire; Thanks For Coming" *Ed Ivey - vocals/bass • Greg Adams-guitar/ vocals • Kenny Craun - drums/vocals*

RIBSY (San Jose)

1982 "Collapse" on *Not So Quiet On The Western Front* comp LP (Alternative Tentacles, VIRUS14)

ROACH MOTEL (Florida)

1980 *Roach Motel* CS **1981** *Roach & Roll* 7" EP (Destroy) "I Hate The Sunshine State; Shut Up; Wetback; Now You're Gonna Die; Creep; More Beer" *Bob Fetz - vocals • Jeff Hodarr - guitar •*

George Tabb - guitar • Paul Miller - bass • Frank Mullen - drums
1982 "Heart Attack," "Fla. Reptile Land," "My Dog's Into
Anarchy" on *We Can't Help It If We're From Florida* comp 7"
(Destroy) **1983** track on *Annoy Your Neighbor With This Tape*
comp CS (Chainsaw) **1984** "Mad
Dog" on *Flipside* comp (Flipside)
1983 *What The Hell, It's Roach
Motel* 7" EP (Destroy)

R.P.A. (Seattle)
1983 "Shoot The Pope" b/w
"Bonecrusher" 7"

RUIN (Philly)
1983 "Proof," "Love Dog" on *Get Off
Our Back* comp LP (Red) **1984** *He-
Ho* (Red) "Alter; Dionysian; Freedom
Has No Bounds; Baby Doll; He - Ho;
Landium; Alarm; Master Song; Where
Fortune; Play With Fire; Twilight;
Proof; Rule Worshipper" *Vosco
Thomas - vocals • Damon Wallis -
lead guitar • Glenn Wallis - rhythm
guitar • Gordy Swope - bass• Rich
Hutchins - drums* **1986** *Fiat Lux* (Red) "You; Make Believe;
Hero; Famous Blue Raincoat; Life After Life; Proof; China;
Taster; White Rabbit; Rain; Great Divide; Real Good Time"
*Vosco Thomas - vocals • Damon Wallis - lead guitar • Glenn
Wallis - rhythm guitar • Paul Della Pella - bass • Rich Hutchins -
drums*

SACCHARINE TRUST (LA) **1980** "Hearts &
Barbarians" on *Cracks In The Sidewalk* comp LP (New Alliance,
NAR 001) **1981** *Pagan Icons* EP (SST 006) "I Have…;
Community Lie; Effort To Waste; Mad At The Co.; I Am Right;
We Don't Need Freedom; Success & Failure; A Human Certainty"
*Joaquin Milhouse Brewer - vocals • Joe Baiza - guitar •
Earl Liberty - bass • Mr. Robert C. Holzman - drums* **1982** "A
Christmas Cry" 7" **1983** "A Human
Certainty" on *The Blasting Concept*
comp LP (SST 013) **1984** *Surviving
You, Always* (SST 024) "The Giver
Takes; Lot's Seed; Sunk; Speak; The
House, The System, The Concrete;
Remnants; The Cat Cracker; Our
Discovery; A Good Night's Bleeding;
Craving The Center; YHWH On Acid;
Peace Frog" *Joaquin Milhouse
Brewer - vocals • Joe Baiza - guitar •
Mark Hodson - bass • Tony Cicero -
drums* **1985** *Worldbroken* (SST 046)
"The Worm's Quest; Just Think;
Merciful Mother; Estuary; Hail Our
Web; In The Sandbox; II Samuel
Chapter 4; The Testimony; Words Left
Unspoken; Fred Presented Himself;
On The Verge Of Finding; No
Compromise Here" *Joaquin
Milhouse Brewer - vocals • Joe Baiza - guitar • Michael Watt -
bass • Tony Cicero - drums* **1986** "Emotions And Anatomy" on
The Blasting Concept Vol II comp LP (SST 043) **1986** *The
Sacramental Element* CS (SST) **1986** *We Became Snakes* (SST
048) We Became Snakes; Drugstore Logic; Frankie On A Pony;
The Need; For Her While; Effort To Waste; The Redeemer;
Longing For Ether; Belonging To October" *Jack Brewer - vocals
• Joe Baiza - guitar • Bob Fitzer - bass • Tony Cicero - drums •
Steve Moss - tenor sax*

SADISTIC EXPLOITS (Philly)
1981 "Apathy b/w "Freedom" 7" **1982** 8-song 7" EP *Bryan K -
vocals • Ped Drick - guitar • Robbie - bass • Howard - drums*

SADO NATION (Portland)
1982 *We're Not Equal* (Brainstorm, 1001) "Messed Up Mixed
Up; Armaggeddon; We're Not Equal; Don't Bother Me; Nuke Up

Now!; On The Wall; Fight Back; Industrial Revolution; Politics &
Passion; Cut Off The Cord; No Use; Johnny Paranoid" *Mish
Bondage - vocals • David Corboy - guitar • Steve Casmano - bass
• Chuck Arjavac - drums* **1983** "Fear Of Failure" on *Copulation*
comp LP (Mystic)

SAMHAIN (NJ)
1984 *Initium* (Plan 9, PL9-04)
1985 *Unholy Passion* EP (PL9 - 05)

SAVAGE CIRCLE (NY)
1982 *Kill Yourself* or *Savage Circle*
7" EP (Savage) "Kill Yourself; We
Don't Have To; Don't Do It; Hardcore
Rules; Kill Corpse" *Javi Savage -
vocals • Carl Frag - guitar • Anthony
Frag - bass • Tommy Olio - drums*

SCAPEGOATS (Santa Cruz)
1982 "Shit Can" on *Not So Quiet On
The Western Front* comp LP
(Alternative Tentacles)

SCREAM (CA)
1982 7" EP (Immortal Nut) "Gov't
Primer; Generation '80; Drainage; Mass Media"

SCREAM (DC)
1982 *Still Screaming* (Dischord, no. 9) "Came Without Warning;
Bedlam; Solidarity; Your Wars; Killer; Piece Of Her Time; Human
Behavior; Stand; Fight; American Justice; New Song; Laissez -
Faire; Influenced; Hygiene; Cry Wolf; Total Mash; Who Knows -
Who Cares?; Amerarockers; U. Suck A.; We're Fed Up" *Peter
Stahl - vocals • Franz Stahl - guitar • Skeeter Thompson - bass •
Kent Stax - drums* **1984** *This Side Up* (Dischord, no.15 1/2)

SECOND WIND (DC)
1984 *Second Wind* 12" EP *Bert Queiroz - bass • Rich Moore-
drums • Steve Hangsen - guitar*

SECTION 8 (Reno)
1982 *Section 8* CS **1982** "Fat,
Drunk & Stupid" on *Not So Quiet
On The Western* Front comp LP
(Alternative Tentacles)

SECRET HATE (LA/OC)
1982 "Deception," "New Routine,"
"Suicide" on *Hell Comes To Your
House* comp (Bemisbrain) **1982**
"Charade" on *You Can't Argue With
Suckcess* comp (Mystic) **1983**
Vegetable Dancing (New Alliance)
"Get On The Bus; Theme Song;
Rixadik; Ballad Of Johnny Butt;
Midas Touch; Edge Marine; Latin
Chongo"

SEDITIONARIES (LA)
1982 "Wherewolf" b/w "Shapes" 7"

SHARP CORNERS (LA)
1980 "Me Too" on *Cracks In The Sidewalk* comp (New Alliance)

SHATTERED FAITH (LA)
1981 "I Love America" b/w "Reagan Country" (Posh Boy)
1981 "I Love America," "Discontent," "Trilogy" on *Who Cares*
comp (American Standard) **1981** "Reagan Country" on *Amercan
Youth Report* comp (Invasion/Thunderbolt) **1981** "Right Is Right"
on *Rodney On The ROQ Vol. 2* comp (Posh Boy) **1981** "Victims
Of Society" on *Is Beautiful - So Why Not Eat Health Food* comp
(New Underground) **1982** *Shattered Faith* (Record Prophet, later
Posh Boy) "Too Tense; U.S.A.; Right Is Right; Mirrors Reflection;
Trilogy; Born To You; Dark Side; Strange Daze; Always The
Same; No Fun No Friends; Hard To Be Free; Final Conflict"
*Spencer Alston - vocals • Dennis McGahey - lead guitar • Kerry
Martinez - rhythm guitar • Bob Tittle - bass • Chris Moon - drums*
1983 "The Omen" on *Life Is Boring - So Why Not Steal This*

Record comp (New Underground) **1983** "Final Conflict" on *Live At The Eastern Front 2* (Enigma) **1983** "Rise & Fall," "Last Name First" on *The Sound Of Hollywood 2* (Mystic) **1983** on *Destroy LA* comp (Mystic) **1983** *Shattered Faith Vol. 2* six-song 12" EP

SHELL SHOCK
(New Orleans) **1981** 7" EP (Vinyl Solution) "Your Way; My Brain Is Jelly; Execution Time" *Greg-vocal • Hatch Boy - guitar • Scott - bass • John - drums* **1985** *Vol. 2* (Slag)

SICK PLEASURE (SF)
1982 *Dolls Under Control* (Subterranean) "Three Seconds Of Pleasure; Get The Muni Driver; Sick Pleasure; I Don't Play Pretty Music; Herpies VIRUS Two; Fools Can't Break Me; Dolls Under Control; Girls Like You *Niki Siki - vocals • Michael Fox - guitar • Dave Chavez - bass • Sal Paradise - drums* **1983** *Speed Rules* EP (Subterranean) "Speed Rules; I Wanna Burn My Parents; Love Song; B.N.S.; Disintegration; Try To Break Me; Time To Change"

SIEGE (Western Mass.)
1984 *Drop Dead* demo CS "Drop Dead; Conform; Life of Hate; Starvation; Armageddon; Walls; Sad But True; Cold War; Grim Reaper"

SILLY KILLERS (Seattle)
1982 7" EP (No Threes) "Not That Time Again; Knife Manual; Social Bitch; Sissy Faggots" *Eddie - vocals • Skats - guitar • Gary - bass; vocals • Tim - drums*

SIN 34 (LA)
1982 "Only Love," "Nuclear War," "Who Needs Them" on *Sudden Death* comp LP (Smoke 7) **1982** *Die Laughing* 7" EP (Spinhead) "American America; Children Shall Not Be Heard; Uniform; 12 Hour Trip; Join The Race" *Julie Lanfeld— vocals • Mike Geek - guitar • Phil - bass • Dave Markey - drums* **1983** track on *The Sound Of Hollywood: Girls* comp LP (Mystic) **1984** *Do You Feel Safe?* (Spinhead) "Do You Feel Safe?; After You; War At Home; Barbie & Ken; Say We Suck; Not; Live Or Die; New Wave Slut; Left Waiting; Forgive & Forget; Two Words; Join The Race; Turn On - Tune In - Drop Out; Nothing Makes Sense; Uncontrollable Urge"

SINS (LA/OC)
1982 *Mood Music* EP (Black Noise) "Fighting In USA; Killing Machine; Indirections; Funeral Hour; Dominant Submission; Mind War; Skin Walk"

SKEWBALD (DC)
1986 *Grand Union* 7" (Dischord) *Ian MacKaye -vocals • Jeff Nelson - drums • Eddie Janney guitar • John Falls - bass*

SLEEPING DOGS (SF)
1982 *Beware* 7" EP (Crass) "Same Old Story; Concrete; Suzy's Song; I Got Mine In El Salvador; Soldier"

SLUGLORDS (SF)
1984 *Trails Of Slime* LP

S.O.A. (DC)
1981 *No Policy* 7" EP (Dischord, no. 2) "Lost In Space; Draw Blank; Girl Problems; Black Out; Gate Crashers; War Zone; Riot; Gang Fight; Public Defender; Gonna Have To Fight" *Henry Garfield - vocals • Michael Hampton - guitar • Wendel Blow - bass • Simon Jacobsen - drums* **1982** "I Hate The Kids," "Disease," "Stepping Stone Party" on *Flex Your Head* comp LP (Dischord, no. 7)

SOCIAL DISTORTION (LA) **1981** "Mainliner" b/w
"Play Pen" (Posh Boy, PBS11) **1981** "1945" on *Rodney On The ROQ Vol. 2* comp LP (Posh Boy, 123) **1982** "Lude Boy" on *Hell*

Comes To Your House comp LP (Bemisbrain, BB123/124) **1982** "Mass Hysteria" on *Someone Got Their Head Kicked In* comp LP (BYO, 001) **1982** "1945" b/w "Under My Thumb," "Play Pen" 7" (Faulty, SD 4501) **1982** "1945" b/w "Under My Thumb" "Play Pen" 12" (13th Floor) **1983** *Mommy's Little Monster* (13th Floor) "The Creeps; Another State Of Mind; It Wasn't A Pretty Picture; Telling Them; Hour Of Darkness; Mommy's Little Monster; Anti - Fashion; All The Answers; Moral Threat" *Mike Ness - guitar; vocals • Dennis Danell - guitar • Brent Liles - bass • Derek O'Brien - drums*

SOCIAL SUICIDE (DC)
1982 "Born Again," "Beat Them," "Foul Appetite," "30- Second Holiday" on *Mixed Nuts Don't Crack* comp LP (Outside)

SOCIAL UNREST (SF)
1981 7" EP (Infra Red) "Making Room For Youth; Join The People Who Joined The Army; Rush Hour" *Creetin K - Os - vocals • Danny Radio Shack - guitar • Doug Logic - guitar • John Bob Vollick - bass • Mark Manslaughter - drums* **1982** "Their Mistakes" on *Not So Quiet On The Western Front* comp LP (Alternative Tentacles) **1982** *Rat In A Maze* (Libertine) "General Enemy; Red, White & Blue; Thinking Of Suicide; Lord's Prayer; Mental Breakdown; Stab Me In The Back; I Love You" **1985** *SU 2000* (Libertine)

SOCIETY DOG (SF)
1980 "Working Class People" b/w "Bad Dream" (Subterranean) *Johnithin Christ - vocals • Joe Dirt - guitar • Jamel Hell - bass • D.D. - drums* **1981** on *SF Underground 2* comp (Subterranean) **1981** *Off The Leash* 7" EP (Subterranean) "How Could I Feel It; The Baby Is Dead; Metropolitian Rush; On The Street" *Johnithin Christ - vocals • Joe Dirt - guitar • James Hell - bass • D.D. - drums*

SOLDIERS OF FORTUNE (SF)
1982 *No Wimps Or Posers (It's The American Way)* 12" EP (Slow Death)

SOLGER (Seattle)
1982 7" EP "American Youth; Dead Soldier; I Hate It; Raping Dead Nuns; Aman" *Kyle - vocals • Paul - guitar • Doug - bass • Tor - drums*

SORRY (Boston)
1984 *Imaginary Friend* (Radiobeat) "My Word; Misanthrope; Doomed From The Start; Where Were You?; Why Do I Have To Look At You?; One More Step; Don't Assume; Bouncer; Imaginary Friend; Listen; No Concern; Unhealthy; On My Own; Buried; Moondance; Dirty Old Man; Honesty; 24" *Jonathan Easley - vocals • David Kleiler - guitar • Chuck Hahn - bass • Andy Burstein - drums* **1986** *Way It Is* (Homestead) "Satellite; Mystery; Anything; Just Making Noise; Read This; Not Today; That's Fine With Me; Stop; Deny; Rise and Fall; Far; In The End"

SQUARE COOLS (SF)
1982 "I Don't Want To Die For My Country" on *Not So Quiet On The Western Front* comp LP (Alternative Tentacles, VIRUS14)

SS DECONTROL, SSD (Boston) **1982** *The Kids Will Have Their Say!* 12" EP (XClaim! #1; Dischord # 7 1/2) "Boiling Point; Fight Them; Do You Ever Care; Not Normal; Wasted Youth; Jock Itch; Fun To You; V.A.; How Much Art; Kids Will Have Their Say; Headed Straight; War Threat; Teach Me Violence; Screw; Who's To Judge; Police Beat; United; The End"
1983 *Get It Away* 12" EP (XClaim!, #3) "Glue; Forced Down Your Throat; Get It Away; Under The Influence; Nothing Done; X Claim; No Reply"

1984 *How We Rock* (Modern Method, MM022) "How We Rock Intro; How We Rock; Words That Kill; The Choice; On The Road; What It Takes; What If I" **1985** *Break It Up* (Homestead, HMS027) "Break It Up; Children Will Rock; Heart Failure; Hit The Bottom; Blood Flood; No Solution; Baby Black; Calender; Screams Of the Night; Feel The Flame" *David Springa Spring - vocals • Francois Levesque - lead guitar • Alan Barile - rhythm guitar • James Sciarappa - bass • Chris Foley - drums*

STAINS (LA)

1983 *The Stains* (SST, 010) "Sick and Crazy; Violent Children; Gang - Related Death; Get Revenge; Germany; Political Scandal; Pretty Girls; Nowhere; Quest the Human Race; I'm Normal; Young Nazis" **1983** "Get Revenge" on *The Blasting Concept* comp (SST, 016) *Rudy Navarro-vocals • Robert Becerra - guitar • Ceasar Viscarra - bass • Gilbert Berumen - drums*

STAINS (Portland, ME)

1980 7" EP (Gutter Worst) "Feel Guilty; Give Ireland Back To The Snakes; Sick Of Being Sick; Submission"

STALAG 13 (LA)

1983 *In Control* LP

STATE (Detroit)

1983 *No Illusions* 7" EP (Statement) "Subvert; New Right; Attention; Hard Line; No Illusions; Police State; Girl Violence" *Preston Woodward - vocals • Art Tendler - guitar • Chris Day - bass • Kier Murray -drums*

STICKMEN WITH RAYGUNS (Dallas)

1981 "Learn To Hate In The 80s" b/w "Scavenger Of Death" (VVV, #004) *as Bobby Soxx* **1982** *Hate In The 80s* (VVV, 05) **1983** "Two Fist" on *VVV—Live At The Hot Club*

STILLBORN CHRISTIANS (NC)

1983 "New Right," "Fred," "Aggression" on *Why Are We Here?* comp 7" (No Core)

STIMULATORS (NY)

1980 "Loud, Fast Rules" b/w "Run, Run, Run" (Stimulator) *Patrick Mack - vocals • Denice Mercedes - guitar • Anne Gustavson - bass • Harley Flanagan - drums* **1982** *Loud Fast Rules* CS (ROIR) "Facts; Crazy House Rock; Dancing In The Front Lines, Hopeless, Blind Ambition; Not The Same, M.A.C.H.I.N.E.; 100X Before; Rock 'N' Roll All Night; Dah Dah Dah; $ick Of George; Got A Right; Loud Fast Rules" *Patrick Mack - vocals • Denice Mercedes - guitar • Nick Marden - bass • Harley Flanagan - drums*

STRANGLEHOLD (Boston)

1984 "She's Not Leavin" 7" (One Step, #3)

STRIKE UNDER (Chicago)

1981 "Fucking Uniforms," "Anarchy Song" on *Busted At Oz* comp LP (Autumn, AU - 2)

SUBHUMANS (Vancouver)

1980 *Incorrect Thoughts* (Quintessence)
1981 "Slave To My Dick" on *Let Them Eat Jellybeans* (Alternative Tentacles) **1983** *No Wishes, No Prayers* (SST)

SUBVERTZ (Chicago)

1981 "March Forth," "State Of The Union" on *Busted At Oz* (Autumn, AU-2) **1981** *Independent Study* EP (Clandestine) "Man For The Job; Radiation Nation; TV Personality; Can't Control Myself" *Brian - vocals • Greg-guitar • Steve- bass • Mike- drums*

SUBURBAN MUTILATION

(Green Bay) **1982** *Daddy Was A Nazi* cassette EP

SUICIDAL TENDENCIES (LA)

1983 *Suicidal Tendencies* (Frontier) "Suicide's An Alternative;

You'll Be Sorry; Two-Sided Politics; I Shot The Devil; Subliminal; Won't Fall In Love Today; Institutionalized; Memories Of Tommorrow; Possessed; I Saw Your Mommy…; Fascist Pig; I Want More; Suicidal Failure" *Mike Muir - vocals • Grant Estes - guitar • Louiche Mayorga - bass • Amery Smith - drums* **1984** "Institutionalized" on *Repo Man* soundtrack (San Andreas/MCA)

SUN CITY GIRLS (Phoenix)

1983 "Bobby Sands Boogie" on *Amuck* comp (Placebo)**1984** *Sun City Girls* (Placebo) **1986** *Midnight Cowboys From Ipanema* CS (Breakfast Without Meat) **1986** Caravan on *More Coffee For The Politicians* comp LP (Placebo) **1986** *Grotto Of Miracles* (Placebo)

SWA (LA)

1985 *Your Future If You Have One* (SST 053) **1985** *S.W.A.* (SST 061) **1986** Mystery Girl on *The Blasting Concept Volume II* (SST 043) **1986** *Sex Dr.* (SST 073) "Catacombs; Sea and Sky; Sex Doctor; The Only One; Oklahoma; Onslaught; Big Ride; Round and Round; The Evil & The Good **1986** Sea & Sky b; w Sex Doctor (SST) *Merrill Ward - vocals • Richard Ford - guitar • Chuck Dukowski - bass • Greg Cameron - drums*

SYMBOL SIX (LA)

1982 *Symbol Six* EP (Posh Boy, PBS 1030) "Ego; Taxation; Symbol Six; Beverlywood"

TALES OF TERROR

(SF) **1984** *Tales Of Terror* (CD Presents, CD015) "Hound Dog; That Girl; Possession; Deathryder; Evil; 13; Romance; Over Elvis Worship; Tales Of Terror; Jim; Chamber Of Horrors; Ozzy" *Rat's Ass - vocals • Luther Storms - guitar; vocals • Capt. Trip Mender - guitar; vocals • Dusty Coffin - bass; vocals • Thopper Jaw-drums* **1985** track on *Them Boners Be Poppin* comp (Boner)

TAR BABIES (Madison)

1982 *Tar Babies-Mecht Mensch* CS (Bone Air) **1982** *Face The Music* EP (Bone Air) **1983** "The Ocean," "Triplets" on *The Master Tape Volume II* (Affirmation, Aff-02) **1985** *Respect Your Nightmares*(Bone Air/Paradise)

TARGET 13 (LA)

1981 "Rodney On The ROQ" on *Rodney On The ROQ Vol. 2* (Posh Boy, PBS-123)

TEEN IDLES (DC)

1981 *Minor Disturbance* 7" EP (Dischord, No.1) "Teen Idles; Sneakers; Get Up & Go; Deadhead; Fleeting Fury; Fiorucci Nightmare; Getting In My Way; Too Young To Rock" *Nathan Strejcek - vocals • Geordie Grindel - guitar • Ian MacKaye - bass; vocals • Jeff Nelson - drums* **1982** "I Drink Milk," "Commie Song," "No Fun" on *Flex Your Head* comp LP (Dischord, No.7)

TOMMY DOG (NY)

1984 *In My Own Words* 7" EP (Lucky Strike) "You're Not Fire; 'Till You're Dead; Welcome To Madam Stranges; Fade To Black; The Monster; An Angel Fell To Death; Church Of Fear; Hex" *Tommy Dog - vocals; guitar • Alex Totino - guitar • Mr. Martian- bass • Jack Rabid-drums*

TONGUE AVULSION (SF)

1982 "Libyan Hit Squad" on *Not So Quiet On The Western Front* (Alternative Tentacles, VIRUS14)

TOXIC REASONS (Dayton)

1981 "Riot Squad" on *Process Of Elimination* comp 7" EP (Touch & Go, T&G4) **1982** "Somebody Help Me" on *Reagan Regime Review* comp (Selfless) **1982** *Independence* (Risky, RI 004) "Mercenary; Drunk & Disorderly; War Hero; Riot Squad; Noiise Boys; Ghost Town; Killer; Somebody Help Me; How Do You Feel; White Noise; The Shape Of Things To Come; Rally Round The Flag, Boy" **1982**

"Mercenary" on *The Master Tape* comp LP (Affirmation, Aff-01) **1983** *Bullets For You* (Treason, TR002) "Tomorrow Tonight; We're The Revolution; Get Out The Gun; Never Give In; It's A Lie; Killing The Future; Breaking Down The War Machine; God Bless America; Can't Get Away; Do What You Can; Gotta Believe" *Bruce Stuckey - guitar/vocals • Terry Howe-guitar/vocals • Bertram (Tufty) Clough - bass/vocals • Jimmy Joe Pearson - drums; vocals* **1984** *Ghost Town* 12" EP (Risky) "Ghost Town; Killer; Noise Boys" *Ed Pittman - vocals • Bruce Stucky - lead guitar • Rob Stout - rhythm guitar • Greg Stout - bass • JJ Pearson - drums* **1984** split 7" EP w/Zero Boys (Selfless) "No Pity; White Noise"

TOXIN III (New Orleans)

1982 *Peer Pressure* EP (Vinyl Solution)

TSOL (LA/OC)

1981 *T.S.O.L.* 12" EP (Posh Boy, PBS 1013) "Superficial Love; Property Is Theft; No Way Out; Abolish Government; Silent Majority; World War III" *Jack Greggors - vocals • Ron Emory - guitar • Mike Roche - bass • Francis Gerald Barnes - drums* **1981** *Dance With Me* (Frontier, FLP004) "Sounds Of Laughter; Code Blue; The Triangle; 80 Times; I'm Tired Of Life; Love Story; Silent Scream; Funeral March; Die For Me; Peace Through Power; Dance With Me" **1981** "Sounds Of Laughter" on *American Youth Report* (Invasion/Thunderbolt) **1982** *Weathered Statues* 7" EP (Alternative Tentacles, VIRUS 10) "Man And Machine; Weathered Statues; Thoughts Of Yesterday; Word Is" *Jack Ladoga - vocals • Ron Emory - guitar • Mike Roche - bass • Todd Scrivener - drums • Greg Kuehn - keyboards* **1982** "Weathered Statues" on *Rat Music For Rat People* comp LP (Go!, GO 003) **1983** "Peace Through Power" on *Posh Hits Volume I* (Posh Boy) **1983** *Beneath The Shadows* (Alternative Tentacles; Faulty, VIRUS 29) "Soft Focus; Forever Old; She'll Be Saying; Beneath The Shadows; Send My Thoughts; Glass Streets; Other Side; Walk Alone; Wash Away; Waiting For You" *Jack Delauge - vocals • Ron Emory - guitar • Mike Roche - bass • Todd Scrivener - drums • Greg Kuehn - keyboards* **1984** *Change Today?* (Enigma) "Black Magic; Just Like Me; In Time; Red Shadows; Flowers By The Door; American Zone; It's Gray; John; Nice Guys; How Do" *Joe Wood - guitar; vocals • Ron Emory - guitar • Mike Roche - bass • Mitch Dean - drums* **1986** *Revenge* (Enigma) No Time; Nothin' For You; Memories; Colors (Take Me Away); Madhouse; Revenge; Change Today; Still The Same; Your Eyes; Everybody's A Cop"

U-BOATS (Florida)

1982 "Government Rip-Off" b/w "Break Out Tonight" (Crow) *Mike Nelson - vocals • Jay Jetmore - guitar • Bob Widenhofer - bass • Hitler - drums* **1983** *Dead & Desperate* 7" EP (Crow) "America Unemployed; VFW Ball; Bad Boy" *Mike Nelson - vocals • Jay Jetmore - guitar • Alex Civiletti - bass • Aaron Knerr - drums*

U-MEN (Seattle)

1984 *U - Men* (Bomb Shelter) **1986** *Stop Spinning* (Homestead) **1986** "Blight," "Shoot Em Down," "Gila" on *Sub Pop 100* CS (Sub Pop) *John Bigley - vocals • Tom Price - guitar • Jim Tillman - bass • Charlie Ryan - drums*

UNDEAD (NY)

1982 "Social Reason," "Nightmare" on *New York Thrash* comp CS (ROIR) **1982** *Nine Toes Later* 7" EP (Stiff; Post/Mortem, PM 1001) "Life Of Our Own; My Kinda Town; When The Evening Comes; I Want You Dead" *Bobby Steele - guitar; vocals • Natz - bass • Patric Blanck - drums* **1985** "Verbal Abuse" b/w "Misfit" 7" (Post Mortem, PM 1002) *Bobby Steele - guitar; vocals • Brain Payne - bass • Bobby Savage - drums* **1985** "Never Say Die" b/w "In 1984" 7" (Post Mortem, PM 1003) **1986** *Never Say Die!*

(Rebel, Germany) *Bobby Steele - guitar; bass; vocals • Steve Zing - drums • Bob Allecca - sax*

UNIFORM CHOICE (LA/OC)

1985 *Screaming For Change* (Wishing Well) **1986** *You Are The One* 7" EP (as Unity) (Wishing Well)

UNITED MUTATION

(DC) **1982** "Out Of Hand," "D.C. Screws The World," "Oh No," "Lice & Fleas," "Vermin" on *Mixed Nuts Don't Crack* comp (Outside)

UNTOUCHABLES (DC)

1982 "Rat Patrol," "Nic Fit," "I Hate You" on *Flex Your Head* comp (Dischord, No. 7) *Alec MacKaye • Bert Quieroz • Chris Bald • Danny Ingram*

URBAN ASSAULT

(Reno/Lake Tahoe) **1982** "SLT" on *Not So Quiet On The Western Front* comp LP (Alternative Tentacles) **1982** *Urban Assault* 7" EP (Fowl) Urban Assault; Shock Value; Join The Army; Product Of Society" *Dagar - vocals • Kevin - guitar • Victoria - bass • James - drums*

URBAN WASTE (NY)

1983 *Urban Waste* 7" EP(Mob Style/Wasteland) "Police Brutality; Public Opinion; No Hope; Wasted Life; Skank; Ignorant; BNC; Regret" *Kenny Ahrens-vocals • Johnny Waste-guitar • Andy Apathy -bass • John Dany-drums*

THE VAINS (Seattle)

1980 7" EP (No Threes) "School Jerks; The Fake; The Loser" *Chris Crass Utting - vocals; guitar • Nico Teen - bass; vocals • Andy Freeze - drums*

VANDALS (LA/OC)

1983 *Peace Thru Vandalism* EP (Epitaph) "Wanna Be Manor; Urban Struggle; Legend Of Pat Brown; Pirate's Life; H.B. Hotel; Anarchy Burger" *Stevo - vocals • Jan Nils Ackermann - guitar • Steve Pfanter - bass • Joseph P. Escalante - drums* **1984** *When In Rome Do As The Vandals* (National Trust, NT884)

VATICAN COMMANDOS (CT)

1983 *Hit Squad For God* 7" EP (Pregnant Nun) "Why Must I Follow; It's So Scary; Housewife On Valium; Hit Squad For God; Your Way; Wunderbread" *Chuck Wheat - vocals • M.H. - guitar • Jim Spar - bass • Charles Moody - drums*

VENGEANCE (SF)

1982 "Fight The System" on *Not So Quiet On The Western Front* comp (Alternative Tentacles, VIRUS14)

VERBAL ABUSE (Houston/SF) **1982** *We're An American Band* (Fowl) **1986** *Rocks Your Liver* (Boner) "V.A. Rocks Your Liver; Metal Melissa The Pissa; Set Me Free; Vengeance; Worth A Try; Can't Stop Us Now; Ratt Pakk; Nothing Changes; The Chase; Time To Go; Best Friends; Saturday Night's Alright For Fighting" *Scott Wilkins - vocals • Joie Mastrokalos - guitar • Dave Koko Chavez - bass • Gregg James - drums*

VERBAL ASSAULT (Providence, RI)

1986 *Learn* (Positive Force, PF7) **1986** Untitled on *Another Shot Of Bracken* comp (Positive Force, PF9) **1987** *Trial* (Giant)

VIOLENT APATHY (Kalamazoo, MI)

1981 "I Can't Take It" on *Process Of Elimination* comp 7" EP (Touch & Go, T&G4) **1983** "Society Rules" on *The Master Tape Vol II* (Affirmation, Aff - 02)

VIRUS (NY)

1984 **Dark Ages** (Rat Cage)

VOID (DC)

1982 "Dehumanized," "Authority," "My Rules" on *Flex Your Head* comp LP (Dischord, no. 7) **1982** *Faith/Void* split LP

(Dischord, no. 8) "Who Are You?; Time To Die; Condensed Flesh; Ignorant People; Change Places; Ask Them Why; Organized Sports; My Rules; Self Defense; War Hero; Think; Explode"

VOODOO IDOLS (LA)

1982 "Dead Air" b/w "We Dig Nixon" 7" (Vee Dee, PMS 121482) *Johnny Yen - mouth • Butchie Necropolis - guitar • Vah Metz - bass • Hughie Whoopie - drums • Merlo - sax*

WARDS (Vermont)

1980 *The World Ain't Pretty And Neither Are We* 7" EP (No Thanks) "Weapons Factory; Ghetto; AFL - CIO; Reagan; Six O' Clock; Digger; Greens; Patrons; Santa's Cadillac; In This World"

WARZONE (NY)

1986 *Lower East Side Crew* EP (Revelation:1) "War Between The Races; Always A Friend For Life; Will You Ever Come Back; Take A Stand; Wound Up; Under 18; We're The Crew" *Raybies - vocals • Todd Youth - guitar • Brad - guitar • Tito & Batmite - bass • Charlie & Tommy - drums*

WARZONE (SF)

1982 *Amerika The Pitiful* 7" EP (Allied) "Immoral Minority; American Business; Multinational Corporations; Election Day; Stuck in 77; Racists Are Dumb Shits" 1982 "Marriage Of Convenience," "Yahoo Song" on *Live At The Eastern Front* comp (ICI/Sandblast, CF3000)

WASTED YOUTH (LA)

1981 *Reagan's In* (ICI) "Reagan's In; Problem Child; Teenage Narc; Un - High Beefrog; Born Deprived; Fuck Authority; You're A Jerk; We Were On Heroin; Punk For A Day; Flush The Bouncers" *Danny Spira - vocals • Chett Lehrer - guitar • Jeff Long - bass • Allen Stiritz - drums* 1983 "We're On Heroin" on *Live At The Eastern Front 2* (Enigma)

WHIPPING BOY (SF)

1982 "Human Farm" on *Not So Quiet On The Western Front* comp (Alternative Tentacles) 1983 *The Sound of No Hands Clapping* (CFY) 1984 *The Third Secret Of Fatima* (CFY, 003) "Lavender Girl; Daddy's Gone; Smokey; Enemy; Rain Dance; The Third Secret; Shades Of Grey; Remember; Something Wrong; Talk To Me; Wisailia" *Eugene Robinson - vocals • Niko Wenner - guitar; vocals • Bart Thurber - guitar; vocals • Ron Isa - bass • Steve Shaughnessy - drums* 1985 *Crow* 7" (CFY, 009) X - Press Train; Cat O'Nine Tails" *Eugene Robinson - vocals • Niko Wenner - guitar • Mark Nichoson - bass • Dan Adams - drums*

WHITE CROSS (Richmond)

1982 *White Cross* 7" EP (Zero Degree, ZD 003) "Fascist; No Straight Edge; Speed of the Presses; American Way; Jump Up; Suburbanite; Nuke Attack; Having Fun" 1983 *What's Going On?* 12 EP (Zero Degree) *Crispy - vocals • Mike Rodriguez - guitar • Dewey Rowell - bass • Rob Mosby - drums*

WHITE FLAG (LA)

1981 *R Is For Rocket* (Gasatanka) 1982 *S Is For Space* (Gasatanka) "Not All Right; Go To God; White Flag; Joey Chip; Mirror, Mirror; Suzy Secret; Hell In A Handbag; Cleocia; Video.d.; Cheze; Gumby; R n R" *Doug Graves • F Fee • Pat Fear • Al Bum • Pick Z. Stix"* 1983 "Shattered Badge" on *Copulation* comp LP (Mystic) 1985 *Third Strike* (Gasatanka) 1986 *Feeding Frenzy* three-sided live bootleg 1986 *Jail Jello* split EP with Necros (Gasatanka) 1986 *R Is For Rad* 7" EP

WHITE TRASH (Denver)

1983 *Wake Up!* 7" EP (Local Anesthetic) "Wake Up; Nazis In My Neighborhood; Ballad Of Ronnie Raygun; I Hate My Toes; Daddy Warbucks" *Louie Largesse - vocal organ • Granville Cleveland, Jr.-guitar • James Clower - guitar • Mat Bischoff - bass • Garret Jon Shavlik - drums*

WILLFUL NEGLECT (Minneapolis)

1982 track on *Kitten Compilation* comp CS (Reflex) 1982 *Willful Neglect* (Neglected, NR001) "EM.S & D; Good Clean Fun; Outta My Mind; Banned; Abort The Mission; Rebel; Gash Abuse; 5 Nice Guys; Geeks; Herpes (Will I Get); Willful Neighbors; Criminals" *Wade Calhoun - vocals • Rory Shoenheider - guitar • Retro Roger DeBace - guitar • James Wallin - bass • Scott Peterson - drums* 1983 LP (Neglected, NR - 002) "(White Collar) Not Guilty; Deprogrammed; Justice For No One; Caskets; Vegetable Zero; Gash Development; Same Old Bullshit; Scratch-n-Sniff; I Was Drunk; Bobbin On Wally; Taint" *Wade Calhoun - vocals • Rory Shoenheider - guitar • Retro Roger DeBace - guitar • James Wallin - bass • Eric Scott - drums*

THE WRECKS (Reno)

1982 *Teenage Jive* CS EP 1982 "Punk's An Attitude" on *Not So Quiet From The Western Front* comp LP (Alternative Tentacles, VIRUS14)

WÜRM (LA)

1982 *I'm Dead* 7" EP (SST 011) "We're Off, I'm Dead, Time Has Come Today" *Ed Danky - vocals • Chuck Dukowski - bass/vocals • Loud Lou - drums* 1983 "I'm Dead" on *The Blasting Concept* comp (SST 014) 1983 "I'm Taking Over" on *Copulation* comp (Mystic, MLP33128) 1984 *Feast* (SST 041) 1986 track on *Program: Annihilator* comp (SST) 1986 "Death Ride" on *The Blasting Concept Volume II* (SST 043)

YDI (Philly)

1983 "Enemy For Life," "I Killed My Family" on *Get Off My Back* comp (Red, PAC 004) 1983 *A Place In The Sun* 7" EP (Blood Bubble)

THE YOUNG AND THE USELESS (NY)

1982 *Real Men Don't Floss* 7" EP (Rat Cage, MOTR 24) "Young & Useless; P.M.H.; The Wave; Home Boy; Rise And Shine; Funky Music" *David Scilken - vocals • Adam O'Keefe - guitar • Art Africano-bass • Adam Trese-drums • (Gabby Abularach-guitar, side 2)*

YOUR FUNERAL (Denver)

1984 *Your Funeral* 7" (Local Anesthetic)

YOUTH BRIGADE (DC)

1981 *Possible* 7" EP (Dischord, #6) "It's About Time That We Had A Change; Full Speed Ahead; Point Of View; Barbed Wire; Pay No Attention; Wrong Decision; No Song; No Song II" *Nathan Strejcek - vocals • Tom Clinton - guitar • Bert Quieroz - bass • Danny Ingram - drums* 1982 Moral Majority, Waste Of Time, Last Word on *Flex Your Head* comp LP (Dischord, no. 7)

YOUTH BRIGADE (LA)

1981 "Violence," "Boys In The Brigade" on *Someone Got Their Head Kicked In* comp (BYO 001) 1982 *Sound & Fury* (BYO 002) "Sink with California; Modest Proposal; Men in Blue (Part 1); Sound and Fury; Fight to Unite; Jump Back; Blown Away; Live Life; What Are You Fighting For; Did You Wanna Die; You Don't Understand; The Circle; Duke of Earl; What Will the Revolution Change" *Shawn Stern - guitar/vocals • Mark Stern/ bass; vocals • Adam Stern - bass/vocals* 1983 *Sound & Fury* (BYO 002B) 1984 *What Price* 7" EP (BYO 006) "What Price Happiness?; Where Are We Going?; Who Can You Believe In?" 1986 *The Dividing Line* (BYO 012) (as The Brigade) "I Scream; The Struggle Within; War For Peace; The Story (Part 1); It's A Wonderful Life; The Dividing Line; The Last Frontier; All Alone; The Hardest Part" *Shawn Stern - vocals/guitar • Mark Stern - vocals/drums • Bob Gnarly Stern - vocals/bass*

YOUTH GONE MAD (LA) 1982 *Oki Dogs* EP (Posh Boy, PBS-36) 1982 "Ode To Darby," "Diaperhead" "Homo Mommy" on *Sudden Death* comp LP (Smoke Seven)

YOUTH PATROL (Detroit)

1981 "America's Power" on *Process Of Elimination* comp 7" EP (Touch & Go,T&G4)

ZERO BOYS (Indianapolis)

1979 *Living In The 80s* 7" EP (Z/ Disc) "I'm Bored; Living In The '80s; Stoned To Death; Piece Of Me" **1982** *Vicious Circle* (Nimrod, #001) "Vicious Circle; Amphetamine Addiction; New Generation; Dirty Alleys; Dirty Minds; Civilization Dying; Livin In The '80s; Drug Free Youth; Down The Drain; Outta Style; You Can Touch Me; Forced Entry; High Time; Charlie's Place; Trying Harder" *Paul - vocals • Terry - guitar • Tufty - bass • Mark - drums* **1982** "High Places," "Human Body", "Mom's Wallet" on *The Master Tape* comp (Affirmation, Aff 01) **1983** "Black Network News," "I Need Energy" on *The Master Tape Volume II* comp (Affirmation, Aff 02) **1985** split 7" w/Toxic Reasons (Selfless) "Black Network," "Blood's Good"

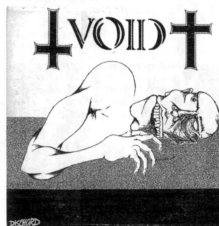

COMPILATIONS:

1980 *The Decline…Of Western Civilization* (soundtrack) (Slash) Black Flag - "White Minority," "Depression," "Revenge"/ Germs - "Manimal"/ Catholic Discipline - "Underground Babylon"/ X - "Beyond & Back," "Johnny Hit & Run Pauline," "We're Desperate"/ Circle Jerks - "Red Tape, "Back Against The Wall," "Wasted," "I Just Want Some Skank," "Beverly Hills"/ Alice Bag Band - "Gluttony"/ Fear -"I Don't Care About You," "I Love Livin InThe City," "Fear Anthem"

1980 *Rodney On The ROQ* (Posh Boy, PBS 106) Brooke Shields - "Introduction"/ Agent Orange - "Bloodstains"/ Adolescents - "Amoeba"/ Circle Jerks - "Wild In The Streets"/ U.X.A. - "Tragedies"/ Lan - "Pushin' Too Hard"/ Black Flag - "No Values"/ Rik L Rik - "The Outback"/ Crowd - "Right Time"/ David Microwave - "I Don't Want To Hold You"/ The Nuns - "Wild"/ Fender Buddies - "Furry Friend"/ Vidiots - "Laurie's Lament"/ Simpletones - "T.V. Love"/ Christina - "Surprise!"

1980 *Cracks In The Sidewalk* (New Alliance, NAR 001) Minutemen - "9:30 May 2"/ Black Flag - "Clocked In"/ Saccharine Trust - "Hearts & Barbarians"/ Kindled Imagination - "Cowboy & Indian Scene"/ Artless Entanglements - "How's The Blood Taste? Pt. 2"/ Sharp Corners - "Me Too"

1981 *Let Them Eat Jellybeans* (Alternative Tentacles, VIRUS 4) Flipper - "Ha Ha Ha"/ DOA - "The Prisoner"/ Black Flag - "Police Story"/ Bad Brains - "Pay To Cum"/ Dead Kennedys - "Nazi Punks Fuck Off"/ Circle Jerks - "Paid Vacation"/ Really Red - "Prostitution"/ The Feederz - "Jesus Entering Through The Rear"/ Subhumans - "Slave To My Dick"/ Geza X - "Isotope Soap"/ B People - "Persecution, That's My Song"/ Wounds - "An Object"/ The Offs - "Everyone's A Bigot"/

Anonymous - "Corporate Food"/ 1/ 2 Japanese - "Fun Again"/ Christian Lunch - "Joke's On You"/ Voice Farm - "Sleep"

1981 *Chunks* (New Alliance, NAR 003) Descendents- "Global Probing"/ Cheifs - "The Lonelys"/ Minutemen - "Clocks"/ Black Flag - "Machine"/ Stains - "Sick & Crazy"/ Peer Group - "I Saw That Movie"/ Vox Pop - "You're My Favorite"/ Ken - "Purposeless Attitudes"/ Slivers - "Sport"/ Saccharine Trust- "A Christmas Cry"/ Artless Entanglements - "Dildos, Bondage & Toys"/ Nig-Heist - "The Nig-Heist"

1981 *Process Of Elimination* 7" EP (Touch and Go, T&G4) Necros - "Bad Dream"/ Meatmen - "Meatmen Stomp"/ Negative Approach - "Lost Cause"/ Youth Patrol - "America's Power"/ Toxic Reasons - "Riot Squad"/ Violent Apathy - "I Can't Take It"/ McDonalds - "Miniature Golf"/ The Fix - "No Idols"

1981 *Busted At Oz* (Autumn, AU 2) Naked Raygun - "Bomb Shelter," "When The Screaming Stops," "Paranoia," "Libido"/ Strike Under - "Fucking Uniiforms," "Anarchy Song"/ Subverts - "March Forth," "State Of The Union"/ Effigies - "Quota," "Guns Or Ballots"/ DA - "Fish Shit," "The Killer"/ Silver Abuse - "Anti-Hot Dog," "Pink Port Now," "Bomb Shelter" "Jigaboo Jump"

1981 *Life Is Beautiful — So Why Not Eat Health Food?* (New Underground) Bags - "We Will Bury You"/ Anti - "Up At Four"/ Shattered Faith - "Victims Of Society"/ Short Haired Thugs - "What Happened"/ China White - "Danger Zone"/ M.I.A. - "Lost Day At The Races," "Missing Or Captured" / Ill Will - "Theme Song," "Mr. Government"/ Germs - "Media Blitz," "What We Do Is Secret"/ Minutemen - "Prelude"/ B People - "I Said Everybody"/ Mood Of Defiance - "Girl In A Painting Part 1"/ Flower Child, "Invisible Chains" "Einstein's Followers"/ Marshall Mellow - "Marshmellow Children"/ Zurich 1916 - "Sugar Sugar"/ Vox Pop - "Good Times Part 1," "Paint It Black"/ Power Trip - "Iron Horse"

1981 *Rodney On The ROQ Vol. 2* (Posh Boy, PBS-123) Target 13 - "Rodney On The ROQ"/ Social Distortion - "1945"/ Shattered Faith - "Right Is Right"/ Black Flag - "Rise Above"/ Minutemen - "Search"/ Red Cross - "Burn Out"/ CH3 - "You Lie"/ Agent Orange - "Mr. Moto"/ Red Rockers - "Dead Heroes"/ Unit 3 w/ Venus - "B.O.Y.S."/ Stepmothers -"Where Is The Dream"/ Gleaming Spires - "Are You Ready For The Sex Girls"/ Little Girls -"Earthquake Song"/ Twisted Roots - "Snaked"/ Geza X - "We Need More Power"

1981 *Public Service* (Smoke 7) Red Cross - "Cease To Exit," "Everyday There's Something New," "Kill Someone You Hate"/ RF7 - "World Of Hate," "Scientific Race," "Long Live The Queen," "Perfect World"/ Circle One - "G.I. Combat," "High School Society," "F.O.," "Destroy Exxon"/ Bad Religion - "Bad Religion," "Slaves," "Drastic Actions"/ Disability - "Battling Against The Police," "White As A Ghost," "Rejection"

1981 *Who Cares* (American Standard) AKA - "Tomorrow's Theme," "Liza Jane"/ Suspects - "Hollywood Nightmare," "Baby Maybe," "I Had Fun," "Make Me"/ Cheifs - "Riot Squad," "No Justice," "Scrapped"/ Political Crap - "On Your Own," "Slow Death," "Rejected"/ Civil Disobedience - "Too Drunk Last Night";

"Campaign Promises"; "Confused"/ Shattered Faith - "I Love America"; "Discontent"; "Trilogy"

1982 *American Youth Report* (Invasion/Thunderbolt)

Modern Warfare - "One For All"/ Bad Religion - "Only Gonna Die"/ Channel 3 - "Catholic Boy"/ Adolescents - "Losing Battle"/ Lost Cause - "Born Dead"/ Legal Weapon - "Pow Wow"/ Flesheaters - "Pony Dress"/ Rhino 39 - "J. Alfred"/ Hypnotics - "Weird People"/ Descendents - "I'm Not A Loser"/ M.I.A. - "Tell Me Why"/ TSOL - "Sounds Of Laughter/ Shattered Faith - "Reagan Country"/ Minutemen - "Working Men Are Pissed"/ RF7 - Jesus Loves You"/ Red Kross - "Notes & Chords"; "Mean Nothing To Me"

1982 *Flex Your Head* (Dischord, No. 7) Teen Idles - "I

Drink Milk" "Commie Song" "No Fun"/ Untouchables - "Rat Patrol" "Nic Fit" "I Hate You"/ S.O.A. - "I Hate The Kids" "Disease" "Stepping Stone Party"/ Minor Threat - "Stand Up" "12XU"/ Government Issue - "Hey, Ronnie" "Lie, Cheat, & Steal"/ Youth Brigade - "Moral Majority" "Waste Of Time" "Last Word"/ Red C - "Jimi 45" "Pressure's On" "Six O'Clock News" "Assassin"/ Void - "Dehumanized" "Authority" "My Rules"/ Iron Cross - "Wargames" "New Breed" "Live For Now"/ Artificial Peace - "Artificial Peace" "Outside Looking In" "Suburban Wasteland"/ Deadline - "Stolen Youth" "Hear The Cry" "Aftermath"

1982 *New York Thrash*

(casette-only) (ROIR) The Mad - "I Hate Music"/ Kraut - "Getaway"/ Heart Attack - "Shotgun"/ Undead - "Social Reason"/ Adrenalin O.D. - "New Year's Eve"/ Even Worse - "Illusion Won Again"/ Fiends - "Cry Now"/ Nihilistics - "Here And Now"/ Undead - "Nightmare"/ False Prophets - "Taxidermist/ Bad Brains - "Regulator (Version)"/ Beastie Boys - "Riot Fight"/ Nihilistics - "Love And Kisses"/ Fiends - "Asian White"/ Kraut - "Last Chance"/ Even Worse - "Emptying The Madhouse"/ Adrenalin O.D. - "Paul's Not Home"/ False Prophets - "Scorched Earth"/ Heart Attack - "God Is Dead"/ The Mad - "The Hell"/ Bad Brains - "Big Take Over"/ Beastie Boys - "Beastie"

1982 *Hell Comes To Your House* (Bemisbrain, BB

123/124) 45 Grave - "Evil" "Concerned Citizen" "45 Grave"/ Christian Death - "Dogs" 100 Flowers - "Reject Yourself"/ Rhino 39 - "Marry It"/ Super Heroines - "Death On The Elevator" "Embalmed Love"/ Social Distortion-"Lude Boy" "Telling Them"/ Legal Weapon - "Daddy's Gone Mad"/ Red Cross - "Puss 'N' Boots"/ Modern Warfare - "Out Of My Head" "Street Fightin' Man"/ Secret Hate -"Deception"; "New Routine," "Suicide"/ Conservatives - "Suburban Bitch" "Just Cuz" "Nervous"

1982 *Life Is Ugly — So Why Not Kill Yourself?*

(New Underground, NU-11) Red Cross - "Rich Brat"/ Descendents - "I Want To Be A Bear"/ Anti - "Fight War Not Wars"; "I Don't Wanna Die"/ Ill Will - "Paranoid" "Midnite Deposit"/ Civil Dismay - "You're So Fucked To Me" "Warhol Genius" "Filch"/ China White - "Criminal" "Solid State"/ Mood Of Defiance -"Empty Me"; "Minutemen - "Shit You Hear At Parties" "Maternal Rite"/ 100 Flowers - "Sensible Virgin"/ Urinals - "She's A Drone"/ Zurich 1916 - "The Children's Song"/ Saccharine Trust - "Disillusion Fool"

1982 *Live At The Eastern Front* (ICI/Sandblast, CF

3000) DOA - "Unknown" "Fucked Up Baby"/ TSOL - "Love Story"/ The Lewd - "Suburban Prodigy"/ Warzone - "Marriage Of Convenience" "Yahoo Song"/ Flipper - "Ever"/ The Offs - "One More Shot"/ The Wounds - "Beach"/ The Tanks - "My Town"/ Toiling Midgets - "Tommorrow Never Knows"

1982 *Big Apple Rotten To The Core* (S.I.N., #2) Ism

- "John Hinckley Jr."/ Squirm - "Fuck You Brook Shields"/ Butch Lust & the Hypocrites - "Smashed Rats"/ The Mob - "Common Criminal"/ Killer Instinct - "Killer Instinct"/ Head Lickers - "House Of Detention"/ Squirm - "Love Someone"/ Ism - "Moon The Moonies"/ Head Lickers - "Hey Mom"/ The Mob - "101"/ Squirm - "Shanghai Go-Go"/ Killer Instinct - "Torture You First"/ Butch Lust & the Hypocrites - "Nervousness & Anger"/ Head Lickers - "1,2,3,4"/ Ism - "Nixon Now More Than Ever"/ Squirm - "Go Die"/ Butch Lust & the Hypocrites -"Degenerate World"

1982 *Not So Quiet On The Western Front*

(Alternative Tentacles, VIRUS 14) Intensified Chaos - "Intensified Chaos"/ Social Unrest - "Their Mistakes"/ Naked Lady Wrestlers - "Dan With The Yellow Hair"/ M.A.D. - "Holocaust"/ Killjoy - "Rich Plastic People"/ Fang - "Fun With Acid"/ Capitol Punishment - "El Salvador"/ Ribsy - "Collapse"/ Crucifix - "Annihilation"/ Square Cools - "I Don't Wanna Die For My Country"/ Los Olvidados - "Pay Salvation"/ Code Of Honor - "What Price Will You Pay?"/ 7 Seconds - "Fuck Your Amerika"/ Unaware - "Race War"/ Frigidettes - "Turmoil"/ 5th Column - "Don't Conform"/ Ghost Dance - "Shrunken Heads"/ Dead Kennedys - "A Child & His Lawn Mower"/ Rebel Truth - "All I Know"/ Pariah - "Learning Process"/ Lennon Burger - "Reagum"/ Impatient Youth - "Praise The Lord & Pass The Ammunition"/ Bad Posture - "GDMF-SOB"/ Demented Youth - "Assasination Attempt"/ MDC - The Only Good Cop …"/ Karnage - The Few, The Proud, The Dead"/ Domino Theory - "Scare"/ NBJ - "Dead Porker"/ Whipping Boy - "Human Farm"/ Angst - "Worker Bee"/ Free Beer - "Premature Enlistment"/ Flipper - "Sacrifice"/ Vengeance - "No One Listens"/ Juvenile Justice - "S&M Nightmare"/ Section 8 - "Fat, Drunk & Stupid"/ Tongue Avulsion - "Libyan Hit Squad"/ Maniax - "Off To War"/ Vicious Circle - "Strike Out"/ UXB - "Breakout"/Scapegoats - "Shitcan"/ Church Police - "The Oven Is My Friend"/ Deadly Reign - "Systems Suck"/ No Alternative - "Dead Men Tell No Lies"/ Wrecks - "Punk Is An Attitude"/ Urban Assault - "SLT"/ Bent Nails - "No More Riots"/ MIA - "New Left"

1982 *Rat Music For Rat People* (Go!, GO-003)

D.O.A. - "America The Beautiful" "Fucked Up Ronnie"/ Flipper - "Life"/ Circle Jerks - "Live Fast, Die Young"/ Bad Brains - "How Low Can A Punk Get?" "You"/ Crucifix - "Steel Case Enclosure"/ Dead Kennedys - "Forward To Death" "The Owl"/Black Flag - "Scream"/ T.S.O.L. - "Weathered Statues" "Sounds Of Laughter"/ Avengers - "Cheap Tragedies"/ Dils - "Blow Up"

1982 *Rodney On The ROQ Vol. 3* (Posh Boy, PBS-

103) Kent State - "Radio Moscow"/ Ill Repute - "Clean Cut American Kid"/ JFA - "Preppy"/ CH3 - "Seperate Peace"/ Catch 22 - "Stop The Cycle"/ Pariah - "Up To Us"/ Red Scare - "Streetlife"/ No Crisis - "She's Into The Scene"/ Rudi - "Crimson"/ Unit 3 w/ Venus - "Pajama Party"/ Bangles - "Bitchin Summer"/ Action Now - "Try"/ Signals - "Gotta Let Go"/ Gayle Wiilsh - "Day Of Age"/ Radio Music - "Johnny Angel"; "New Dance"/ David Hines - "Land Of 1,000 Dances"

1982 *Someone Got Their Head Kicked In!*

(Better Youth Records, BYO-001) Youth Brigade - "Violence"/ Agresion - "Intense Energy" (1:30)/ Battalion Of Saints - "Beefmasters"/ Joneses - "Pill Box"/ Bad Religion - "In The Night"/ Agression - "Dear John Letter"/ Blades - "Don't Wanna Dance With You"/ Battalion Of Saints - "No More Lies"/ Adolescents - "Who Is Who"/ Social Distortion - "Mass Hysteria"/ Joneses - "Graveyard Rock"/ Youth Brigade - "Boys In The Brigade"/ Blades - "False Face"/ Aggression - "Rat Race"/

Adolescents - "Wrecking Crew"/ Blades - "Had Enough"/ Youth Brigade - "Look In The Mirror"/ Battalion Of Saints -"Cops Are Out"

1982 Mixed Nuts Don't Crack (Outside) Media Disease - "Unwritten Laws" "Life Unfulfilled" "Redneck Asshole"; "Sit Down"; "Religion"; "Concentration Camp"/ Chalk Circle - "The Slap"; "Subversive Pleasure"/ Social Suicide - "Born Again" "Beat Them"; "Foul Appetite"; "30-Second Holiday"/ United Mutation - "Out Of Hand" "D.C. Screws The World" "Oh No"; "Lice & Fleas & Vermin"/ Nuclear Crayons - "Nuclear Crayons"; "Catwalk"; "Blitz Beauty"; "Man InThe Big Hat"/ Hate From Ignorance - "Instrumental"; "Through Posterity"; "What Do You Say"

1982 Sudden Death (Smoke 7, SMK7-105) Jody Foster's Army - "Low Rider" "American Buttfuckers"/ Sin 34 - "Only Love" "Nuclear War" "Who Needs Them"/ Moral Decay - "America" "T.V. News"/ Crankshaft - "Life Is Getting Faster" "Massacre Killer"/ Sadist Faction - "Twisted Cross" "Peace Corps"/ The Sins - "Rat Society" "All Your Tommorrows"/ The Demented - "Back To The Bed" "Deadly Game" "How Can I Kill You"/ Redd Kross - "Tatum O'Neil and the Fried Vegetables"/ Youth Gone Mad - "Ode To Darby"; "Diaperhead"; "Homo Mommy"/ Naughty Women - "Linda Is A Monster""Jealousy"/ Dead Youth - "Phantom Citizen" "Kern County"

1982 The Master Tape
(Affirmation, Aff-01) Toxic Reasons - "Mercenary" "Drunk & Disorderly"/ Slammies - "Frustrated" "P.U.S."/ "Manager Breakdown"/ Battered Youth - "New Patriot" "We'll Love You When You're Dead"/Delinquents - "Bible School" "System Pressure"/ Zero Boys - "High Places" "Human Body" "Mom's Wallet"/ Articles Of Faith - "Buried Alive" "False Security"/ Repellents-"Think For Yourself" "LiveLike An Animal"/Learned Helplessness - "Vegis"/ F.U.'s - C.E.T.A. Suckers" "Death Wish"/ Pattern - "Unnatural Silence" "Michelob"/ Die Kreuzen - "On The Street" "All White" "Fighting"

1982 This Is Boston Not L.A. (Modern Method, MM012) Jerry's Kids - "Straight Jacket" "Uncontrollable" "Wired" "Desperate" "Pressure""I Don't Wanna"/The Proletariat- "Options" "Religion is the Opium of the Masses""Allegiance"/The Groinoids - "Angel"/ The F.U.'s - "Preskool Dropou" "Radio UNIX USA" "Green Beret" "Time Is Money"/ Gang Green - "Snob" "Lie Lie" "I Don't Care" "Rabies" "Narrow Mind" "Kill A Commie""Have Fun"/ Decadence - "Slam"/ The Freeze - "Broken Bones" "Idiots at Happy Hour" "Now or Never" "Sacrifice not Suicide" "It's Only Alcohol" "Trouble if You Hide" "Time Bomb" "Boston not L.A."

1982 Unsafe At Any Speed 7" EP (Modern Method, MM014) Gang Green - "Selfish"/ The Groinoids - "Empty Skull"/ The Proletariat - "Voodoo Economics"/ Jerry's Kids - "Machine Gun"/ F.U.'s - "CETA Suckers"/ The Freeze-"Refrigerator Heaven"

1982 No Core CS (No Core) w/ Corrosion Of Conformity, No Labels, No Rock Stars, Colcor

1982 You Can't Argue With Suckcess (Mystic, MLP33102) F Troop - "Last Rites" "We're The Young" "Death Bed"/ Crewd - "Shit" "Bobby Sands""Little Boy Blue"/ Red Beret - "Saturnon" "I Can't Take It"/ Nuclear Baby Food - "Sex Fix" "Dad's Growing Older" "Suburbia"/ Mad Society - "Riot Squad"; "Napalm" "Little Devil"/ Secret Hate - "Charade" "Misery Chord"; "Rich Man's Son"/ No Crisis - "Change Your Name"/ The Conservatives - "Confusion" "Nuclear Madness" "Beaver Cleaver"/ Even Worse - "Contaminated Waste" "We Suck"

1982 Reagan Regime Review (Selfless) The Fix - "Vengeance"/ Meatmen - "1 Down, 3 To Go"/ Negative Approach - "Can't Tell No One"/ Toxic Reasons - "Somebody Help Me"/ McDonalds -"Untitled"

1983 The Blasting Concept (SST 013) Minutemen - "Paranoid Chant," "The Maze,""Boiling,""Games"/ Meat Puppets - "Tumblin' Tumbleweeds" "Meat Puppets"/ Saccharine Trust - "A Human Certainty"/ Black Flag - "Nervous Breakdown""Jealous Again" "I've Heard It Before"/ Overkill - "Hell's Getting Hotter"/ Stains-"Get Revenge"/Würm-"I'm Dead"/Hüsker Dü-"Real World"

1983 The Master Tape Vol. II (Affirmation, Aff-02) Violent Apathy - "Society Rules" "Desperation Takes Hold"; "Ignorance Is Bliss"/ Malignant Growth -"Hopelessness" "Killing Time" "Tired Of Life"/ Idiot Savants - "Try & Get Out" "School's Prison"/ Sand In The Face- "Teenage Life" "I Wanna Be Dead"/ Poison Center - "Pencil Pusher" "Typical Chick"/ Sacred Order - "Hate Them Okay" "I Just Do"/ No Labels - "Tortured Thought" "Society's Problem"/ Front Line - "D.W.I." "Front Line"/ End Result-"Slash""Children Die In Pain"/ Repellents - "Lash Out" "New Image" "My Motel"/ Killing Children-"Happy Mutants"; "Certain Death"/ The Fetish -"Surf Bandits"; "Before Not After"/ Mecht Mensch- "Killer Klowns" "What D'Ya Feel"/ Gynecologists-"Infant Doe"/ Zero Boys-"Black Network News" "I Need Energy"/ Delinquents -"Blind Patriot" "Under Age" "Death From Above"/ Tar Babies -"The Ocean" "Triplets"/ Wasted Talent-"Junta Man" "Not Anymore" "Off To War"/ Anti-Bodies- "Gun Control" "Seeds Of Destruction"

1983 Get Off My Back (Red, PAC-004) YDI - "Enemy For Life" "I Killed My Family"/ F.O.D. - "Murder Castle" "Suburban Cowboy"/ "Blunder Boys - "Conspiracy" "I'm Afraid Of The Night" "Middle Class Morals"/ Little Gentlemen - "No Justice No Law" "No Crime No Flaw"/ Autistic Behavior - "T.V. Messiah" "Powerhead"/ Ruin - "Proof" "Love Dog"/ Informed Sources - "Right & Wrong" "Dense Pack"/ Seeds Of Terror - "Brain Down" "Straight Edge"/ Mc Rad - "Inflation Dub" "Ejected"/ Heathens - "Oohleigh At Great Adventure" "My Twin From Hell"

1983 Life Is Boring — So Why Not Steal This Record? (New Underground, NU-55) Germs - "Strange Notes" "Caught In My Eye"/ Minutemen - "Base King"/ Redd Kross - "Out Of Focus"/ Modern Warfare - "Moral Majority"/ Shattered Faith - "The Omen"/ Anti - "Without Love We Will Die"/ Mood Of Defiance-"American Love Song"/ Har-Kari - "Prey For Peace"/ Sin 34 - "Forced Education"/ Artistic Decline - "Friday Punk"/ Modern Torture - "Fascist Media"/ Invisible Chains - "Paisley Douche/Cactus Juice"/ Slivers - "Restraint For Style"/ Vox Pop - "Jumble Bug"/ Marshall Mellow -"Marshmellow Children"/ Carl Stone - "Jang"/ Doo Doo ettes - "Red Wrec Said"/ Zurich 1916 - "No Canvas"/ Tone Deaf - "Story of a T.V. Murder"/ Diet Of Nature - "And It Got Hit By A Truck" "Your Life Means Nothing"

1983 Posh Hits Vol 1 (Posh Boy, PBS-8138) Circle Jerks - "Wild In The Streets"/ Agent Orange - "Everything Turns Grey"/ Social Distortion - "Moral Threat"/ Crowd - "Modern Machine"/ U.X.A. - "Immunity"/ Red Cross - "Annette's Got The Hits" "Cover Band"/ F-Word! - "Shutdown"/ Los Microwaves - "Time To Get Up"/ Channel 3 - "You Make Me Feel Cheap"/ Black Flag - "Louie Louie"/ Simpletones - "I Like Drugs"/ Shattered Faith - "I Love America"/ TSOL - "Peace Through Power"/ Stepmothers - "Push Comes To Shove"/ Nuns - "Suicide Child"

1983 Live At The Eastern Front 2 (Enigma, E-1015) Chron-Gen-"Clouded Eyes" "Reality"; Breaking Down"/ Channel 3 - "Mannequin"/ Free Beer - "My Money Or My Car"/ Wasted Youth-"We're On Heroin"/ Battallion Of Saints - "Fighting Boys"/ The Lewd - "M17"/ Shattered Faith - "Final Conflict"/ JFA - "Low Rider"/ Circle One - "Red Machine"/ Fartz - "Buried Alive"

1983 *Copulation* (Mystic, MLP33128) Dr. Know- "Egomaniac"/ Sado Nation - "Fear Of Failure"/ S.V.D.B.- "Your Friendly Local Police"/ The Authorities - I Hate Cops"/ Government Issue - "No Rights"/ Ill Repute - "Lust Bust"/ Mentors - "Police Hotel"/ Black Flag - "Police Story"/ White Flag - "Shattered Badge"/ Agression - "Slamming At The Club"/ The Stains- "Flashing Reds"/ America's Hardcore- "Cops Are Criminals"/ Würm- "I'm Taking Over"/ Manifest Destiny- "Protect And Serve"/Aryan Disgrace - "LAP.D"/ The Grim - "Government Man"/ Crankshaft - "License To Kill"/ New Regime - "Night Stix"

1983 *Why Are We Here?* 7" EP (No Core) Bloodmobile- "Drug-Related Death" "Little Boy Blue" "The Smiths"/ COC - "Poison Planet" "Indifferent" "Too Cool"/ Stillborn Christians - "New Right" "Fred" "Aggression"/No Labels-"Changes" "Compromises"

1983 *Noise From Nowhere Vol.. 1* (Toxic Shock) Kent State-"Breakout Breakfree"/Modern Industry-"Out Of Focus"/ Moslem Birth - Horror Snores"/ Manson Youth - "Penis Brain"

1983 *Big City Ain't So Pretty* 7" EP (Big City) XKI-"I Hate Everything"/ "Betrayed - "Self-Oppression"/ "Ultra Violence - "I Don't Wanna Work"/ Savage Circle - "We Don't Have To"/ No Thanks - Are You Ready"/ Armed Citizens - "Thrill Of It All"/ Fathead Suburbia - "The Masses

1983 *Hardcore Takes Over* (Dirt, DR-003) TMA - "I'm In Love With Nancy Reagan" "Herpes II"/ Phil Scalzo Band - "Savage Truth"; "Death House Riot"/ Mourning Noise - "Progress For The People"; "Radical"/ Mad Daddys - "Cool & Wild"; "Acid Rain Dark"/ Stetz - "East Coast Slang"/ "Ain't Gonna Be In No Army"/ Sand In The Face - "Auschwitz"; "Laughing At Me"/ B-Day Vacation - "She Fucks For Drugs"; "Tear Down The Wall"/ Genocide - "Stillborn" "Never Nothing"

1983 *The Sound Of Hollywood 2* (Mystic,MLP 33124) SVDB - "Chain Reaction"/ Shattered Faith-"Rise & Fall"/ Still Life - Tearin' Me Up"/ F-Beat -"Oughta Be Dancing"/ Red Scare - "Drag The Lake"/ Bad Religion - "Waiting For the Fire" "Every Day"/ Red Scare - "Keep America Beautiful"/ Circle One - "Hate, Lust, Filth & Greed"/ Battalion Of Saints - "Sweaty Little Girls"/ 10,000 Hurts - "Fruit Loops"; "Abandon"/ F-Beat - "Sharin'/ SVDB -"Melt Down"/ Würm - "Black Swan"/ Shattered Faith - "Last Name First"

1983 *Hell Comes To Your House II* (Bemisbrain/Enigma) The Joneses - "I'm Bad" "She's So Filthy"/ Mau Maus-"Sex Girls In Uniforms" "We All Fall Down"/ Cambridge Apostles - "Can't Fight The Feeling"/ Blood In The Saddle - "I Wish I Was A Single Girl Again" "Ghost In My Heart"/ Tex & the Horseheads - "Short Train" "Go West Young Man" "Slip Away"/ Minutemen- "Corona"/ Screamin' Sirens - "Your Good Girl's Gonna Go Bad" "Runnin' Kind"/ Lotus Lame & the Lame Flames - "Bad Sex"

1983 *VVV - Live At The Hot Club* (VVV, 06) The Doo - "Victim Of His Age"/ The Telefones - "You Really Got It Bad"/ The Ralphs- "Drug Induced State"/ Fort Worth Cats - "Raison D'Etre"/ Ejectors - "Fade With The Summer"/ NCM - "Mental Case"/ Hugh Beaumont Experience - "Let's Go Join The Army"; "My Country"/ Stickmen With Rayguns - "Two Fist"/ The Devices - "Soldier Of Fortune"/ The Frenetics - "Anamation"/ NCM - "No Can Do"

1983 *We Can't Help It If We're From Florida* 7" EP (Destroy) Hated Youth - "Hardcore Rules" "Ted Bundy" "Army Dad"/ Morbid Opera - "Eat The Rich" "White Flag" "Polyester Pig"/ Rat Cafeteria - "Kill" "Tax Revolt"/ Roach Motel

- "Heart Attack" "Fla. Reptile Land" "My Dog's Into Anarchy"/ Sector 4 - "White House" "Plaid Space Ship"

1984 *Repo Man* soundtrack (San Andreas/MCA, SAR-39019) Black Flag- "TV Party"/ Suididal Tendencies - "Institutionalized"/ Circle Jerks - "Coup D'Etat"/ Iggy Pop - "Repo Man"/ The Plugz - "El Cavo Y La Cruz"/ Burning Sensations - "Pablo Picasso"/ Fear - "Let's Have A War"/ Circle Jerks - "When The Shit Hits The Fan"/ The Plugz - "Hombre Secreto (Secret Agent Man)"/ Juicy Bananas - "Bad Man"/ The Plugz - "Reel Ten"

1984 *Something To Believe In* (BYO, BYO-004) Nils - "Scratches & Needles"/ Rigor Mortis - "Silent Scream"/ Big Boys - "History"/ Unwanted-"Tanks Keep Rolling"/ Tourists - "Memories"/ Kraut - "Pyramids"/ Youth Brigade - "Care"/ Youth Youth Youth - "Domination"/SNFU - "Womanizer"/Personality Crisis - "Piss On You"/ Channel 3 - "Indian Summer"/ Young Lions-"In A Field"/ Zeroption - "Realpolitik"/ D.O.A.-"Tits On The Beach"/ 7 Seconds - "Out Of Touch"/ Stretch Marks - "Foreign Policies"

1984 *Nice & Loud* 7" EP (Big City) No Control- "Johnny"/ Disorderly Conduct - "Enemy"/ Ultra Violence - "No Help"/ Reflex From Pain - "The Scream"/ Vatican Commandos - "Us & Them"/ CIA - "I Hate The Radio"

1985 *When Men Were Men And Sheep Were Scared* (Bemisbrain, 72027) Rhino 39 - "Hurry Up & Waste" "Sleepwalking"/ The Vandals - "Dachau Cabana" "Frog Stomp"/ Red Beret - "Look Behind" "Roller Coaster Ride"/ Crewd - "Audobon Baby" "Lady of the Night"/ Falling Idols - "Defeat The Purpose" "Cut It Out"/ Secret Hate-"Bomb Chic" "Death In The Desert"/ Nip Drivers -"Rio," "E.Y.O.B."/ Target Of Demand-"Air Head" "Target Of Demand"

1985 *New Jerseys' Got It* (Buy Our Records, BOR-12-003) Bedlam - "Mongoofy,""Burn One"/ Bodies In Panic - "Spiders & Cameras" "Wendy O"/ Cyanamid - "N.J. Is A Mall" "Support"/ Pleased Youth - "I'd Rather Be An Asshole""Obedience School"/ Children In Adult Jails - "Fishing For Compliments""Dog Day"/ Stetz - "Kidds Habits""M.A.D.D."/ My 3 Sons - "People Who Bleed," "Untitled 13"/ Sacred Denial - "What Religion" "Our Friend"/ Adrenalin O.D. - "Crowd Control" "Infiltrate"

1986 *Another Shot For Bracken* (Positive Force, # 9) Flag Of Democracy - "The Family Knows"/ Scream - "Green Eyed Lady"/ Short Dogs Grow - "Grandstand Play"/ Dissonance - "Cruise Control"/ Verbal Asault - untitled/ Entirely Distorted - "I Could See Myself"/ The Brigade - "The Last Frontier"/ Outcry - "Someday"/ White Flag - "Suicide King"/7 Seconds - "When One Falls"/5 Balls Of Power - "Radio Station A.S.O.L."/ Adrenalin O.D. - "Anarchy In The U.S.A." (live)/ Scram - "Imagine"/ Care Unit - "Little Circus Man"/ Youth Of Today - "We Just Might"/ Action Figure - "Use Your Head"/ The Sins - "Crazy River"

1986 *The Blasting Concept Vol. II* (SST 043) Saint Vitus - "Look Behind You"/ DC3 - "Theme From An Imaginary Western"/ SWA - "Mystery Girl"/ Black Flag - "I Can See You"/ Gone - "Watch The Tractor"/ Würm - "Death Ride"/ Overkill - "Over The Edge"/ Saccharine Trust - "Emotions And Anatomy"/ Painted Willie - "The Big Time"/ Angst - "Just Me"/ Meat Puppets - "I Just Want To Make Love To You"/ Minutemen - "Ain't Talkin' 'Bout Love"/ Hüsker Dü - "Erase Today"/ October Faction - "I Was Grotesque"/ Tom Troccoli's Dog - "Todo Para Mi"

Steven Blush promoted Hardcore shows in
Washington, DC throughout the early 80s. In 1986
he founded *Seconds* magazine, publishing it
until 2000. His writing has appeared in *Spin,
Interview, Village Voice, Details* and *High Times.* He
currently lives in Manhattan, serves as senior editor
at *Paper,* and throws the weekly party Röck Cändy.

In this 1981 Edward Colver photograph of Fear
singer Lee Ving, Mr. Blush can be seen in the lower
left corner, circled.

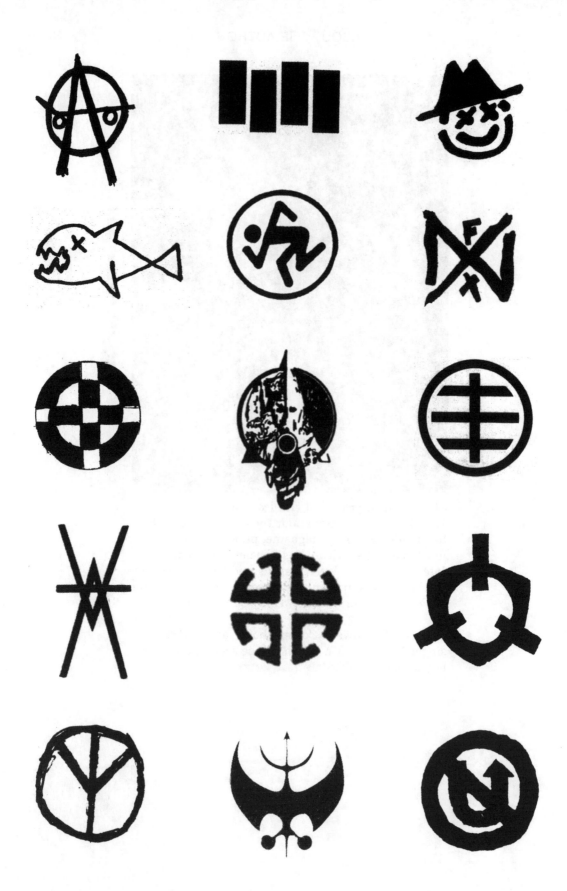

Also available from Feral House

LEXICON DEVIL
THE SHORT LIFE AND FAST TIMES OF DARBY CRASH AND THE GERMS

Don Bolles and Brendan Mullen

Lexicon Devil reveals a largely secret part of L.A. history – an impossible occurrence in an improbable time. Darby Crash is to now what the Velvet Underground and the Stooges were to earlier rock generations: a legendary, but little understood icon, a brilliant and strangely charismatic Sun God, sacrificed on the altar of Rock and Roll. Darby's never-before-told story, involving skate-punks, chickenhawks, violence, suicide and occasional brilliance, is as tragic as any Pasolini film, yet as absurdly hilarious as "*Beyond The Valley Of the Dolls*" – and, like the mythos of Jack Parsons, James Dean, Charles Manson and Jim Morrison, it's a story that could only have happened in Los Angeles. Authors Don Bolles played drums for The Germs, and Brendan Mullen managed the notorious urine-stained basement, The Masque, circle one of the original Los Angeles punk scene.

Paperback original ◆ extensively illustrated
ISBN: 0-922915-70-9 ◆ $16.95

BUBBLEGUM MUSIC IS THE NAKED TRUTH
THE DARK HISTORY OF PREPUBESCENT POP, FROM THE BANANA SPLITS TO BRITNEY SPEARS

Edited by Kim Cooper and David Smay

"Bubblegum music" is rediscovered and reinvigorated by this remarkably fun and thorough cyclopedia about a vilified genre and its Faustian pursuit of the perfect pop song.

"*Bubblegum Music is the Naked Truth* sticks to your heart and not to your shoe. The talented writers are clever without a touch of meanness; when the heads of their subjects float to the clouds they remember to push the down button on the elevator. This is a wise, witty and important book. Read it, or else!"—Rod McKuen

7 x 10 ◆ 344 pages ◆ illustrated
ISBN: 0-922915-69-5 ◆ $19.95

LORDS OF CHAOS
THE BLOODY RISE OF THE SATANIC METAL UNDERGROUND

Michael Moynihan and Didrik Søderlund

"An unusual combination of true crime journalism, rock and roll reporting and underground obsessiveness, *Lords of Chaos* turns into one of the more fascinating reads in a long time . . ."
—David Thomas, *Denver Post*

". . . this is gripping stuff, a book about scary rock that is really scary."
—Mike Tribby, *Booklist*

Lords of Chaos won the Firecracker Award for Best Music Book of 1998.

6 x 9 ◆ 358 pages ◆ illustrated
ISBN 0-922915-48-2 ◆ $16.95

To order from Feral House: Domestic orders add $4.50 shipping for first item, $2.00 each additional item. Amex, MasterCard, Visa, checks and money orders are accepted. (CA state residents add 8% tax.) Canadian orders add $9 shipping for first item, $6 each additional item. Other countries add $11 shipping for first item, $9 each additional item. Non-U.S. originated orders must be international money order or check drawn on a U.S. bank only. Send orders to: Feral House, P.O. Box 13067, Los Angeles, CA 90013

www.feralhouse.com